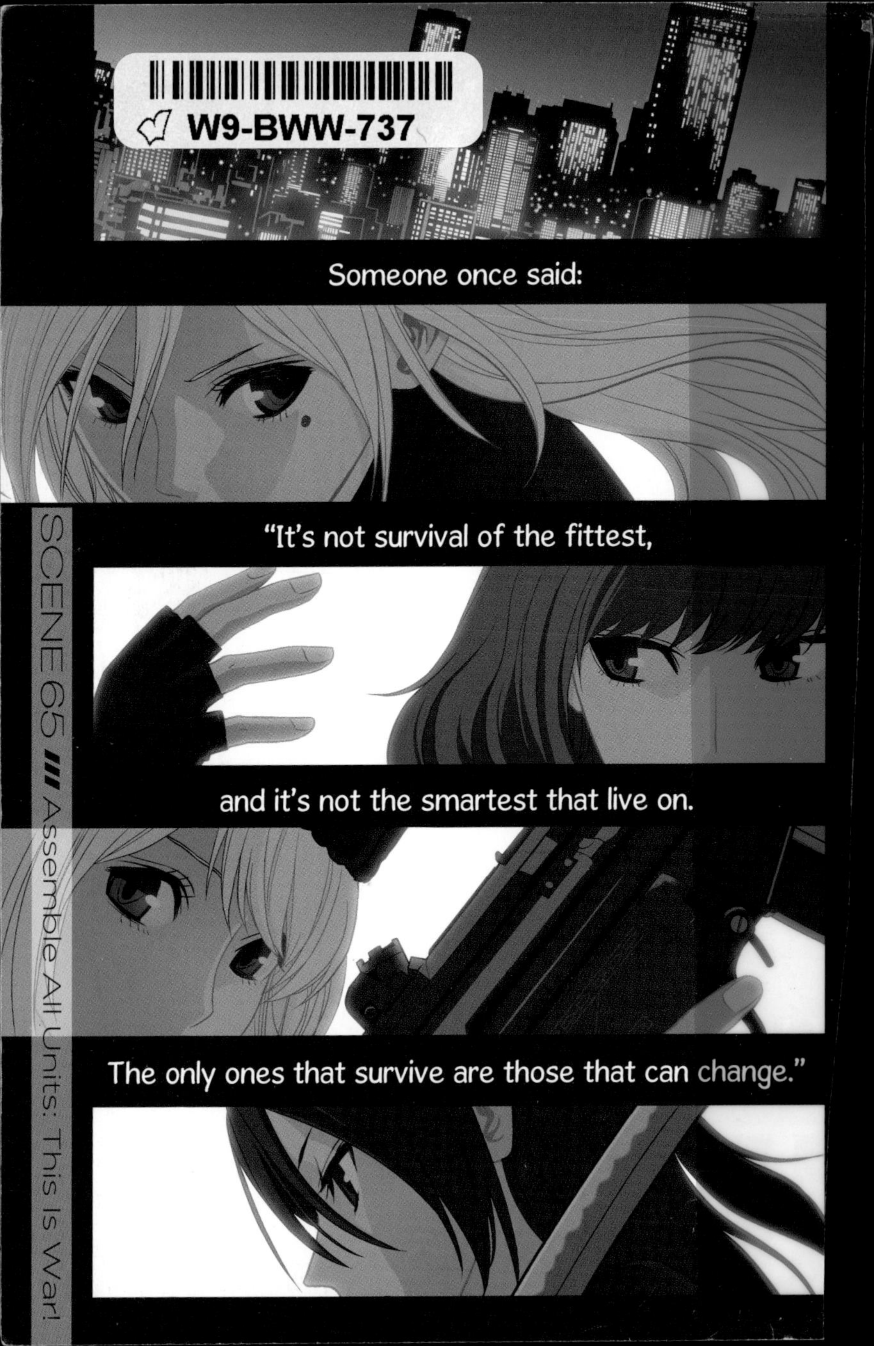
Someone once said:
"It's not survival of the fittest,
and it's not the smartest that live on.
The only ones that survive are those that can change."
SCENE 65 /// Assemble All Units: This Is War!

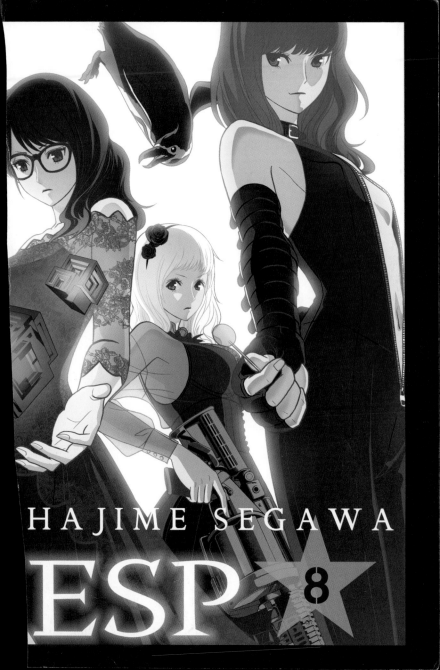

HAJIME SEGAWA

ESP ★8

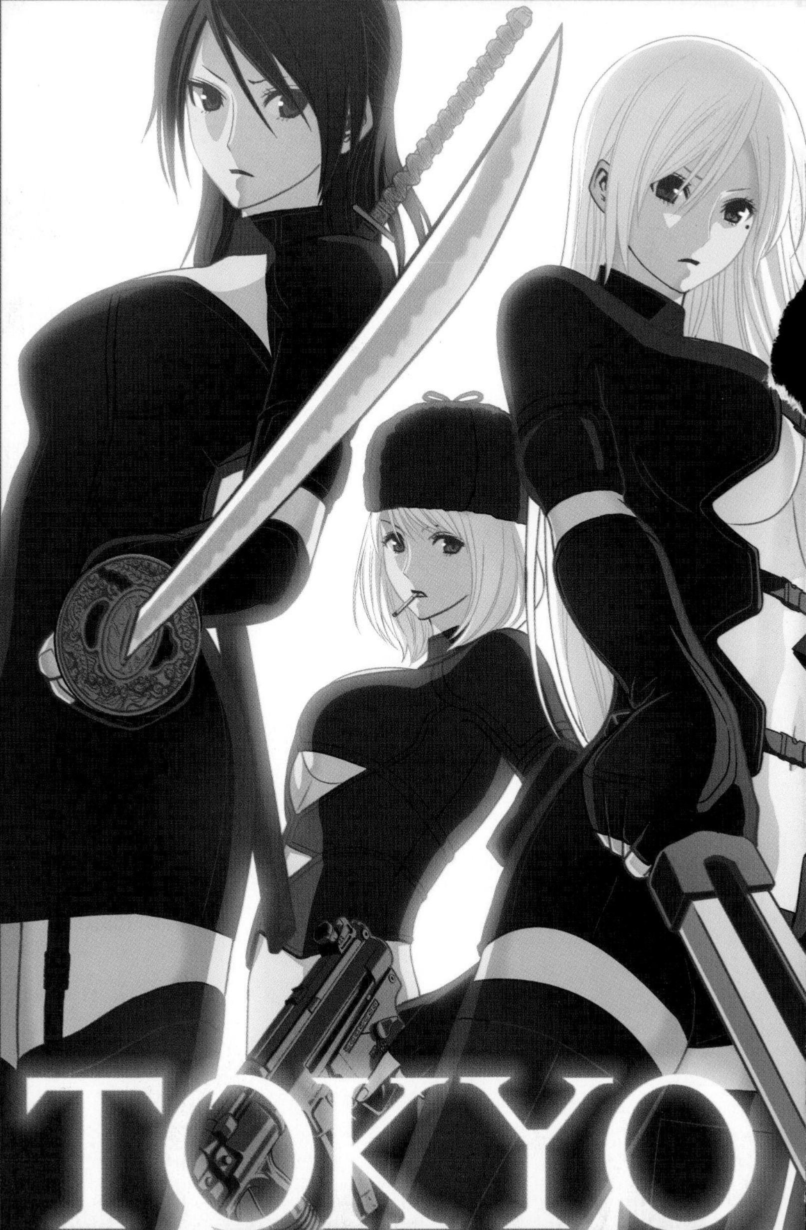
TOKYO

CONTENTS 8

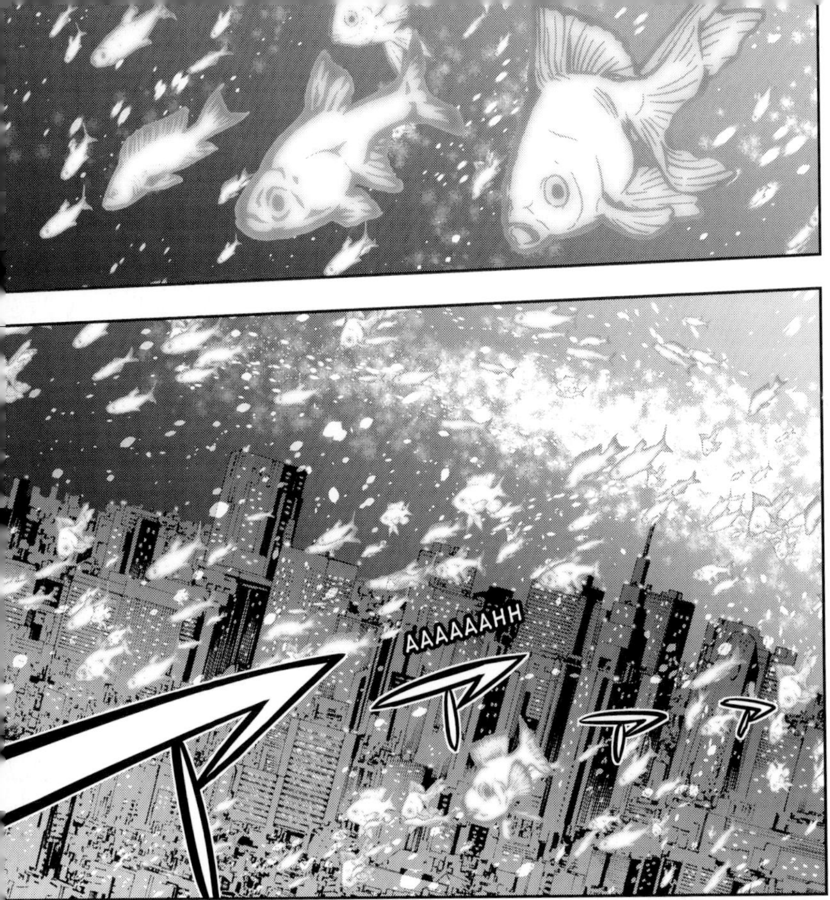
AAAAAAHH

SCENE 65 /// Assemble All Units: This Is War!

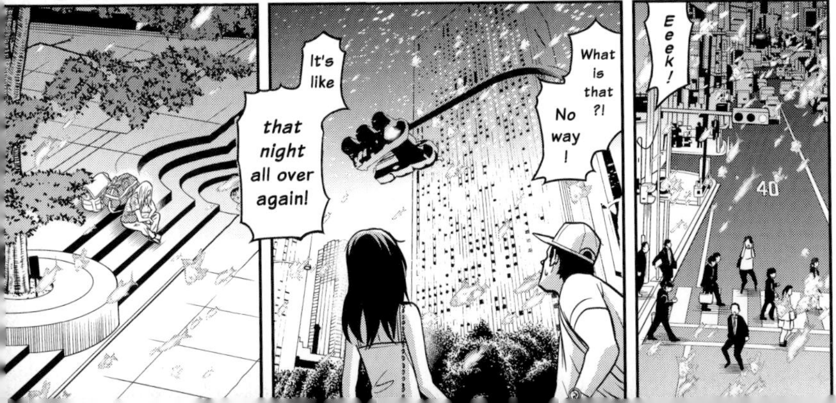
Eeek!
What is that?!
No way!
It's like that night all over again!

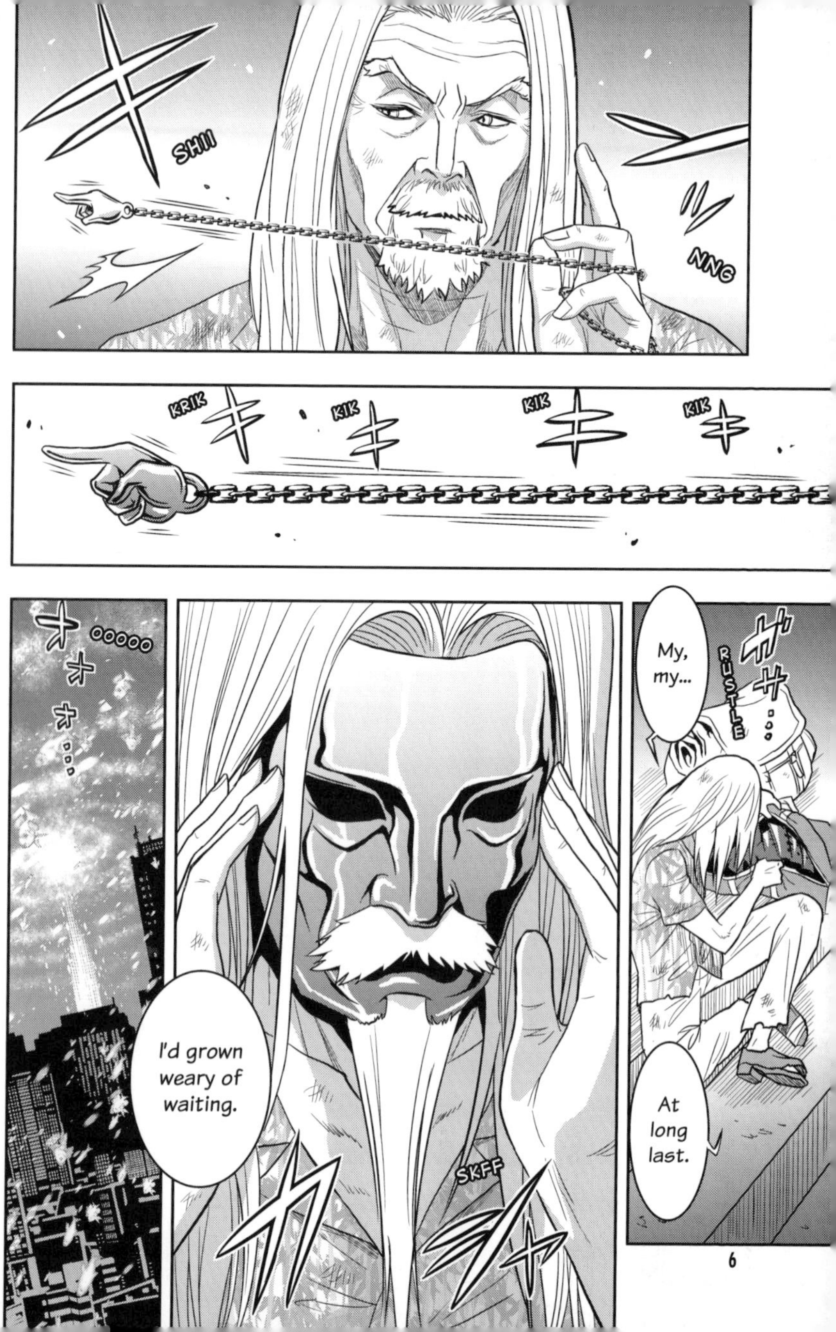
NNG
SHII
KIK
KIK
KIK
KRIK
RUSTLE
My, my...
At long last.
I'd grown weary of waiting.
SKFF
OOOOO

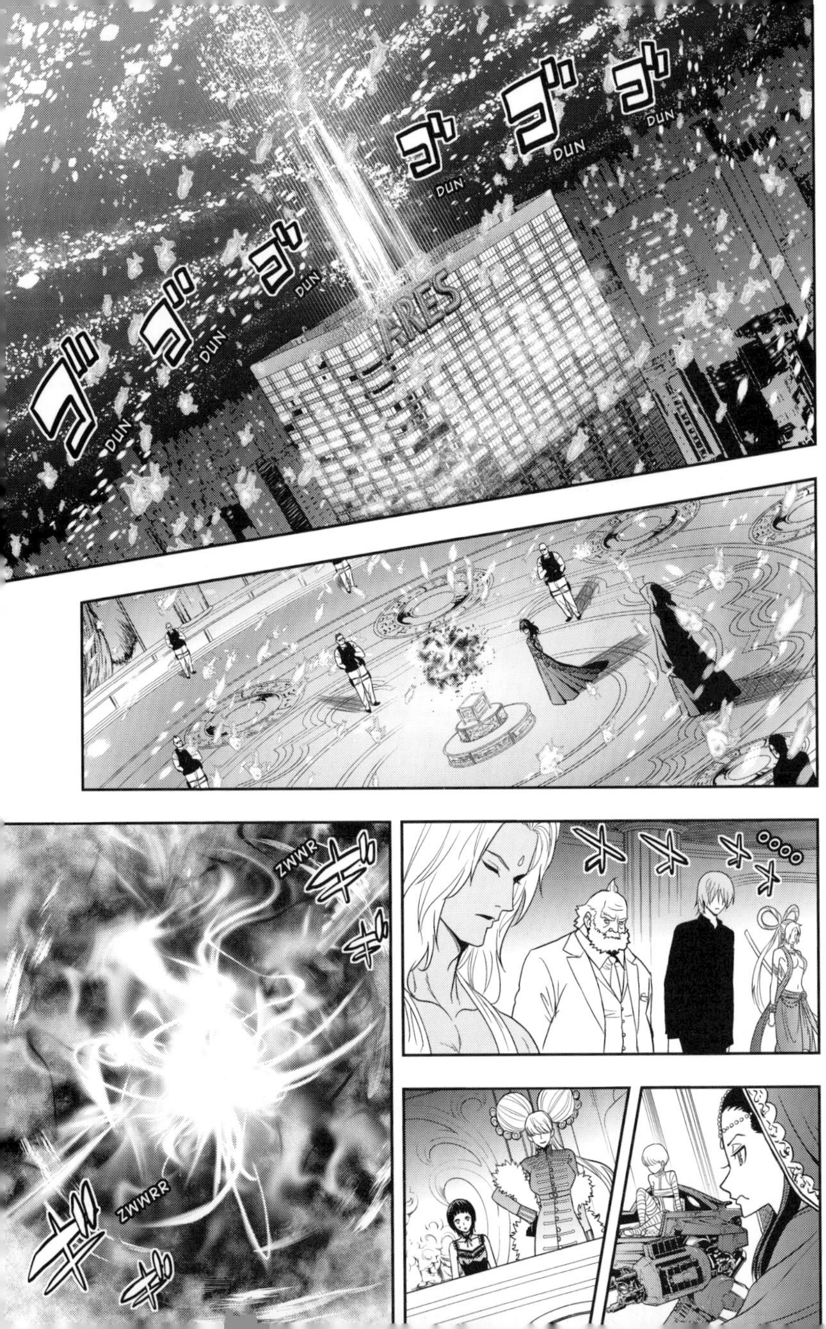

DUN
DUN
DUN
DUN
DUN
DUN
ARES
ZWWRR
ZWWRR

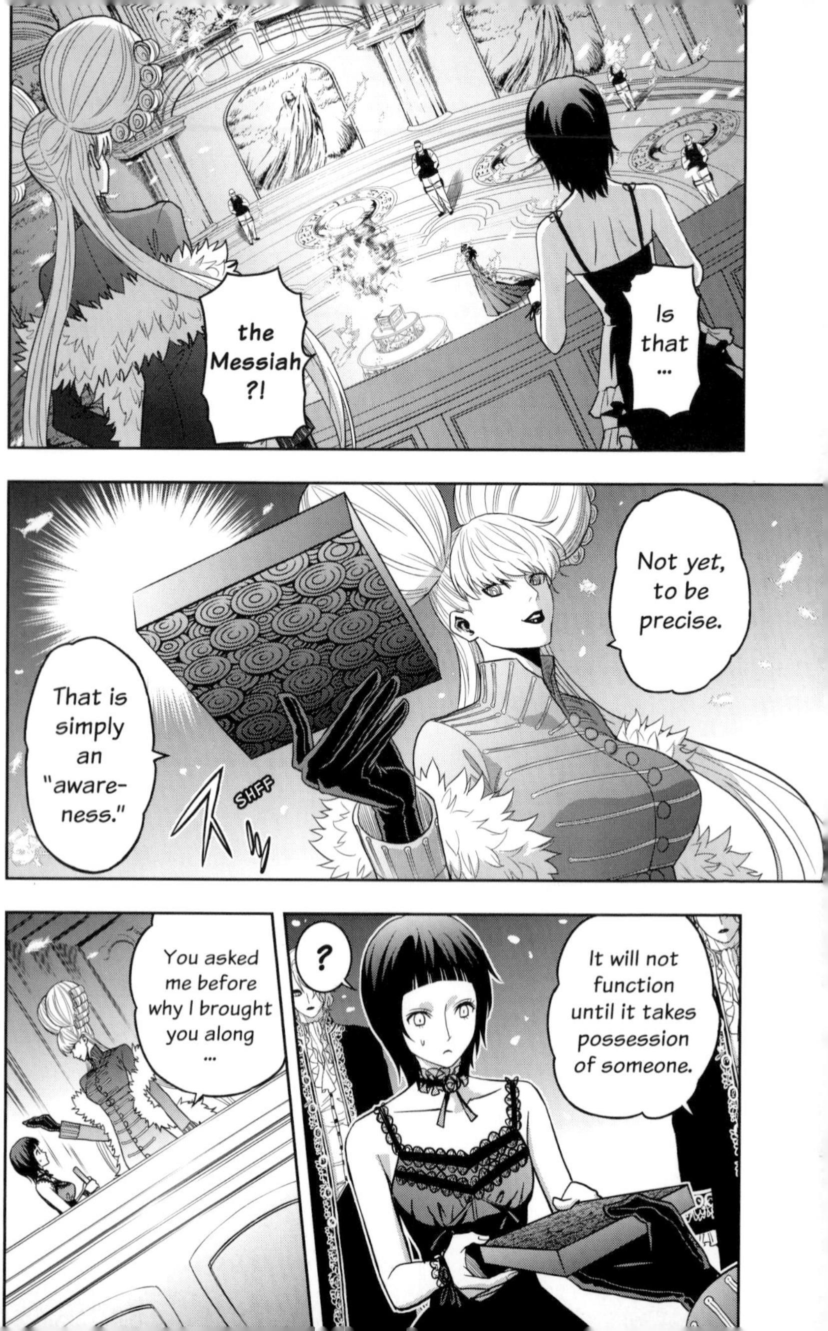
Is that ...
the Messiah?!
Not yet, to be precise.
SHFF
That is simply an "awareness."
It will not function until it takes possession of someone.
?
You asked me before why I brought you along ...

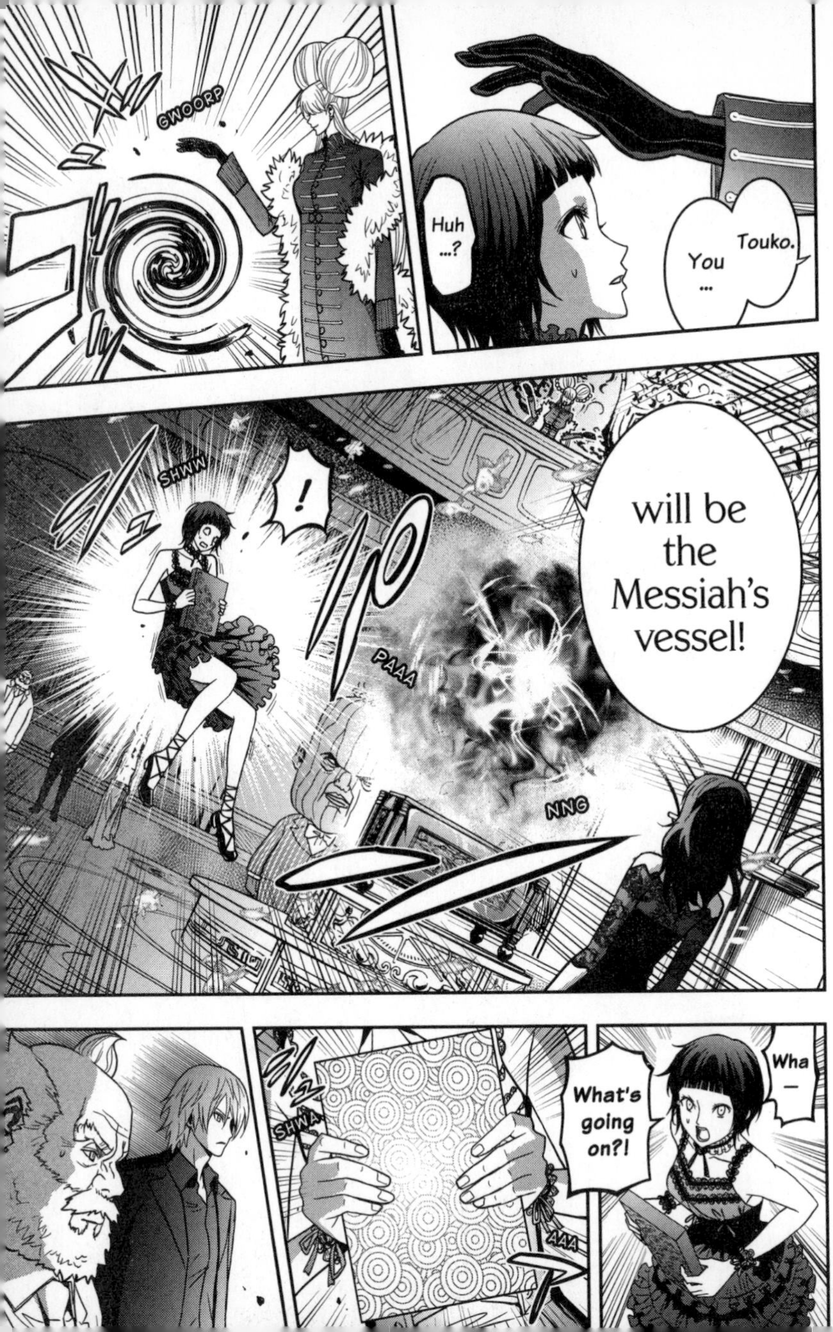
Touko.
You ...
Huh ...?
GWOORP
will be the Messiah's vessel!
!
SHWW
PAAA
NNG
Wha —
What's going on?!
SHWA
AAA

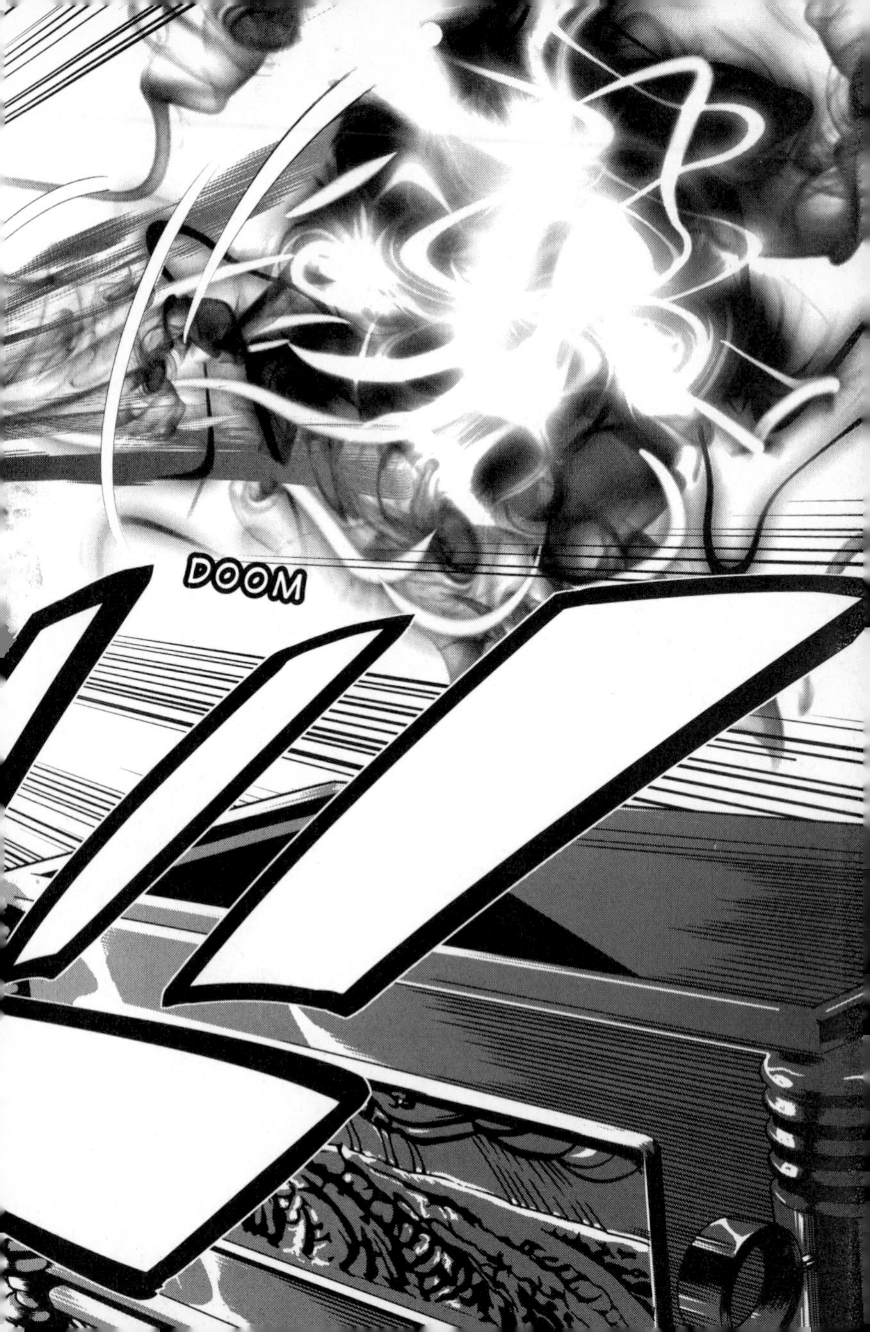
DOOM

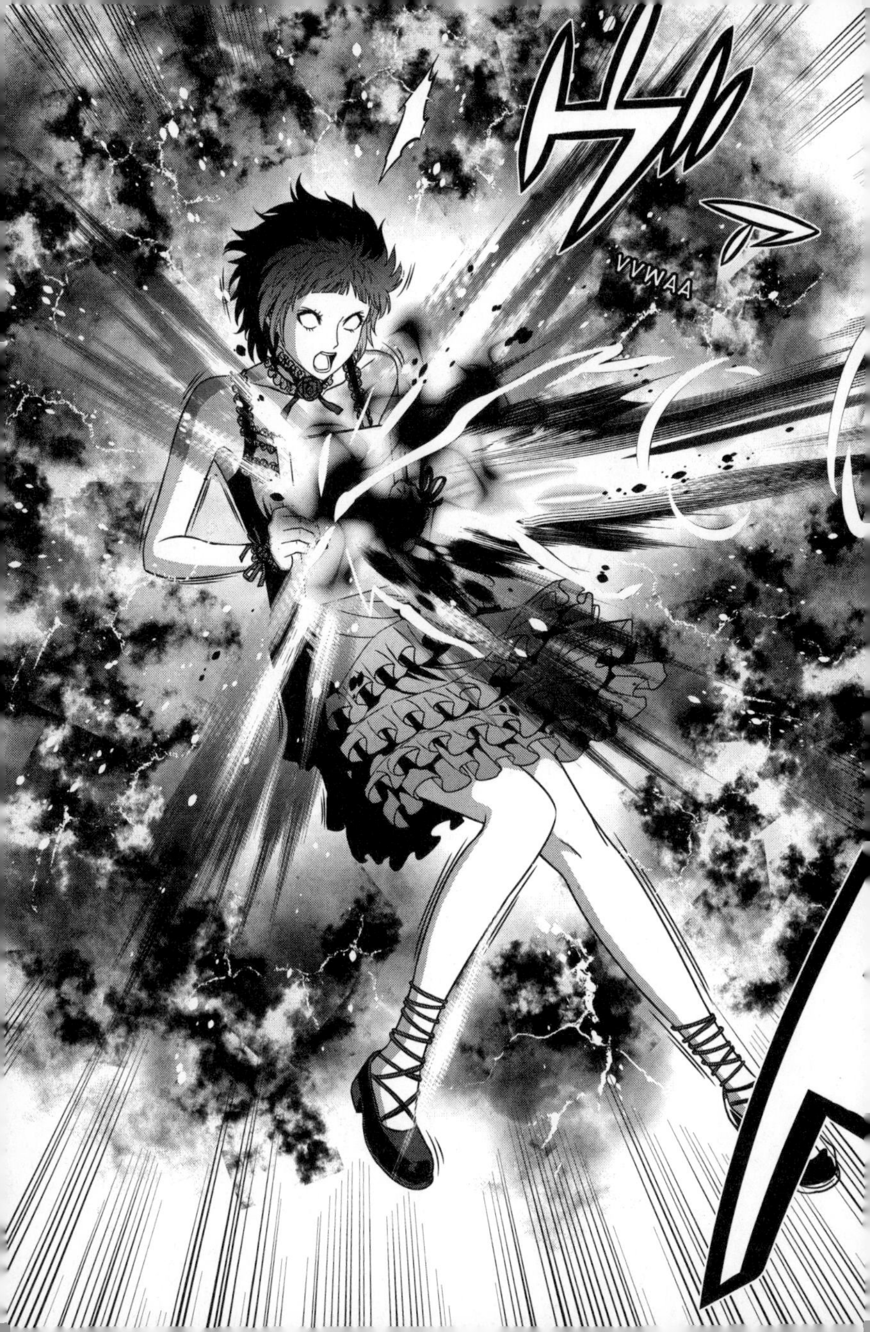
VVWAA

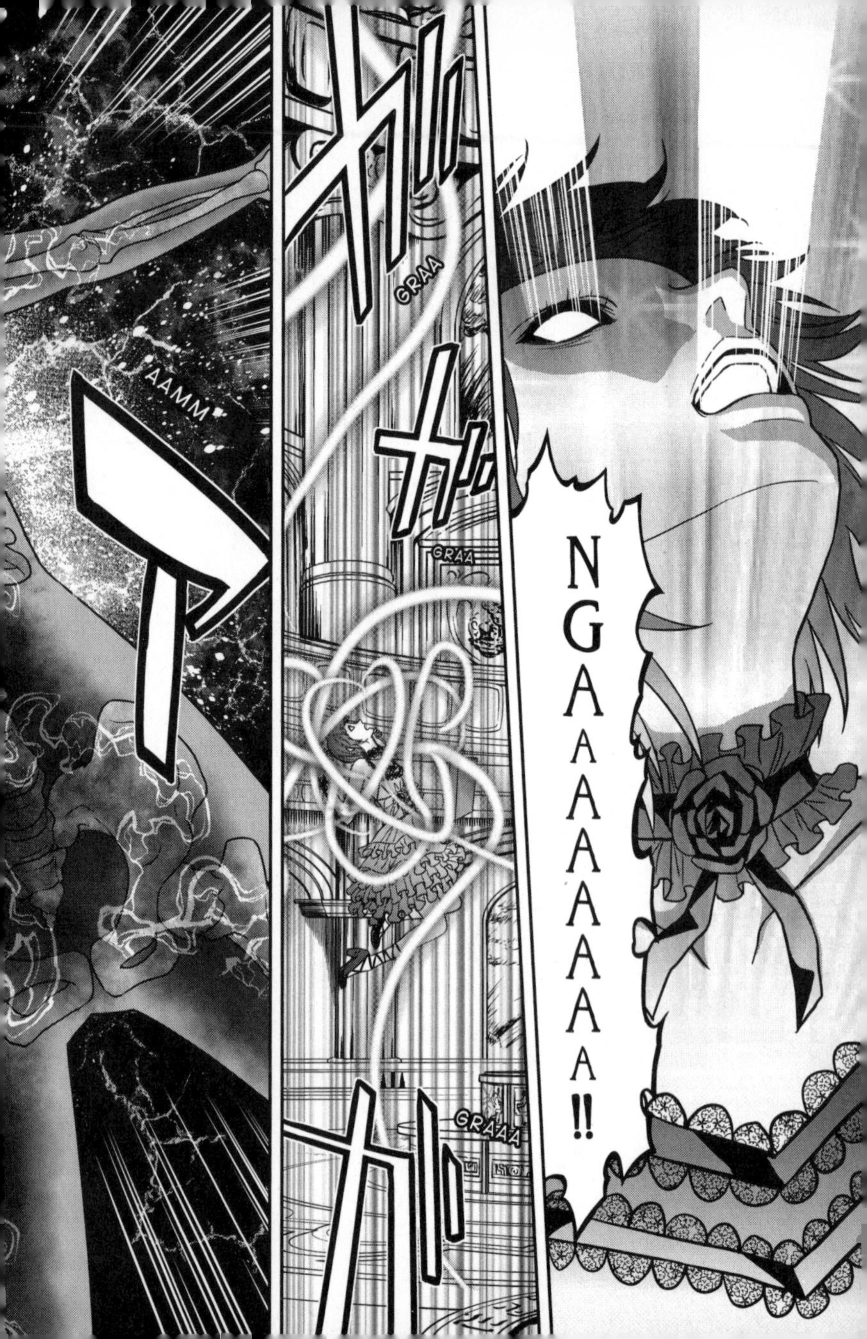
NGAAAAAAAA!!
GRAA
GRAA
GRAAA
AAMM

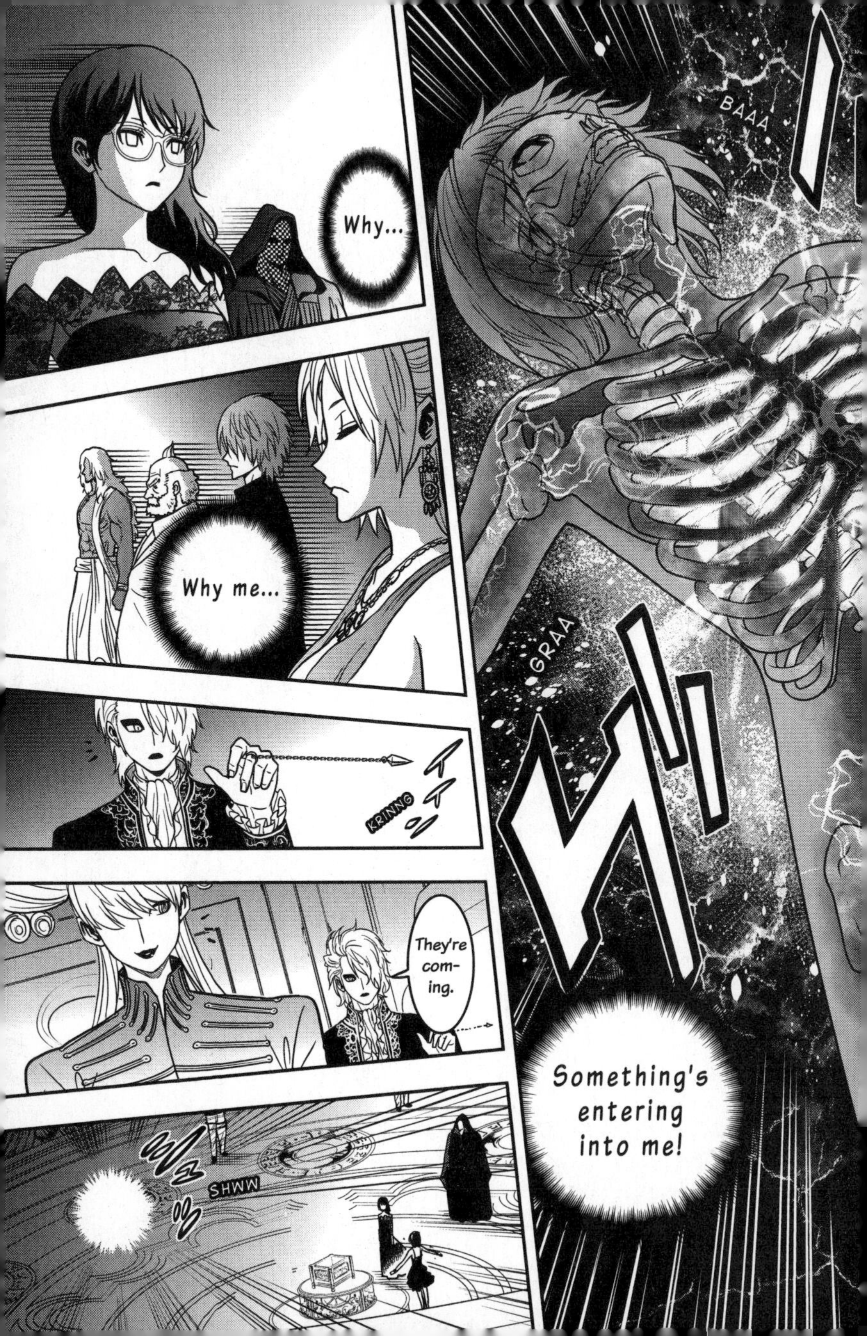
BAAA
GRAA
Something's entering into me!
Why...
Why me...
KRINNG
They're coming.
SHWW

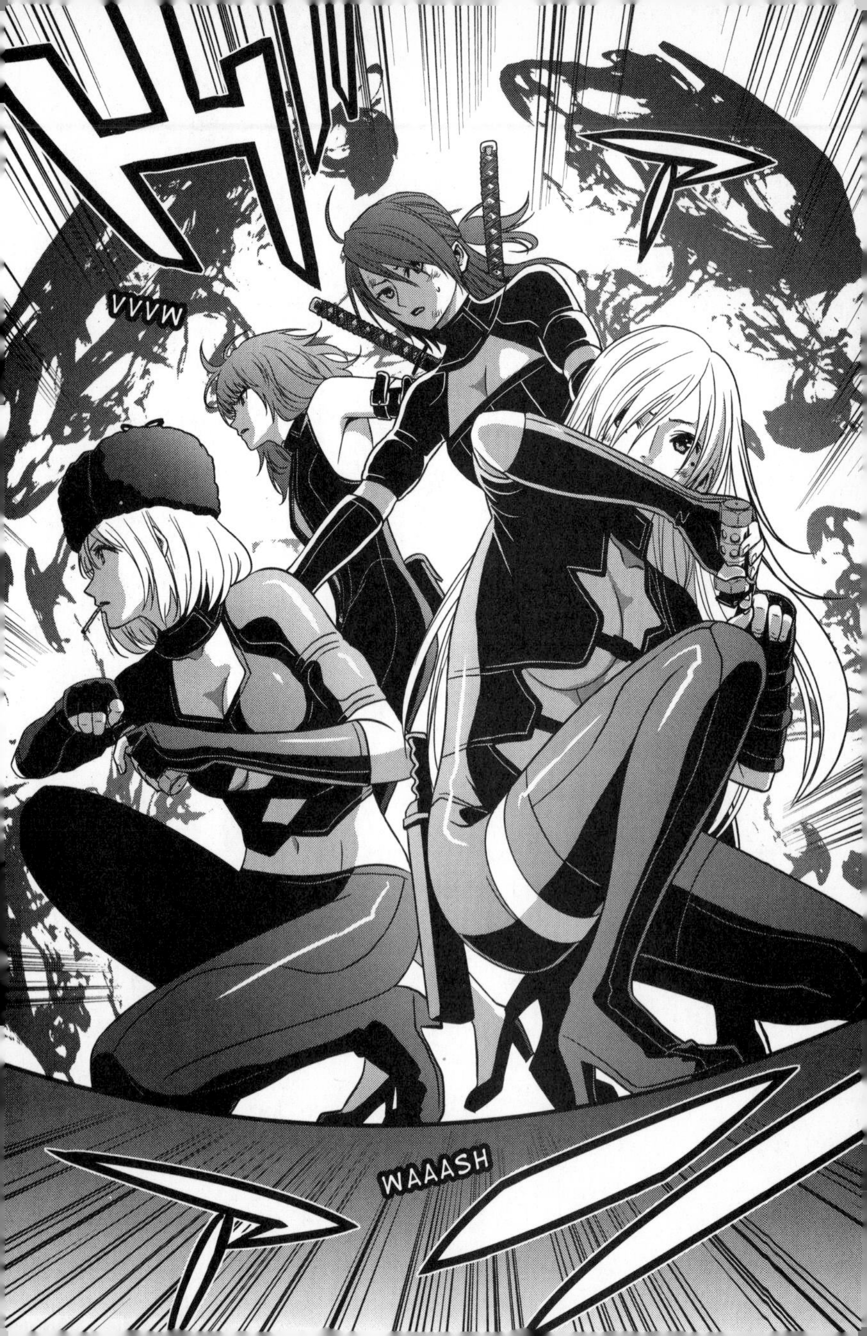
VVVW
WAAASH

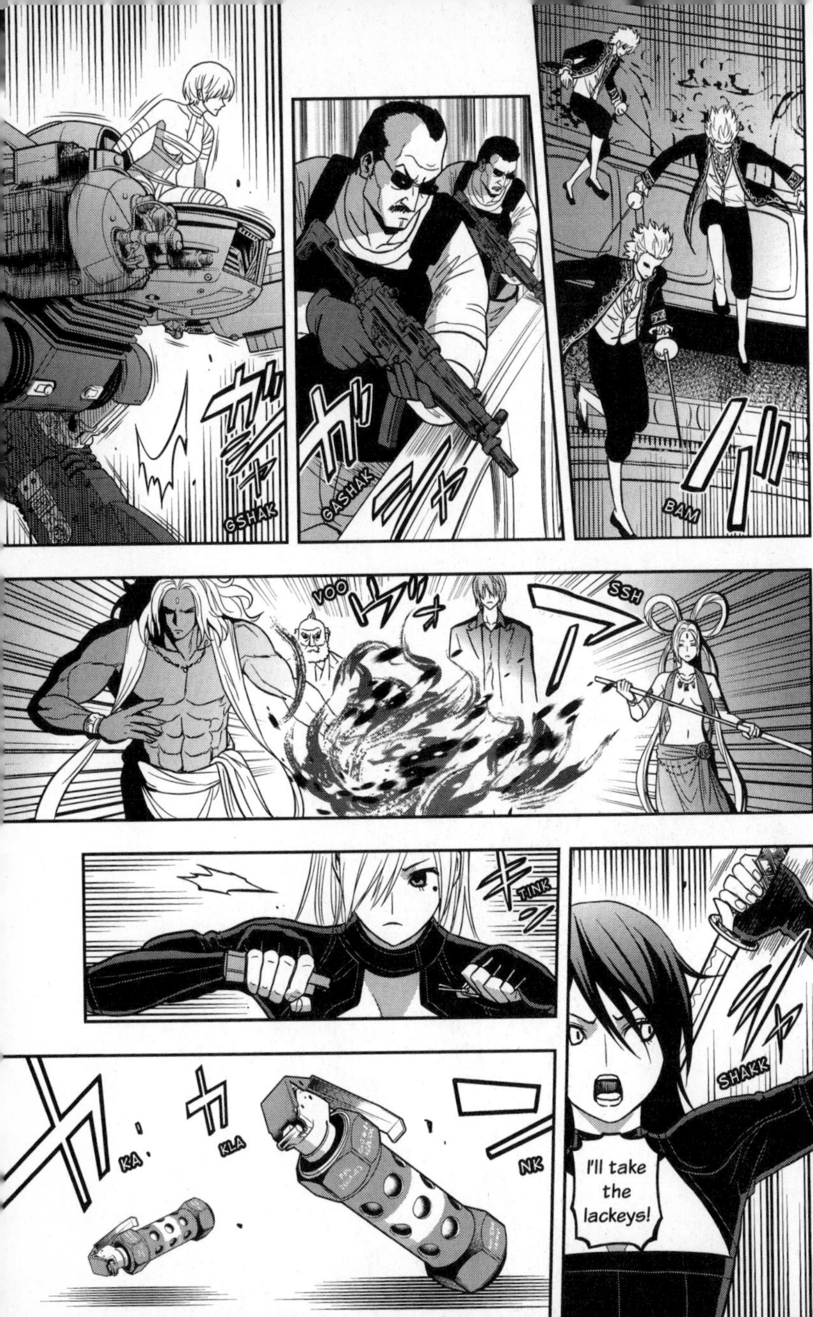
BAM
GASHAK
GSHAK
SSH
VOO
SHAKK
I'll take the lackeys!
TINK
KA KLA NK

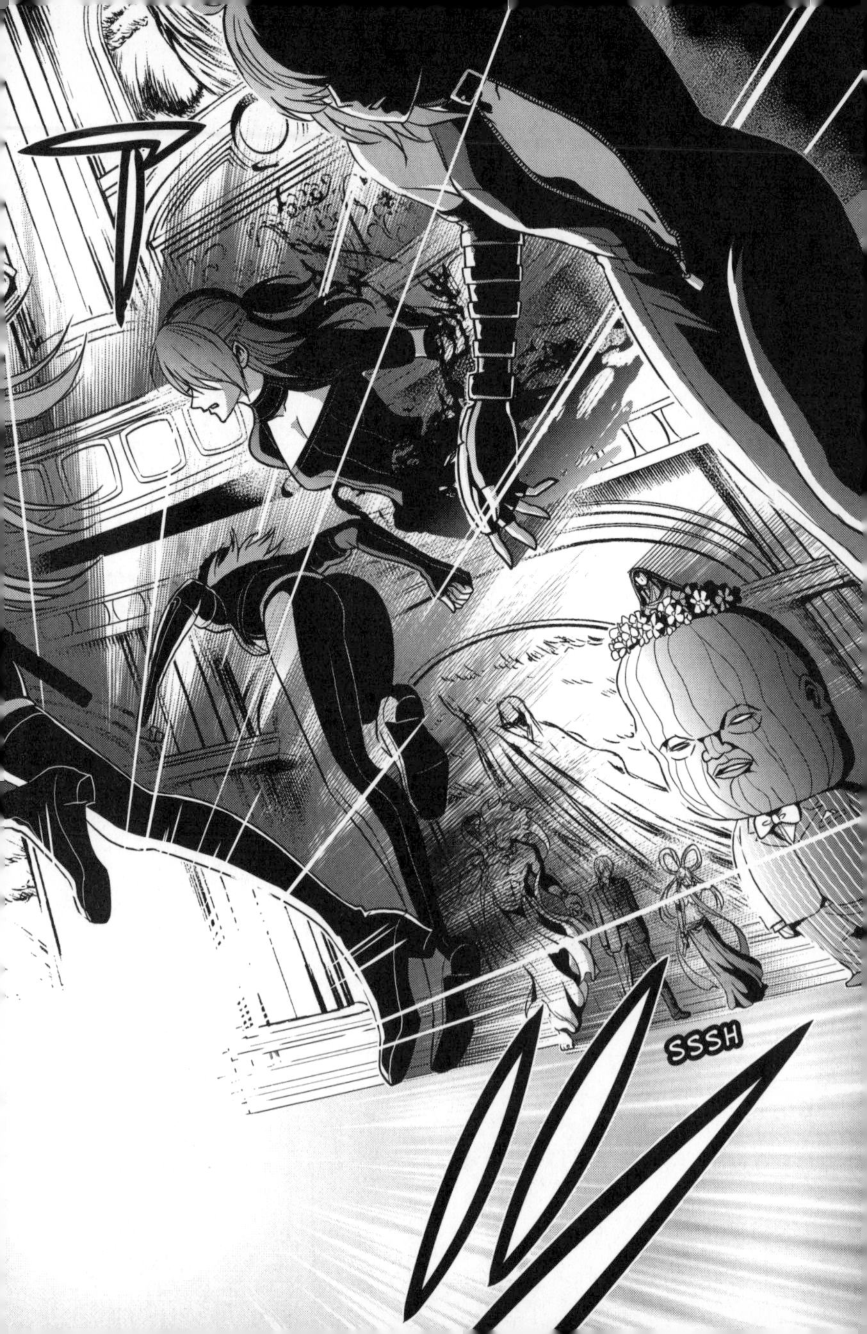
SSSH

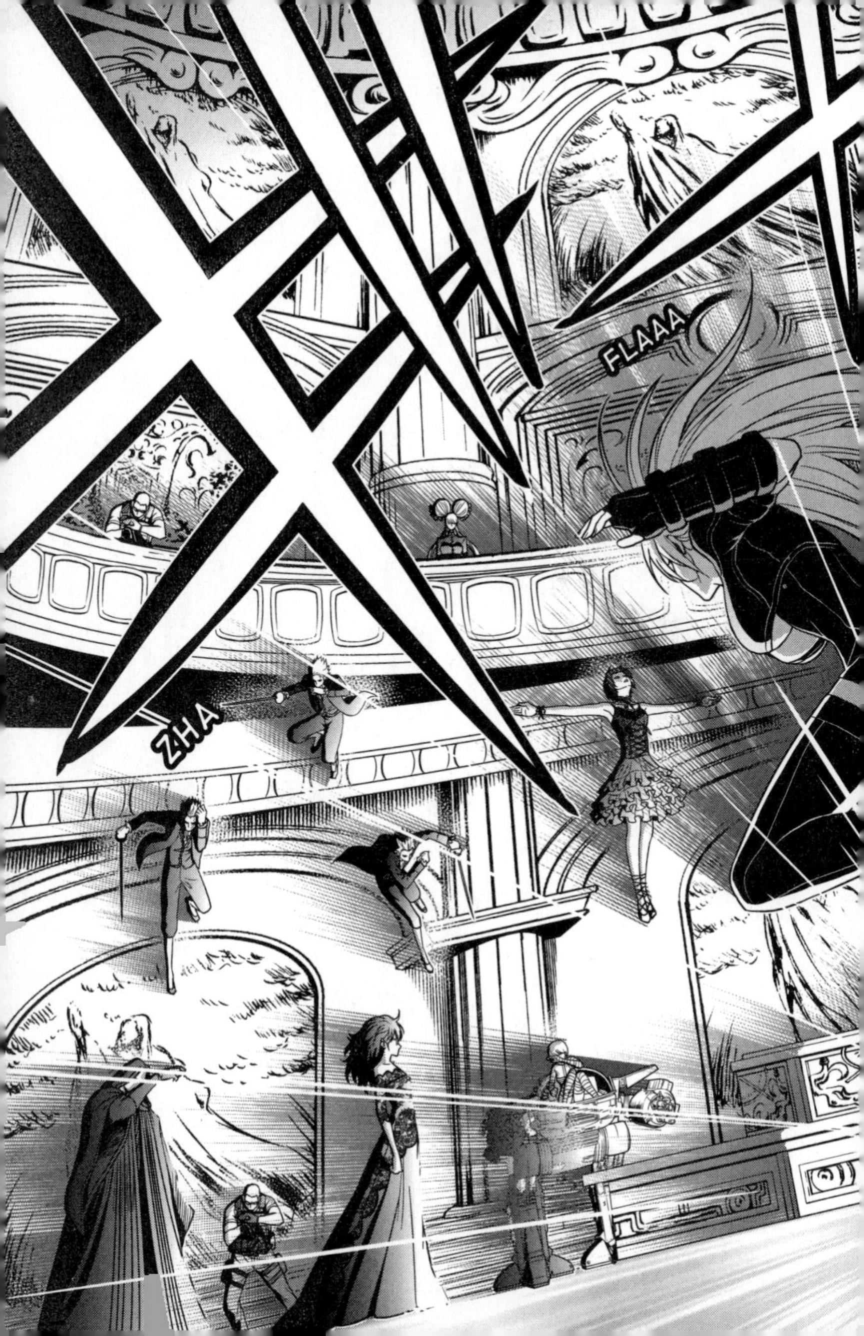
FLAAA
ZHA

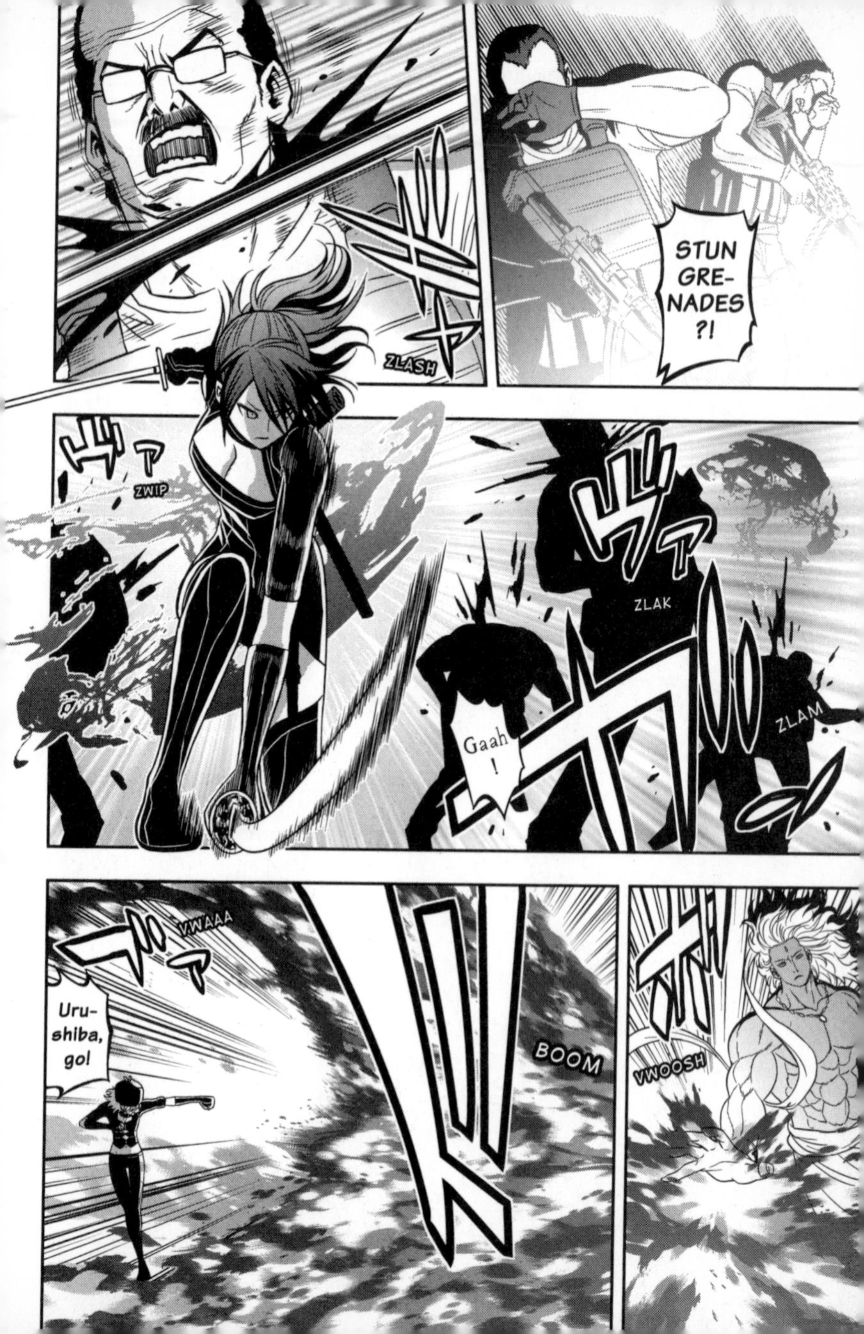
STUN GRE- NADES ?!
ZLASH
ZLAK
ZLAM
Gaah !
ZWIP
VWOOSH
BOOM
VWAAA
Uru- shiba, go!

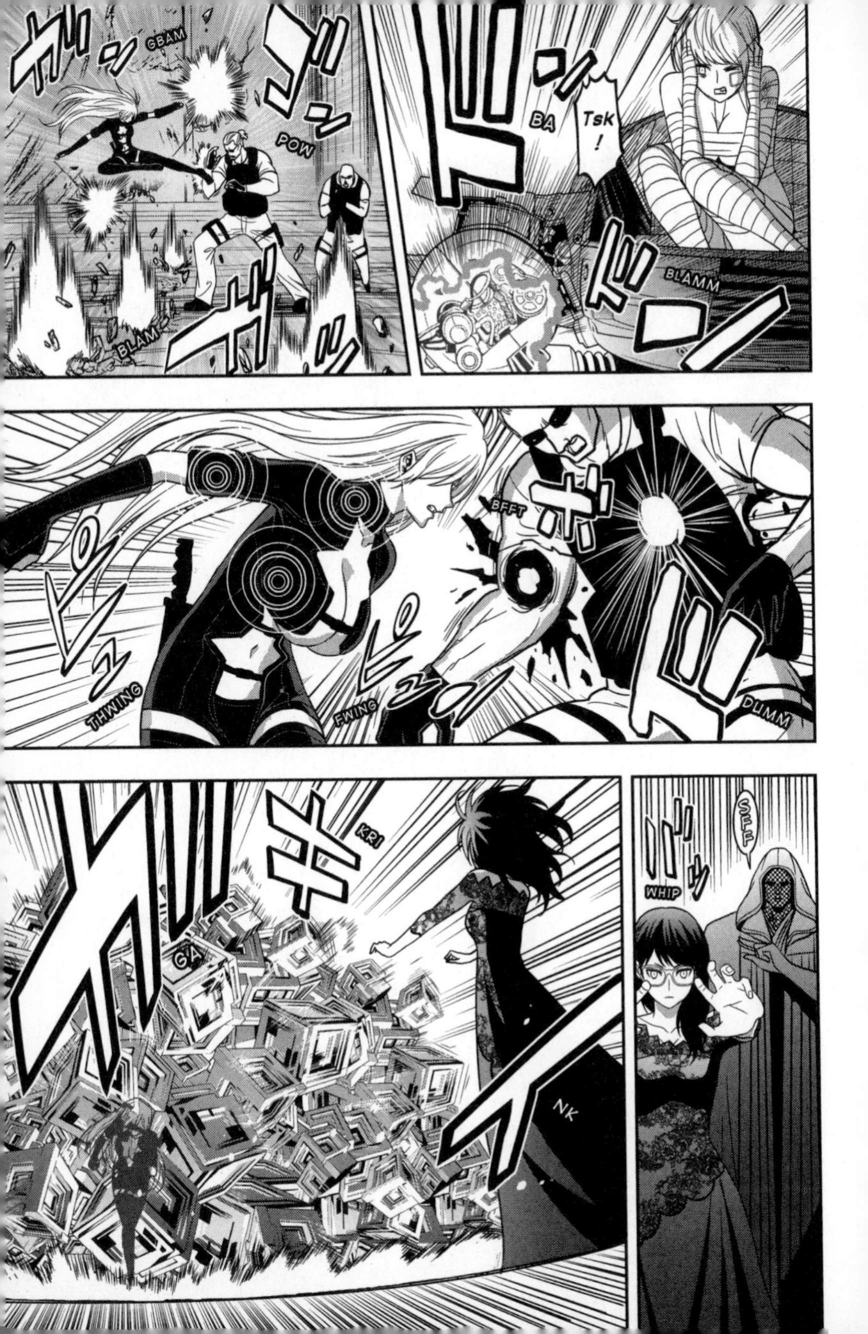
BA
Tsk!
BLAMM
GBAM
POW
BLAM
BFFT
DUMM
FWING
THWING
SFF
WHIP
KRI
GA
NK

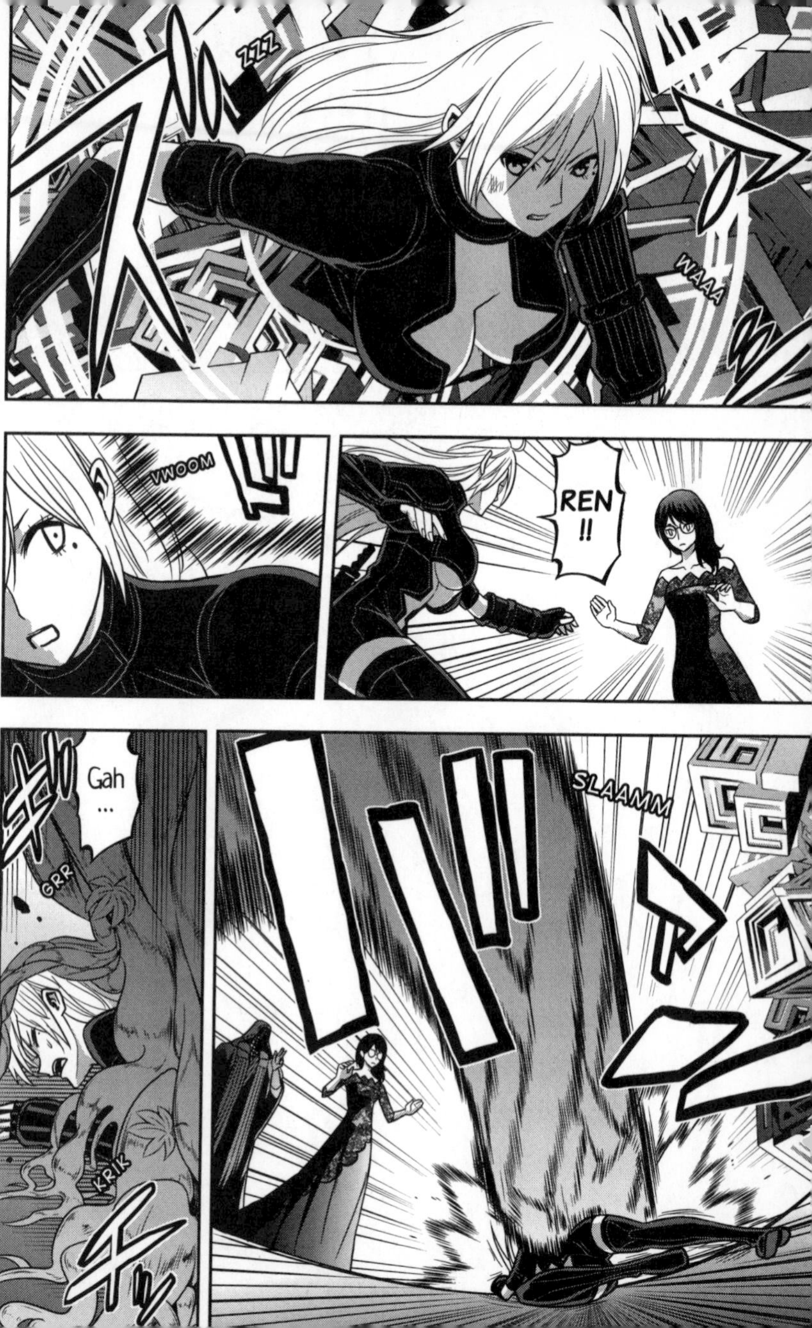
ZZZ
WAAA
REN !!
VWOOM
SLAAMM
Gah ...
GRR
KRIK

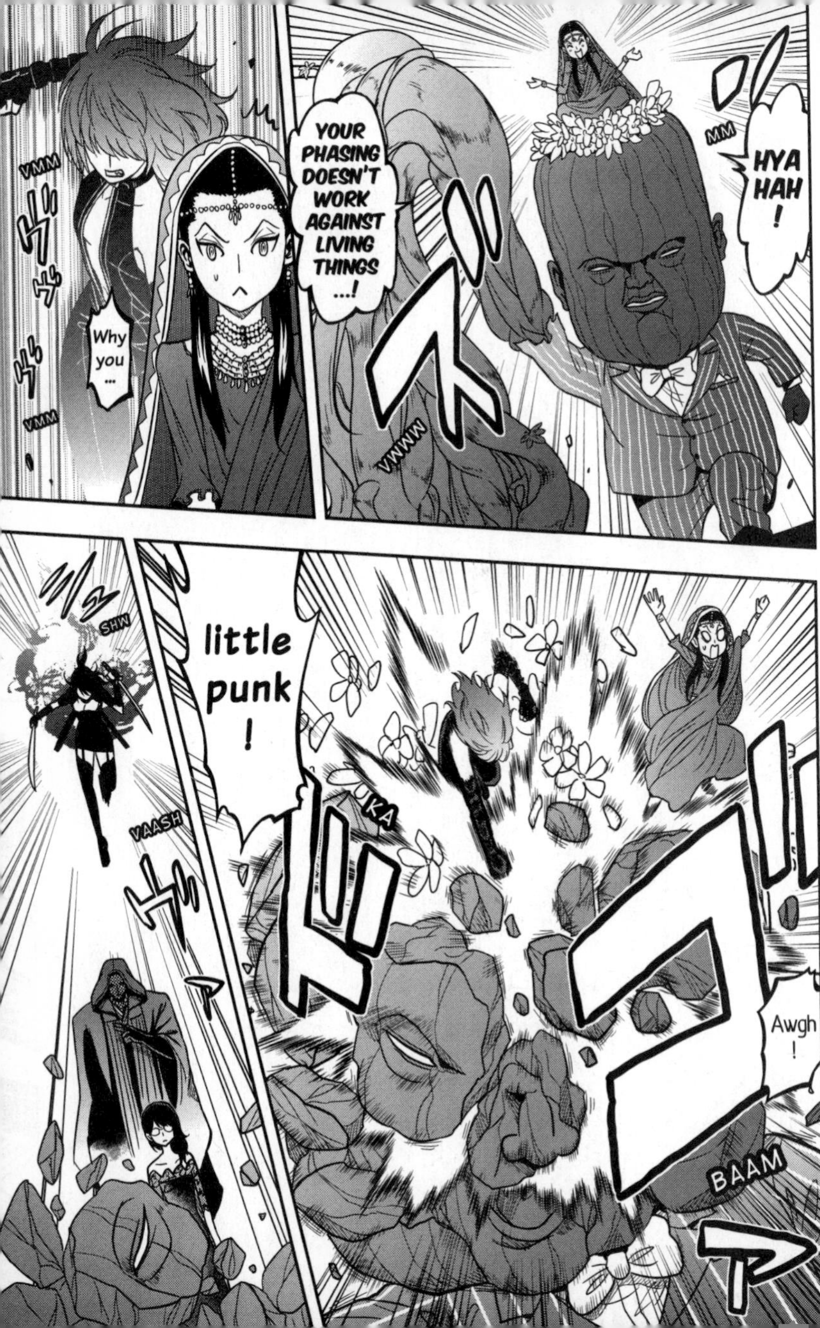

MM
HYA HAH!
YOUR PHASING DOESN'T WORK AGAINST LIVING THINGS ...!
VMM
Why you ...
VMM
Awgh!
BAAM
KA
little punk!
SHW
VAASH

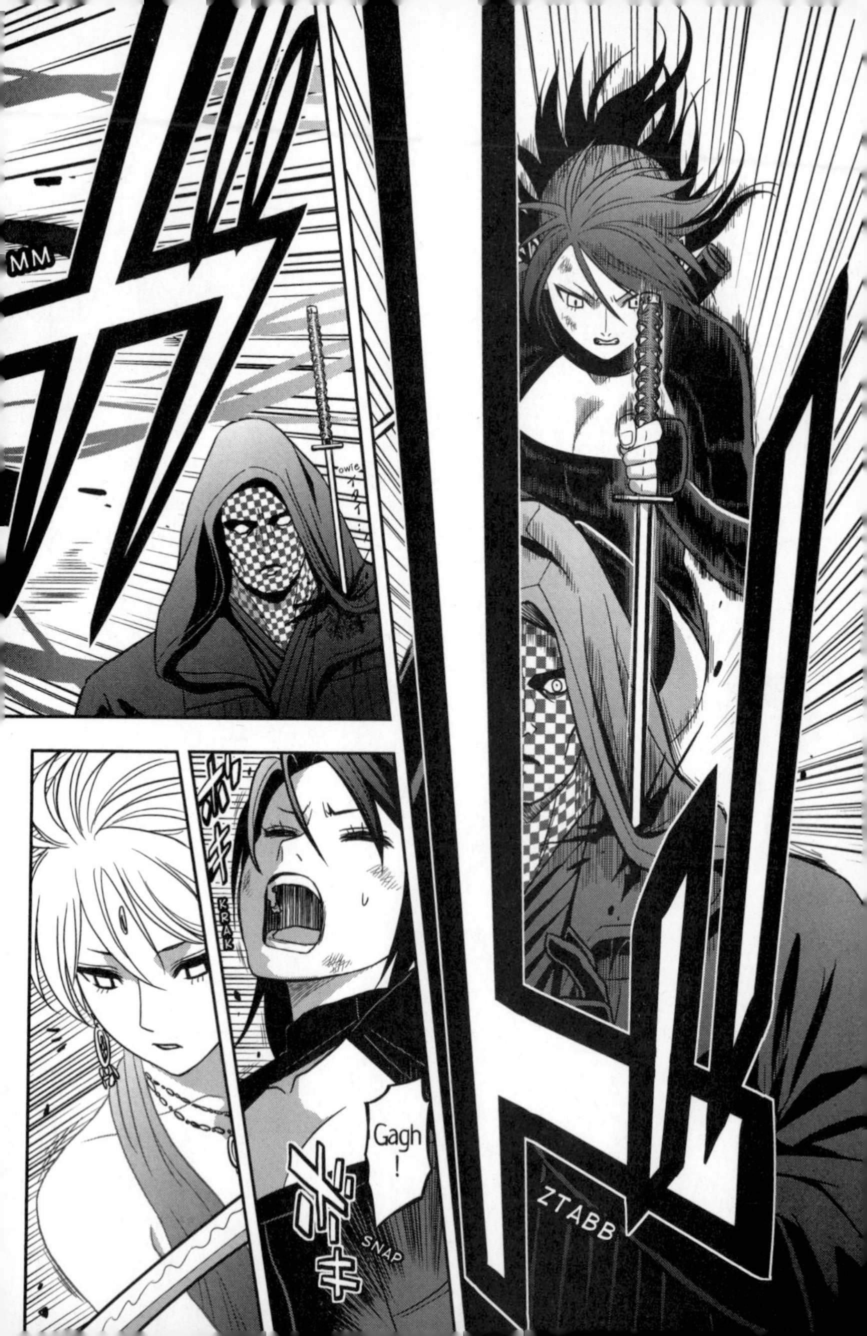
ZTABB
MM
owie
Gagh!
SNAP
KRAK

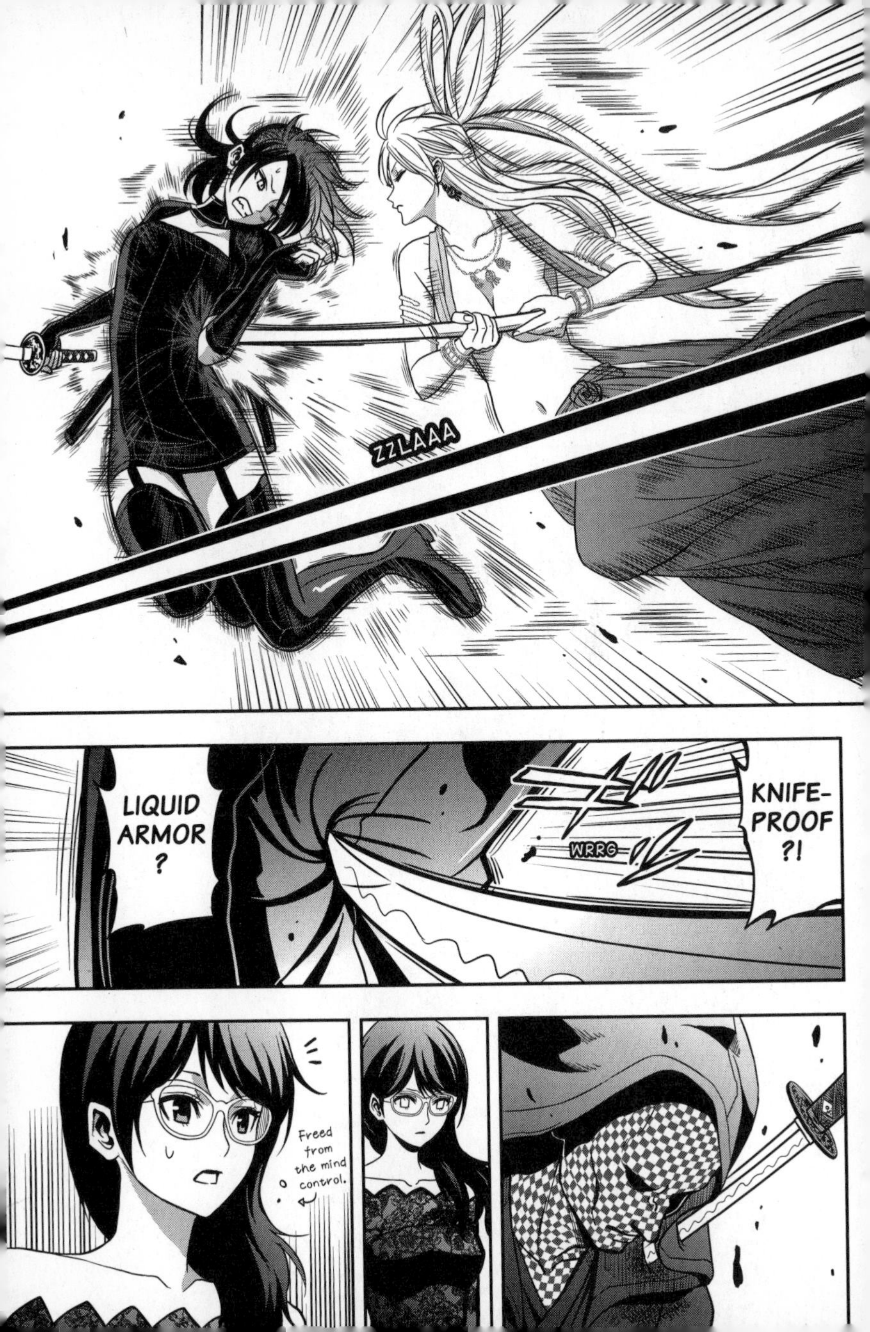
ZZLAAA
KNIFE-PROOF ?!
WRRG
LIQUID ARMOR ?
Freed from the mind control.

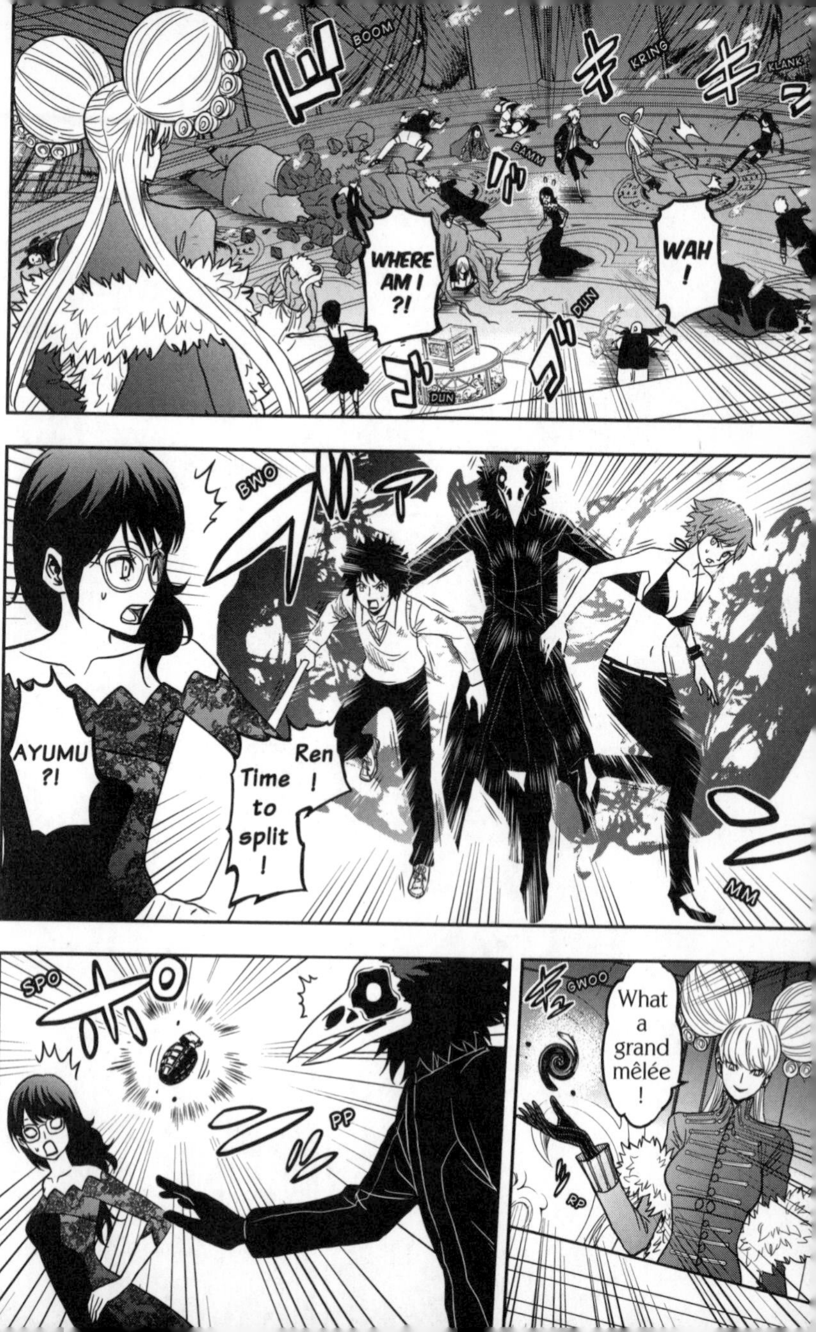
KLANK
KRING
BOOM
WAH !
BAMM
WHERE AM I ?!
DUN
DUN
BWO
Ren ! Time to split !
AYUMU ?!
MM
GWOO
What a grand mêlée !
RP
SPO
PP

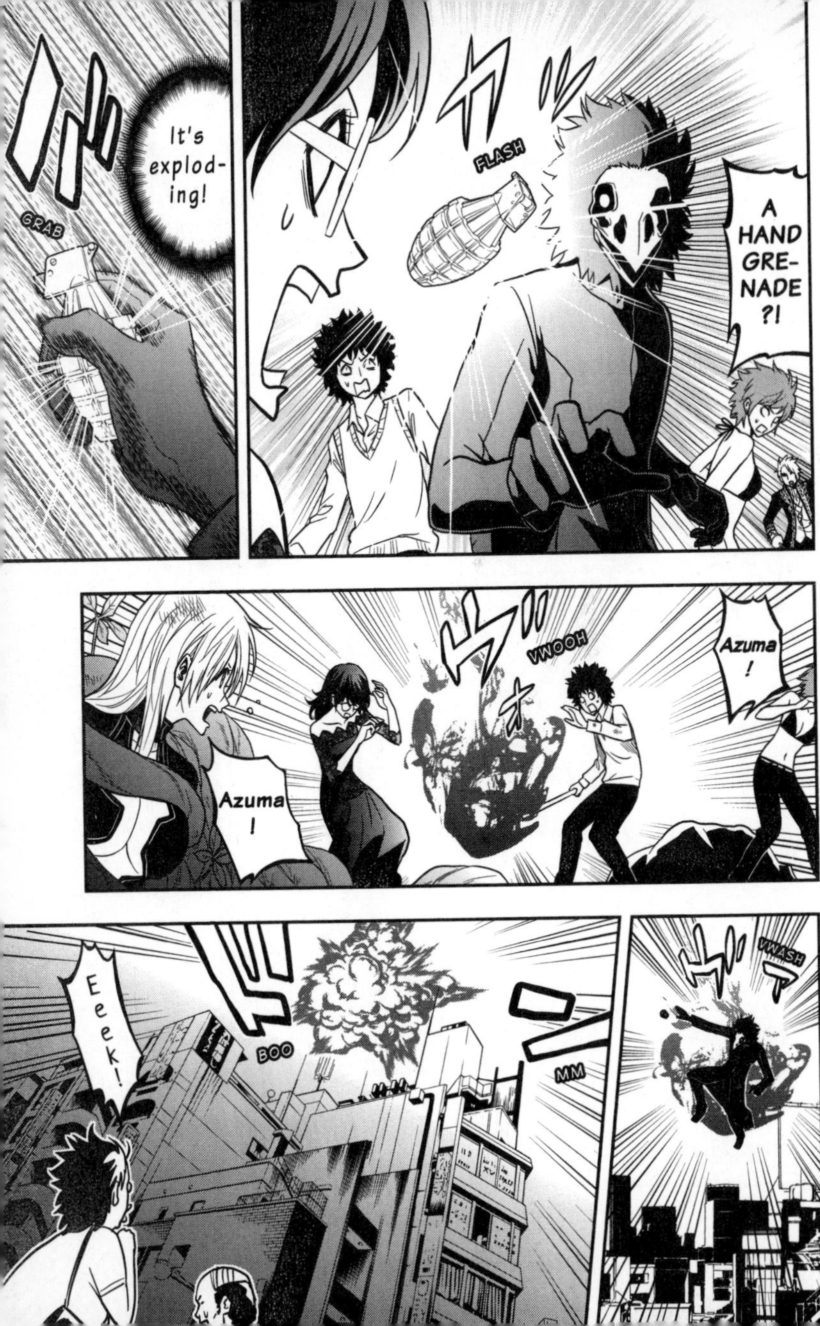

A HAND GRE-NADE?!
FLASH
It's explod-ing!
GRAB
Azuma!
VWOOH
Azuma!
VWASH
BOO
MM
Eeek!

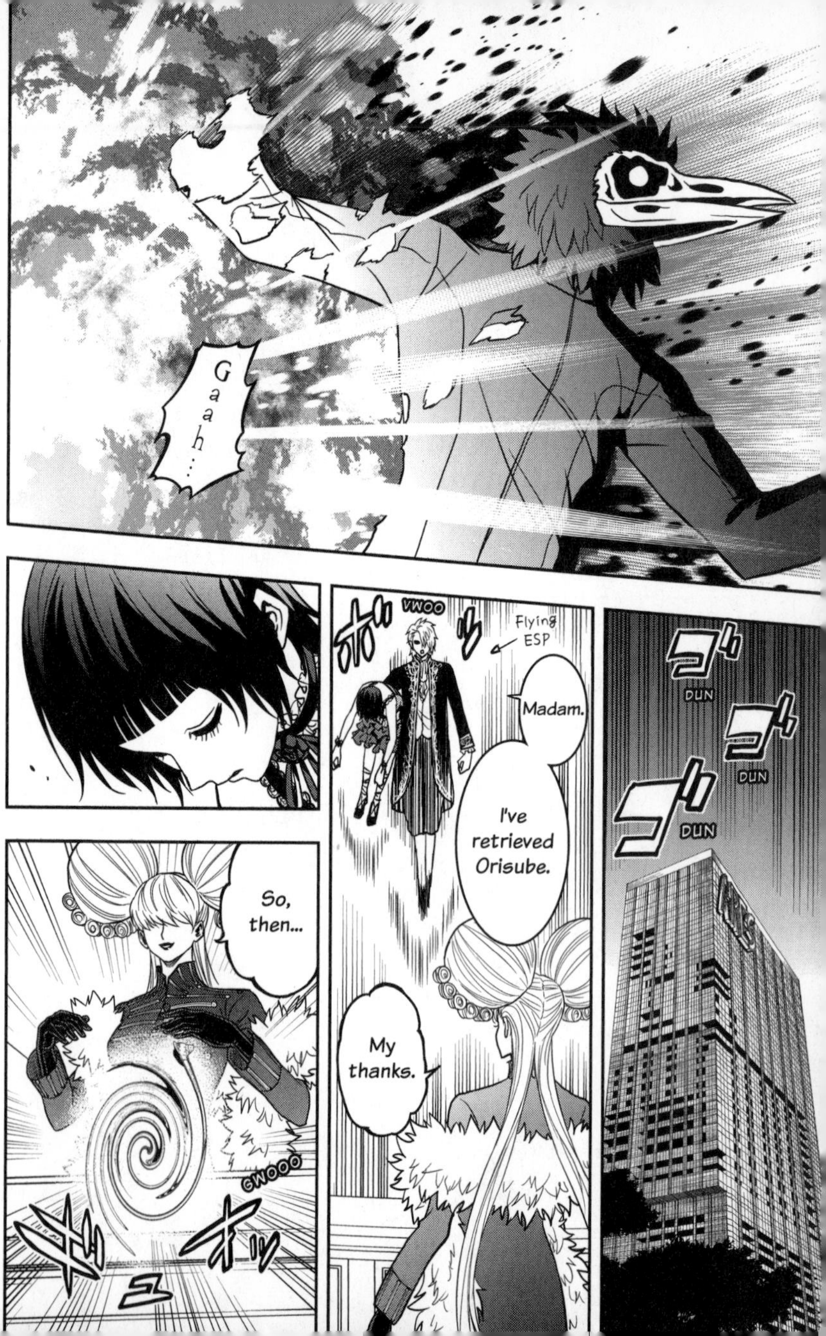
Gaah...
DUN
DUN
DUN
VWOO
Flying ESP
Madam.
I've retrieved Orisube.
My thanks.
So, then...
GWOOO

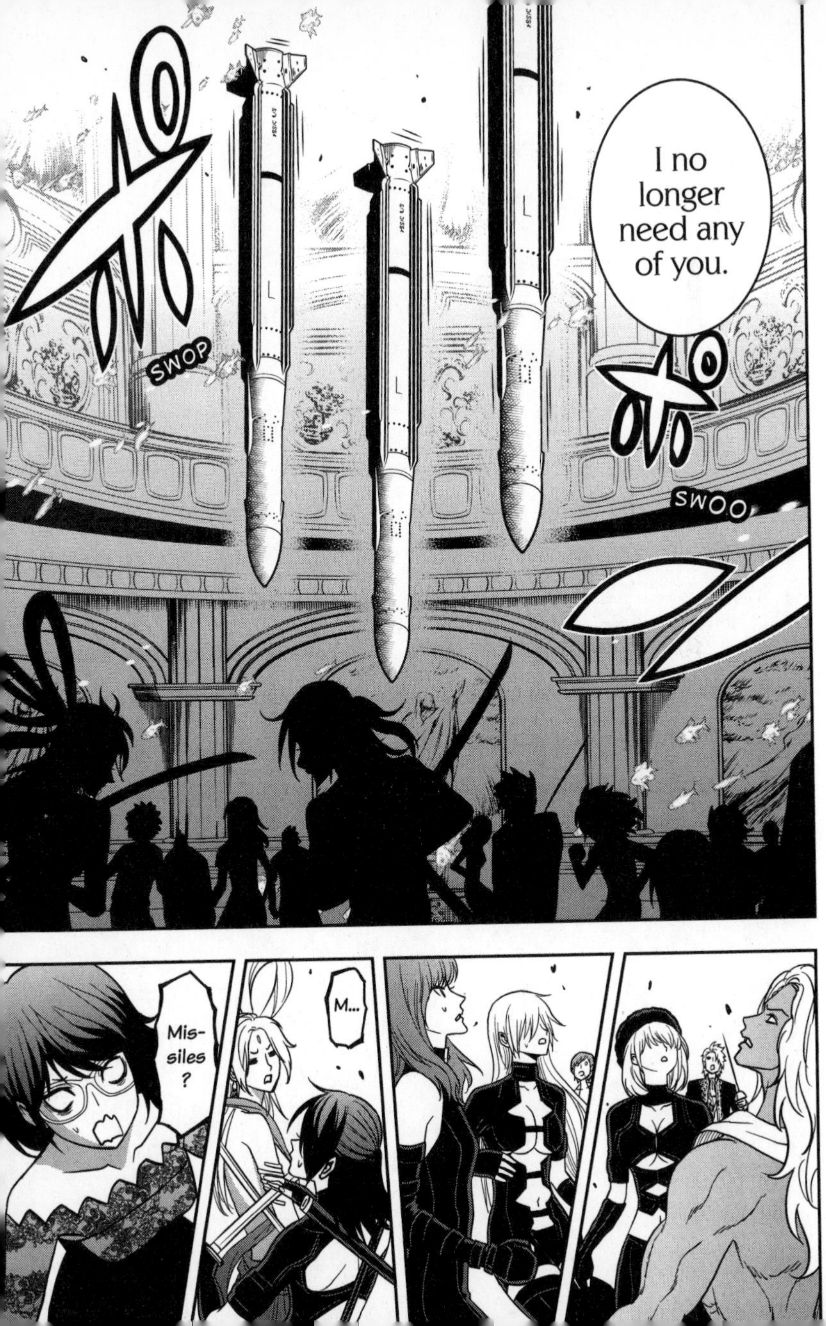
I no longer need any of you.
SWOO
SWOP
M...
Mis-siles?

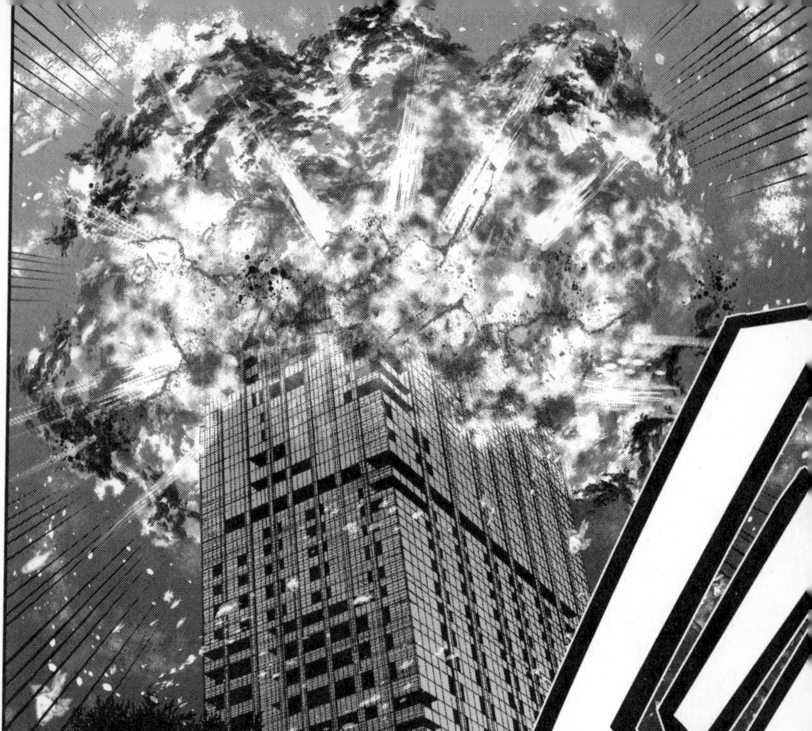
BOOOM
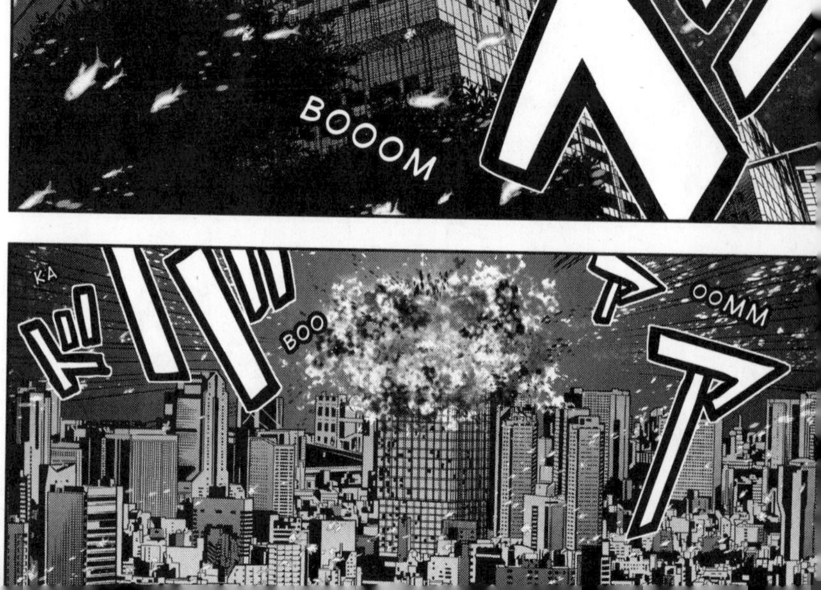
KA BOO OOMM

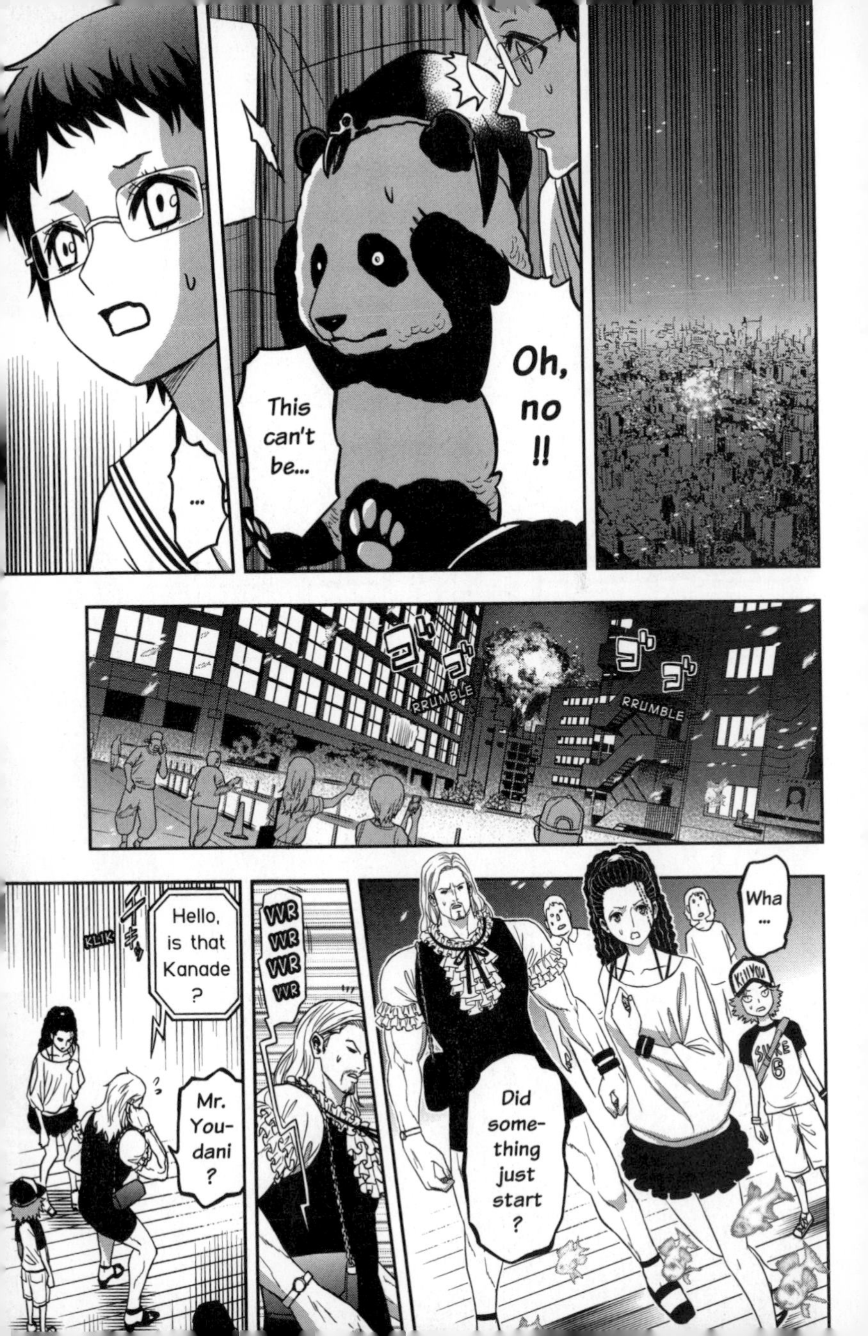
Oh, no !!
This can't be...
...
RRUMBLE
RRUMBLE
Wha...
Did something just start?
VVR VVR VVR VVR
Hello, is that Kanade?
KLIK
Mr. You-dani?

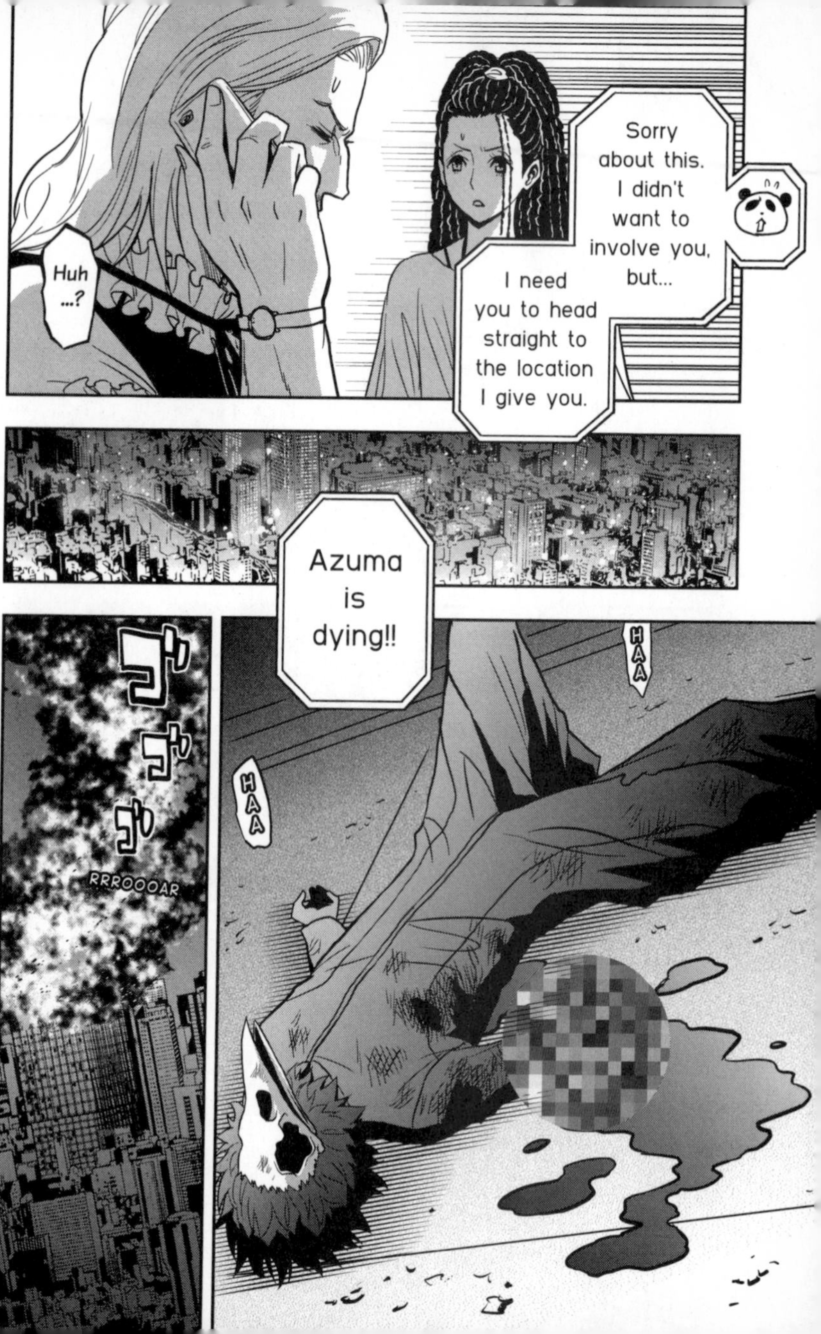
Sorry about this. I didn't want to involve you, but...
I need you to head straight to the location I give you.
Huh ...?
Azuma is dying!!
HAA
HAA
ゴゴゴゴ
RRROOOAR

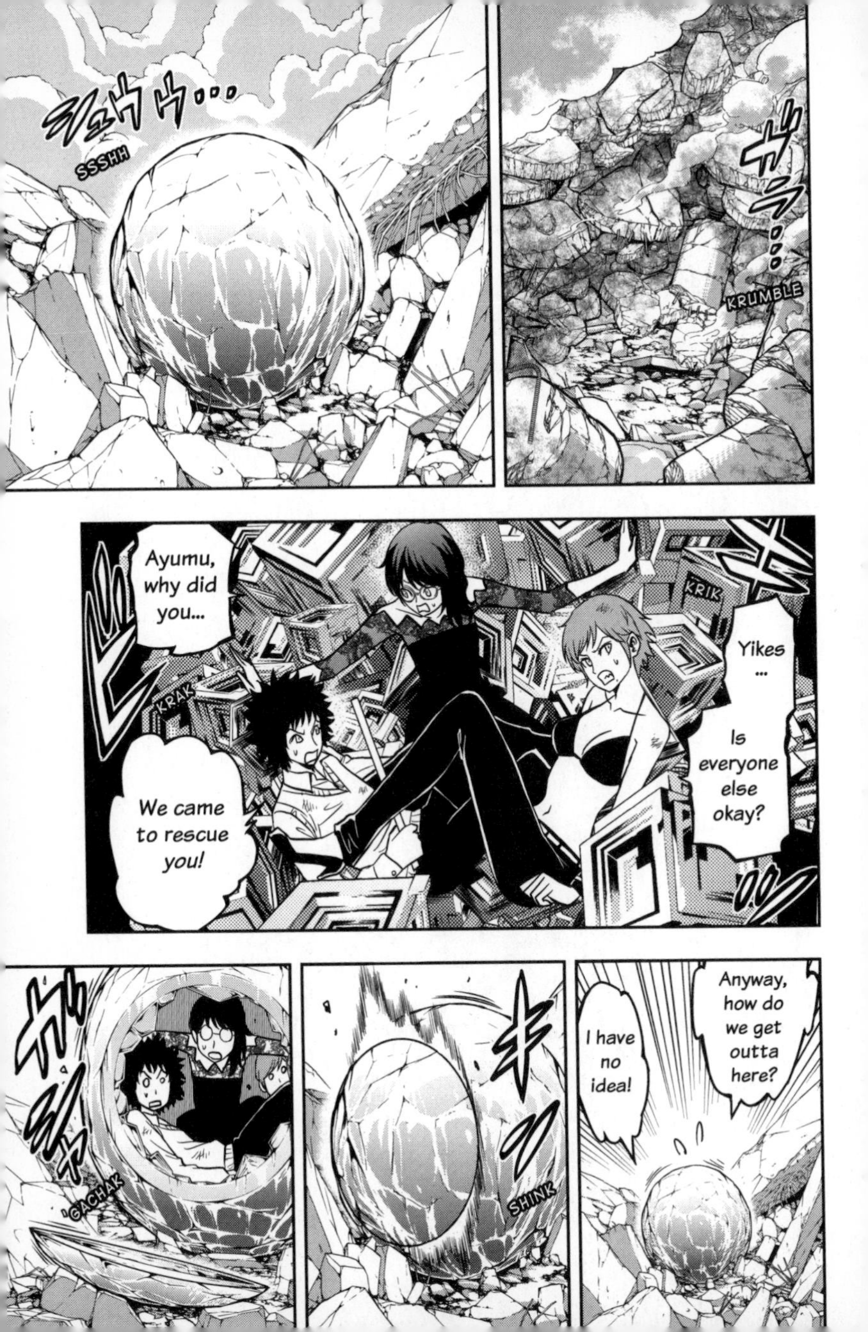
KRUMBLE
SSSHH
Yikes
...
Is everyone else okay?
KRIK
Ayumu, why did you...
KRAK
We came to rescue you!
Anyway, how do we get outta here?
I have no idea!
SHINK
GACHAK

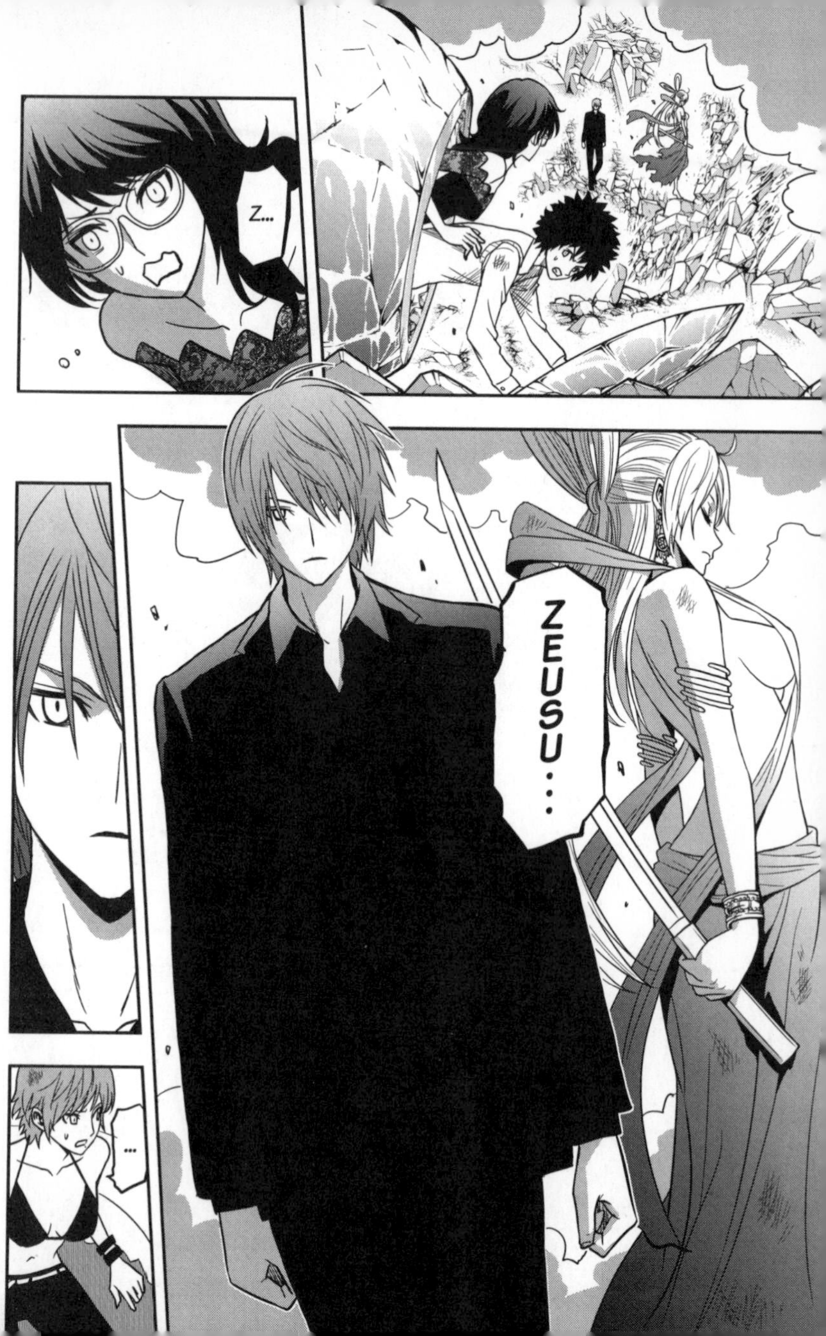
Z...
ZEUSU...
...

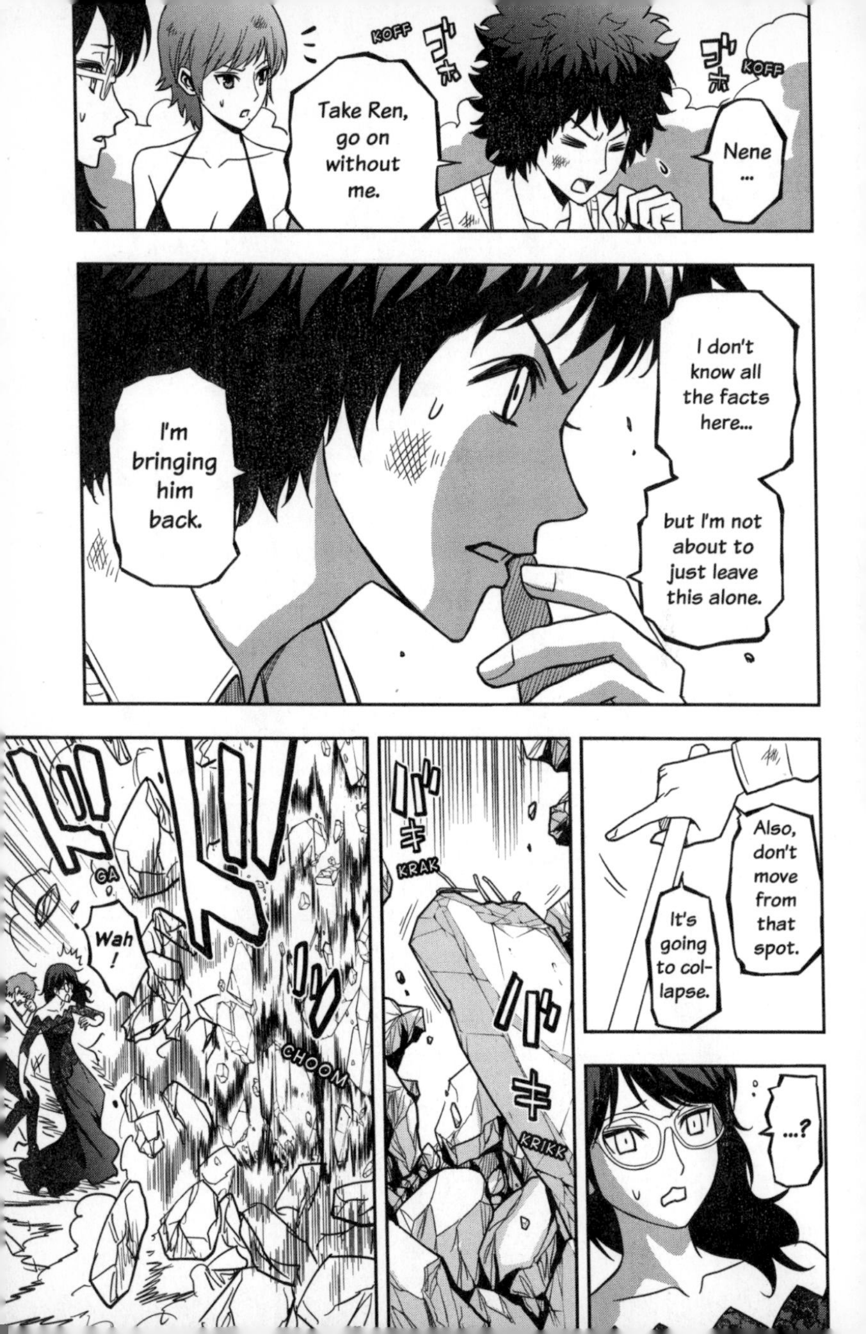
KOFF
Nene ...
KOFF
Take Ren, go on without me.
I don't know all the facts here...
but I'm not about to just leave this alone.
I'm bringing him back.
Also, don't move from that spot.
It's going to col-lapse.
...?
KRAK
KRIKK
GA
Wah!
CHOOM

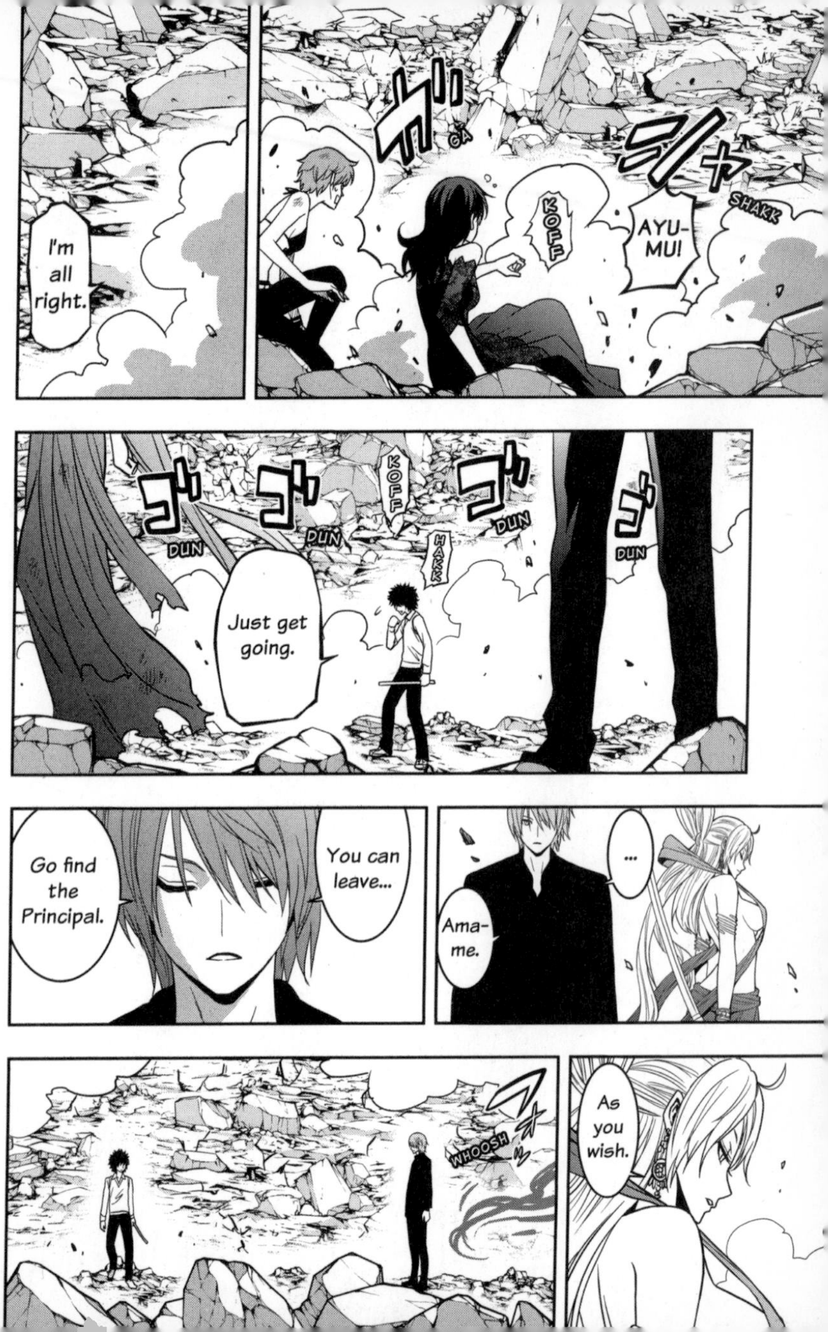
SHAKK
AYU-MU!
KOFF
GA
I'm all right.
DUN
DUN
KOFF
HAKK
DUN
Just get going.
DUN
...
Ama-me.
You can leave...
Go find the Principal.
As you wish.
WHOOSH

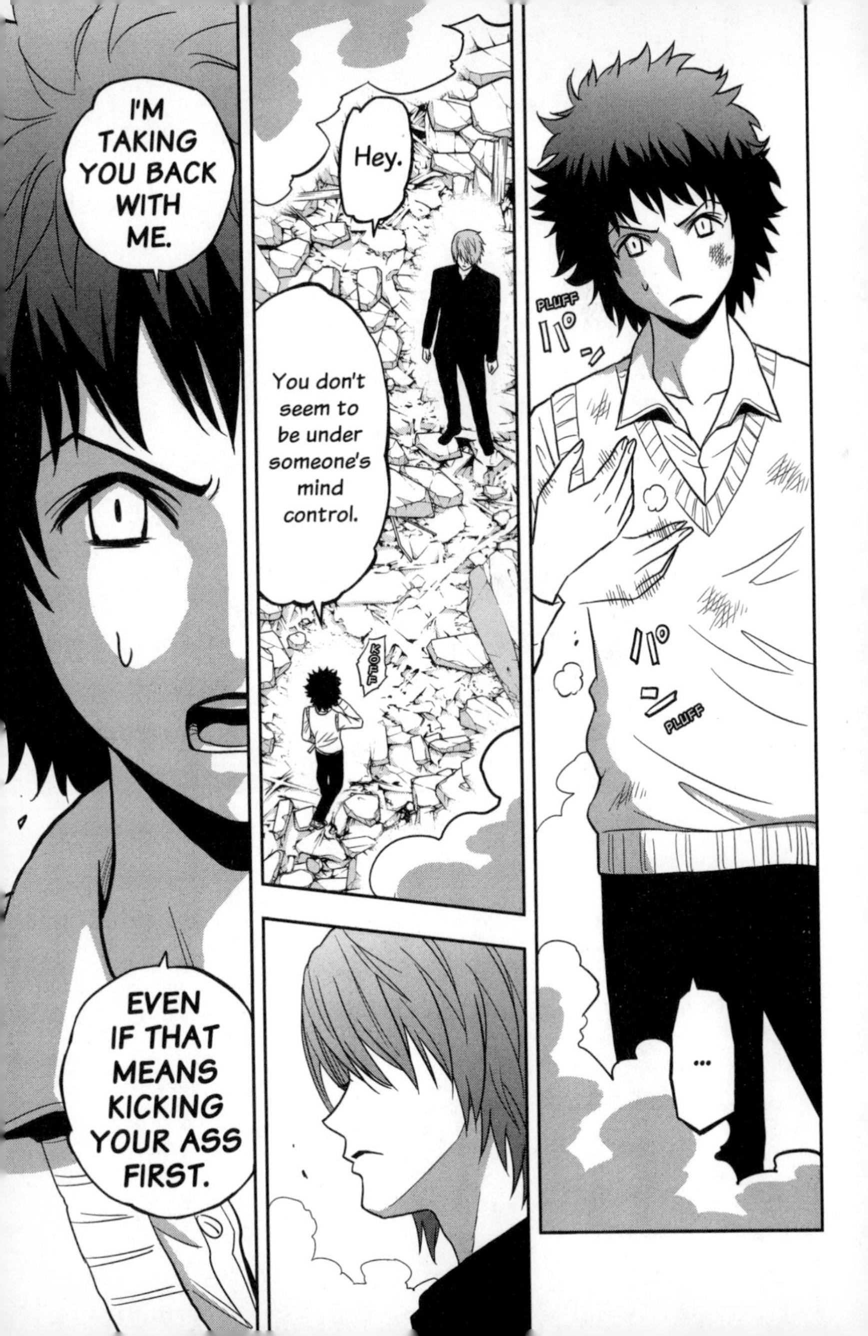
PLUFF
PLUFF
...
Hey.
You don't seem to be under someone's mind control.
KOFF
I'M TAKING YOU BACK WITH ME.
EVEN IF THAT MEANS KICKING YOUR ASS FIRST.

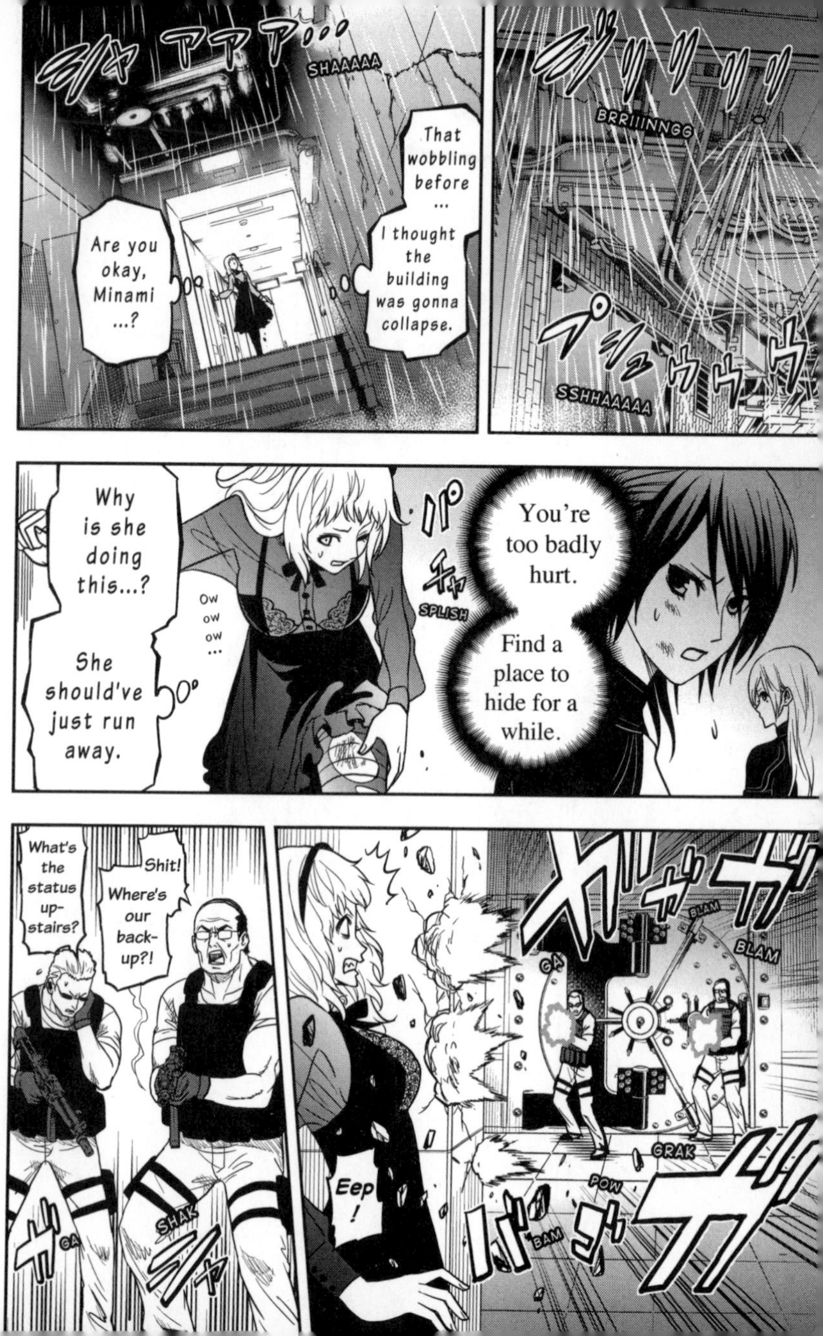
BRRIIINNGG
SSHHAAAAA
SHAAAAA
That wobbling before ... I thought the building was gonna collapse.
Are you okay, Minami ...?
You're too badly hurt.
Find a place to hide for a while.
SPLISH
Ow ow ow ...
Why is she doing this...?
She should've just run away.
BLAM
BLAM
GA
GRAK
POW
BAM
Eep!
Shit!
Where's our back-up?!
What's the status up-stairs?
SHAK
GA

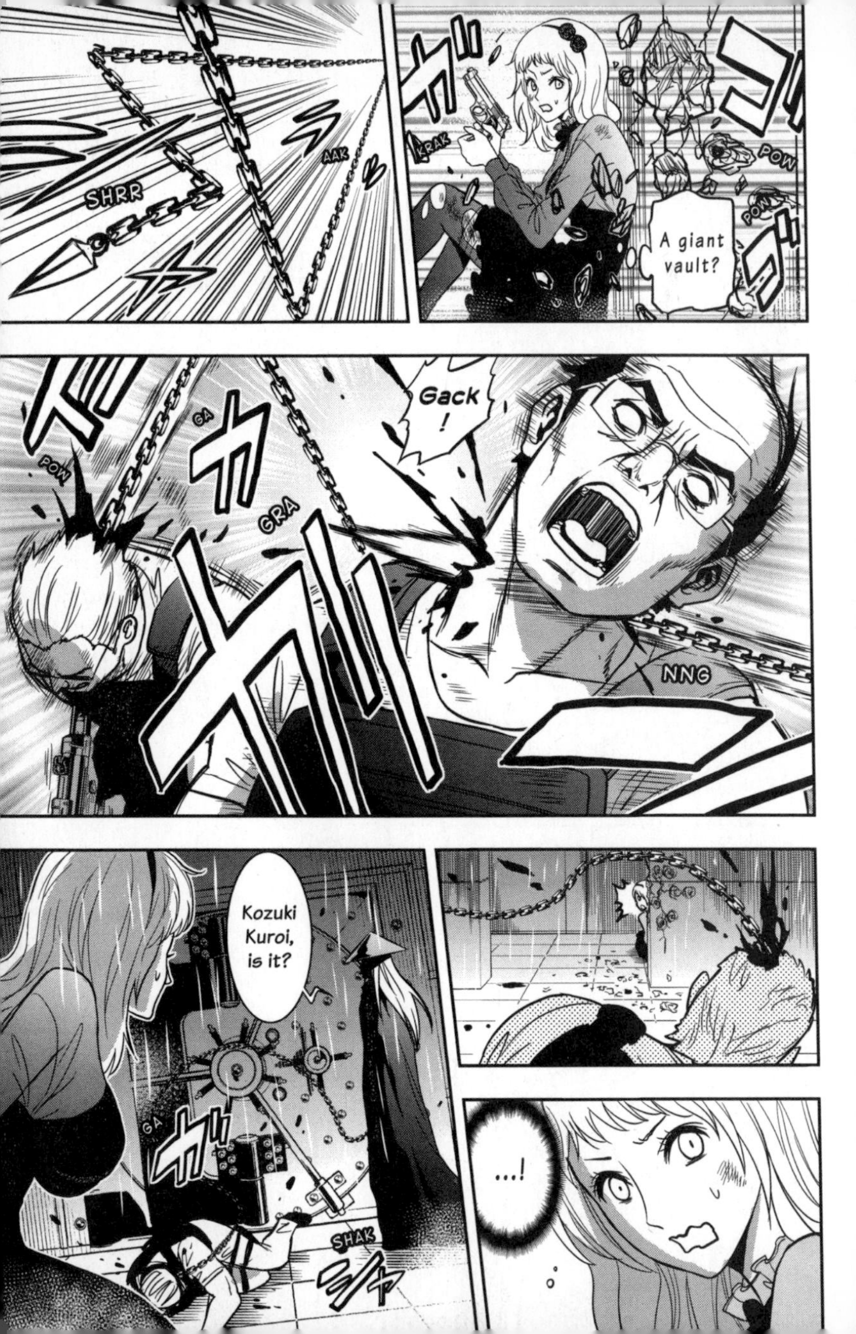
POW
POW
A giant vault?
KRAK
AAK
SHRR
Gack!
NNG
GA
GRA
POW
...!
Kozuki Kuroi, is it?
SHAK
GA

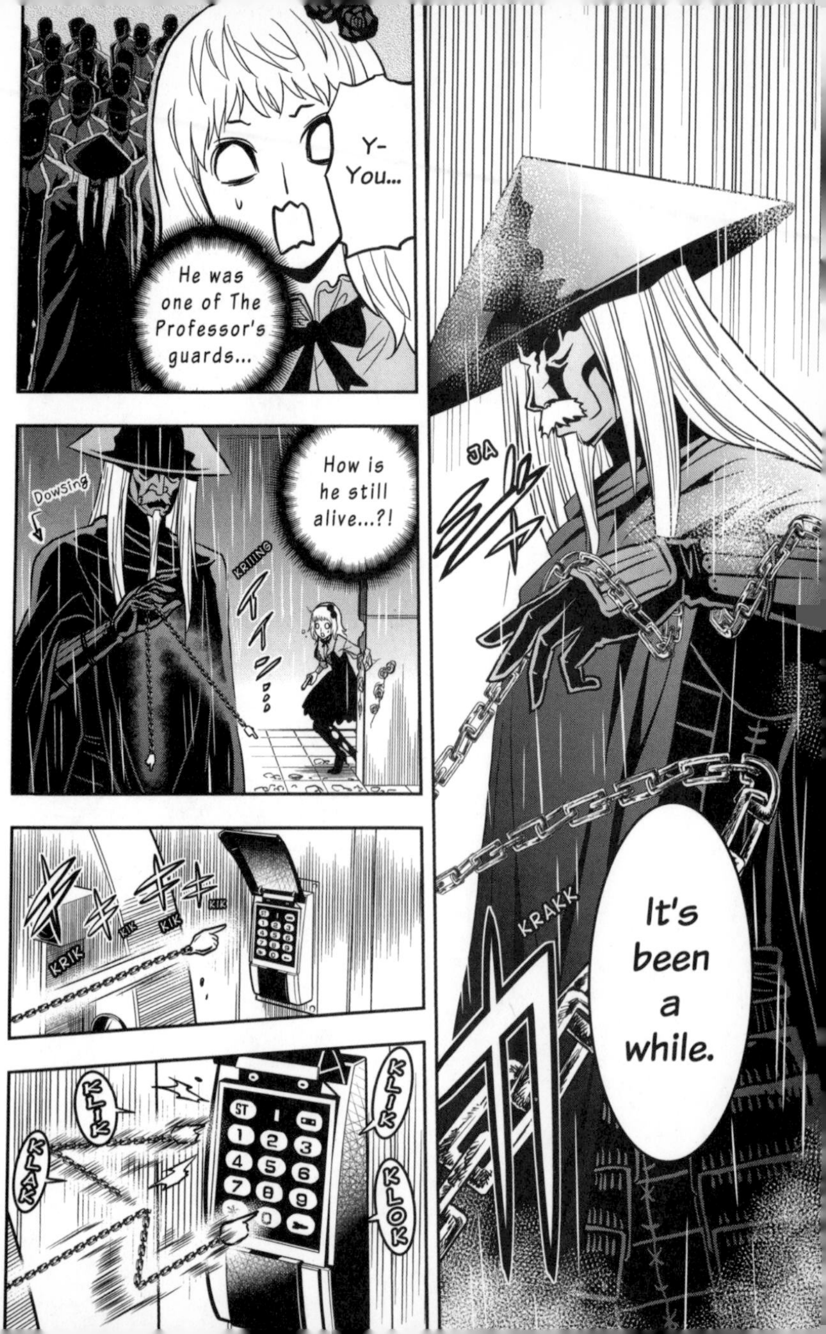
JA
KRAKK
It's been a while.
Y- You...
He was one of The Professor's guards...
How is he still alive...?!
KRIIING
Dowsing
KIK
KIK
KIK
KRIK
KLIK
KLOK
KLIK
KLAK

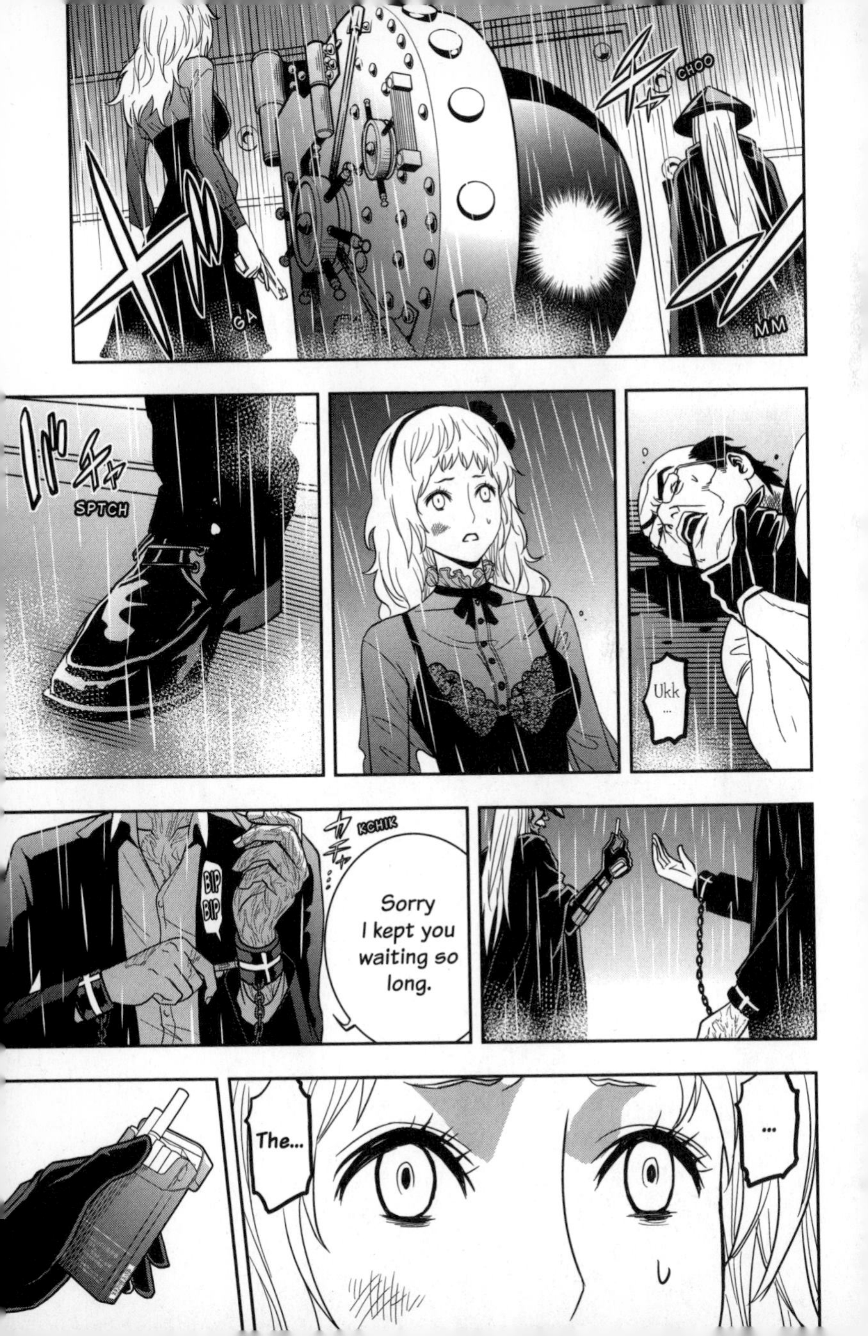
CHOO
MM
GA
Ukk ...
SPTCH
KCHIK
Sorry I kept you waiting so long.
BIP BIP
...
The...

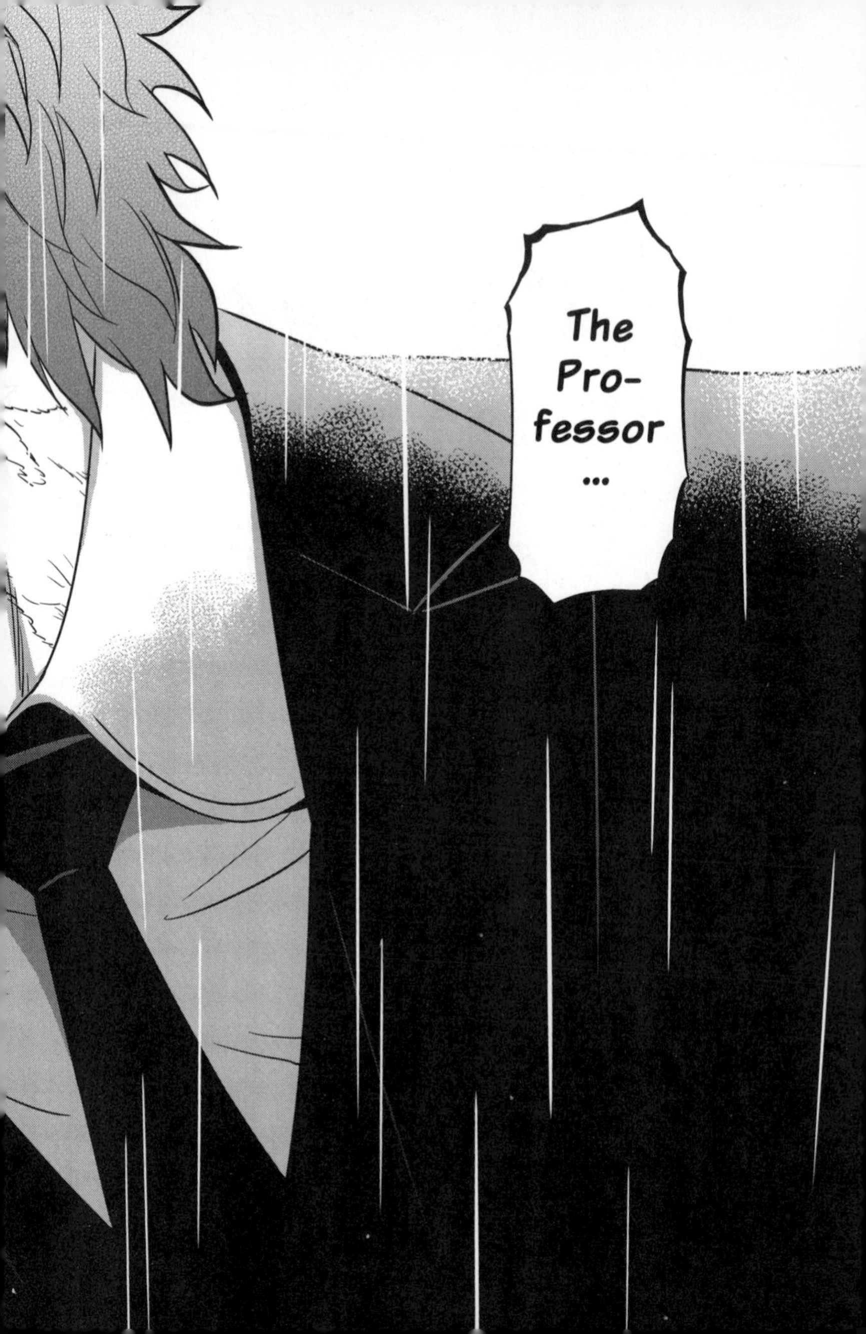
The Pro-fessor...

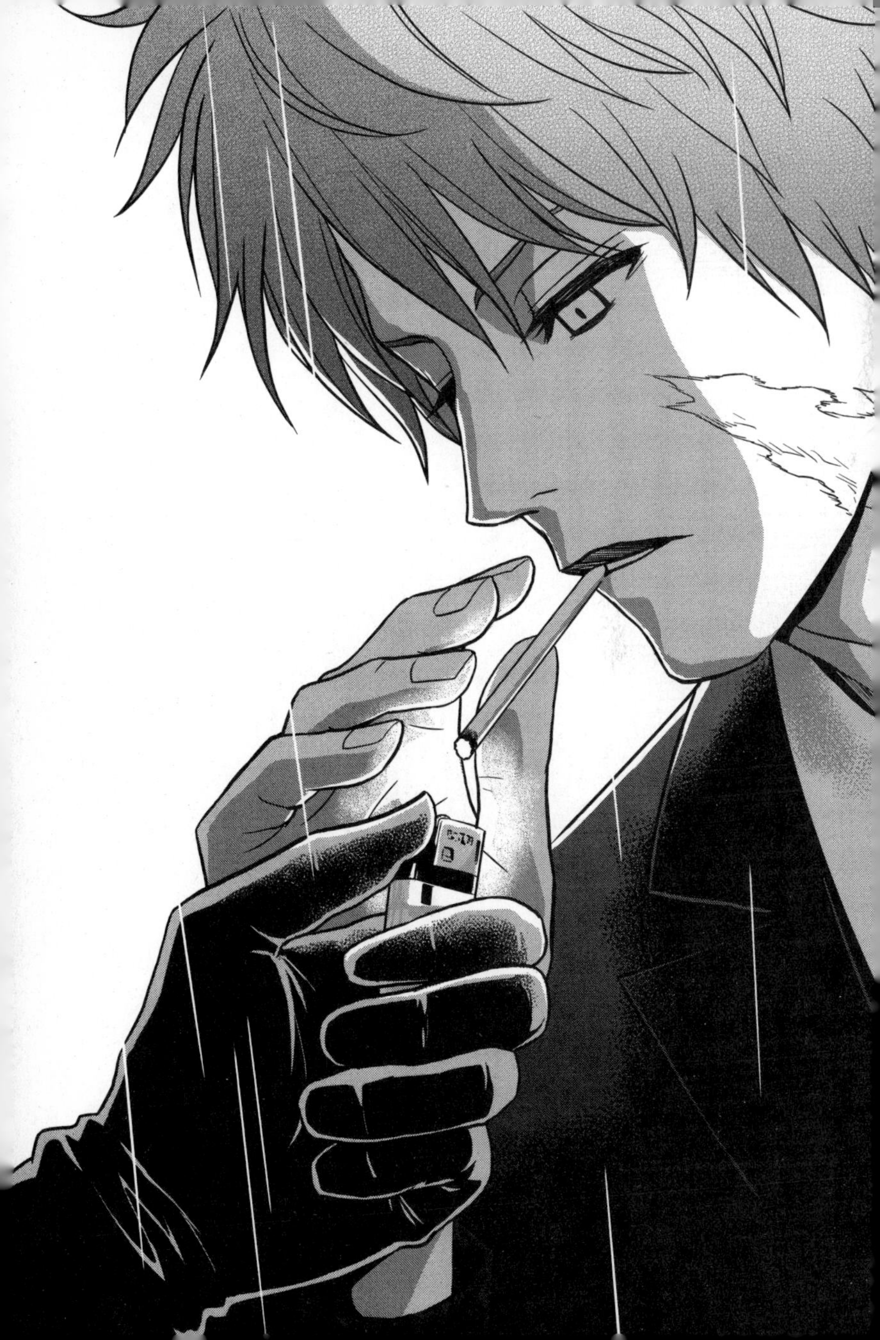

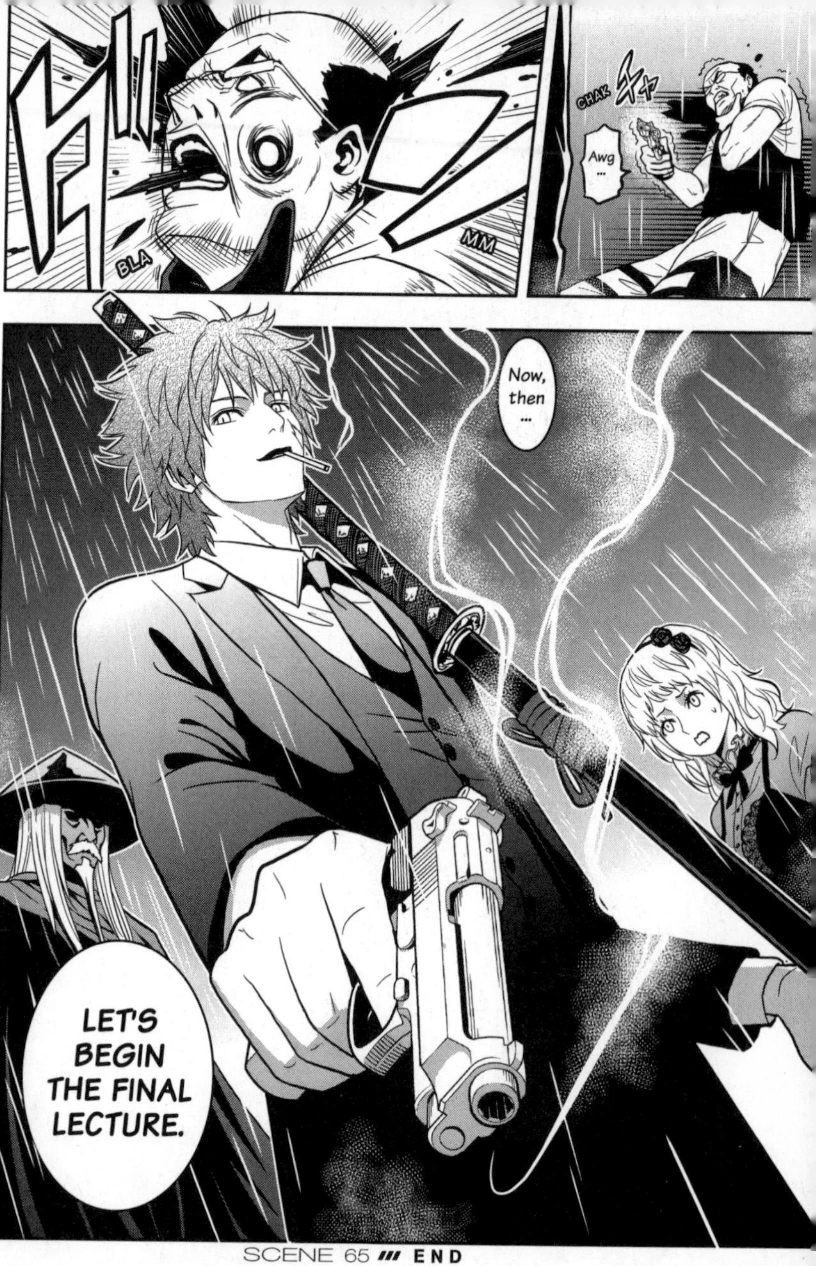
CHAK
Awg ...
BLA
MM
Now, then ...
LET'S BEGIN THE FINAL LECTURE.

SCENE 65 /// END

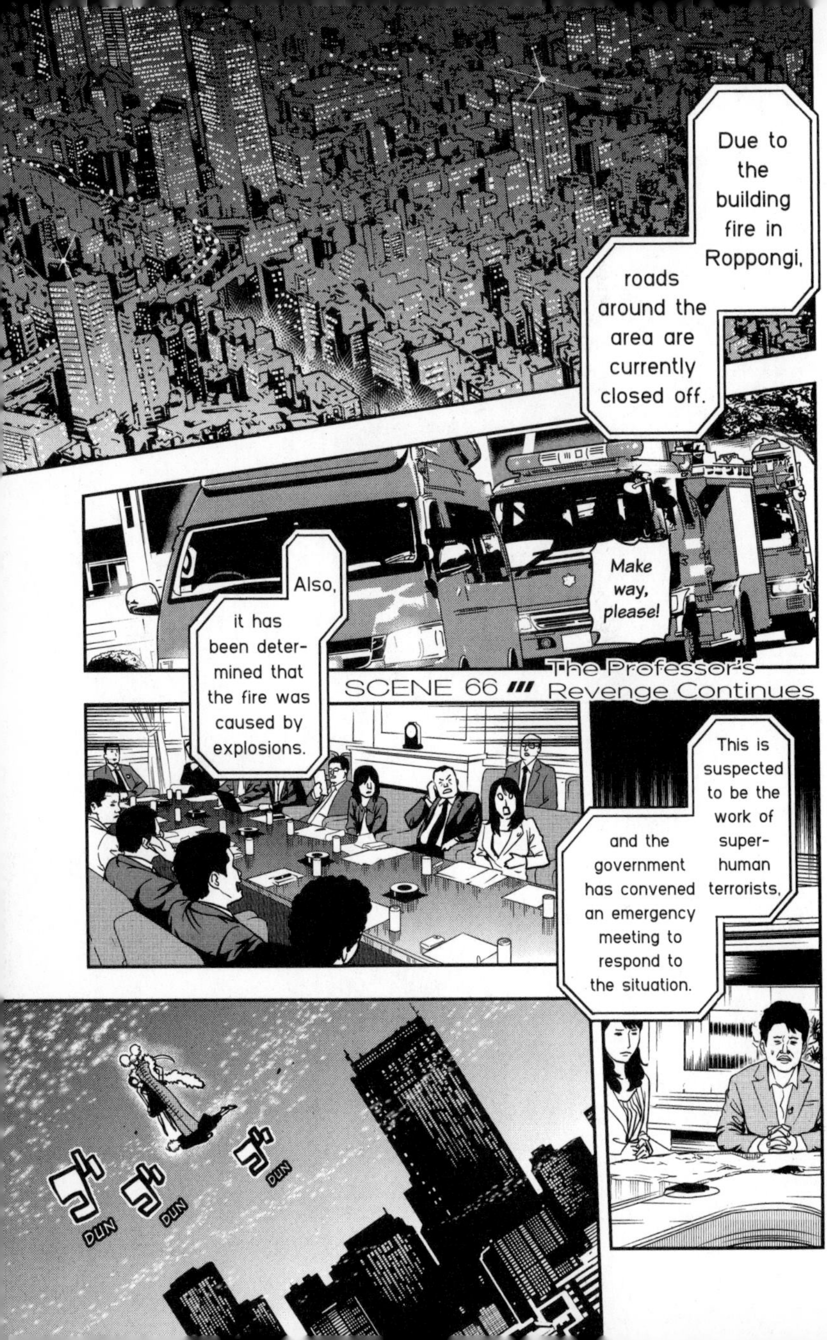
Due to the building fire in Roppongi,
roads around the area are currently closed off.
Make way, please!
Also,
it has been determined that the fire was caused by explosions.
SCENE 66 The Professor's Revenge Continues
This is suspected to be the work of super-human terrorists,
and the government has convened an emergency meeting to respond to the situation.
DUN
DUN
DUN

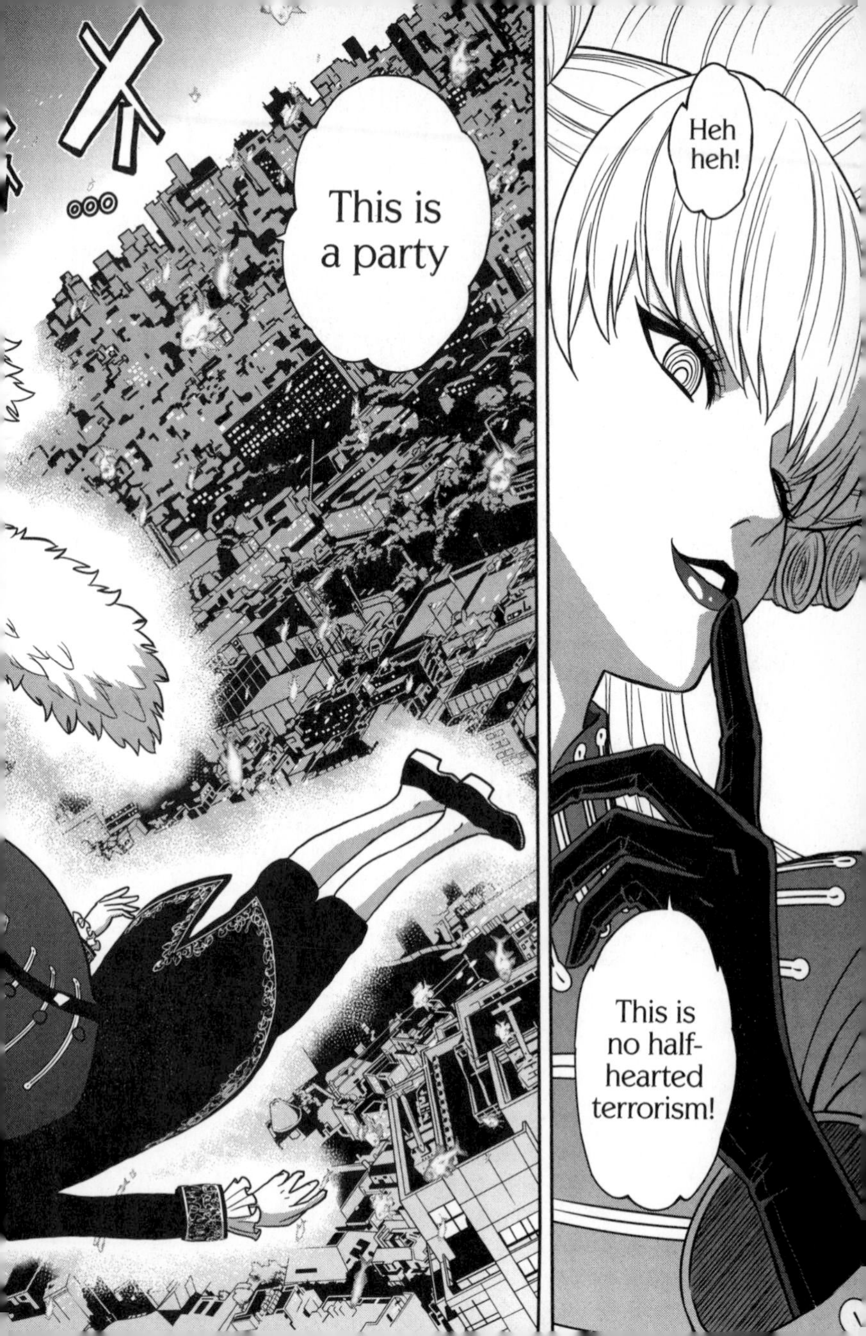
Heh heh!
This is no half-hearted terrorism!
This is a party

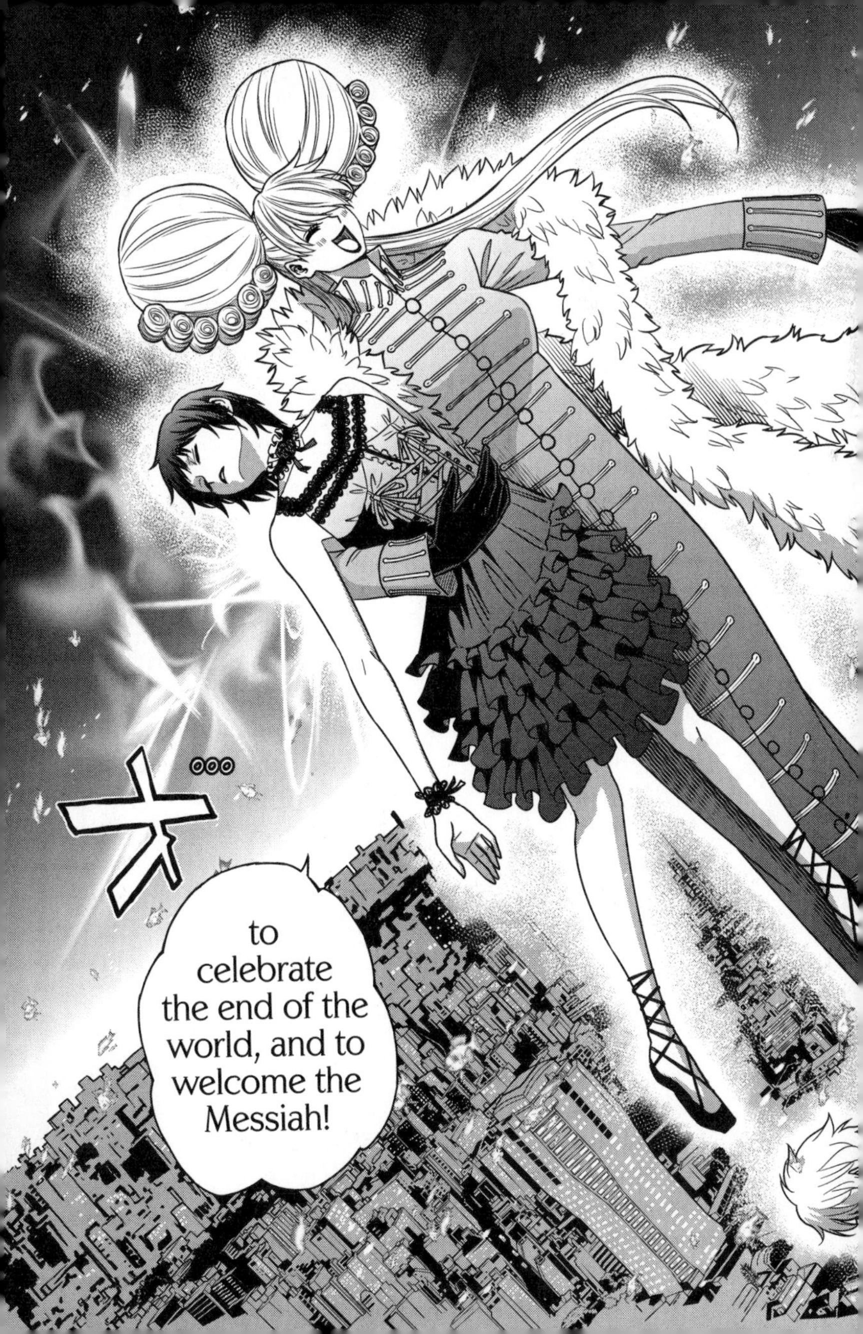
to celebrate the end of the world, and to welcome the Messiah!

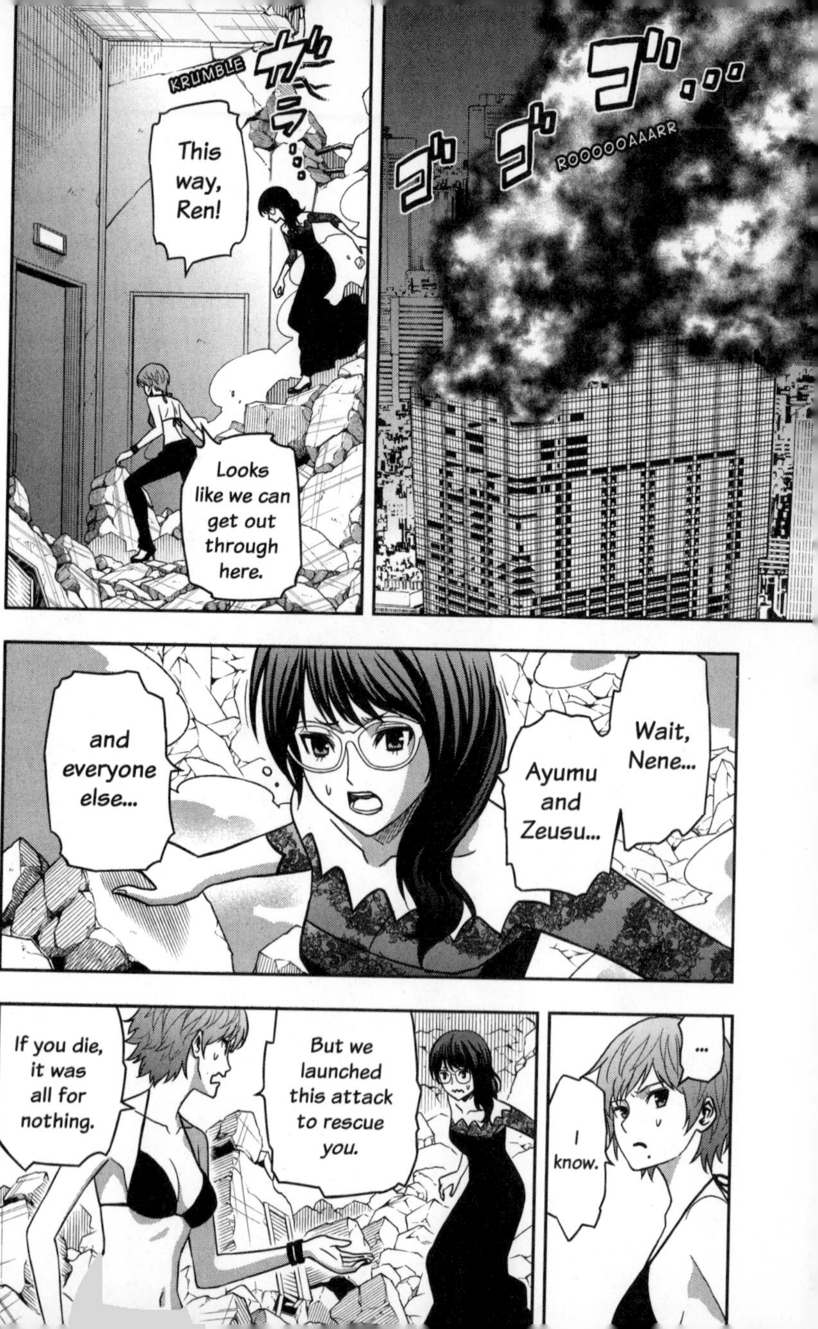
ROOOOOAAARR
KRUMBLE
This way, Ren!
Looks like we can get out through here.
Wait, Nene...
Ayumu and Zeusu...
and everyone else...
...
I know.
But we launched this attack to rescue you.
If you die, it was all for nothing.

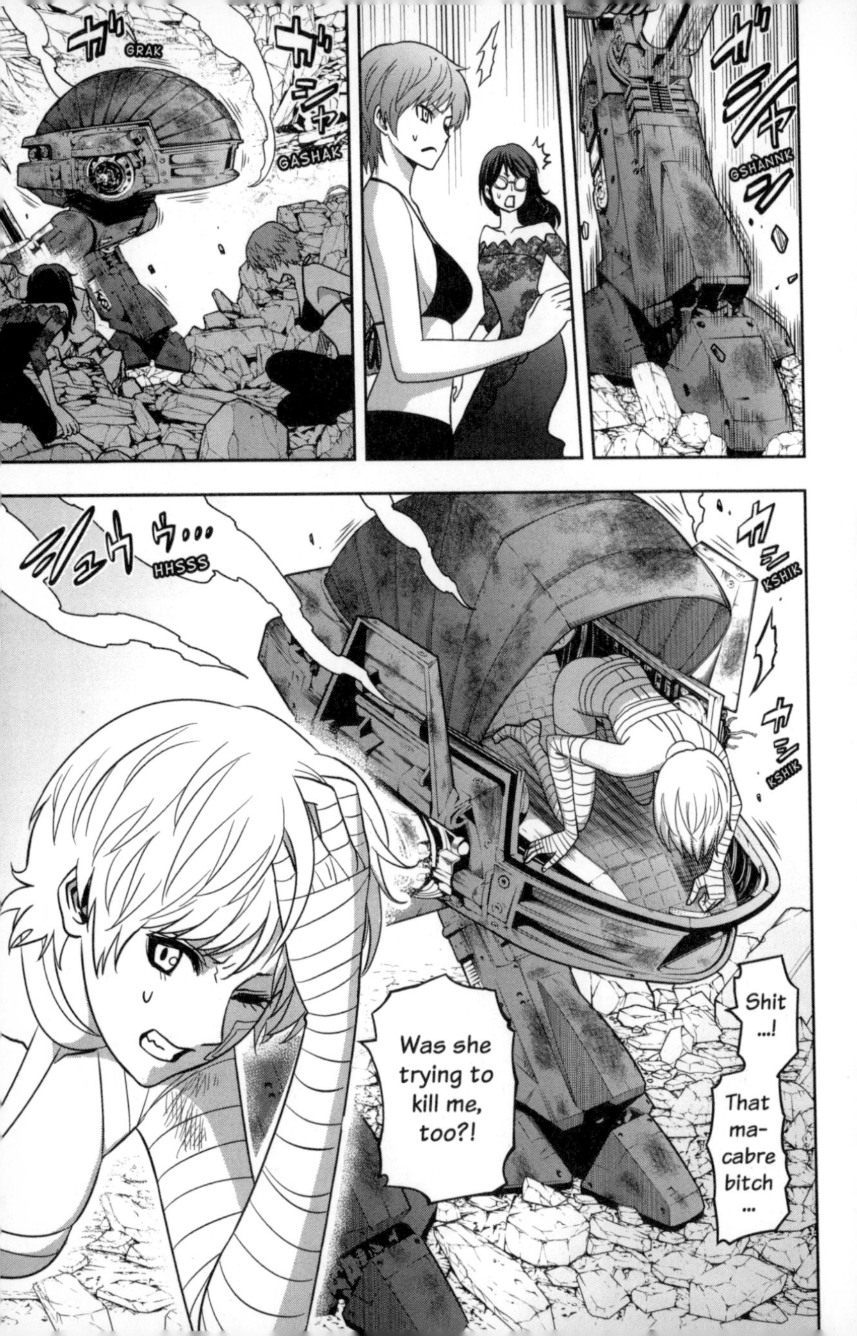
GSHANNK
GRAK
GASHAK
KSHIK
KSHIK
HHSSS
Shit ...! That ma-cabre bitch ...
Was she trying to kill me, too?!

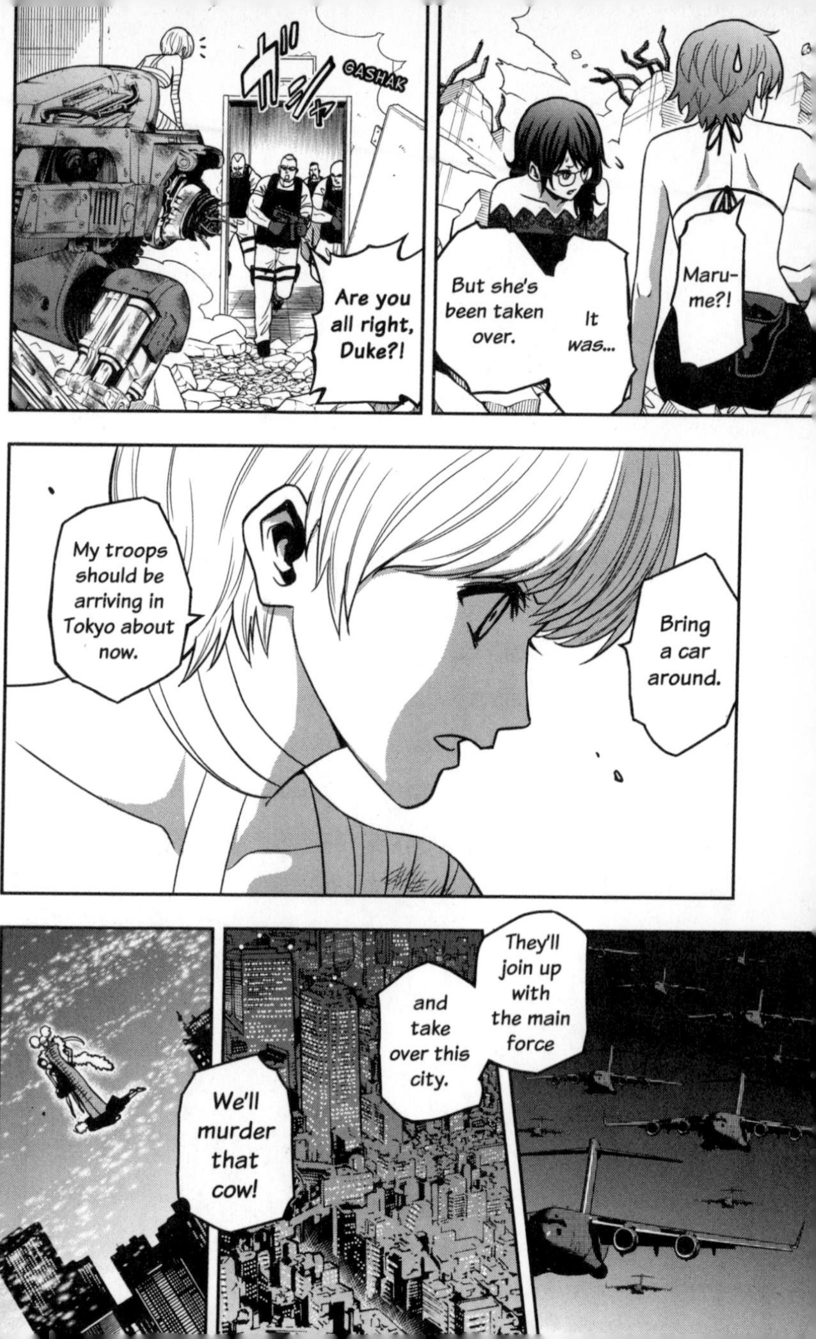
Maru-me?!
It was...
But she's been taken over.
GASHAK
Are you all right, Duke?!
Bring a car around.
My troops should be arriving in Tokyo about now.
They'll join up with the main force
and take over this city.
We'll murder that cow!

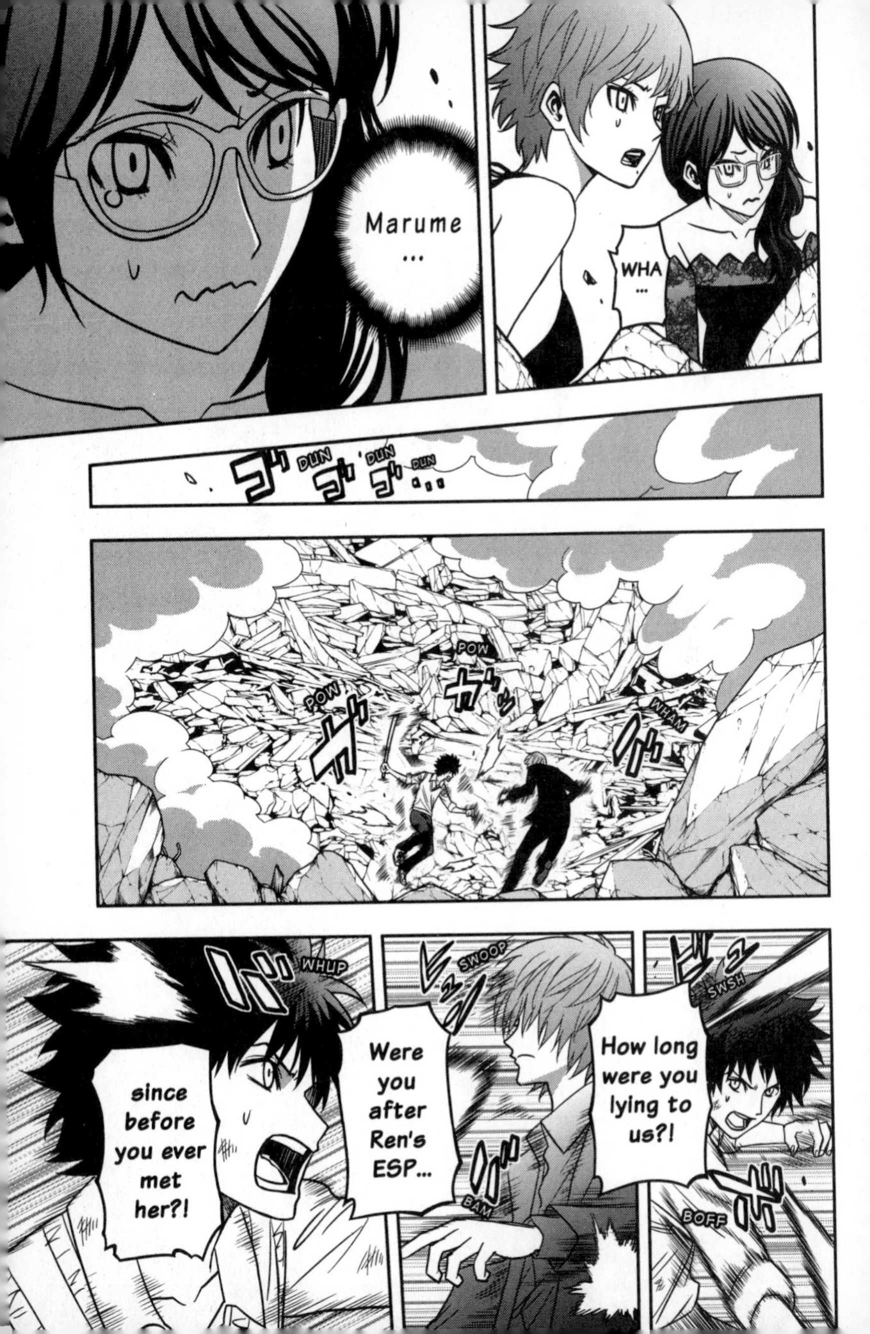
WHA ...
Marume ...
DUN
DUN
DUN
POW
WHAM
POW
SWSH
How long were you lying to us?!
BOFF
SWOOP
Were you after Ren's ESP...
BAM
WHUP
since before you ever met her?!

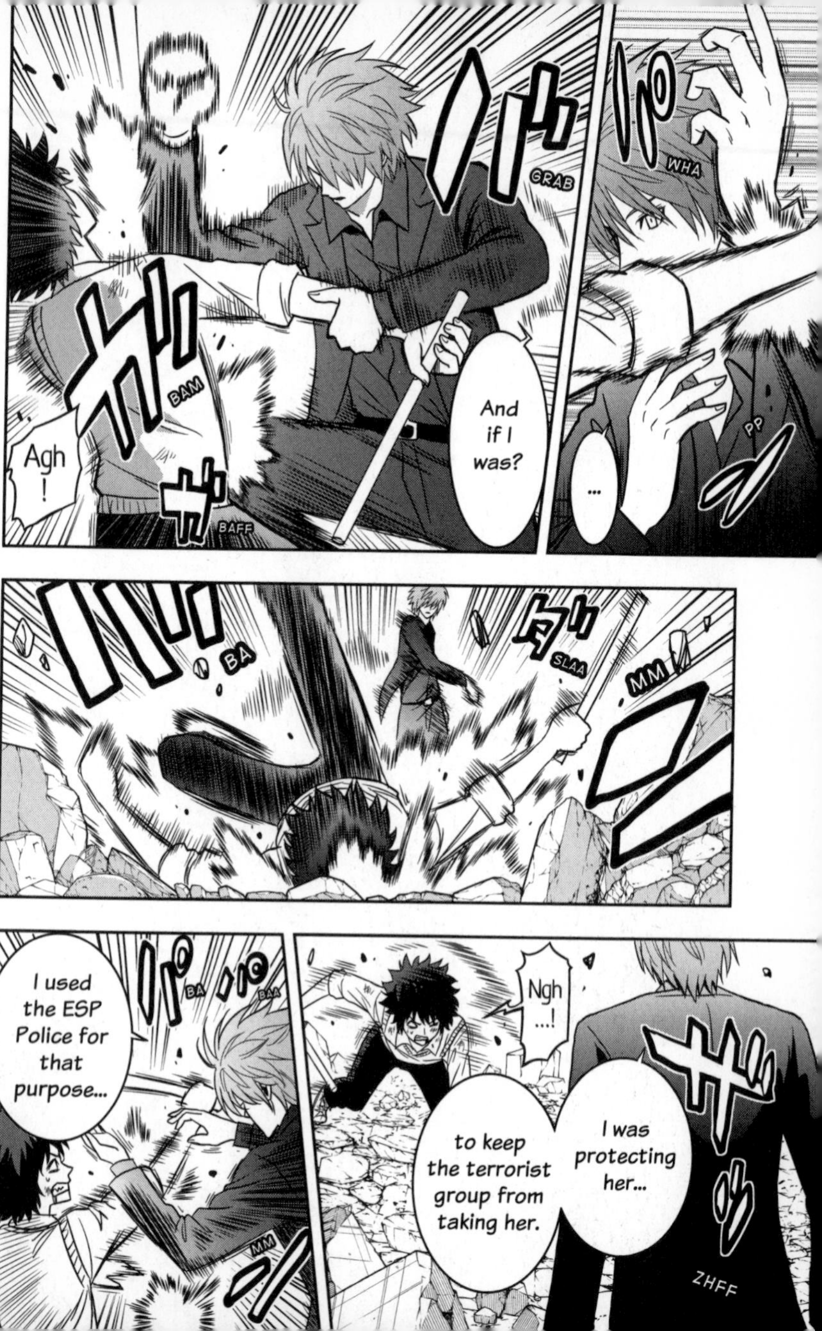
WHA
PP
...
GRAB
And if I was?
BAM
Agh!
BAFF
MM
SLAA
BA
Ngh...!
I was protecting her...
to keep the terrorist group from taking her.
ZHFF
BAA
BA
I used the ESP Police for that purpose...
MM

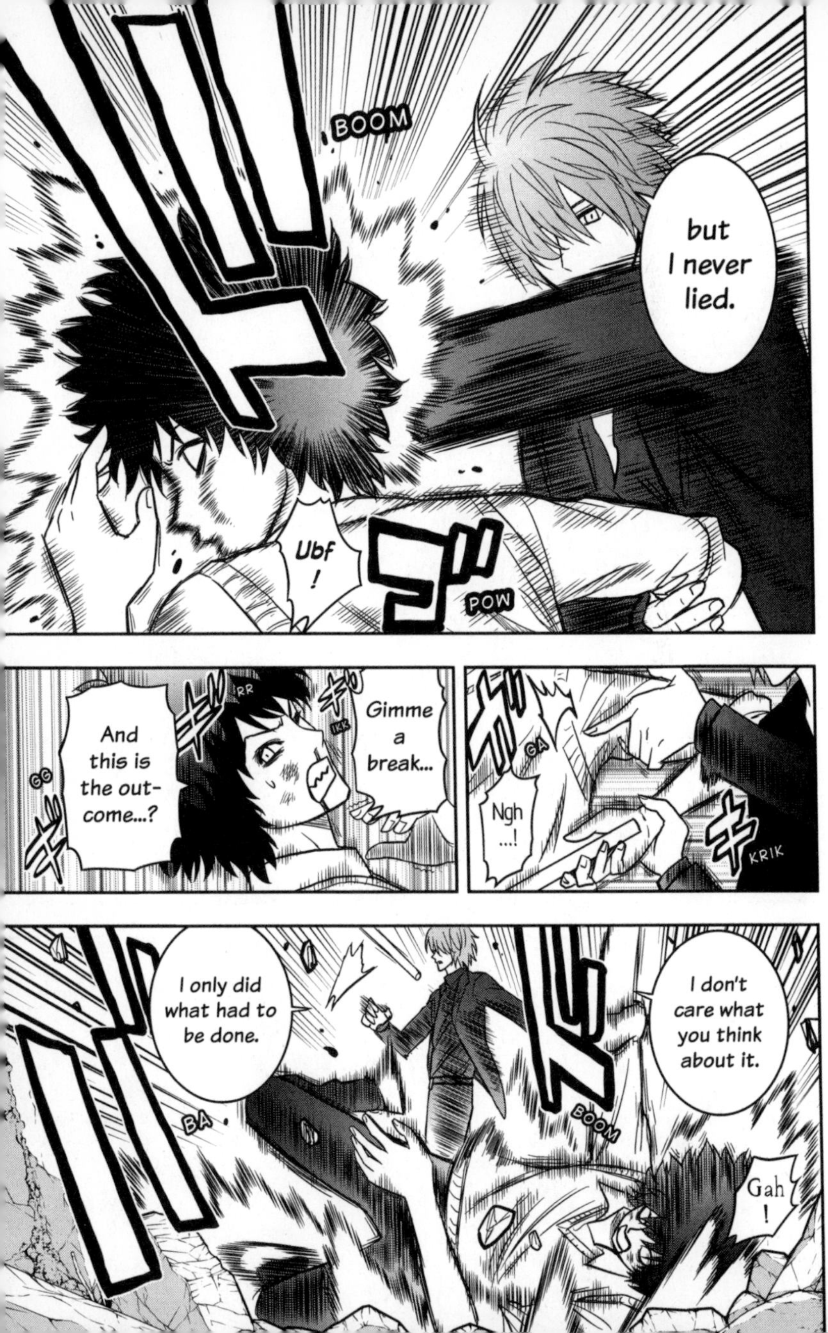
but I never lied.
BOOM
Ubf !
POW
GA
Ngh ...!
KRIK
Gimme a break...
IKK
RR
And this is the out-come...?
GG
I don't care what you think about it.
BOOM
Gah !
I only did what had to be done.
BA

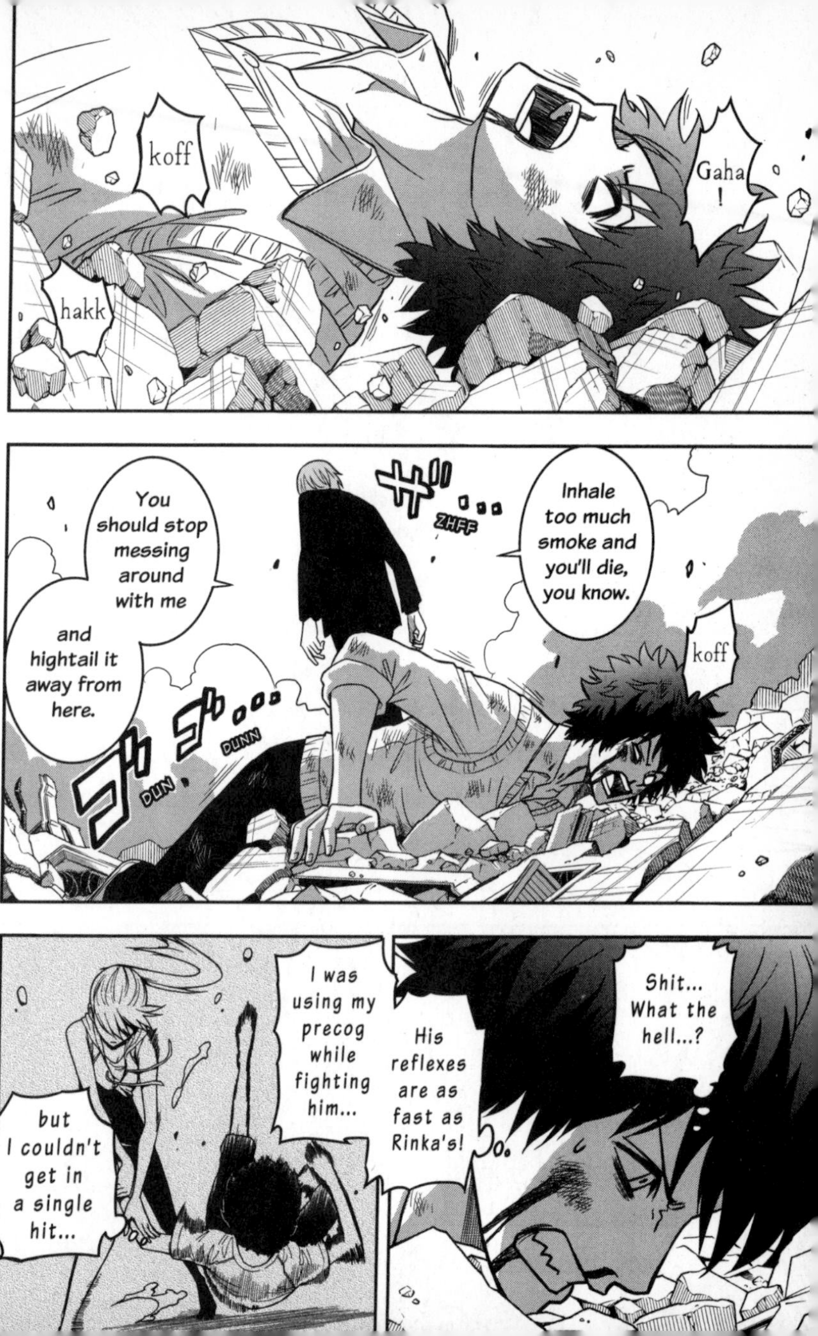
Gaha !
koff
hakk
Inhale too much smoke and you'll die, you know.
ZHFF
You should stop messing around with me
koff
and hightail it away from here.
DUNN
DUN
Shit... What the hell...?
I was using my precog while fighting him...
but I couldn't get in a single hit...
His reflexes are as fast as Rinka's!

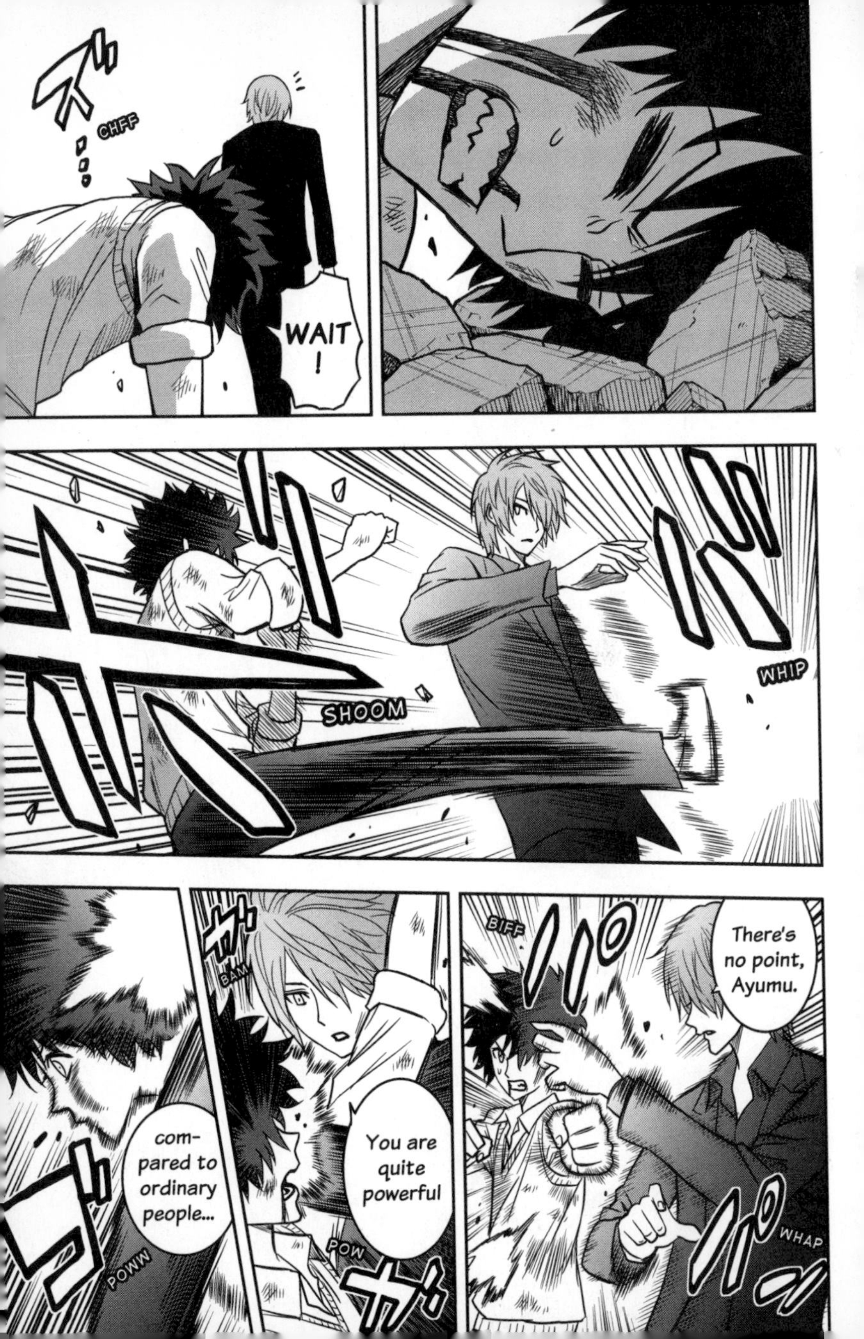
CHFF
WAIT!
WHIP
SHOOM
BIFF
There's no point, Ayumu.
WHAP
BAM
You are quite powerful
POW
com-pared to ordinary people...
POWW

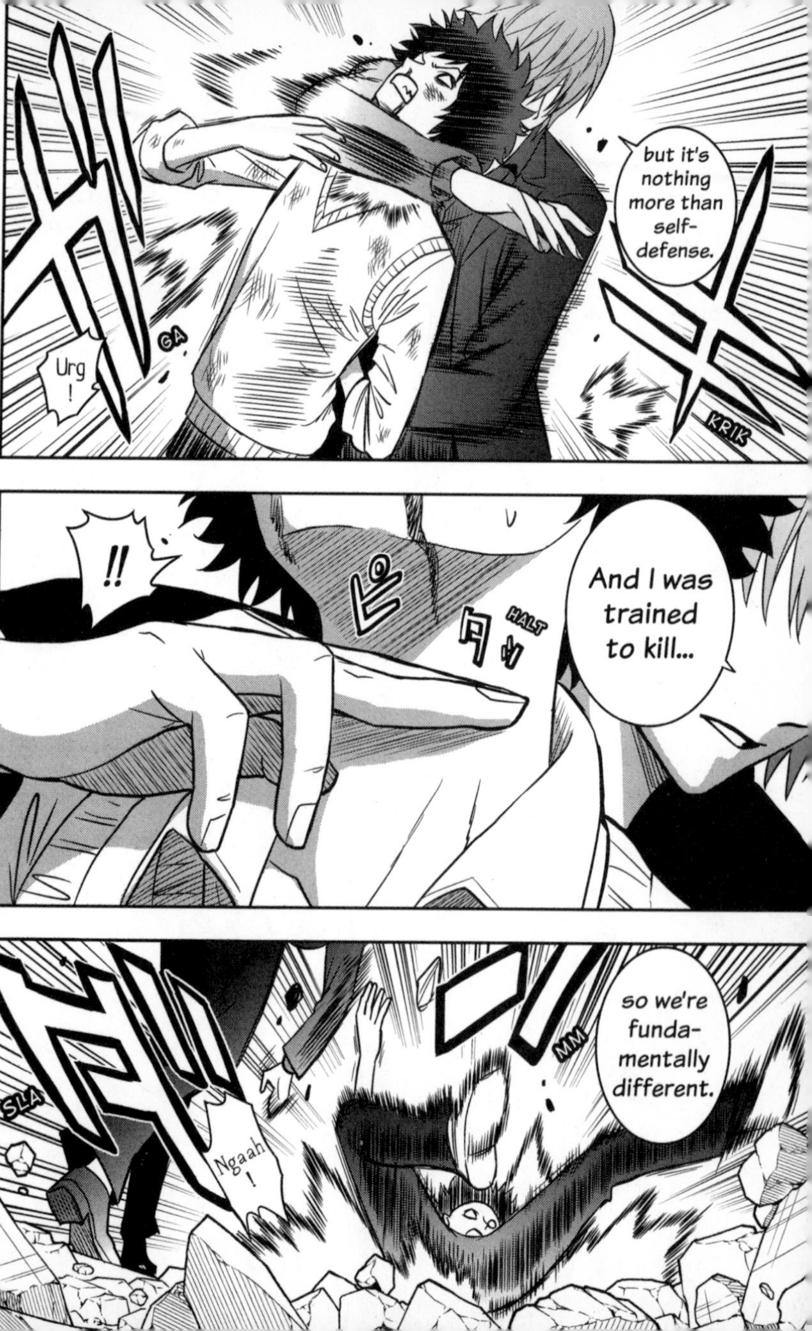
but it's nothing more than self-defense.
KRIK
GA
Urg!
And I was trained to kill...
HALT
!!
so we're funda-mentally different.
MM
SLA
Ngaah!

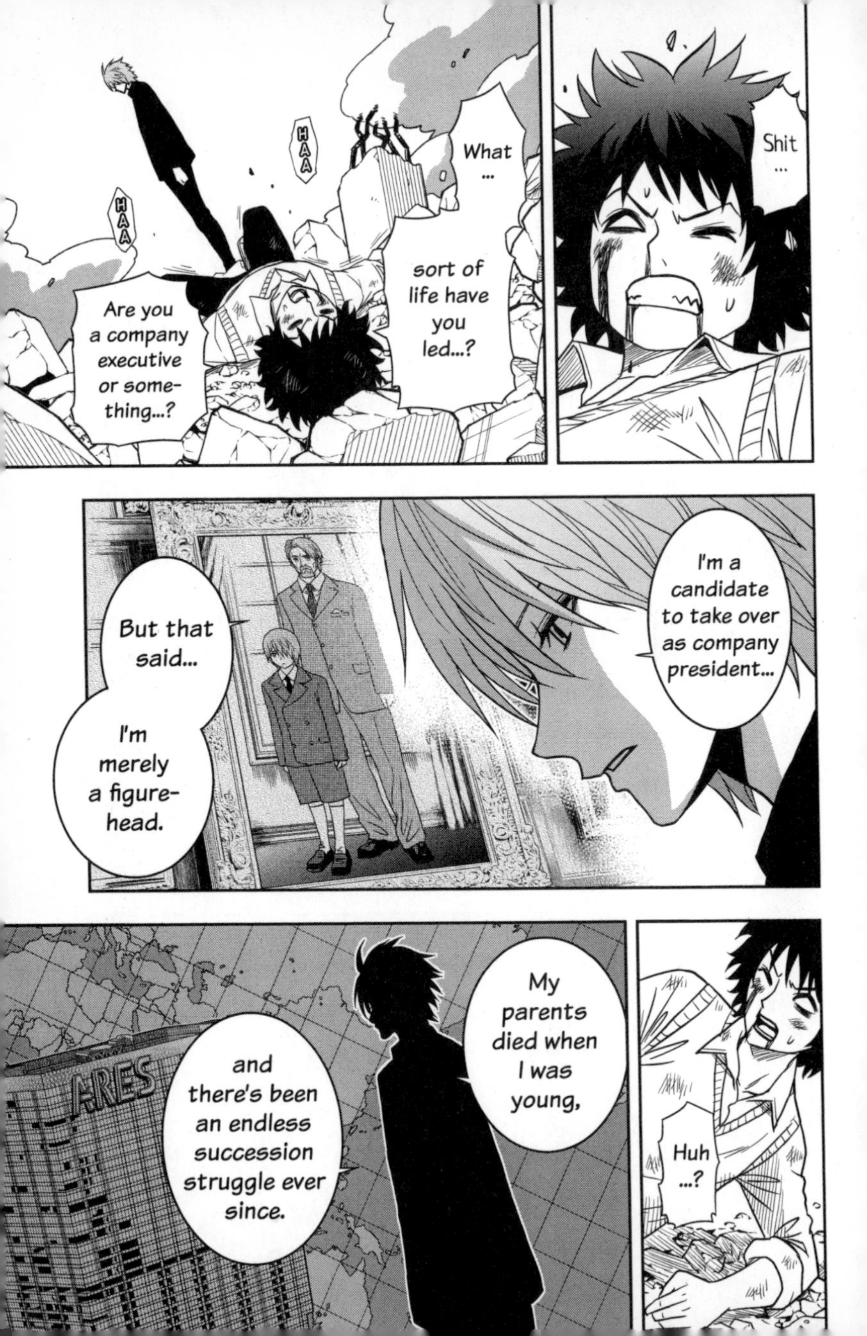
Shit ...
What ...
HAA
sort of life have you led...?
HAA
Are you a company executive or some-thing...?
I'm a candidate to take over as company president...
But that said...
I'm merely a figure-head.
Huh ...?
My parents died when I was young,
and there's been an endless succession struggle ever since.
ARES

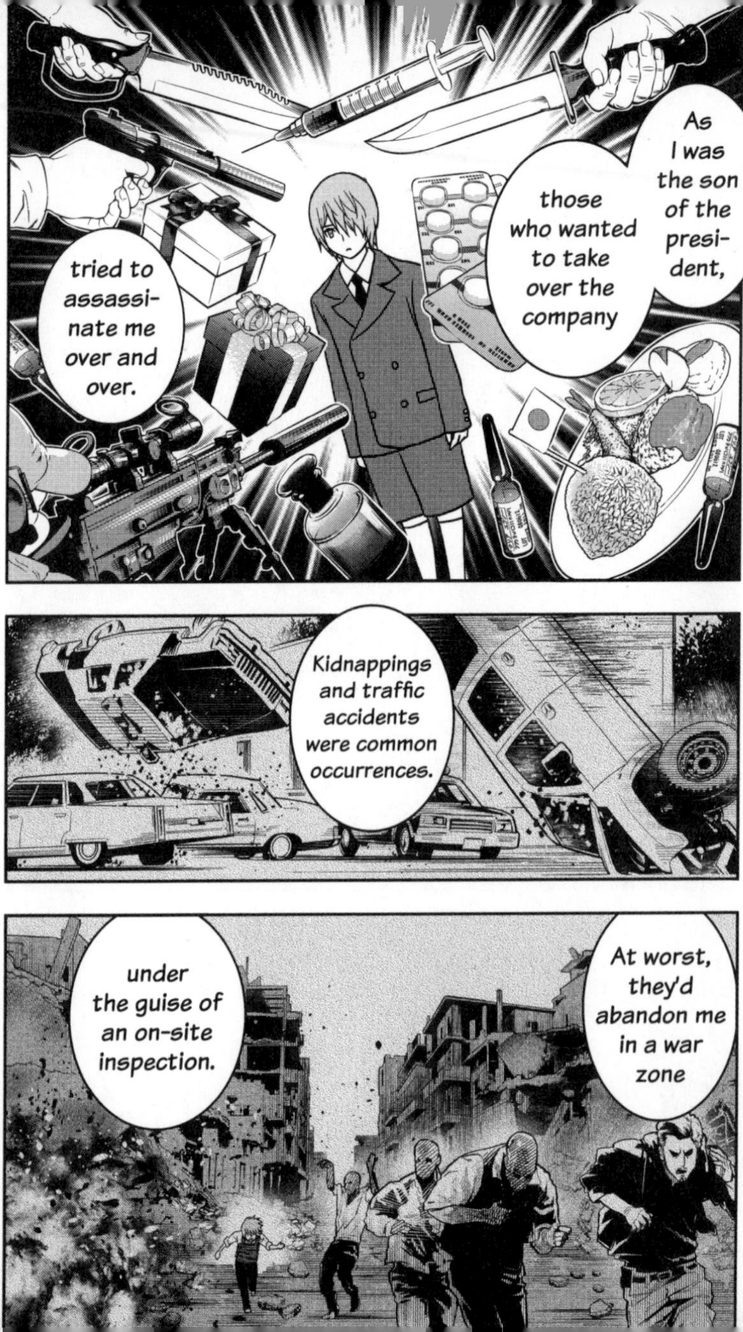
As I was the son of the presi-dent,
those who wanted to take over the company
tried to assassi-nate me over and over.
Kidnappings and traffic accidents were common occurrences.
At worst, they'd abandon me in a war zone
under the guise of an on-site inspection.

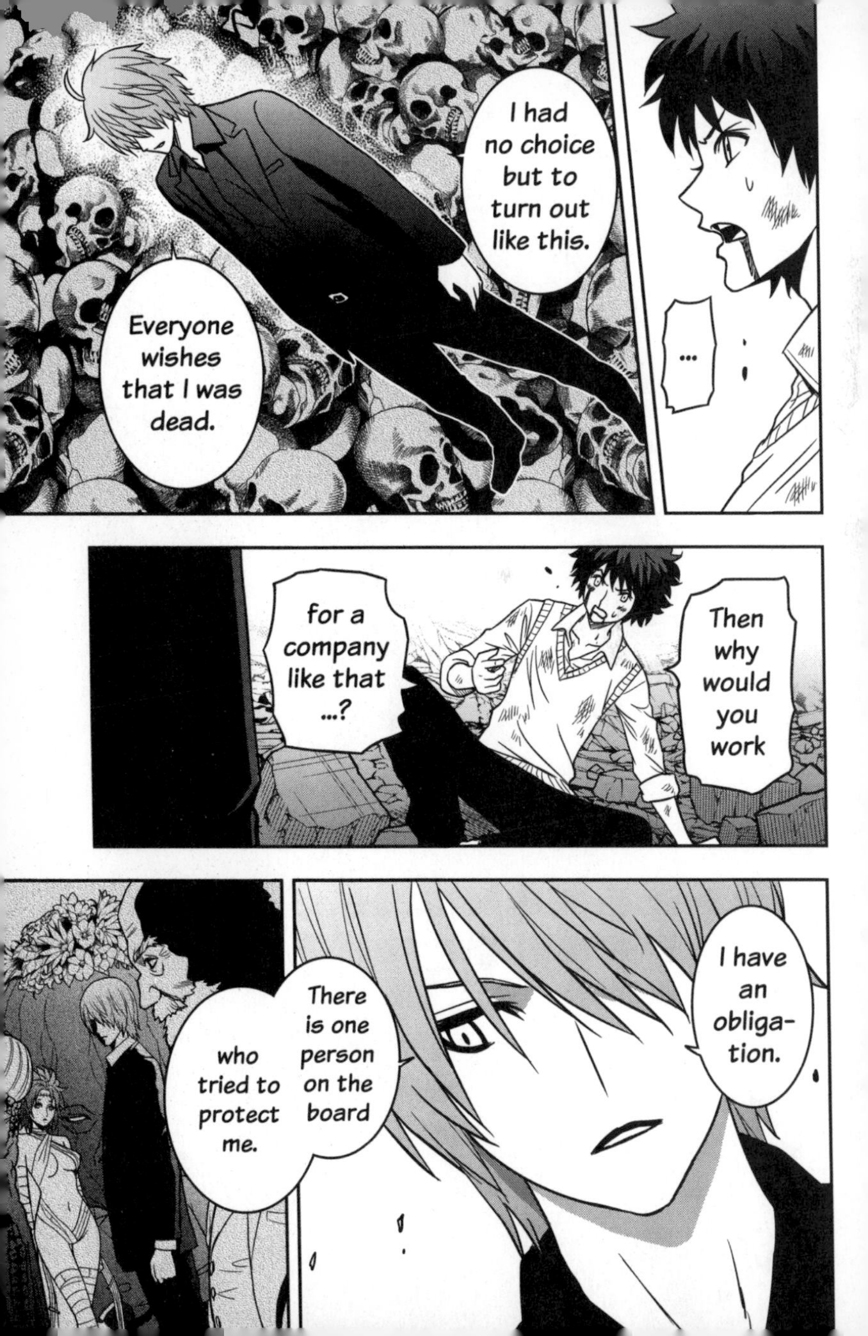
...
I had no choice but to turn out like this.
Everyone wishes that I was dead.
Then why would you work
for a company like that ...?
I have an obligation.
There is one person on the board
who tried to protect me.

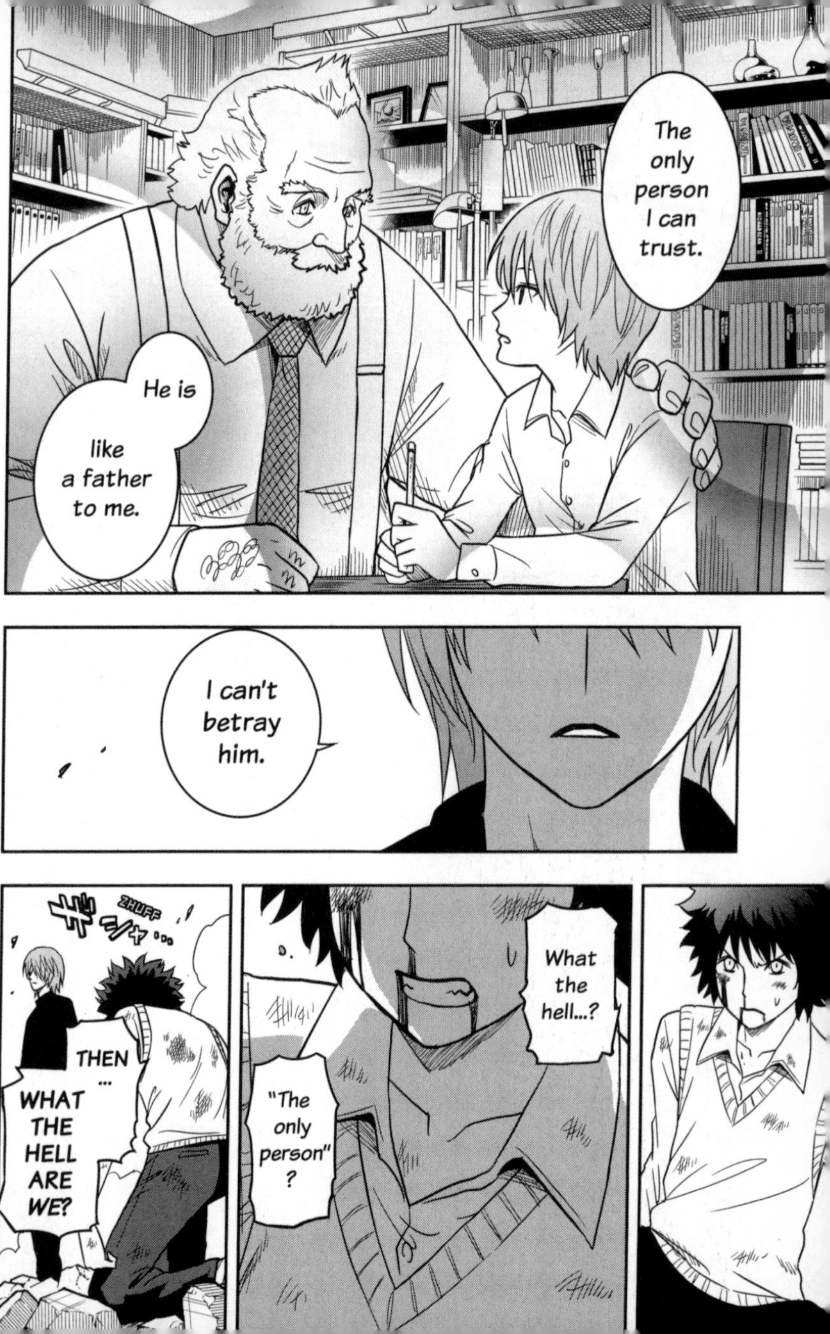
The only person I can trust.
He is like a father to me.
I can't betray him.
What the hell...?
"The only person"?
ZHUFF
THEN... WHAT THE HELL ARE WE?

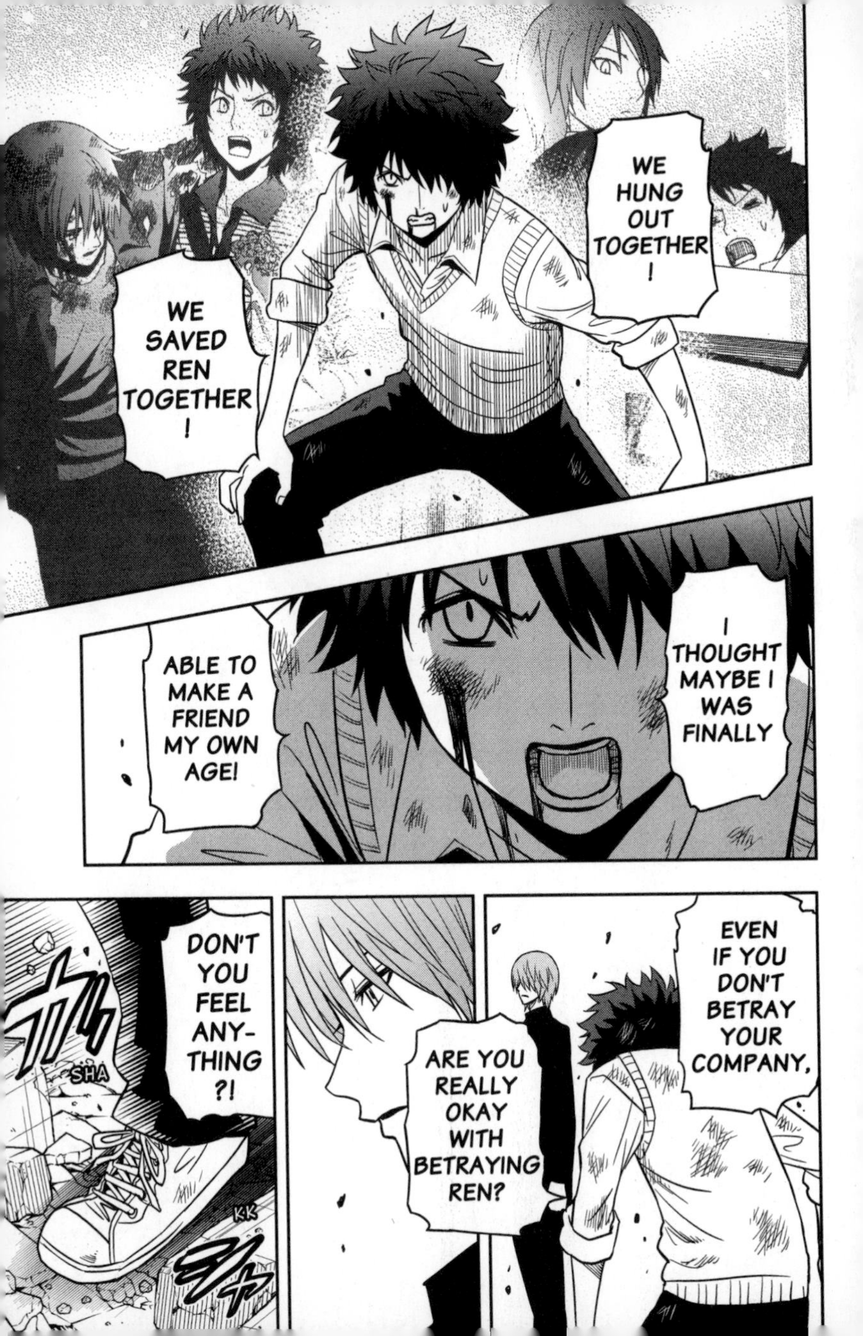
WE HUNG OUT TOGETHER!
WE SAVED REN TOGETHER!
I THOUGHT MAYBE I WAS FINALLY
ABLE TO MAKE A FRIEND MY OWN AGE!
EVEN IF YOU DON'T BETRAY YOUR COMPANY,
ARE YOU REALLY OKAY WITH BETRAYING REN?
DON'T YOU FEEL ANY-THING?!
SHA
KK

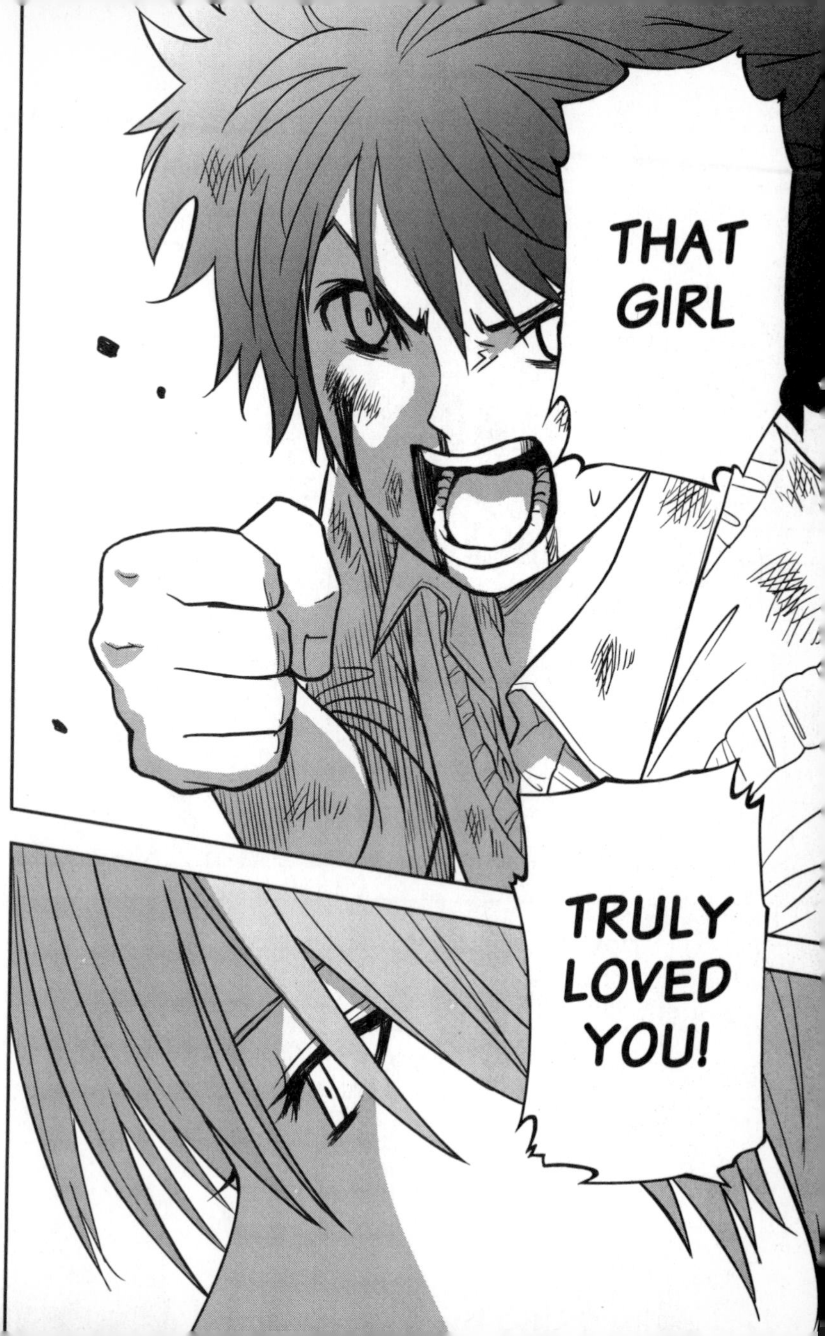
THAT GIRL
TRULY LOVED YOU!

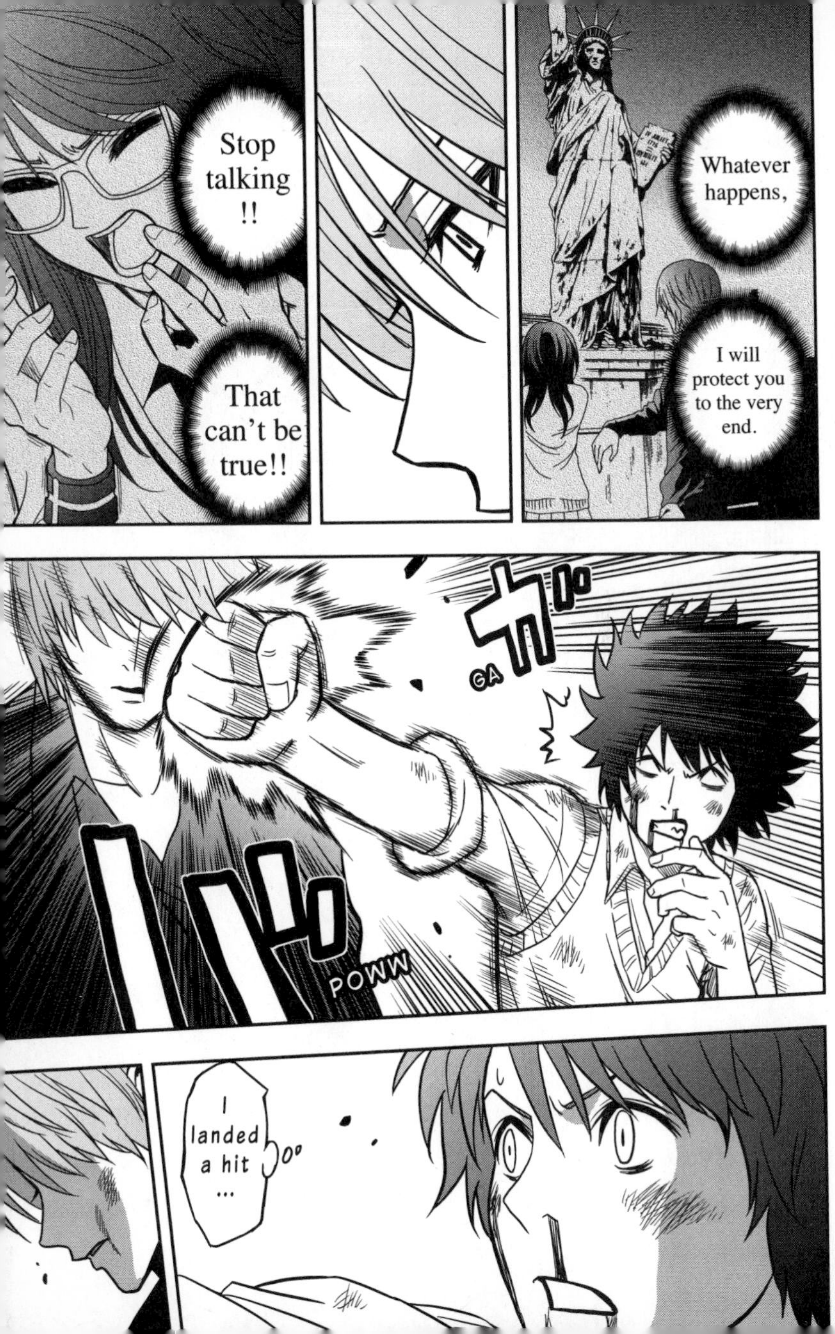
Whatever happens,
I will protect you to the very end.
Stop talking!!
That can't be true!!
GA
POWW
I landed a hit ...

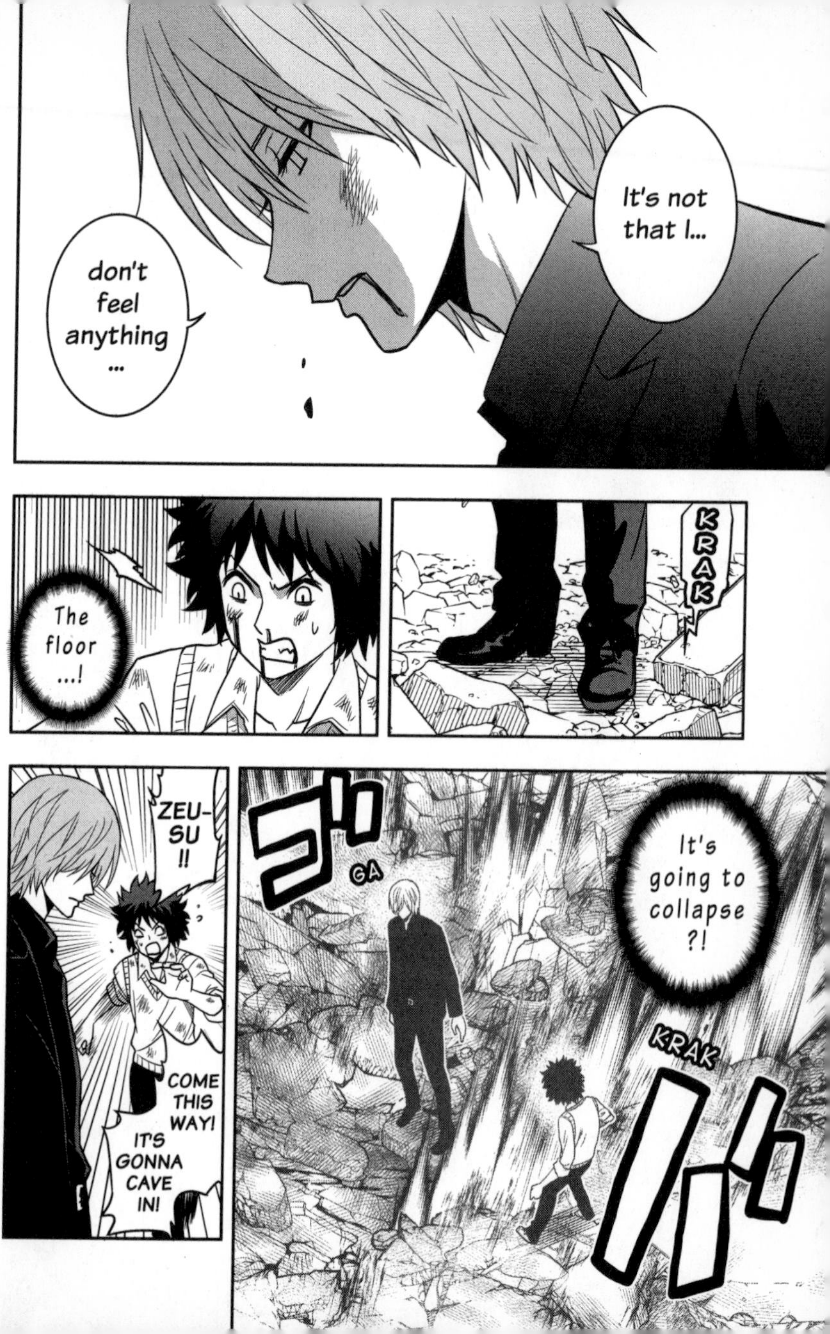
It's not that I...
don't feel anything ...
KRAK
The floor ...!
It's going to collapse ?!
GA
KRAK
ZEU-SU !!
COME THIS WAY!
IT'S GONNA CAVE IN!

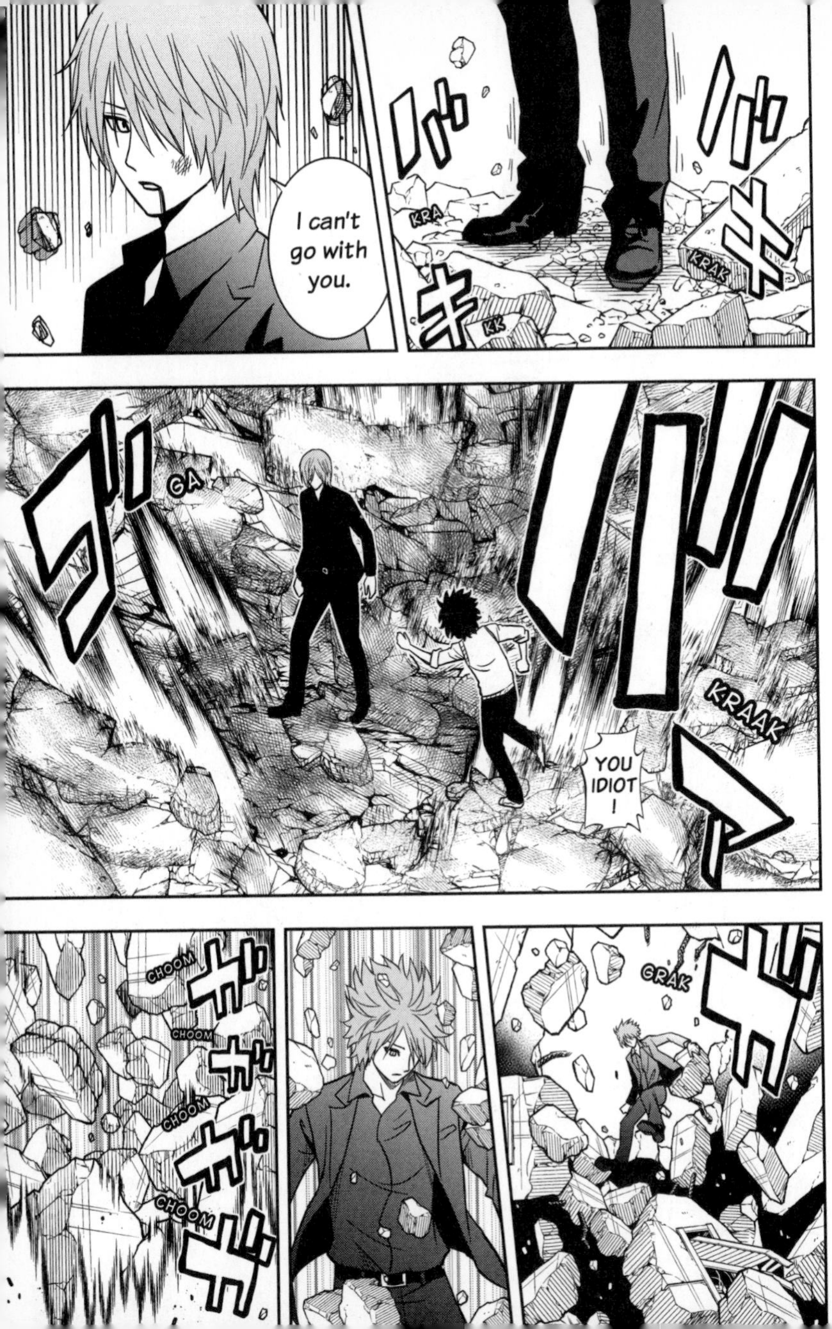
KRAK
KRA
KK
I can't go with you.
KRAAK
YOU IDIOT !
GA
GRAK
CHOOM
CHOOM
CHOOM
CHOOM

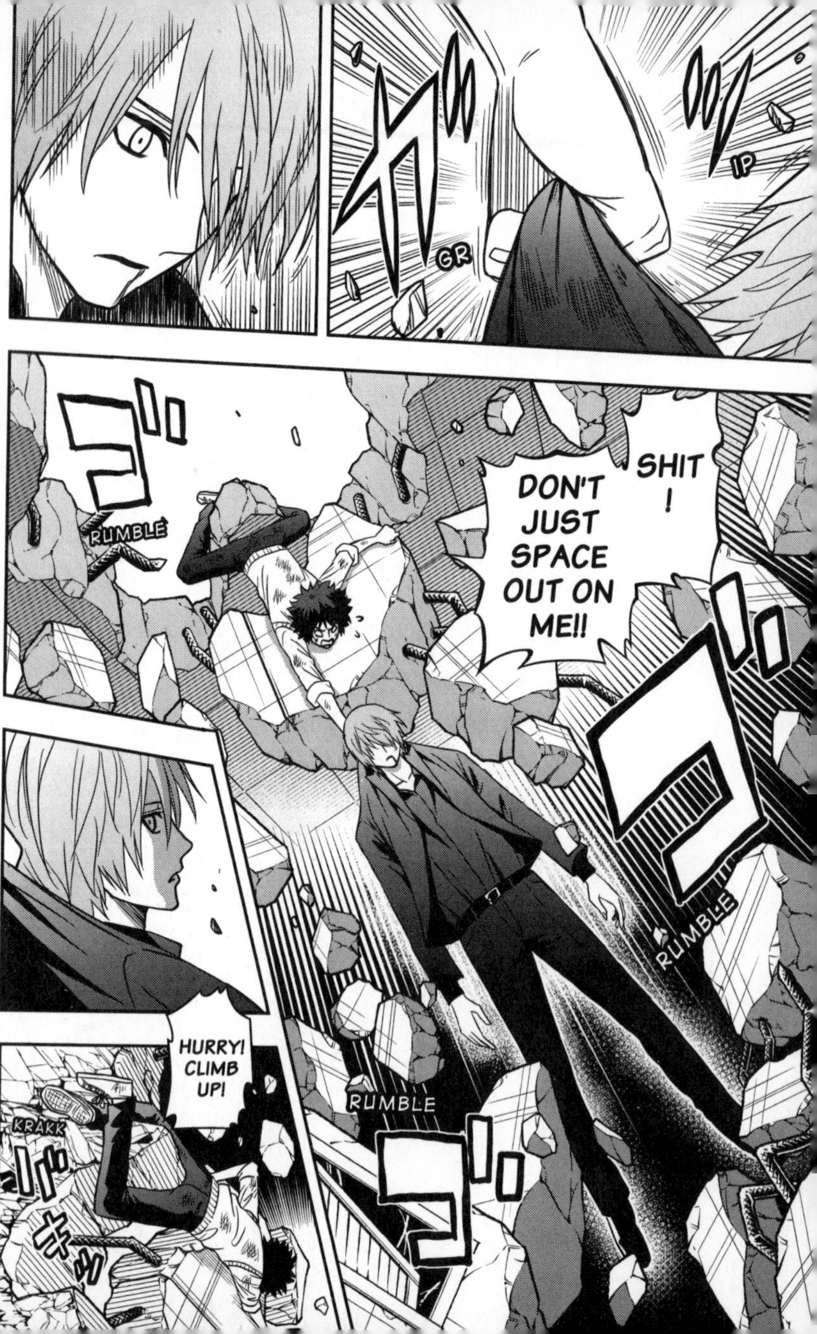
GR
IP
RUMBLE
SHIT!
DON'T JUST SPACE OUT ON ME!!
RUMBLE
RUMBLE
RUMBLE
HURRY! CLIMB UP!
KRAKK

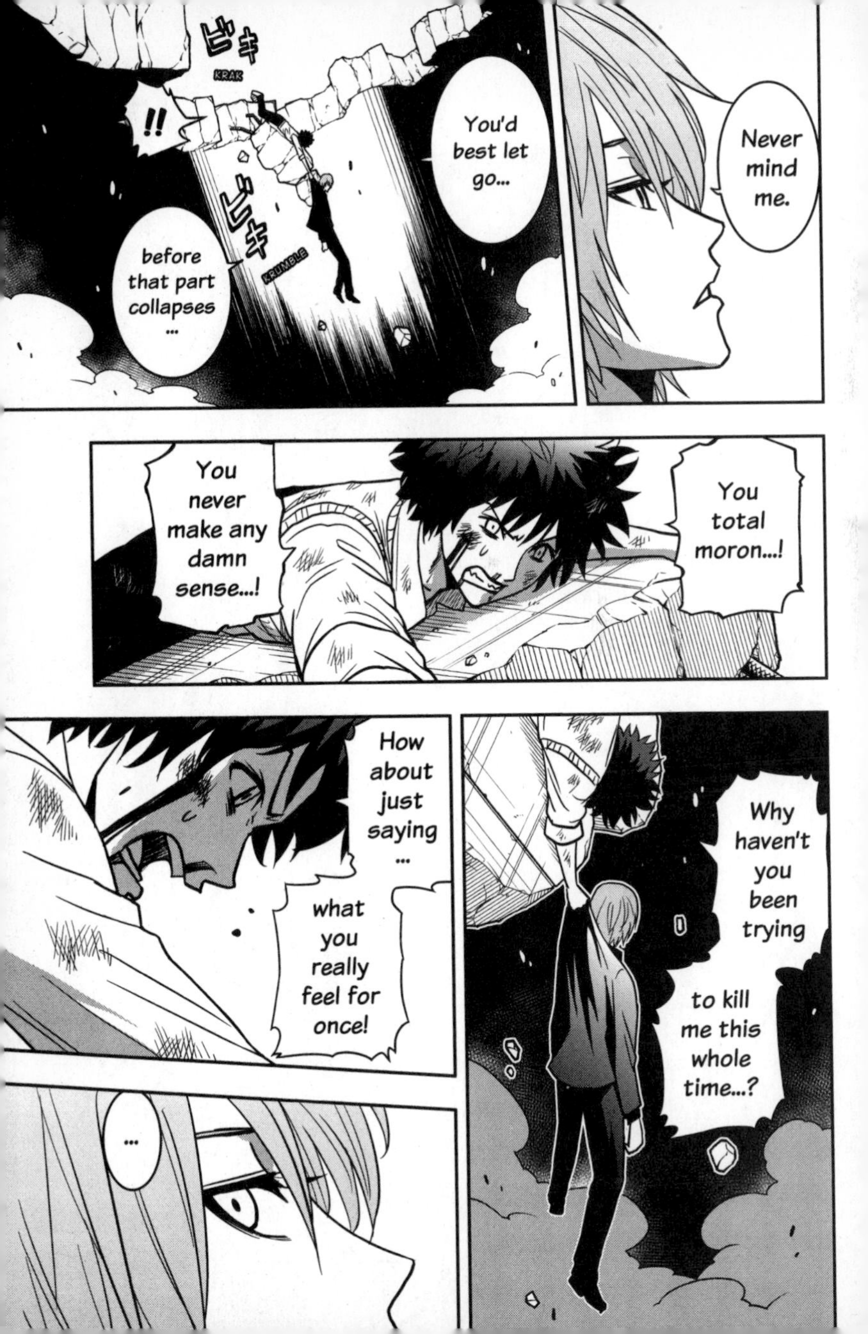
Never mind me.
You'd best let go...
ビキ KRAK
!!
before that part collapses ...
ビキ KRUMBLE
You total moron...!
You never make any damn sense...!
Why haven't you been trying
to kill me this whole time...?
How about just saying ...
what you really feel for once!
...

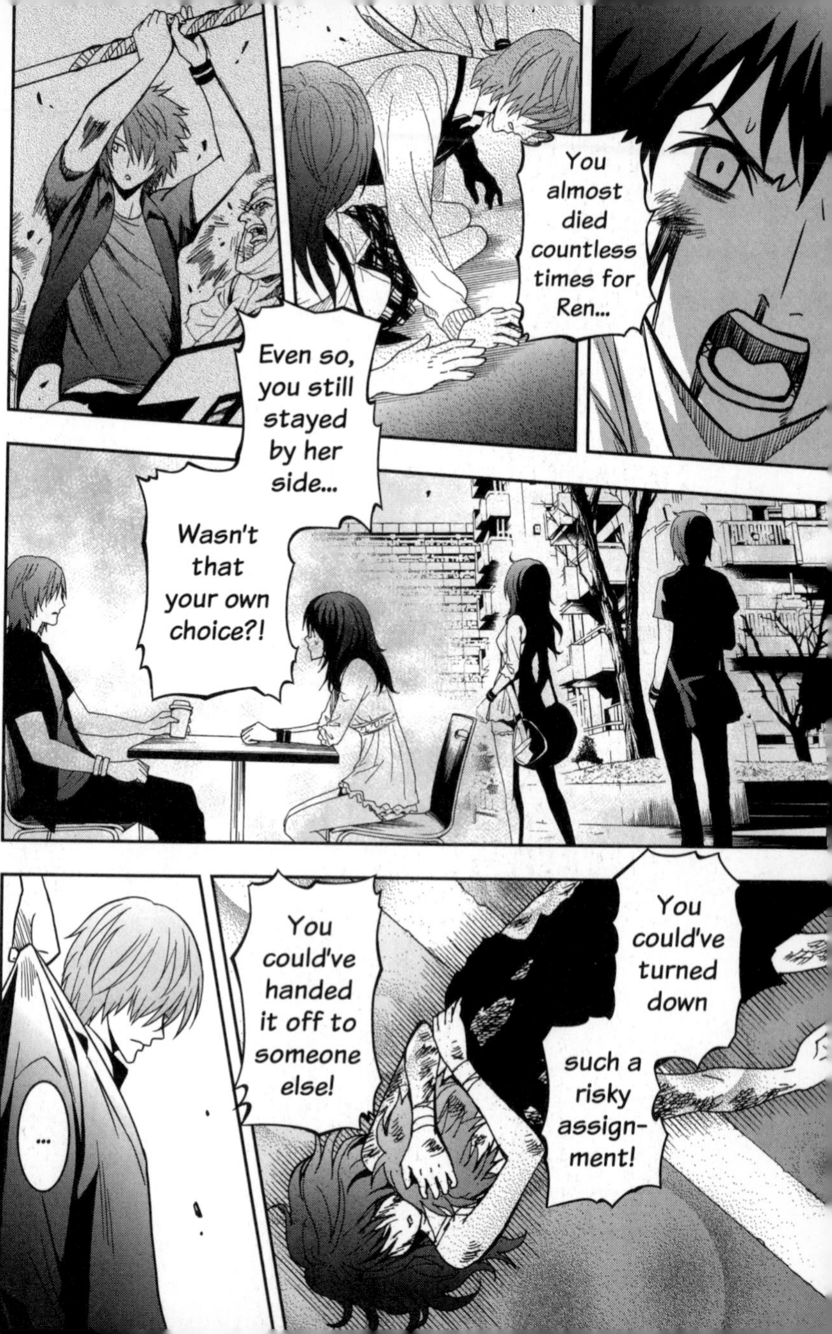
You almost died countless times for Ren...
Even so, you still stayed by her side...
Wasn't that your own choice?!
You could've turned down such a risky assignment!
You could've handed it off to someone else!
...

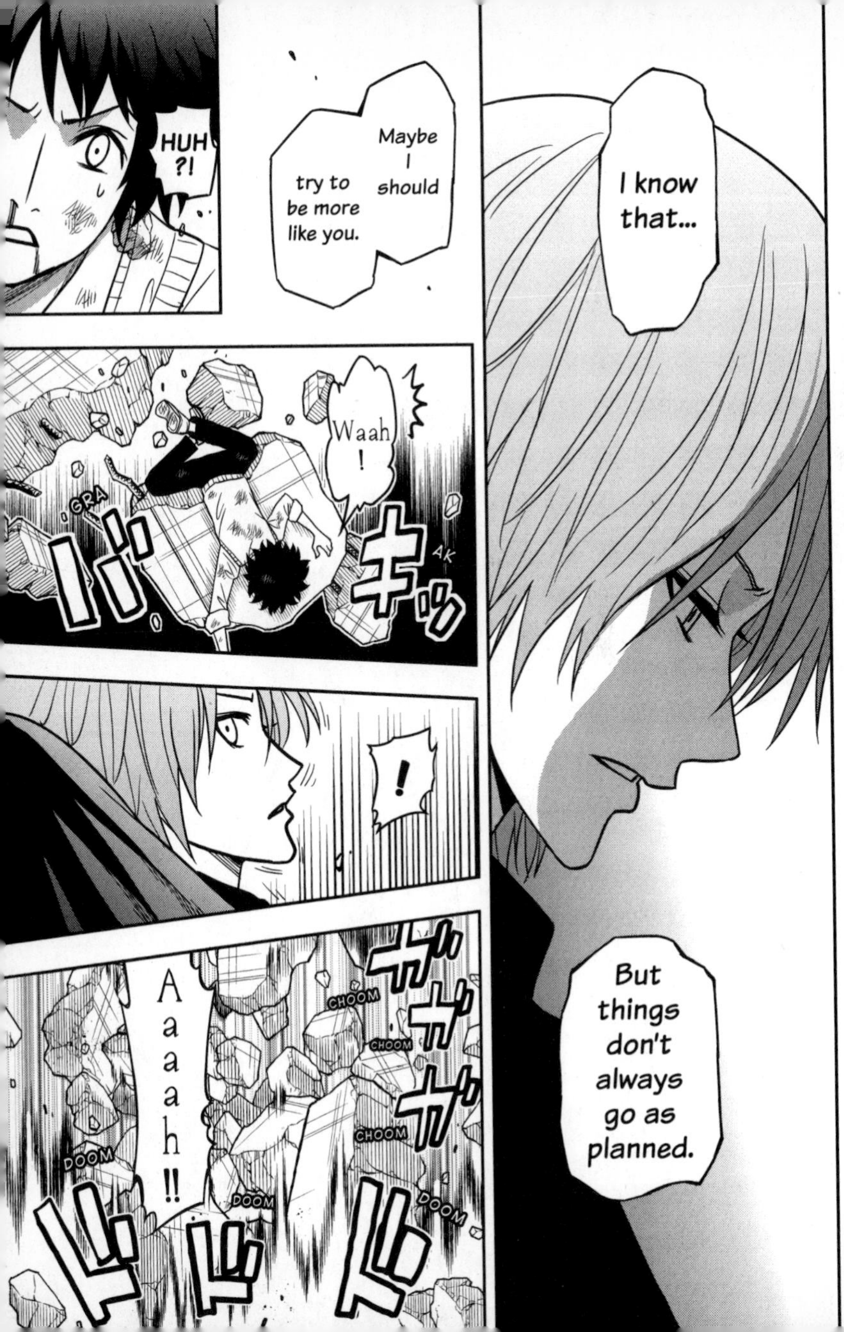
I know that...
But things don't always go as planned.
Maybe I should try to be more like you.
HUH ?!
Waah!
GRA
AK
!
Aaaah!!
CHOOM
CHOOM
CHOOM
DOOM
DOOM
DOOM

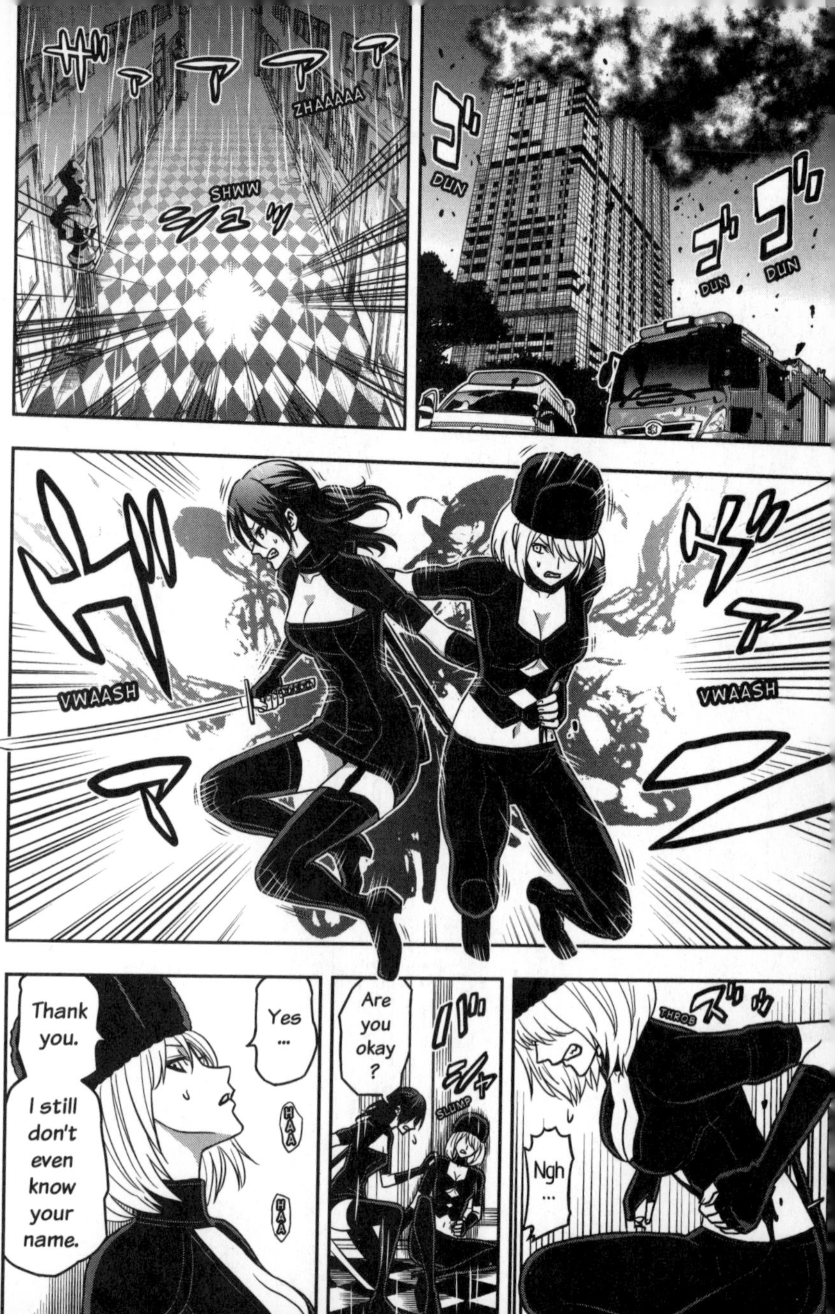
DUN
DUN
DUN
ZHAAAAA
SHWW
VWAASH
VWAASH
THROB
Ngh ...
Are you okay ?
SLUMP
HAA
HAA
Yes ...
Thank you.
I still don't even know your name.

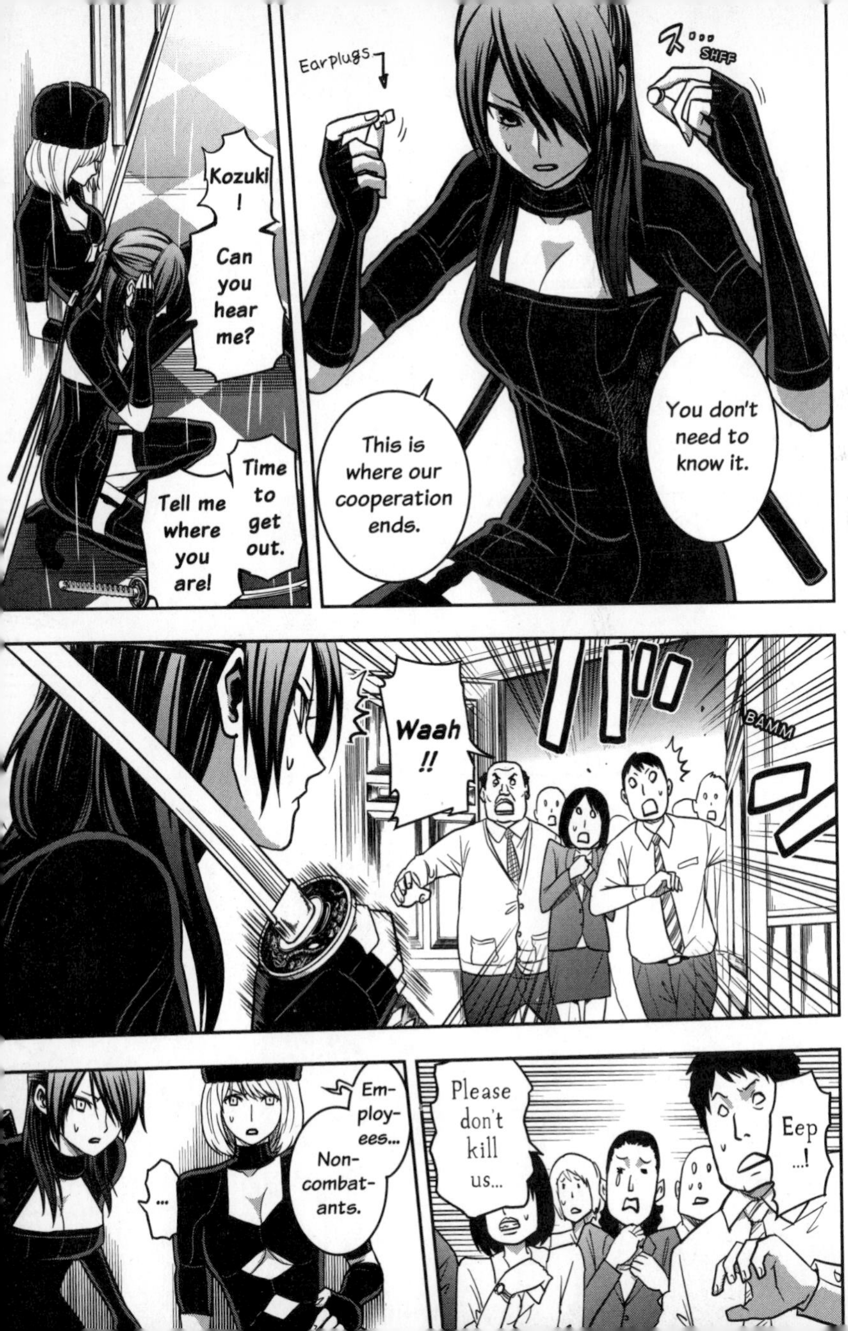
ス... SHFF
Earplugs
You don't need to know it.
This is where our cooperation ends.
Kozuki!
Can you hear me?
Time to get out.
Tell me where you are!
BAMM
Waah!!
Eep...!
Please don't kill us...
Em-ploy-ees... Non-combat-ants.
...

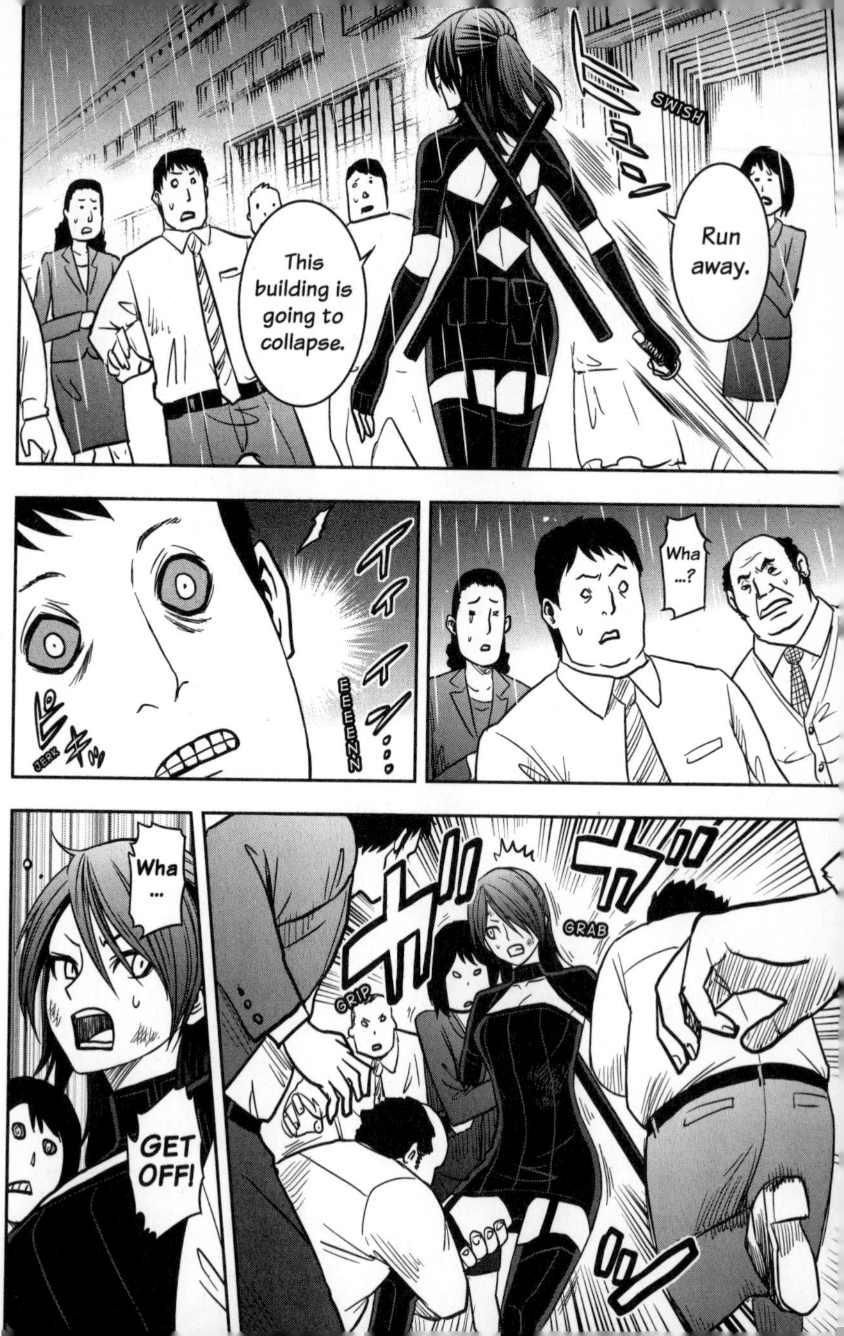
SWISH
Run away.
This building is going to collapse.
Wha ...?
EEEENN
JERK
GRAB
GRIP
Wha ...
GET OFF!

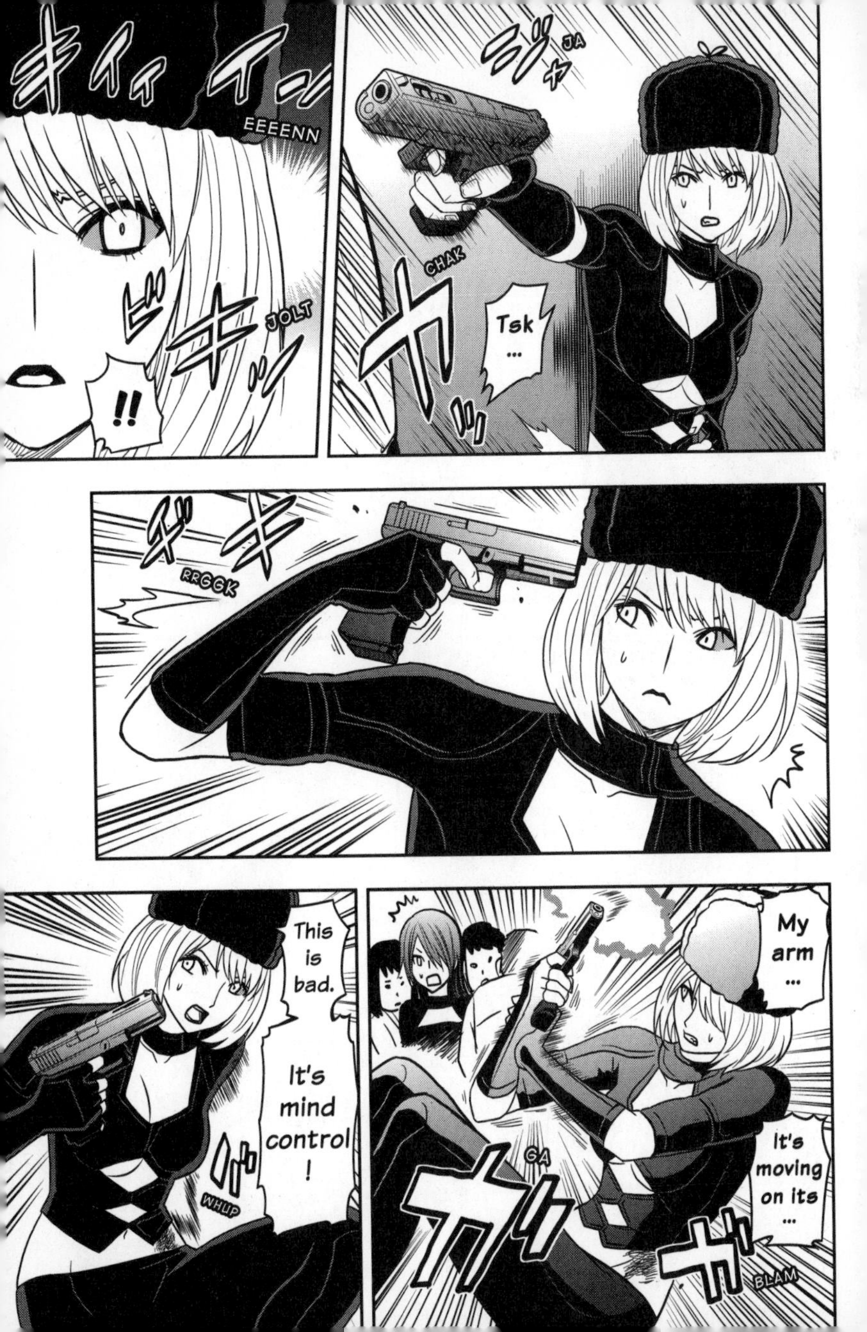
JA
CHAK
Tsk ...
EEEENN
JOLT
!!
RRGGK
My arm ...
GA
It's moving on its ...
BLAM
This is bad.
It's mind control !
WHUP

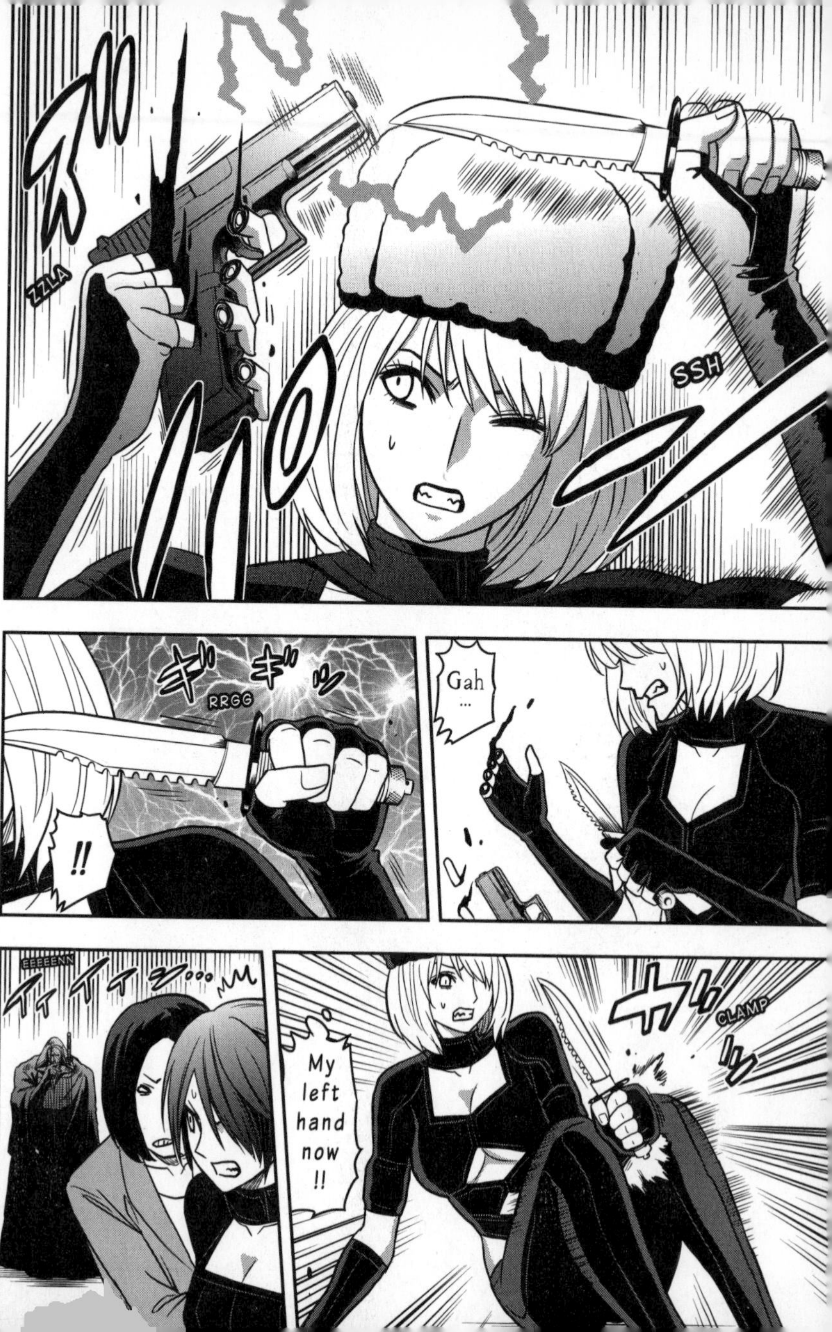

SSH
ZZLA
Gah ...
RRGG
!!
My left hand now !!
CLAMP
EEEEEENN

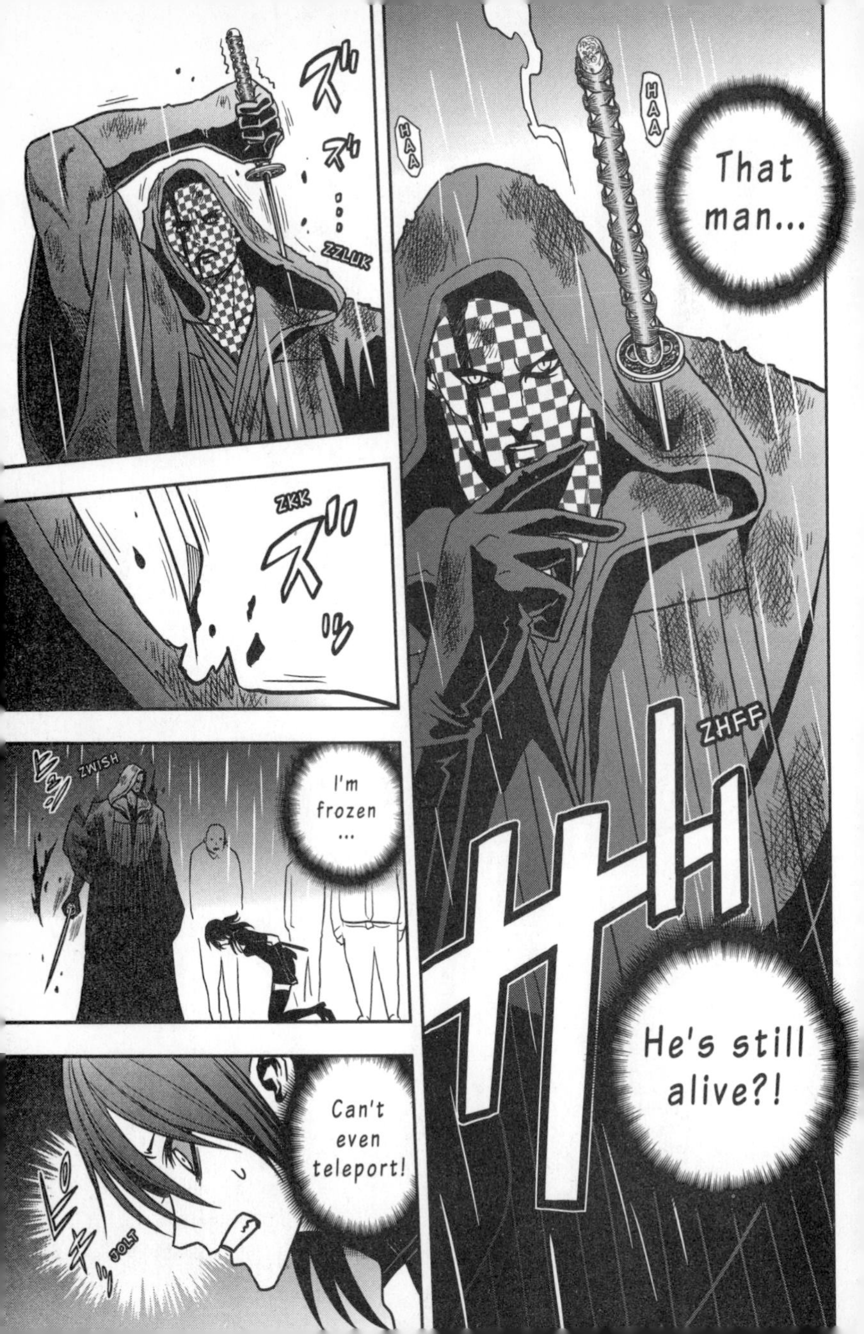
HAA
HAA
That man...
ZHFF
He's still alive?!
ZZLUK
ZKK
ZWISH
I'm frozen ...
Can't even teleport!
JOLT

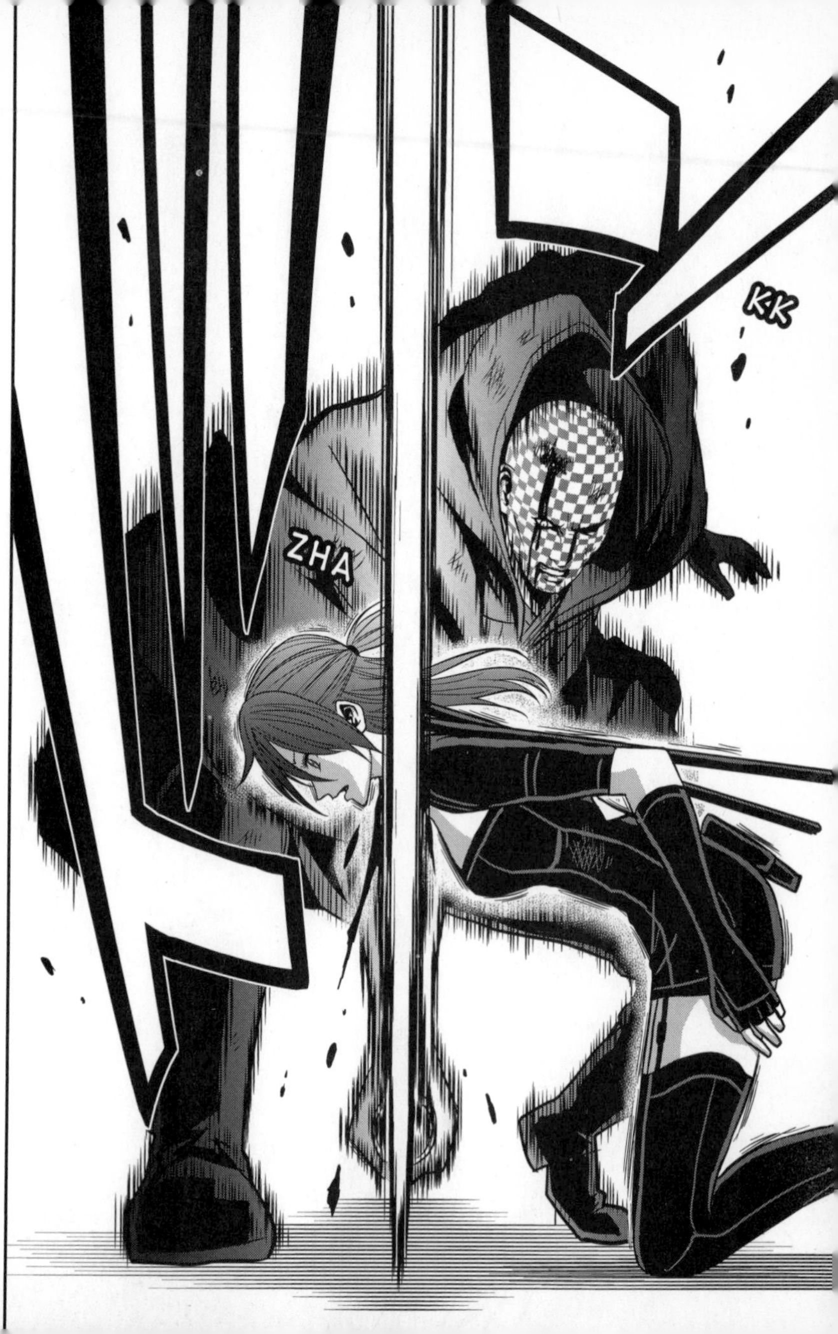
KK
ZHA

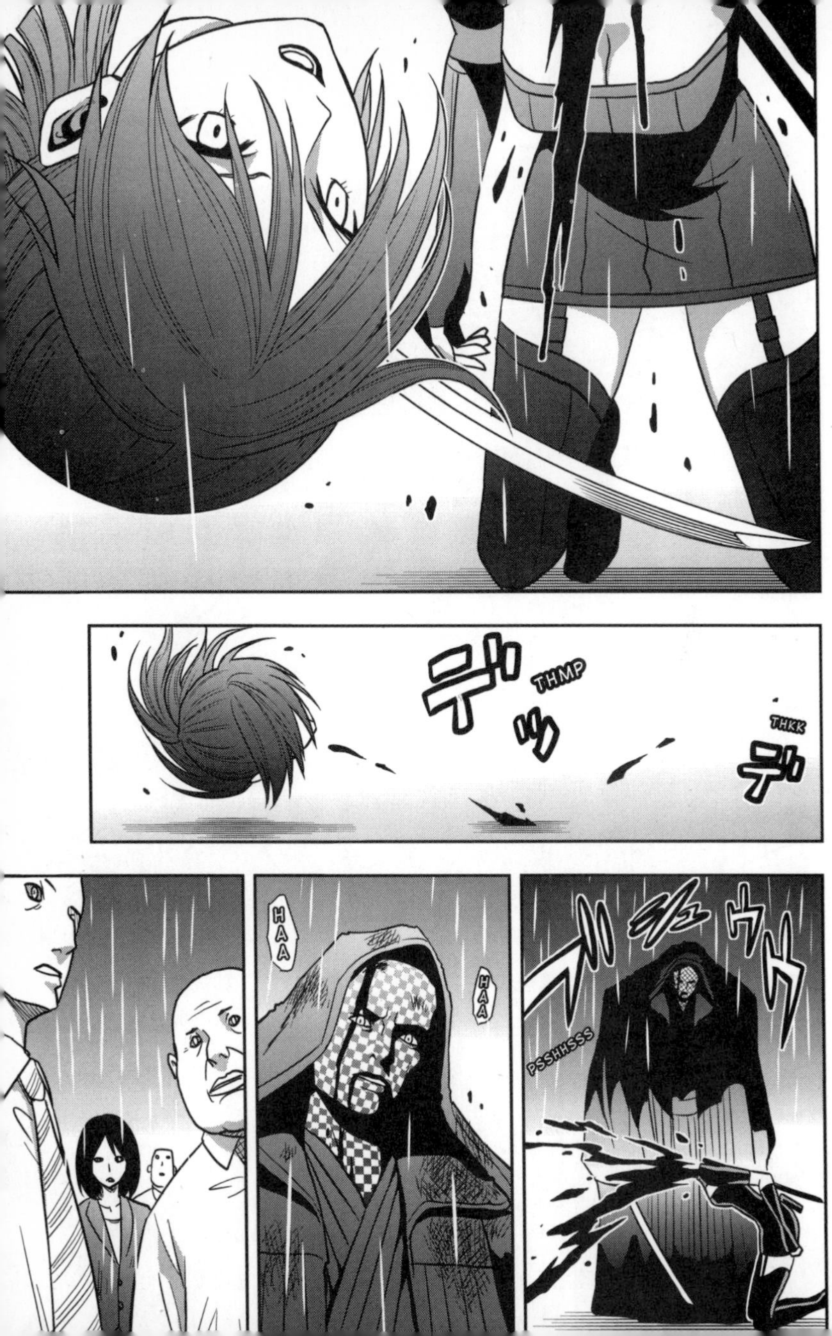
THKK
THMP
PSSHHSSS
HAA
HAA

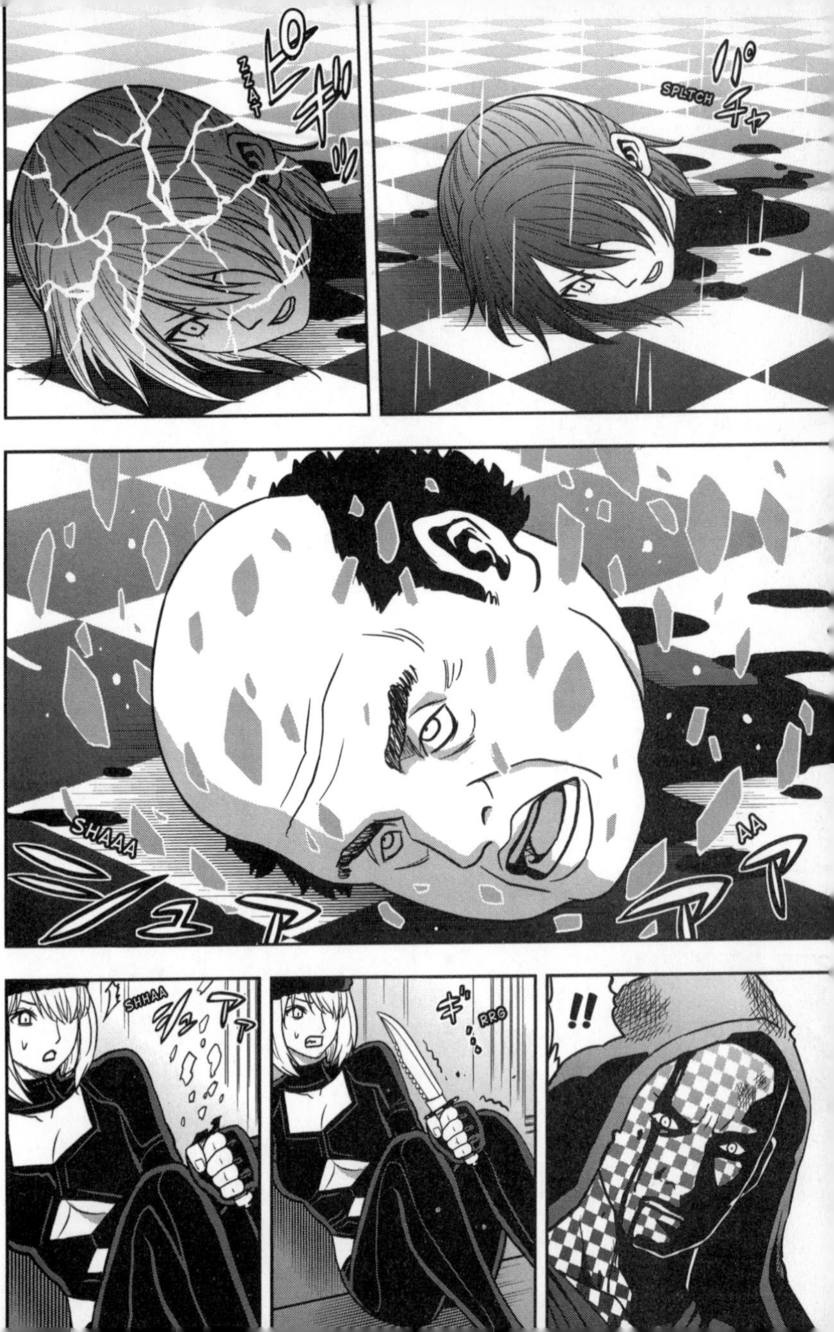

SPLTCH
ZZAT
AA
SHAAA
!!
RRG
SHHAA

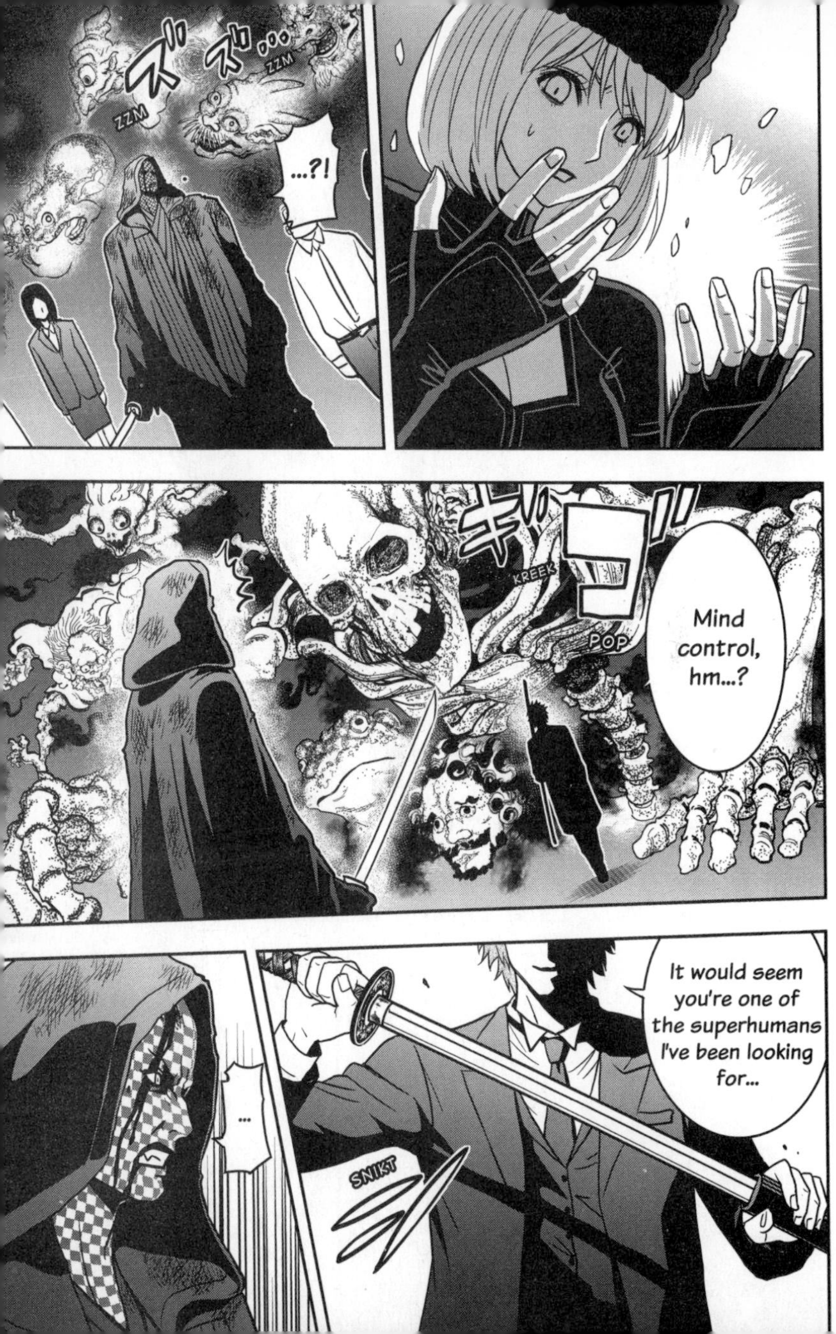
...?!
ZZM
ZZM
KREEK
POP
Mind control, hm...?
It would seem you're one of the superhumans I've been looking for...
SNIKT
...

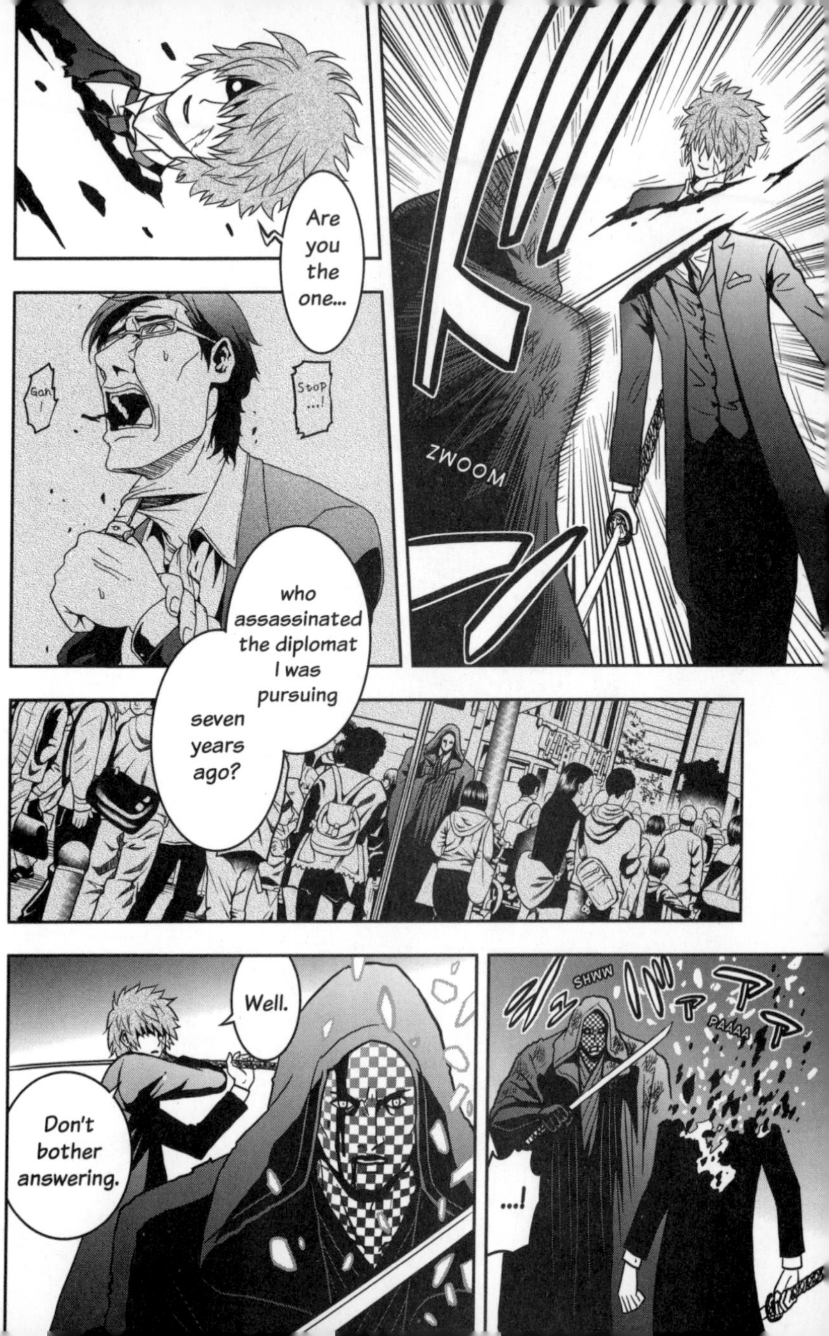
ZWOOM
Are you the one...
Stop ...!
Gah!
who assassinated the diplomat I was pursuing
seven years ago?
SHWW
PAAAA
...!
Well.
Don't bother answering.

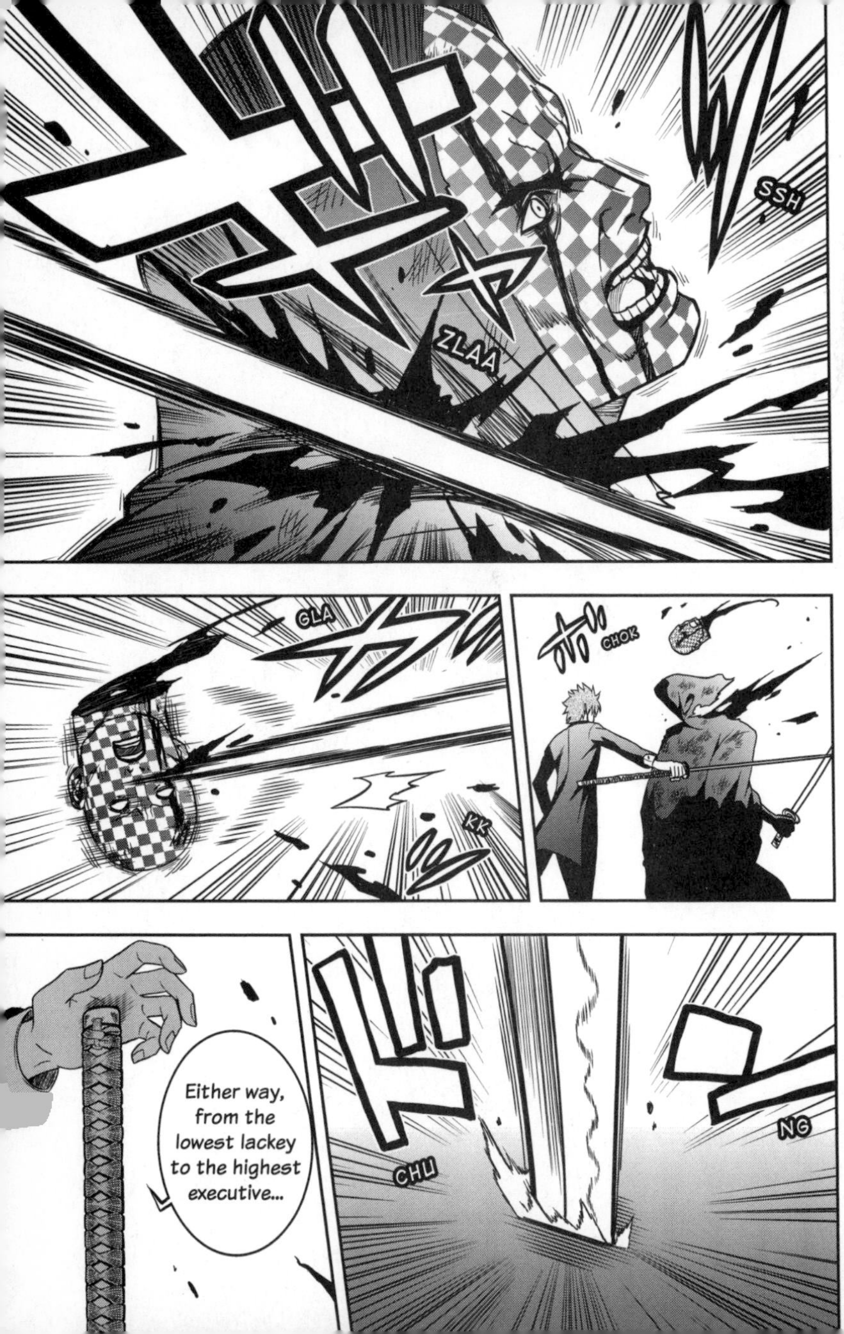
SSH
ZLAA
CHOK
GLA
KK
NG
CHU
Either way, from the lowest lackey to the highest executive...

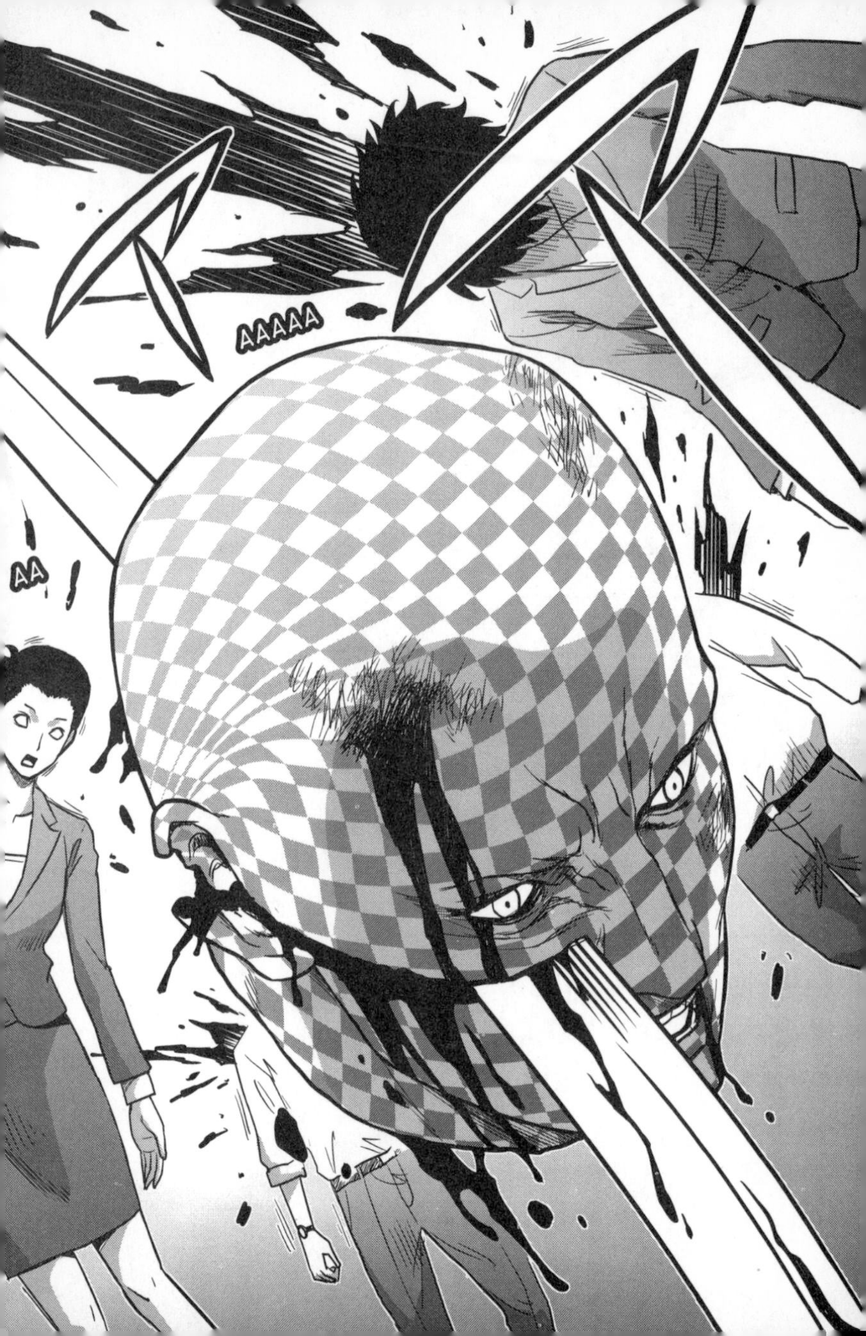
AAAAA
AA

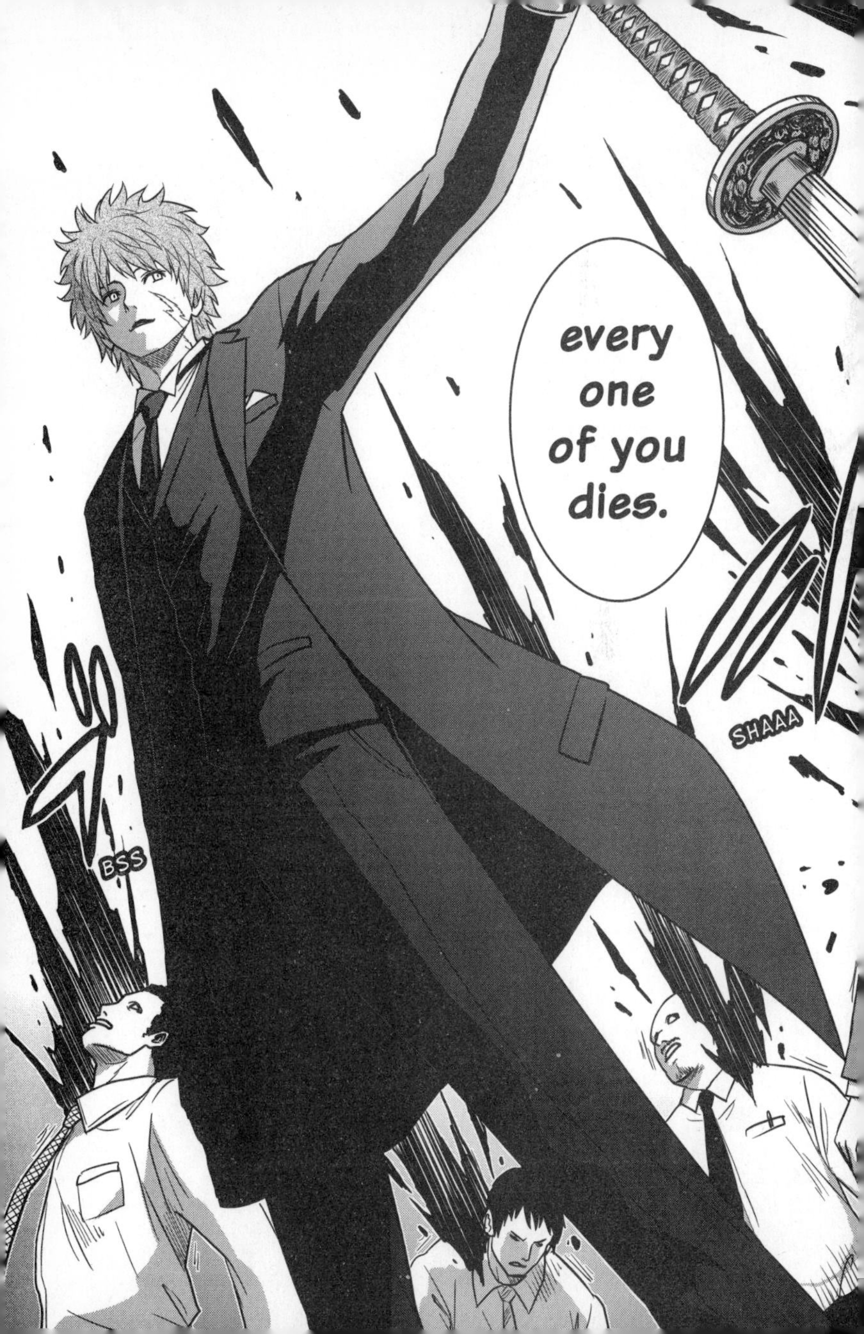
every one of you dies.
SHAAA
BSS

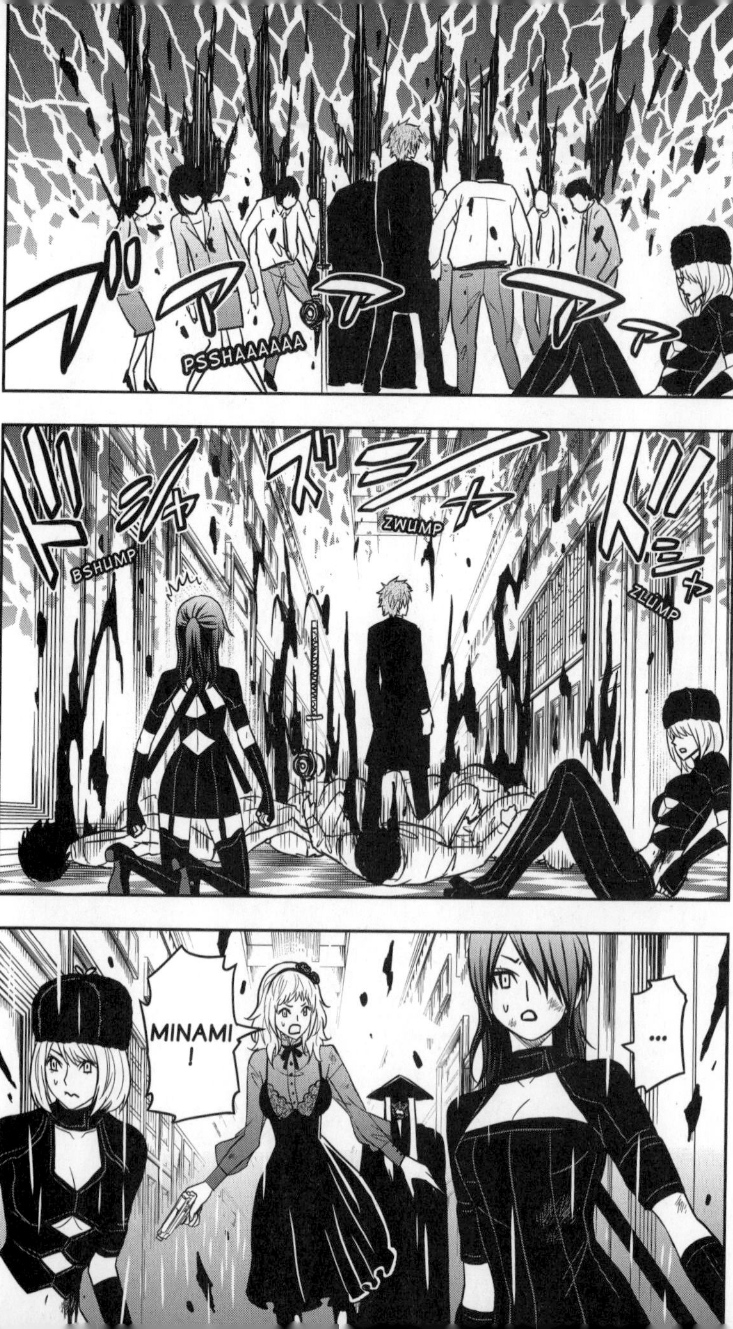
PSSHAAAAAA
ZLUMP
ZWUMP
BSHUMP
...
MINAMI!

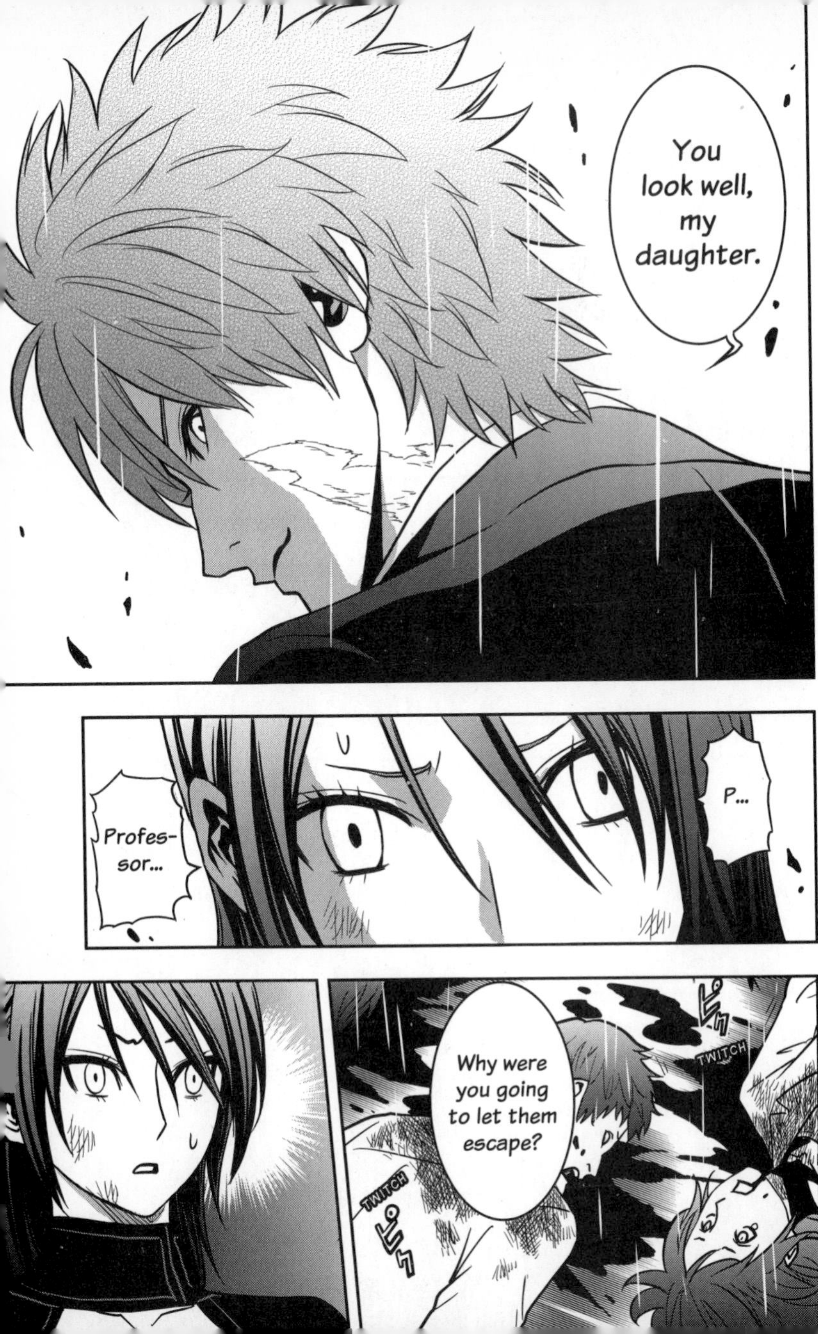
You look well, my daughter.
P...
Profes-sor...
TWITCH
Why were you going to let them escape?
TWITCH

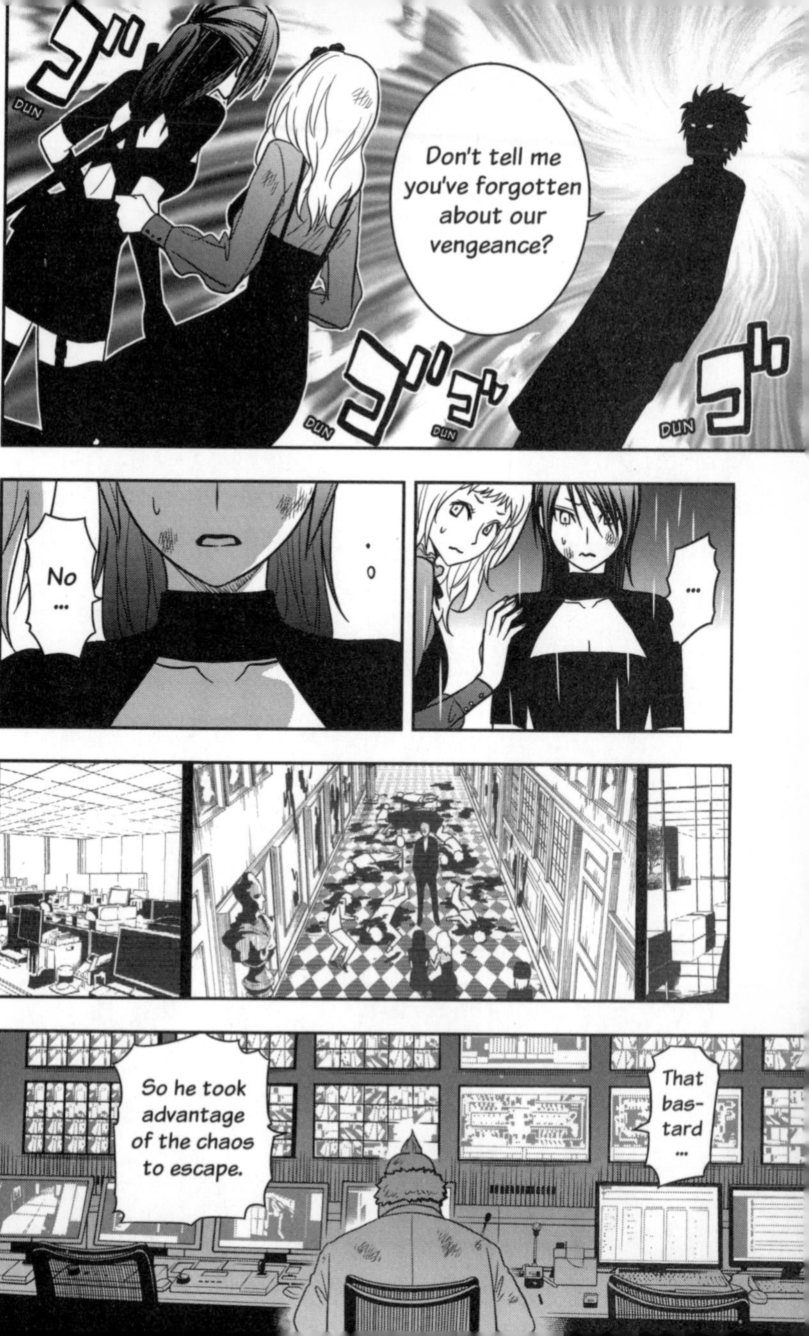

Don't tell me you've forgotten about our vengeance?
DUN
DUN
DUN
DUN
...
No ...
That bas- tard ...
So he took advantage of the chaos to escape.

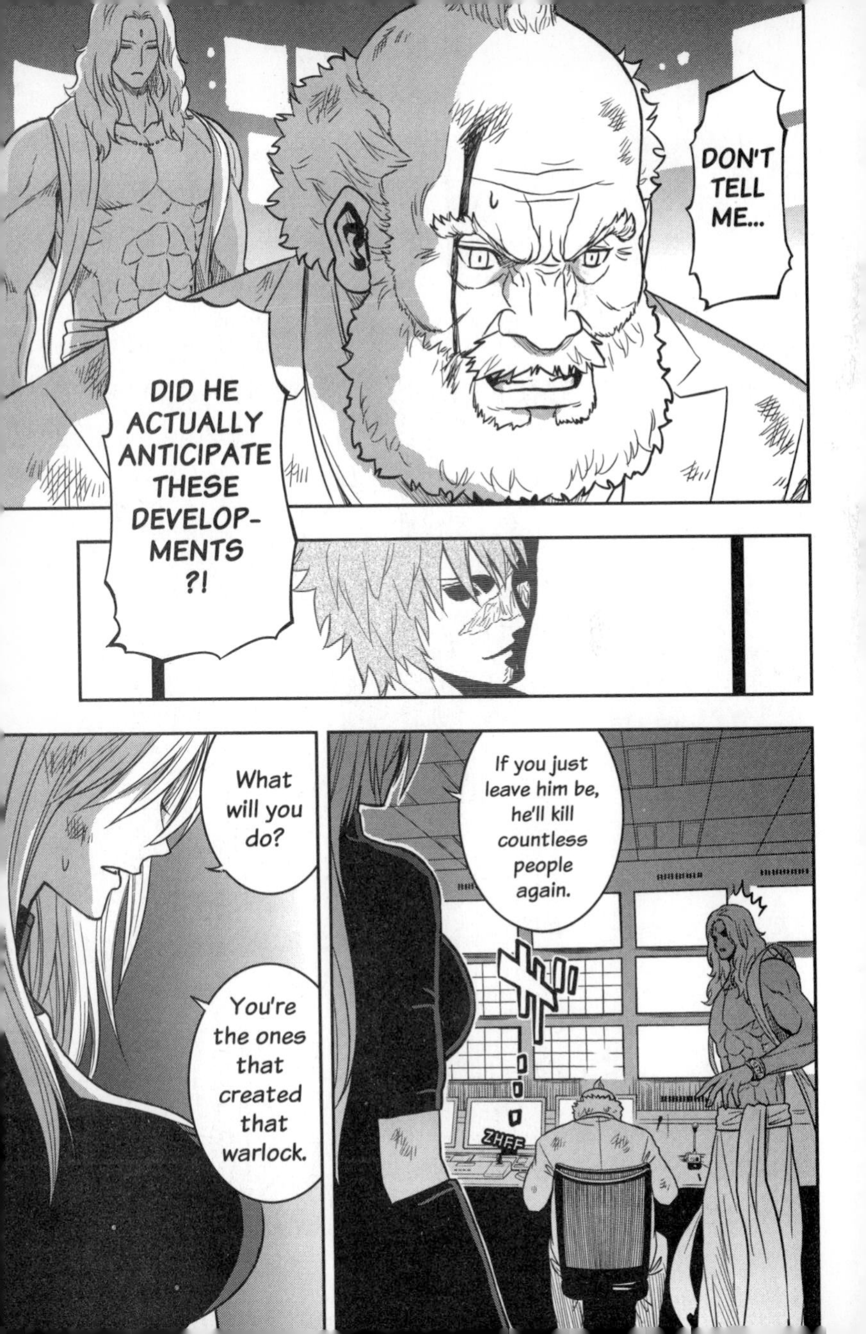
DON'T TELL ME...
DID HE ACTUALLY ANTICIPATE THESE DEVELOP-MENTS?!
If you just leave him be, he'll kill countless people again.
ZHFF
What will you do?
You're the ones that created that warlock.

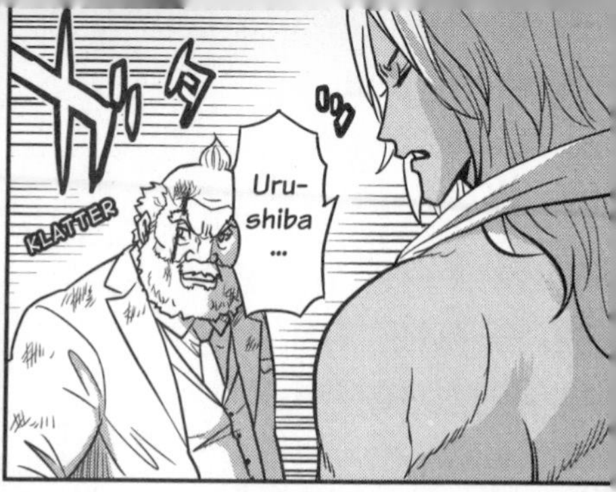
KLATTER
Uru-shiba ...
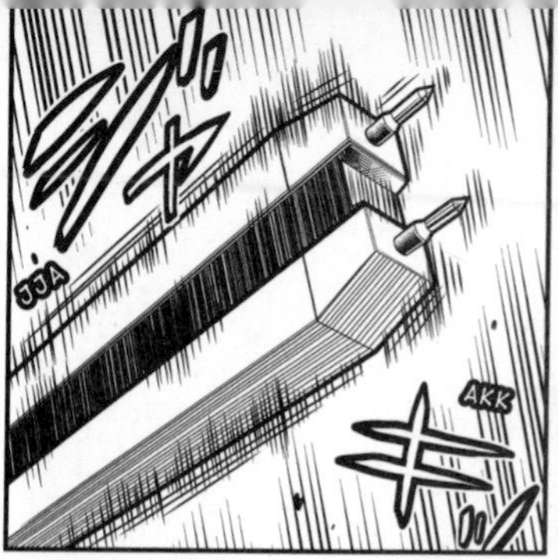
JJA
AKK
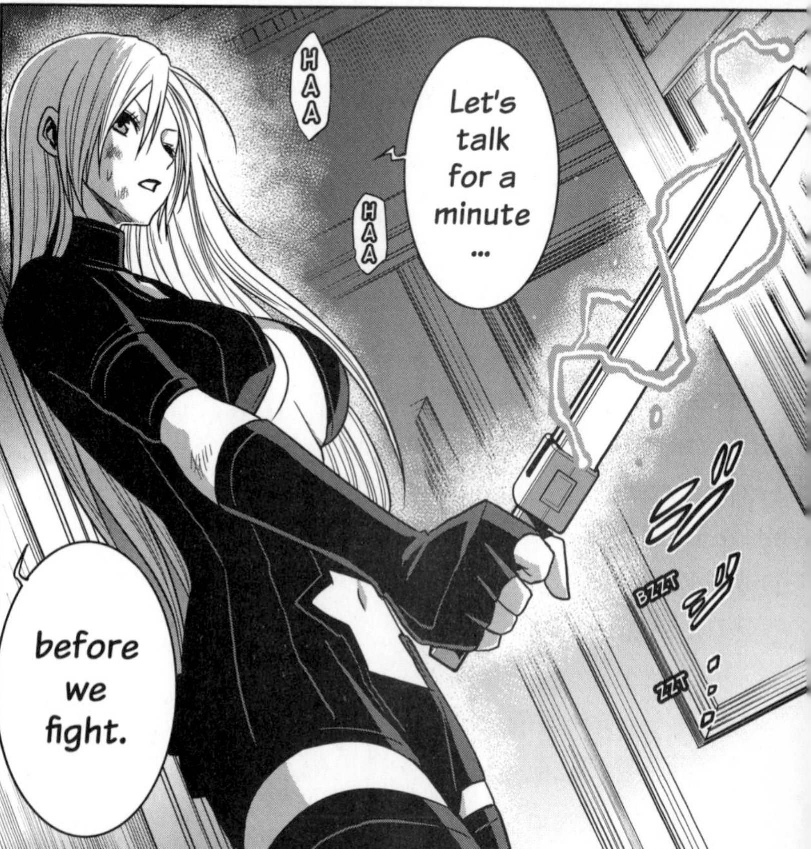
HAA
Let's talk for a minute ...
HAA
BZZT
ZZT
before we fight.

SCENE 66 /// END

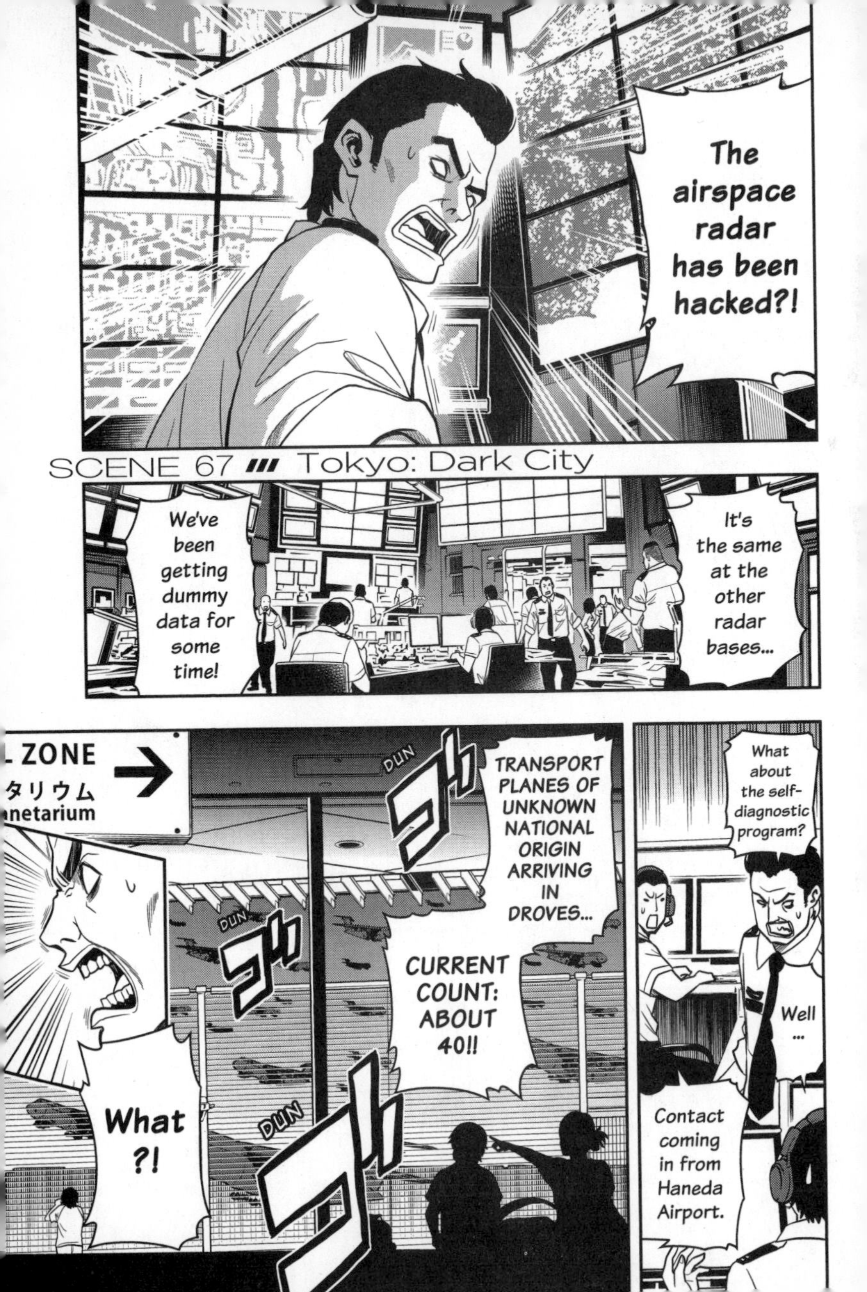
The airspace radar has been hacked?!
SCENE 67 /// Tokyo: Dark City
It's the same at the other radar bases...
We've been getting dummy data for some time!
What about the self-diagnostic program?
Well ...
Contact coming in from Haneda Airport.
TRANSPORT PLANES OF UNKNOWN NATIONAL ORIGIN ARRIVING IN DROVES...
DUN
CURRENT COUNT: ABOUT 40!!
DUN
DUN
What ?!

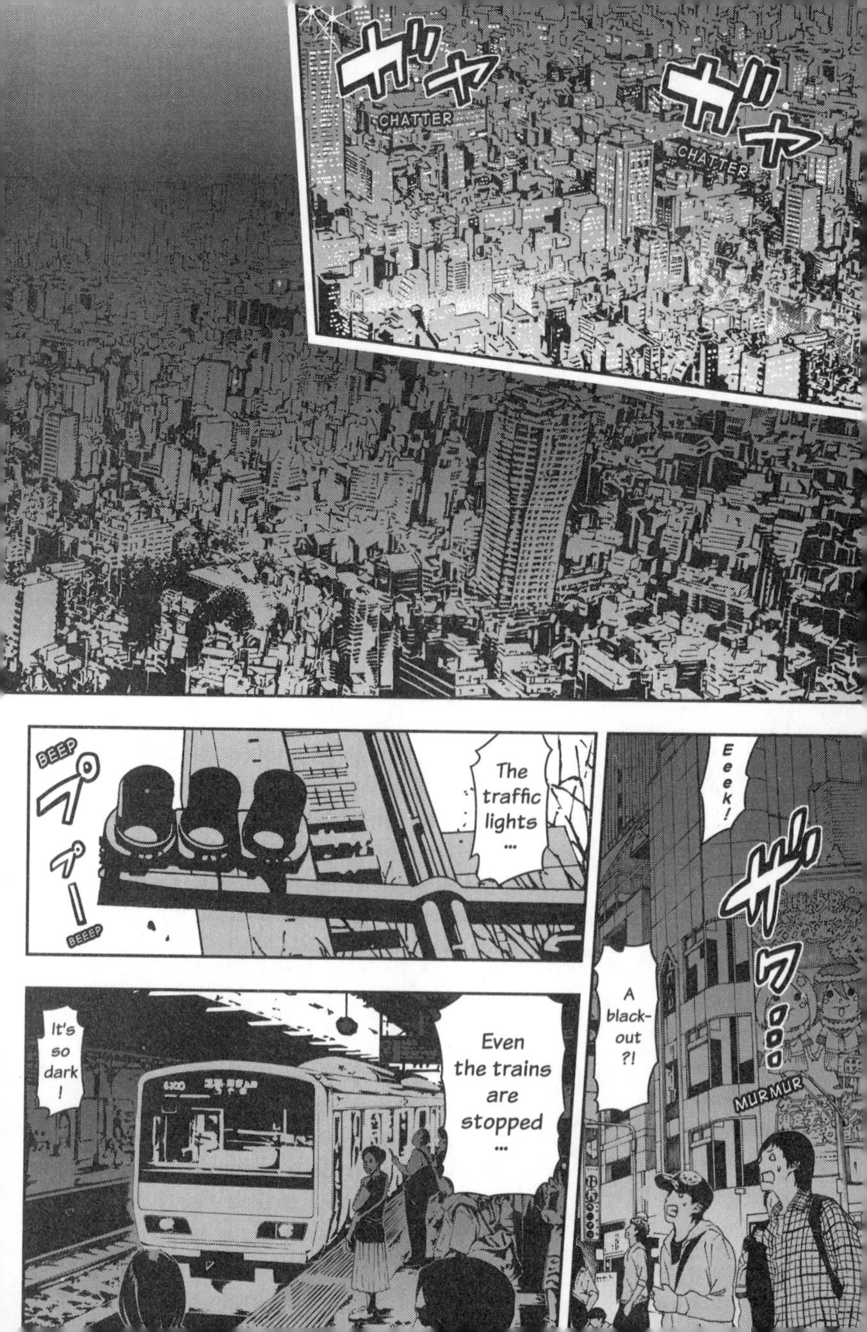

CHATTER
CHATTER
Eeek!
MURMUR
A black-out?!
The traffic lights...
BEEP
BEEEP
Even the trains are stopped...
It's so dark!

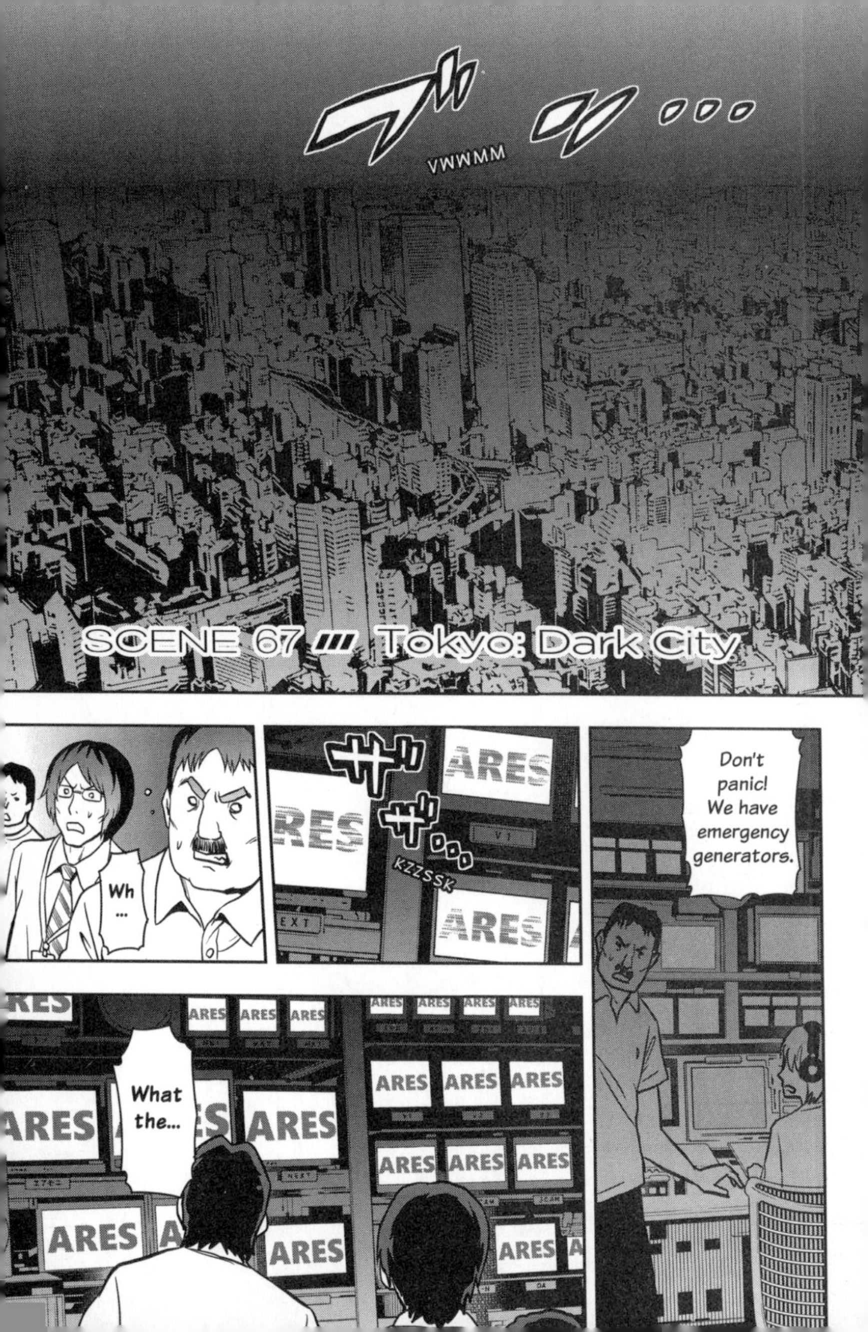
VWWMM
SCENE 67 /// Tokyo: Dark City
Don't panic! We have emergency generators.
ARES
KZZSSK
Wh ...
What the...

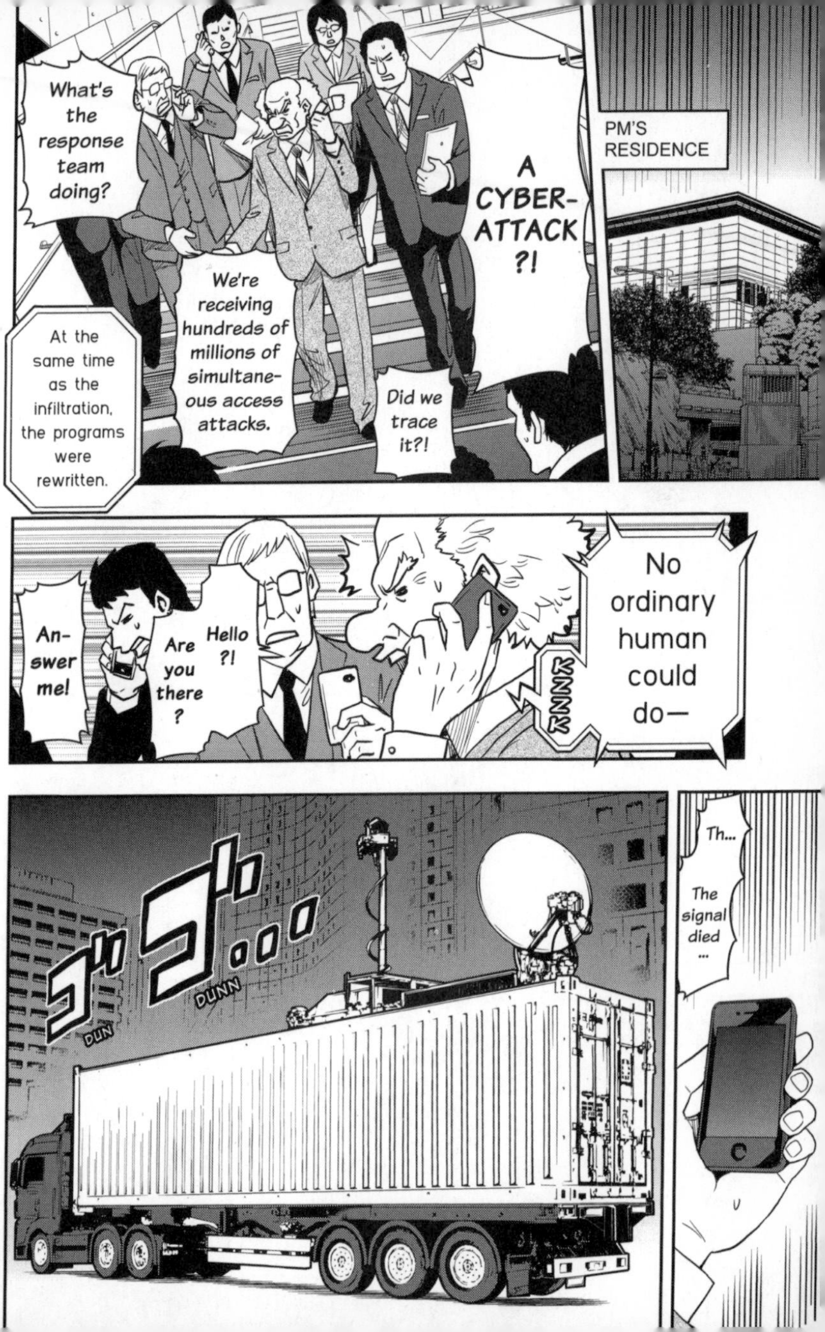
PM'S RESIDENCE
A CYBER-ATTACK?!
What's the response team doing?
Did we trace it?!
We're receiving hundreds of millions of simultaneous access attacks.
At the same time as the infiltration, the programs were rewritten.
No ordinary human could do—
KNNNK
Hello?!
Are you there?
Answer me!
Th...
The signal died...
DUNN
DUN

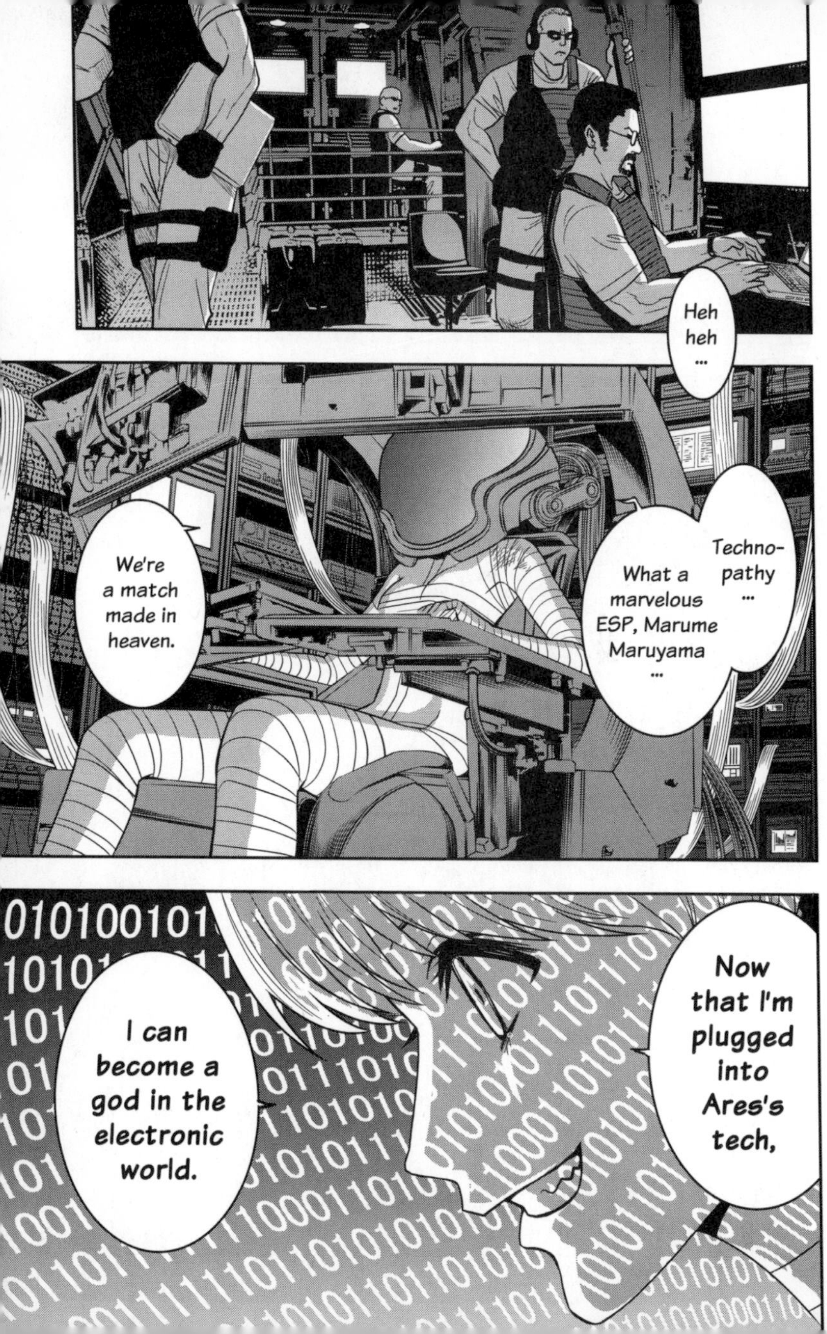
Heh heh ...
Techno-pathy ...
What a marvelous ESP, Marume Maruyama ...
We're a match made in heaven.
Now that I'm plugged into Ares's tech,
I can become a god in the electronic world.

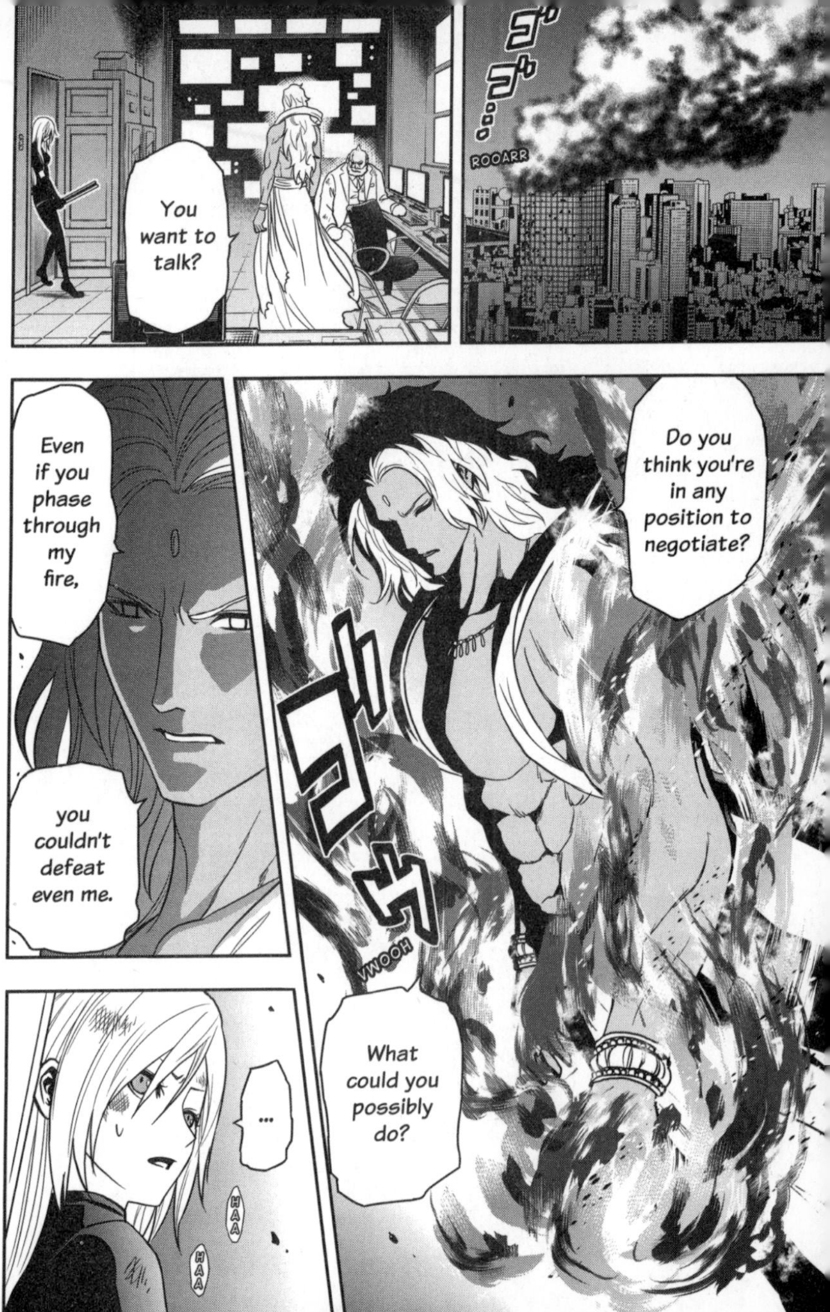
ROOARR
You want to talk?
Do you think you're in any position to negotiate?
VWOOH
What could you possibly do?
Even if you phase through my fire,
you couldn't defeat even me.
...
HAA
HAA

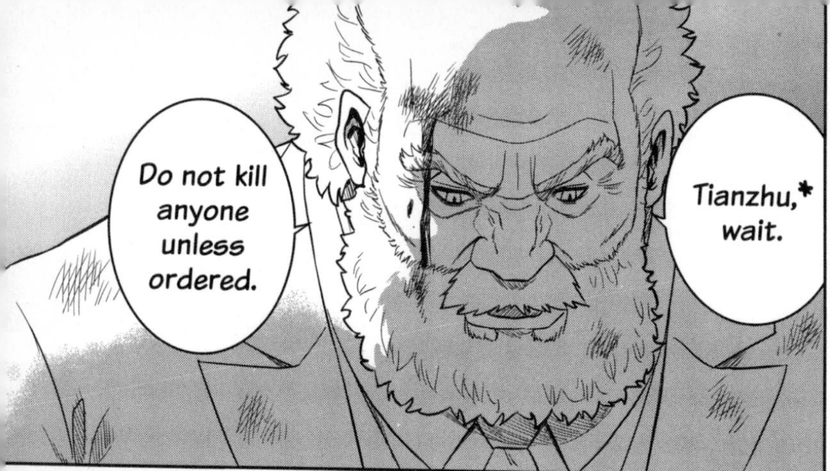
Tianzhu,* wait.
Do not kill anyone unless ordered.

*Literally, "Heavenly Master."

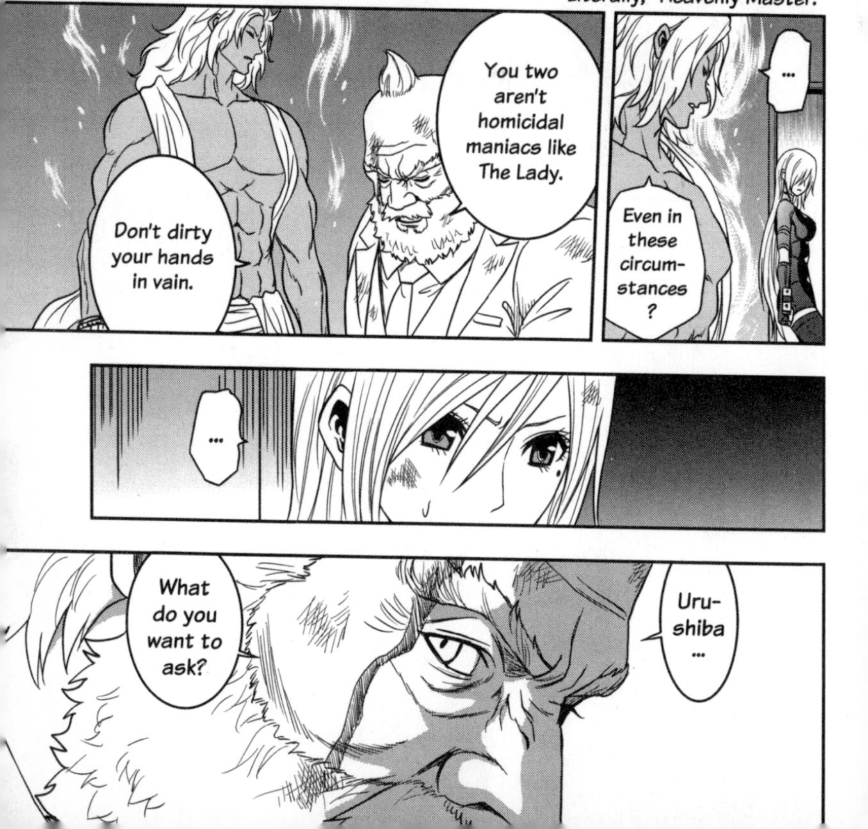
...
Even in these circumstances?
You two aren't homicidal maniacs like The Lady.
Don't dirty your hands in vain.
...
Uru-shiba...
What do you want to ask?

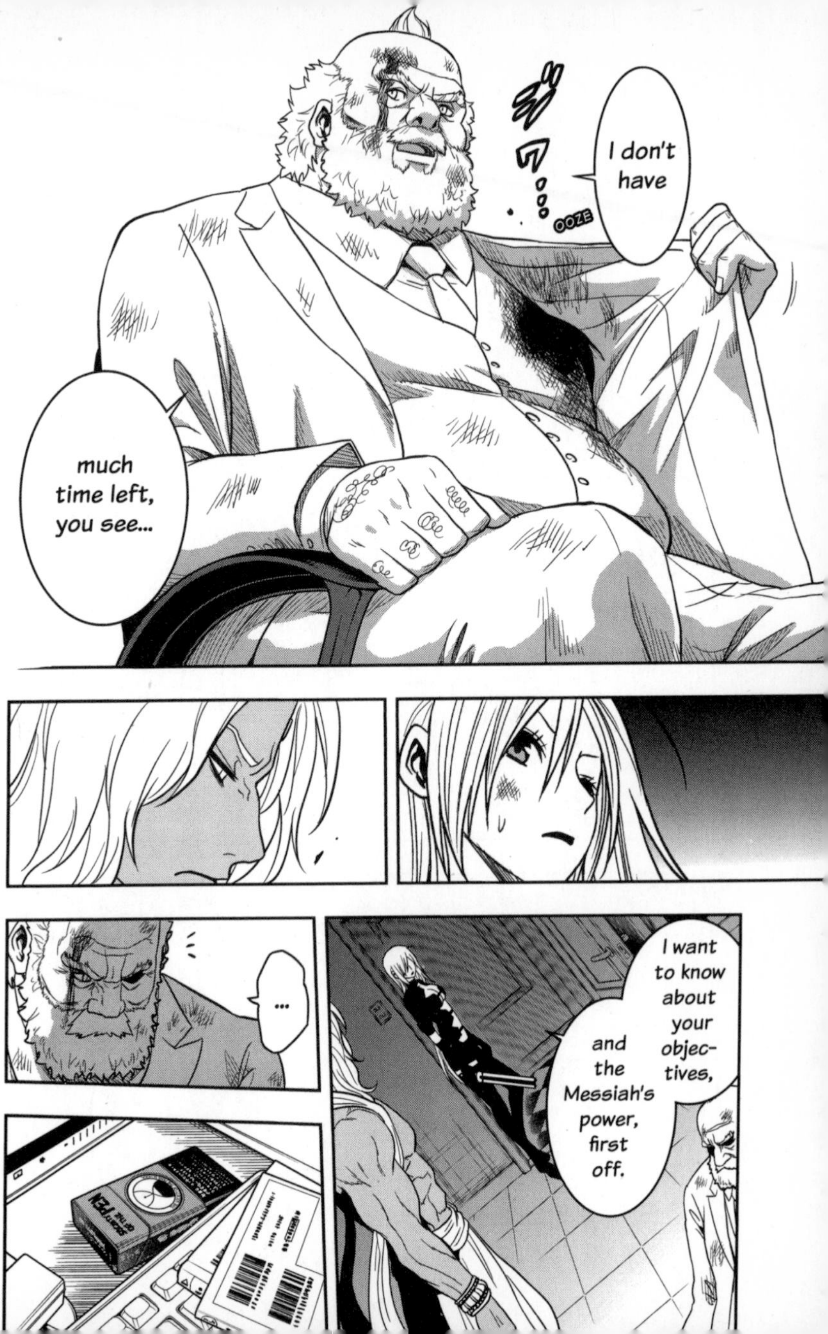
I don't have
much time left, you see...
OOZE
I want to know about your objectives, and the Messiah's power, first off.
...

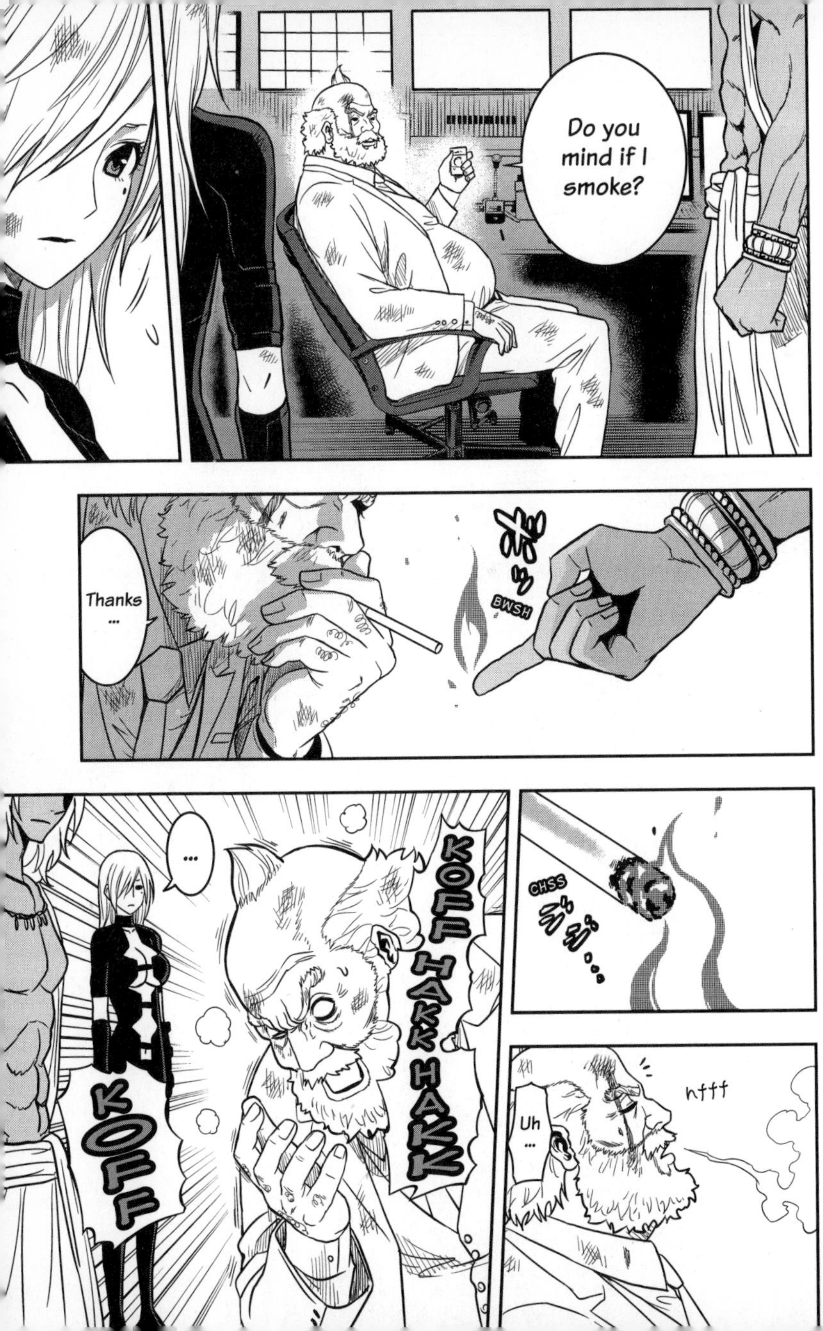
Do you mind if I smoke?
Thanks ...
BWSH
CHSS
Uh ...
hfff
...
KOFF HAKK HAKK
KOFF

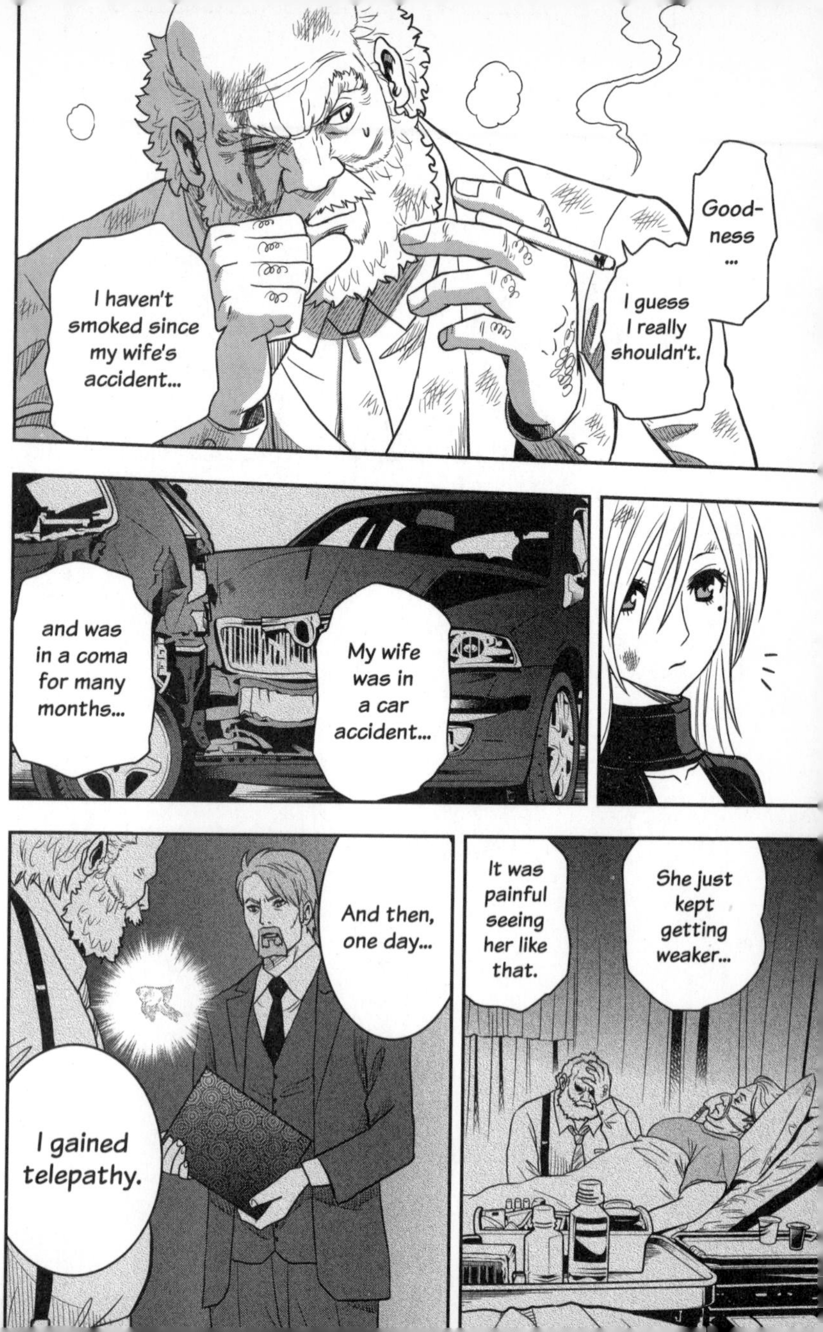
Goodness... I guess I really shouldn't.
I haven't smoked since my wife's accident...
My wife was in a car accident...
and was in a coma for many months...
She just kept getting weaker...
It was painful seeing her like that.
And then, one day...
I gained telepathy.

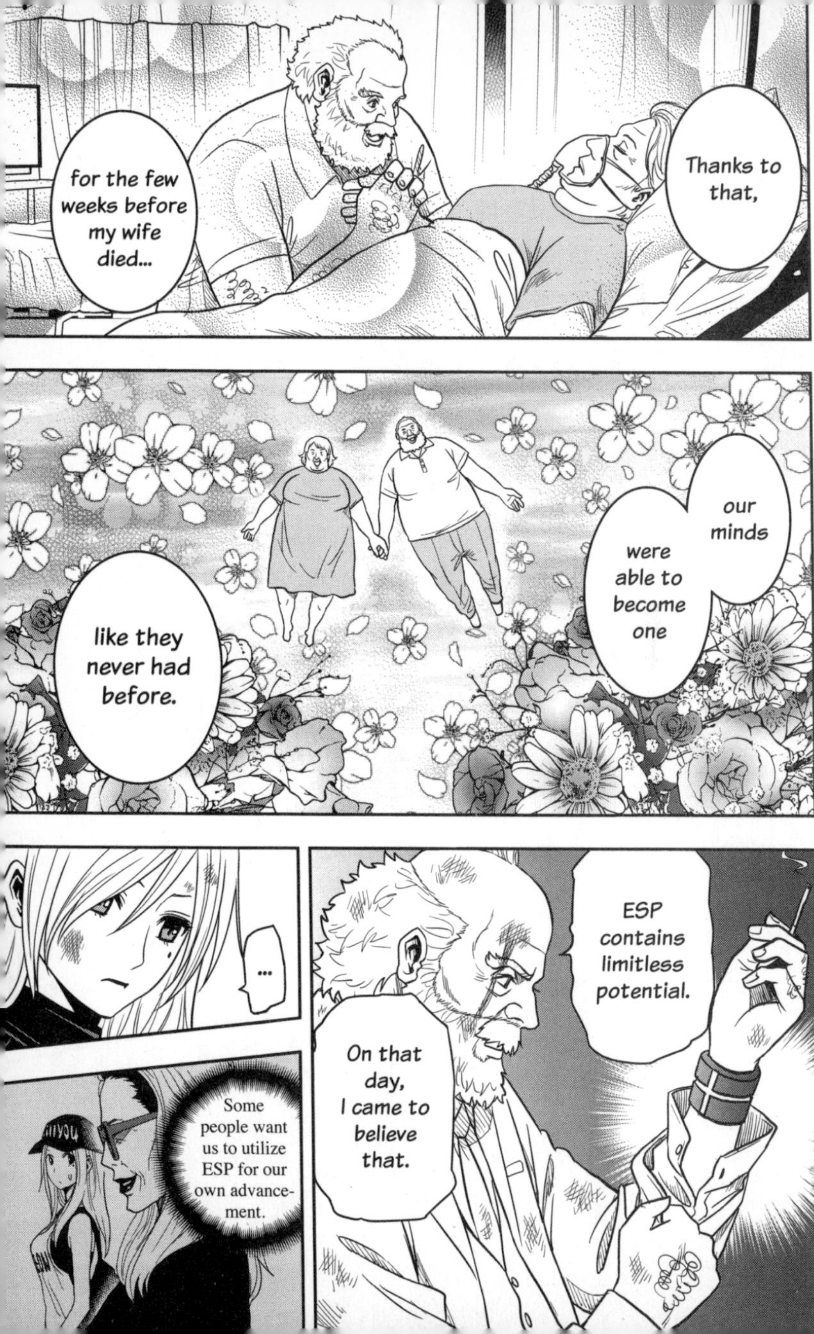
Thanks to that,
for the few weeks before my wife died...
our minds were able to become one
like they never had before.
ESP contains limitless potential.
On that day, I came to believe that.
...
Some people want us to utilize ESP for our own advancement.

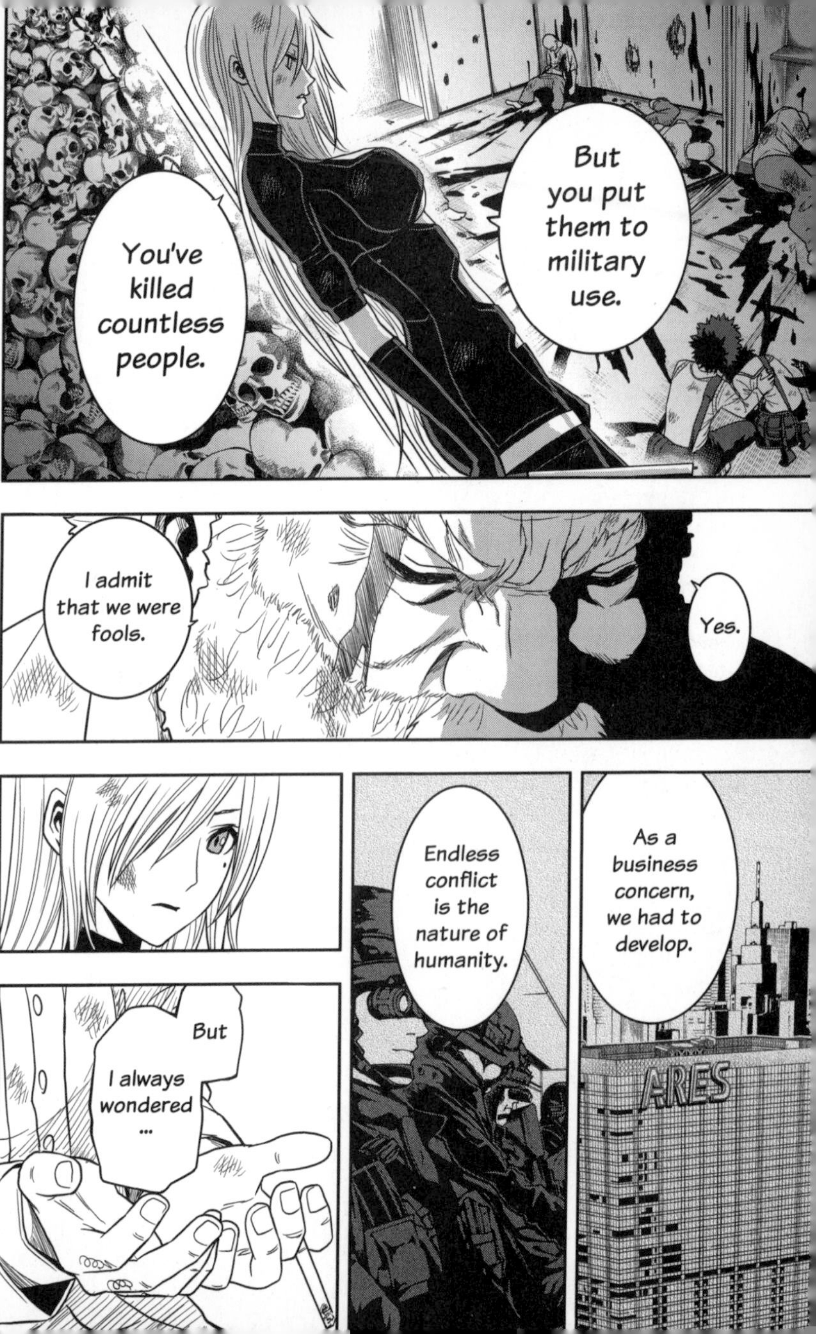
But you put them to military use.
You've killed countless people.
Yes.
I admit that we were fools.
As a business concern, we had to develop.
ARES
Endless conflict is the nature of humanity.
But I always wondered ...

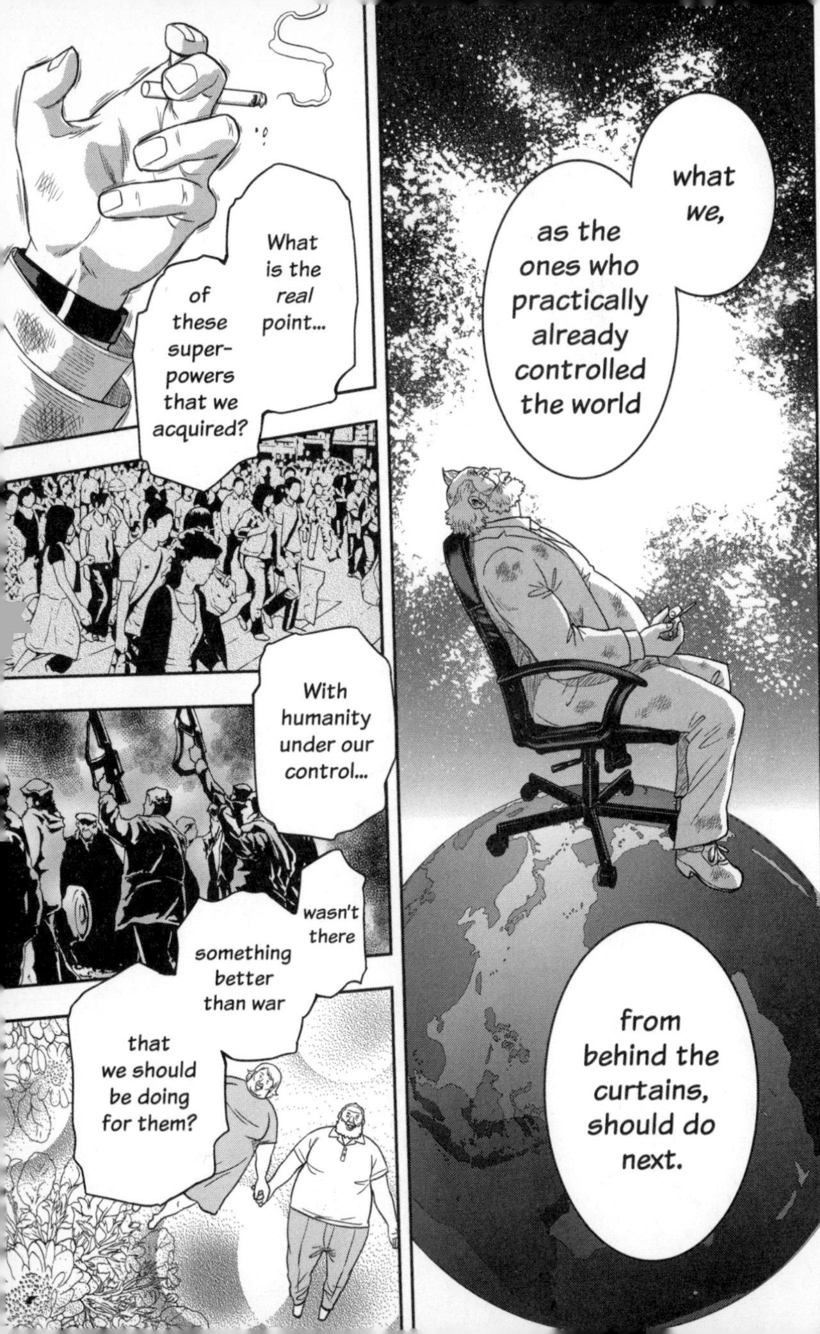
what we,
as the ones who practically already controlled the world
from behind the curtains, should do next.
What is the real point...
of these super-powers that we acquired?
With humanity under our control...
wasn't there
something better than war
that we should be doing for them?

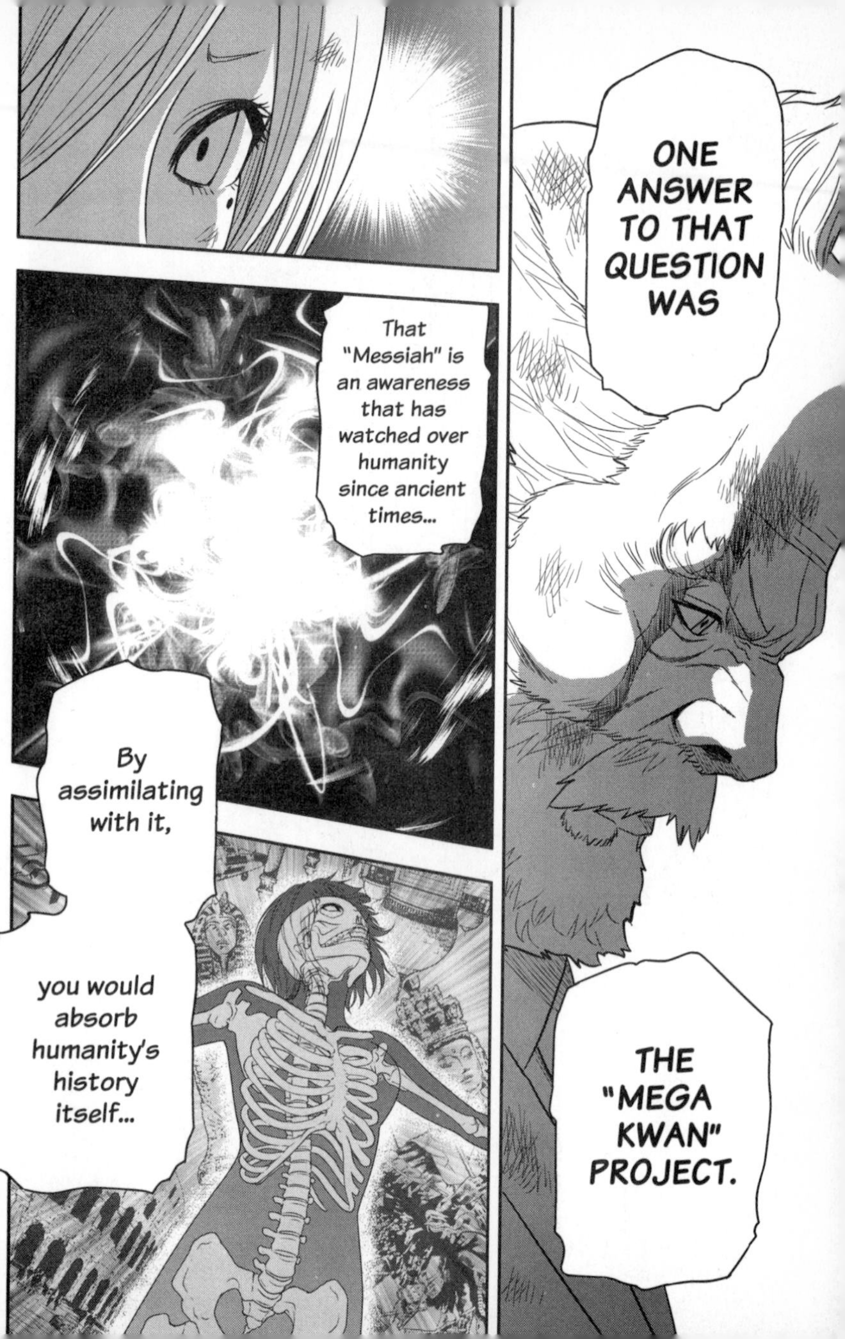
ONE ANSWER TO THAT QUESTION WAS
THE "MEGA KWAN" PROJECT.
That "Messiah" is an awareness that has watched over humanity since ancient times...
By assimilating with it,
you would absorb humanity's history itself...

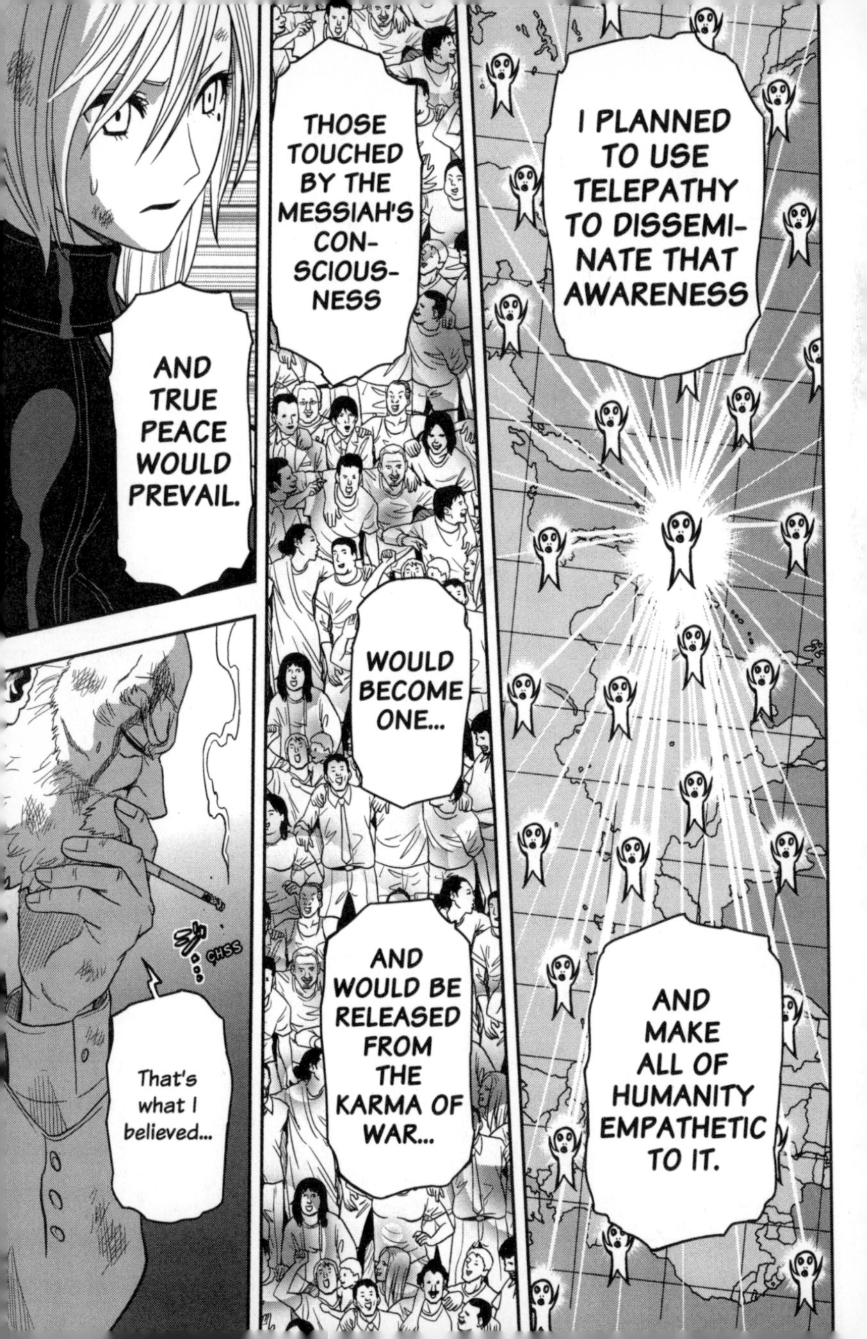
I PLANNED TO USE TELEPATHY TO DISSEMINATE THAT AWARENESS
AND MAKE ALL OF HUMANITY EMPATHETIC TO IT.
THOSE TOUCHED BY THE MESSIAH'S CONSCIOUSNESS
WOULD BECOME ONE...
AND WOULD BE RELEASED FROM THE KARMA OF WAR...
AND TRUE PEACE WOULD PREVAIL.
CHSS
That's what I believed...

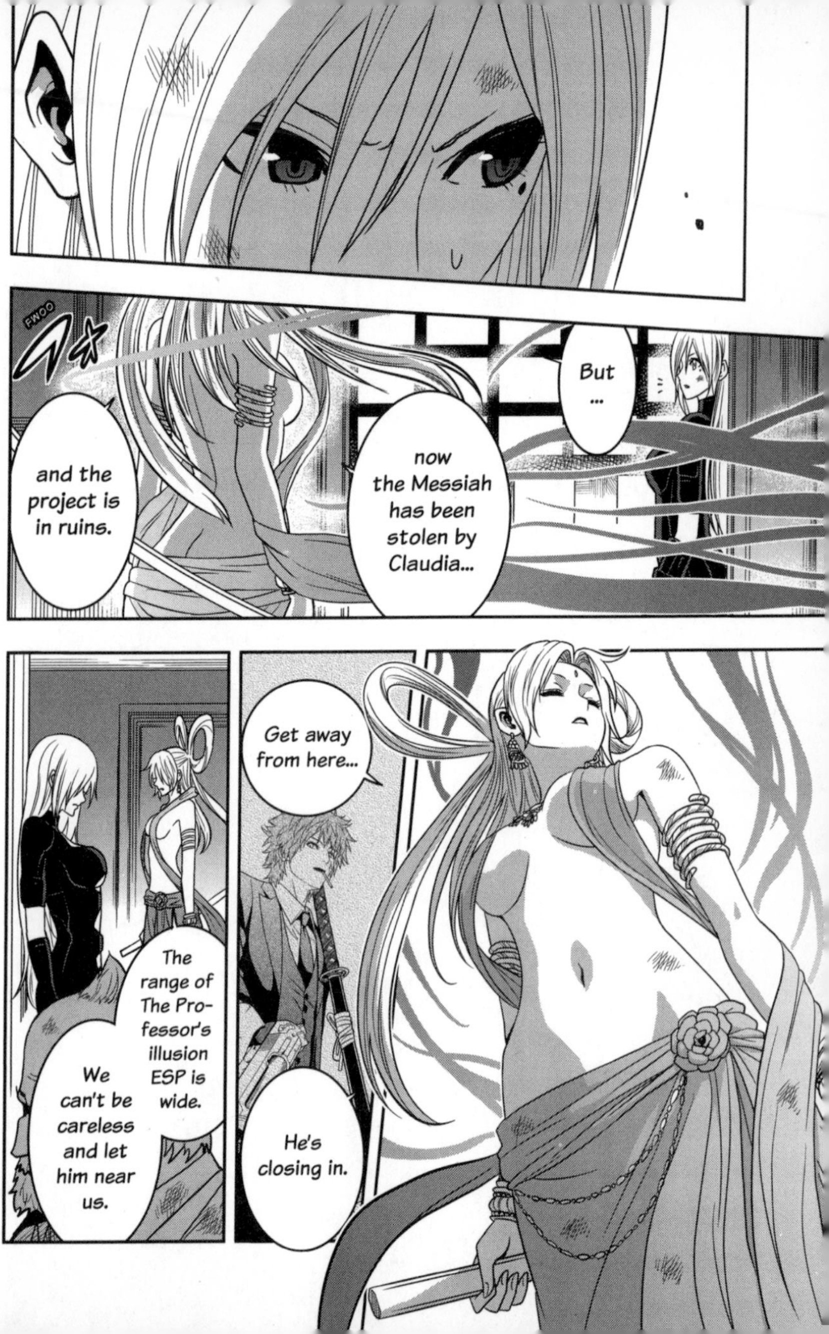
FWOO
But ...
now the Messiah has been stolen by Claudia...
and the project is in ruins.
Get away from here...
He's closing in.
The range of The Professor's illusion ESP is wide.
We can't be careless and let him near us.

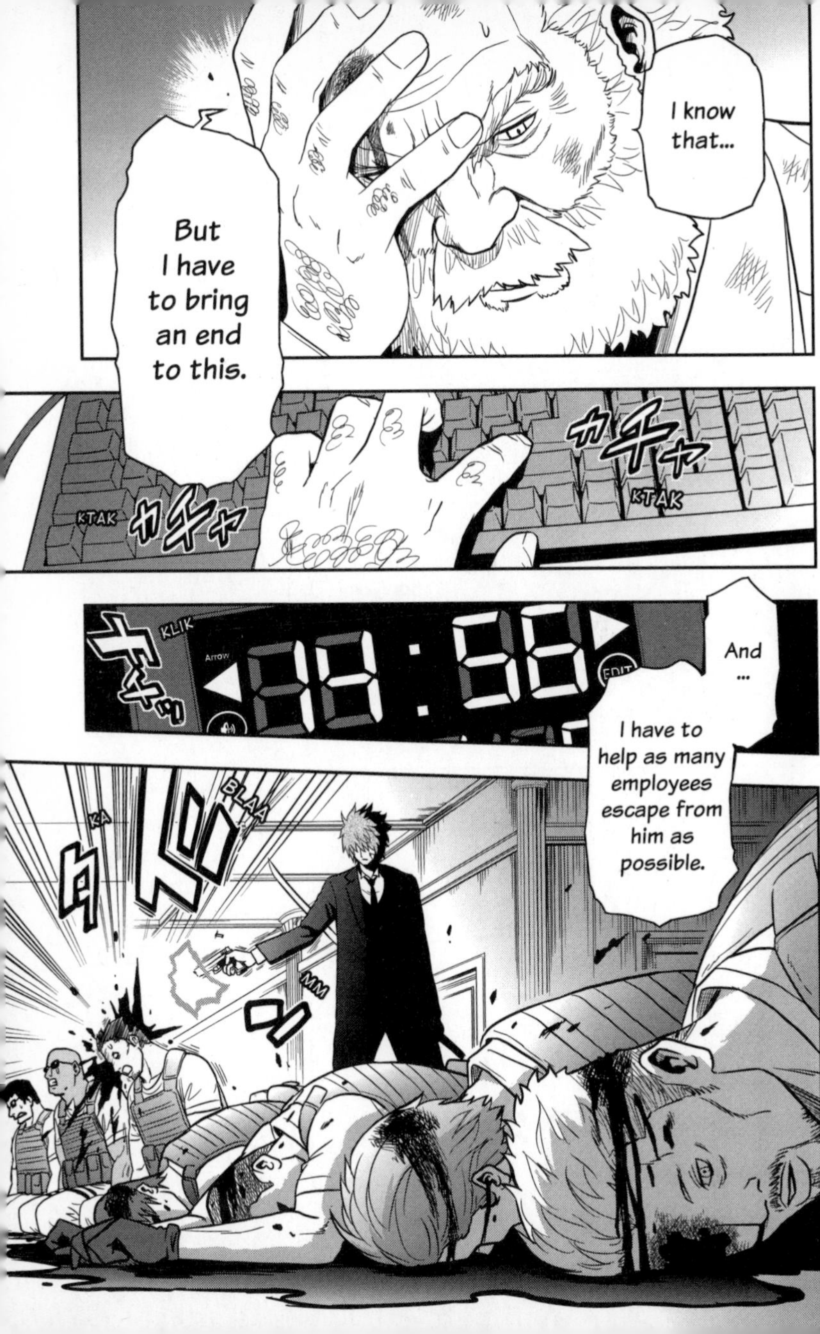
I know that...
But I have to bring an end to this.
KTAK
KTAK
KLIK
Arrow
EDIT
And...
I have to help as many employees escape from him as possible.
BLAA
KA
MM

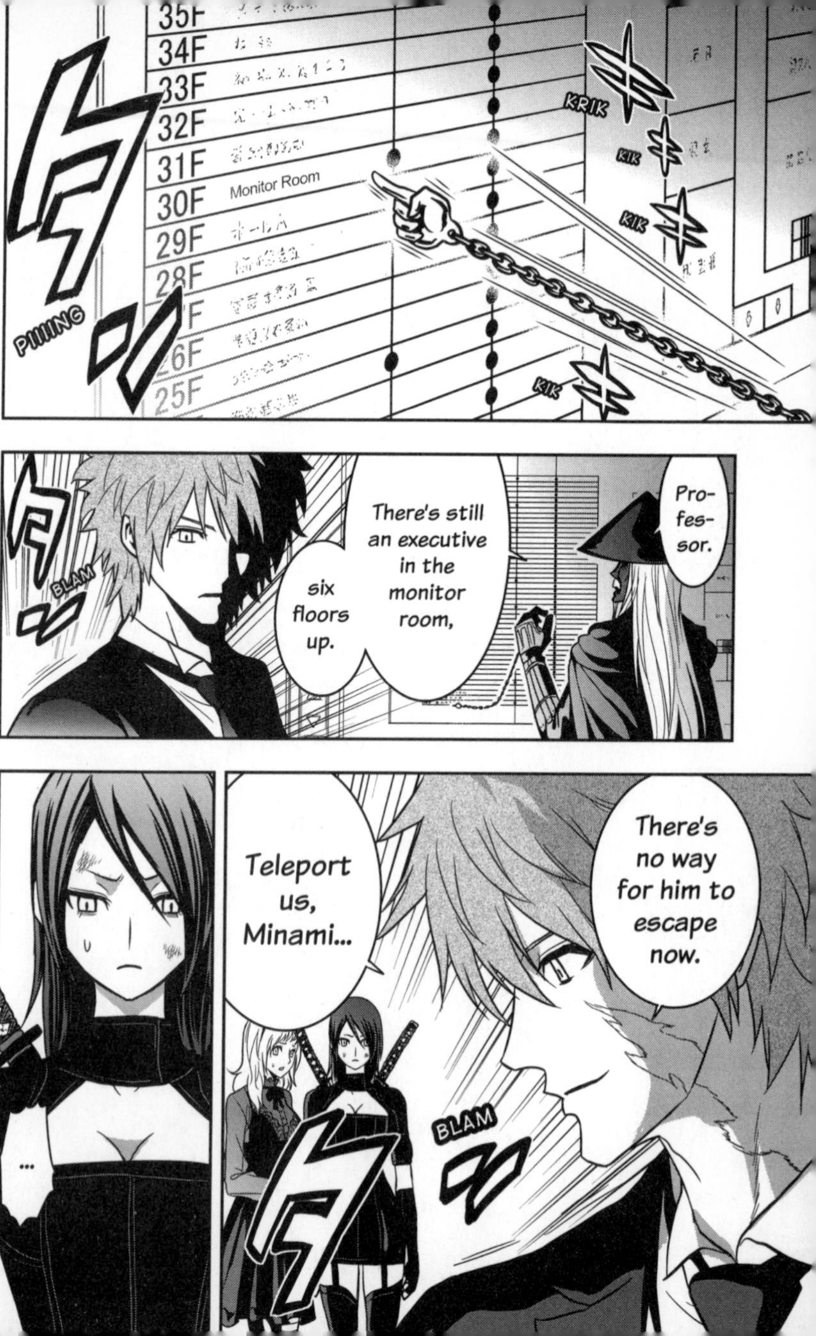
35F
34F
33F
32F
31F
Monitor Room
30F
29F
28F
26F
25F
KRIK
KIK
KIK
KIK
PIIIING
Pro-fes-sor.
There's still an executive in the monitor room,
six floors up.
BLAM
There's no way for him to escape now.
Teleport us, Minami...
BLAM
...

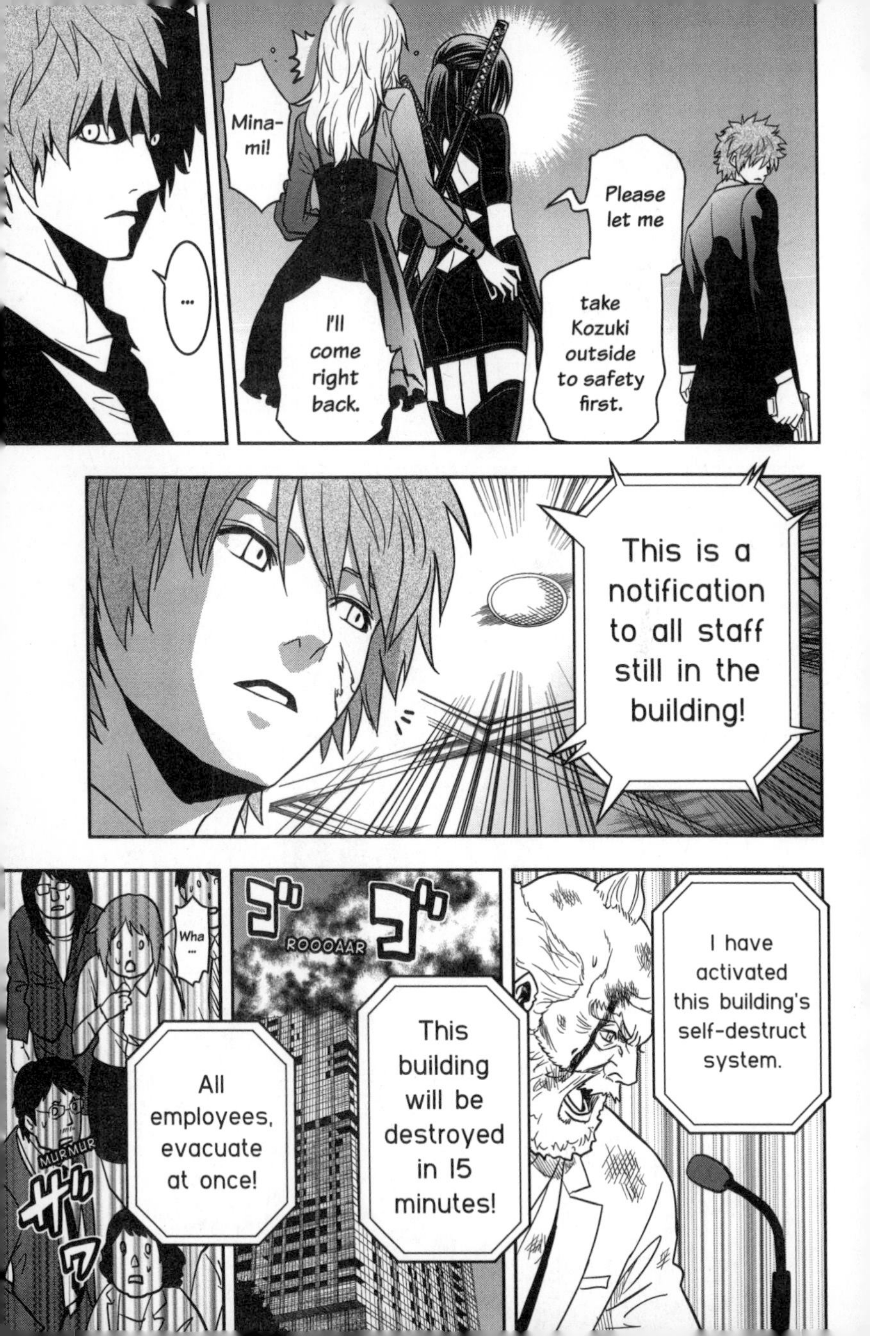
Please let me
take Kozuki outside to safety first.
I'll come right back.
Mina-mi!
...
This is a notification to all staff still in the building!
I have activated this building's self-destruct system.
ゴゴ
ROOOOAAR
This building will be destroyed in 15 minutes!
Wha...
All employees, evacuate at once!
MURMUR
ザワ

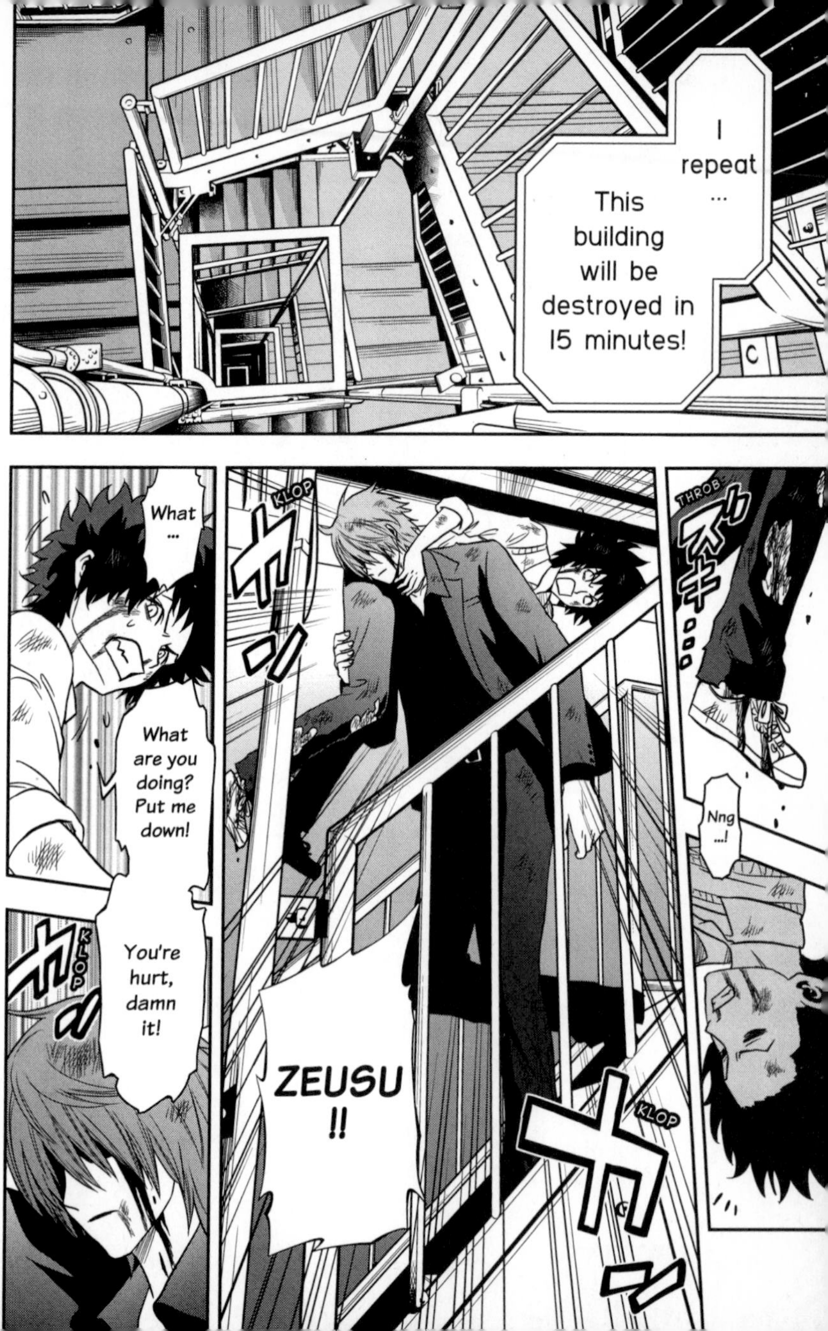

I repeat ...
This building will be destroyed in 15 minutes!
THROB
Nng ...!
KLOP
ZEUSU !!
KLOP
What ...
What are you doing? Put me down!
KLOP
You're hurt, damn it!

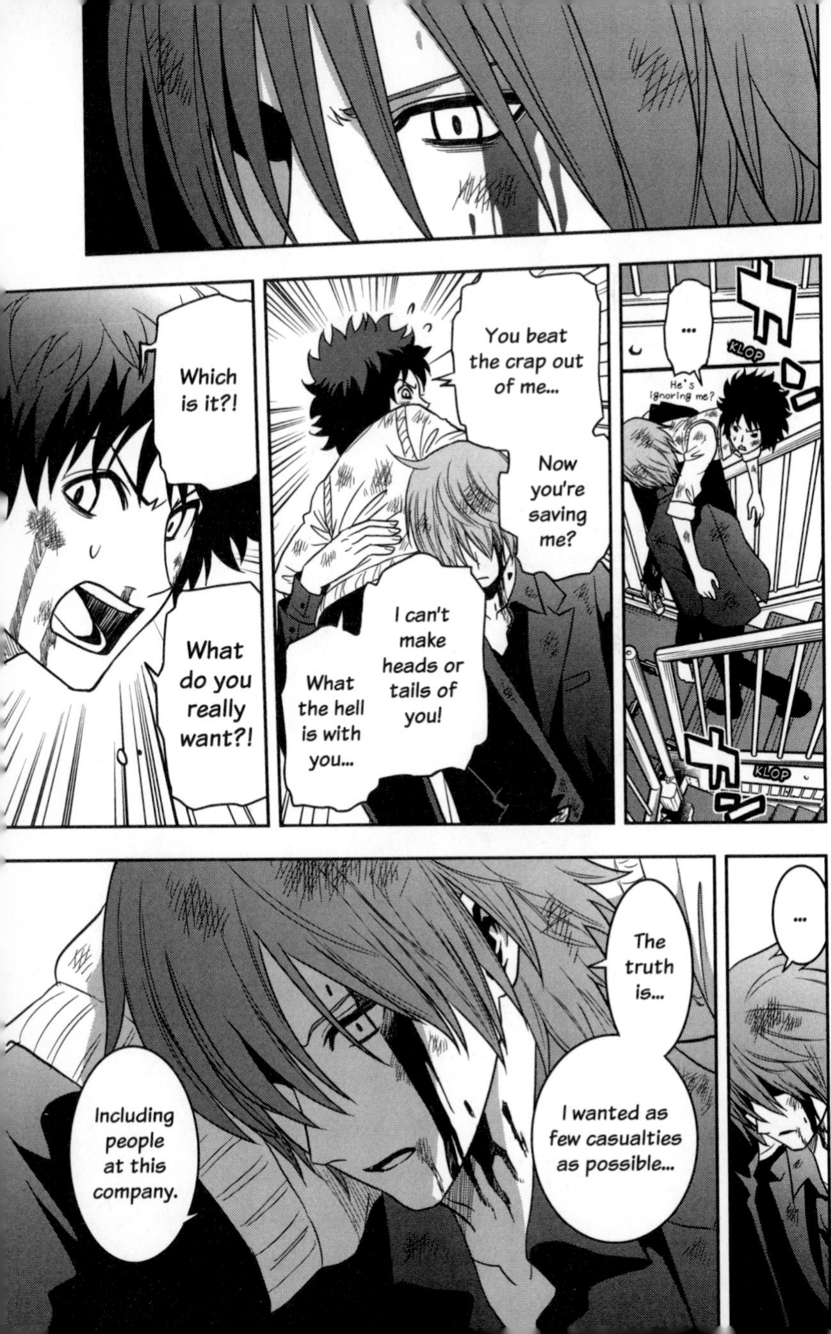
...
KLOP
He's ignoring me?
KLOP
You beat the crap out of me...
Now you're saving me?
I can't make heads or tails of you!
What the hell is with you...
Which is it?!
What do you really want?!
...
The truth is...
I wanted as few casualties as possible...
Including people at this company.

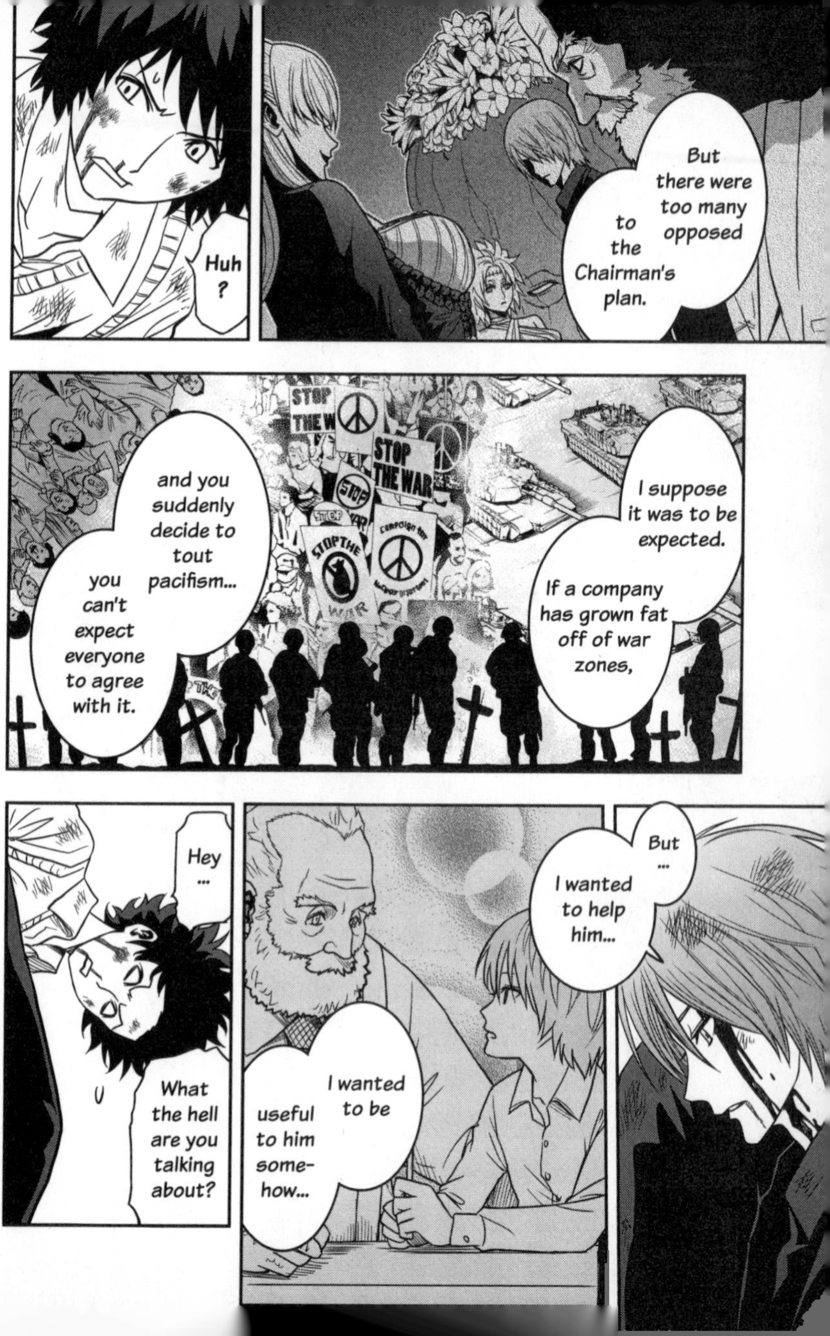

But there were too many opposed to the Chairman's plan.
Huh?
I suppose it was to be expected.
If a company has grown fat off of war zones,
and you suddenly decide to tout pacifism...
you can't expect everyone to agree with it.
STOP THE WAR
STOP THE WAR
But...
I wanted to help him...
I wanted to be useful to him somehow...
Hey...
What the hell are you talking about?

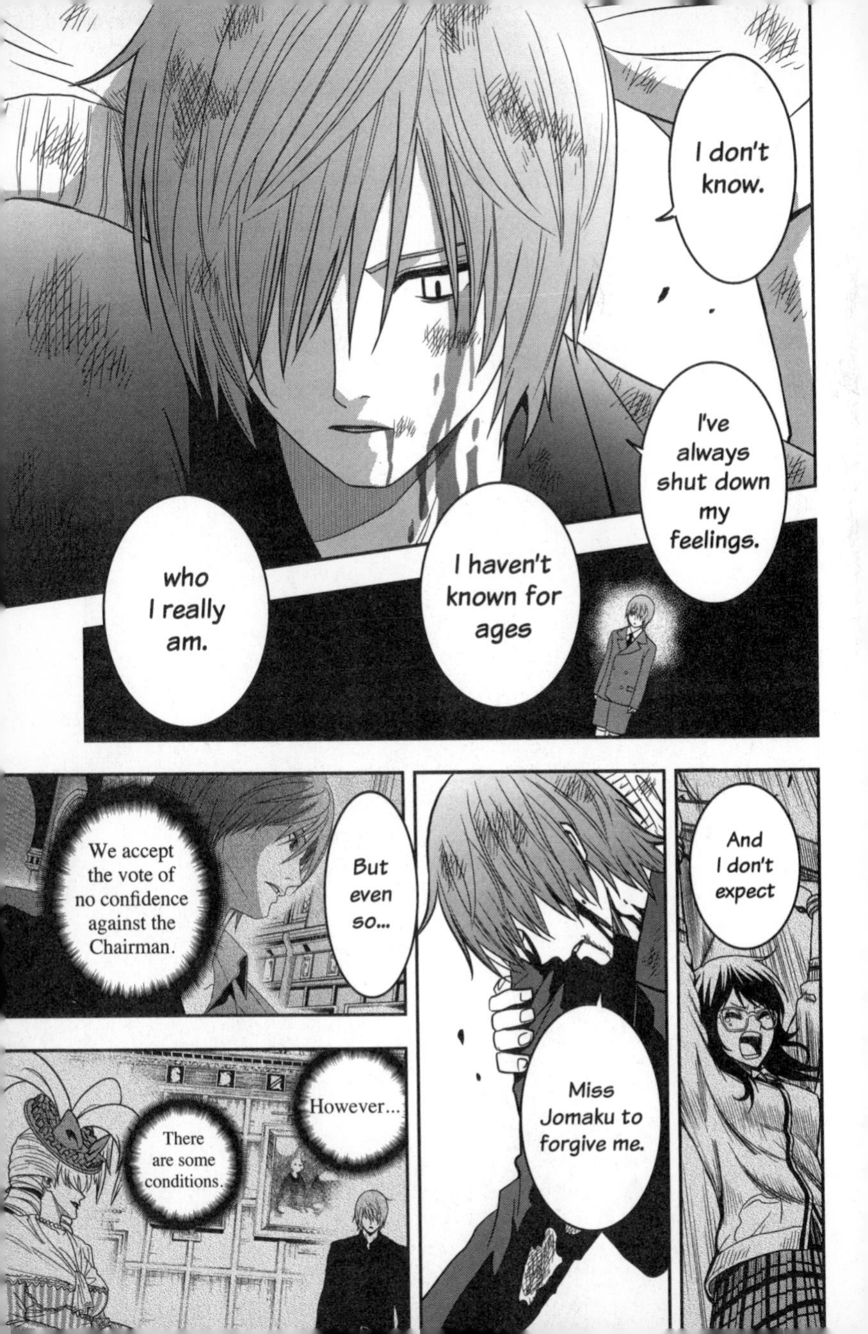
I don't know.
I've always shut down my feelings.
I haven't known for ages
who I really am.
And I don't expect
Miss Jomaku to forgive me.
But even so...
We accept the vote of no confidence against the Chairman.
However...
There are some conditions.

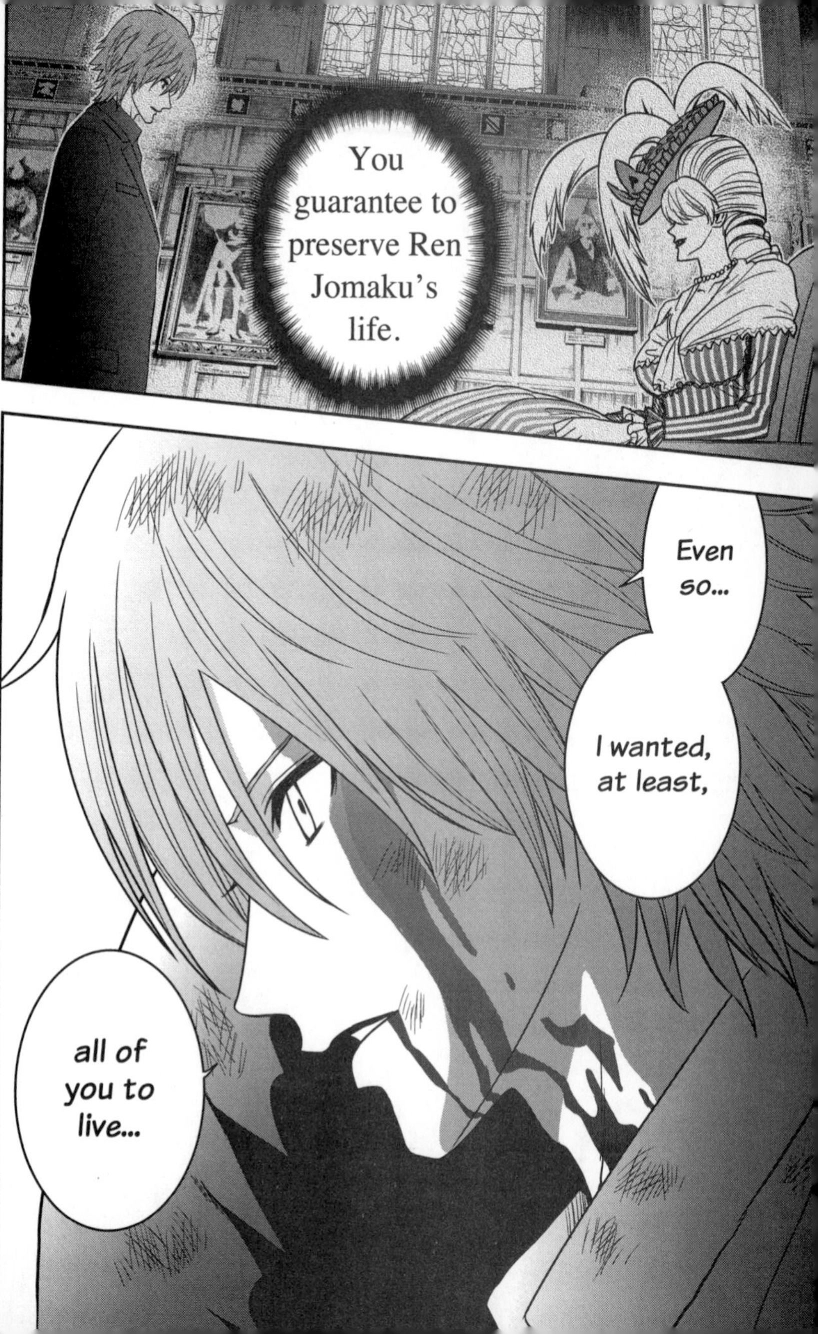
You guarantee to preserve Ren Jomaku's life.
Even so...
I wanted, at least,
all of you to live...

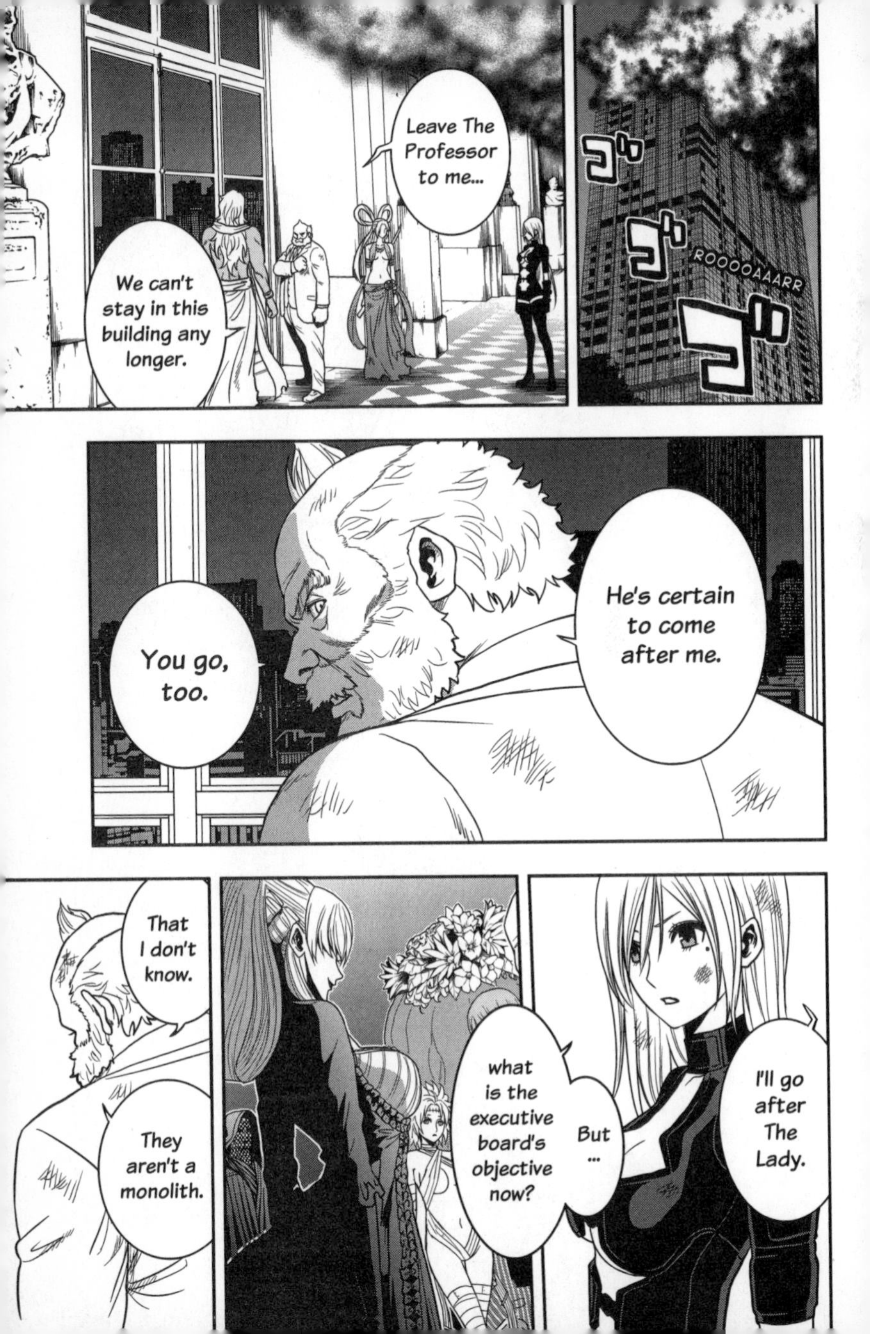
ROOOOAAARR
Leave The Professor to me...
We can't stay in this building any longer.
He's certain to come after me.
You go, too.
I'll go after The Lady.
But ...
what is the executive board's objective now?
That I don't know.
They aren't a monolith.

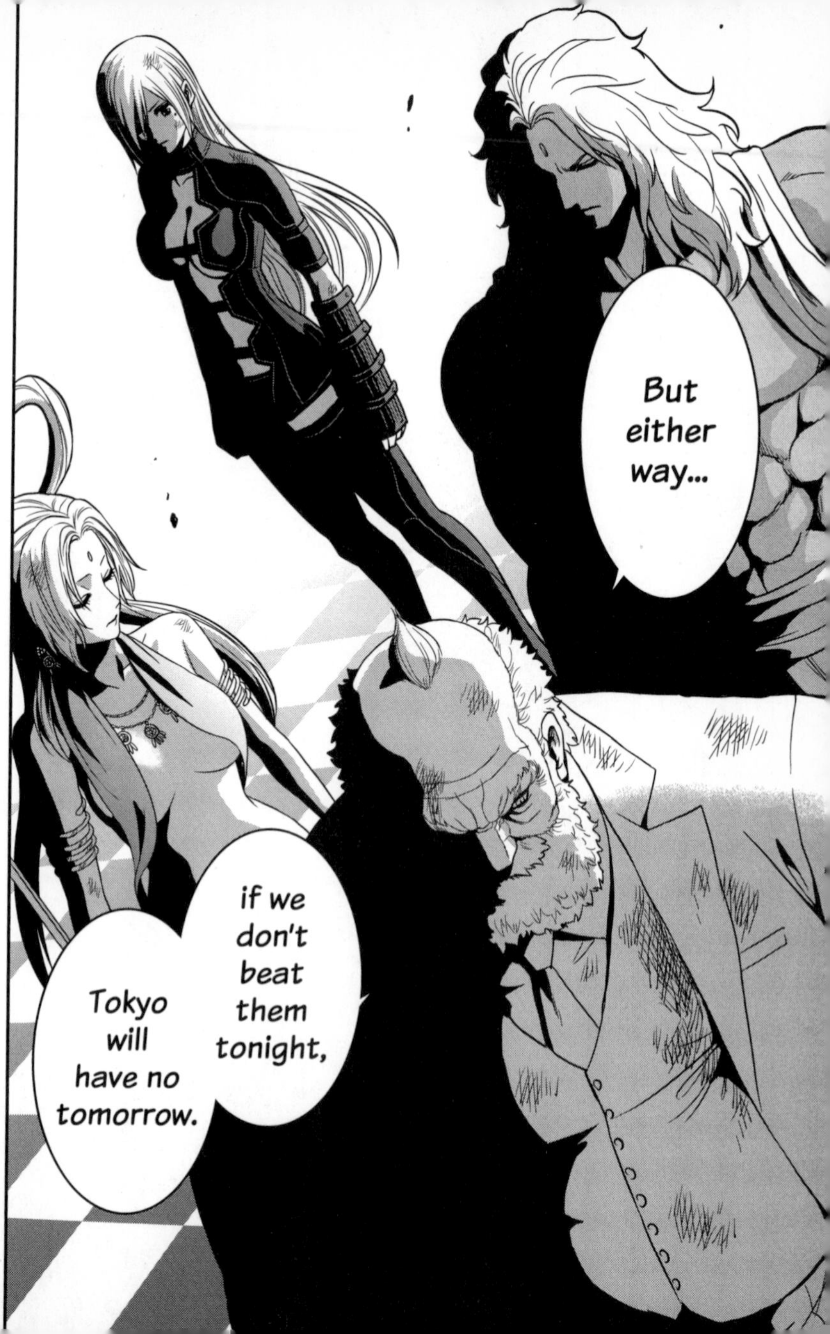
But either way...
if we don't beat them tonight,
Tokyo will have no tomorrow.

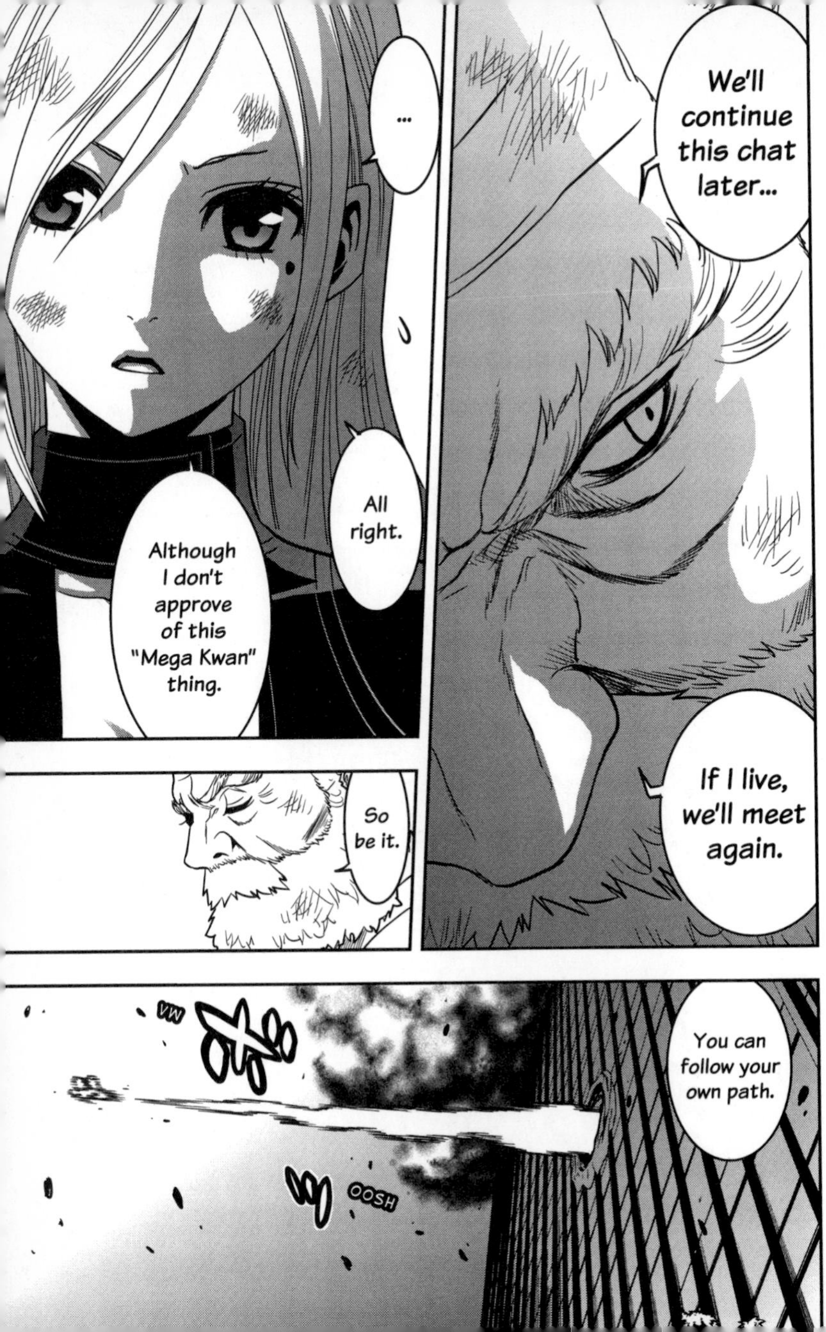
We'll continue this chat later...
If I live, we'll meet again.
...
All right.
Although I don't approve of this "Mega Kwan" thing.
So be it.
You can follow your own path.
VW
OOSH

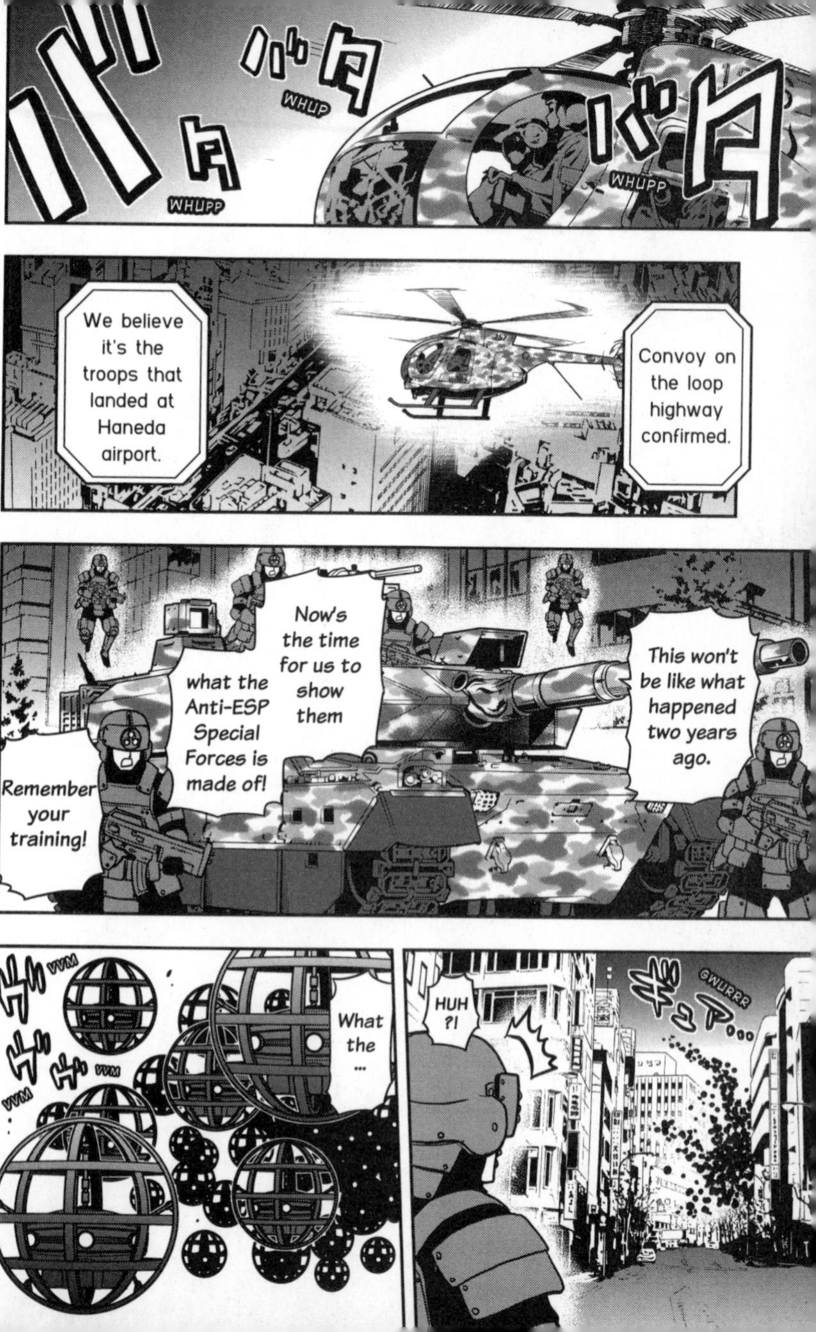

WHUPP
WHUP
WHUPP
Convoy on the loop highway confirmed.
We believe it's the troops that landed at Haneda airport.
This won't be like what happened two years ago.
Now's the time for us to show them
what the Anti-ESP Special Forces is made of!
Remember your training!
GWURRR
HUH ?!
VVM
What the ...
VVM
VVM

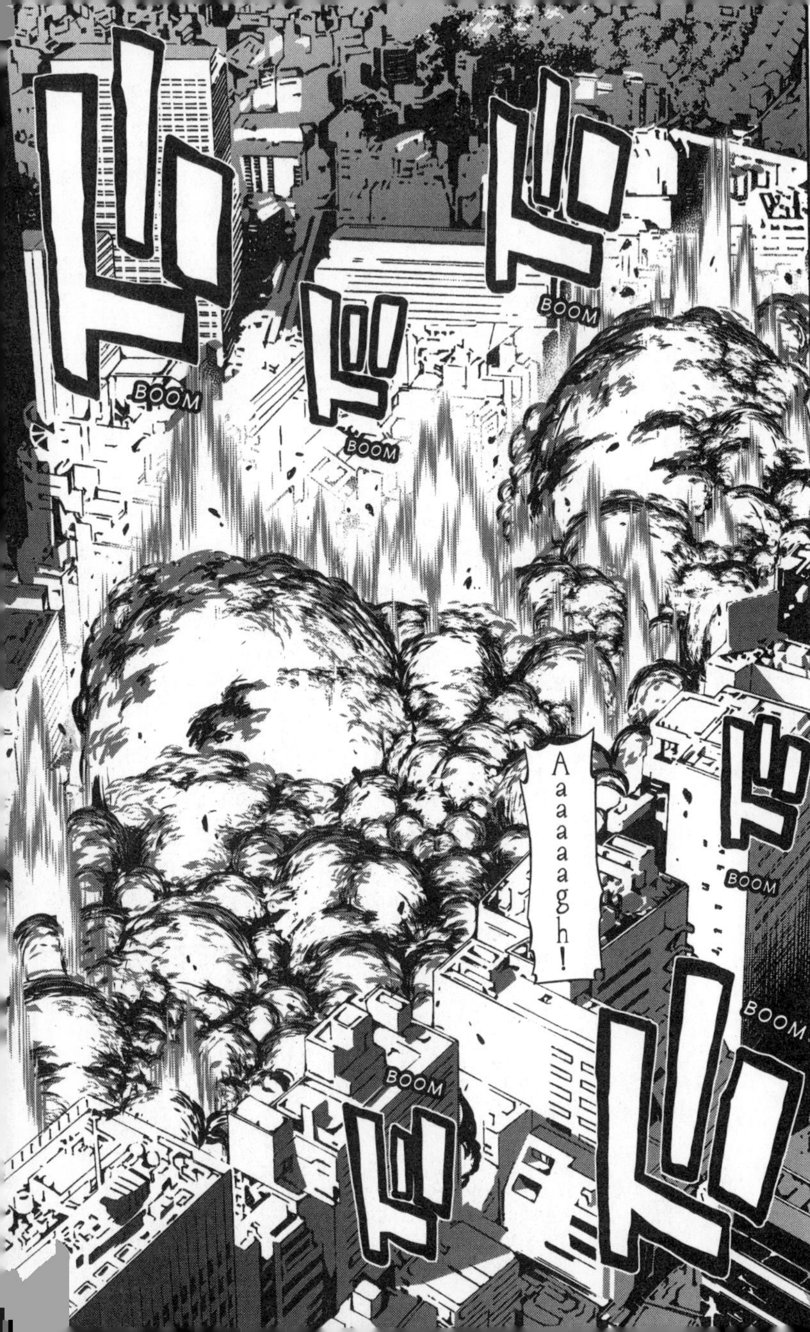
BOOM
BOOM
BOOM
Aaaaaagh!
BOOM
BOOM.
BOOM

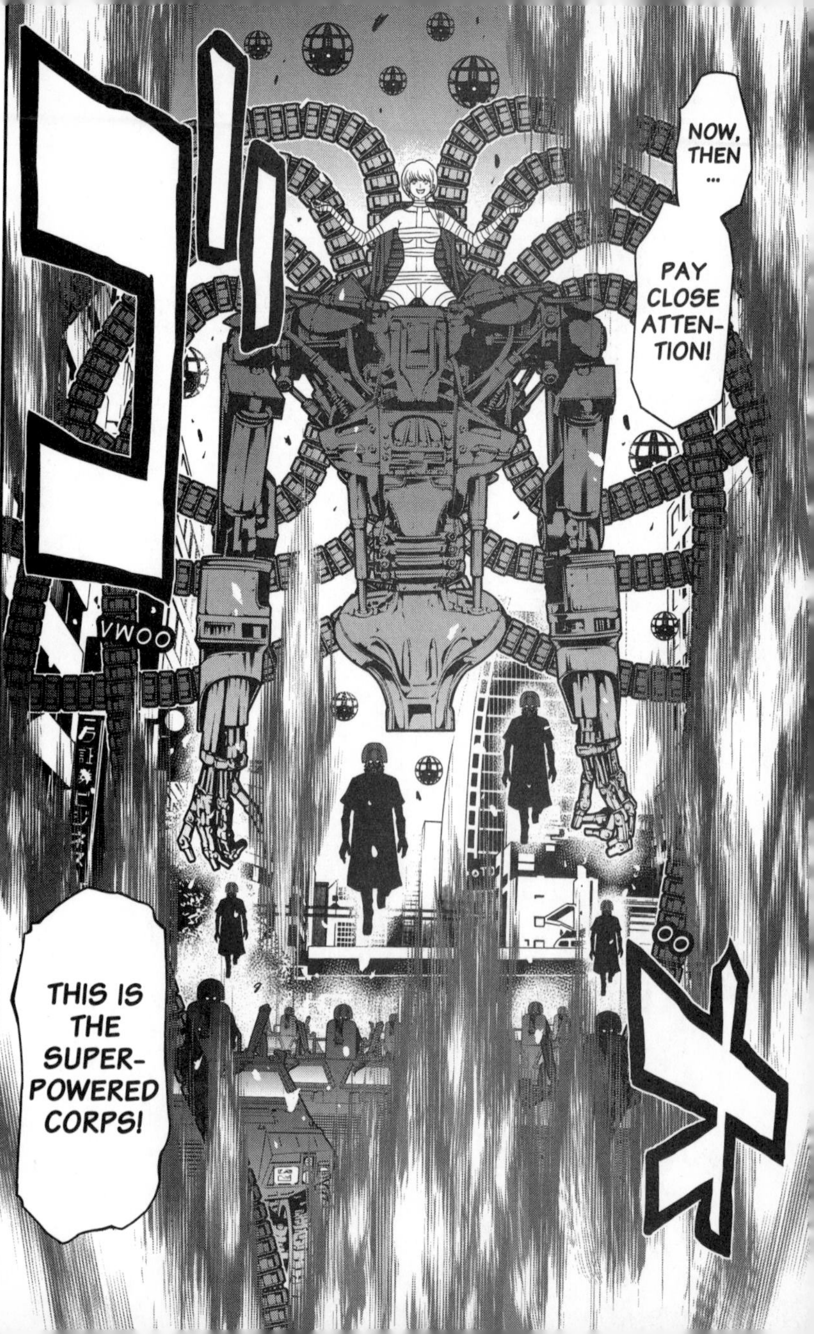
NOW, THEN ...
PAY CLOSE ATTEN-TION!
VWOO
THIS IS THE SUPER-POWERED CORPS!

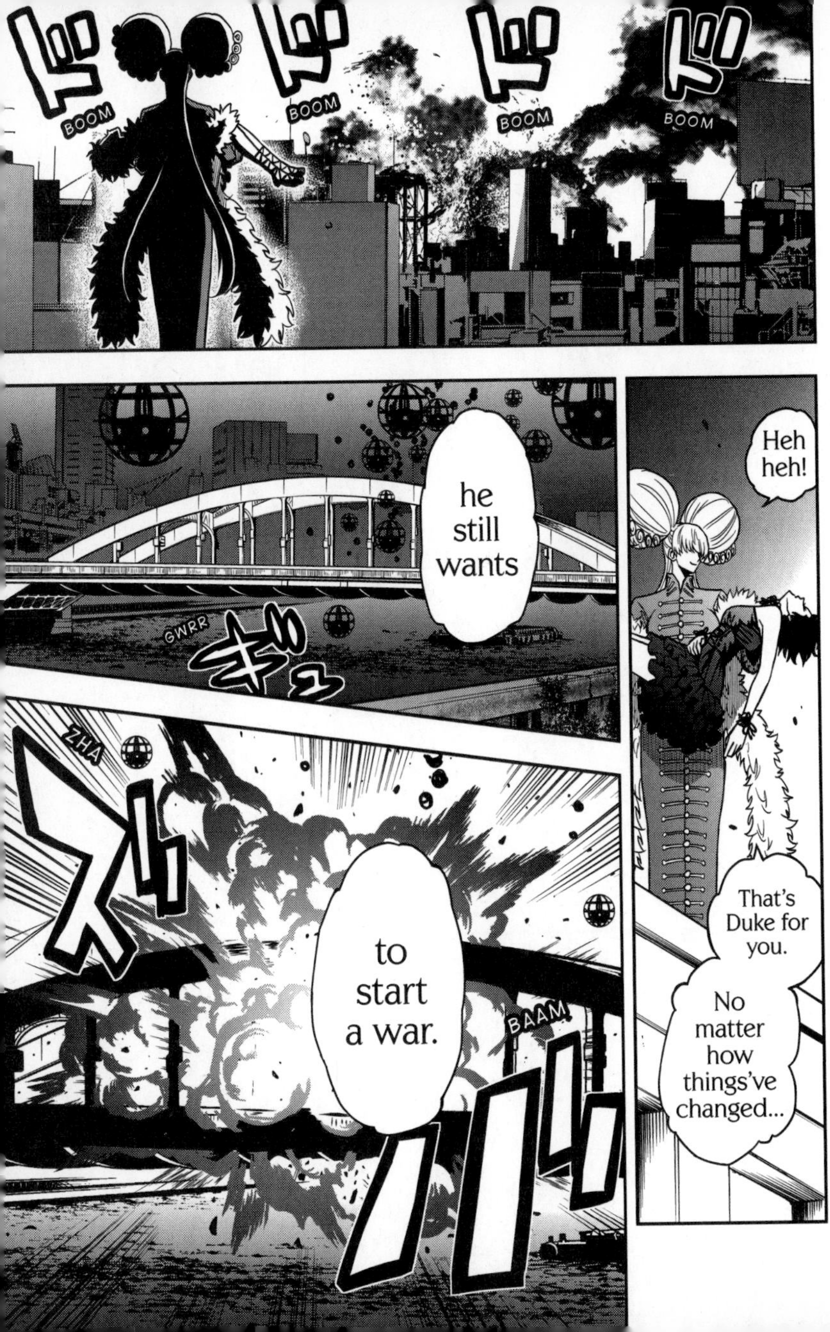

ドッ
BOOM
ドッ
BOOM
ドッ
BOOM
ドッ
BOOM
Heh heh!
That's Duke for you.
No matter how things've changed...
he still wants
GWRR
to start a war.
ZHA
BAAM

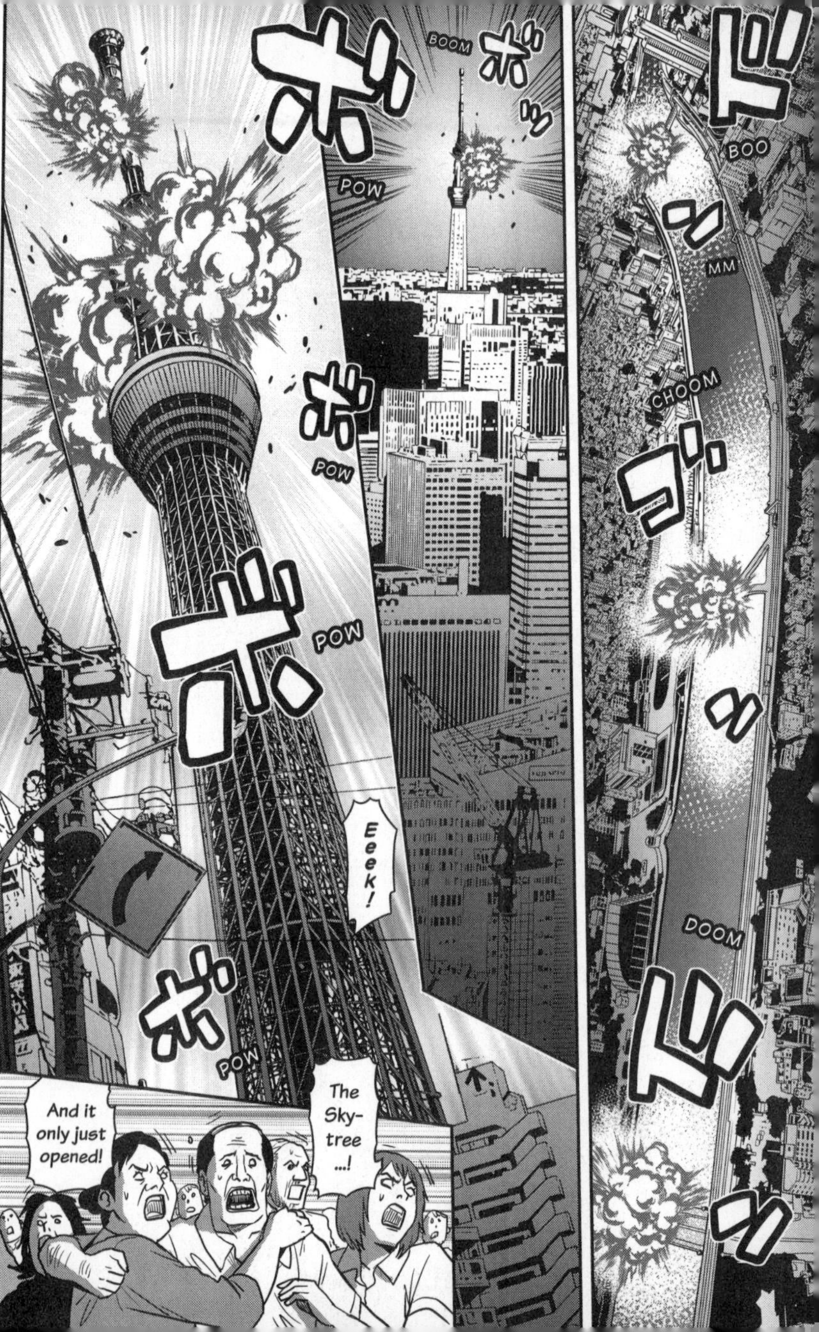
BOO
MM
CHOOM
DOOM
BOOM
POW
POW
POW
Eeeek!
POW
The Sky-tree ...!
And it only just opened!

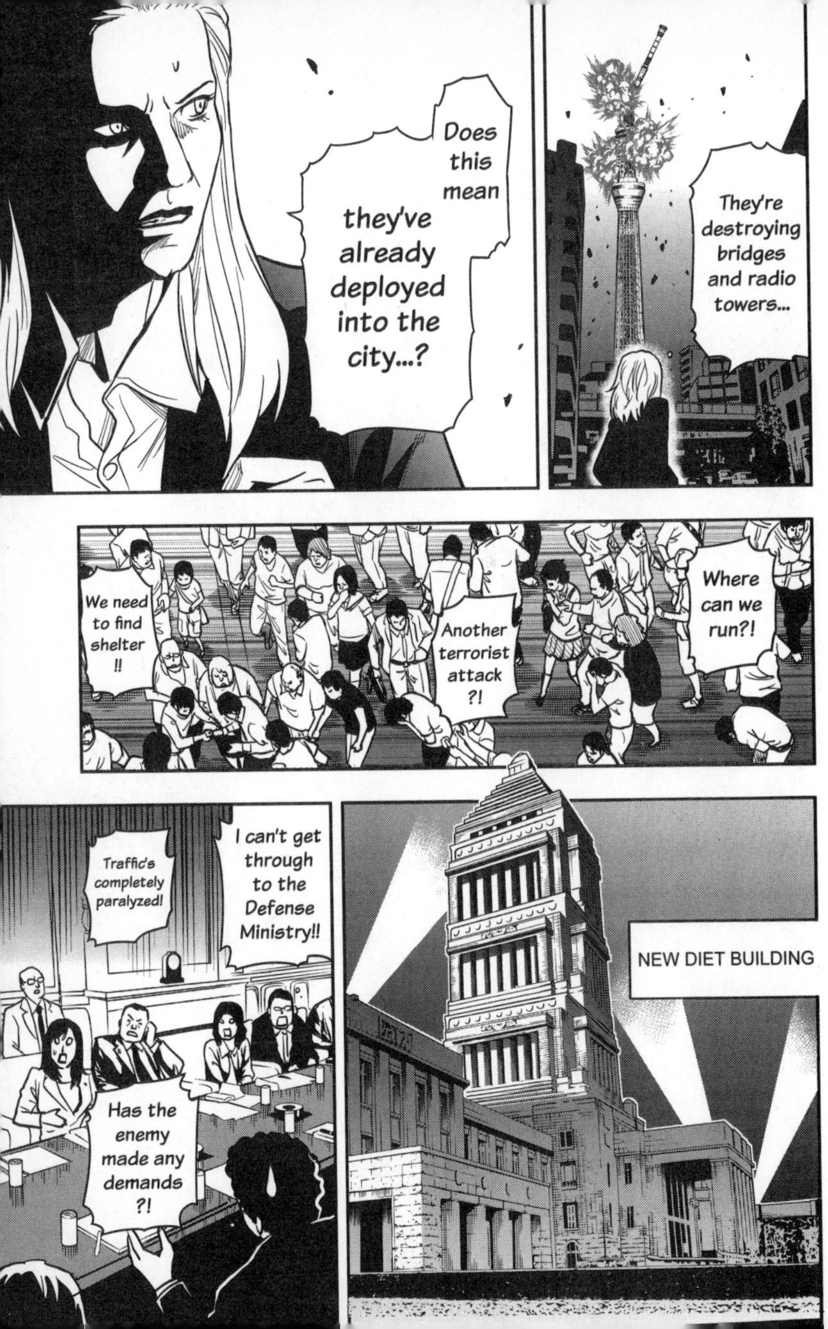
They're destroying bridges and radio towers...
Does this mean they've already deployed into the city...?
Where can we run?!
Another terrorist attack ?!
We need to find shelter !!
NEW DIET BUILDING
I can't get through to the Defense Ministry!!
Traffic's completely paralyzed!
Has the enemy made any demands ?!

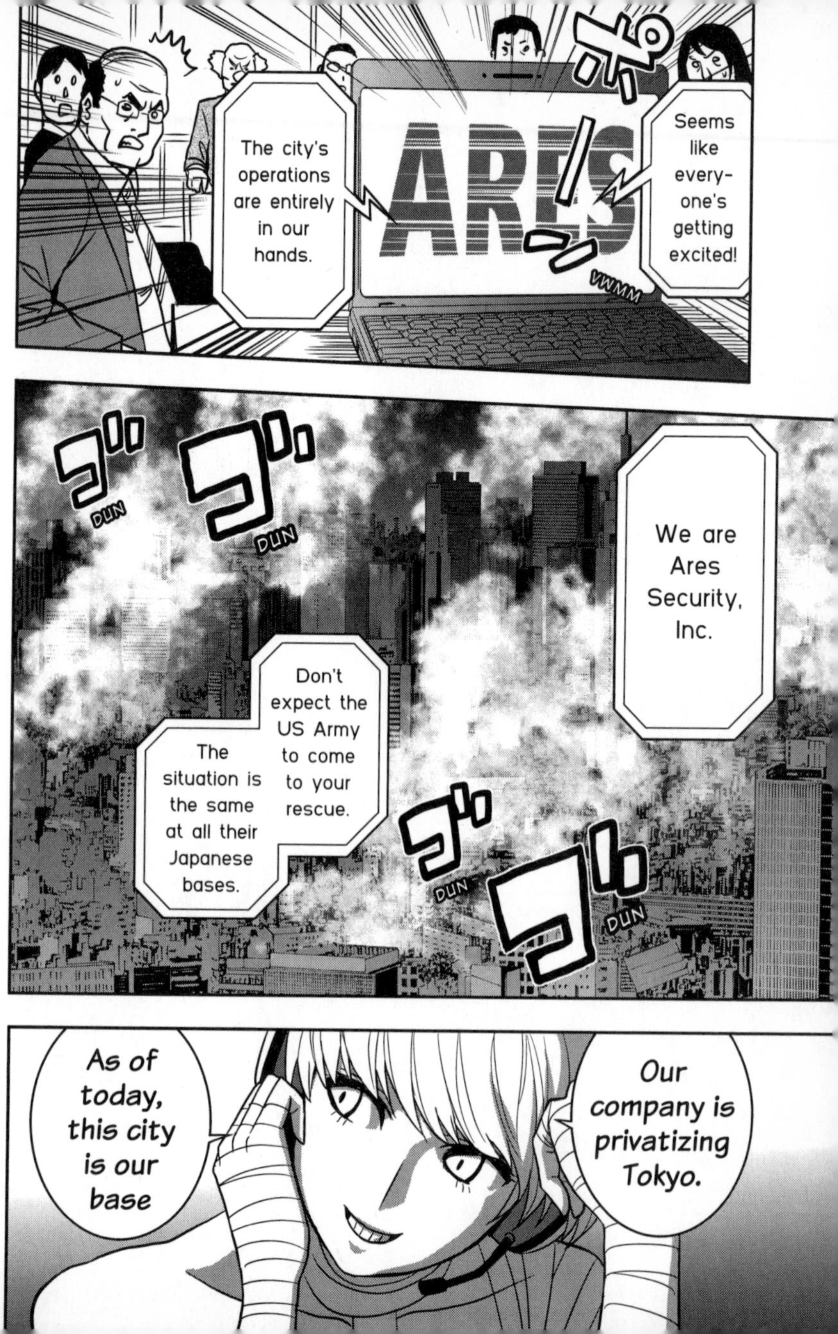
Seems like every-one's getting excited!
ARES
VWMM
The city's operations are entirely in our hands.
We are Ares Security, Inc.
Don't expect the US Army to come to your rescue.
The situation is the same at all their Japanese bases.
DUN
DUN
DUN
DUN
Our company is privatizing Tokyo.
As of today, this city is our base

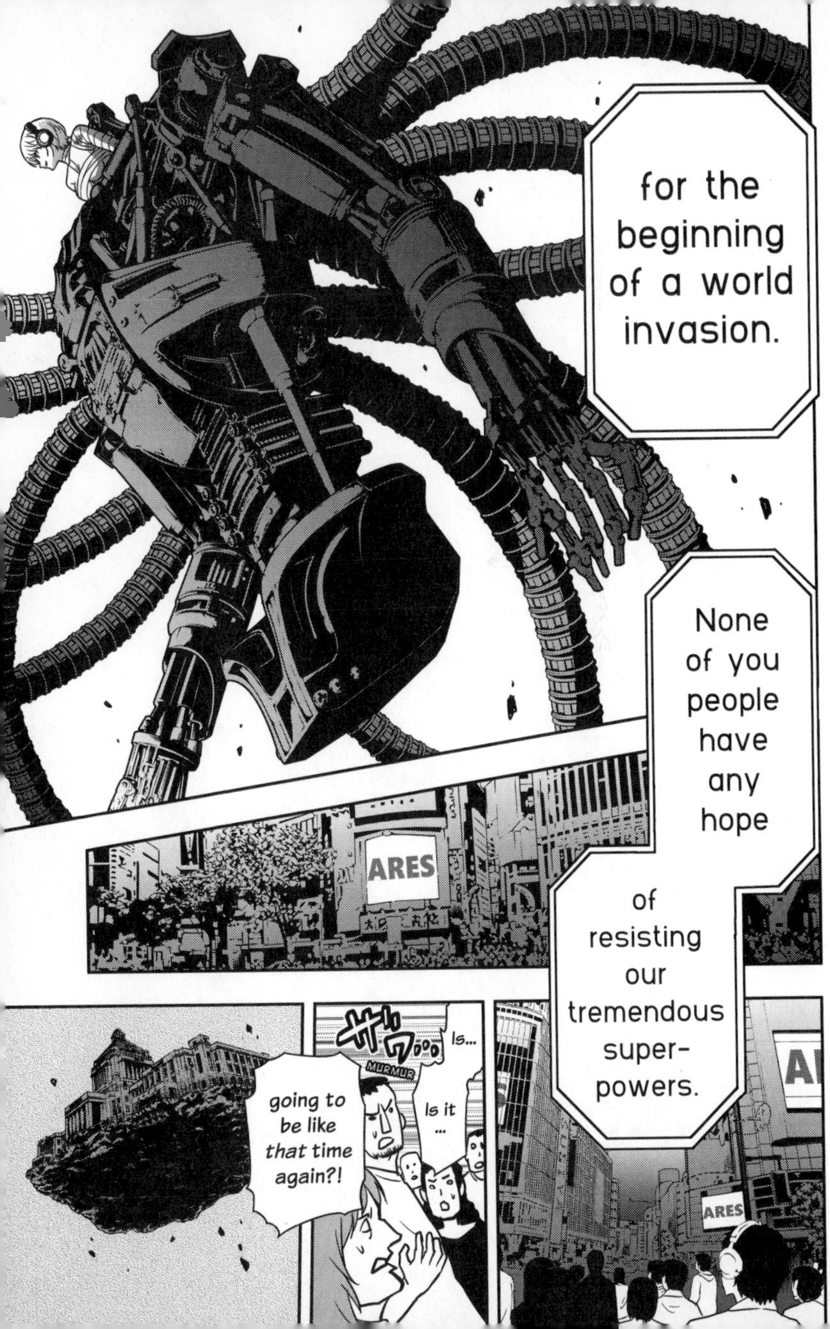
for the beginning of a world invasion.
None of you people have any hope
of resisting our tremendous super-powers.
ARES
ARES
MURMUR
Is...
Is it ...
going to be like *that* time again?!

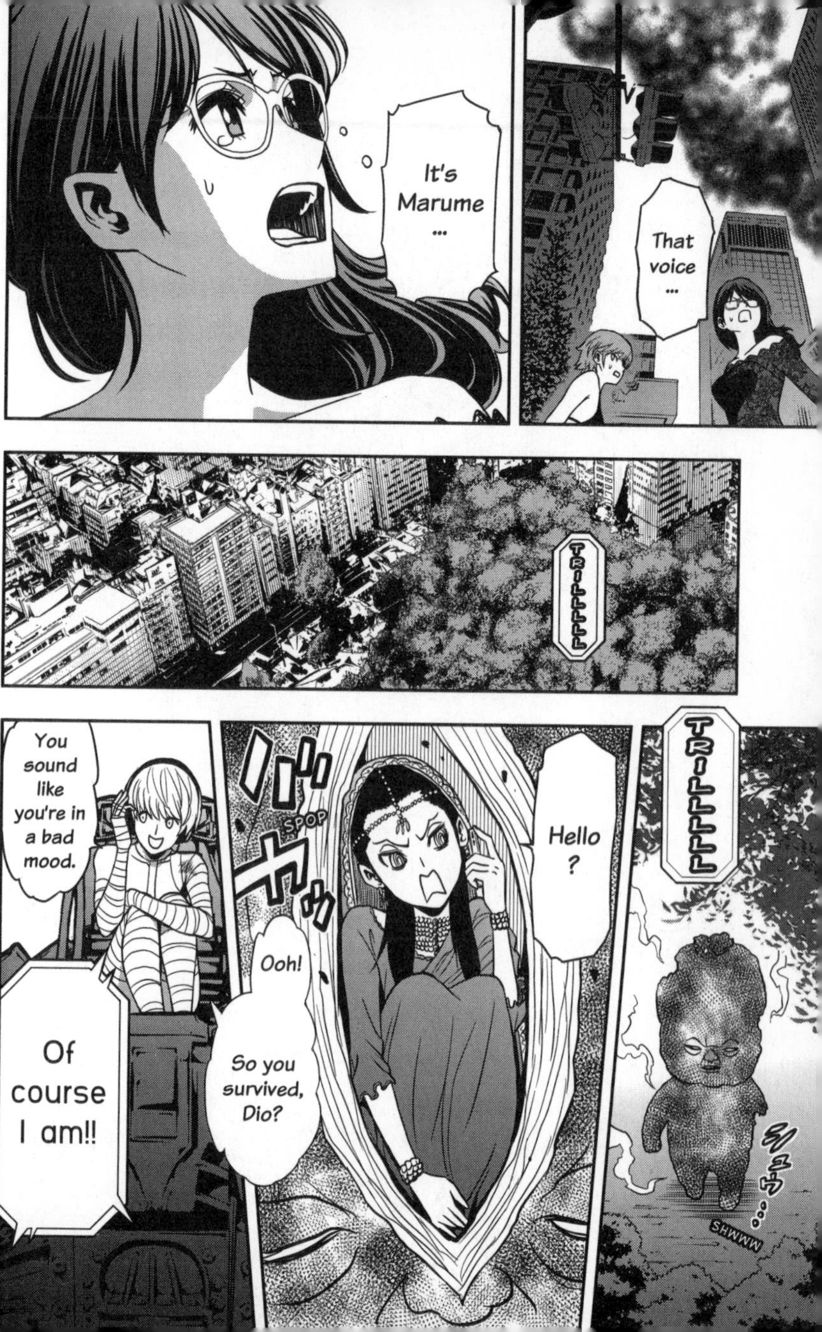
That voice ...
It's Marume ...
TRILLLLL
TRILLLLLL
SHWMM
Hello ?
SPOP
Ooh!
So you survived, Dio?
You sound like you're in a bad mood.
Of course I am!!

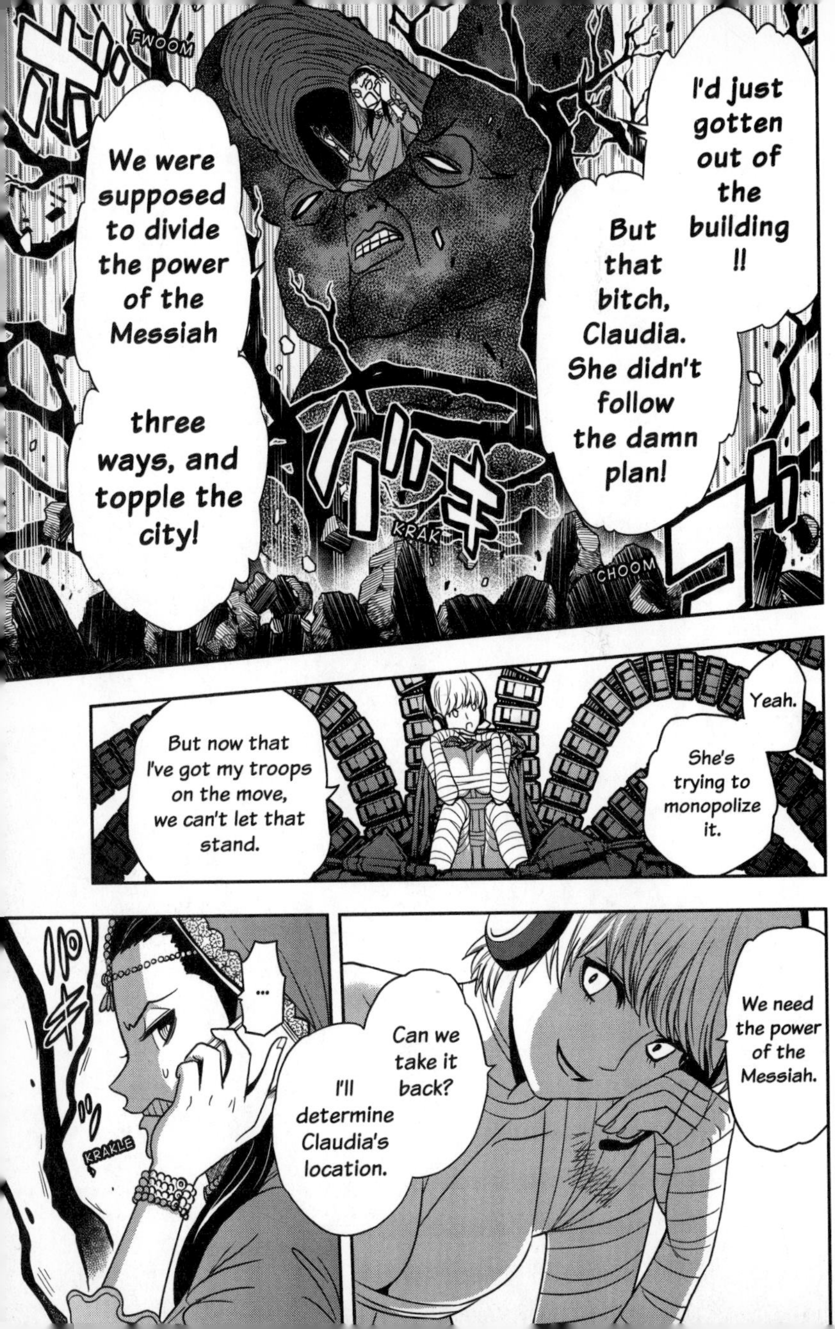
FWOOM
I'd just gotten out of the building !!
But that bitch, Claudia. She didn't follow the damn plan!
CHOOM
KRAK
We were supposed to divide the power of the Messiah
three ways, and topple the city!
Yeah.
She's trying to monopolize it.
But now that I've got my troops on the move, we can't let that stand.
We need the power of the Messiah.
Can we take it back?
I'll determine Claudia's location.
...
KRAKLE

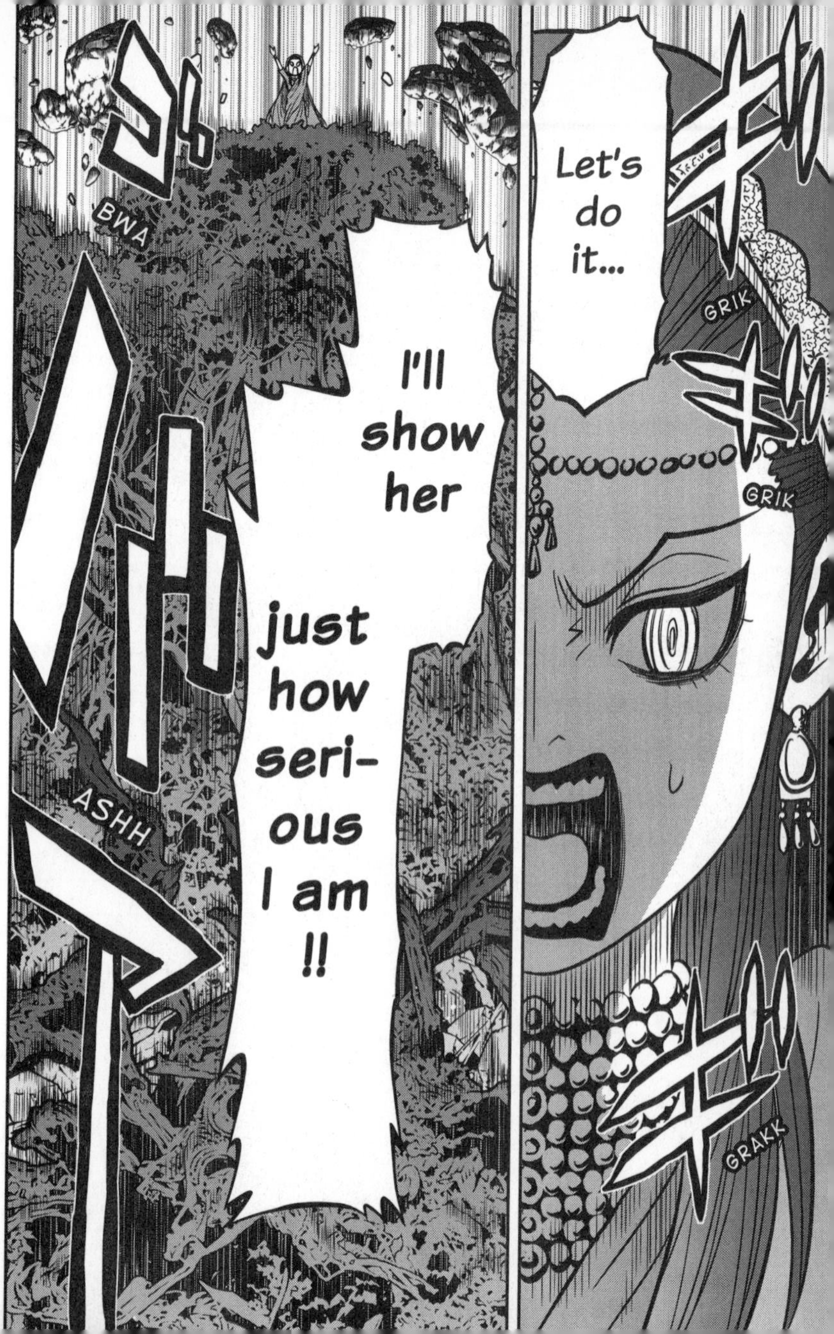
Let's do it...
GRIK
GRIK
GRAKK
BWA
I'll show her just how seri-ous I am!!
ASHH

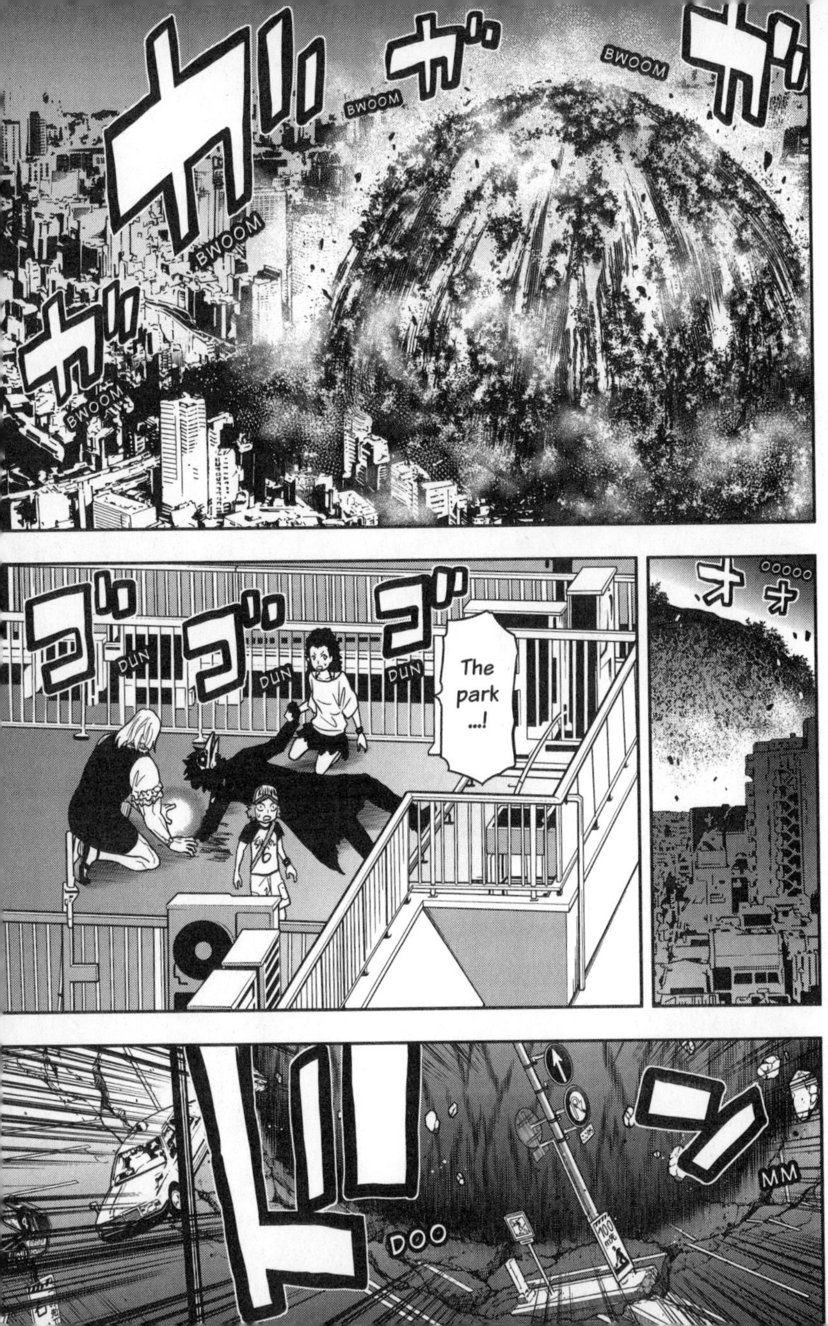
BWOOM
BWOOM
BWOOM
BWOOM
OOOOO
The park ...!
DUN
DUN
DUN
MM
DOO

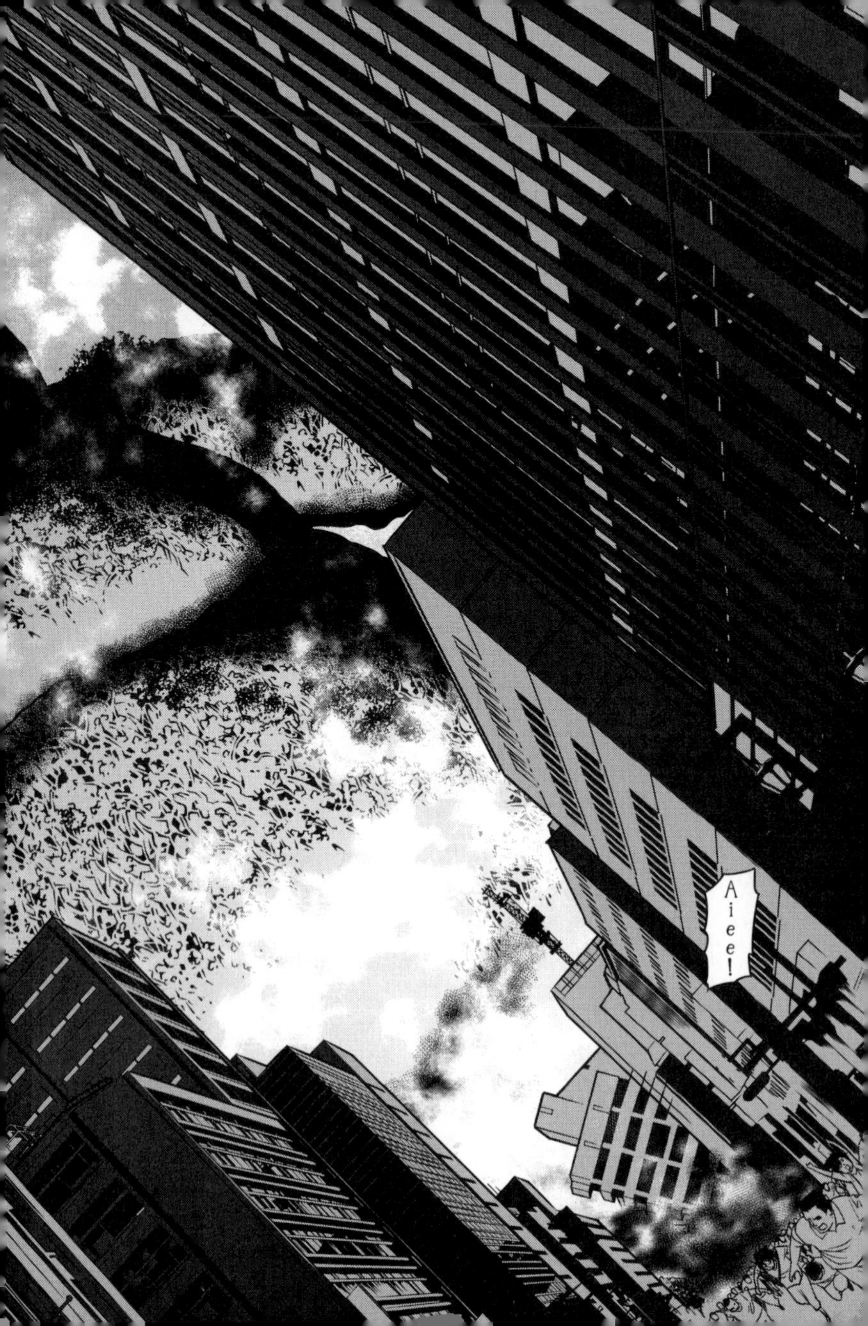
Aiee!

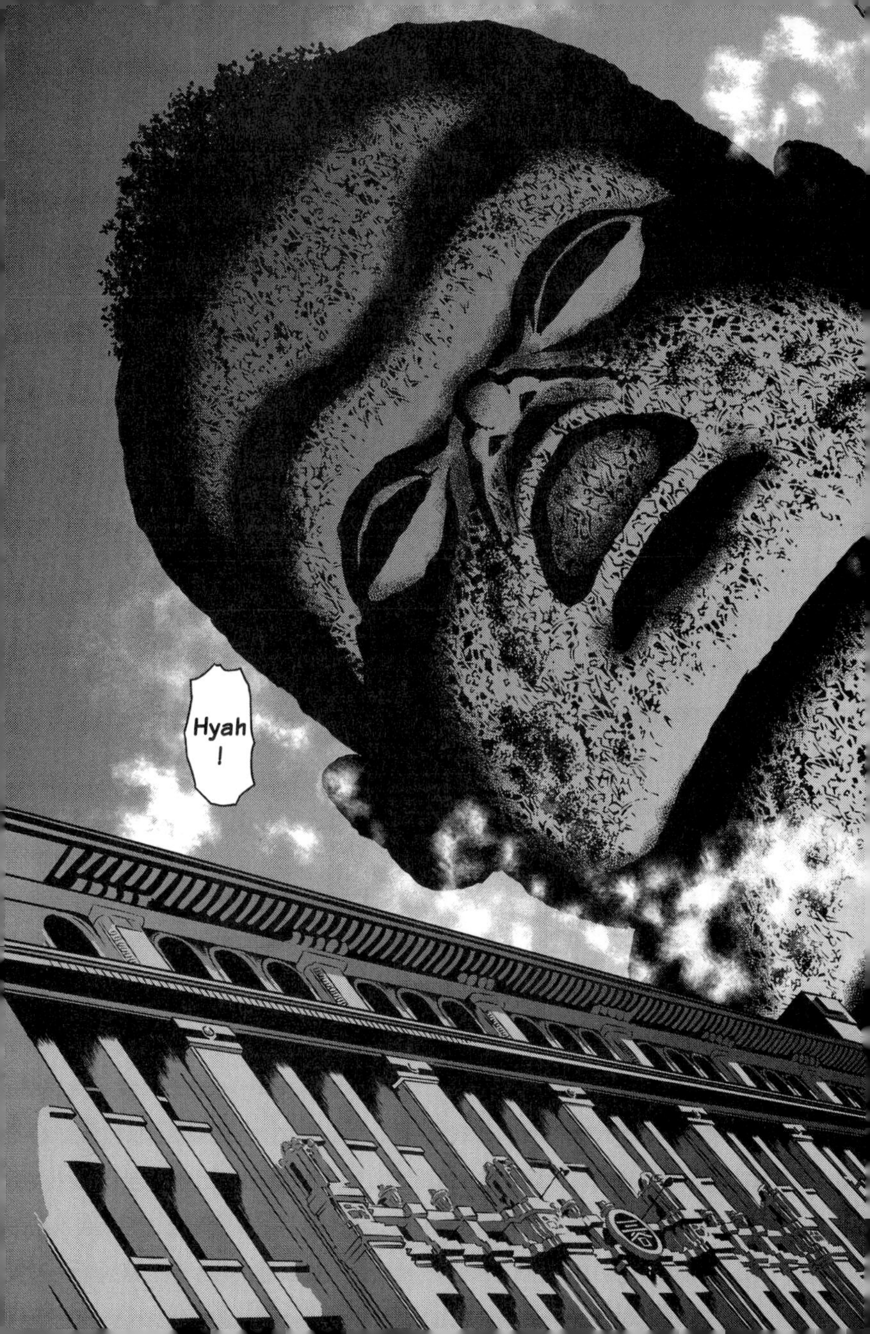
Hyah!

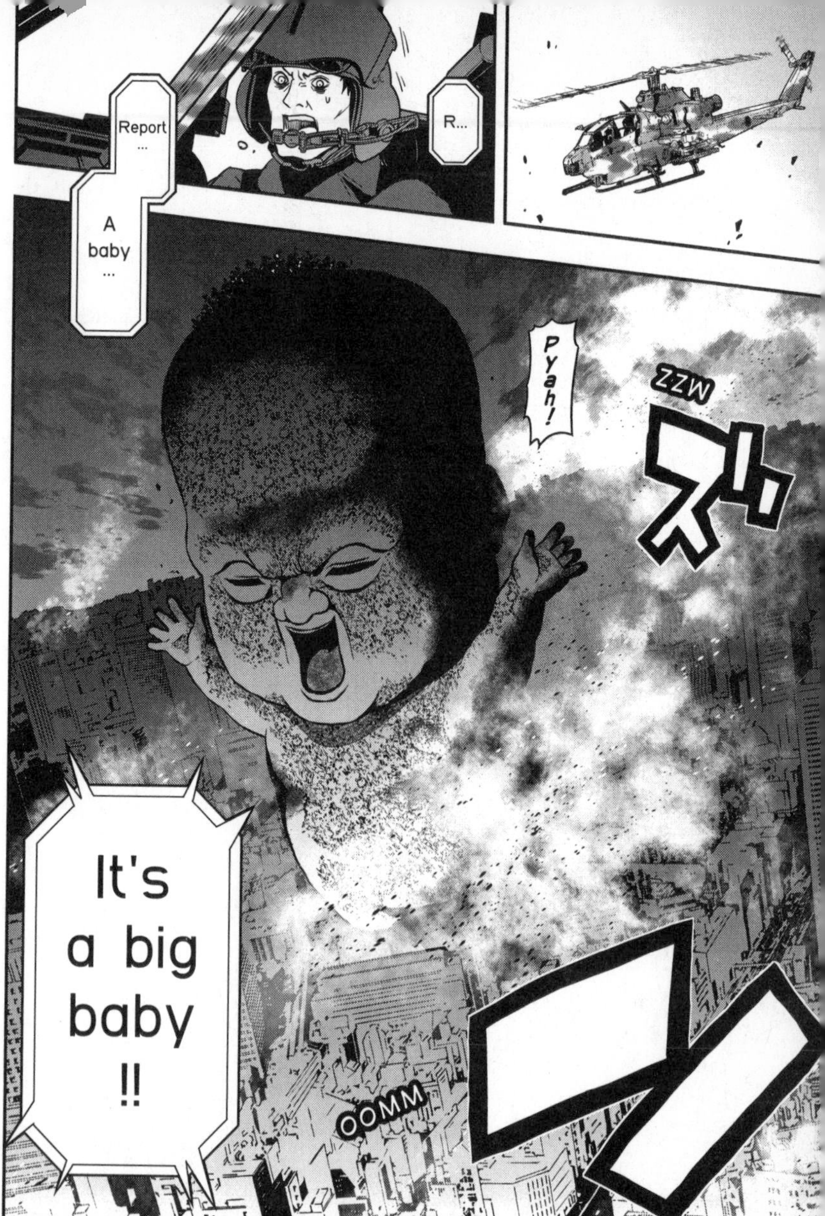
R...
Report ...
A baby ...
ZZW
Pyah!
It's a big baby !!
OOMM

SCENE 67 /// END

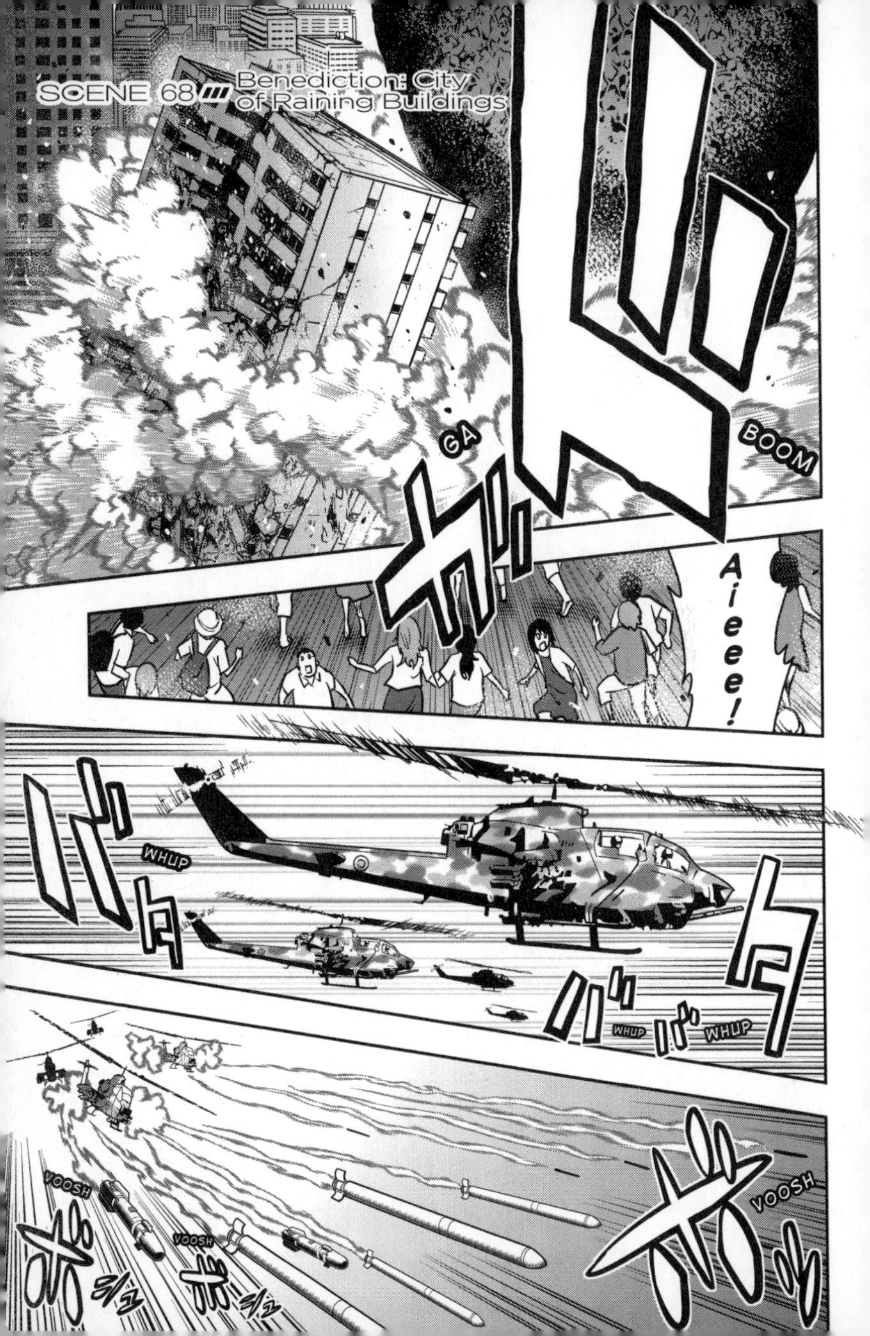
SCENE 68 /// Benediction: City of Raining Buildings
BOOM
GA
Aieeee!
WHUP
WHUP
WHUP
VOOSH
VOOSH
VOOSH

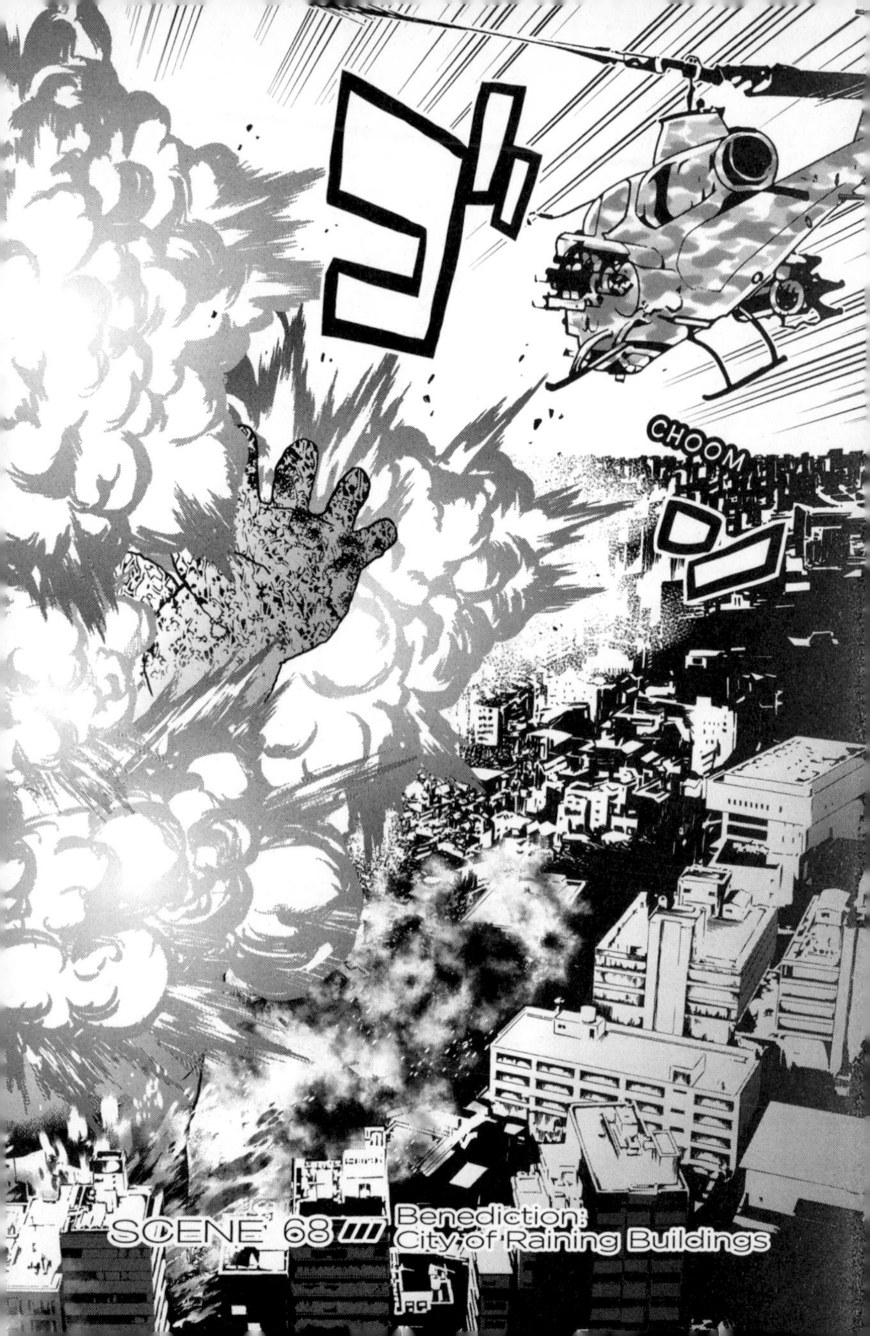
CHOOM

SCENE 68 Benediction: City of Raining Buildings

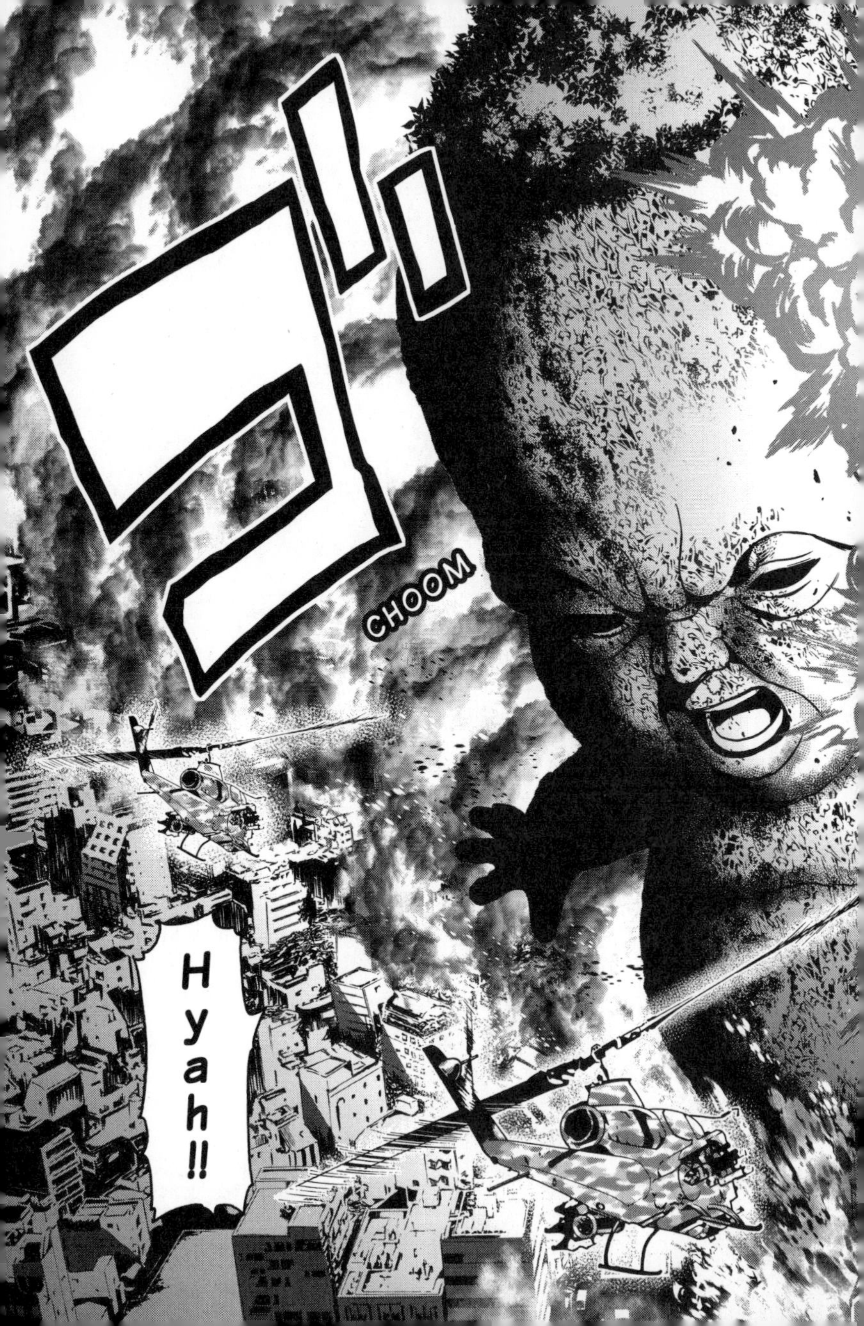
CHOOM
Hyah!!

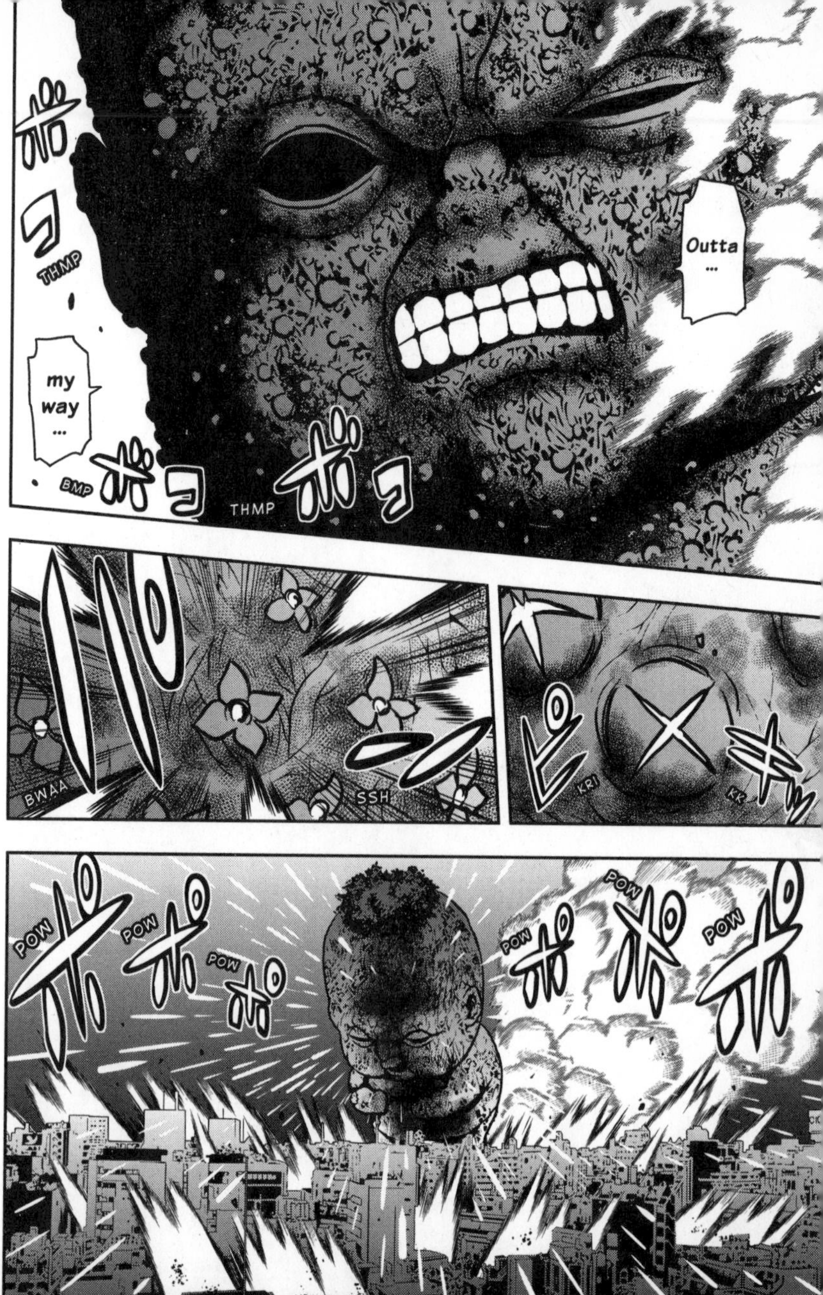
Outta ...
THMP
my way ...
THMP
BMP
KRI
KK
SSH
BWAA
POW
POW
POW
POW
POW
POW

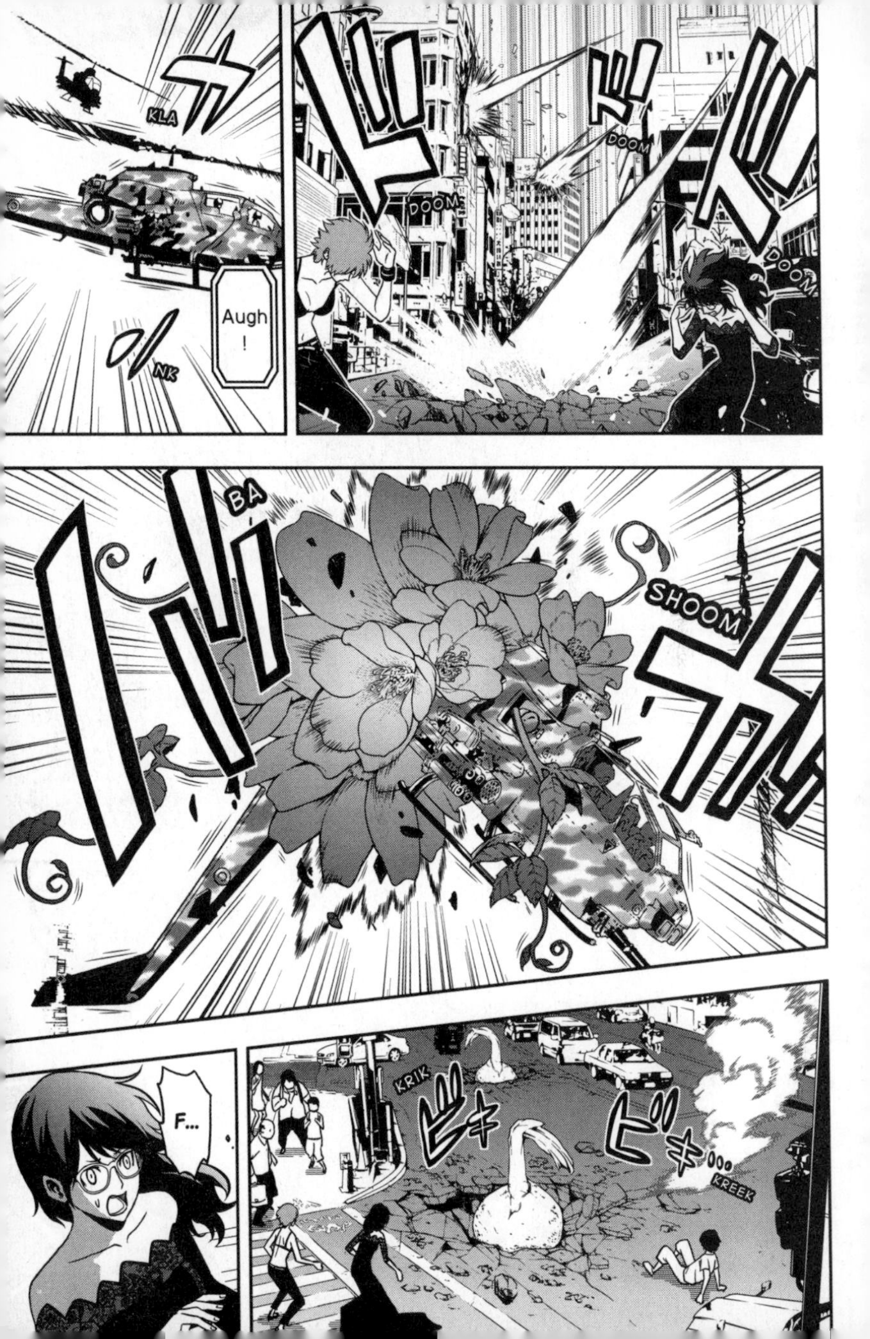
DOOM
DOOM
DOOM
KLA
Augh!
NK
BA
SHOOM
KRIK
KREEK
F...

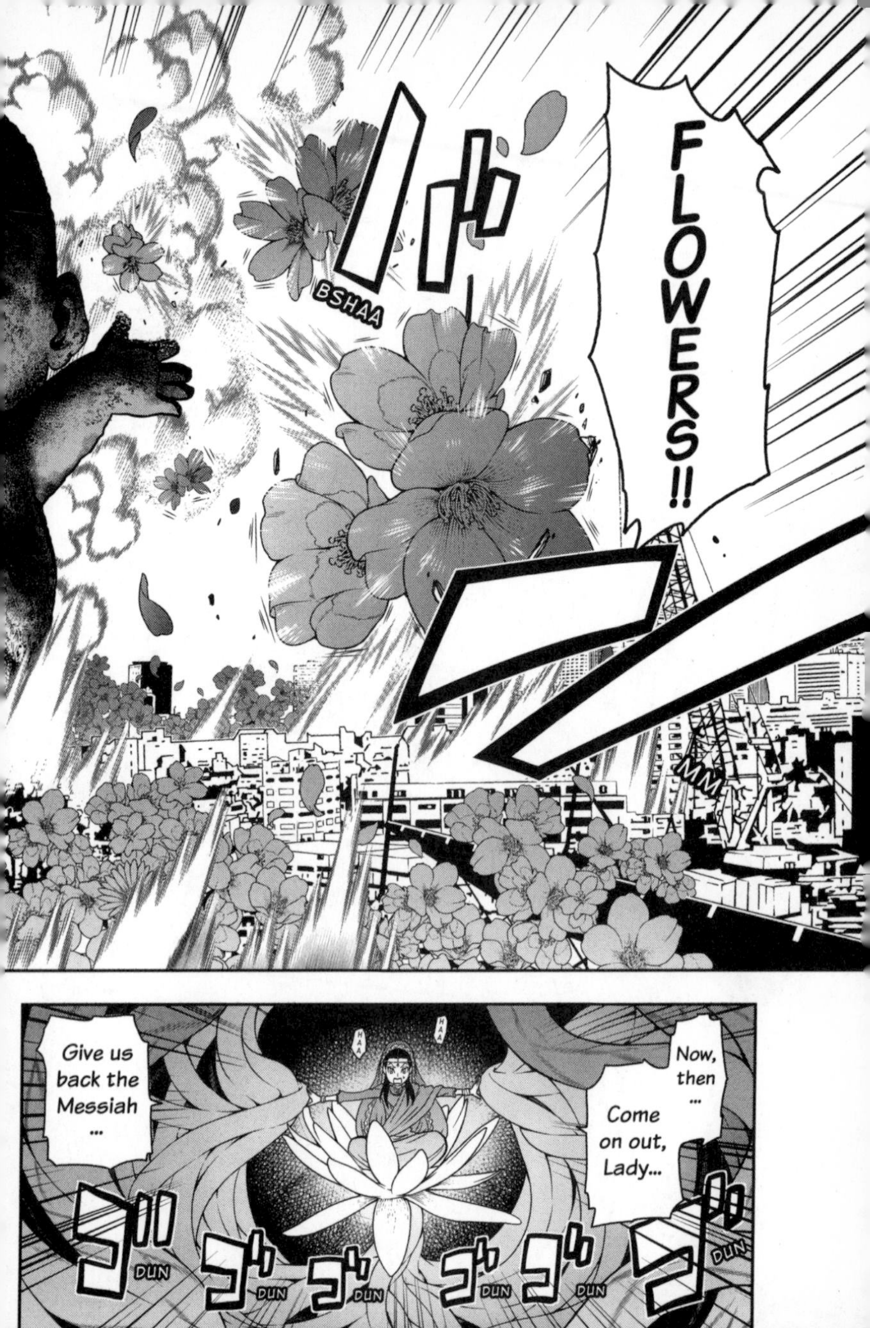
FLOWERS!!
BSHAA
MM
Now, then ...
Come on out, Lady...
HAA
HAA
Give us back the Messiah ...
DUN
DUN
DUN
DUN
DUN
DUN

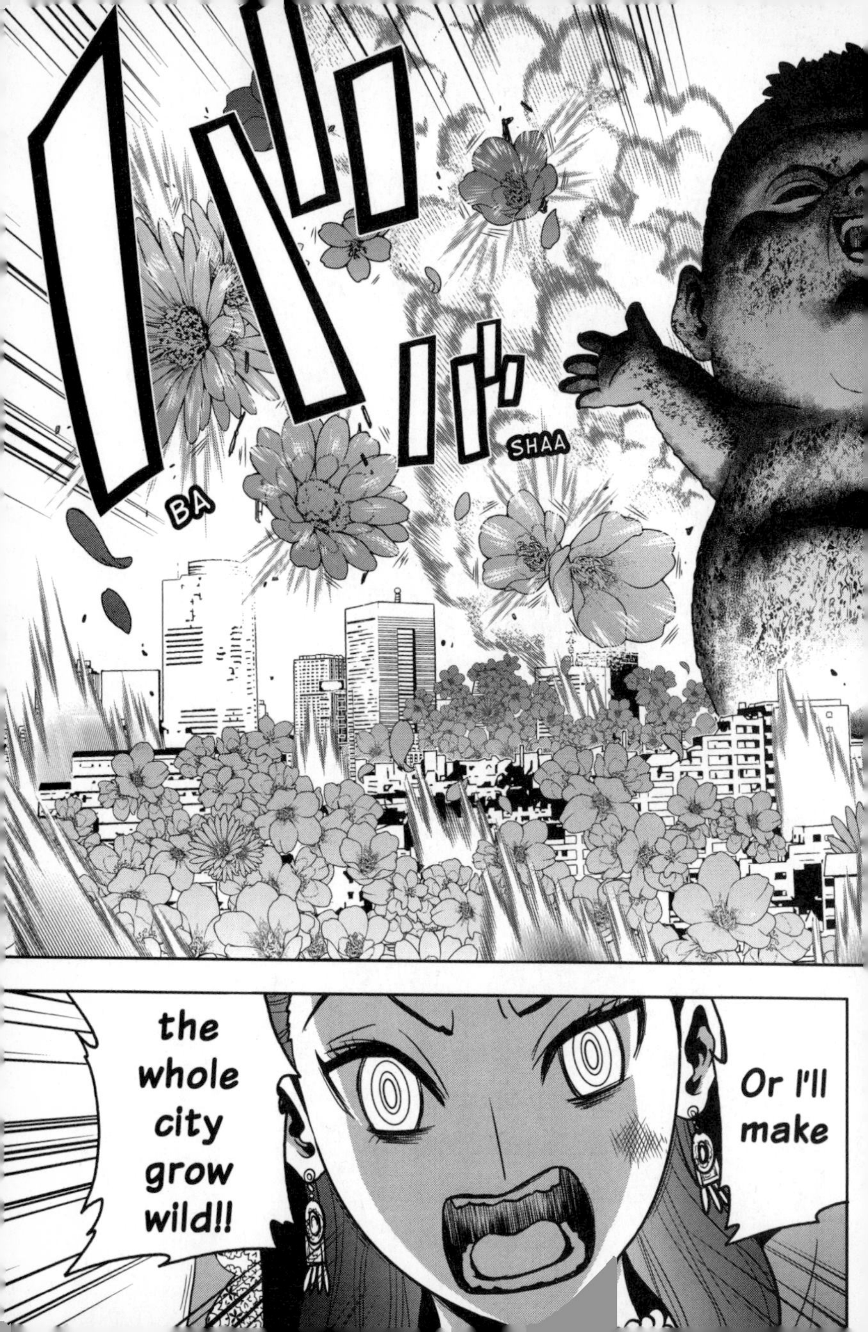
SHAA
BA
Or I'll make
the whole city grow wild!!

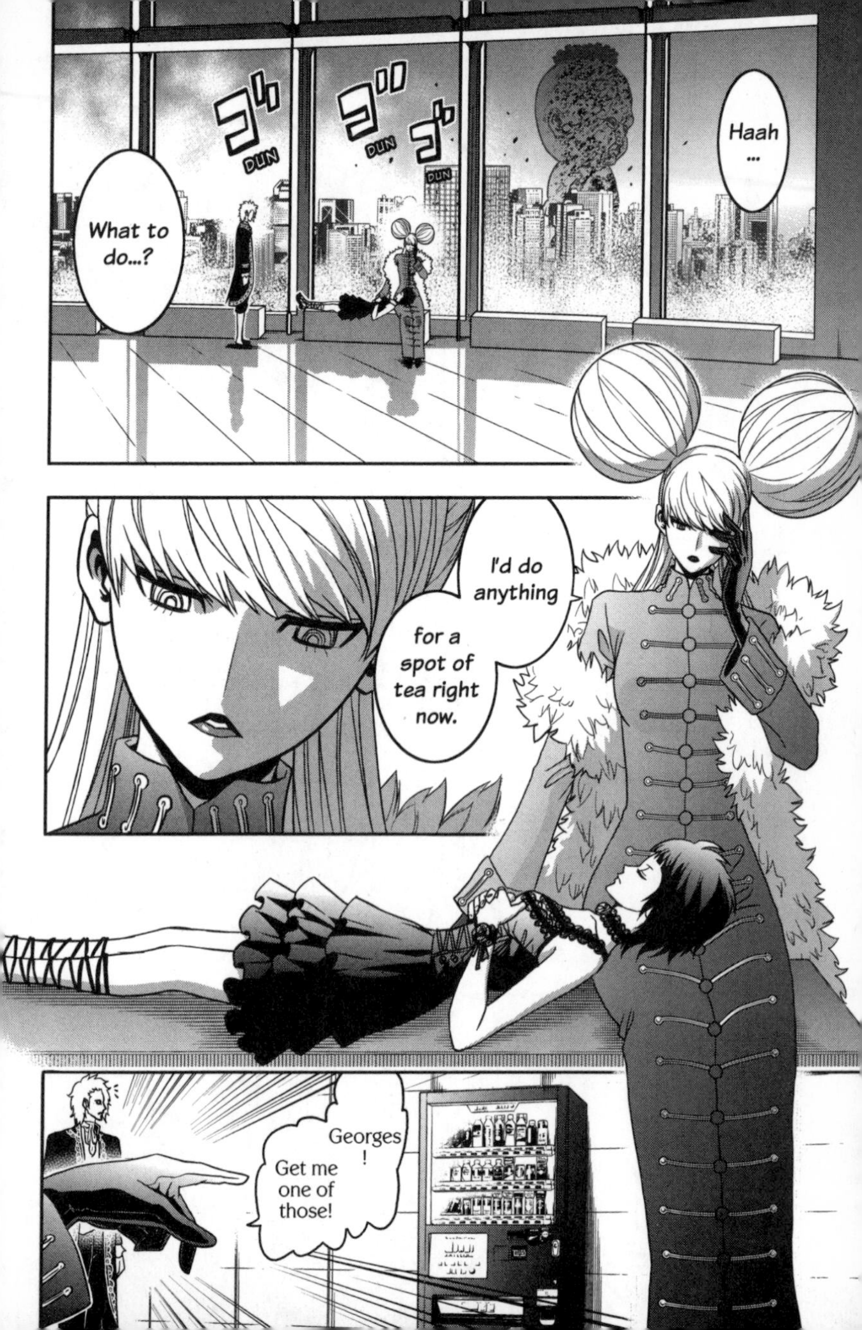
Haah ...
ゴ DUN
ゴ DUN
ゴ DUN
What to do...?
I'd do anything for a spot of tea right now.
Georges!
Get me one of those!

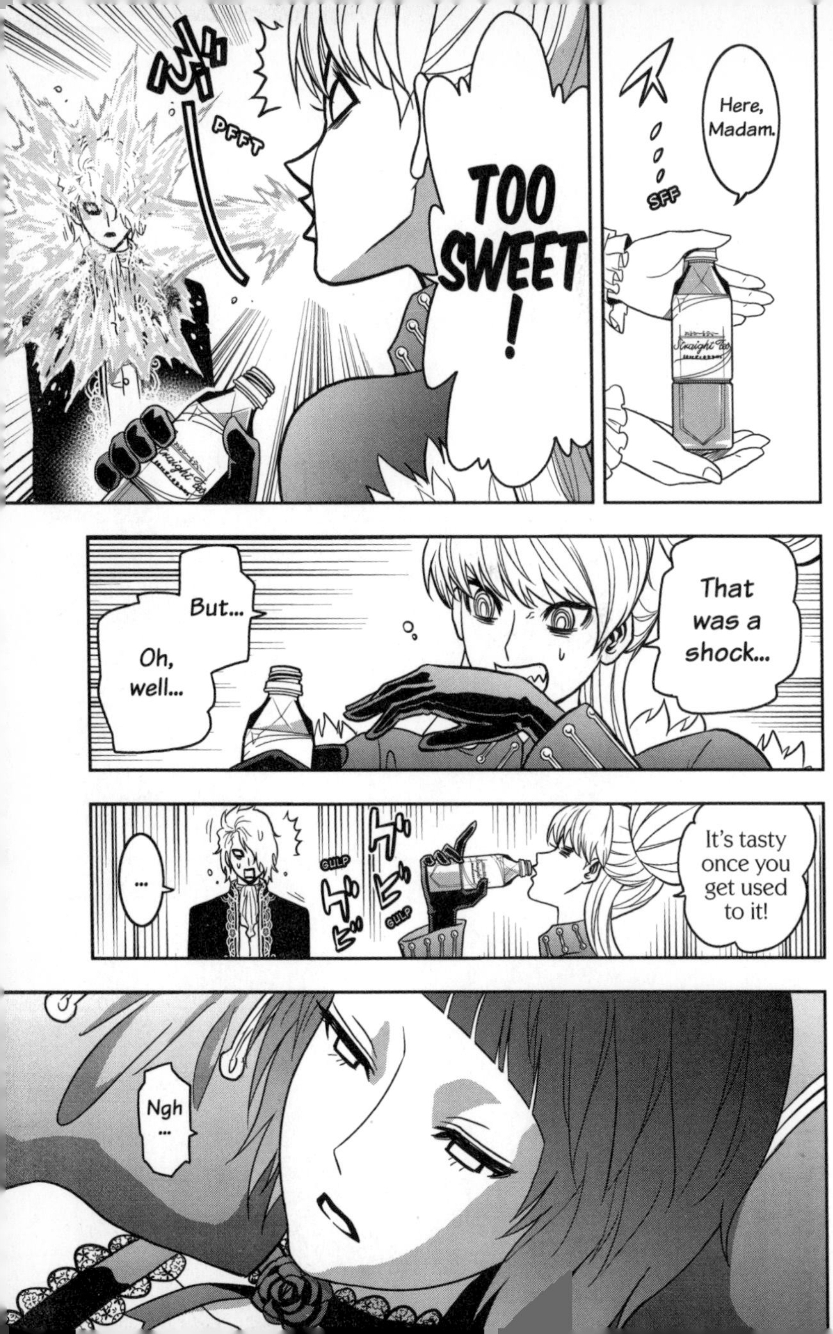
Here, Madam.
SFF
TOO SWEET!
PFFT
That was a shock...
But...
Oh, well...
It's tasty once you get used to it!
GULP
GULP
...
Ngh ...

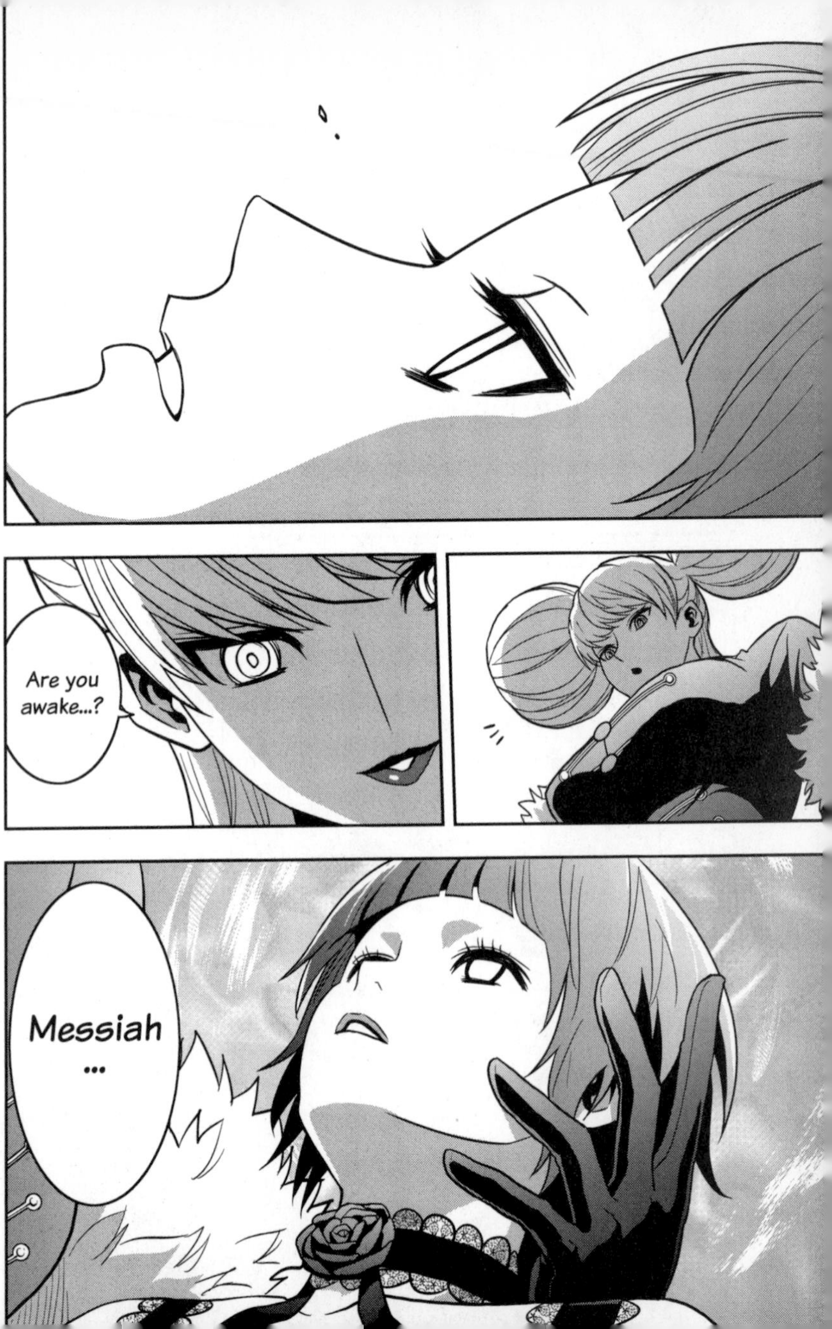
Are you awake...?
Messiah ...

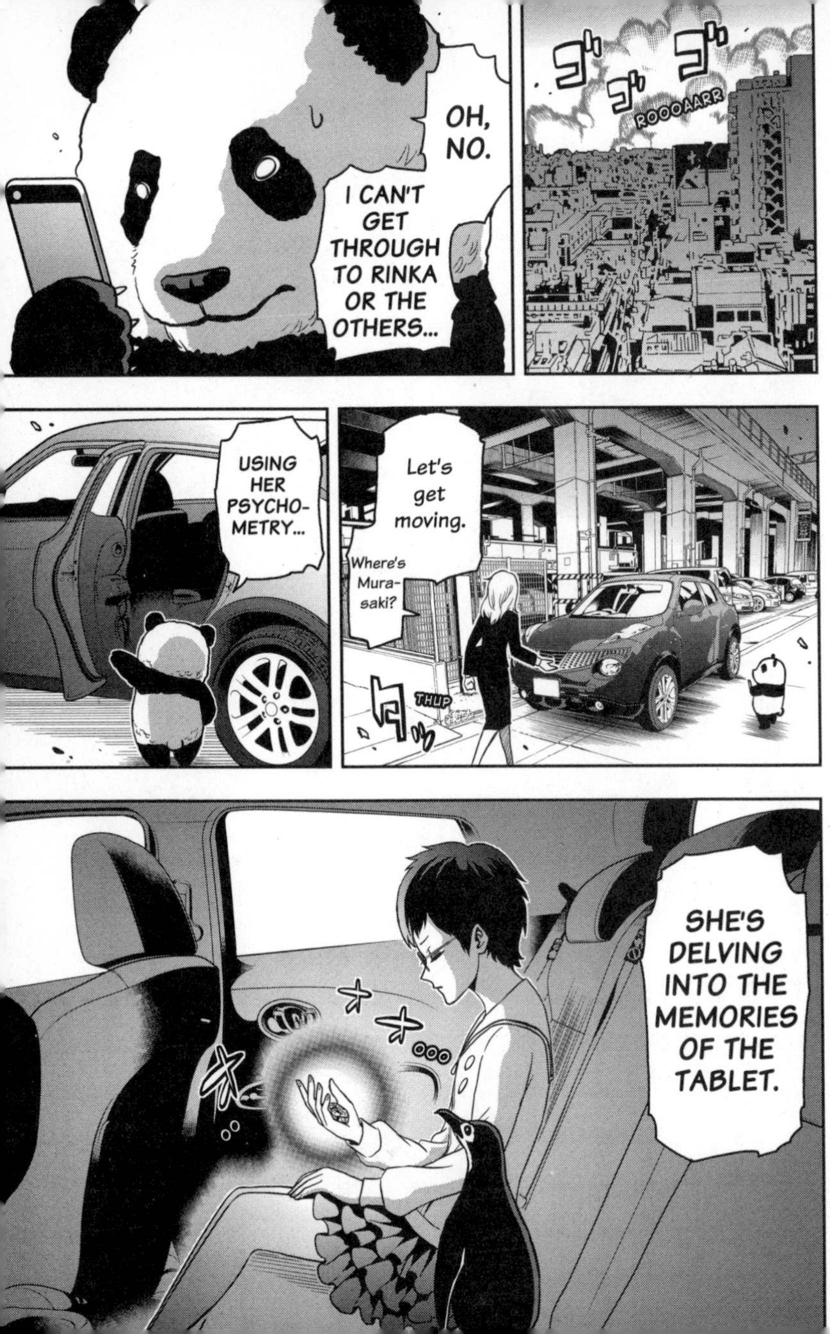
ゴゴゴ
ROOOAARR
OH, NO.
I CAN'T GET THROUGH TO RINKA OR THE OTHERS...
Let's get moving.
Where's Mura-saki?
THUP
USING HER PSYCHO-METRY...
SHE'S DELVING INTO THE MEMORIES OF THE TABLET.

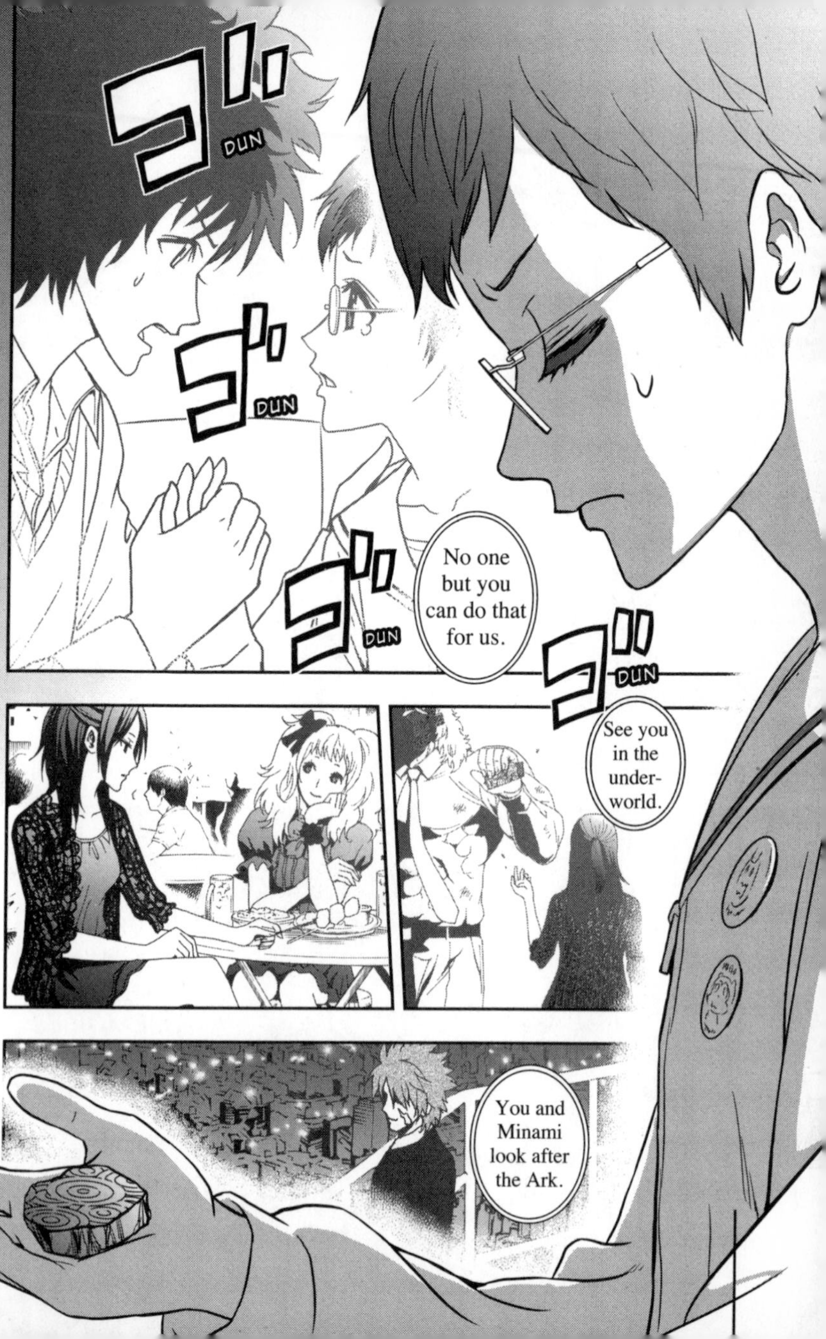
DUN
DUN
DUN
No one but you can do that for us.
DUN
See you in the under-world.
You and Minami look after the Ark.

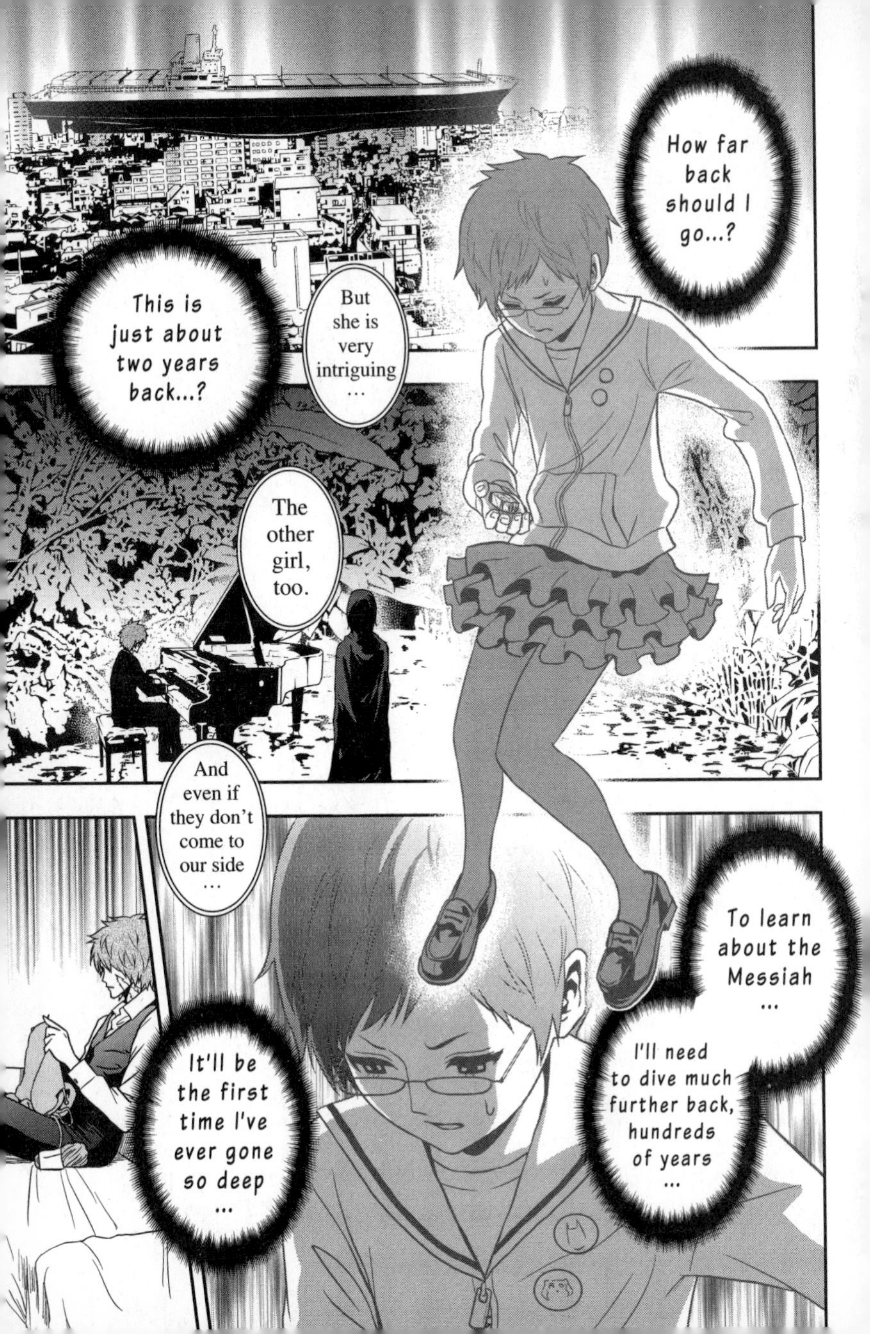

How far back should I go...?
This is just about two years back...?
But she is very intriguing …
The other girl, too.
And even if they don't come to our side …
To learn about the Messiah …
I'll need to dive much further back, hundreds of years …
It'll be the first time I've ever gone so deep …

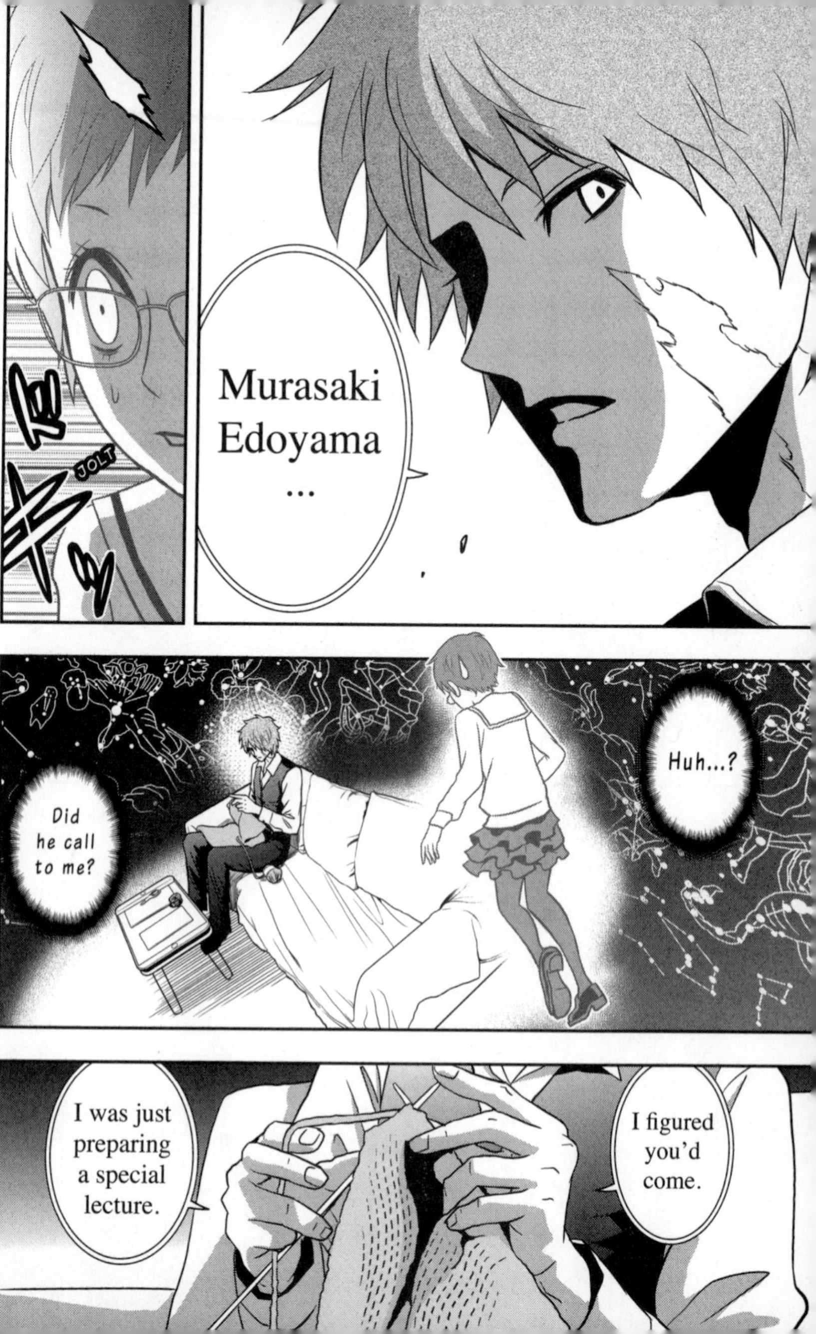
Murasaki Edoyama ...
JOLT
Huh...?
Did he call to me?
I figured you'd come.
I was just preparing a special lecture.

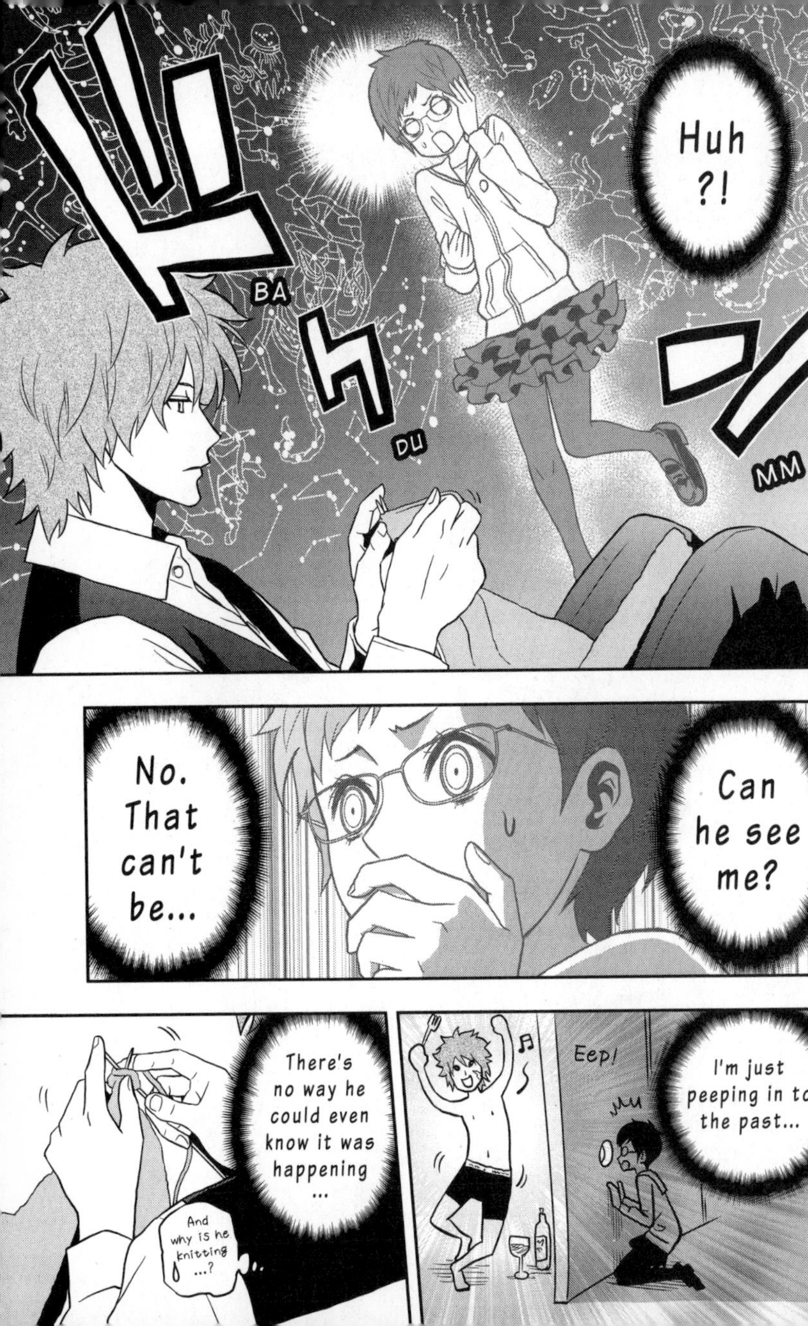
Huh ?!
BA DU MM
Can he see me?
No. That can't be...
I'm just peeping in to the past...
Eep!
There's no way he could even know it was happening ...
And why is he knitting ...?

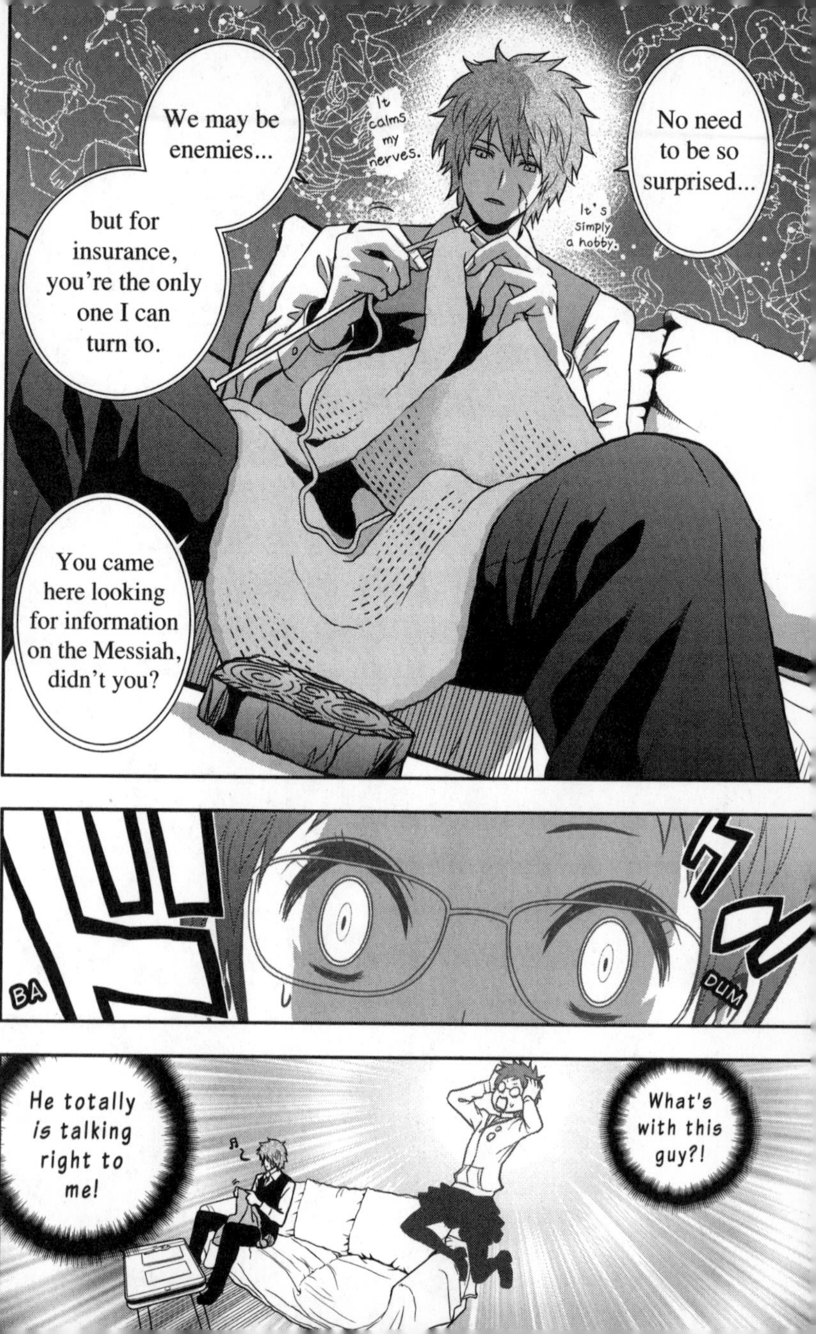
No need to be so surprised...
It's simply a hobby.
It calms my nerves.
We may be enemies...
but for insurance, you're the only one I can turn to.
You came here looking for information on the Messiah, didn't you?
BA
DUM
What's with this guy?!
He totally *is* talking right to me!

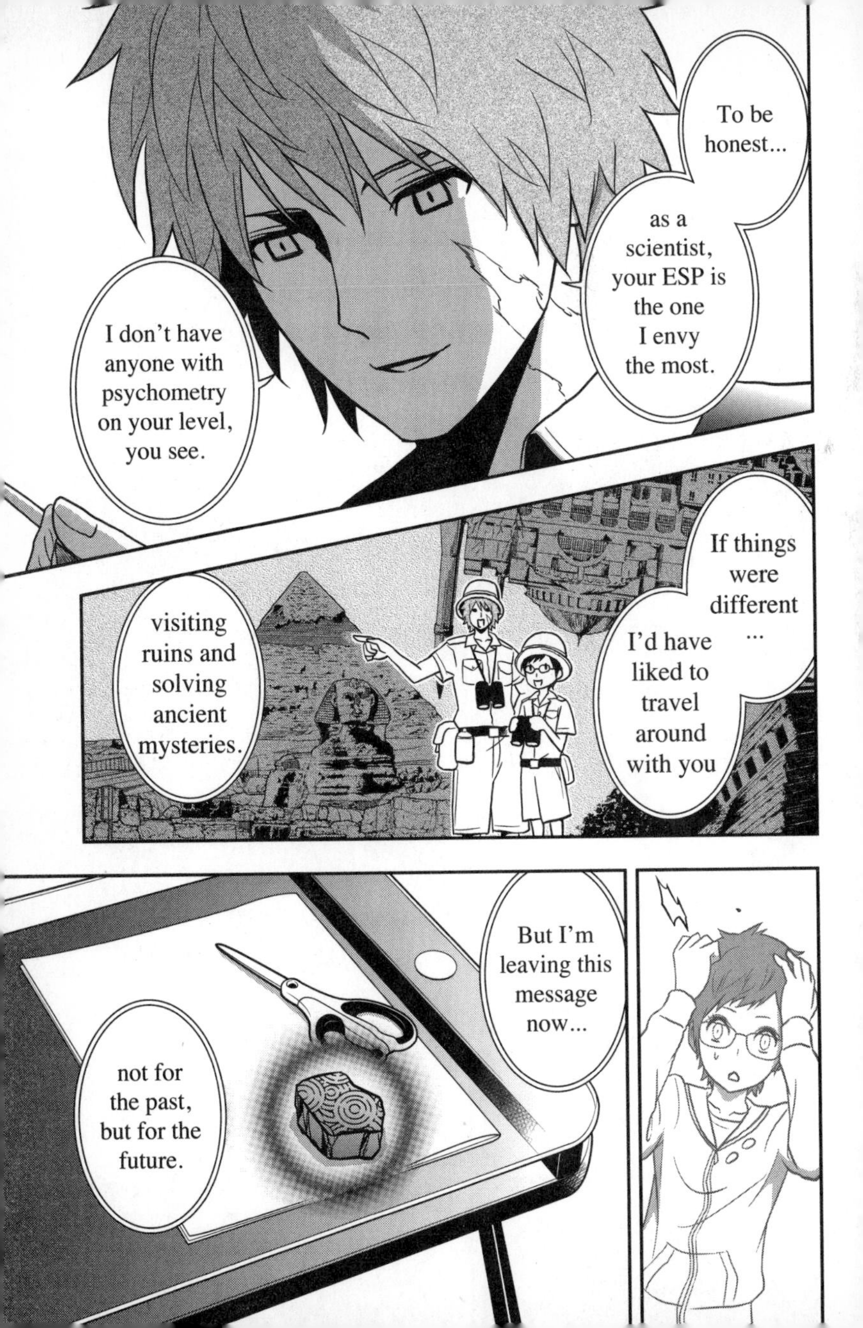
To be honest...
as a scientist, your ESP is the one I envy the most.
I don't have anyone with psychometry on your level, you see.
If things were different ...
I'd have liked to travel around with you
visiting ruins and solving ancient mysteries.
But I'm leaving this message now...
not for the past, but for the future.

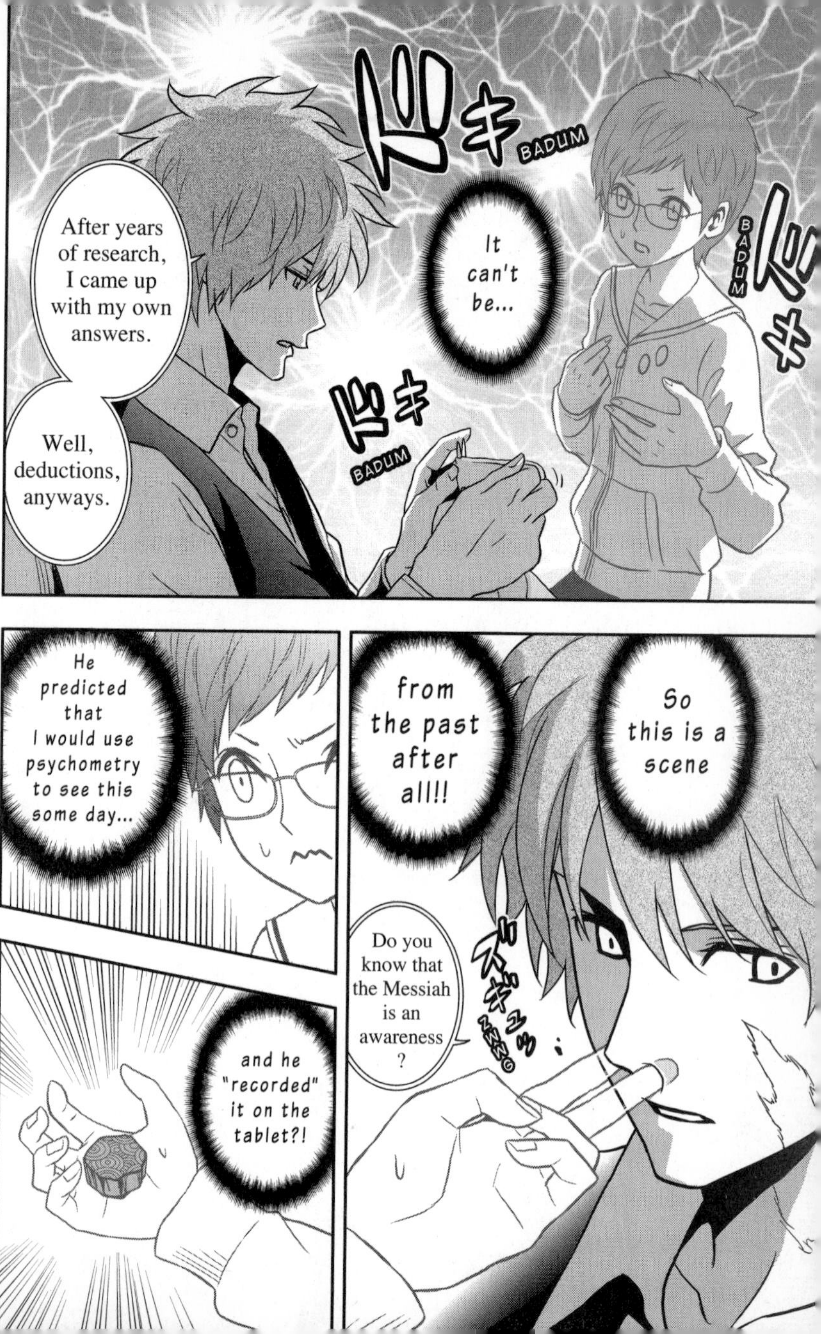
ドキ
BADUM
ドキ
BADUM
It can't be...
After years of research, I came up with my own answers.
Well, deductions, anyways.
ドキ
BADUM
So this is a scene
from the past after all!!
Do you know that the Messiah is an awareness?
ズギュッ
NNNG
He predicted that I would use psychometry to see this some day...
and he "recorded" it on the tablet?!

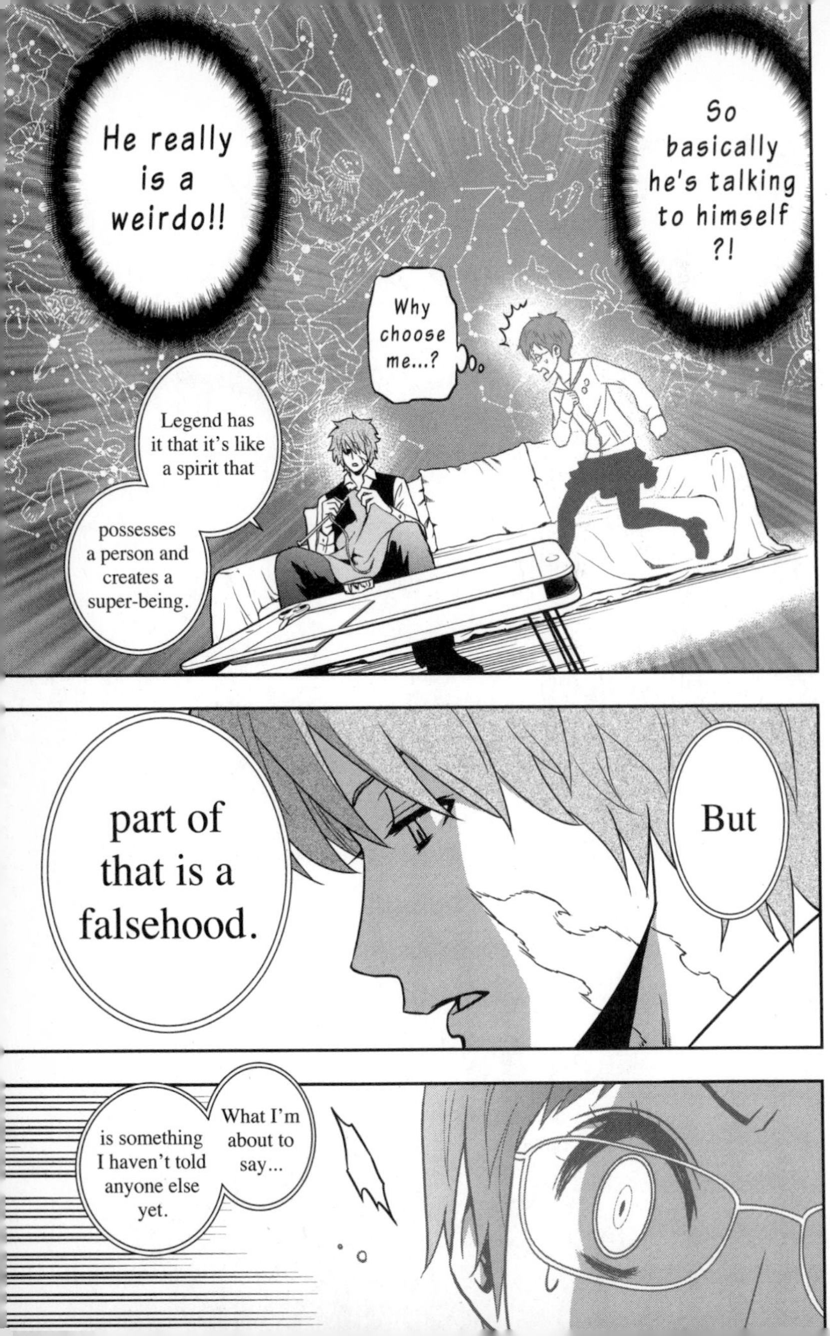
So basically he's talking to himself ?!
He really is a weirdo!!
Why choose me...?
Legend has it that it's like a spirit that
possesses a person and creates a super-being.
But
part of that is a falsehood.
What I'm about to say...
is something I haven't told anyone else yet.

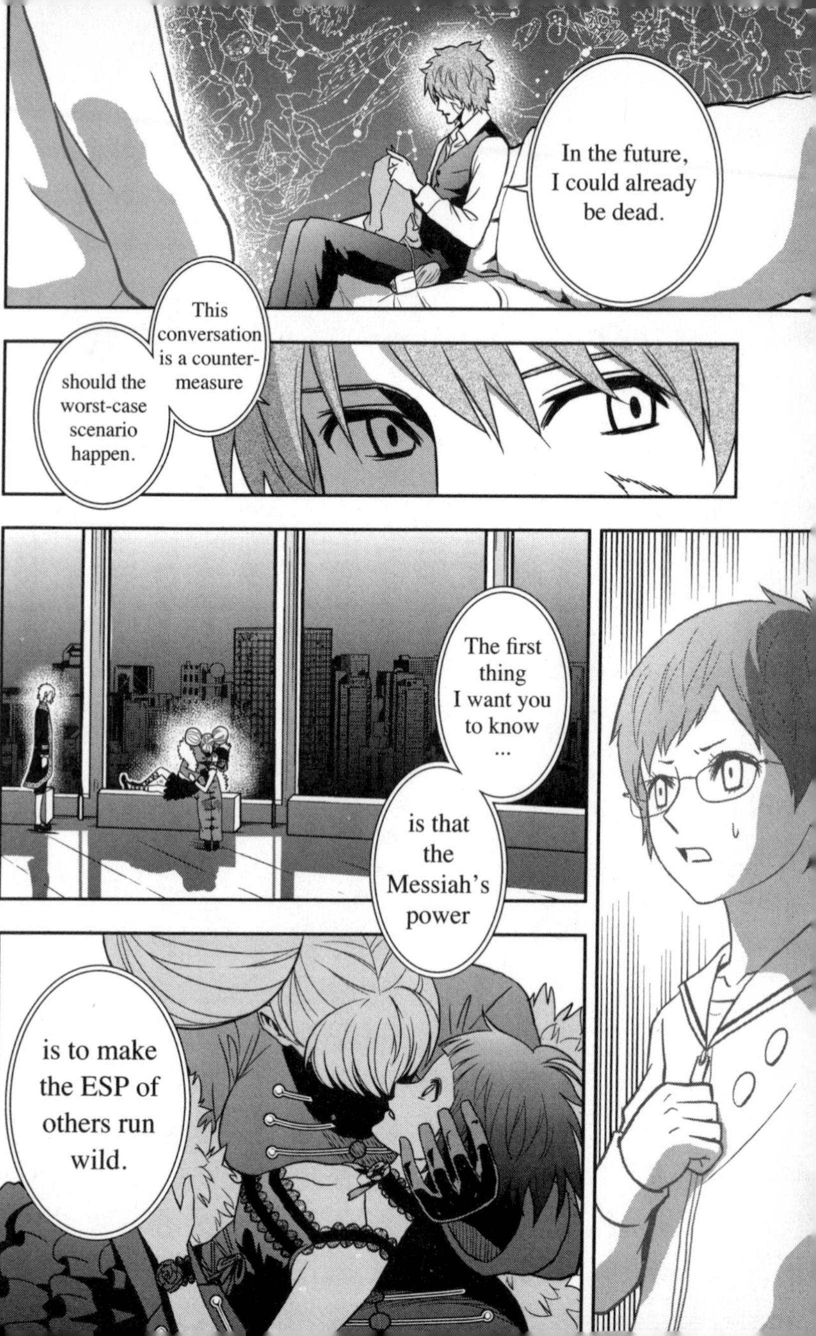
In the future, I could already be dead.
This conversation is a counter-measure
should the worst-case scenario happen.
The first thing I want you to know ...
is that the Messiah's power
is to make the ESP of others run wild.

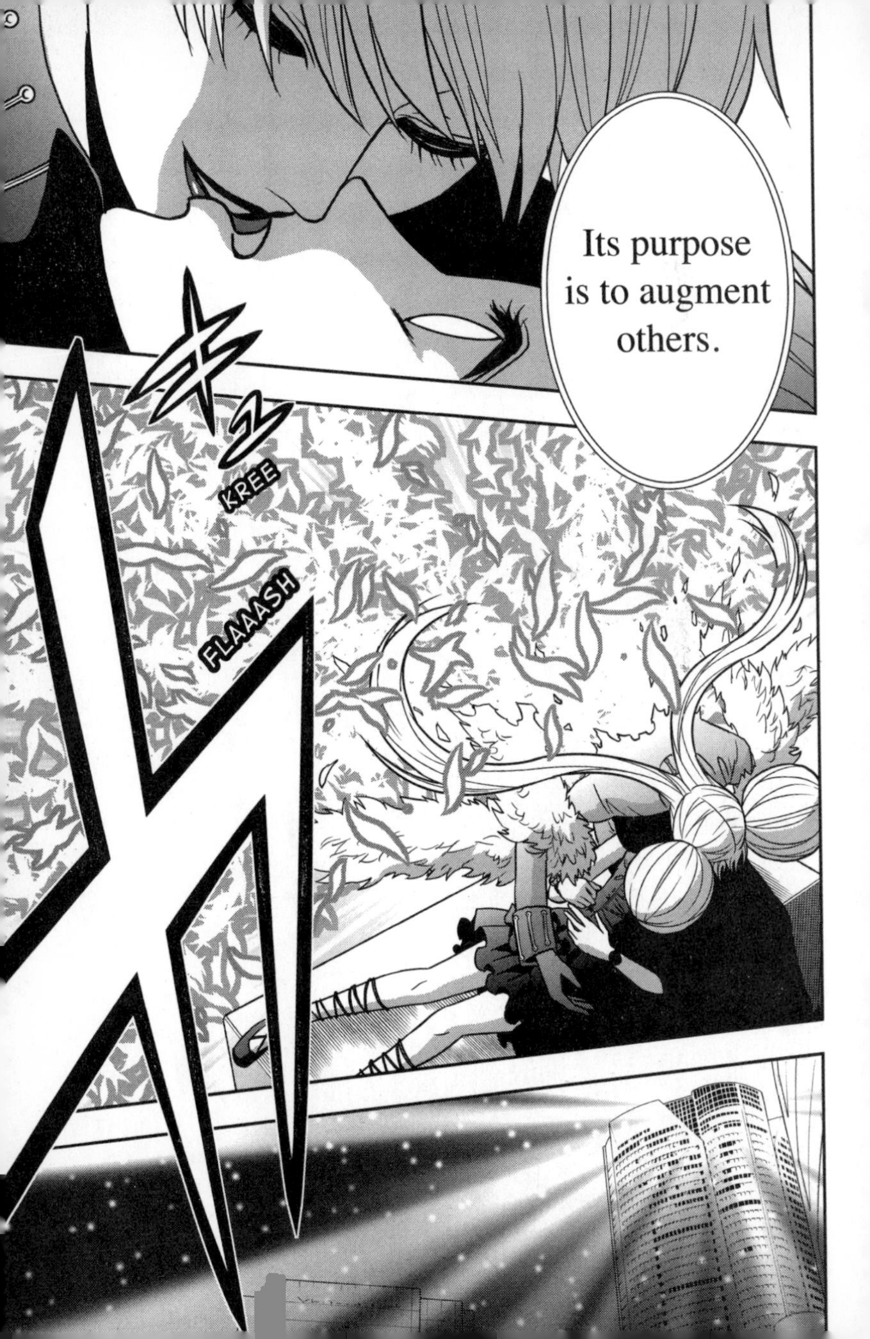
Its purpose is to augment others.
KREE
FLAAASH

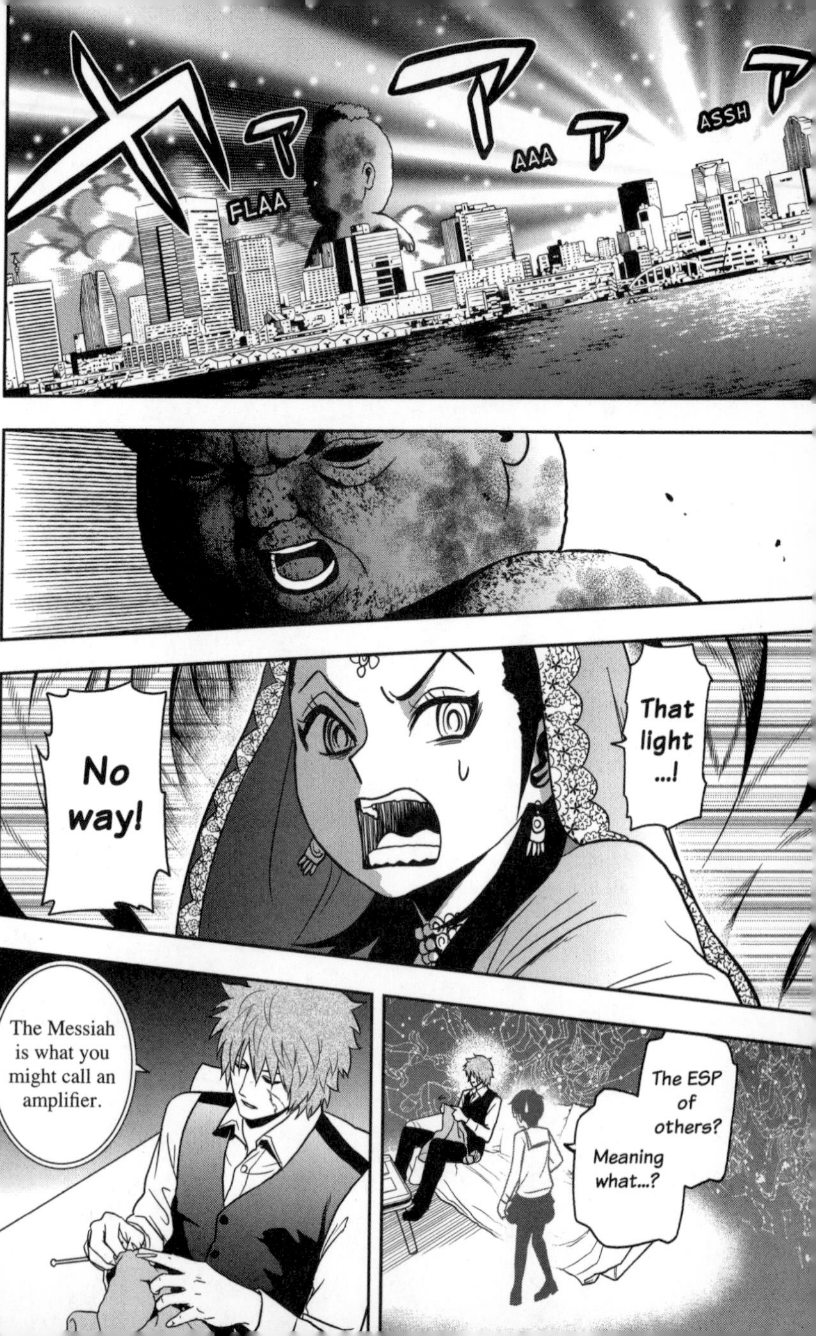
FLAA AAA ASSH
That light ...!
No way!
The ESP of others?
Meaning what...?
The Messiah is what you might call an amplifier.

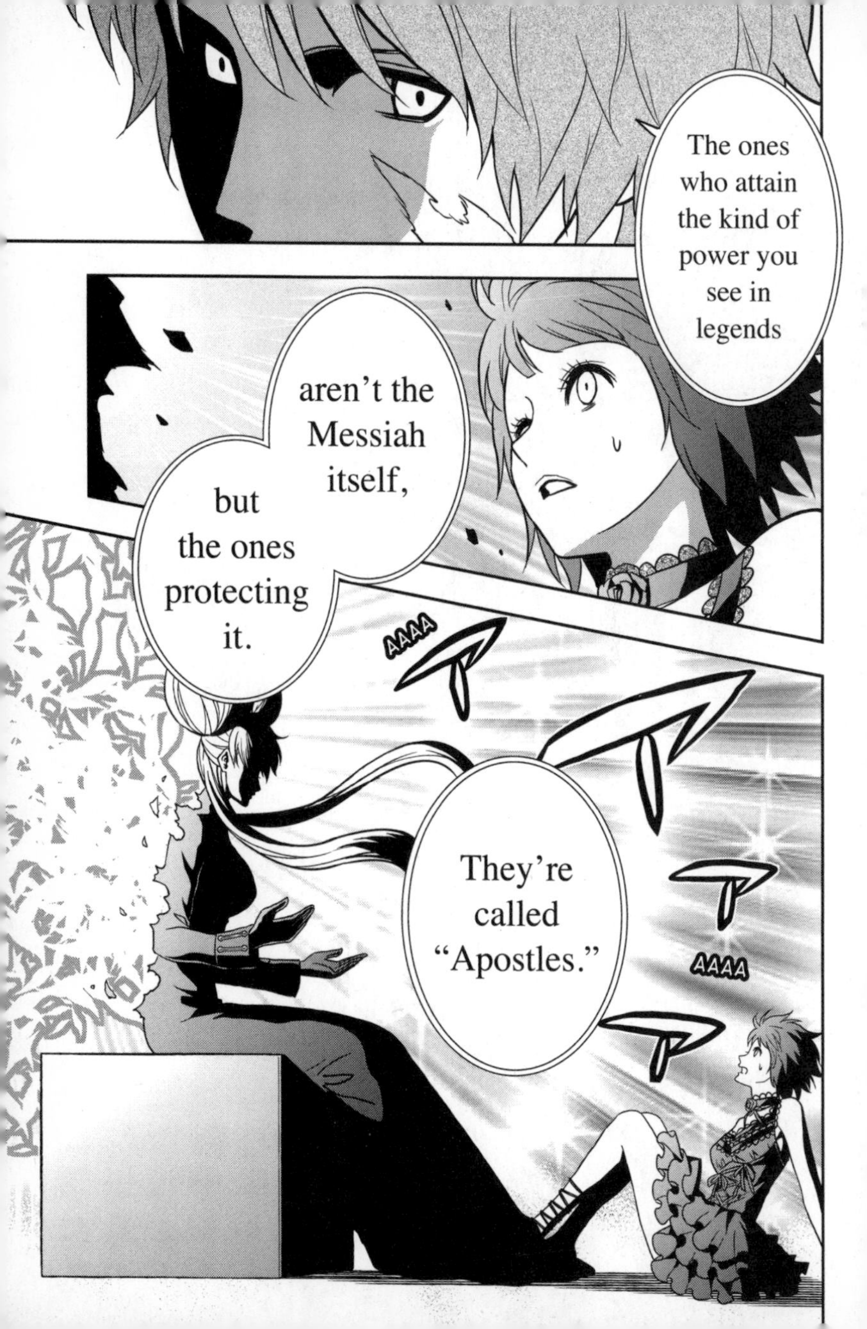
The ones who attain the kind of power you see in legends
aren't the Messiah itself,
but the ones protecting it.
AAAA
They're called "Apostles."
AAAA

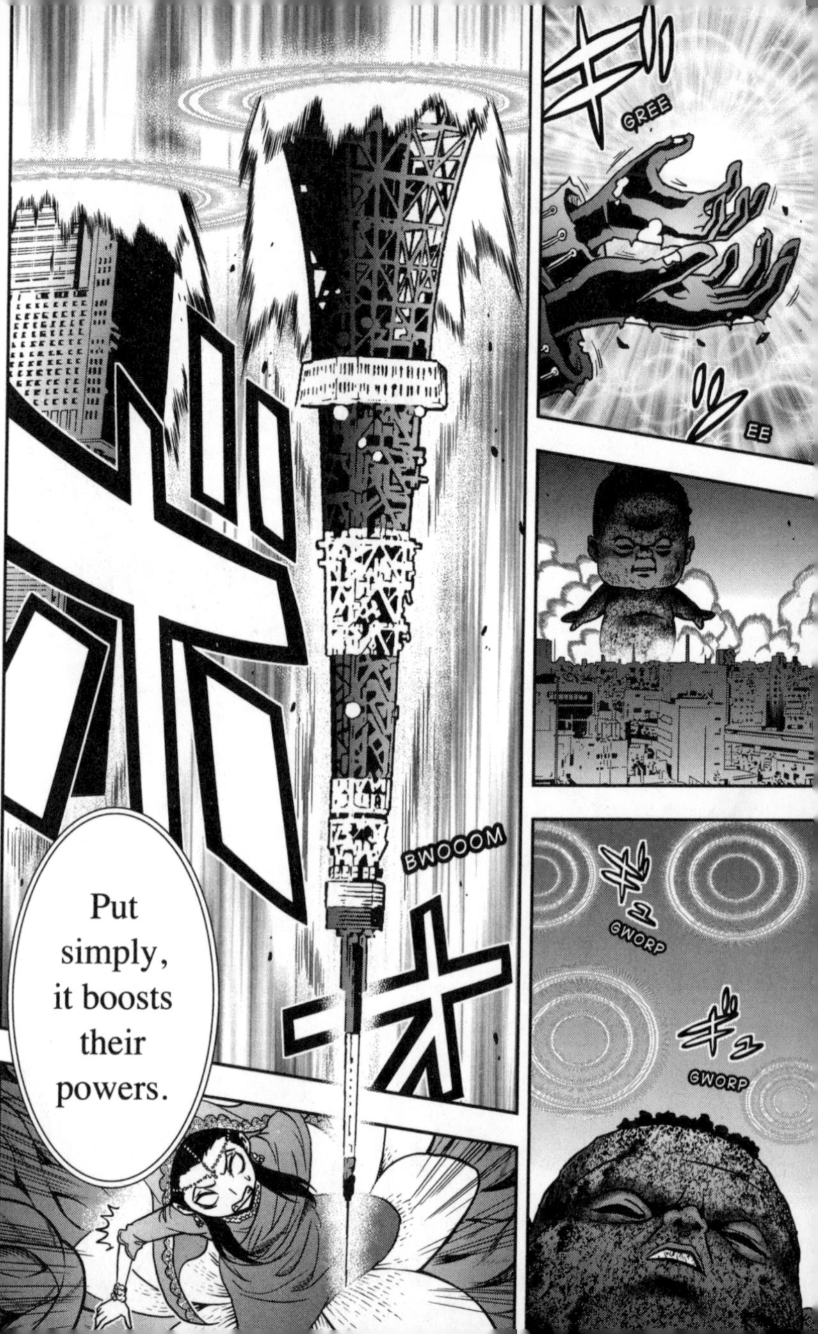
GREE
EE
GWORP
GWORP
BWOOOM
Put simply, it boosts their powers.

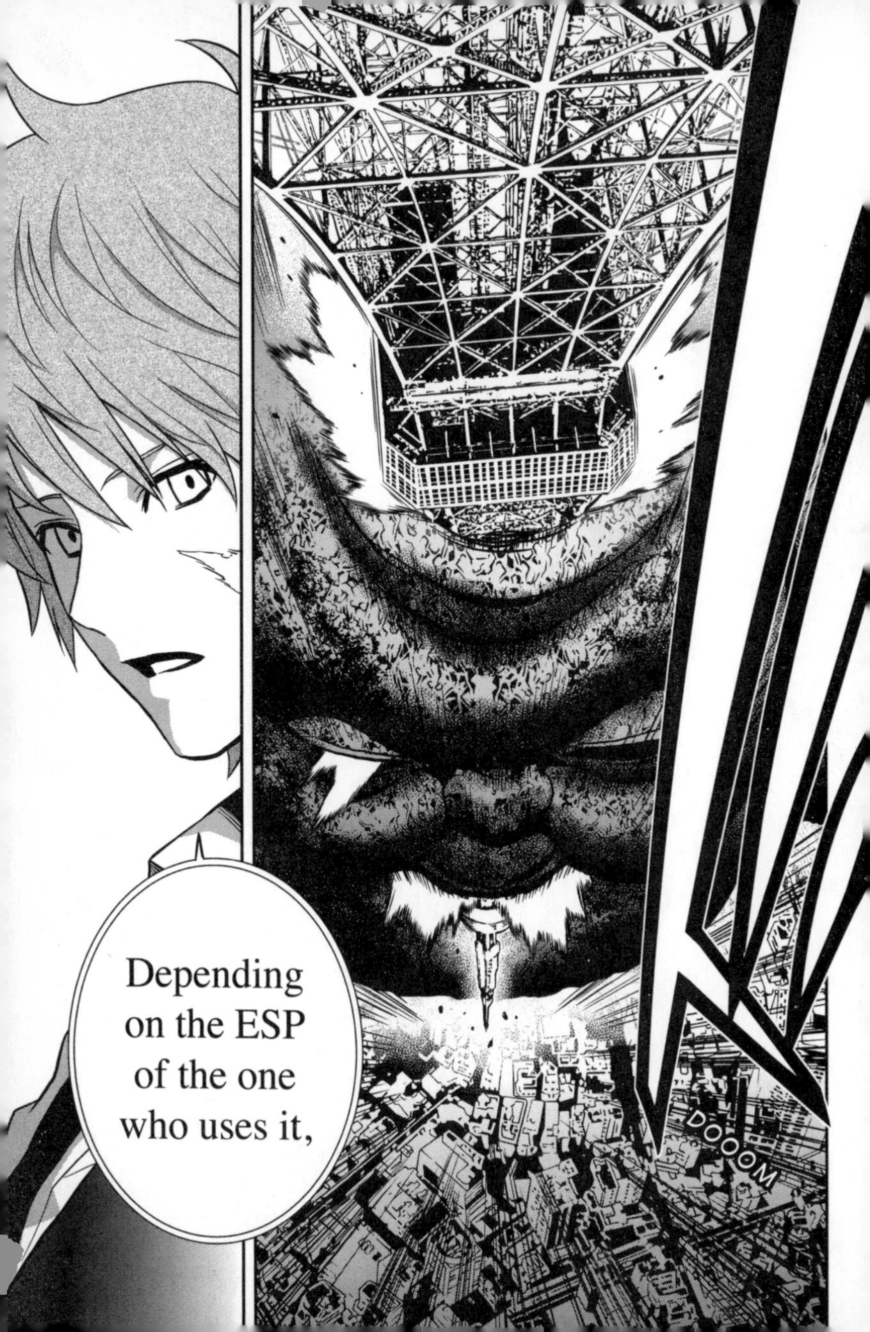
DOOOM
Depending on the ESP of the one who uses it,

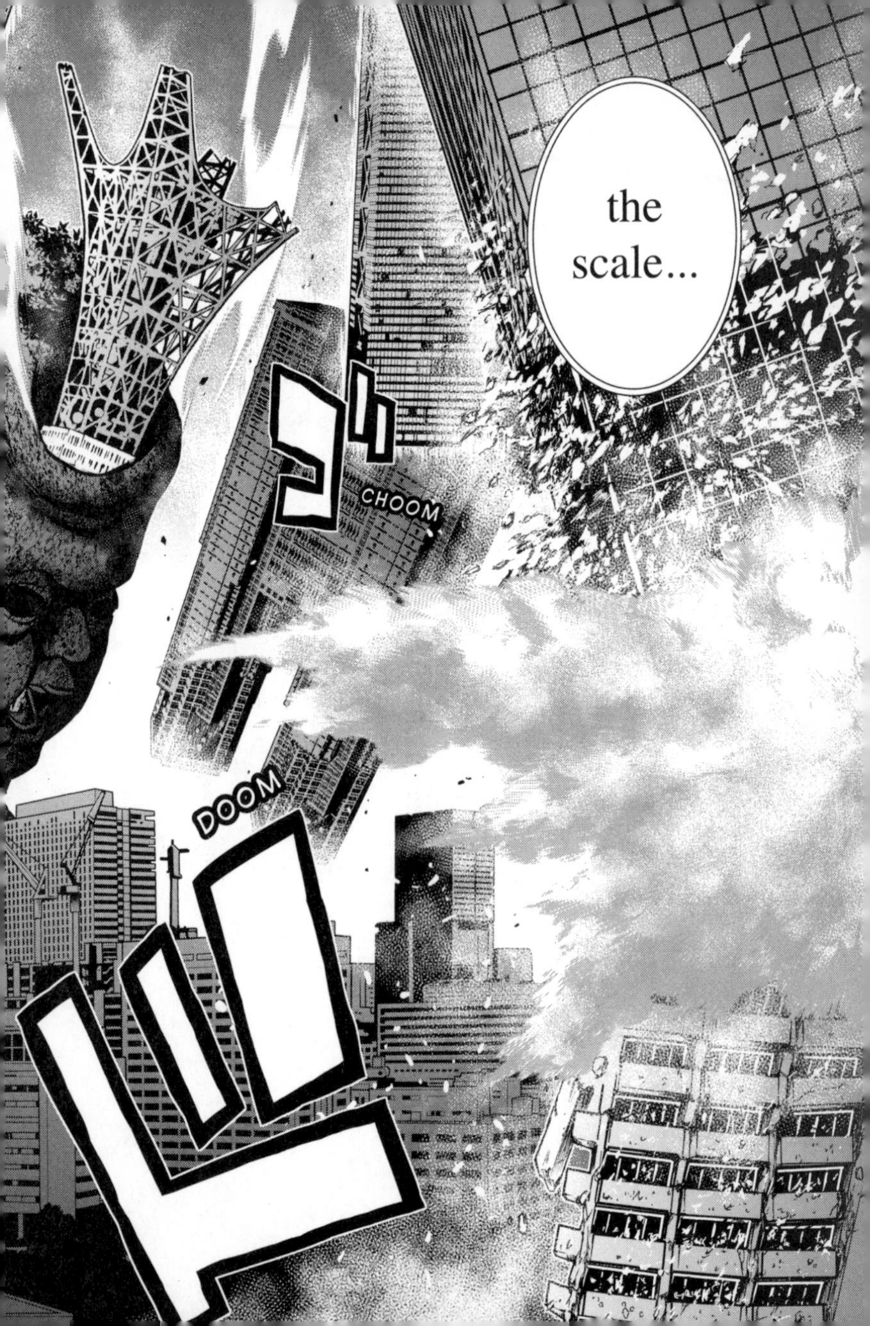
the scale...
CHOOM
DOOM

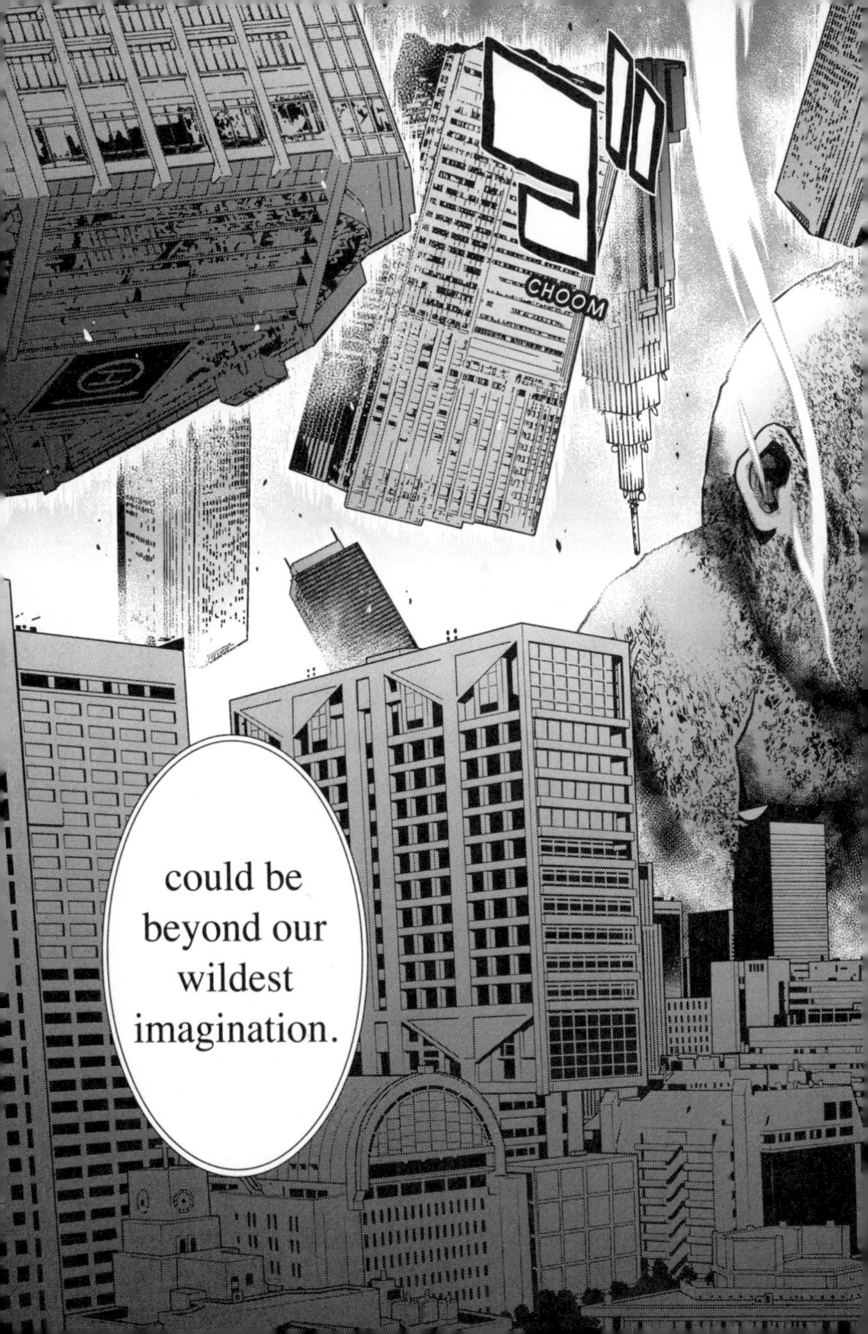
CHOOM
could be beyond our wildest imagination.

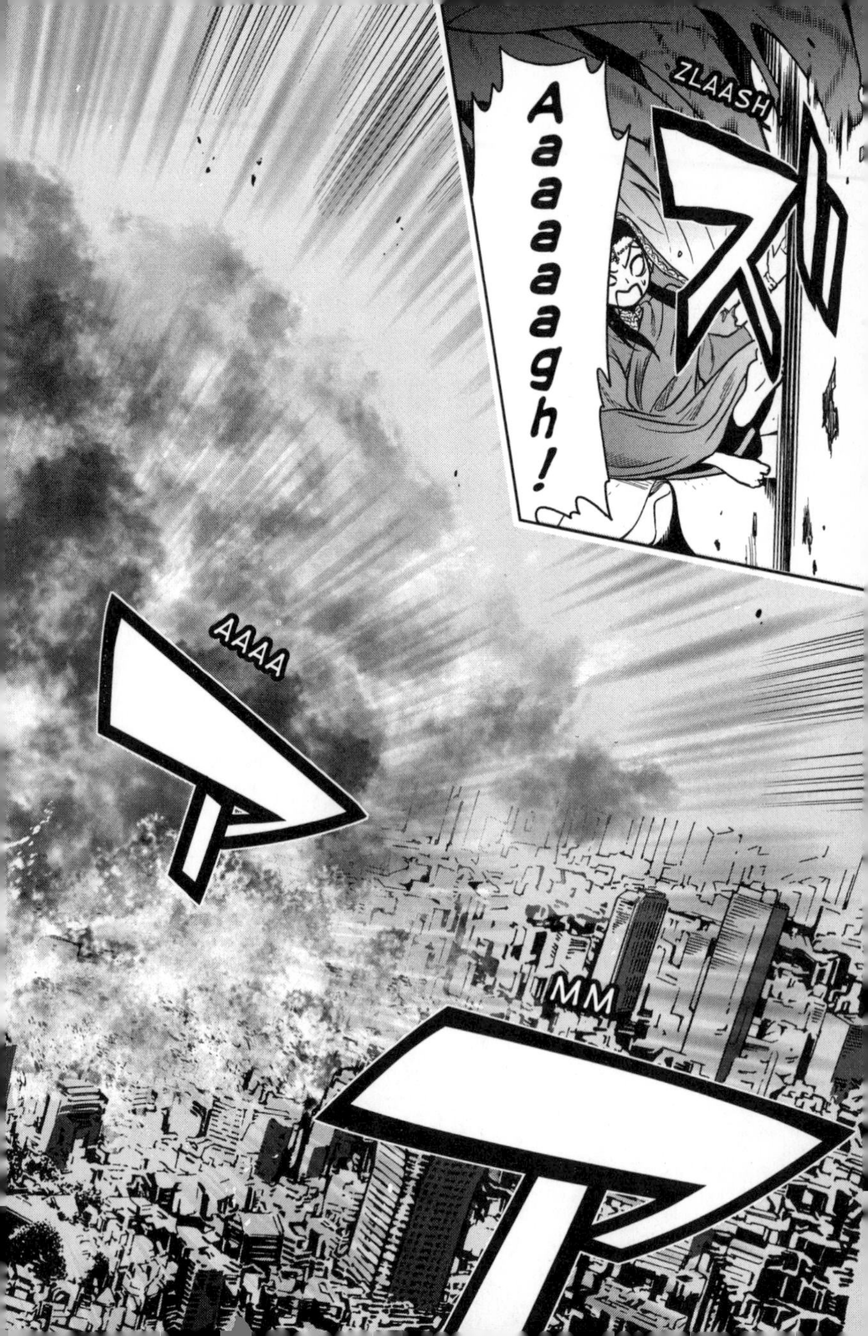
ZLAASH
Aaaaaaagh!
AAAA
MM

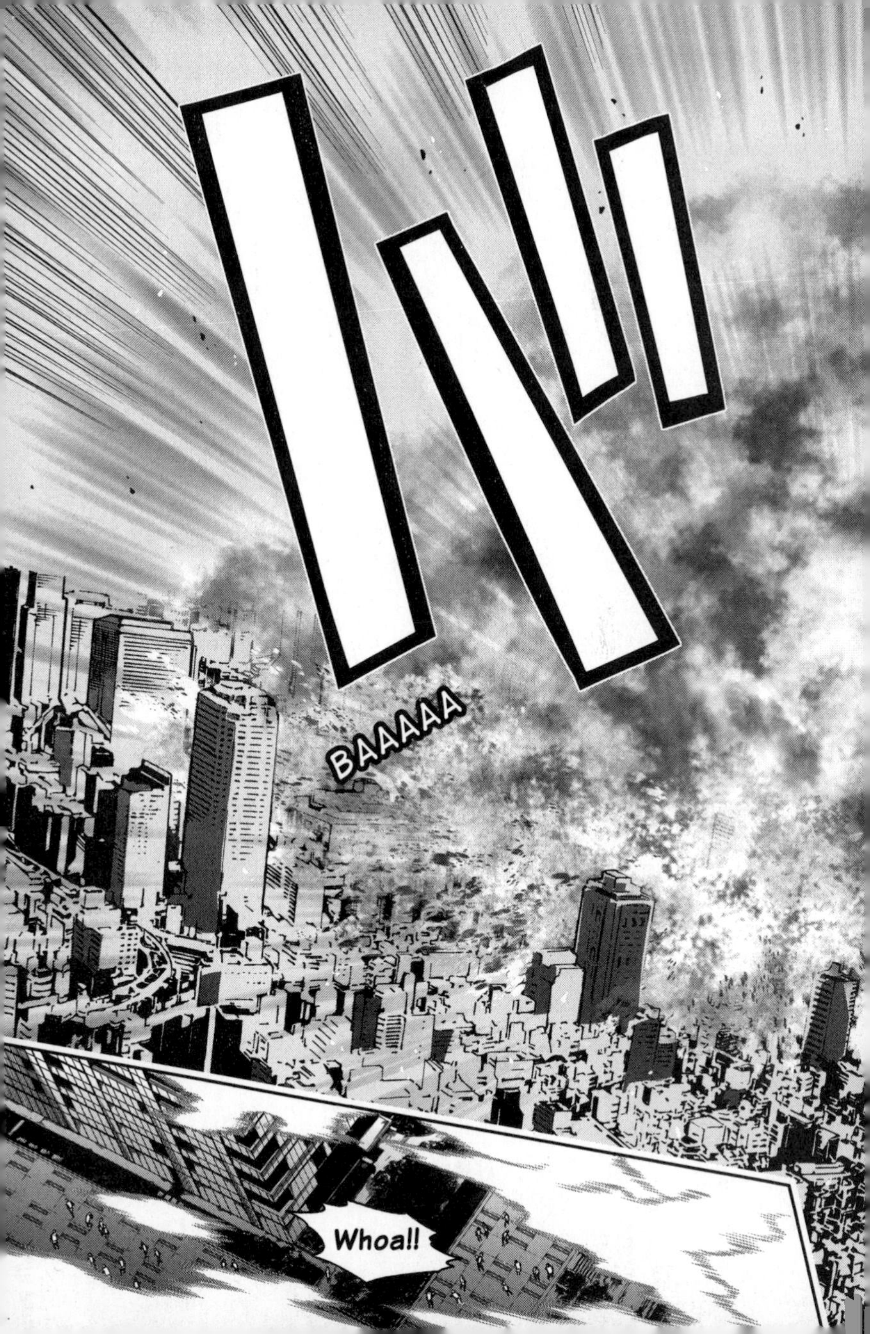
BAAAAA
Whoa!!

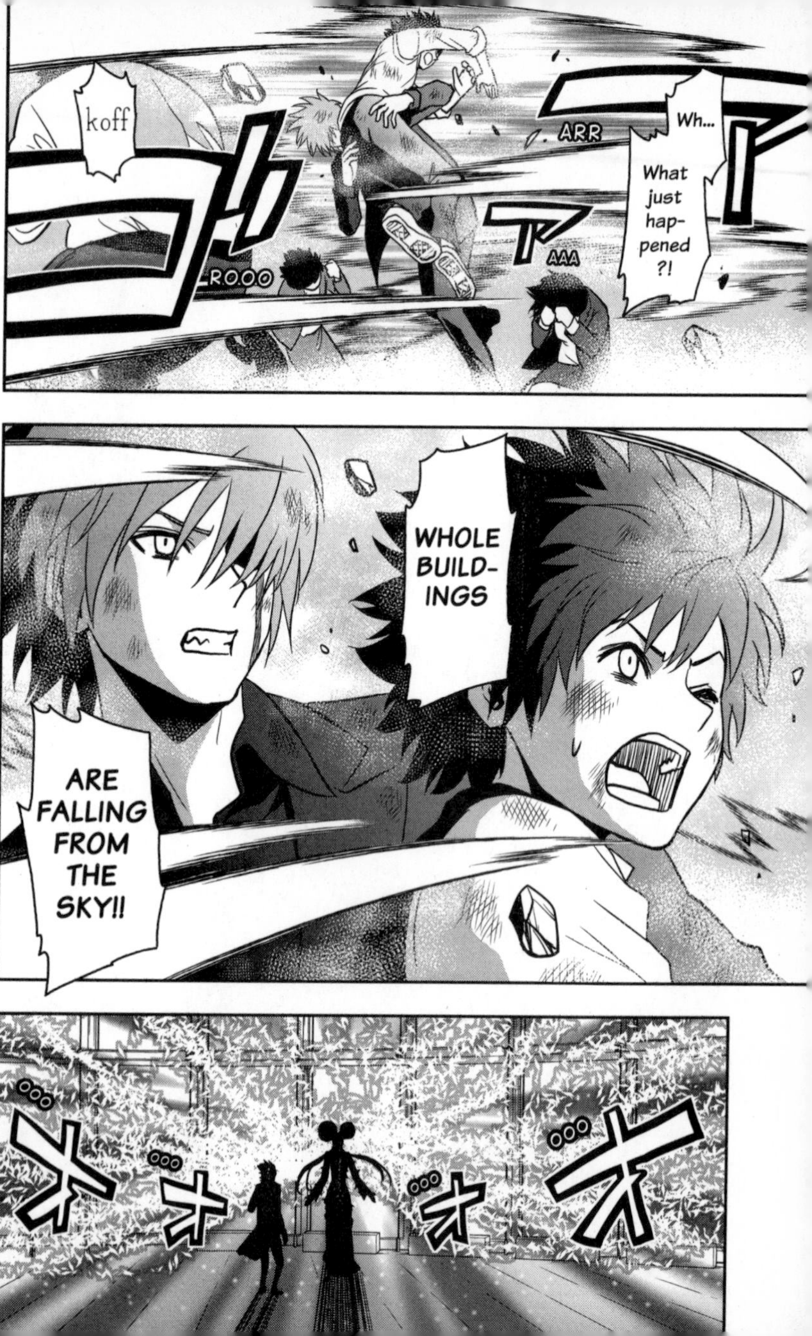
Wh...
What just hap-pened?!
ARR
koff
AAA
ROOO
WHOLE BUILD-INGS
ARE FALLING FROM THE SKY!!
OOO
OOO
OOO
OOO

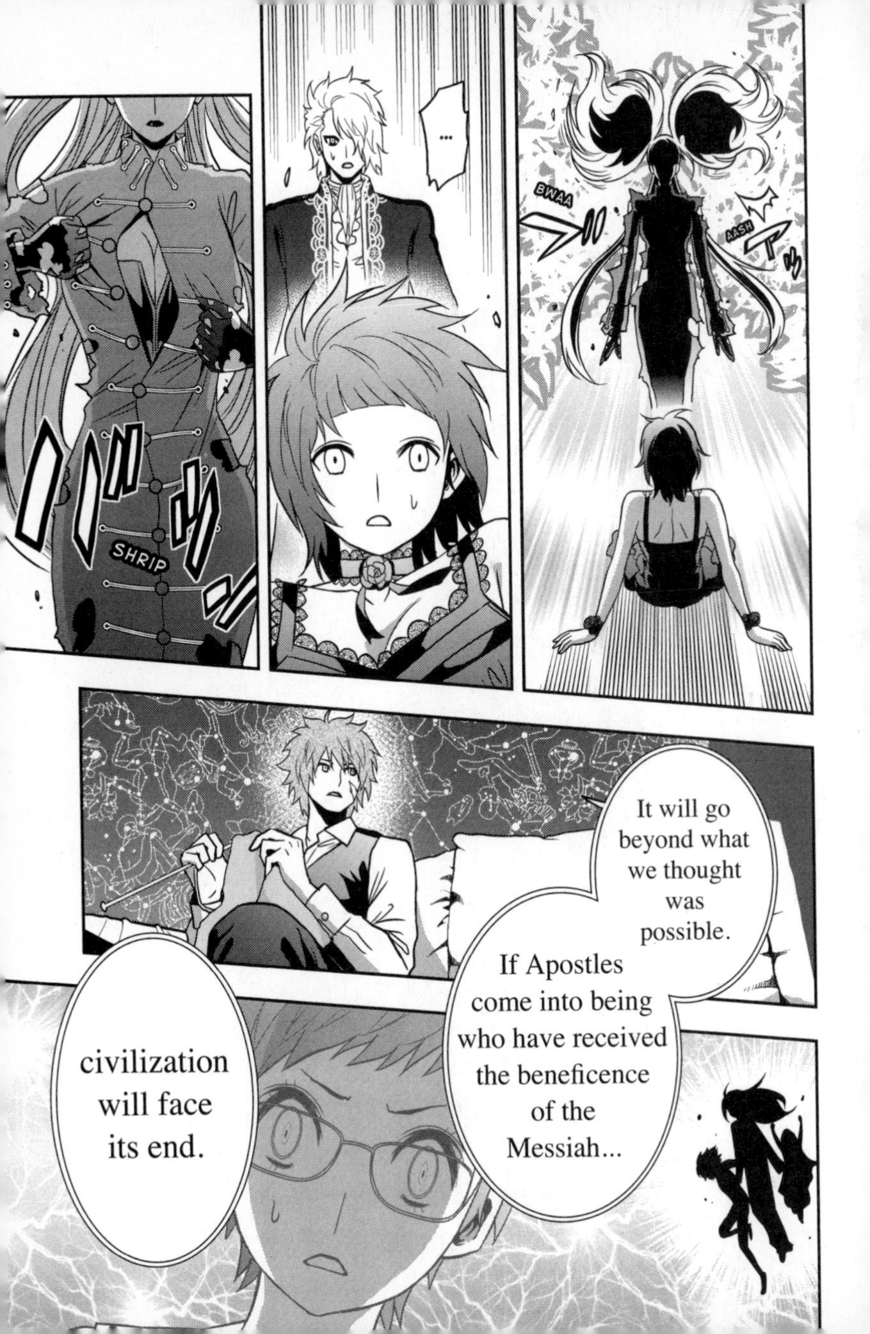
BWAA
AASH
...
SHRIP
It will go beyond what we thought was possible.
If Apostles come into being who have received the beneficence of the Messiah...
civilization will face its end.

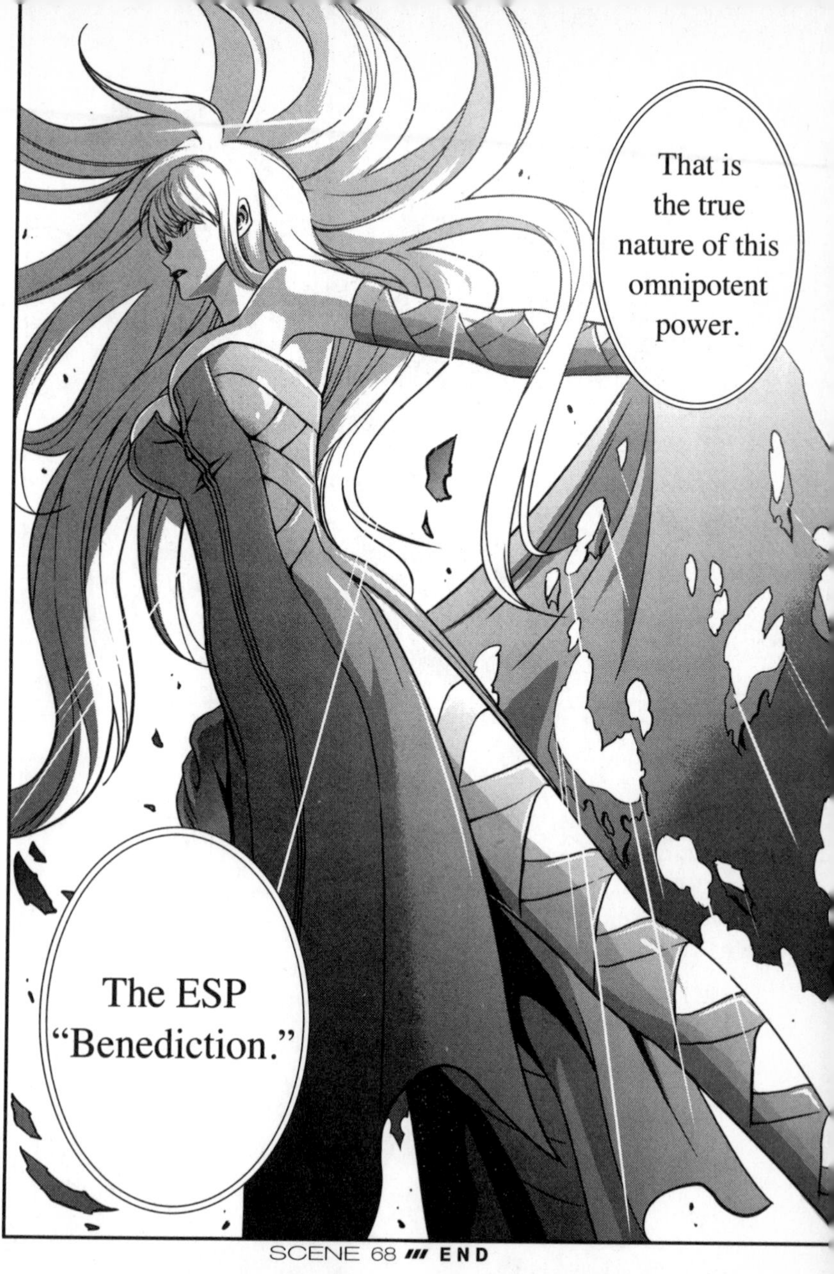
That is the true nature of this omnipotent power.
The ESP "Benediction."

SCENE 68 /// END

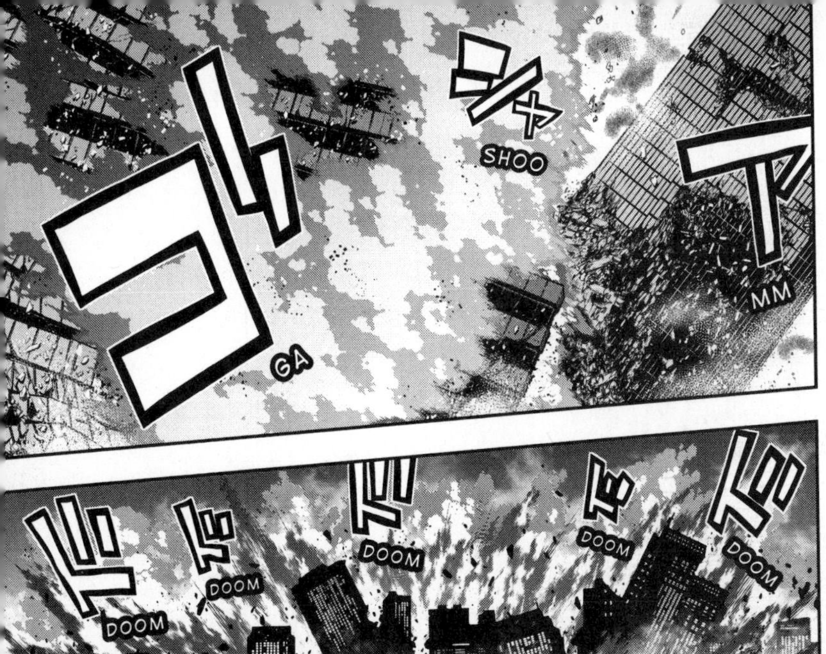
MM
SHOO
GA
DOOM
DOOM
DOOM
DOOM
DOOM

SCENE 69 /// Fragments of Justice

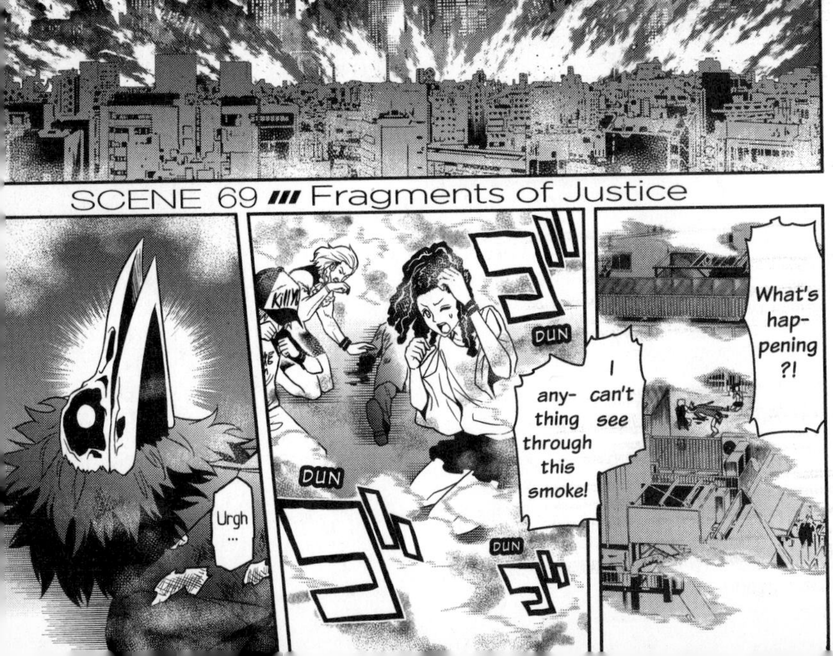
What's hap-pening?!
DUN
I can't see anything through this smoke!
DUN
DUN
Urgh ...

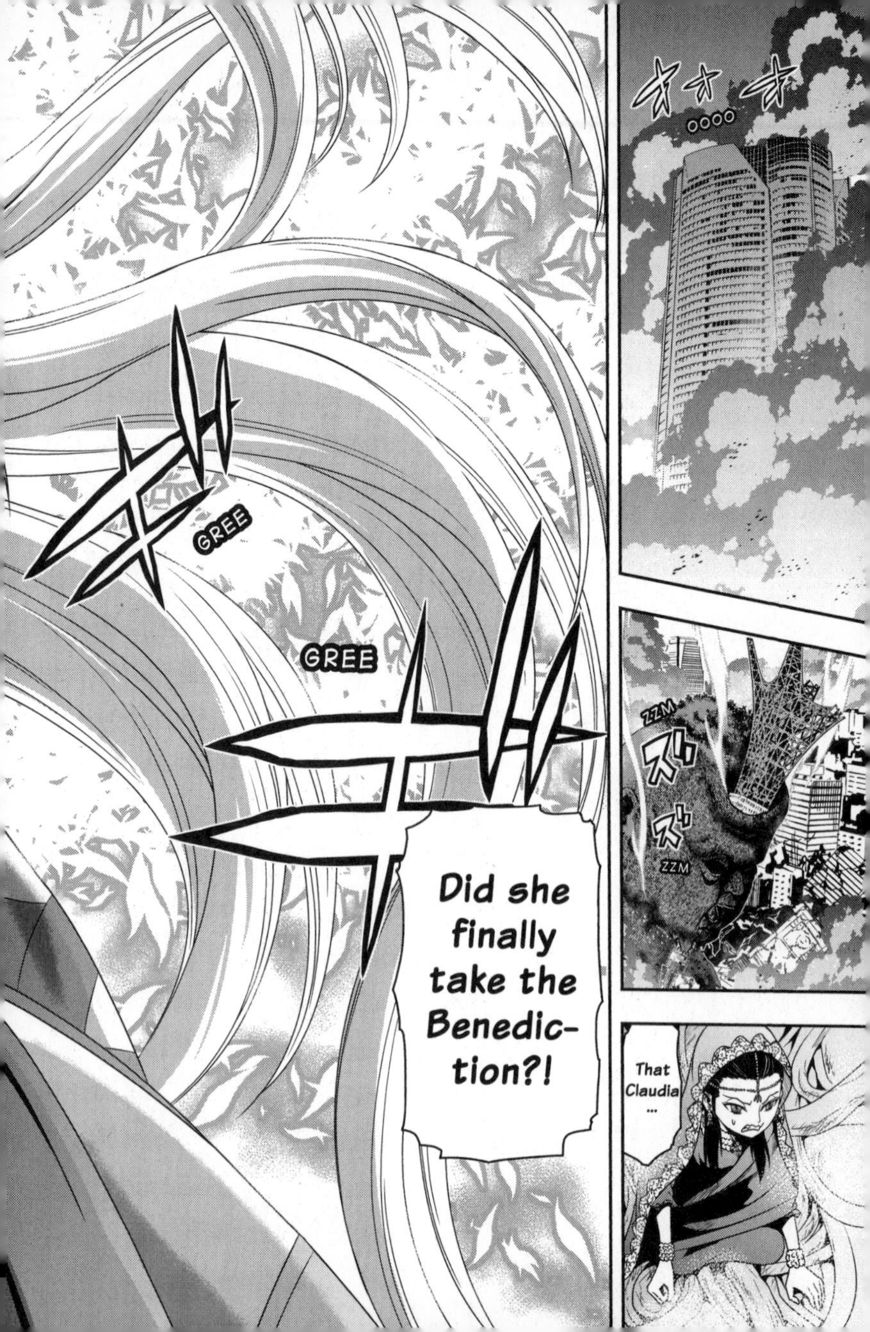
oooo
ZZM
ZZM
That Claudia ...
GREE
GREE
Did she finally take the Benediction?!

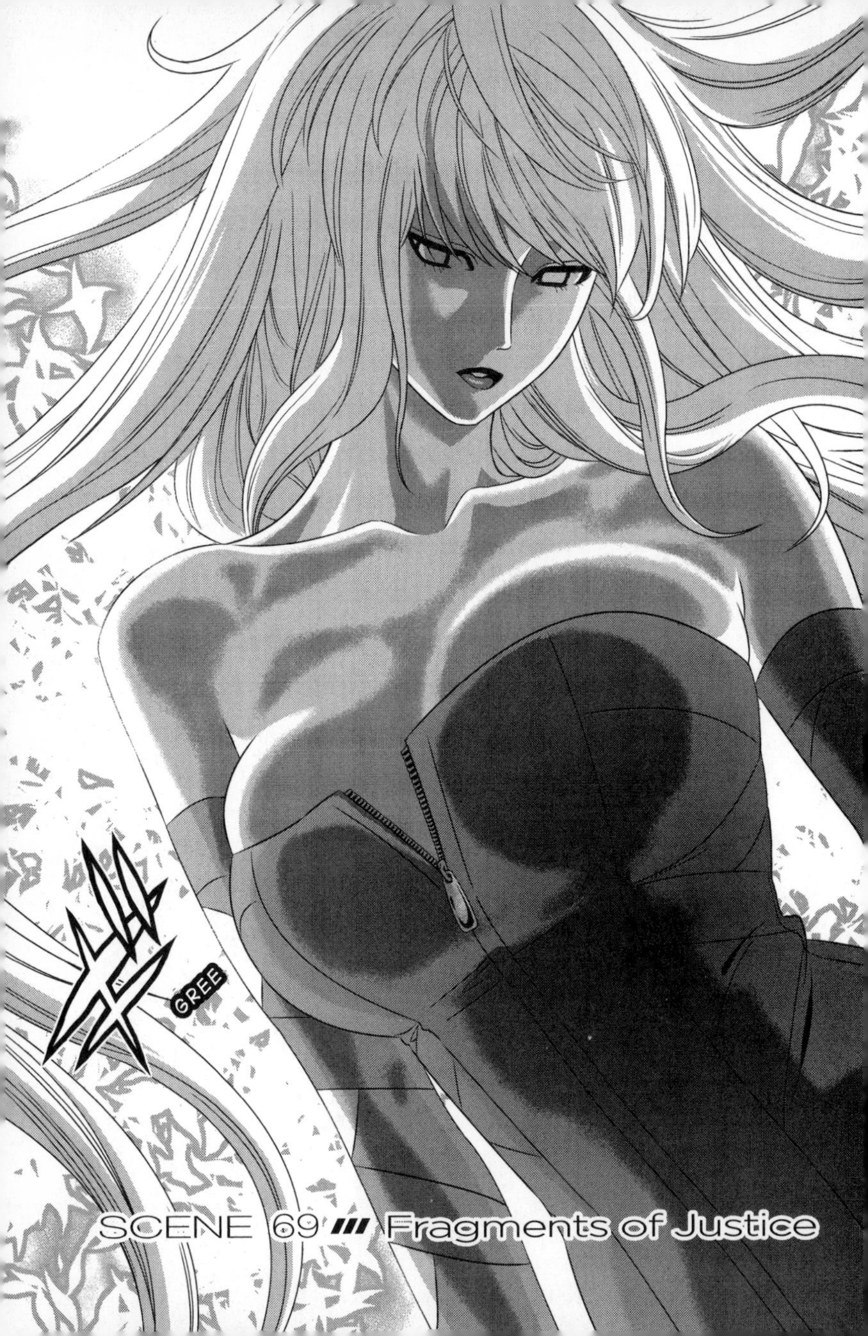
GREE
SCENE 69 /// Fragments of Justice

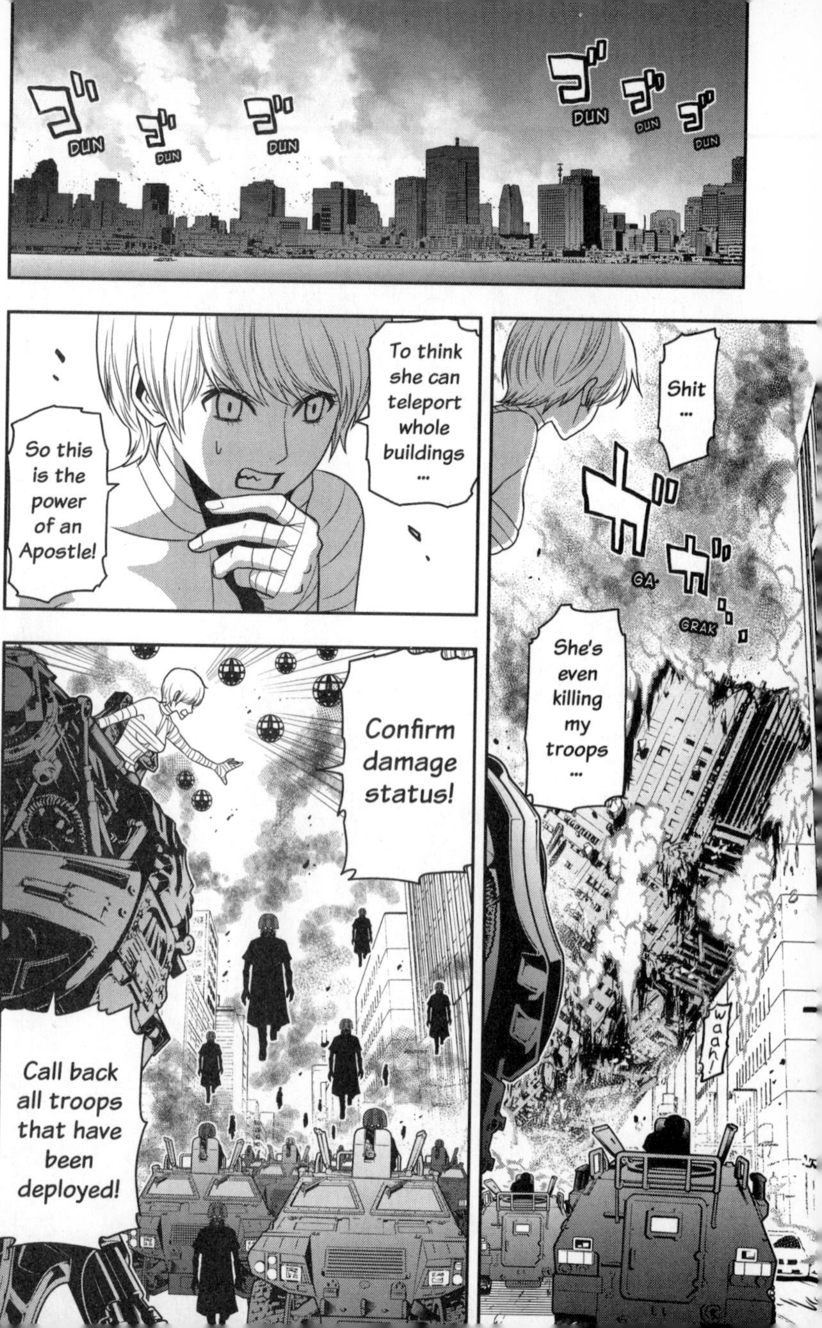
DUN
DUN
DUN
DUN
DUN
DUN
Shit ...
GA
GRAK
She's even killing my troops ...
Waah!
To think she can teleport whole buildings ...
So this is the power of an Apostle!
Confirm damage status!
Call back all troops that have been deployed!

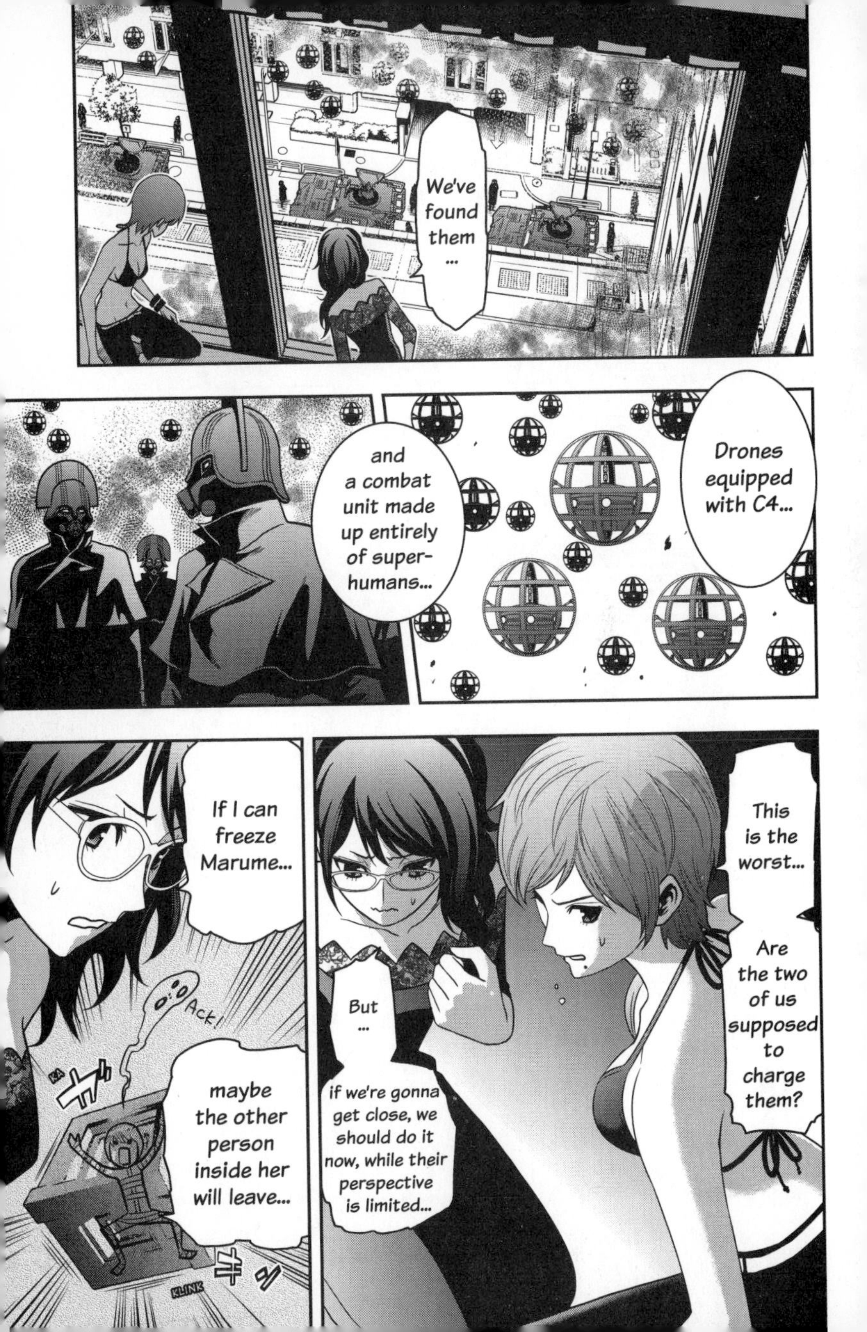
We've found them ...
Drones equipped with C4...
and a combat unit made up entirely of super-humans...
This is the worst...
Are the two of us supposed to charge them?
But ...
if we're gonna get close, we should do it now, while their perspective is limited...
If I can freeze Marume...
maybe the other person inside her will leave...
Ack!
KA
KLINK

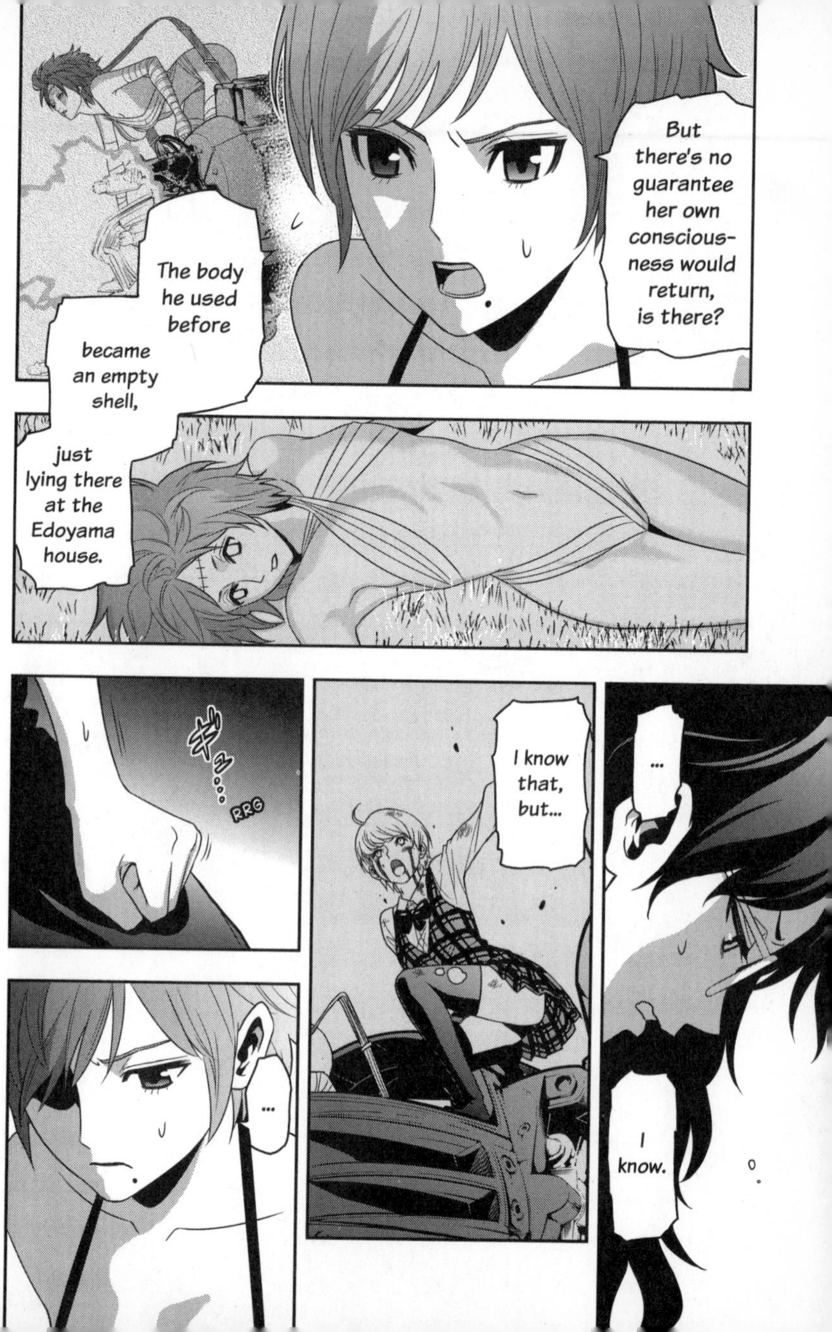

But there's no guarantee her own conscious-ness would return, is there?
The body he used before
became an empty shell,
just lying there at the Edoyama house.
...
I know.
I know that, but...
RRG
...

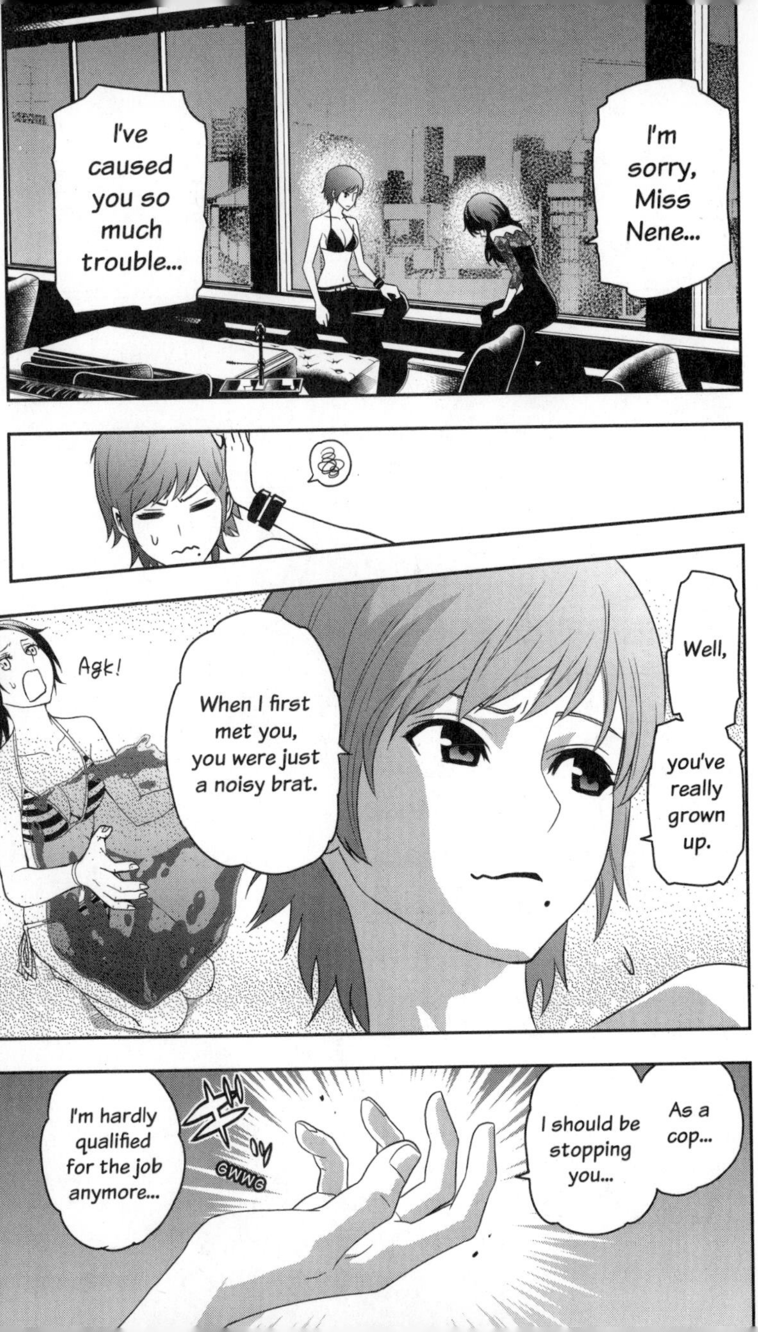
I'm sorry, Miss Nene...
I've caused you so much trouble...
Well, you've really grown up.
When I first met you, you were just a noisy brat.
Agk!
As a cop...
I should be stopping you...
I'm hardly qualified for the job anymore...
GWWG

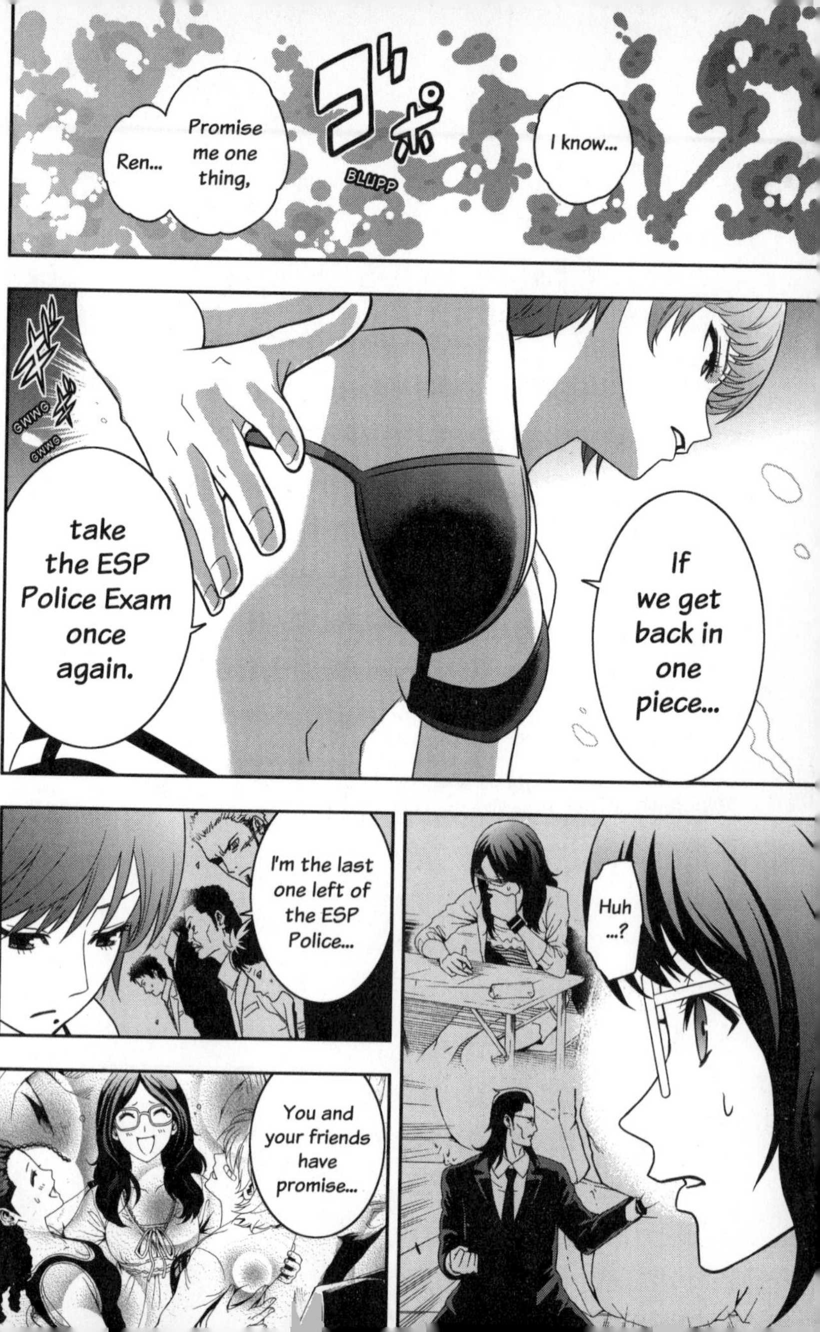
I know...
ゴポ
BLUPP
Ren... Promise me one thing,
If we get back in one piece...
take the ESP Police Exam once again.
GWNG GWNG
Huh ...?
I'm the last one left of the ESP Police...
You and your friends have promise...

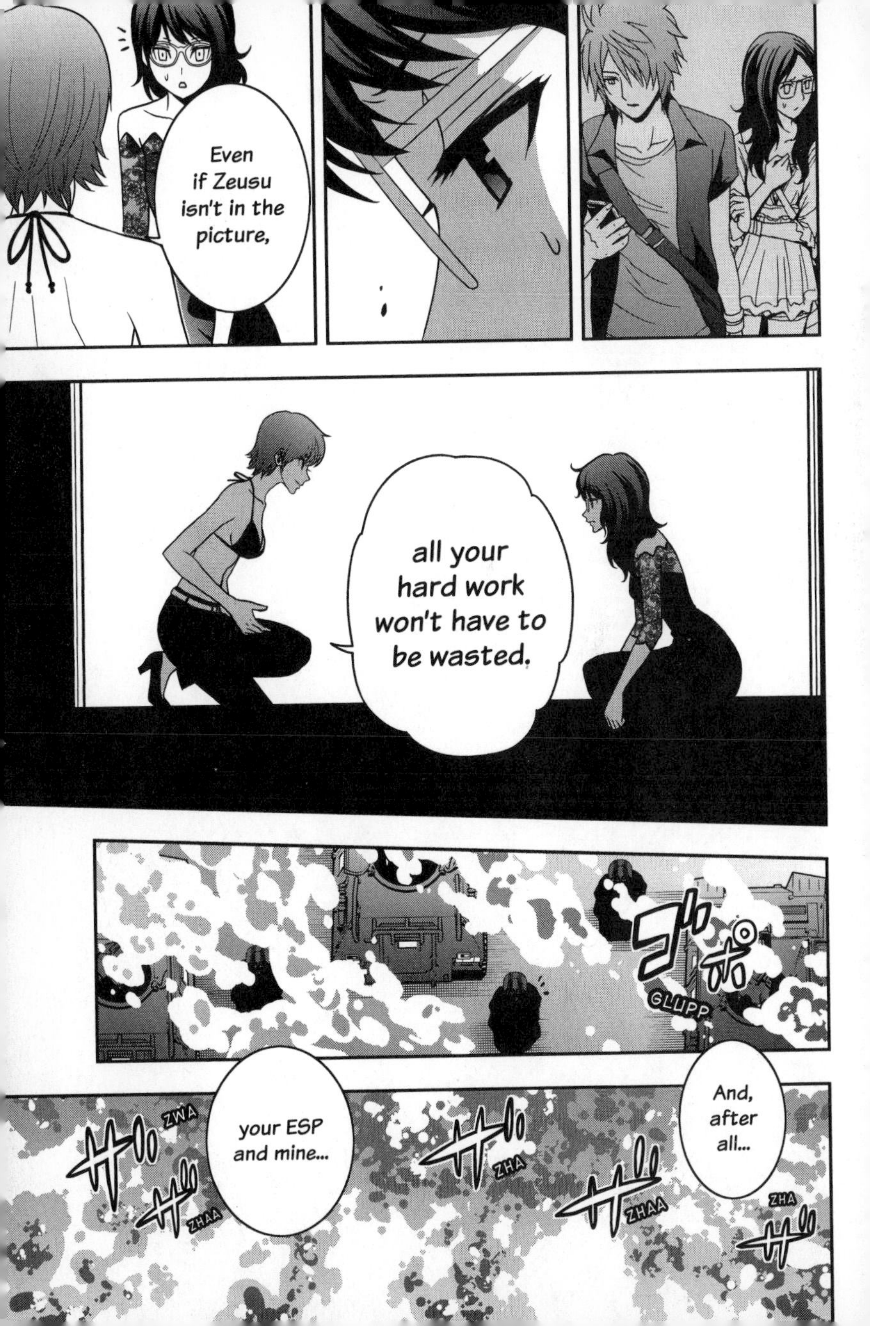
Even if Zeusu isn't in the picture,
all your hard work won't have to be wasted.
GLUPP
And, after all...
ZHA
ZHAA
ZHA
your ESP and mine...
ZWA
ZHAA

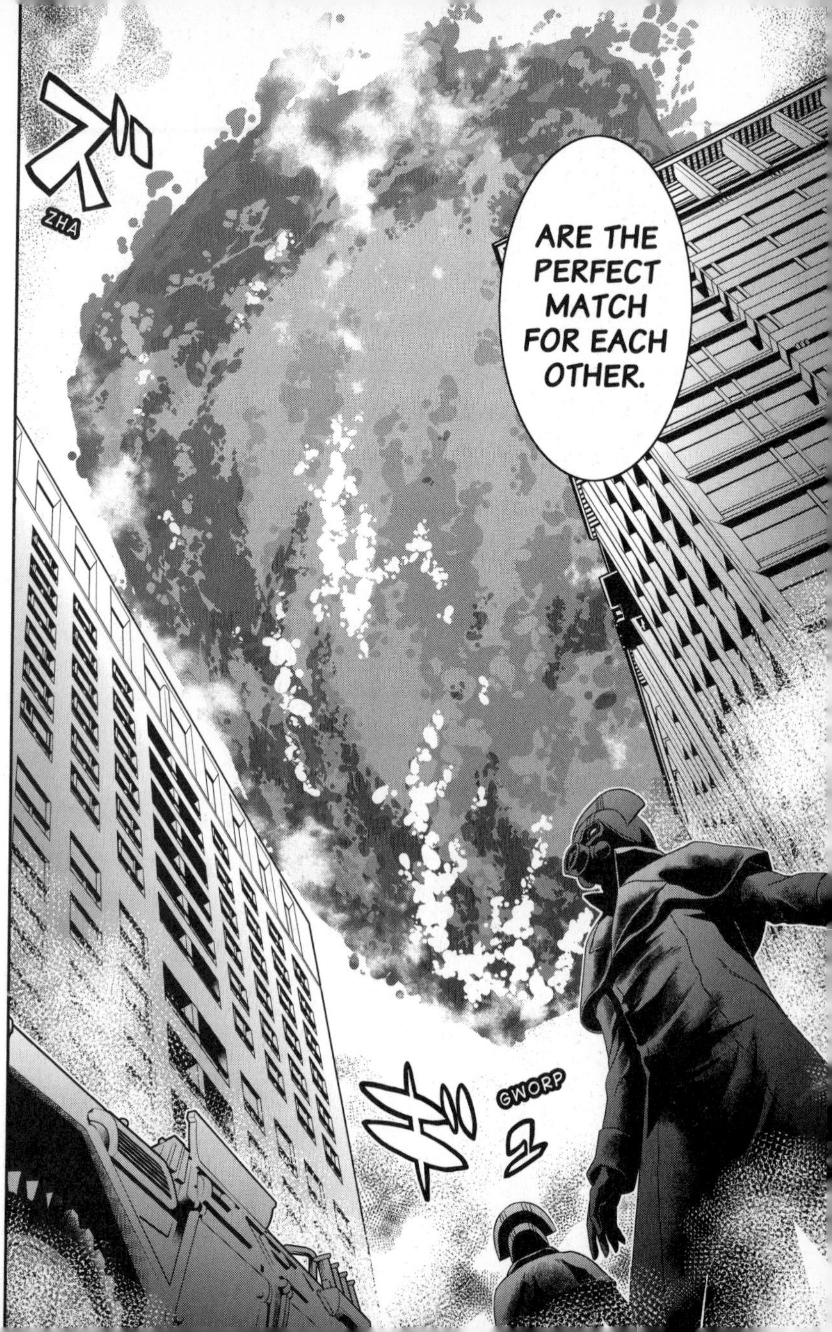
ARE THE PERFECT MATCH FOR EACH OTHER.
ZHA
GWORP

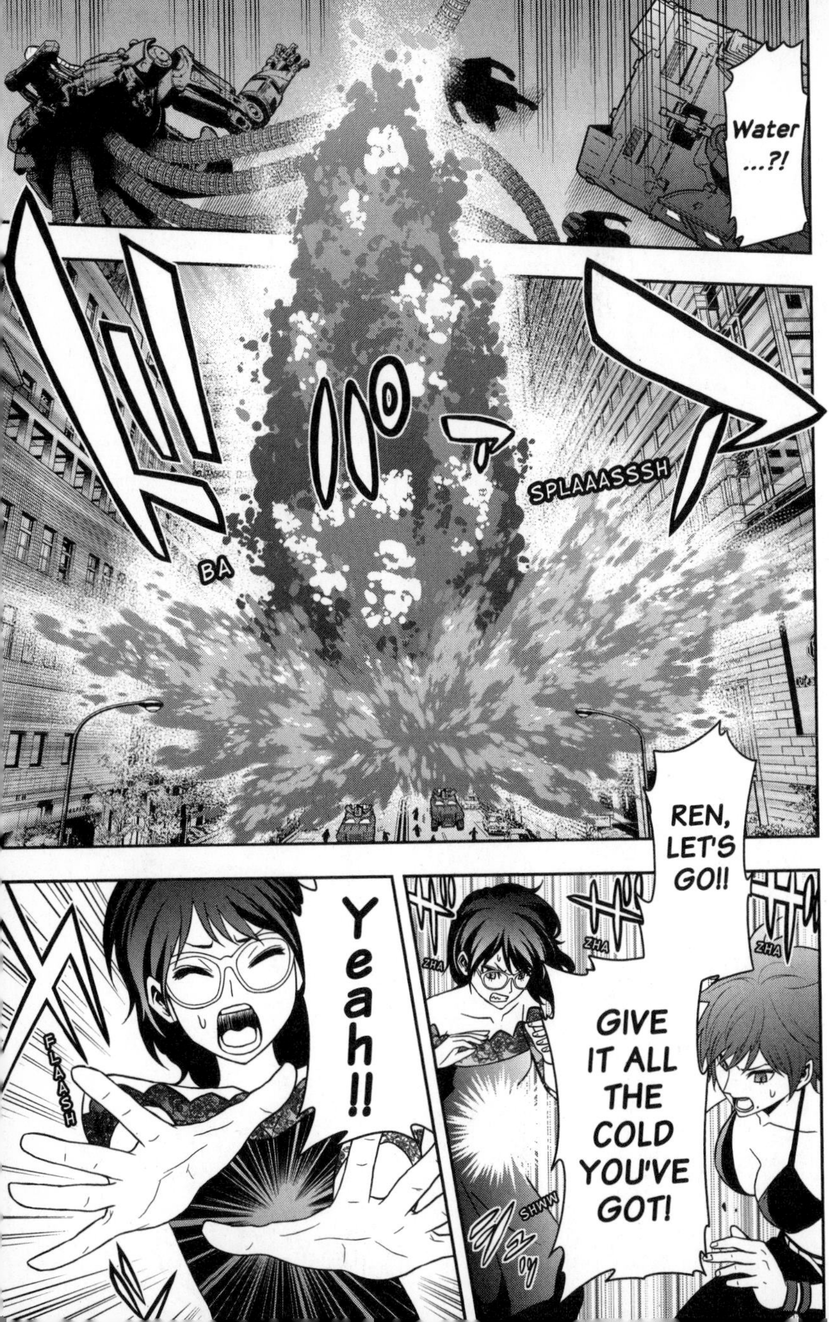
Water ...?!
SPLAAASSSH
BA
REN, LET'S GO!!
ZHA
ZHA
ZHA
GIVE IT ALL THE COLD YOU'VE GOT!
SHWW
Yeah!!
FLAAASH

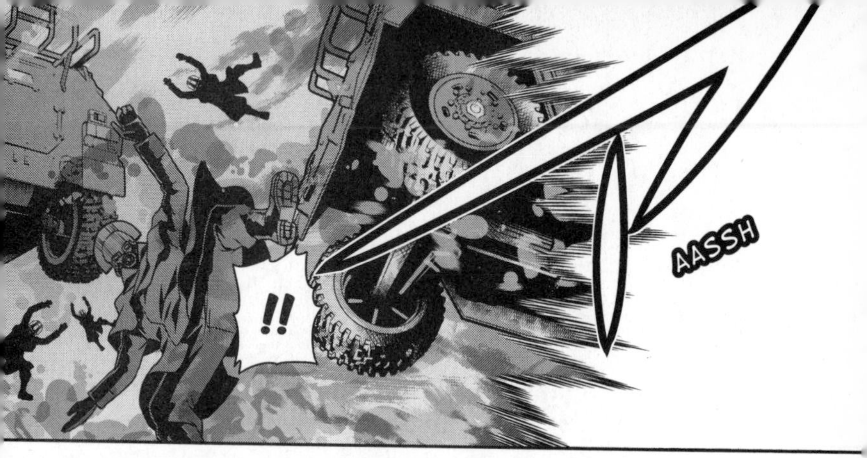
AASSH
!!

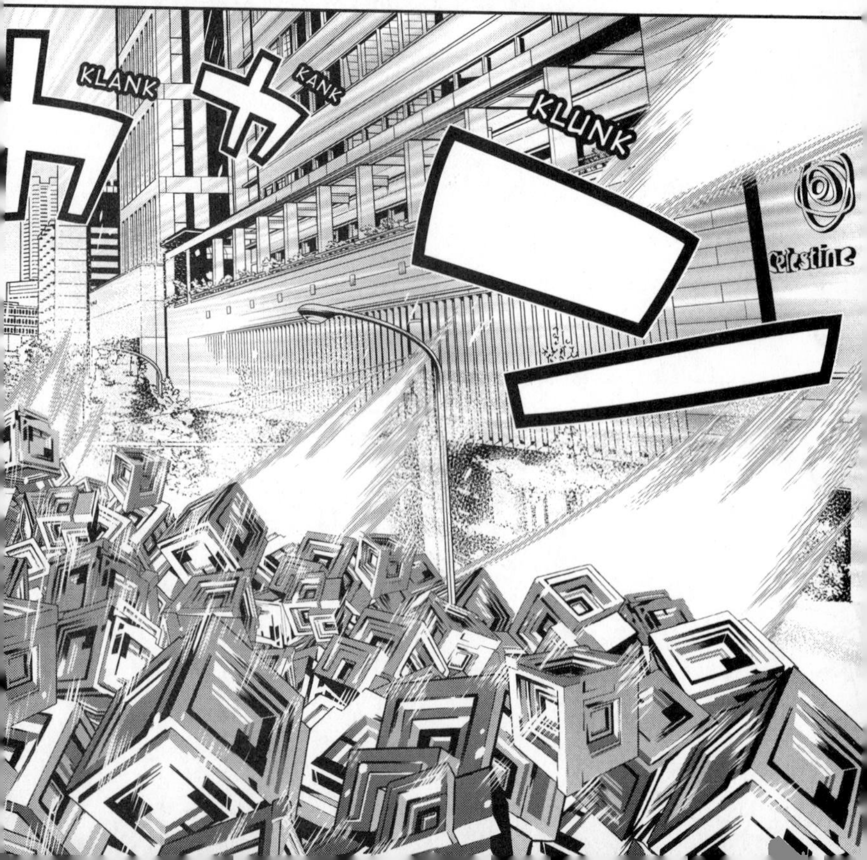
celestine
KLUNK
KANK
KLANK

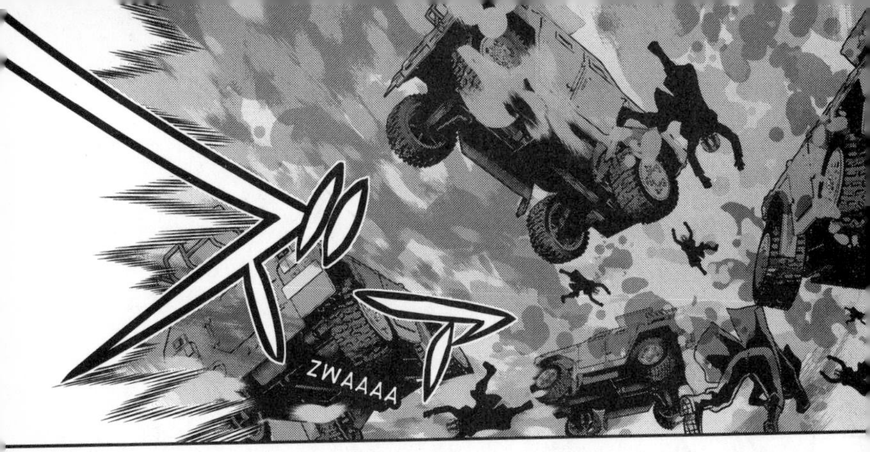
ZWAAAA
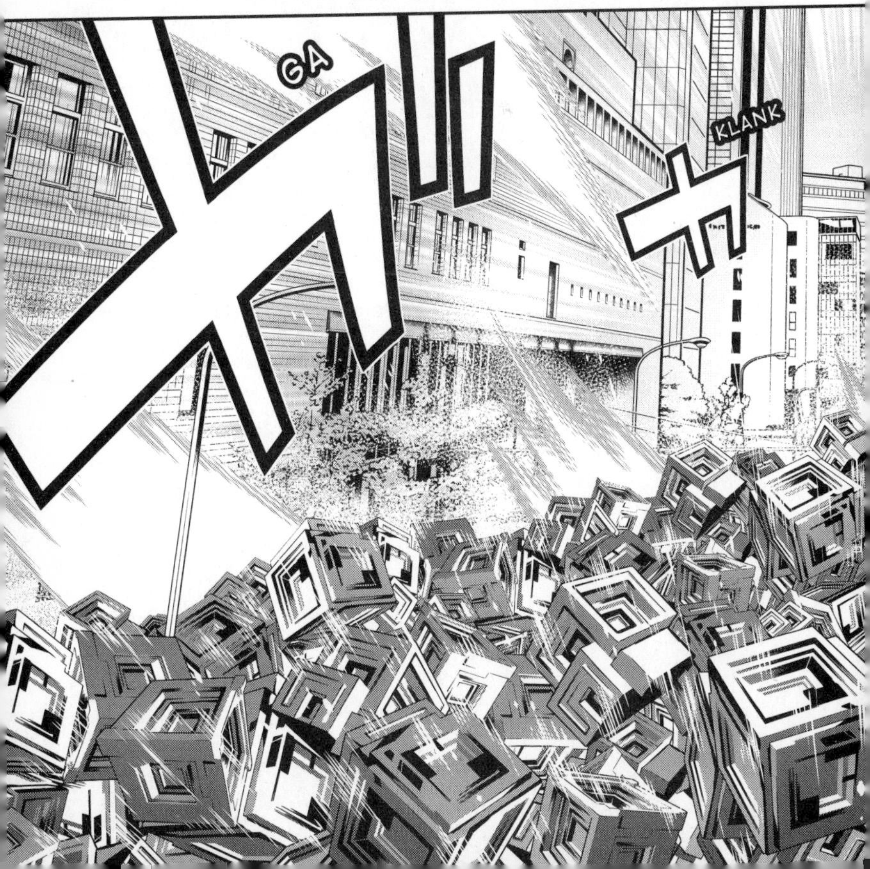
GA
KLANK

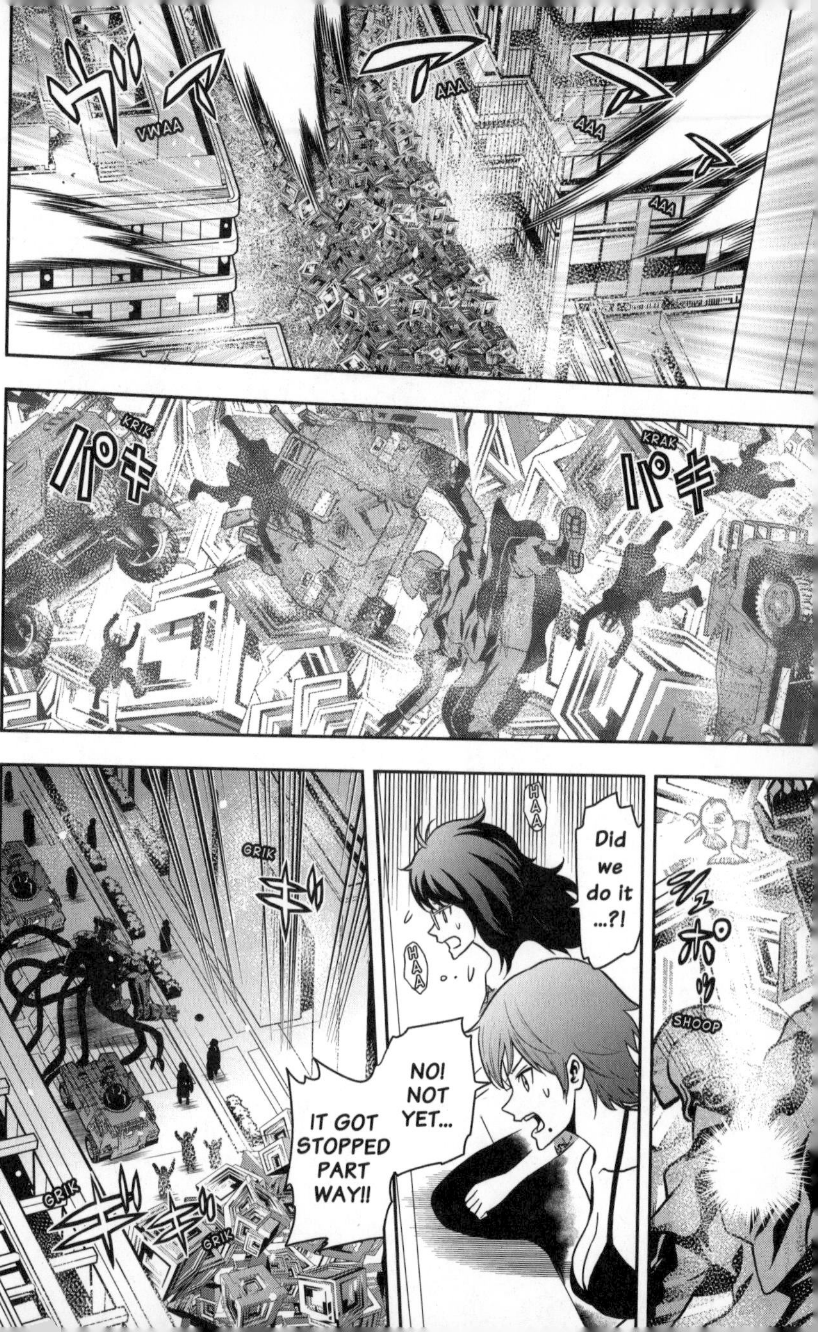
VWAA
AAA
AAA
AAA
KRAK
KRIK
SHOOP
HAA
Did we do it ...?!
HAA
NO! NOT YET...
IT GOT STOPPED PART WAY!!
GRIK
GRIK
GRIK

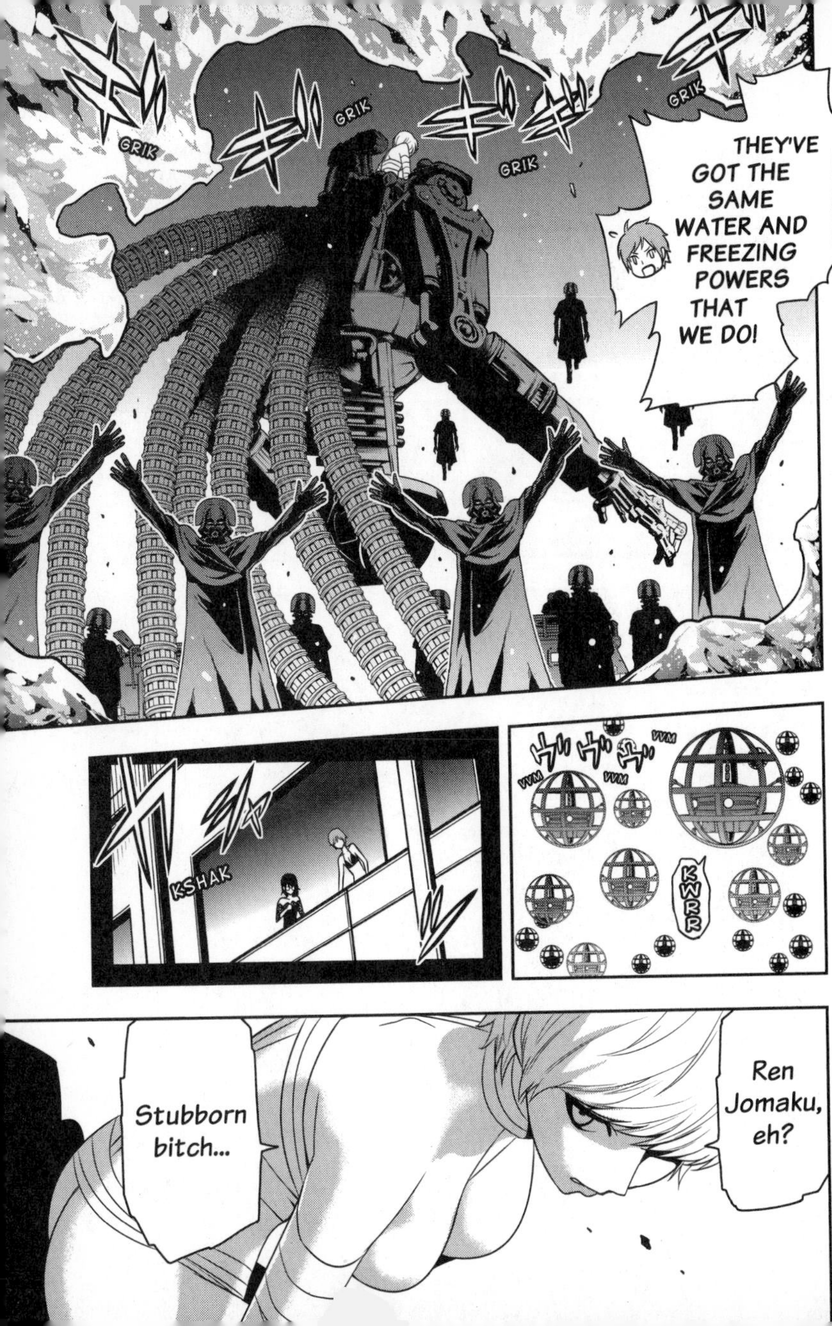
GRIK
GRIK
GRIK
GRIK
THEY'VE GOT THE SAME WATER AND FREEZING POWERS THAT WE DO!
VVM
VVM
VVM
KWRR
KSHAK
Ren Jomaku, eh?
Stubborn bitch...

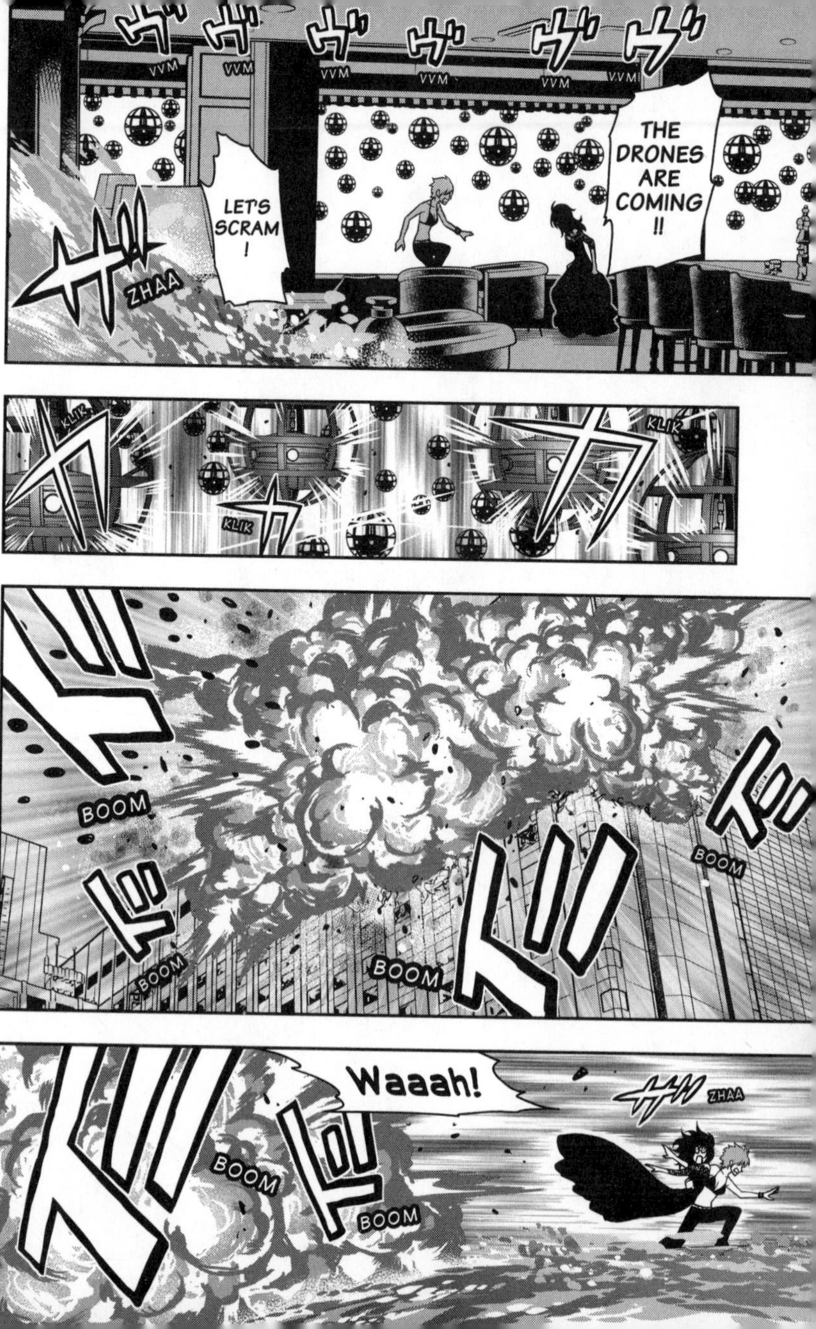
VVM
VVM
VVM
VVM
VVM
VVM
THE DRONES ARE COMING !!
LET'S SCRAM !
ZHAA
KLIK
KLIK
KLIK
BOOM
BOOM
BOOM
BOOM
ZHAA
Waaah!
BOOM
BOOM

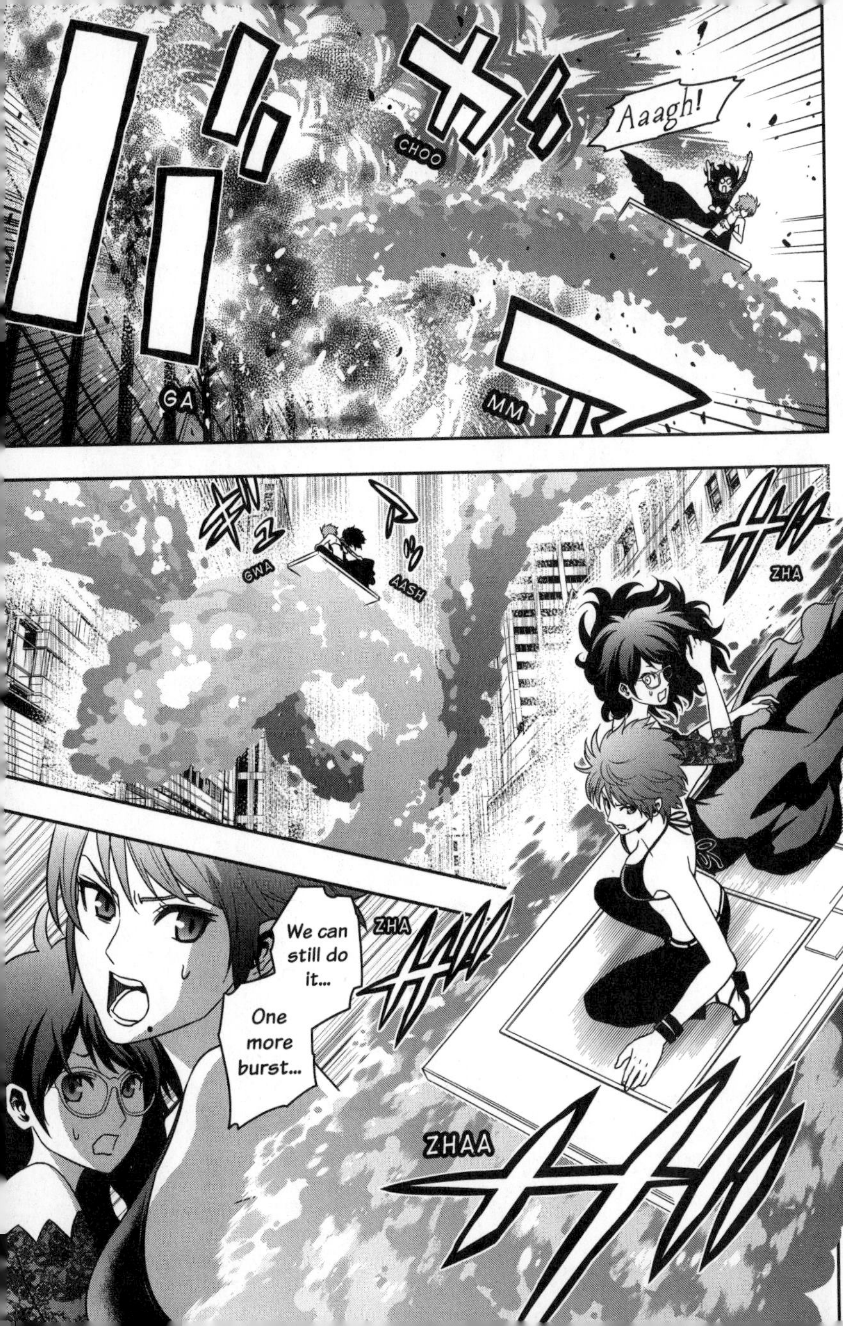
Aaagh!
GA
CHOO
MM
ZHA
GWA
AASH
We can still do it...
One more burst...
ZHA
ZHAA

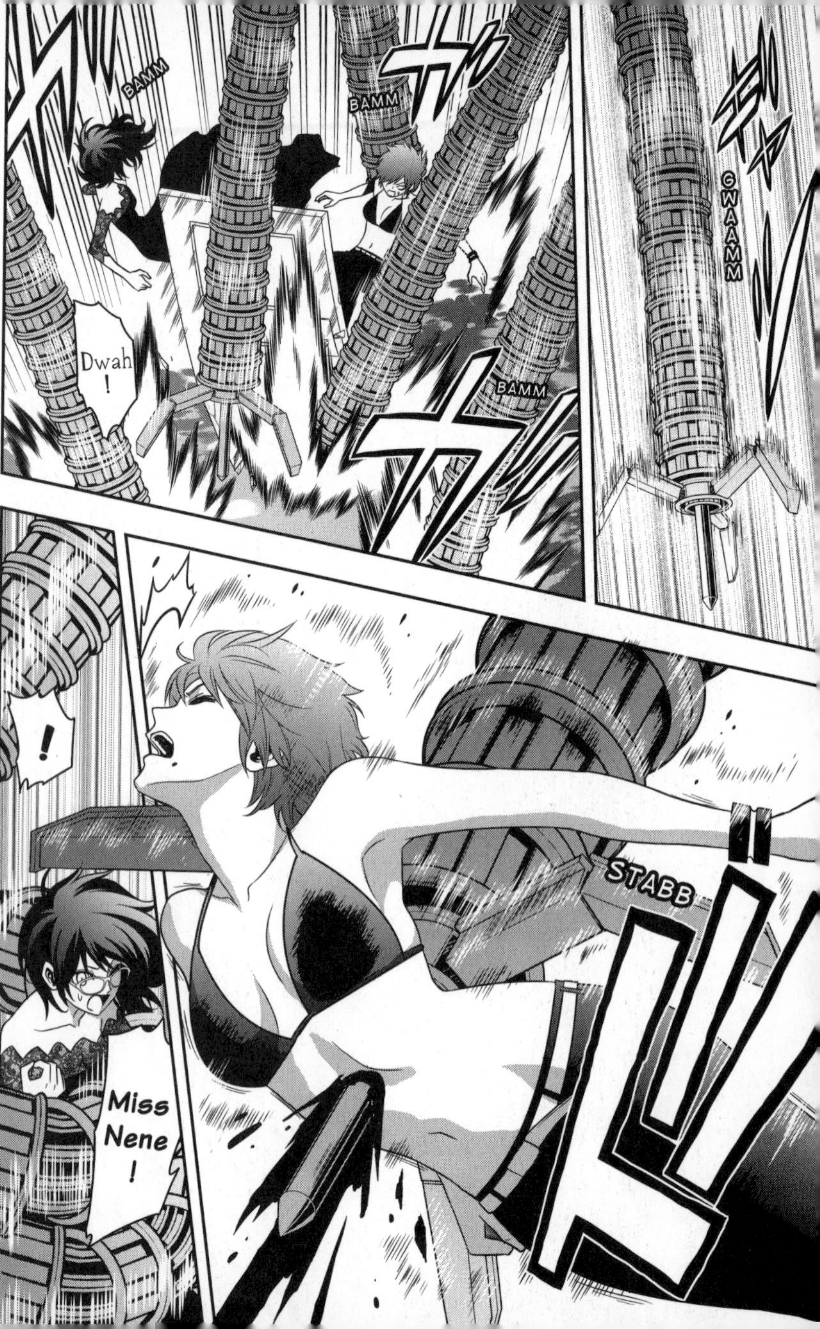
GWAAAMM
BAMM
BAMM
BAMM
Dwah!
STABB
!
Miss Nene!

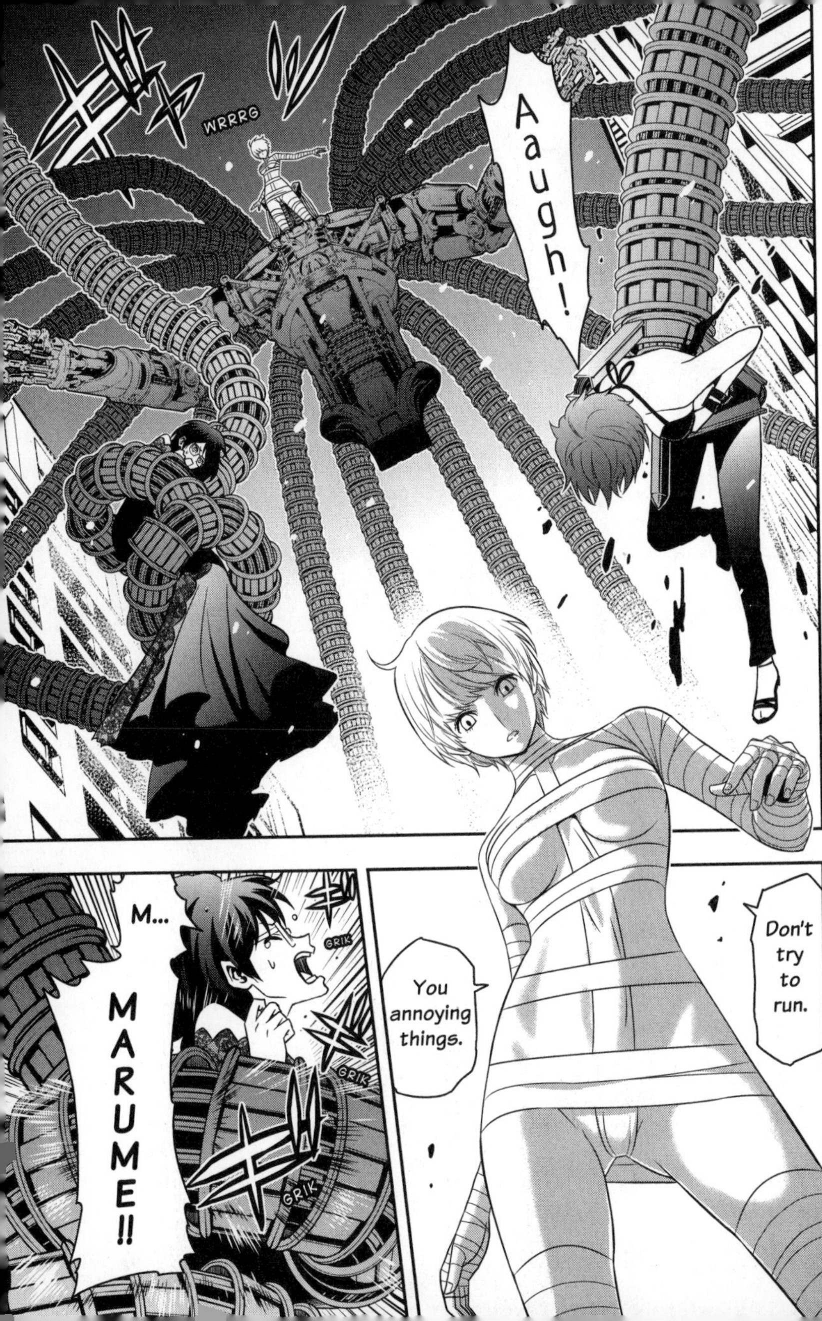
Aaugh!
WRRRG
Don't try to run.
You annoying things.
M...
MARUME!!
GRIK
GRIK
GRIK

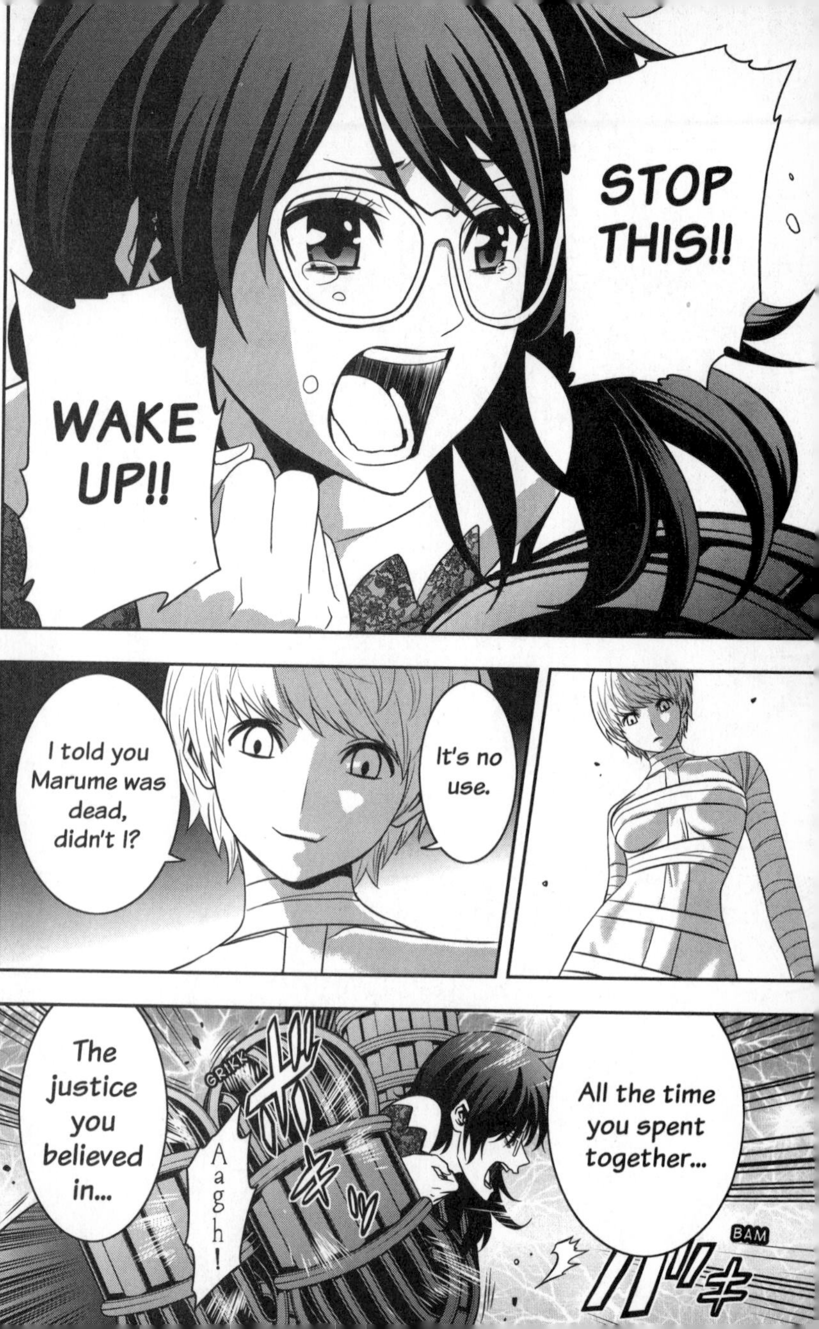
STOP THIS!!
WAKE UP!!
It's no use.
I told you Marume was dead, didn't I?
All the time you spent together...
BAM
GRIKK
Aagh!
The justice you believed in...

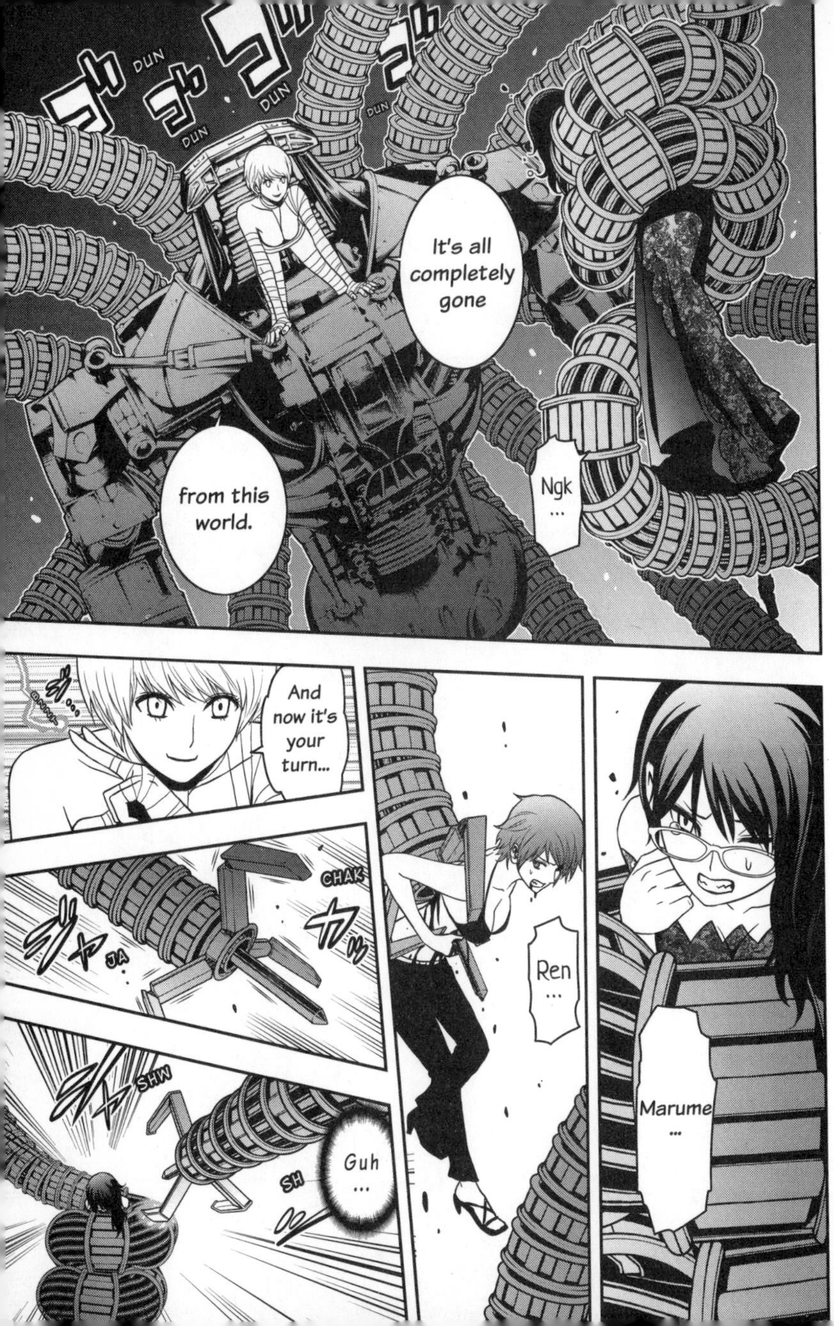
DUN
DUN
DUN
DUN
It's all completely gone
from this world.
Ngk ...
Marume ...
Ren ...
And now it's your turn...
CHAK
JA
SHW
SH
Guh ...

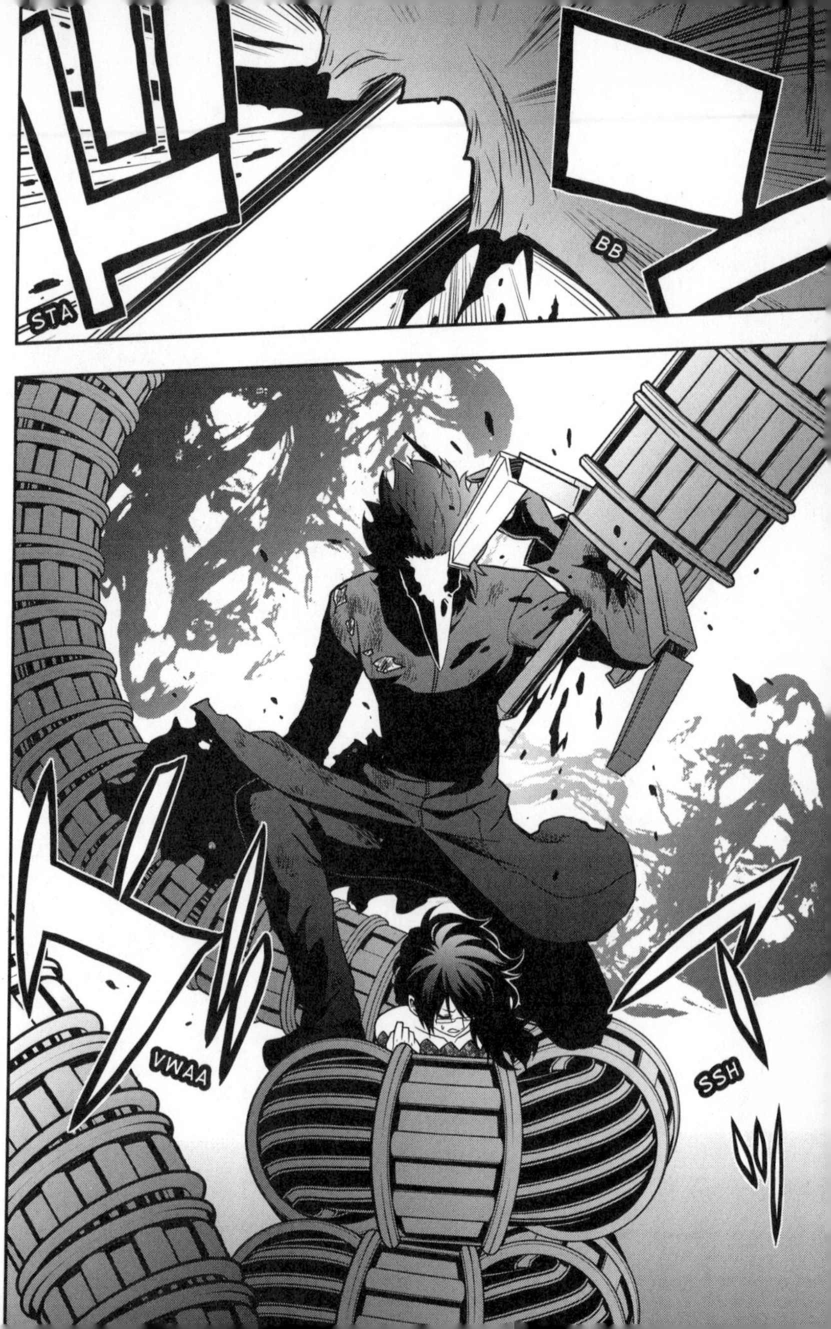
BB
STA
SSH
VWAA

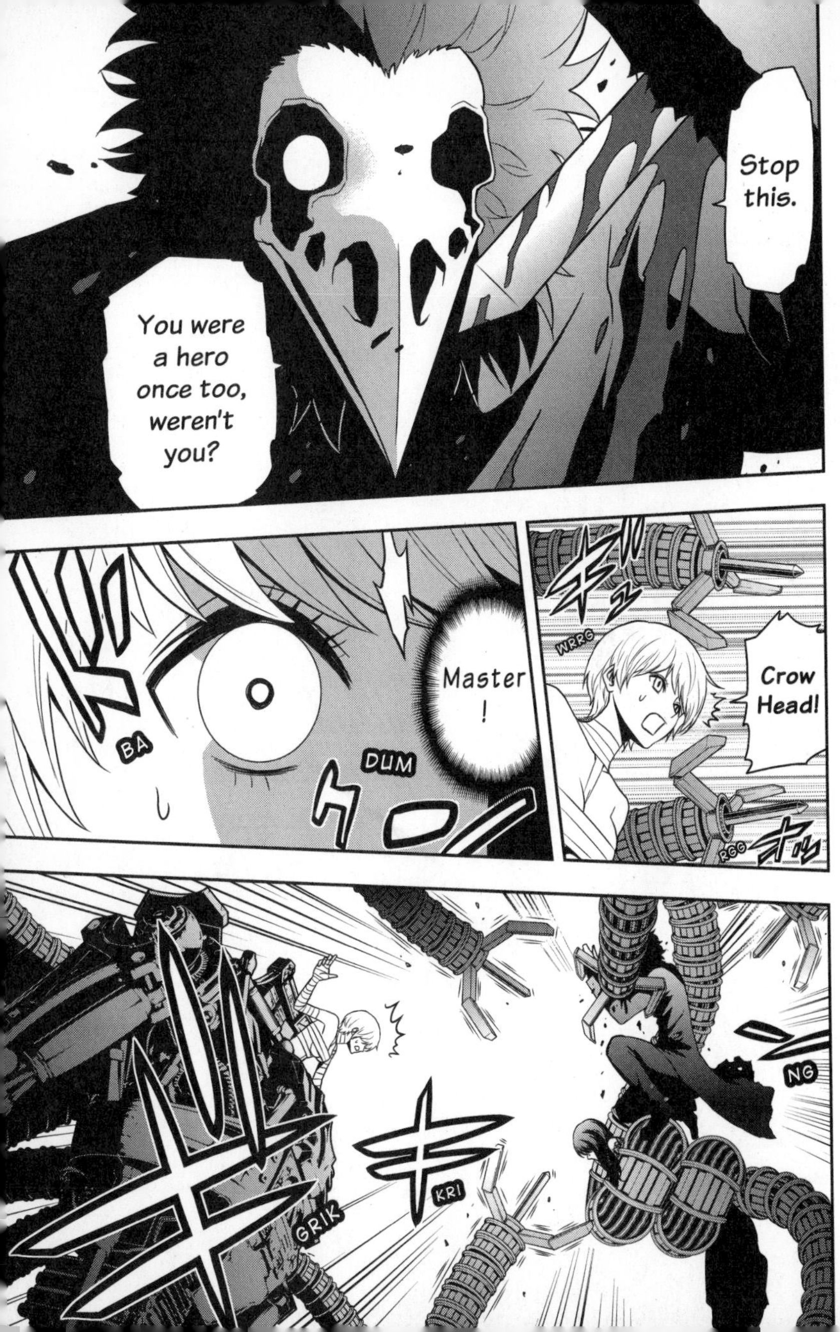
Stop this.
You were a hero once too, weren't you?
WRRG
Crow Head!
RGG
Master!
BA
DUM
NG
KRI
GRIK

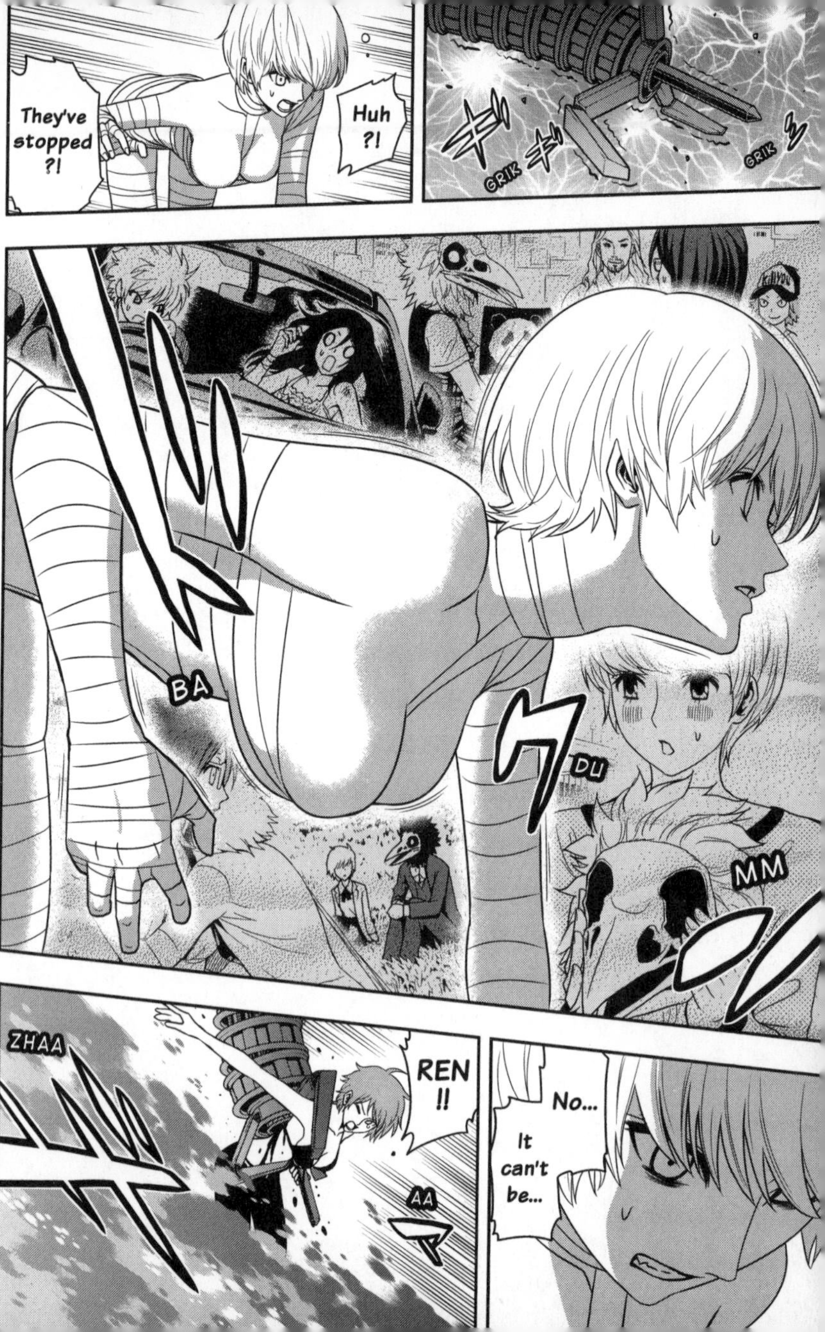
GRIK
GRIK
Huh ?!
They've stopped ?!
MM
DU
BA
No...
It can't be...
REN !!
ZHAA
AA

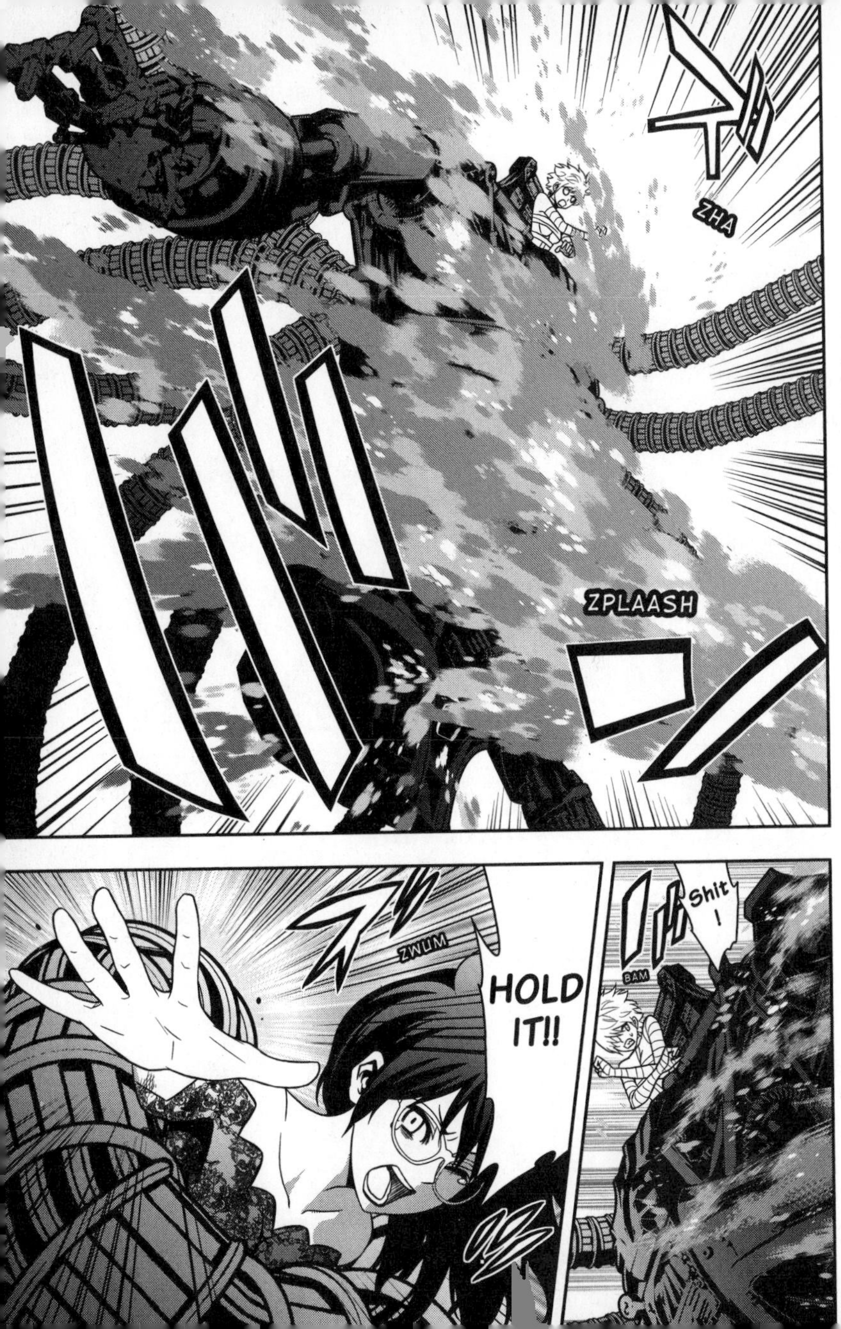
ZHA
ZPLAASH
Shit !
BAM
ZWUM
HOLD IT!!

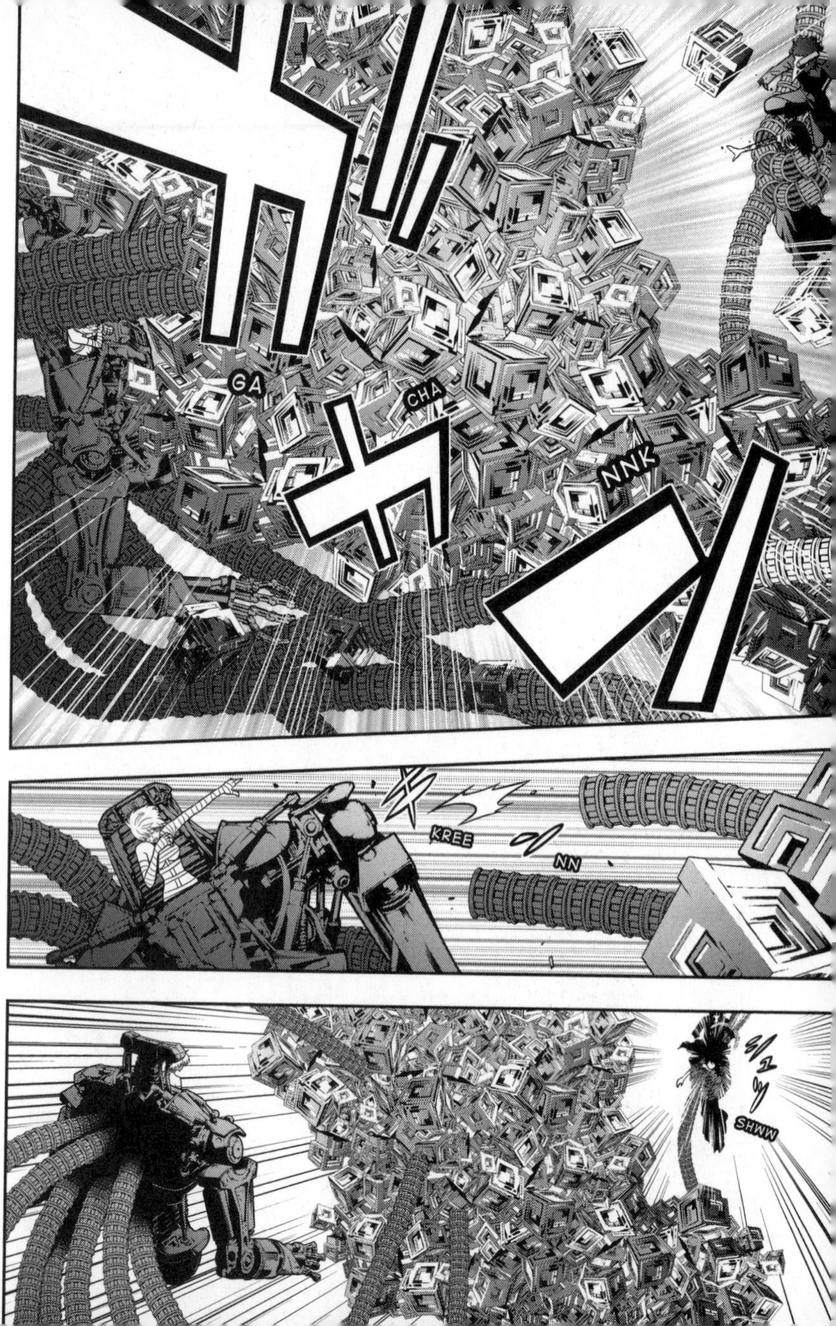
GA
CHA
NNK
KREE
NN
SHWW

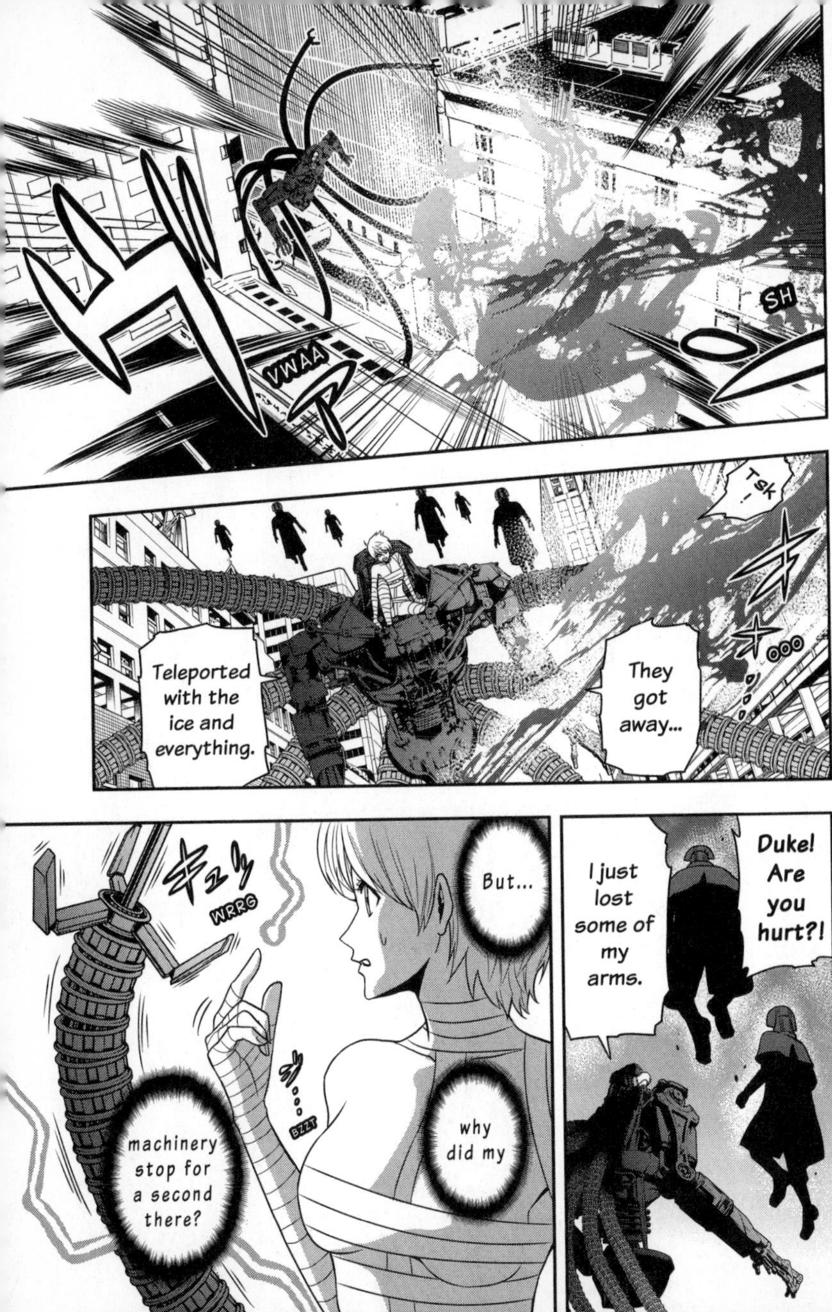
SH
VWAA
Tsk!
ooo
They got away...
Teleported with the ice and everything.
Duke! Are you hurt?!
I just lost some of my arms.
But...
WRRG
why did my
BZZT
machinery stop for a second there?

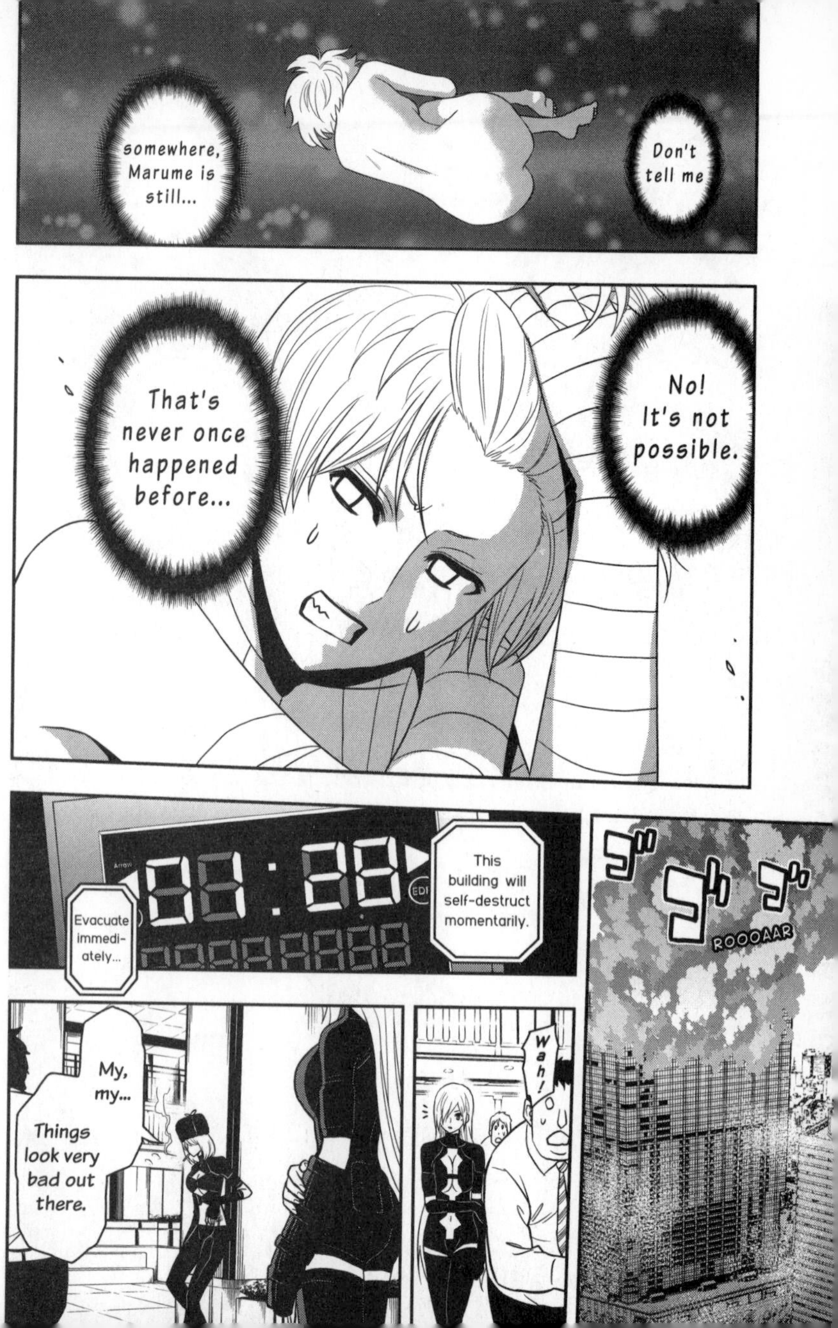
Don't tell me
somewhere, Marume is still...
No! It's not possible.
That's never once happened before...
ゴゴゴ
ROOOAAR
This building will self-destruct momentarily.
Evacuate immediately...
Wah!
My, my...
Things look very bad out there.

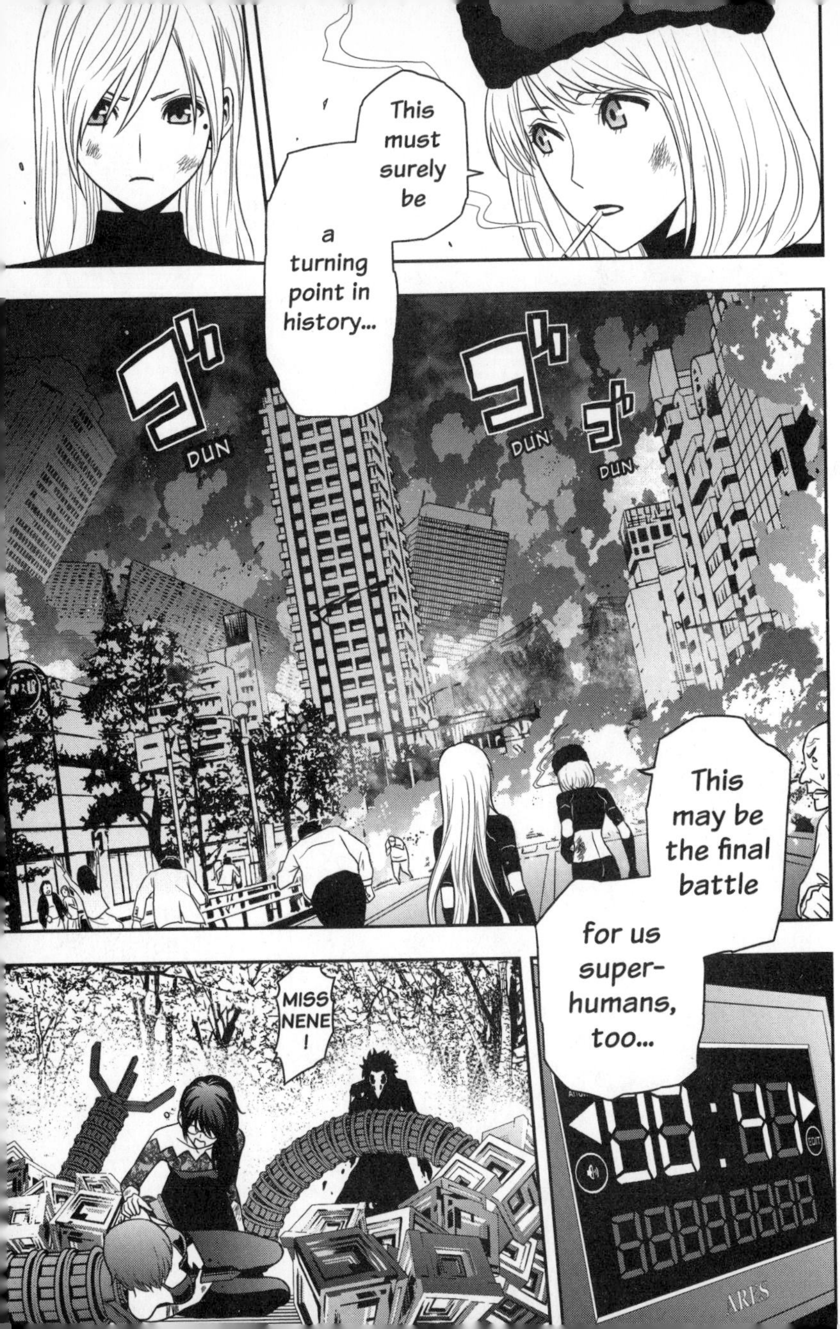
This must surely be a turning point in history...
DUN
DUN
DUN
This may be the final battle for us super-humans, too...
MISS NENE!

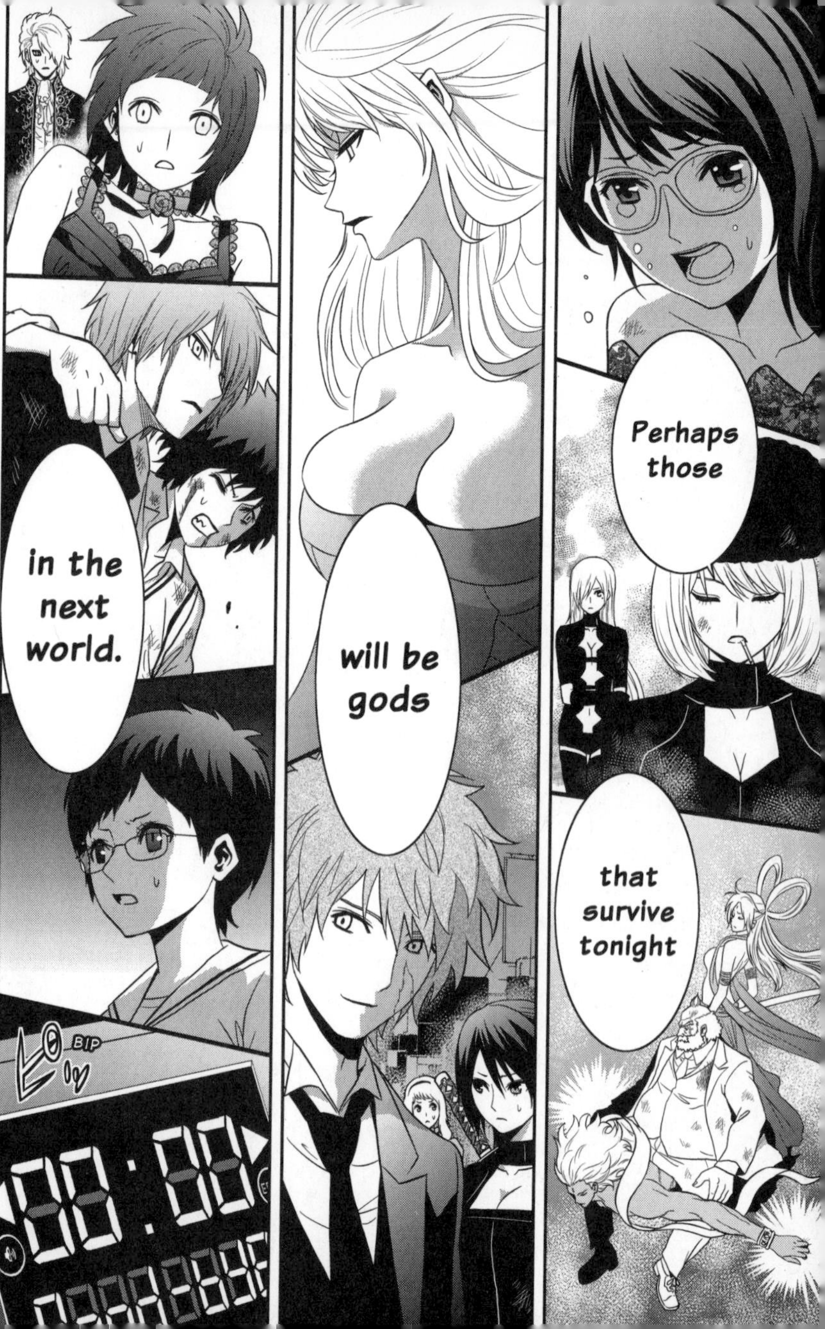
Perhaps those
that survive tonight
will be gods
in the next world.
BIP

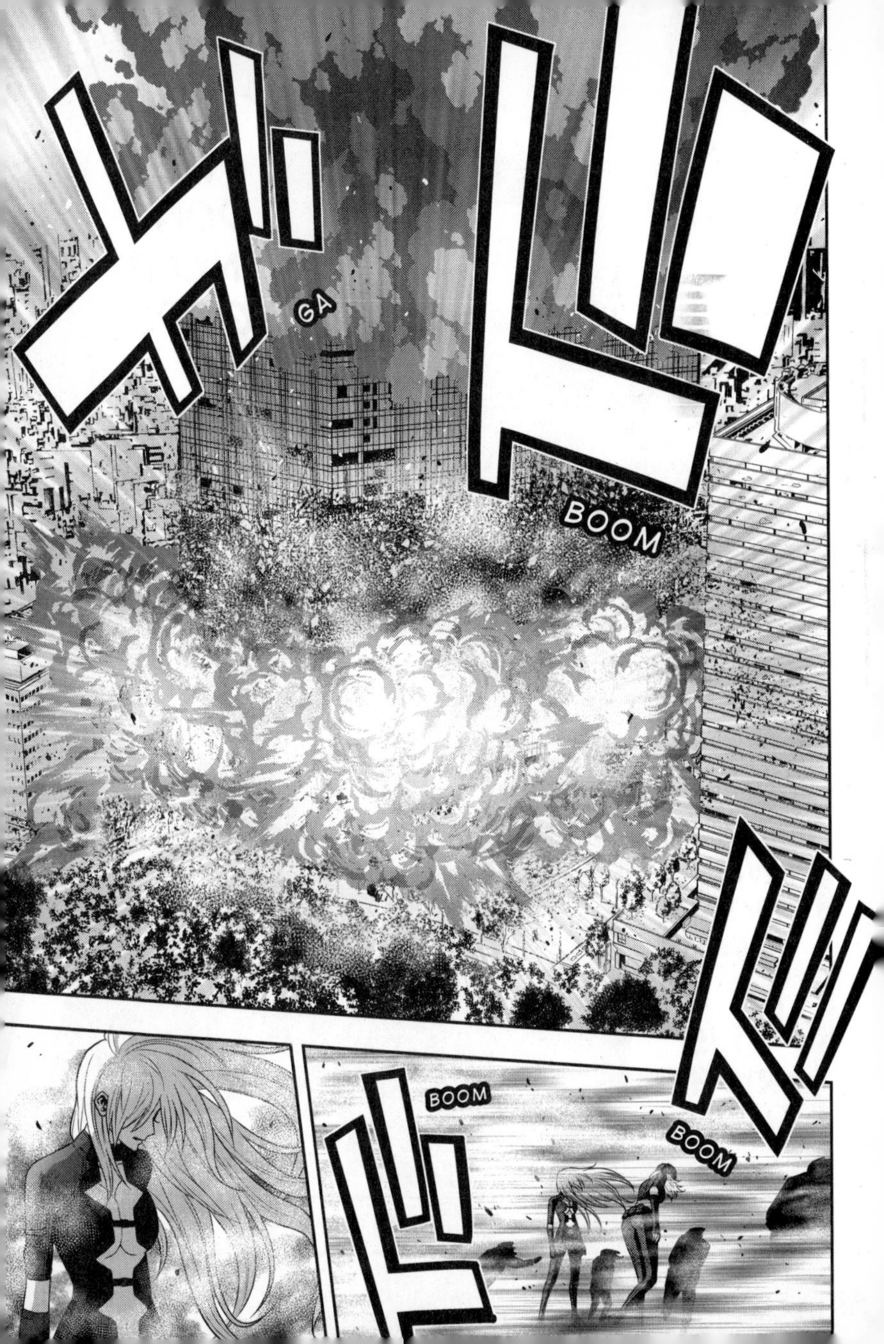
GA
BOOM
BOOM
BOOM

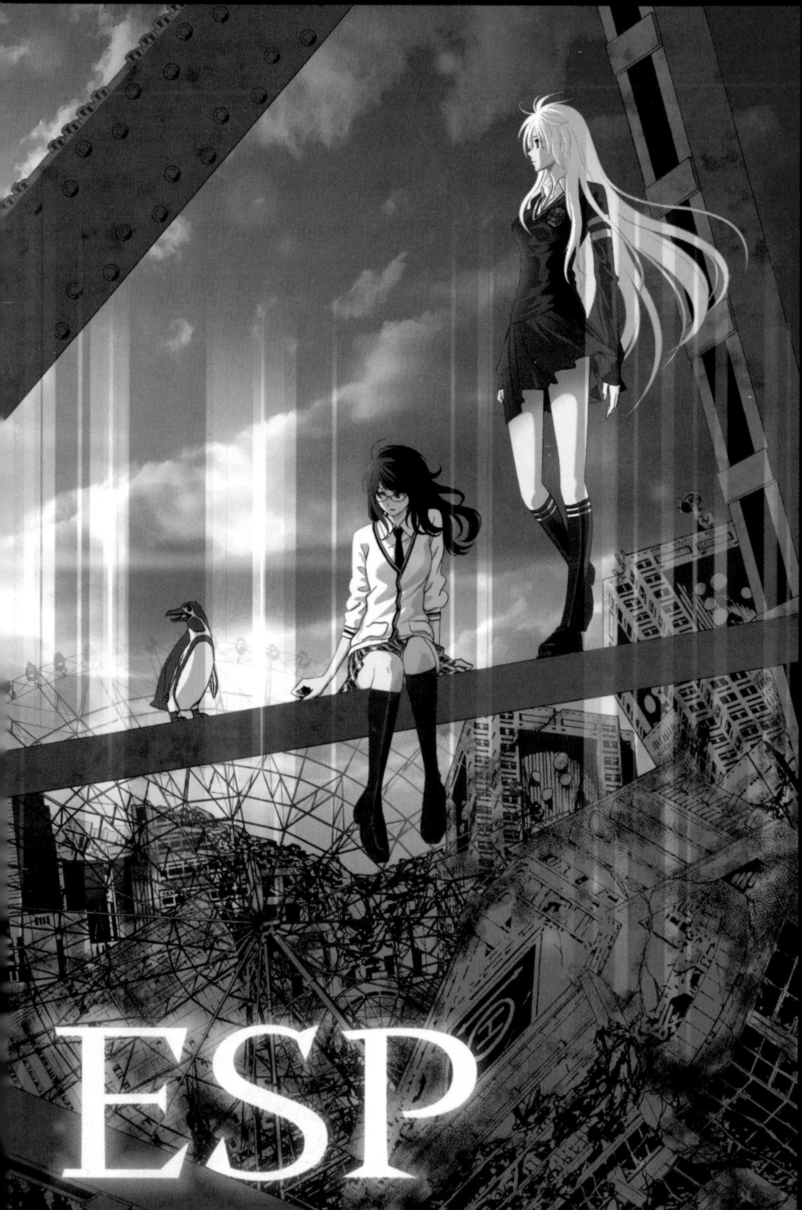
ESP

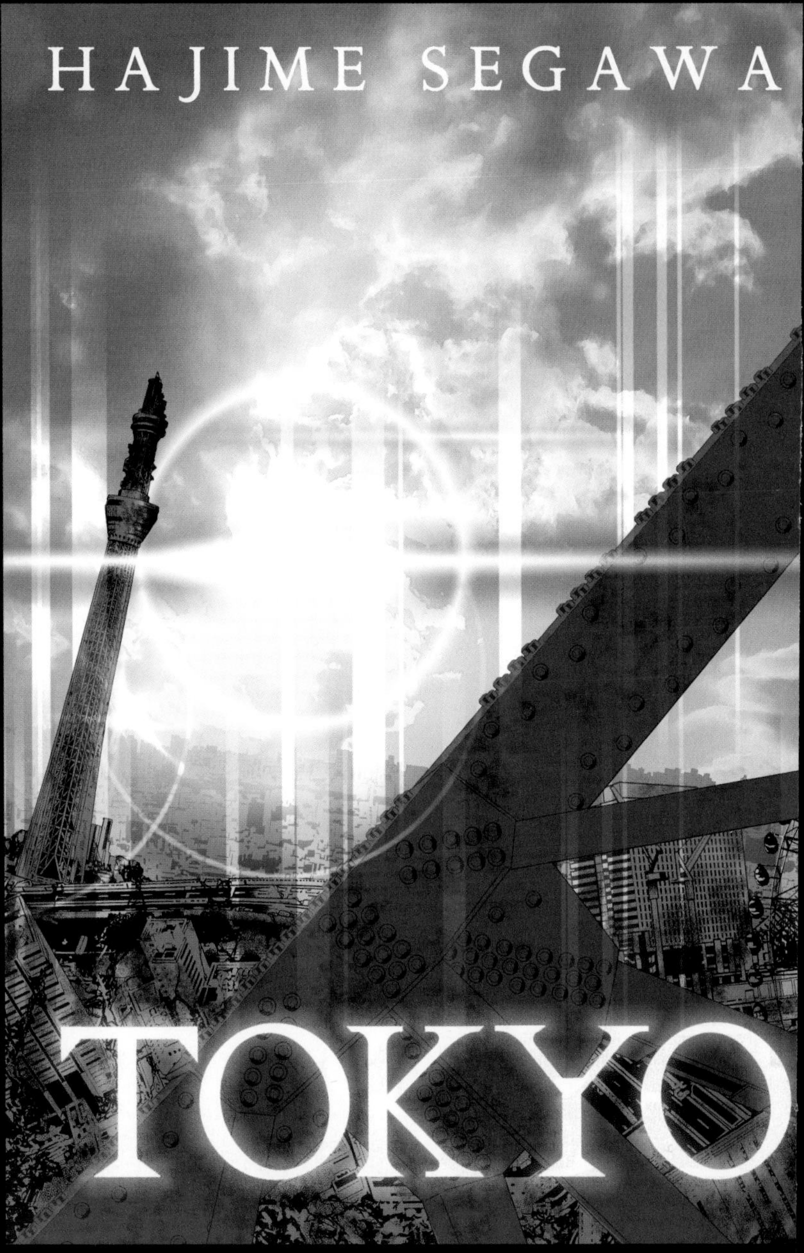
HAJIME SEGAWA
TOKYO

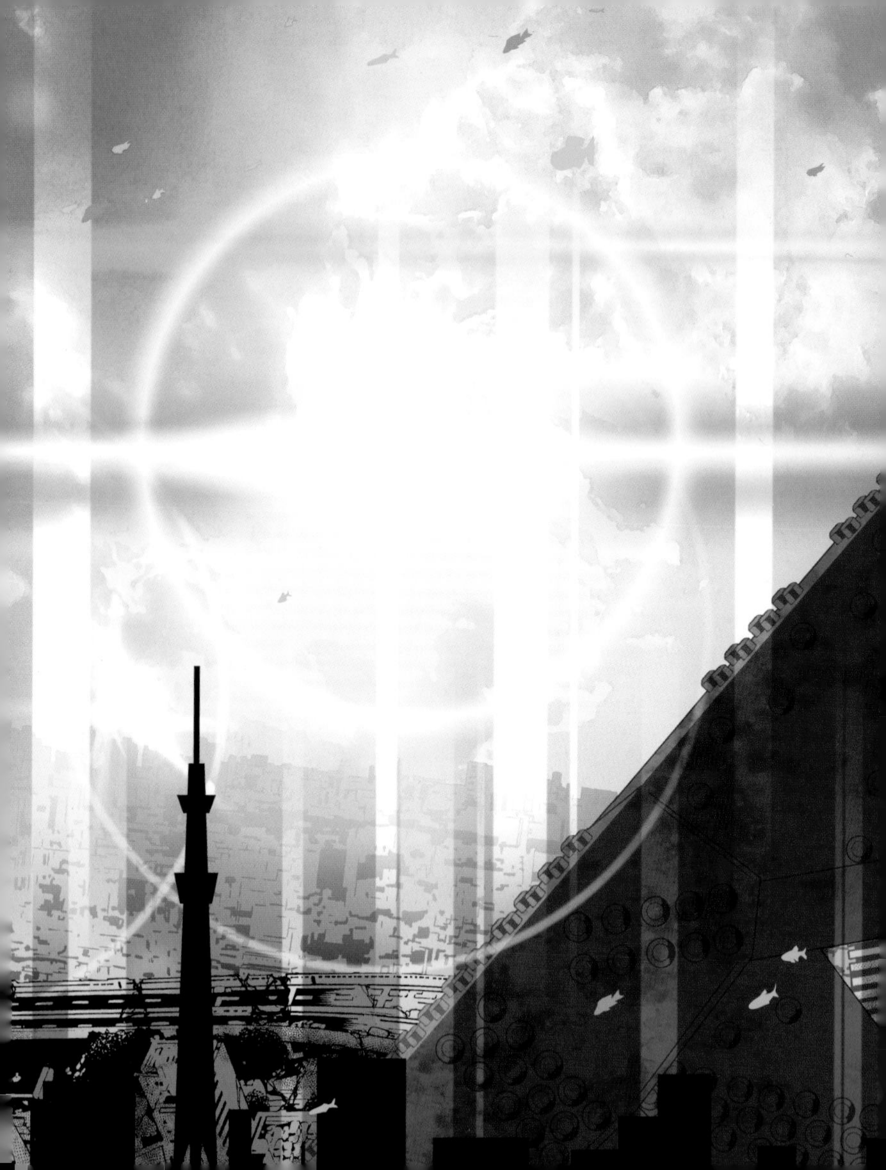

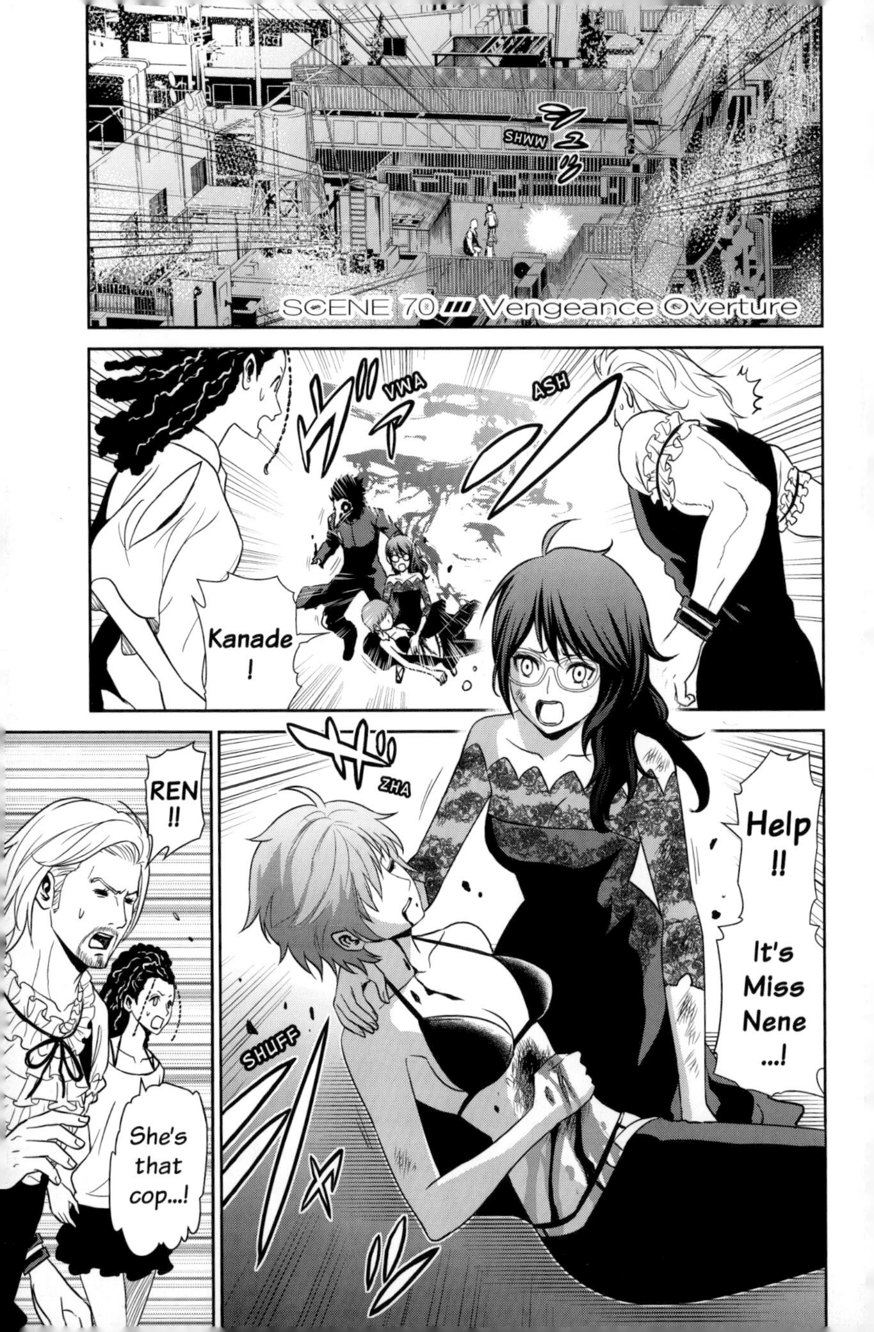
SHWW
SCENE 70 /// Vengeance Overture
ASH
VWA
Kanade !
ZHA
Help !!
It's Miss Nene ...!
SHUFF
REN !!
She's that cop...!

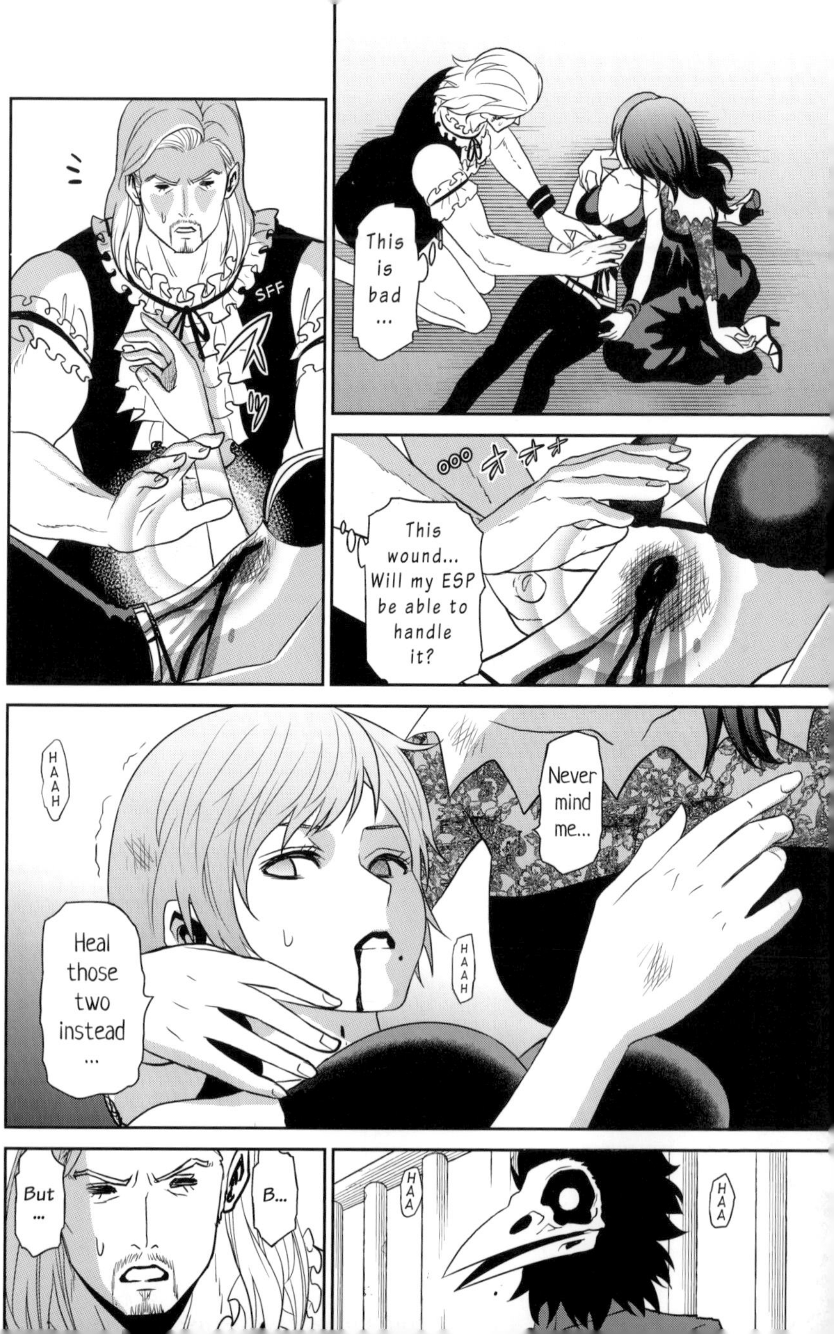
This is bad ...
ooo
This wound... Will my ESP be able to handle it?
SFF
Never mind me...
HAAH
HAAH
Heal those two instead ...
HAA
HAA
B...
But ...

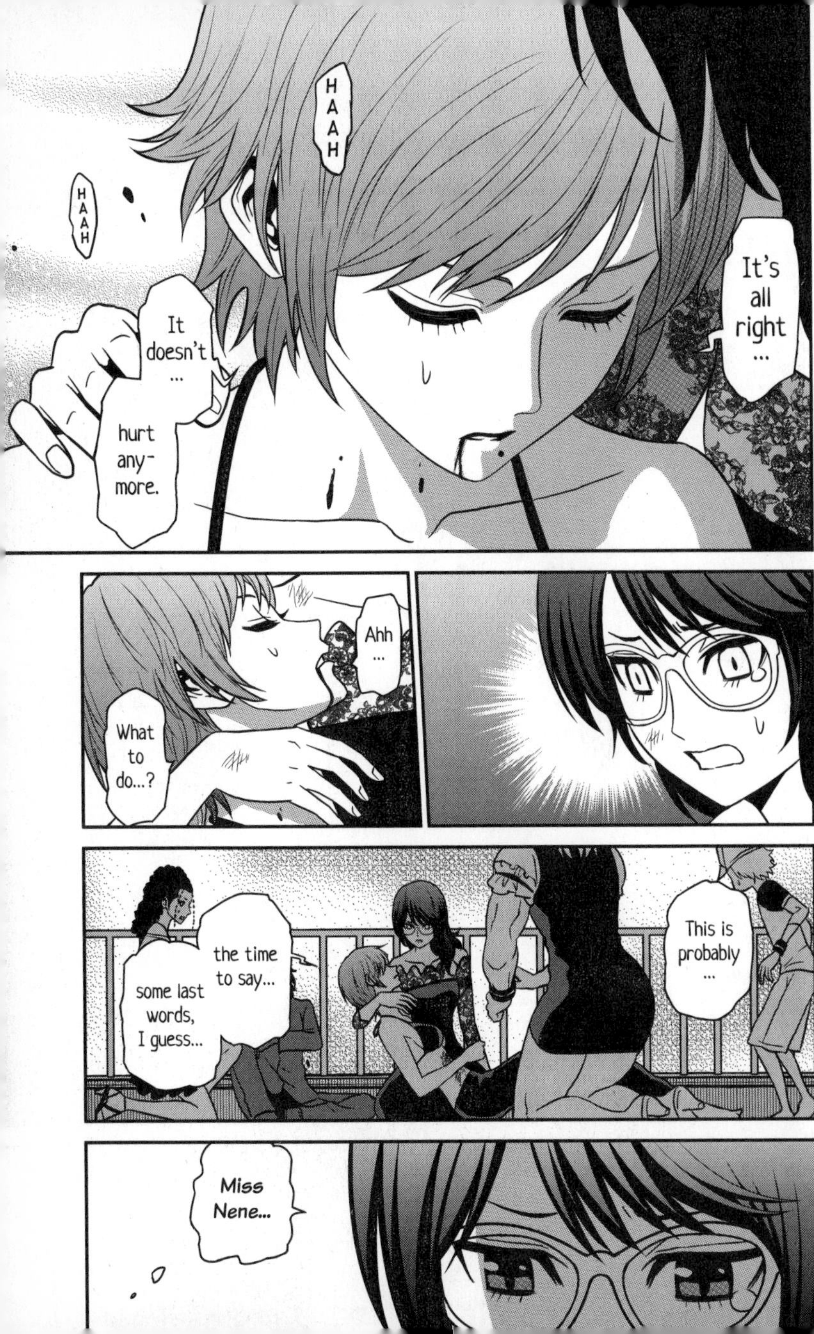
It's all right ...
HAAH
HAAH
It doesn't ...
hurt any- more.
Ahh ...
What to do...?
This is probably ...
the time to say...
some last words, I guess...
Miss Nene...

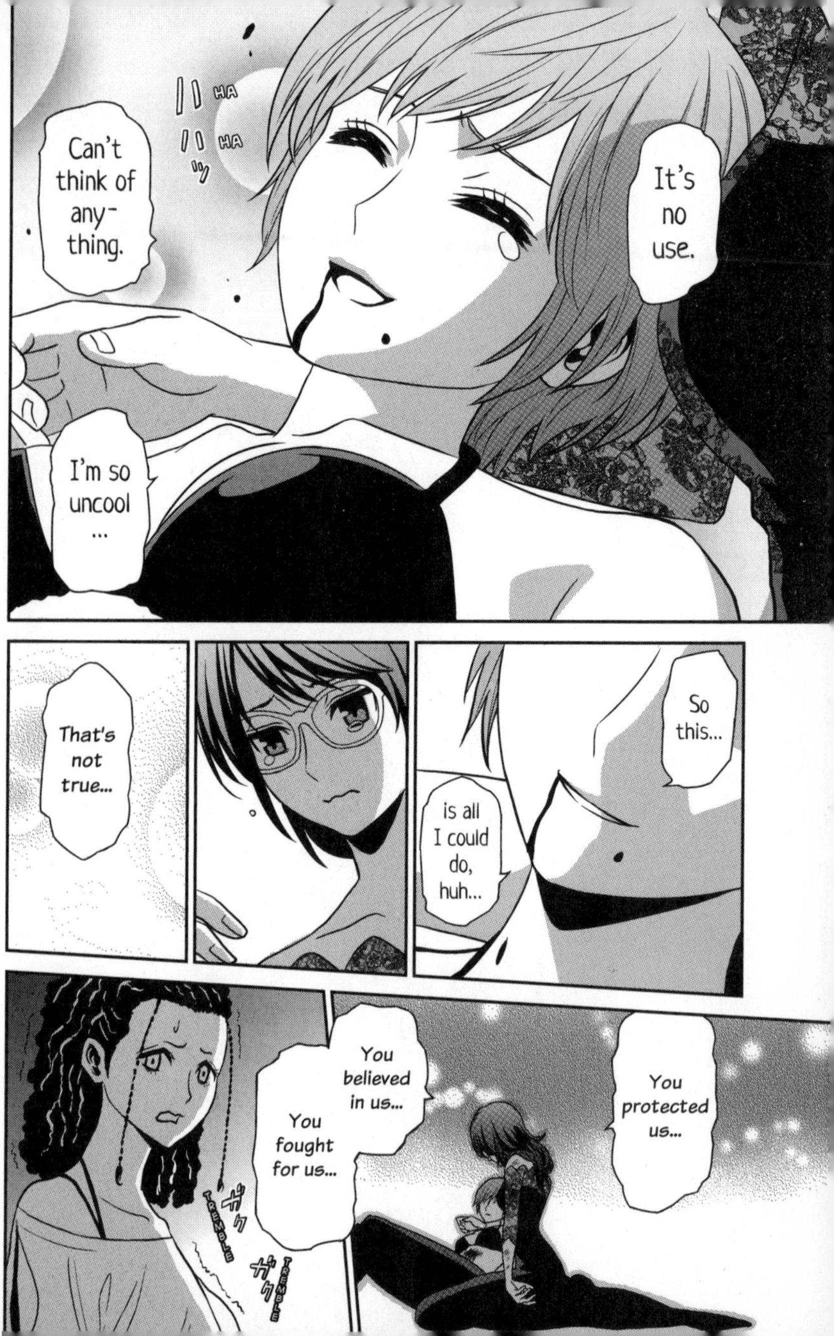

HA
HA
It's no use.
Can't think of any-thing.
I'm so uncool ...
So this...
is all I could do, huh...
That's not true...
You protected us...
You believed in us...
You fought for us...
TREMBLE
TREMBLE

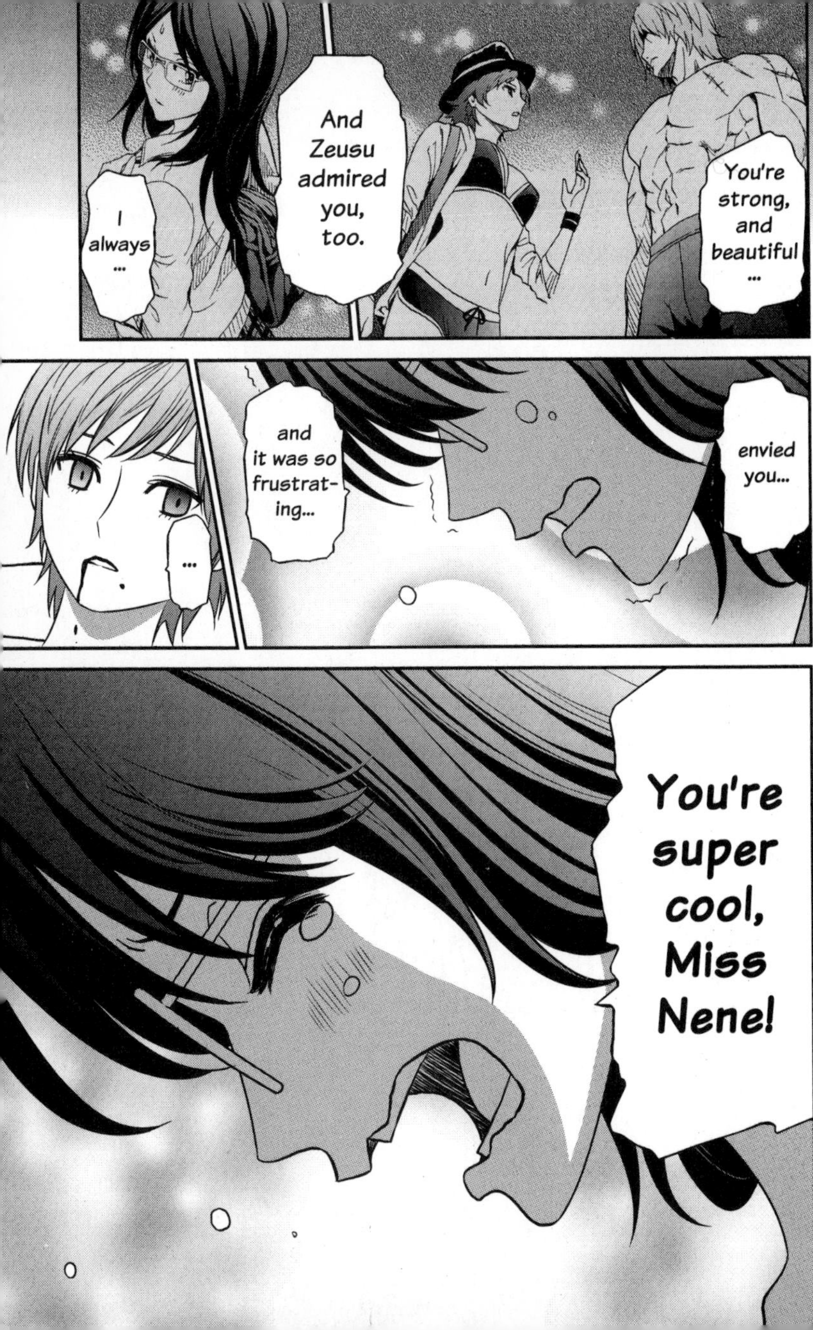
You're strong, and beautiful ...
And Zeusu admired you, too.
I always ...
envied you...
and it was so frustrat-ing...
...
You're super cool, Miss Nene!

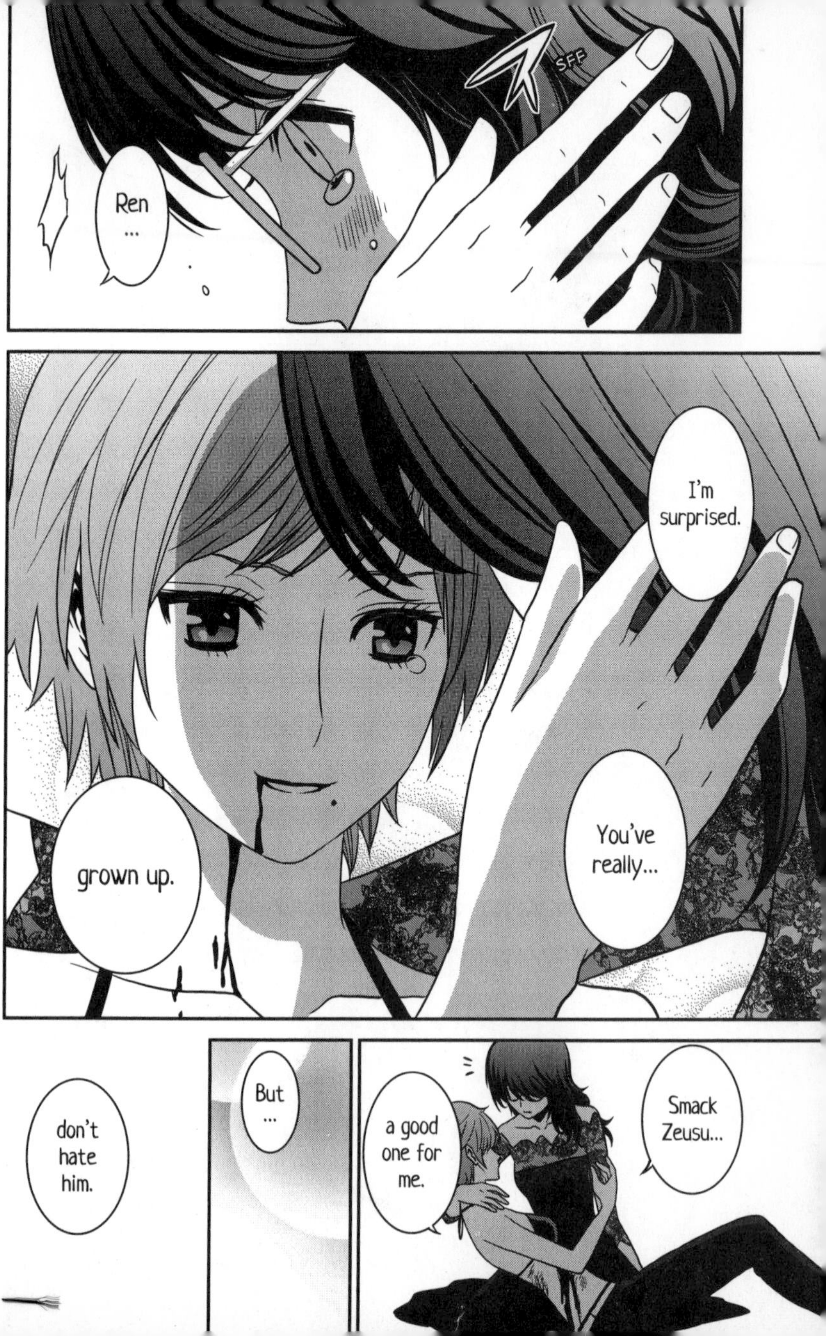
SFF
Ren ...
I'm surprised.
You've really...
grown up.
Smack Zeusu...
a good one for me.
But ...
don't hate him.

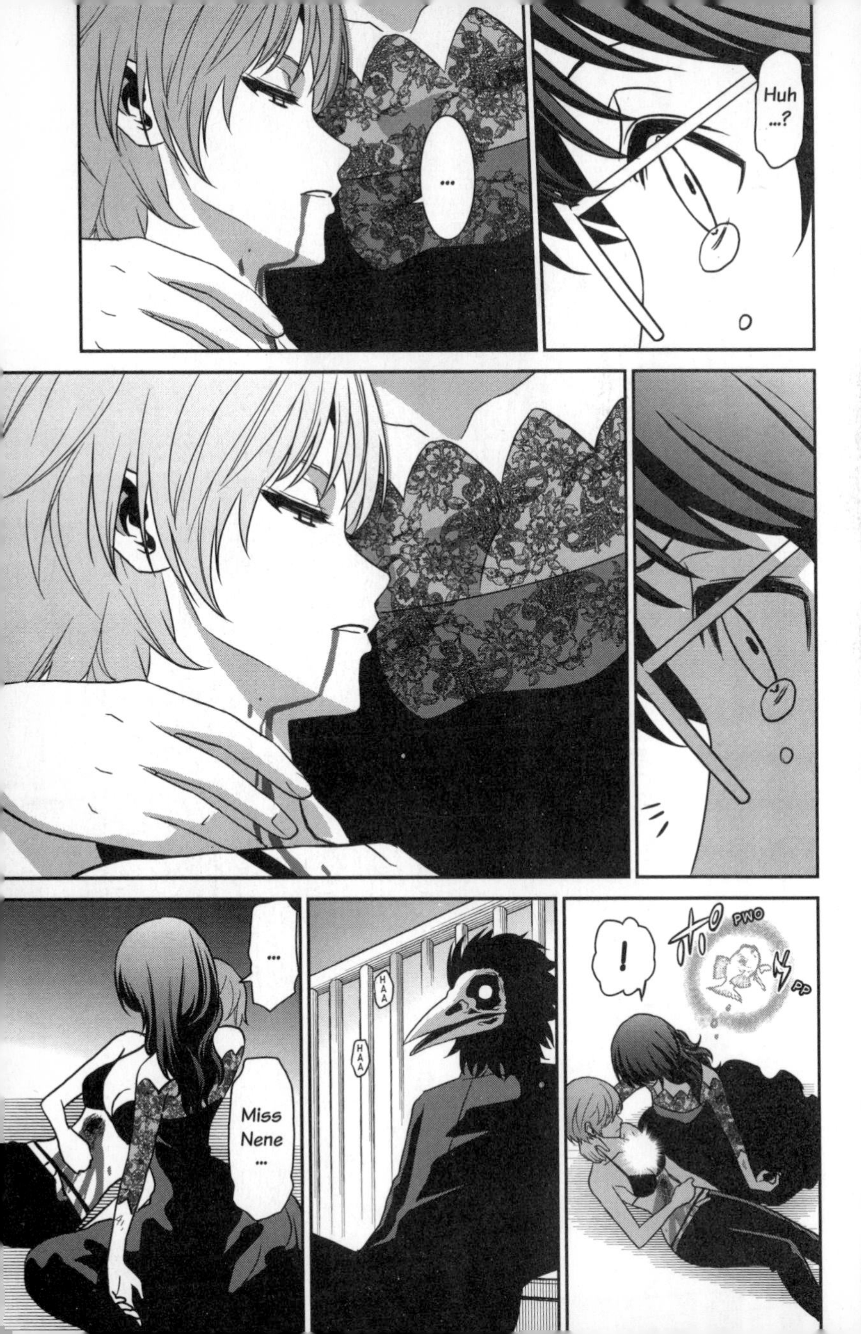
Huh ...?
...
!
PWO
PP
HAA
HAA
...
Miss Nene ...

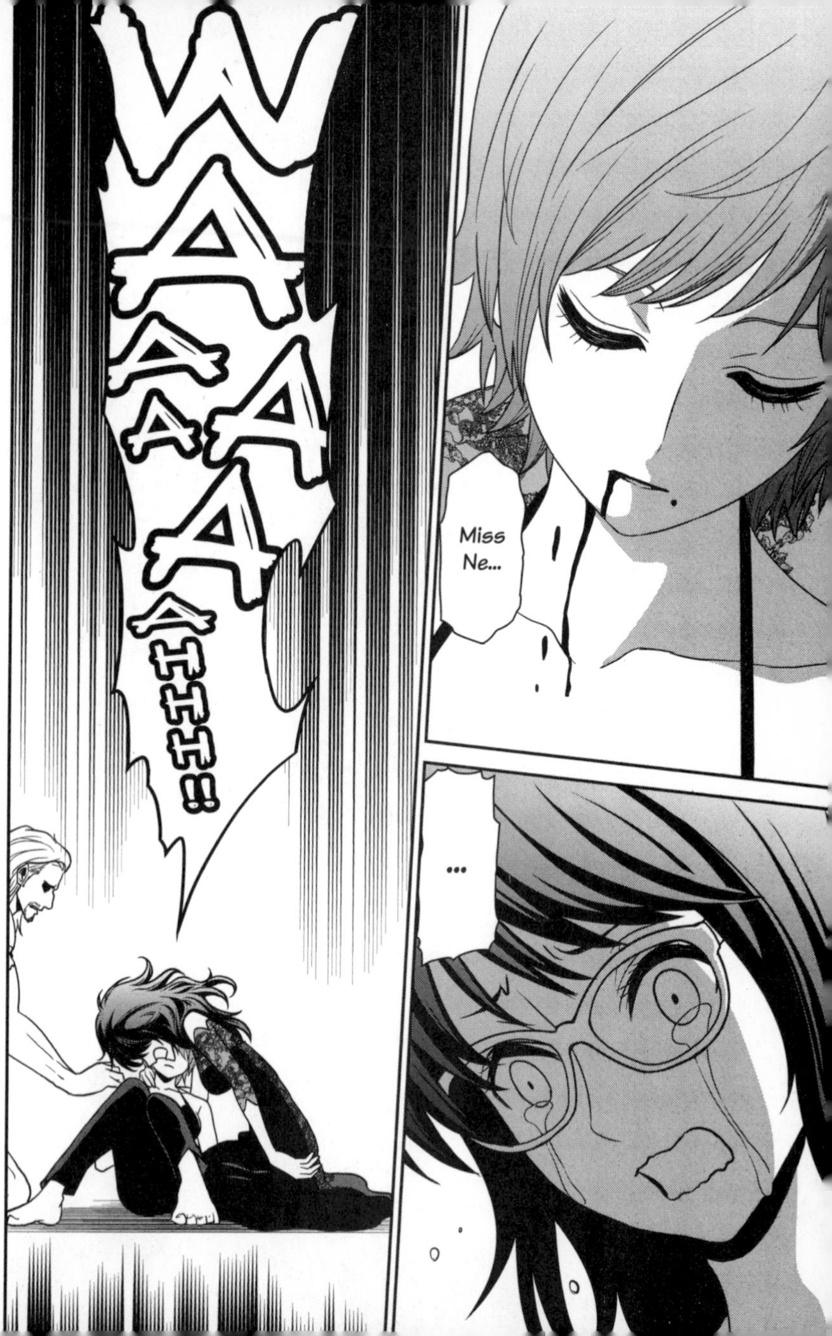
Miss Ne...
...
WAAAA!!

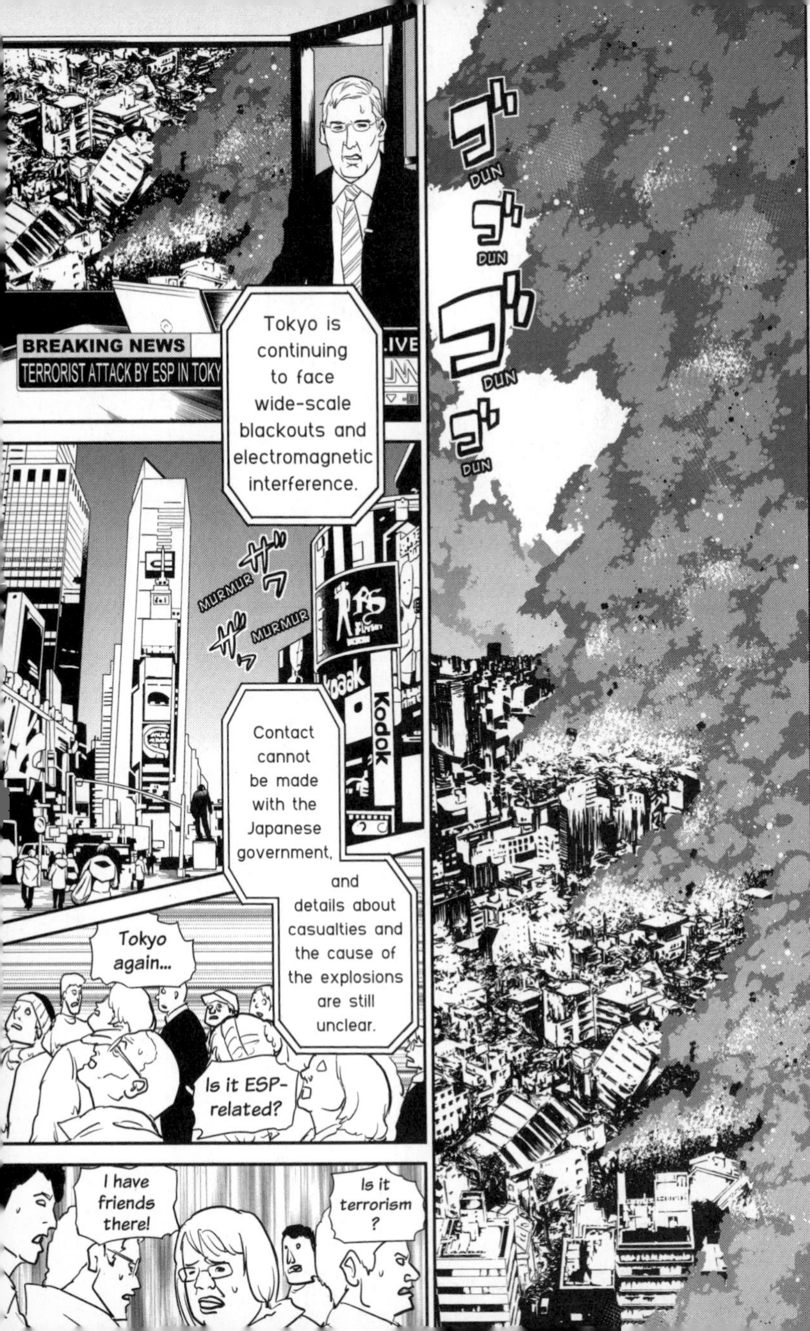

ゴゴ DUN
ゴゴ DUN
ゴゴ DUN
ゴゴ DUN
BREAKING NEWS
TERRORIST ATTACK BY ESP IN TOKY
LIVE
Tokyo is continuing to face wide-scale blackouts and electromagnetic interference.
ザワ MURMUR
ザワ MURMUR
Contact cannot be made with the Japanese government,
and details about casualties and the cause of the explosions are still unclear.
Tokyo again...
Is it ESP-related?
Is it terrorism?
I have friends there!

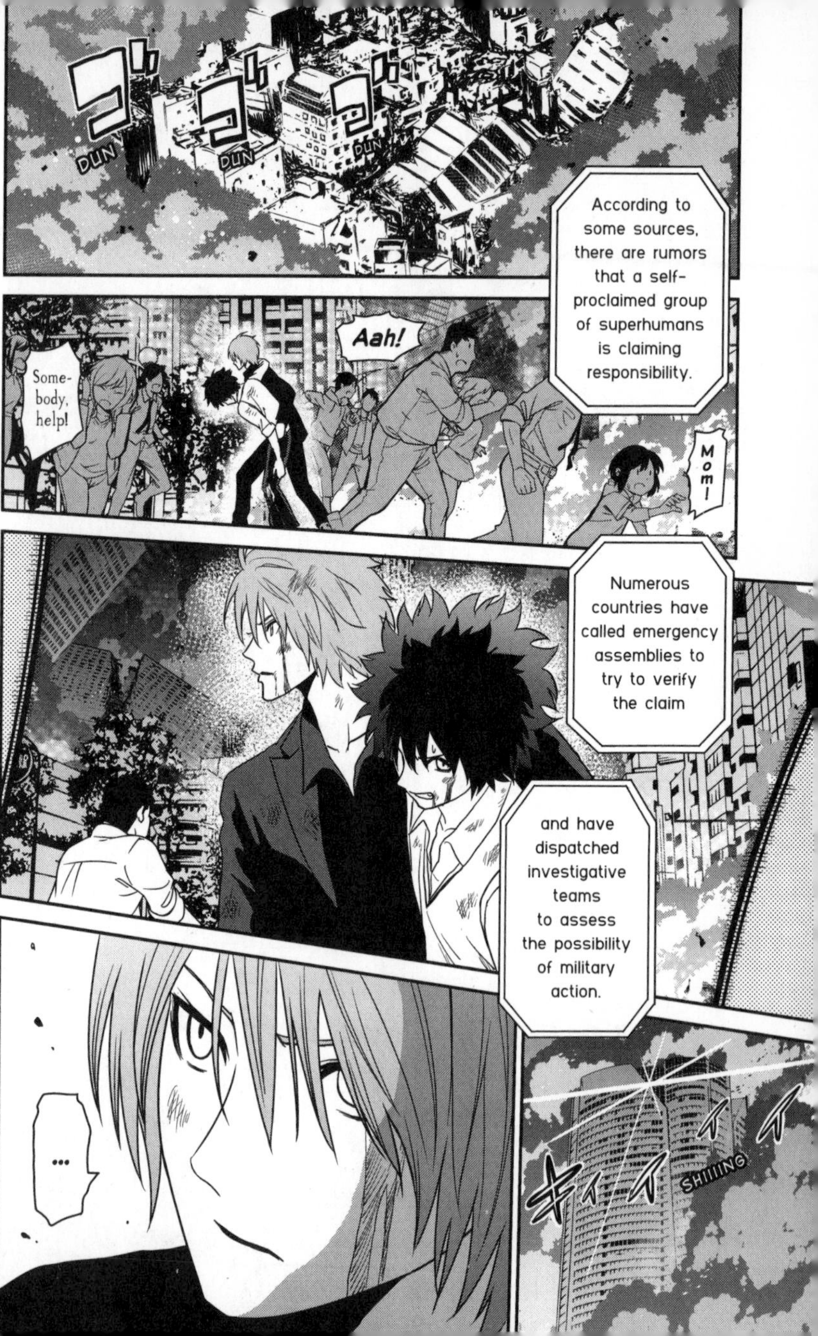
DUN
DUN
DUN
According to some sources, there are rumors that a self-proclaimed group of superhumans is claiming responsibility.
Mom!
Aah!
Somebody, help!
Numerous countries have called emergency assemblies to try to verify the claim
and have dispatched investigative teams to assess the possibility of military action.
SHIIIING
...

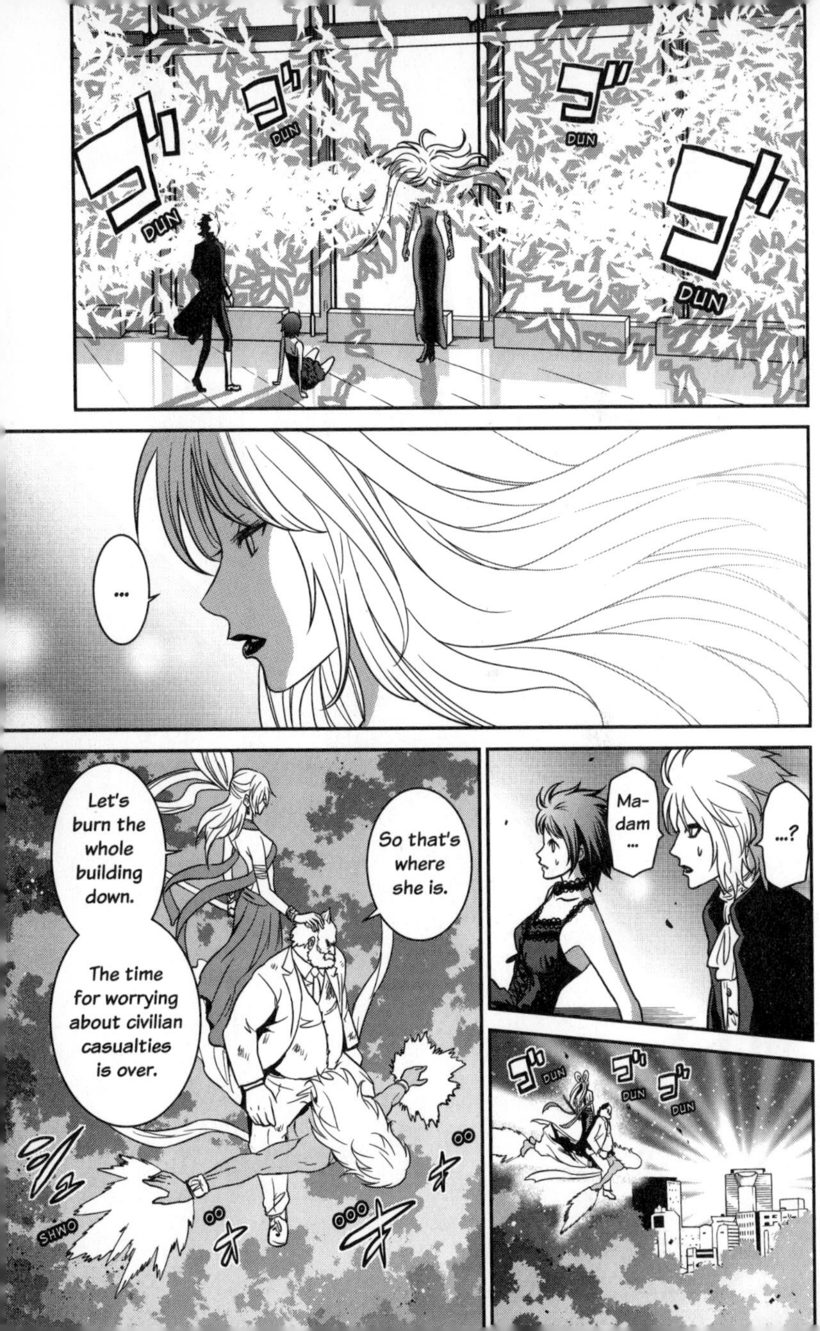
DUN
DUN
DUN
DUN
...
...?
Ma-dam ...
DUN
DUN
DUN
So that's where she is.
Let's burn the whole building down.
The time for worrying about civilian casualties is over.
OO
OOO
OO
SHWO

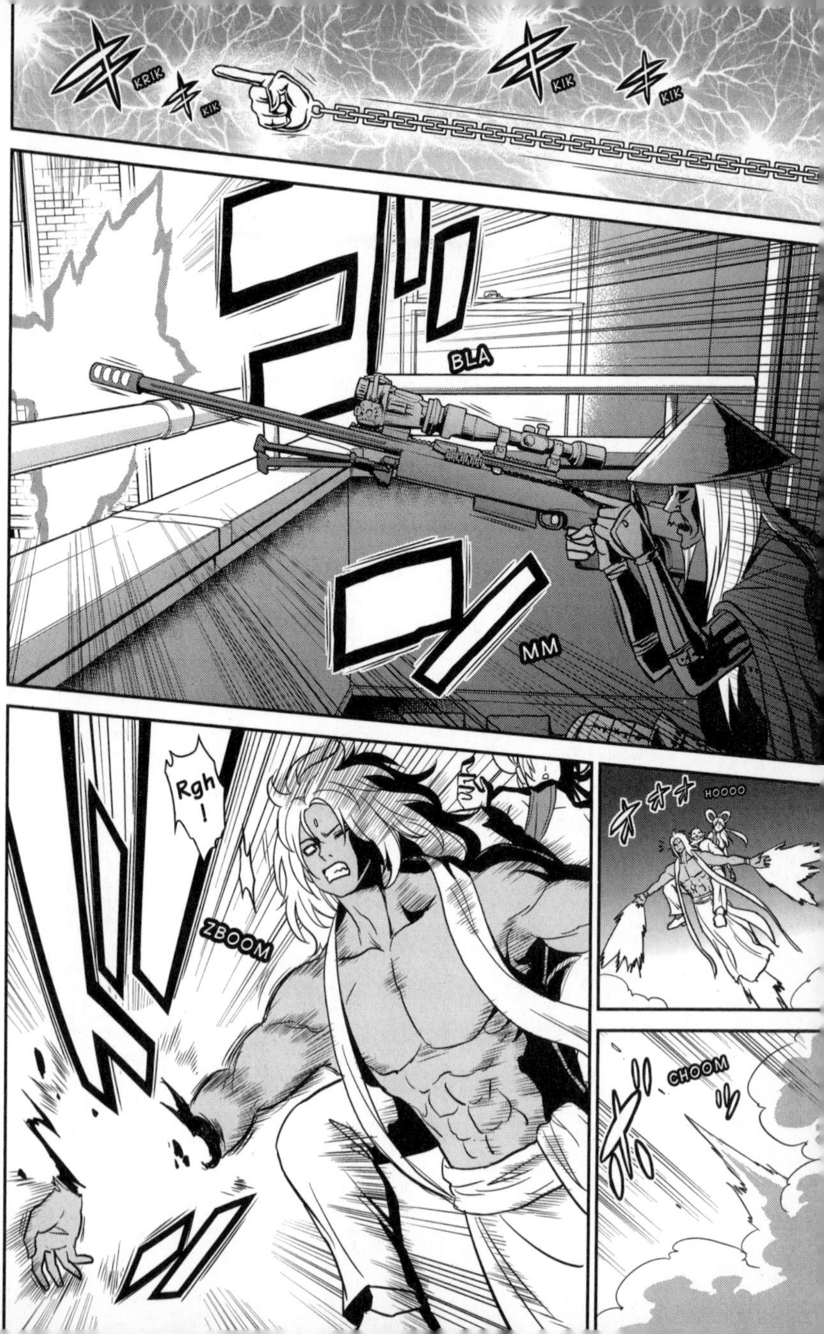
KIK
KIK
KIK
KRIK
BLA
MM
HOOOO
CHOOM
Rgh!
ZBOOM

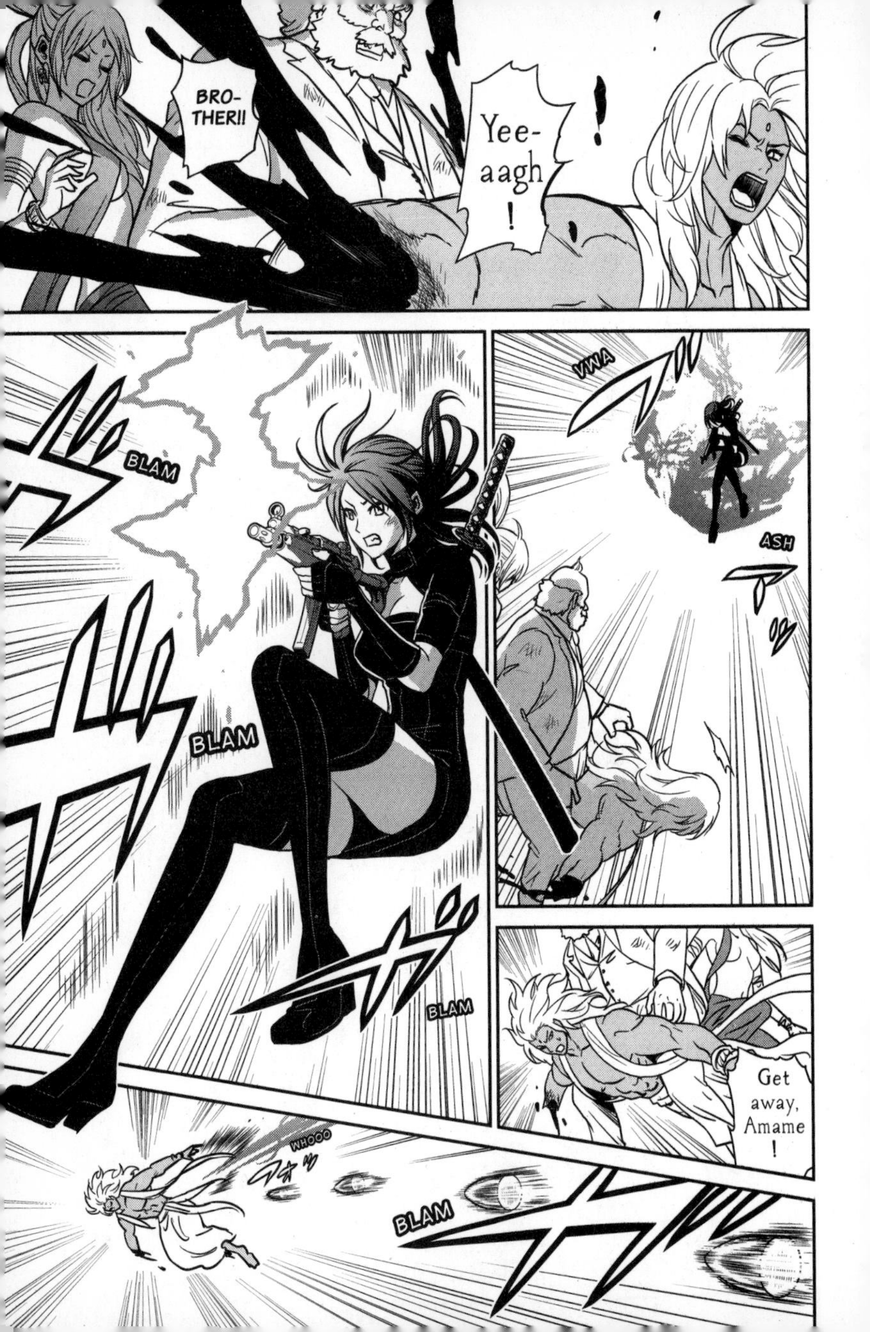
Yee-aagh!
BRO-THER!!
VWA
ASH
Get away, Amame!
BLAM
BLAM
BLAM
WHOOO
BLAM

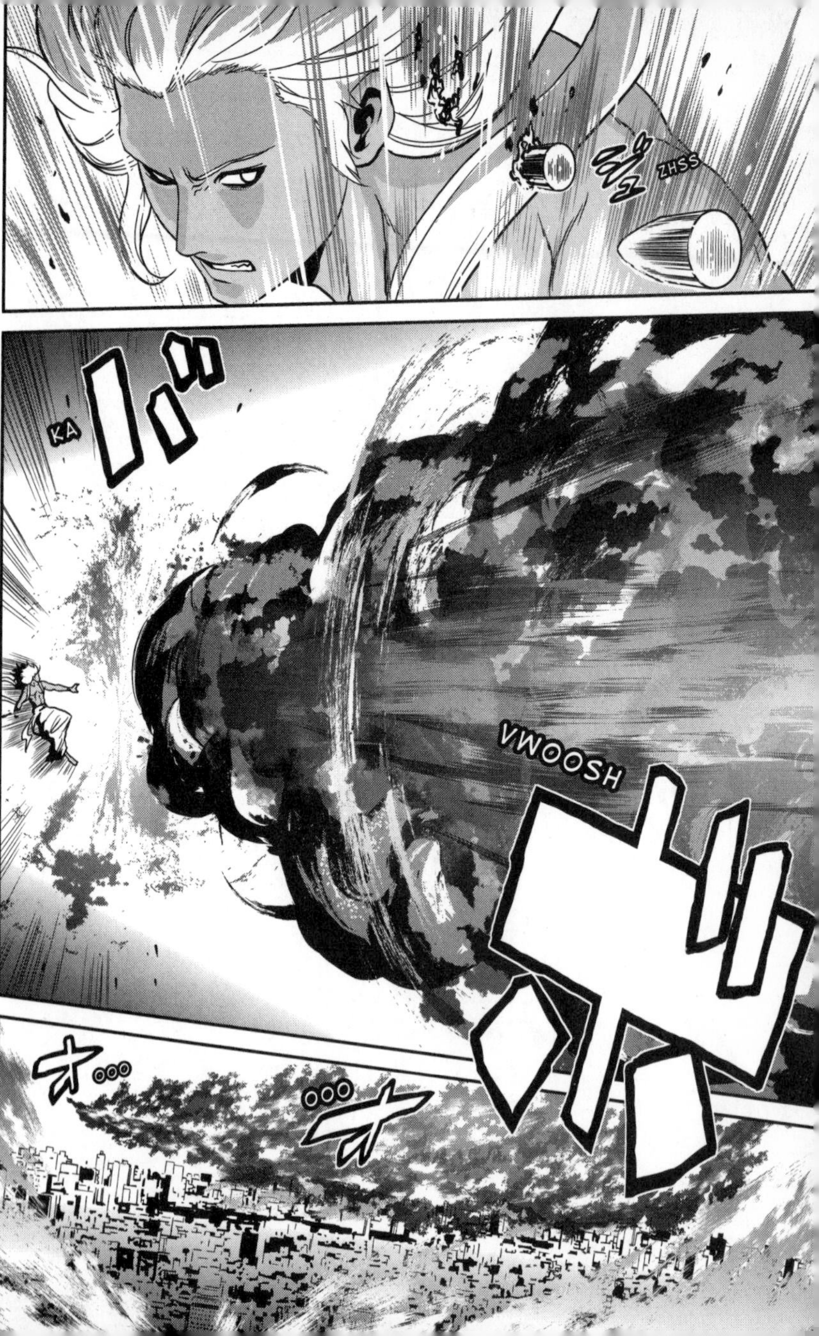
ZHSS
VWOOSH
KA

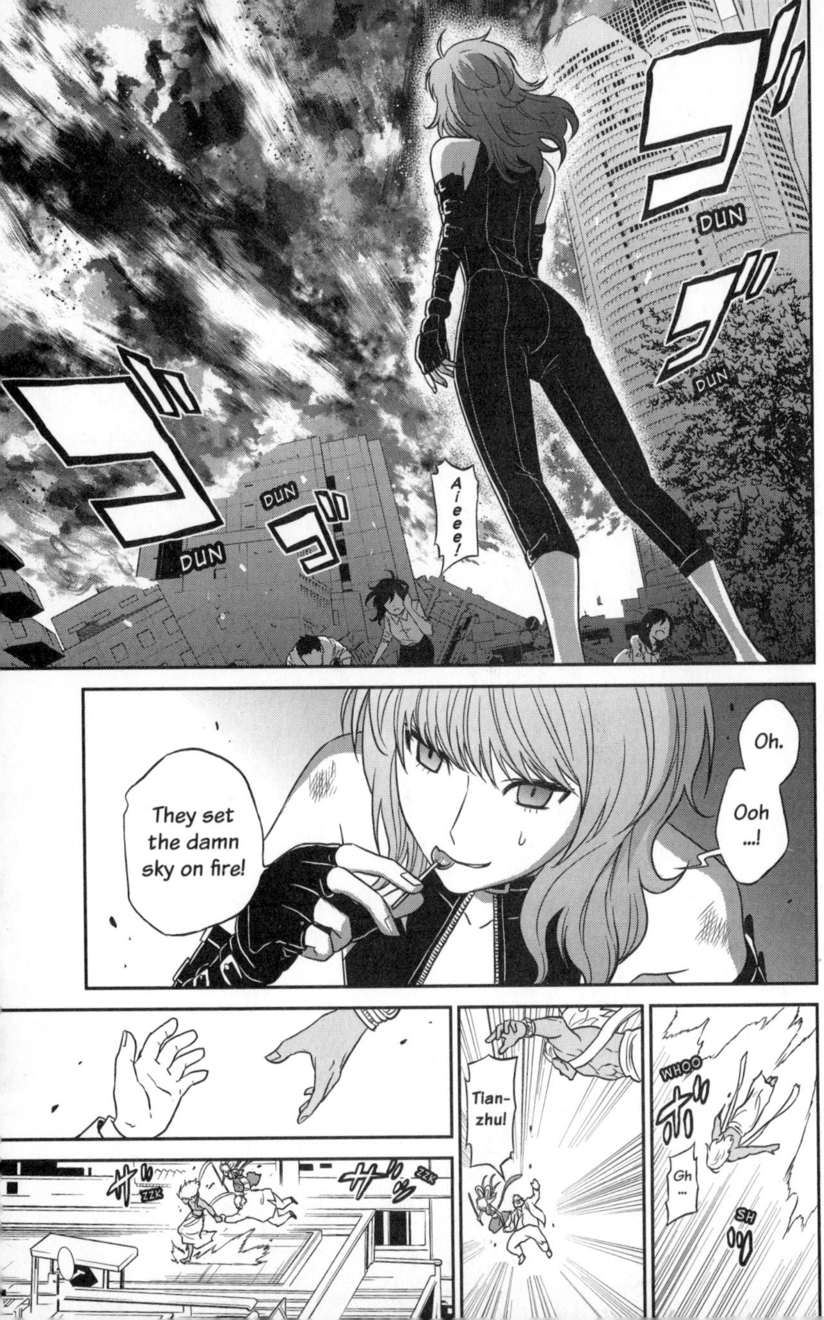
DUN
DUN
Aieee!
DUN
DUN
Oh.
Ooh ...!
They set the damn sky on fire!
WHOO
Gh ...
SH
Tian-zhu!
ZZK
ZZK

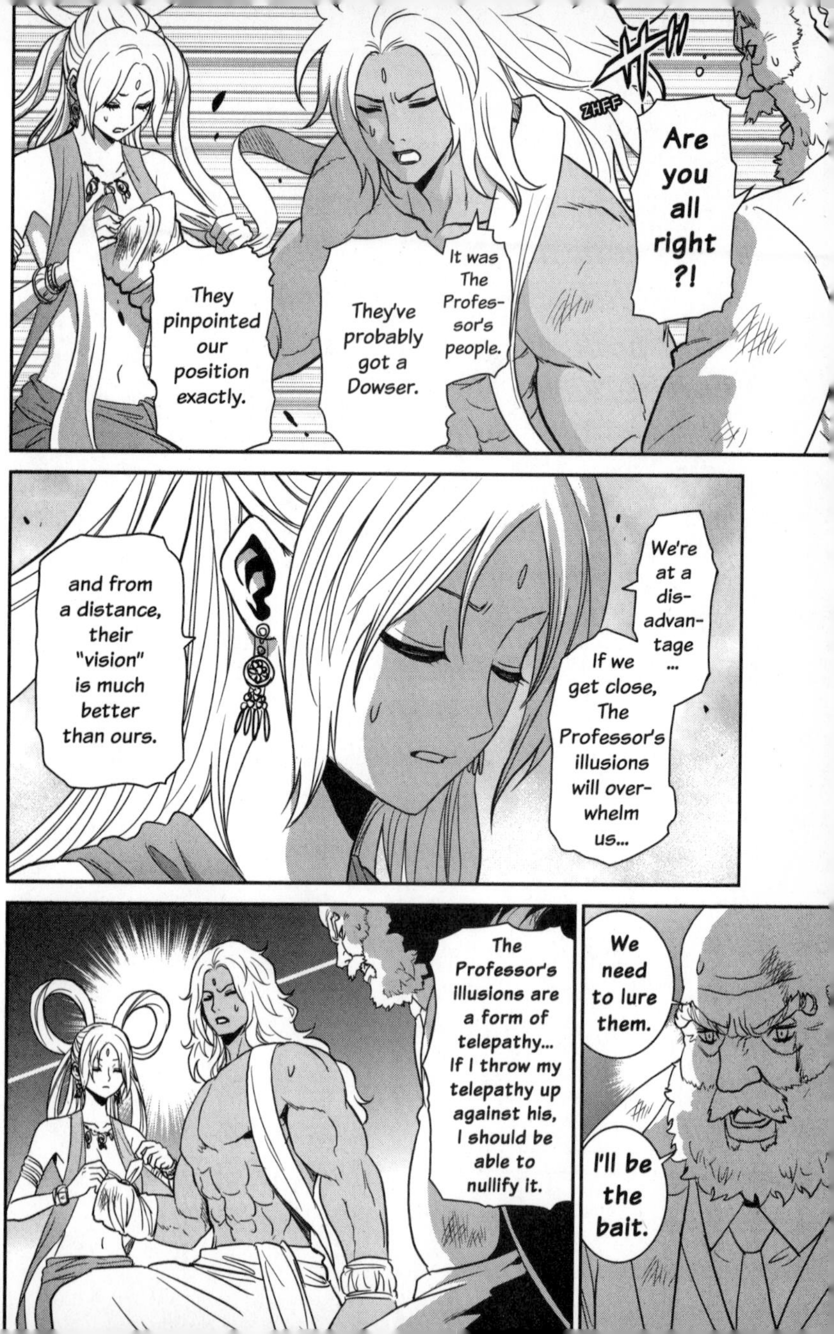
ZHFF
Are you all right?!
It was The Professor's people.
They've probably got a Dowser.
They pinpointed our position exactly.
We're at a disadvantage...
If we get close, The Professor's illusions will overwhelm us...
and from a distance, their "vision" is much better than ours.
We need to lure them.
I'll be the bait.
The Professor's illusions are a form of telepathy... If I throw my telepathy up against his, I should be able to nullify it.

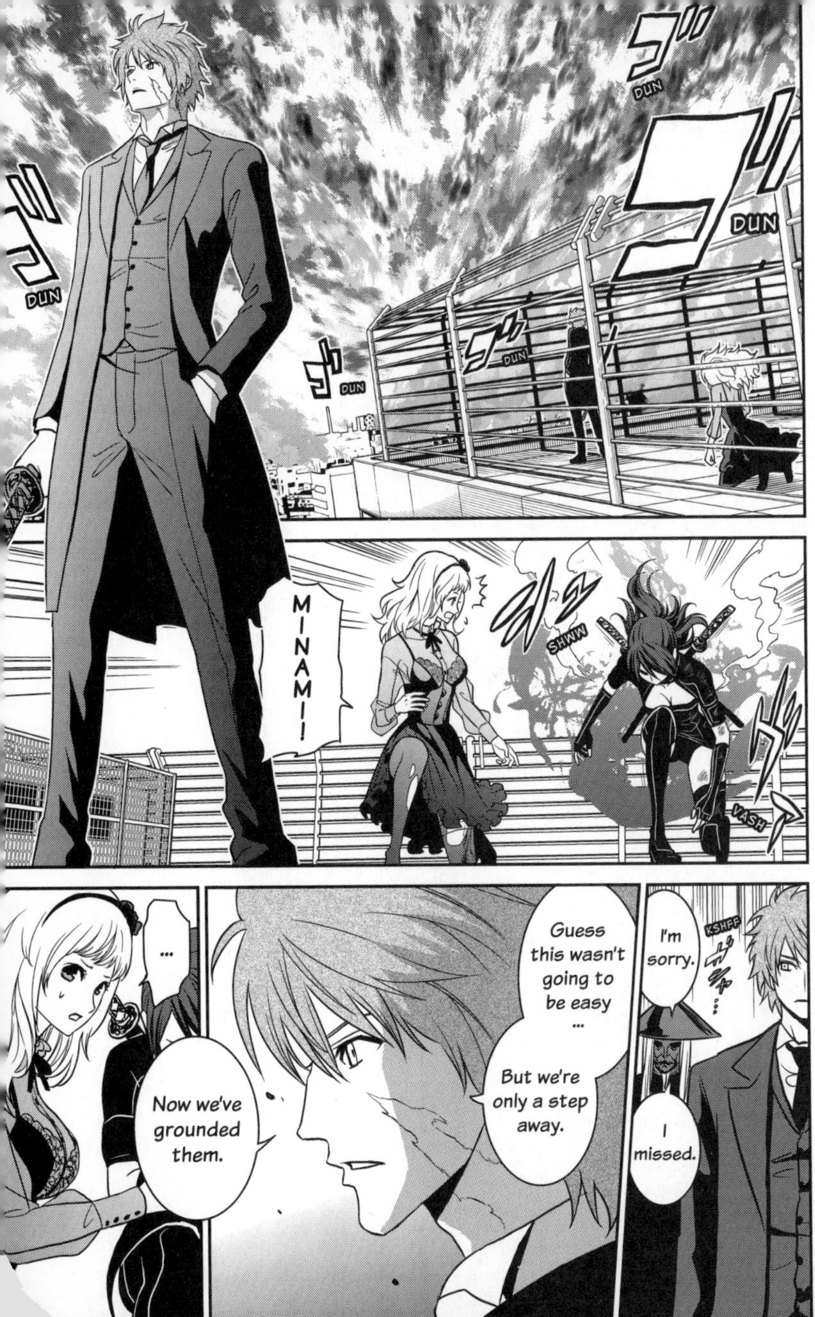
DUN
DUN
DUN
DUN
SHWW
VASH
MINAMI!!
DUN
I'm sorry.
KSHFF
I missed.
Guess this wasn't going to be easy ...
But we're only a step away.
...
Now we've grounded them.

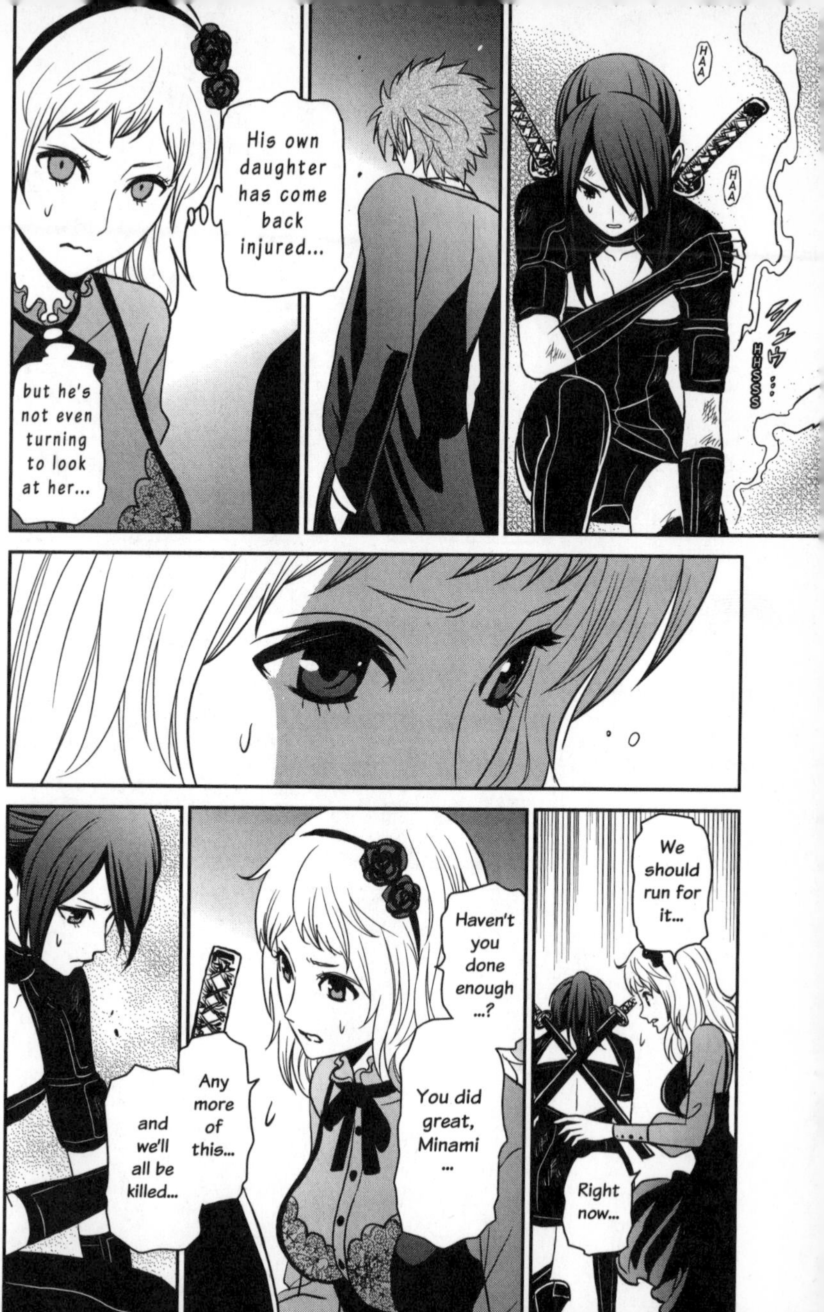
HAA
HAA
HSSSS...
His own daughter has come back injured...
but he's not even turning to look at her...
We should run for it...
Right now...
Haven't you done enough ...?
You did great, Minami ...
Any more of this...
and we'll all be killed...

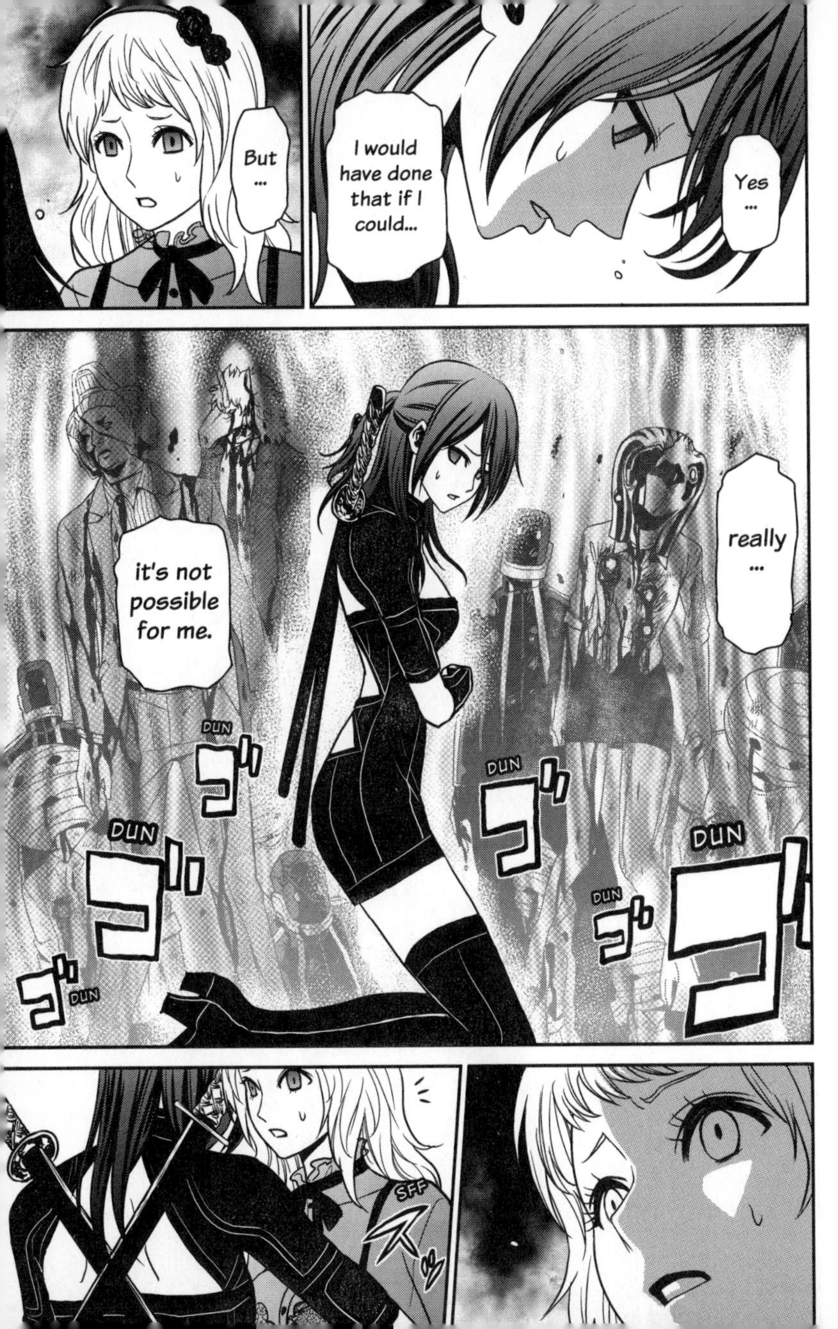

Yes ...
I would have done that if I could...
But ...
really ...
it's not possible for me.
DUN
DUN
DUN
DUN
DUN
DUN
SFF

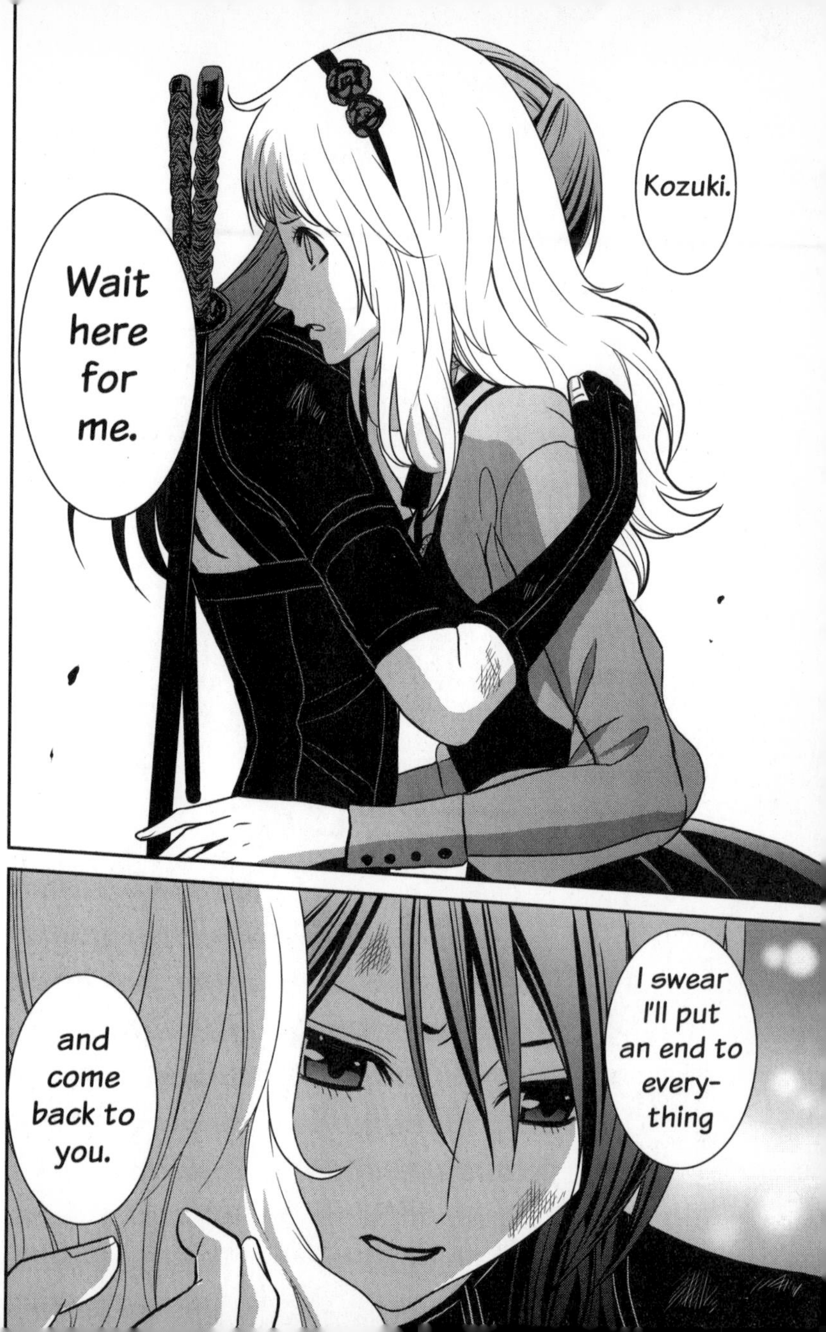
Kozuki.
Wait here for me.
I swear I'll put an end to every-thing
and come back to you.

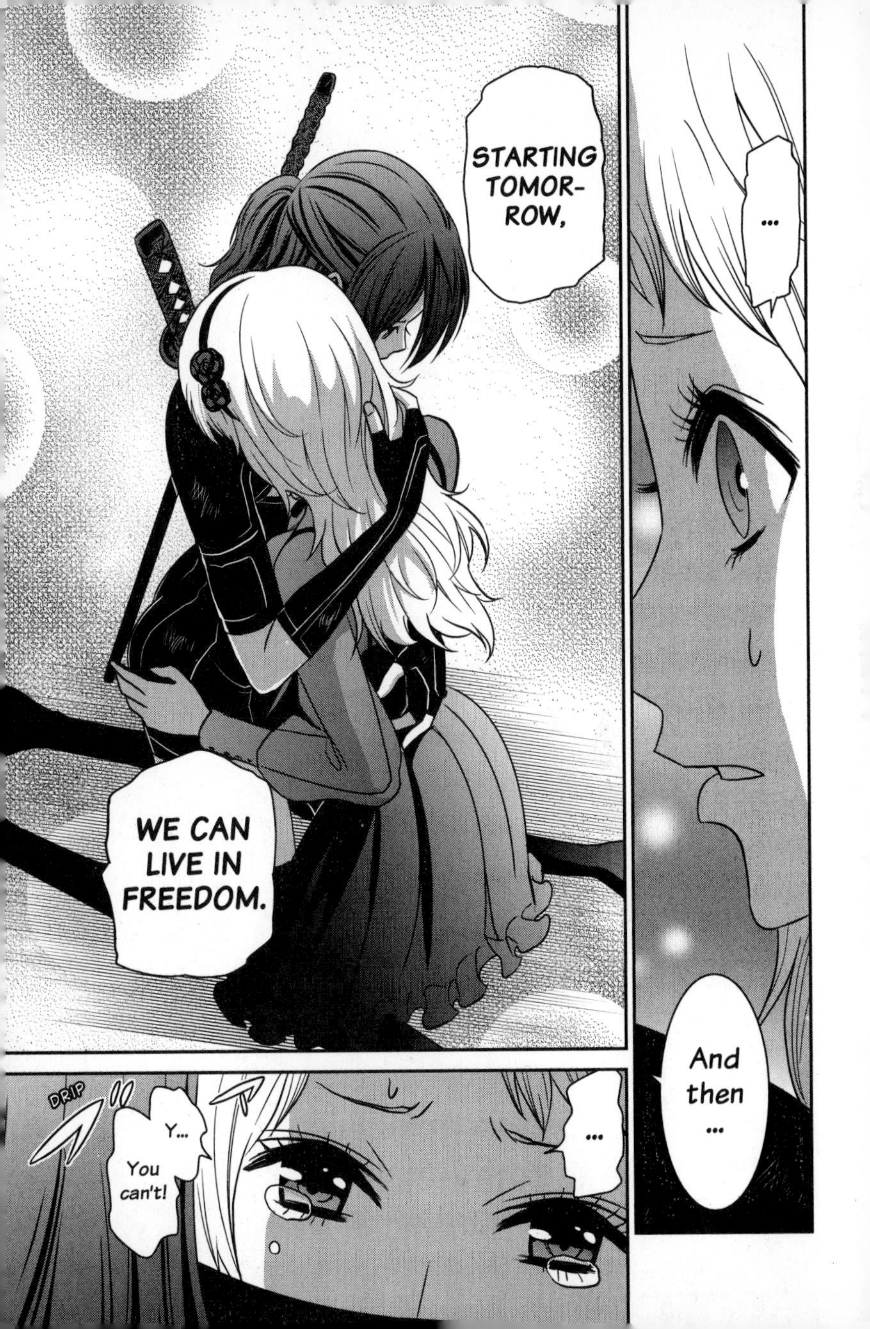
...
And then ...
STARTING TOMORROW,
WE CAN LIVE IN FREEDOM.
...
Y... You can't!
DRIP

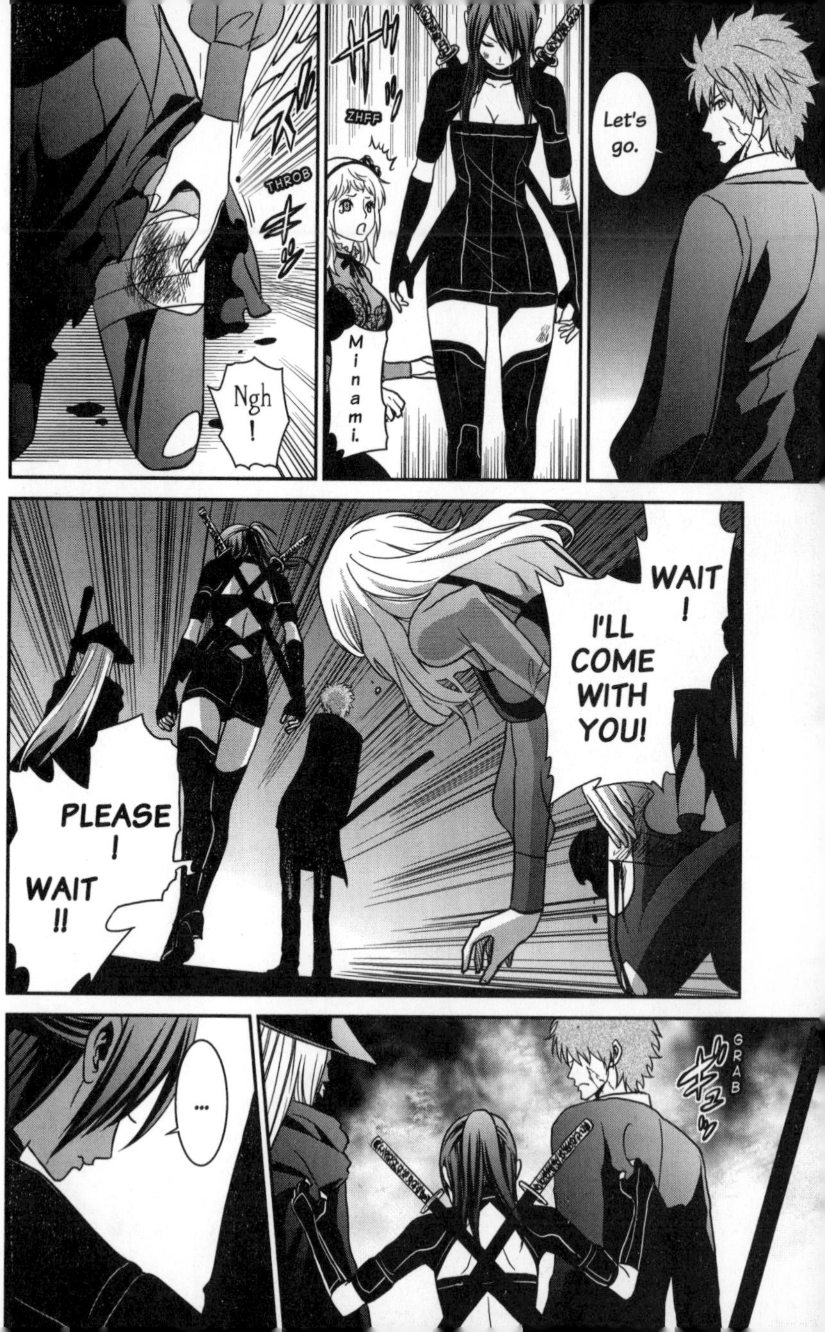
Let's go.
ZHFF
Minami.
THROB
Ngh!
WAIT!
I'LL COME WITH YOU!
PLEASE!
WAIT!!
GRAB
...

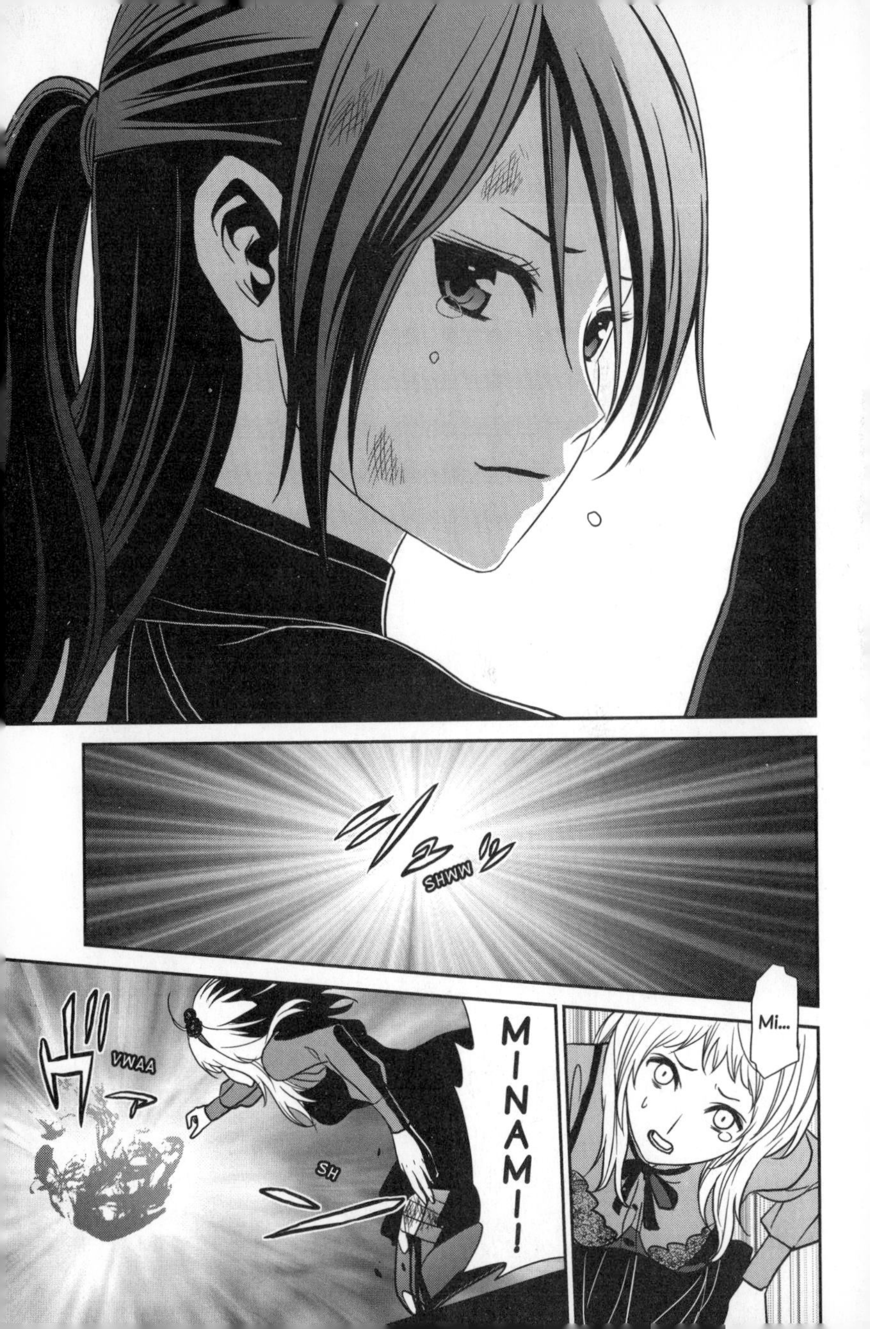
SHWW
Mi...
MINAMI!!
VWAA
SH

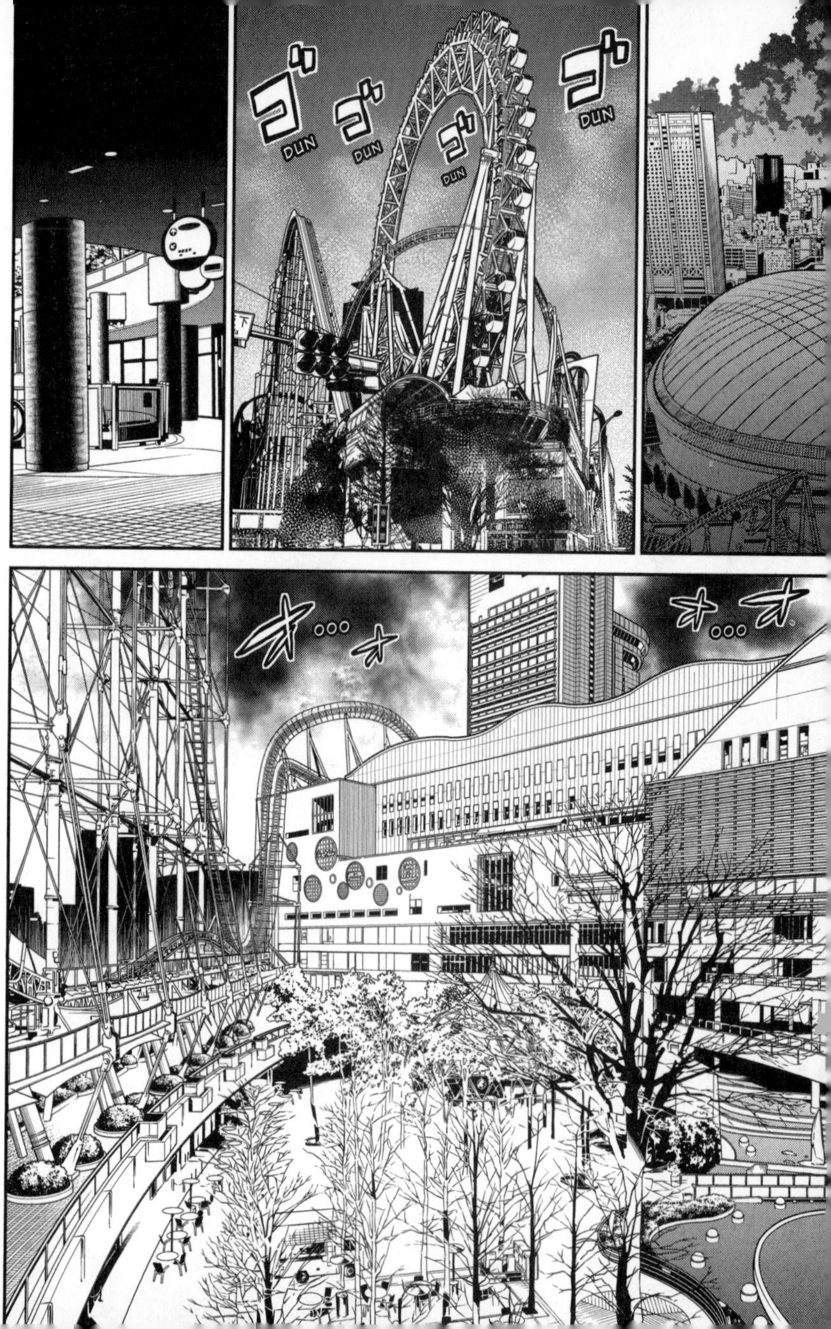
ゴ DUN
ゴ DUN
ゴ DUN
ゴ DUN
オ...オ
オ...オ

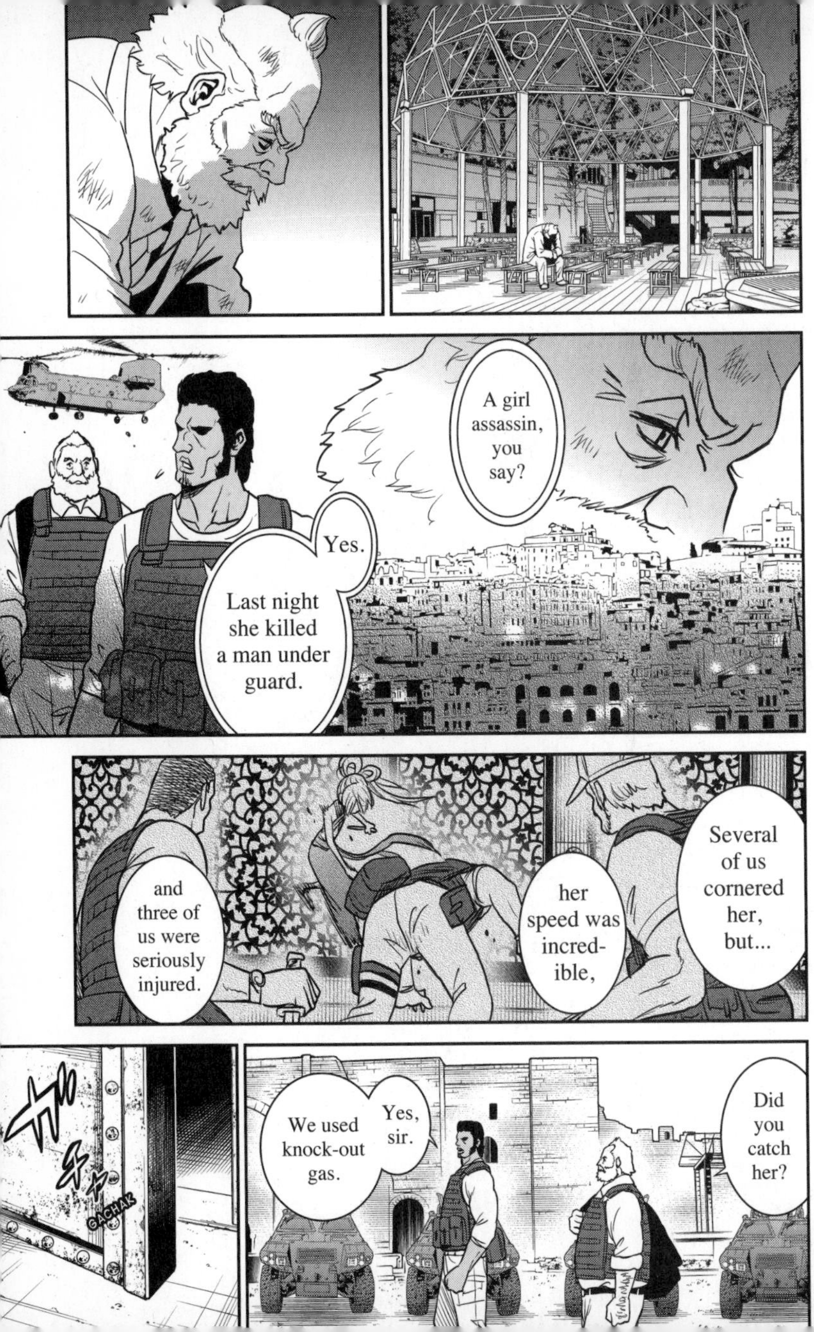
A girl assassin, you say?
Yes.
Last night she killed a man under guard.
Several of us cornered her, but...
her speed was incred-ible,
and three of us were seriously injured.
Did you catch her?
Yes, sir.
We used knock-out gas.
GACHAK

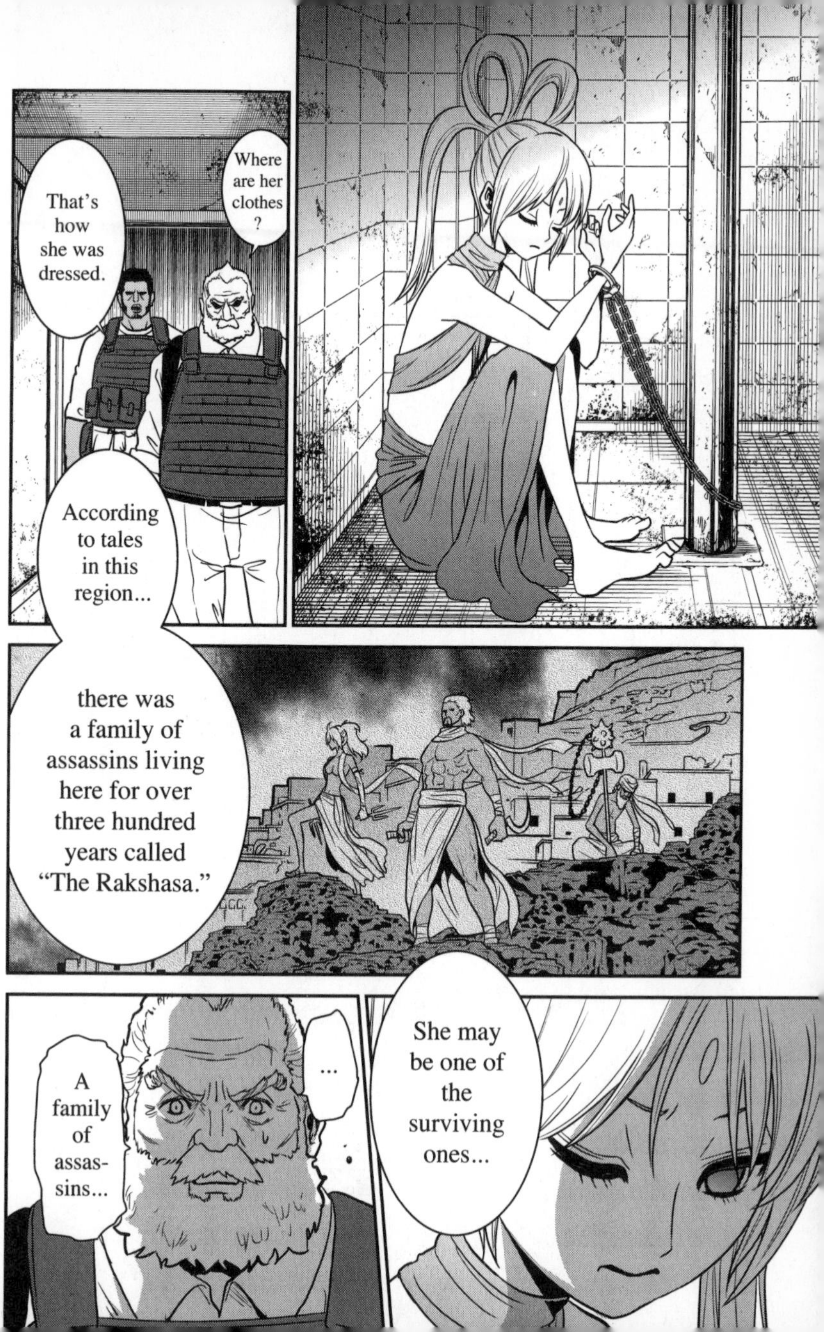
Where are her clothes?
That's how she was dressed.
According to tales in this region...
there was a family of assassins living here for over three hundred years called "The Rakshasa."
She may be one of the surviving ones...
...
A family of assas-sins...

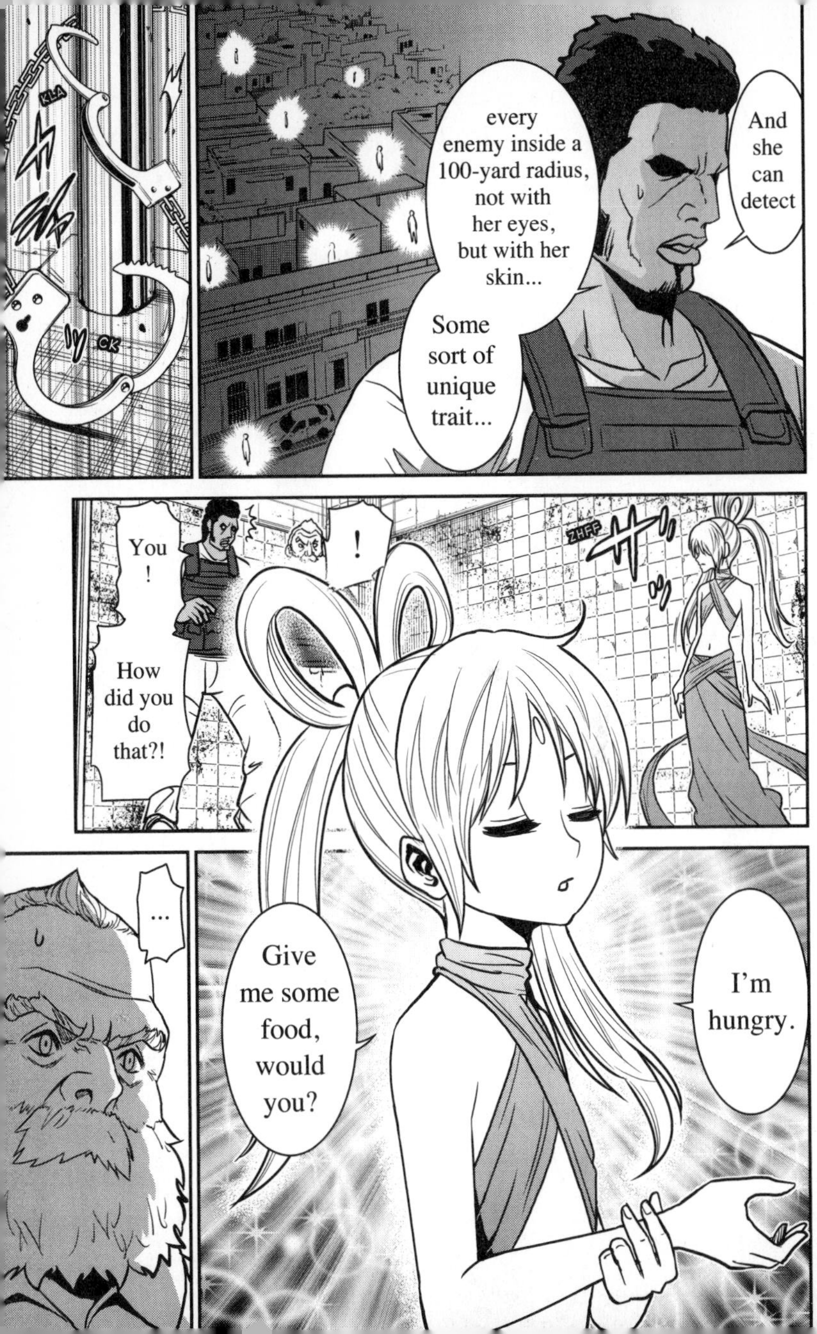
And she can detect
every enemy inside a 100-yard radius, not with her eyes, but with her skin...
Some sort of unique trait...
KLA
CK
ZHFF
!
You!
How did you do that?!
I'm hungry.
Give me some food, would you?
...

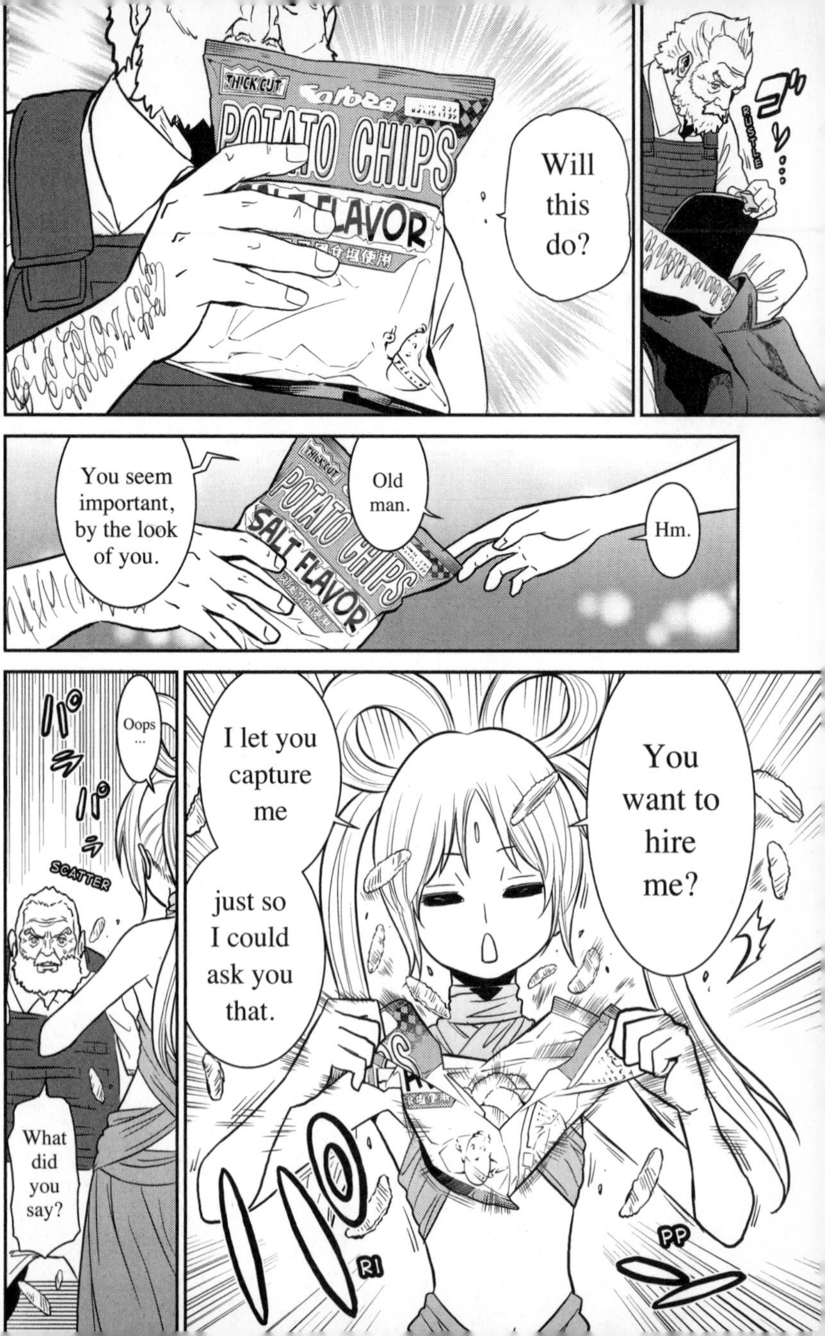
RUSTLE
THICK CUT
POTATO CHIPS
SALT FLAVOR
Will this do?
Hm.
Old man.
You seem important, by the look of you.
You want to hire me?
I let you capture me
just so I could ask you that.
RI
PP
Oops ...
SCATTER
What did you say?

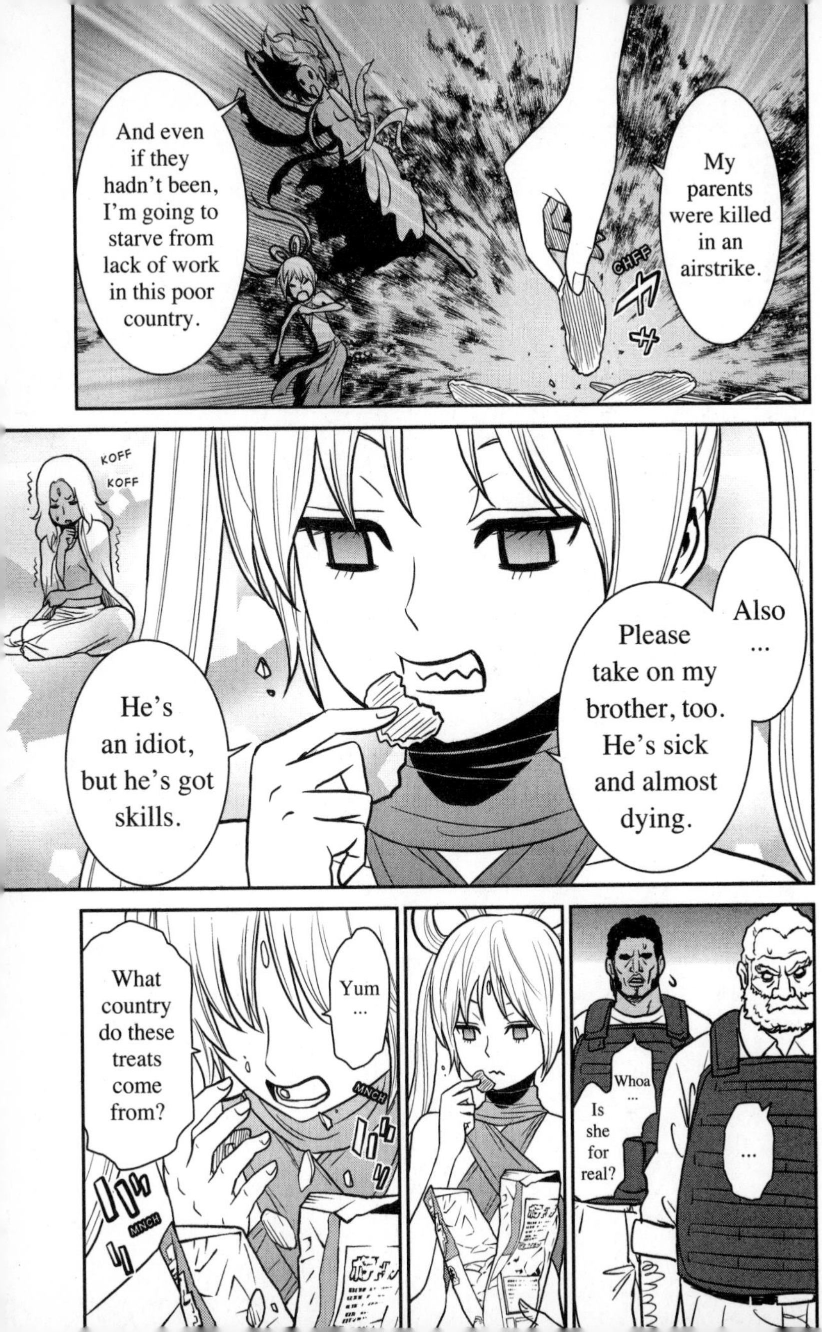
My parents were killed in an airstrike.
CHFF
And even if they hadn't been, I'm going to starve from lack of work in this poor country.
Also ...
Please take on my brother, too. He's sick and almost dying.
KOFF KOFF
He's an idiot, but he's got skills.
Whoa ... Is she for real?
...
Yum ...
MNCH
What country do these treats come from?
MNCH

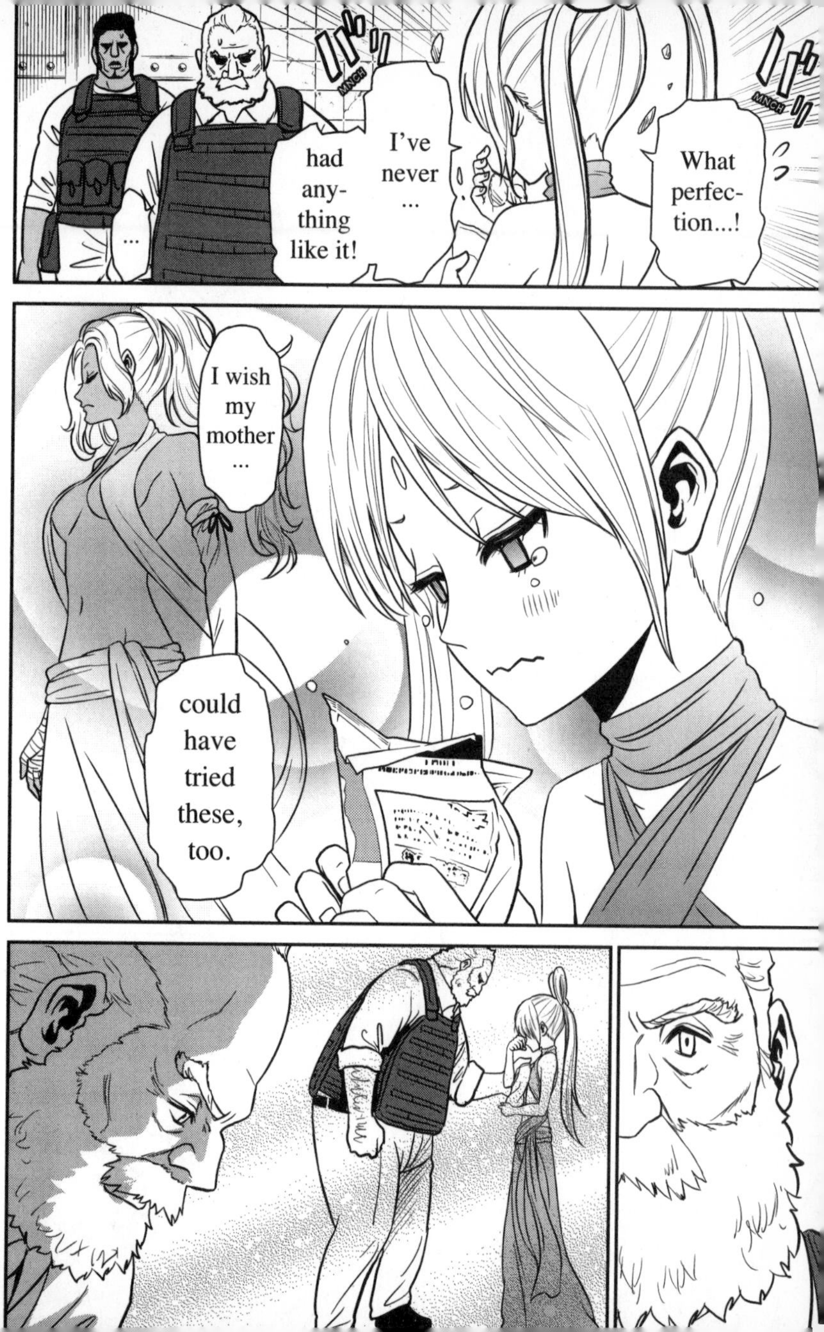
MNCH
What perfection...!
I've never ...
had anything like it!
MNCH
...
I wish my mother ...
could have tried these, too.

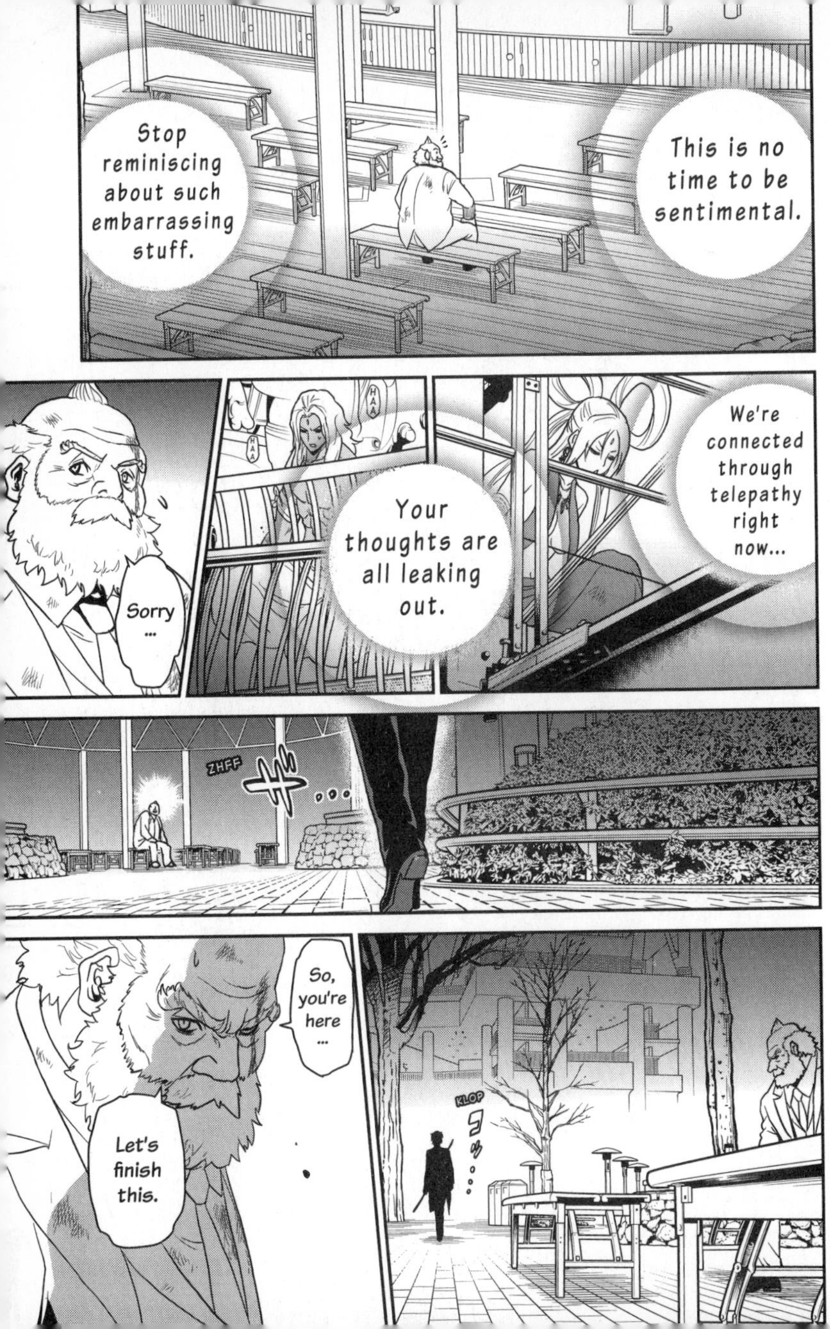
This is no time to be sentimental.
Stop reminiscing about such embarrassing stuff.
We're connected through telepathy right now...
Your thoughts are all leaking out.
HAA
HAA
Sorry ...
ZHFF
KLOP
So, you're here ...
Let's finish this.

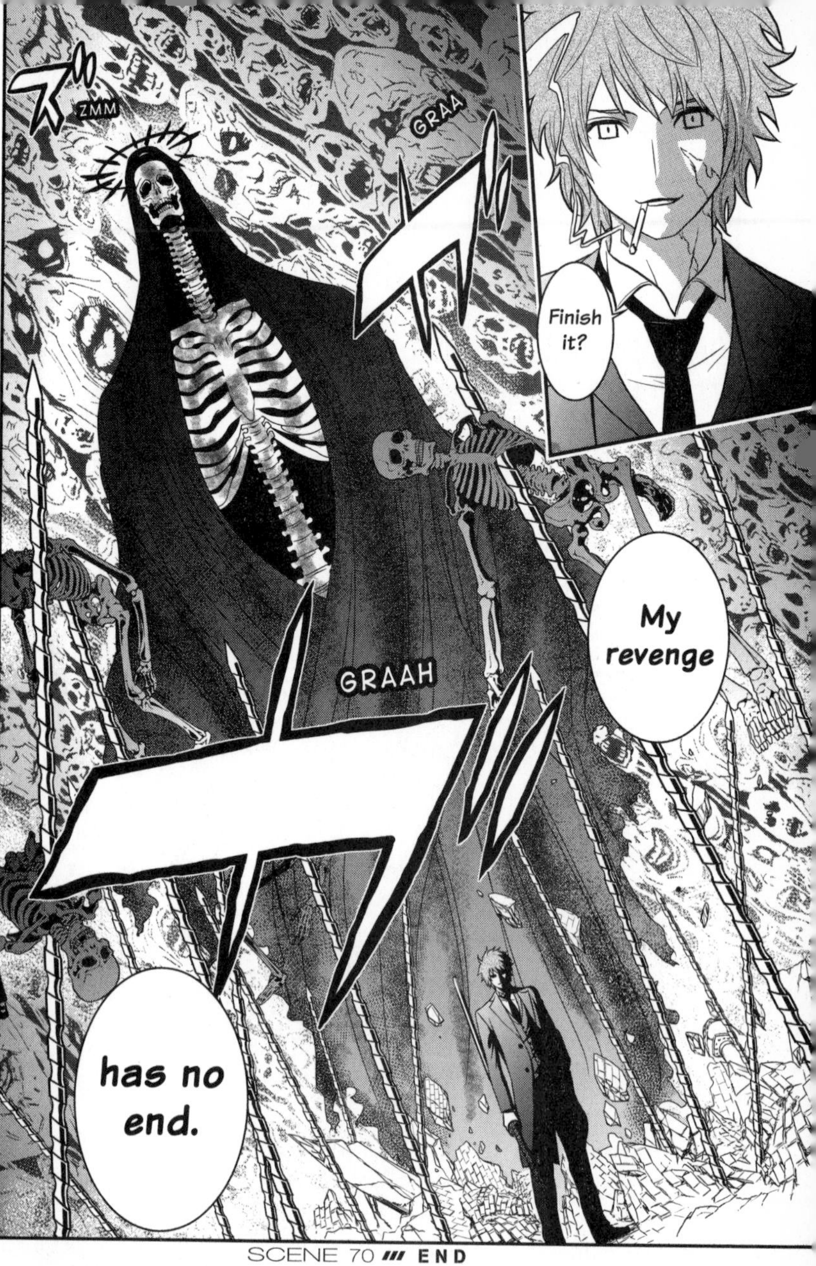
Finish it?
GRAA
ZMM
My revenge
GRAAH
has no end.

SCENE 70 /// END

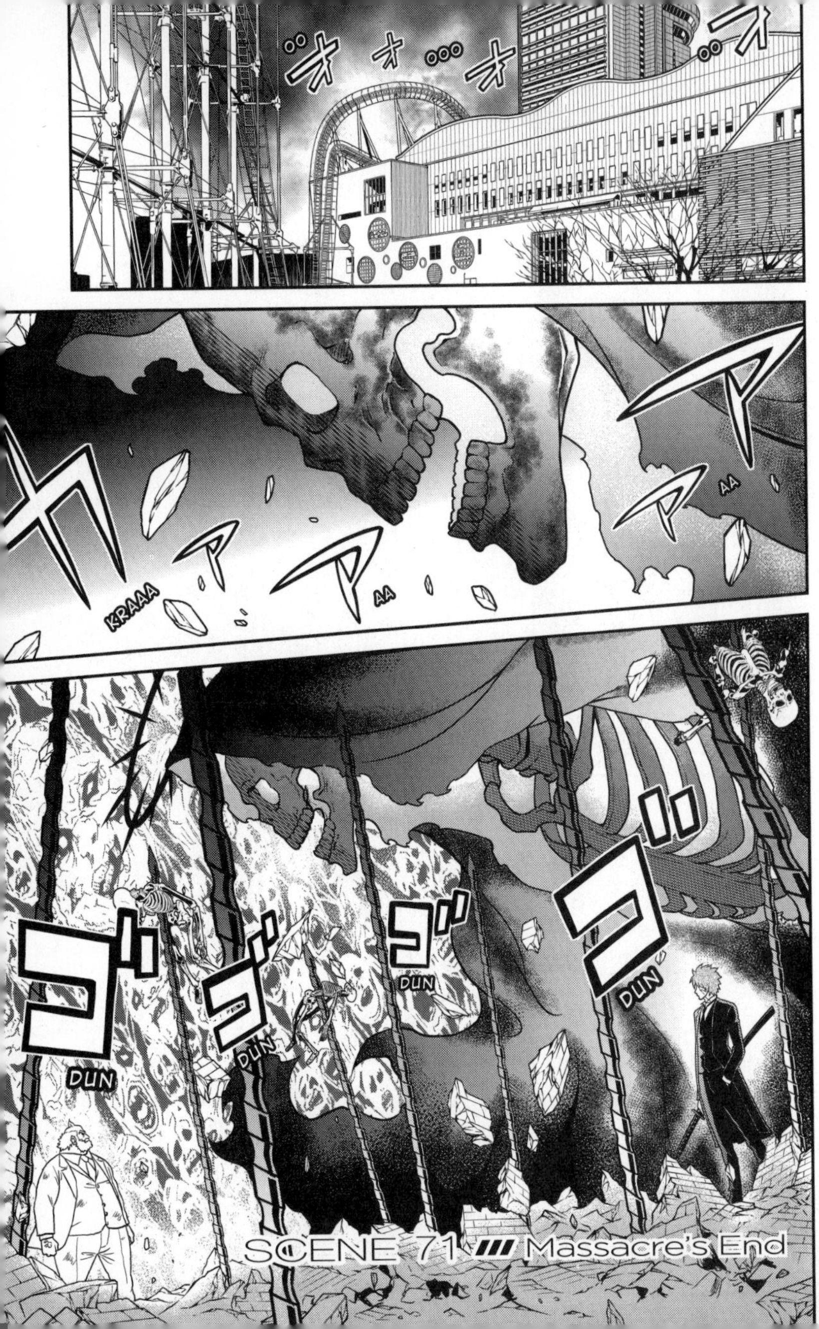
AA
AA
KRAAA
DUN
DUN
DUN
DUN
SCENE 71 /// Massacre's End

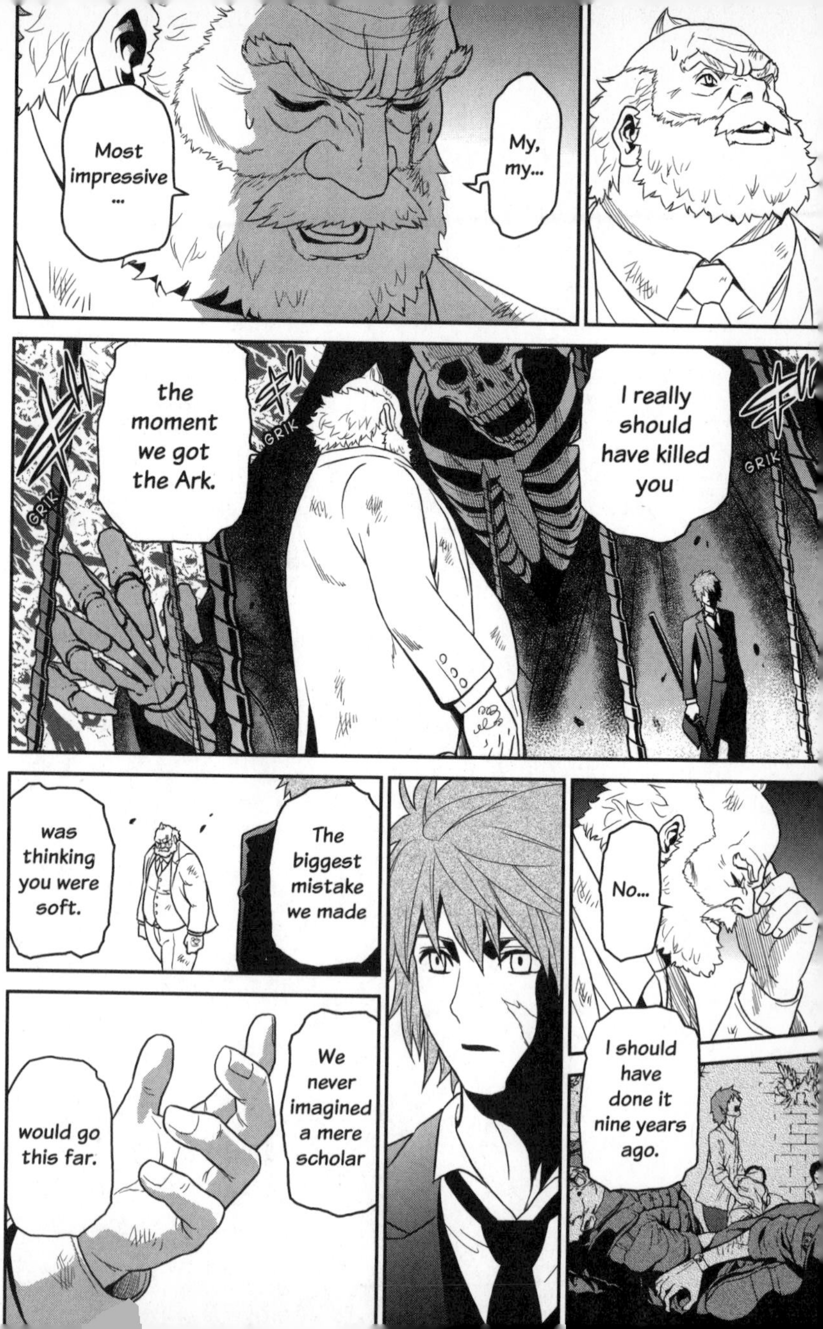
My, my...
Most impressive ...
I really should have killed you
GRIK
GRIK
the moment we got the Ark.
GRIK
No...
I should have done it nine years ago.
The biggest mistake we made
was thinking you were soft.
We never imagined a mere scholar
would go this far.

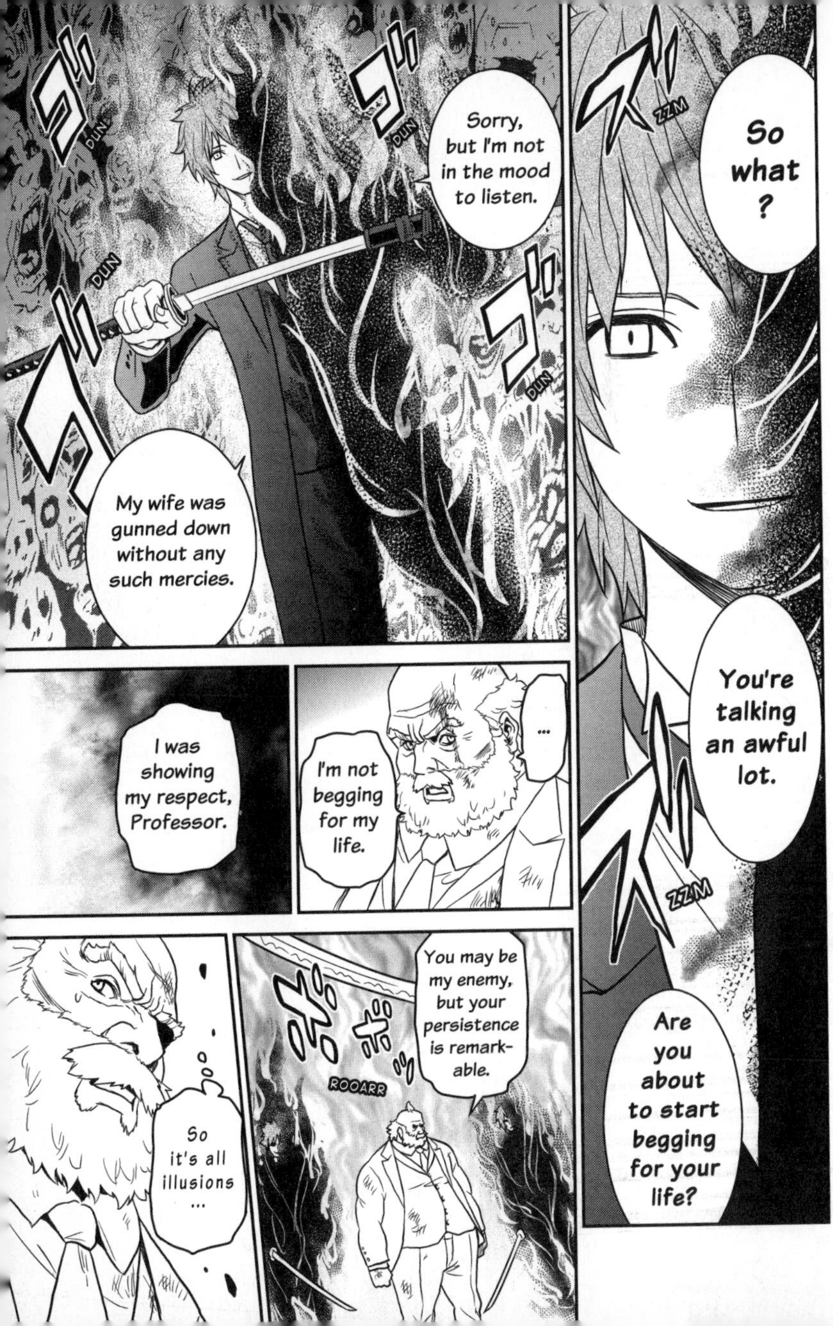
ZZM
So what?
You're talking an awful lot.
ZZM
Are you about to start begging for your life?
DUN
DUN
Sorry, but I'm not in the mood to listen.
DUN
DUN
My wife was gunned down without any such mercies.
...
I'm not begging for my life.
I was showing my respect, Professor.
You may be my enemy, but your persistence is remark-able.
ROOARR
So it's all illusions ...

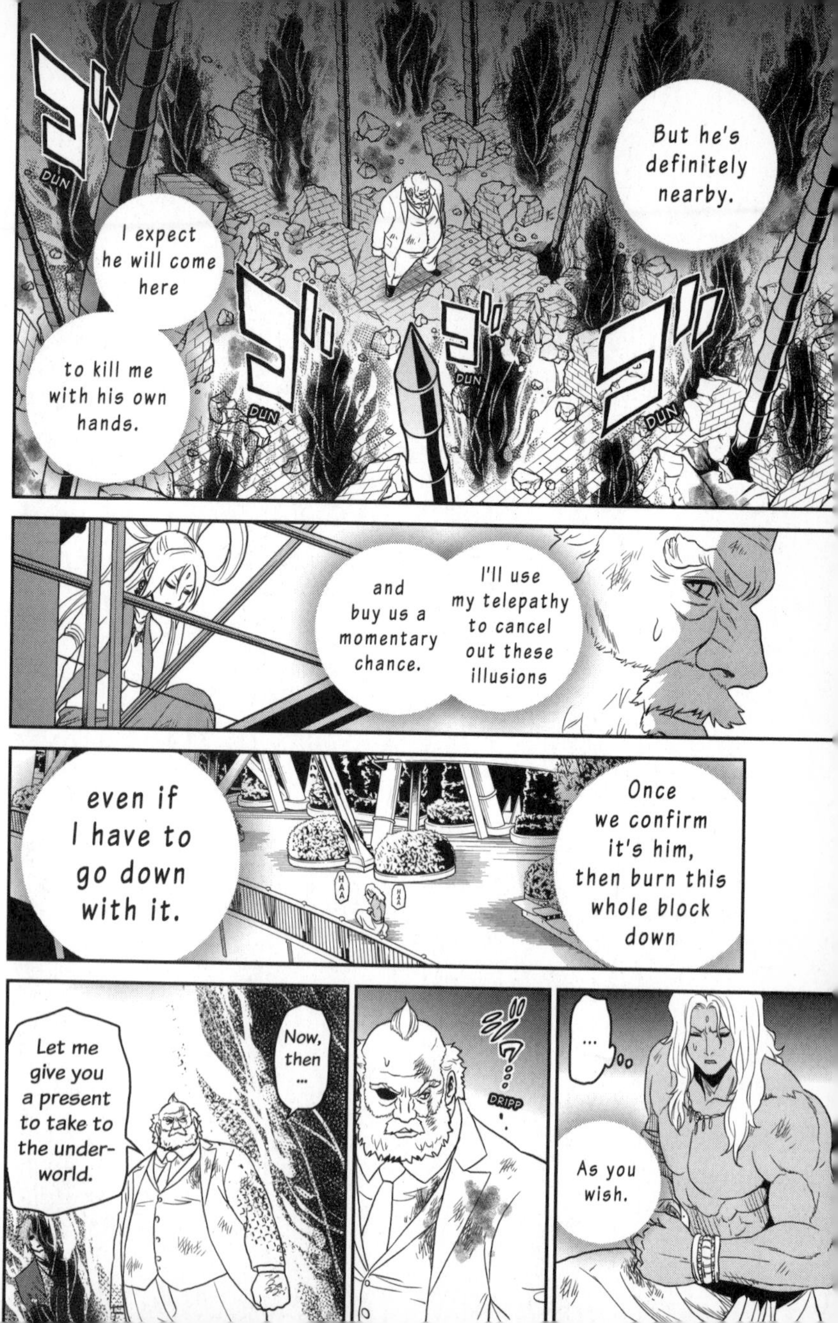
DUN
But he's definitely nearby.
I expect he will come here
to kill me with his own hands.
DUN
DUN
DUN
I'll use my telepathy to cancel out these illusions
and buy us a momentary chance.
Once we confirm it's him, then burn this whole block down
even if I have to go down with it.
HAA
HAA
...
As you wish.
DRIPP
Now, then ...
Let me give you a present to take to the under-world.

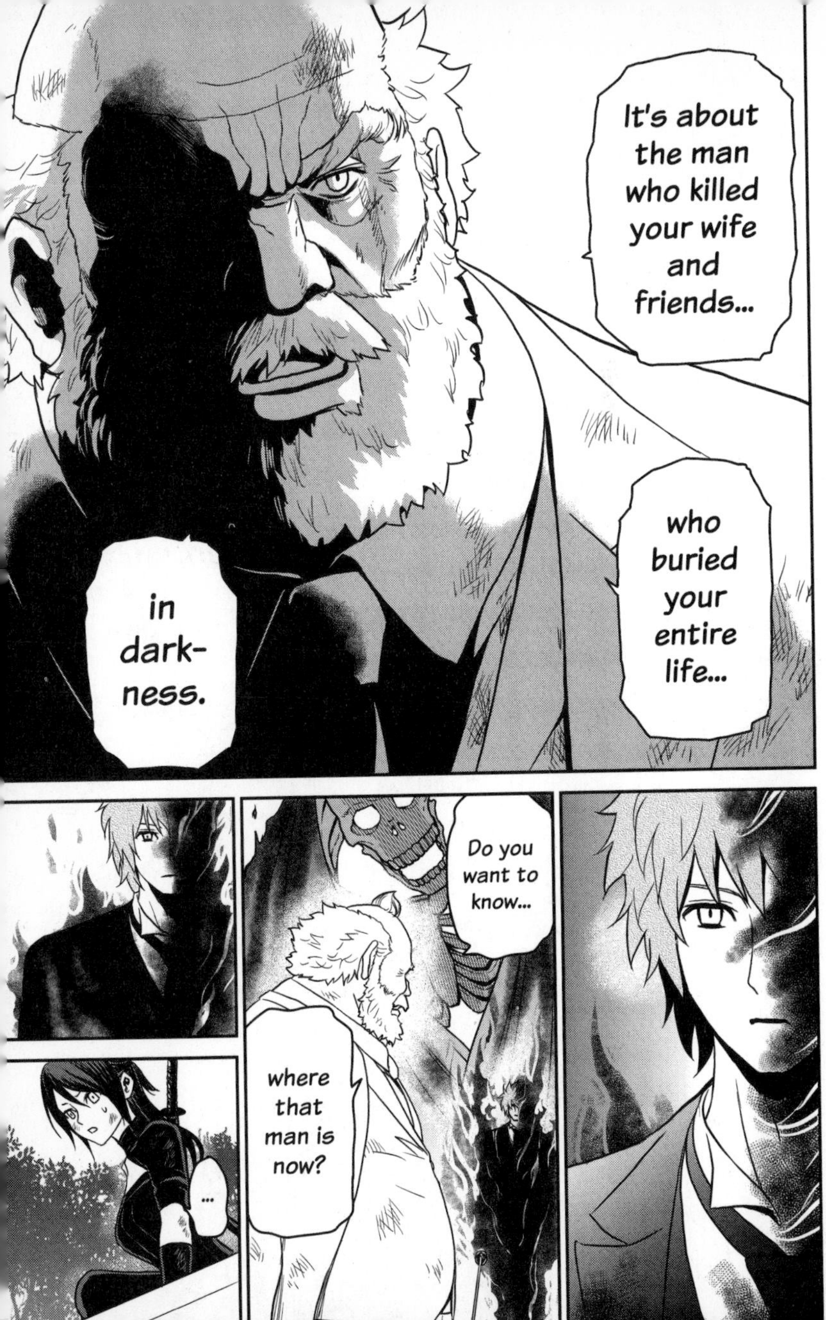
It's about the man who killed your wife and friends...
who buried your entire life...
in dark-ness.
Do you want to know...
where that man is now?
...

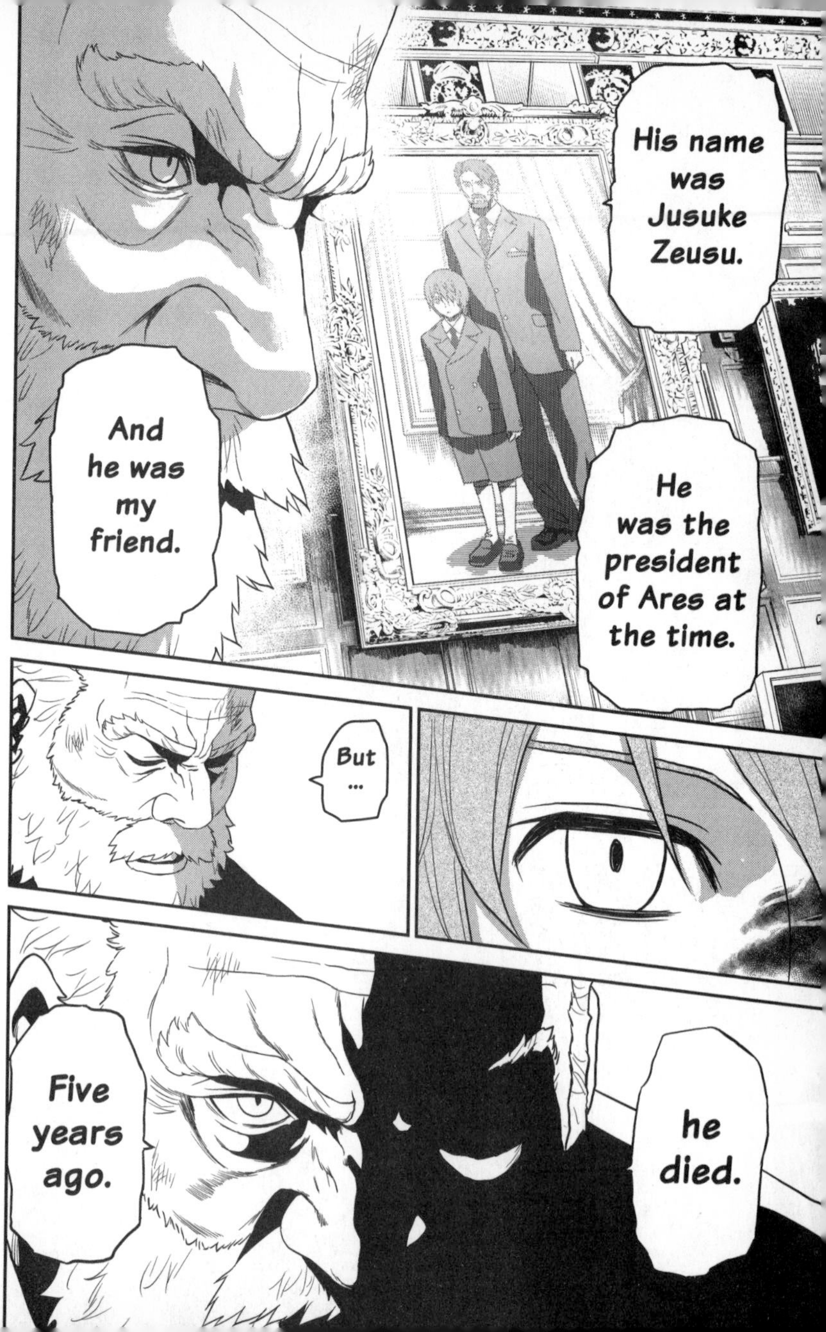
His name was Jusuke Zeusu.
He was the president of Ares at the time.
And he was my friend.
But ...
Five years ago.
he died.

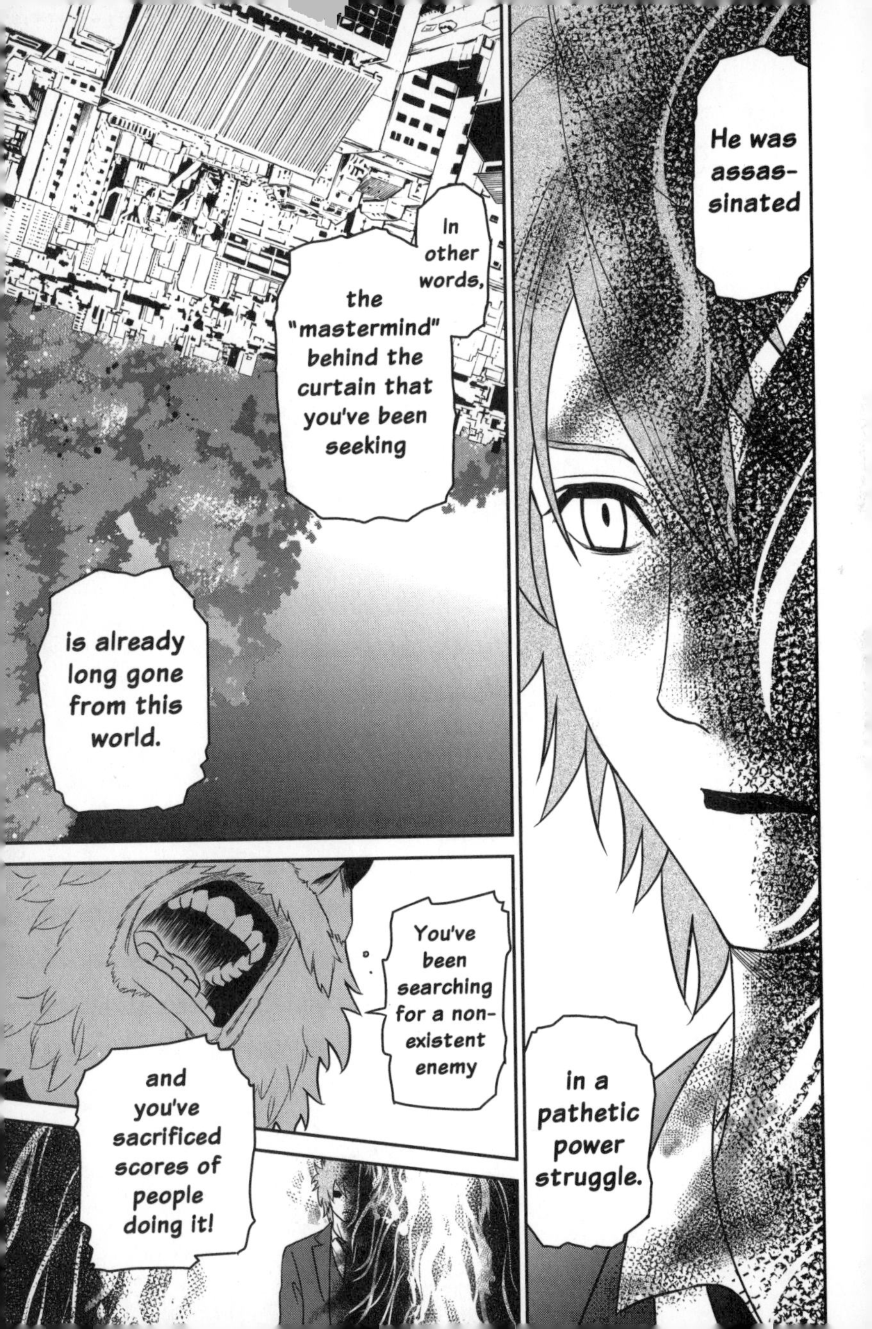
He was assas-sinated
in a pathetic power struggle.
In other words,
the "mastermind" behind the curtain that you've been seeking
is already long gone from this world.
You've been searching for a non-existent enemy
and you've sacrificed scores of people doing it!

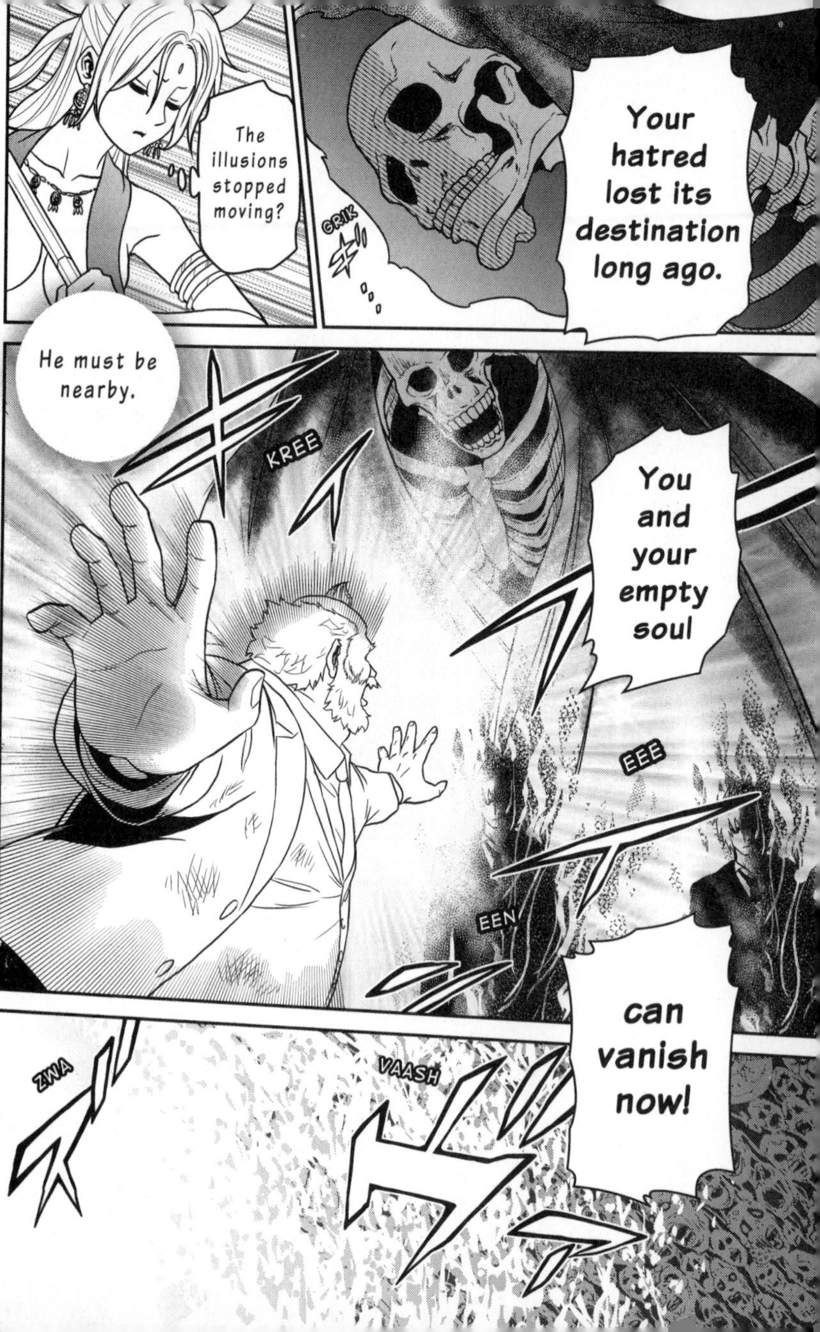

Your hatred lost its destination long ago.
CRIK
The illusions stopped moving?
He must be nearby.
KREE
You and your empty soul
EEE
EEN
can vanish now!
VAASH
ZNA

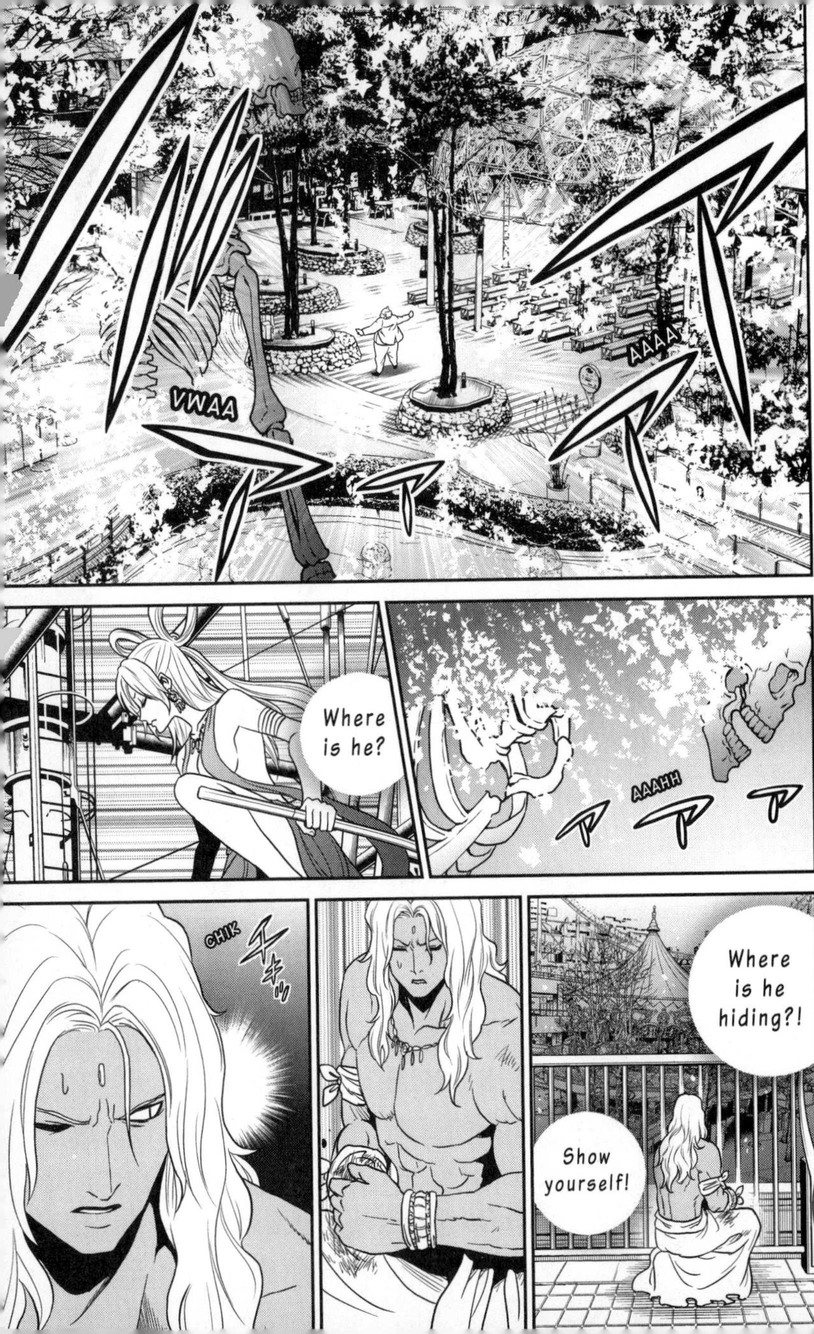
AAAA
VWAA
AAAHH
Where is he?
Where is he hiding?!
Show yourself!
CHIK

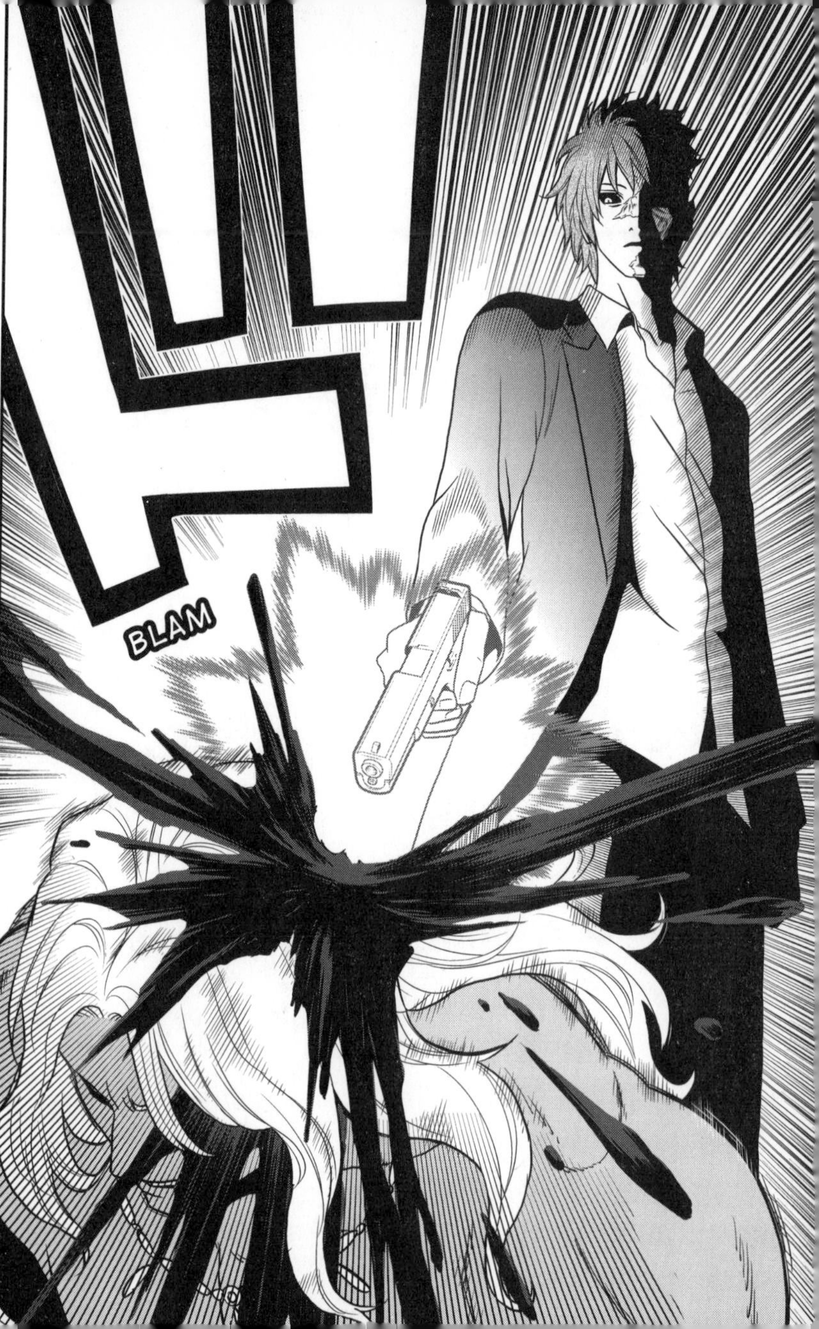
BLAM

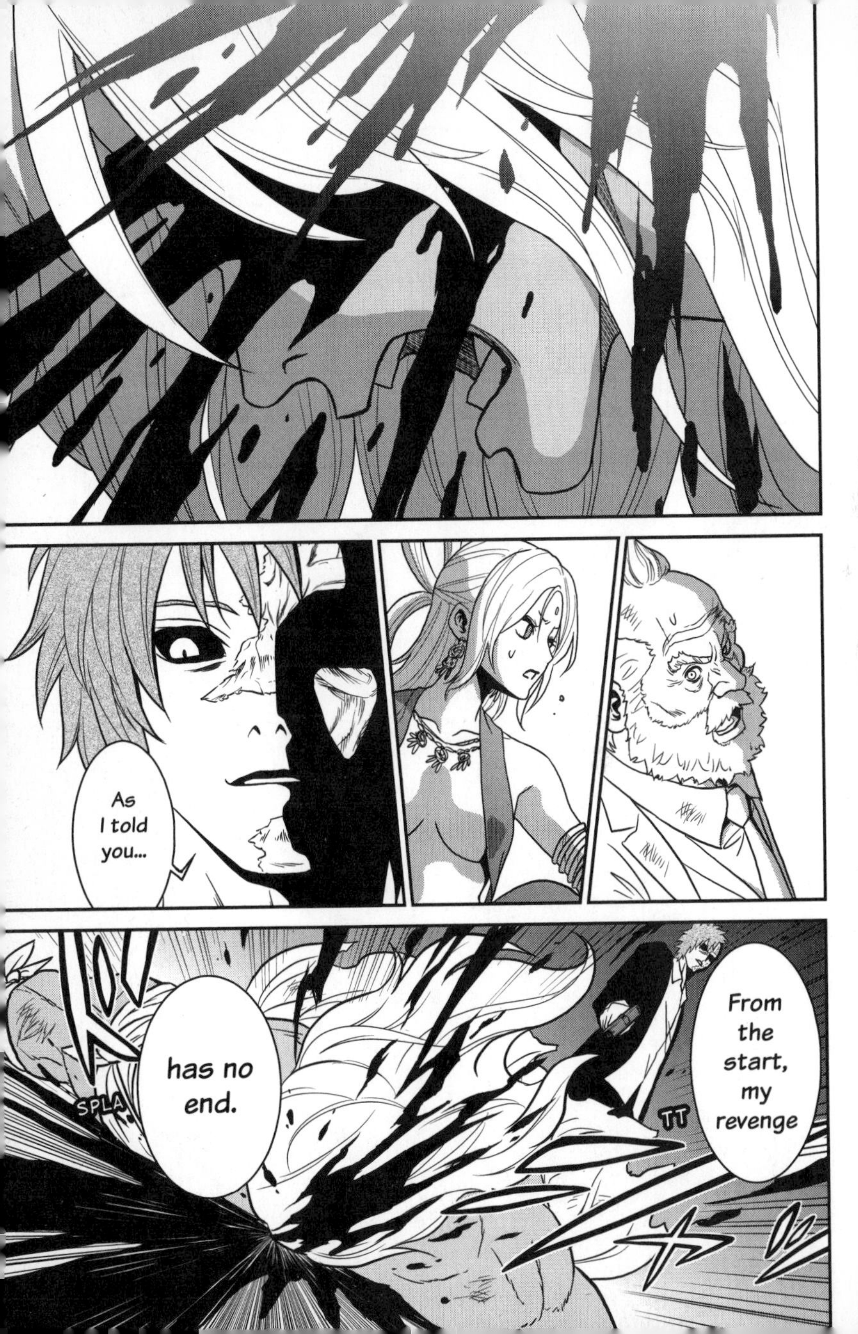
As I told you...
From the start, my revenge
TT
has no end.
SPLA

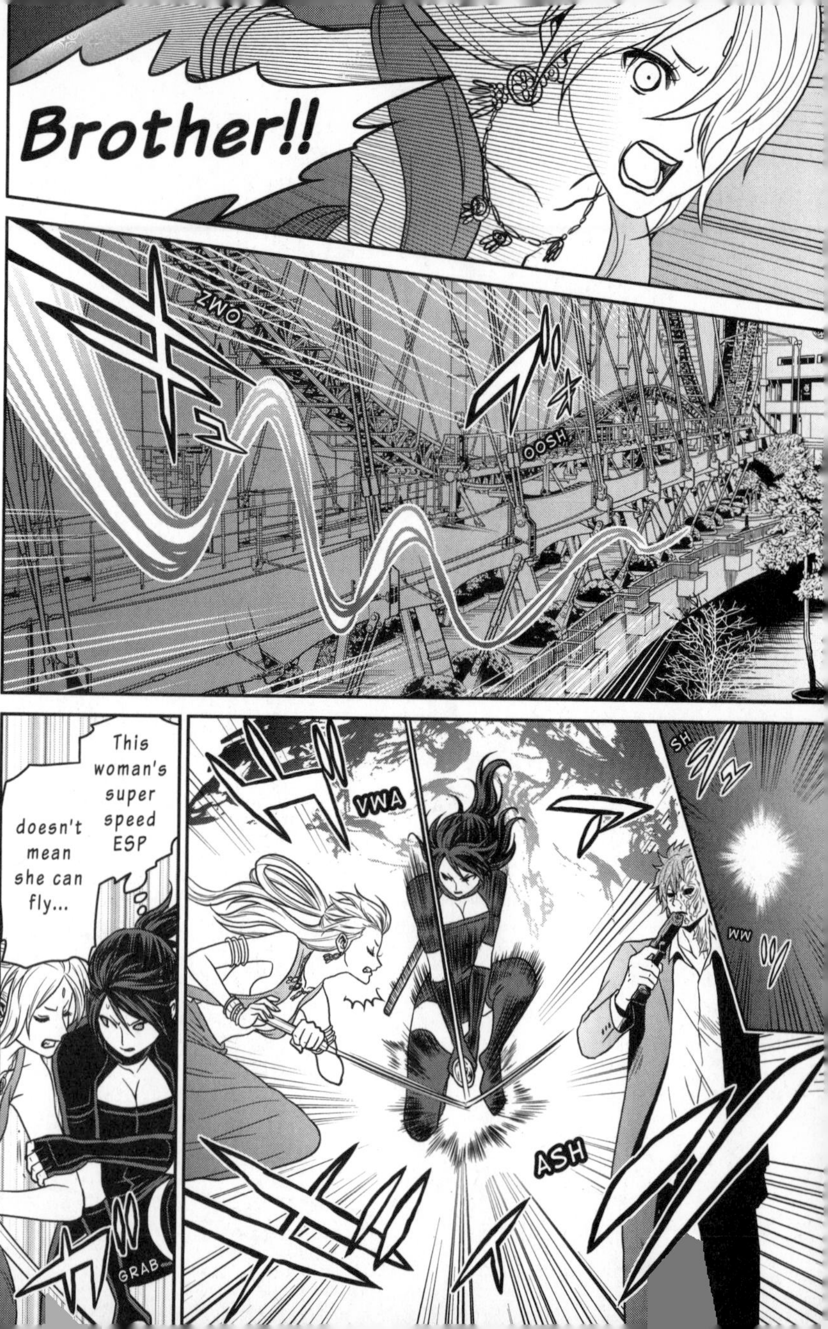
Brother!!
ZWO
OOSH
SH
VWA
WW
ASH
This woman's super speed ESP
doesn't mean she can fly...
GRAB

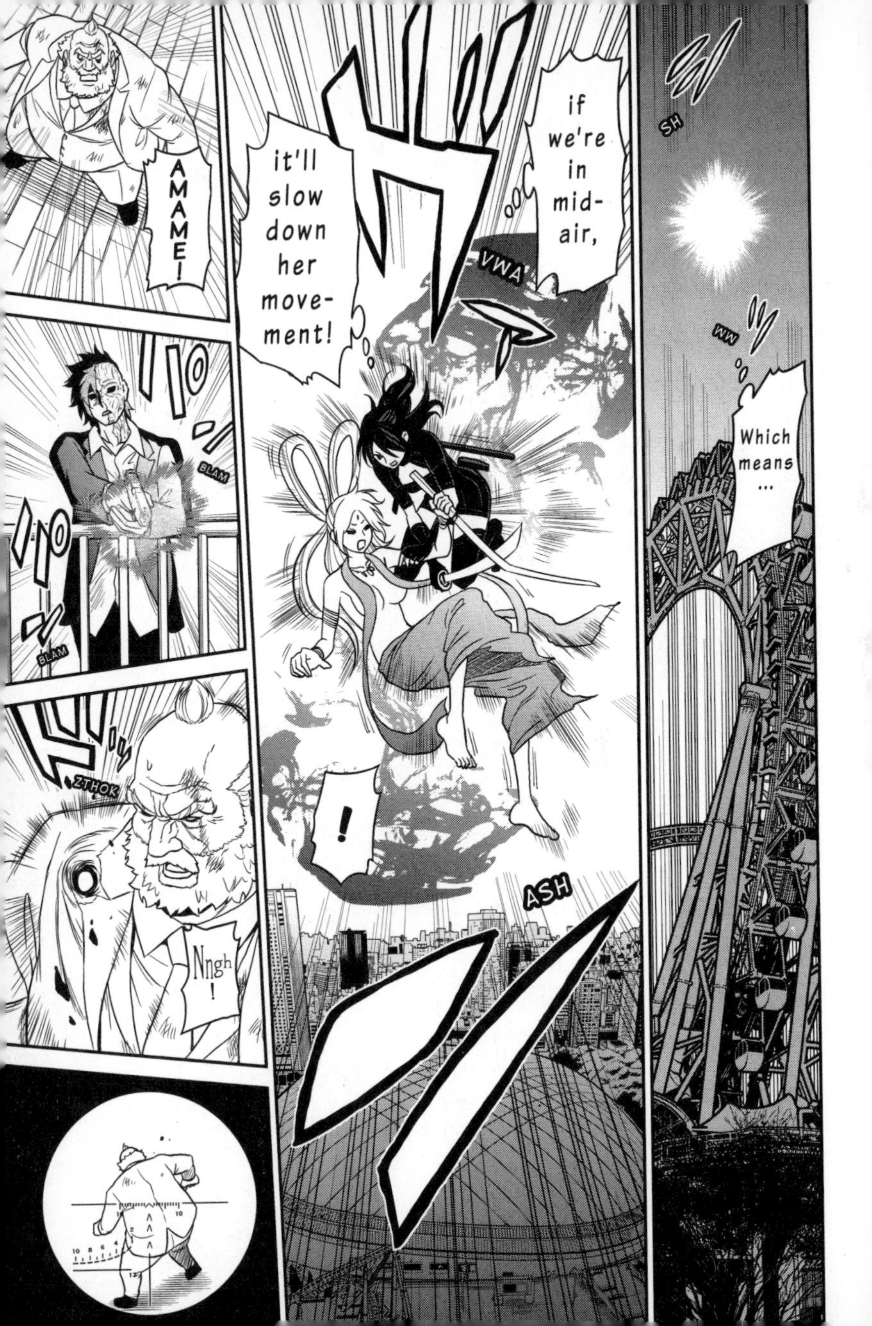
SH
WW
Which means...
if we're in mid-air,
it'll slow down her movement!
VWA
!
ASH
AMAME!
BLAM
BLAM
ZTHOK
Nngh!

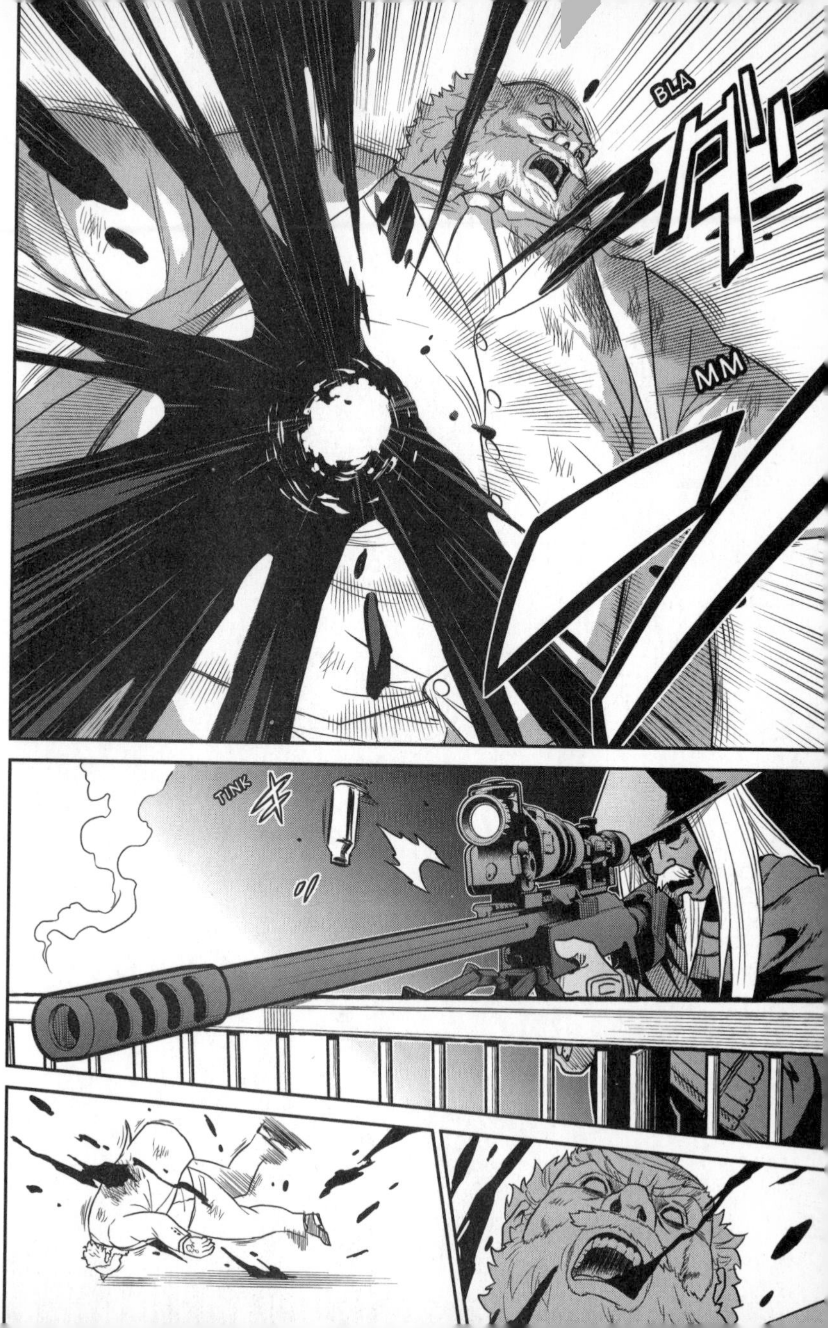
BLA
MM
TINK

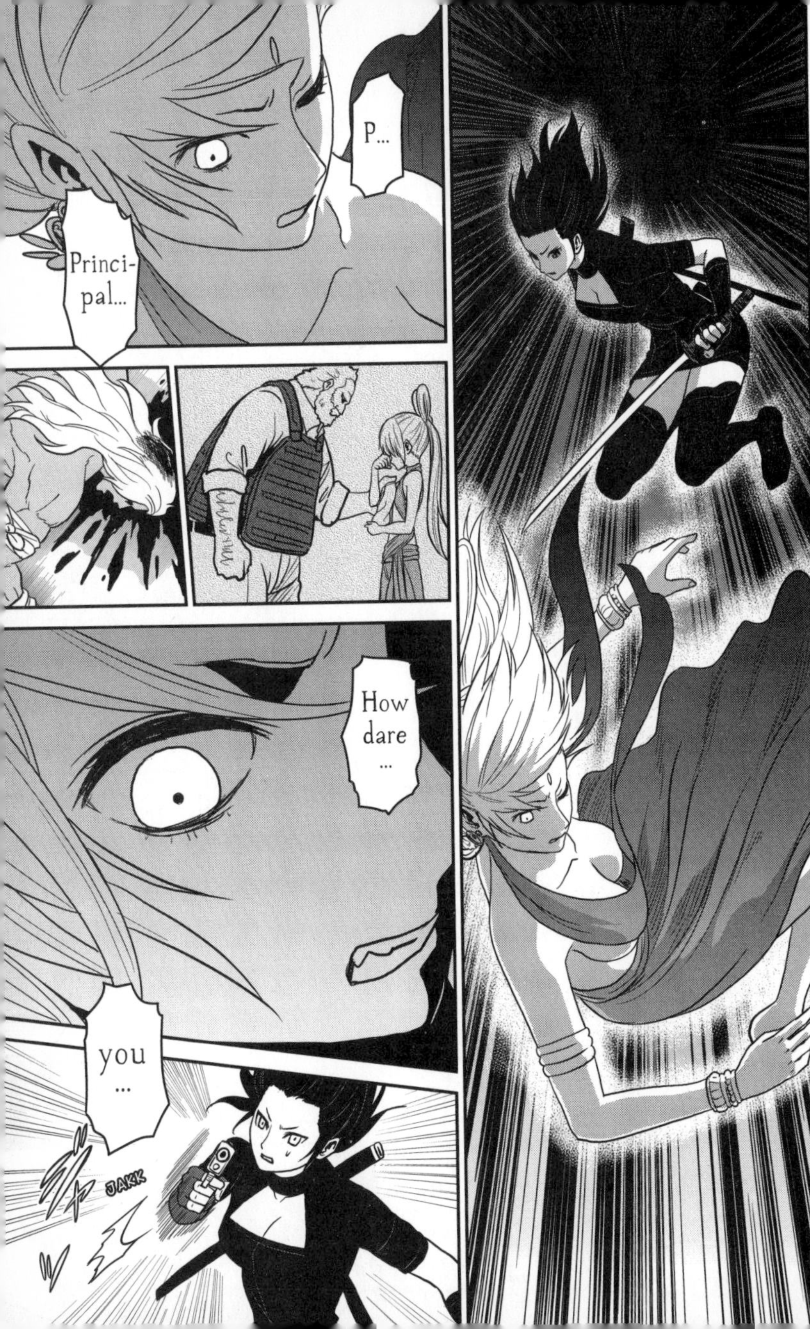
P...
Princi-pal...
How dare ...
you ...
JAKK

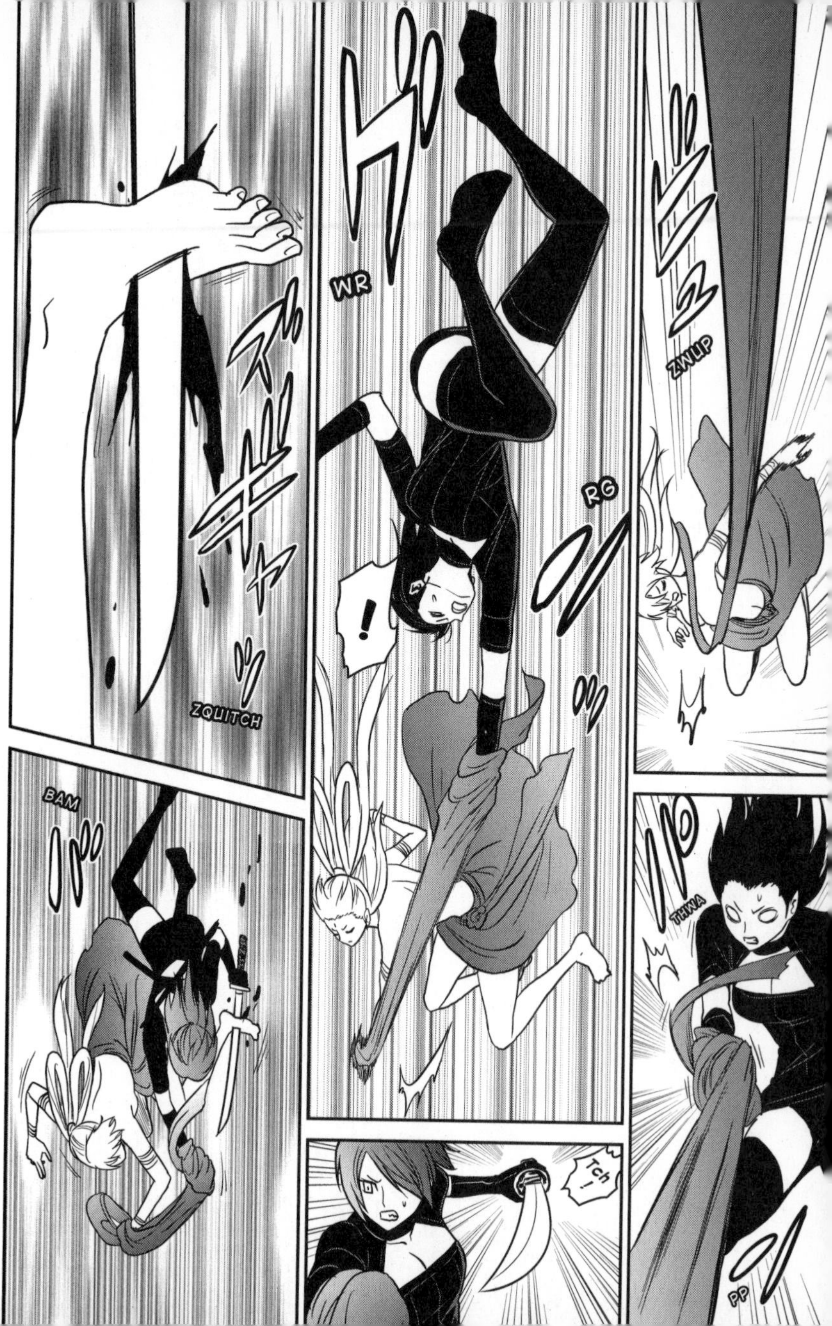
ZWUP
THWA
PP
WR
RG
!
Tch!
ZQUITCH
BAM

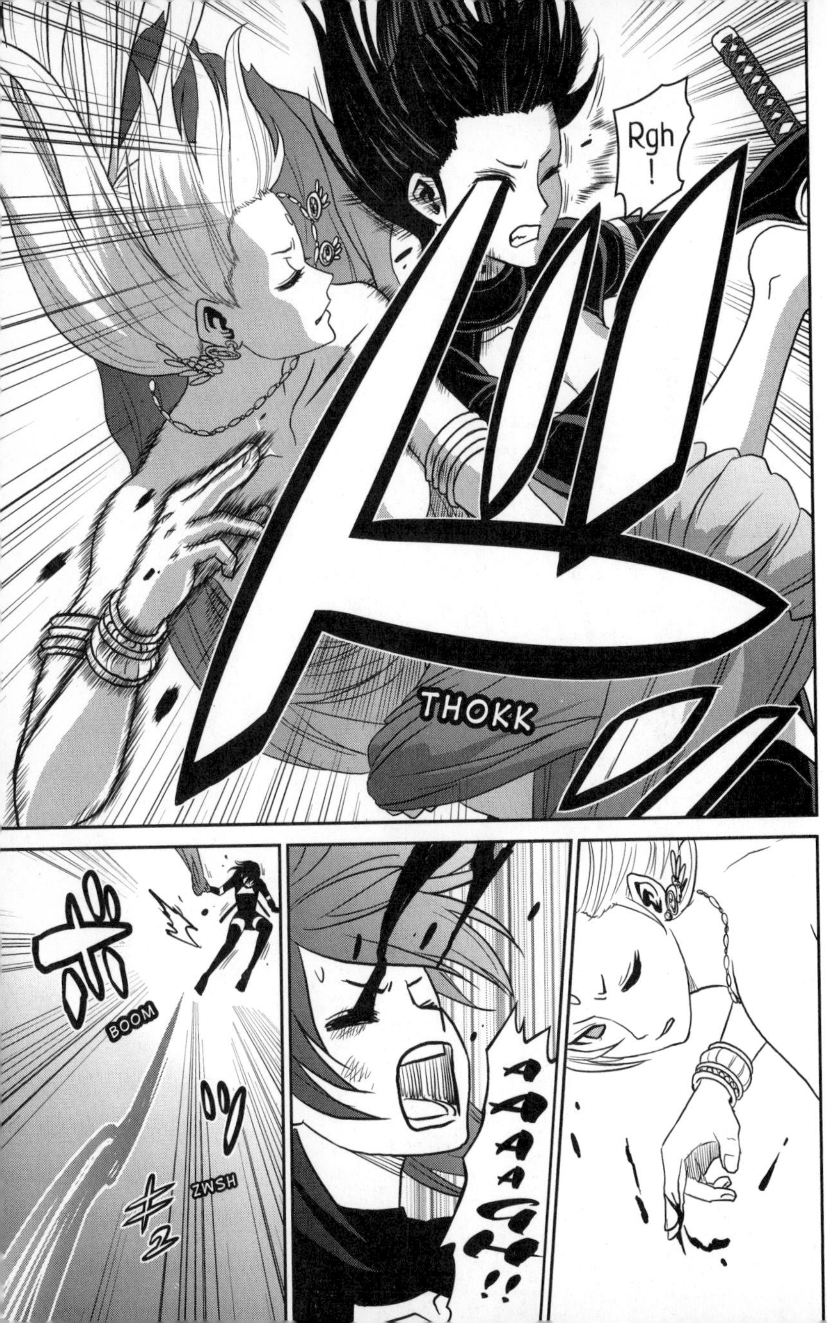
Rgh
!
THOKK
AAAAAAGG!!
BOOM
ZWSH

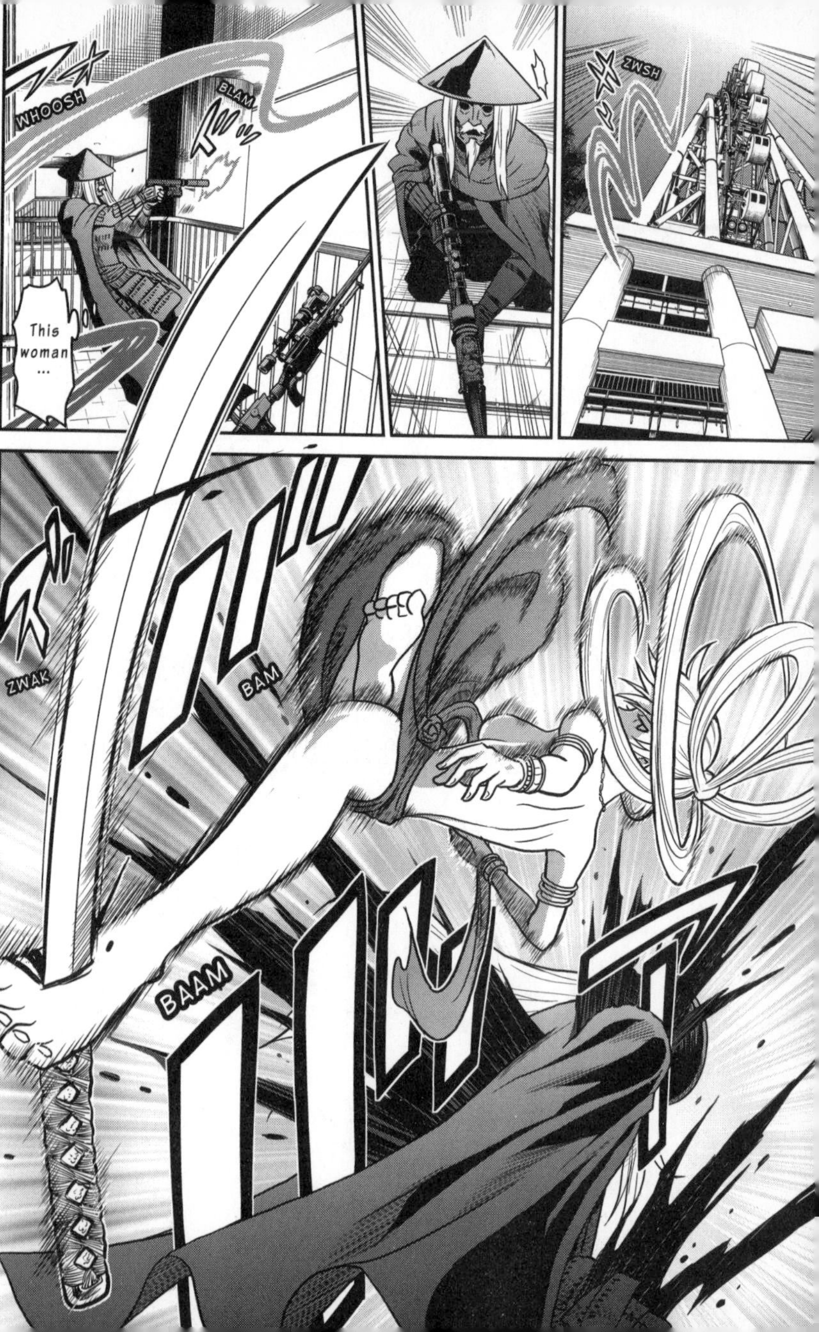
ZWSH
BLAM
WHOOSH
This woman ...
BAM
ZWAK
BAAM

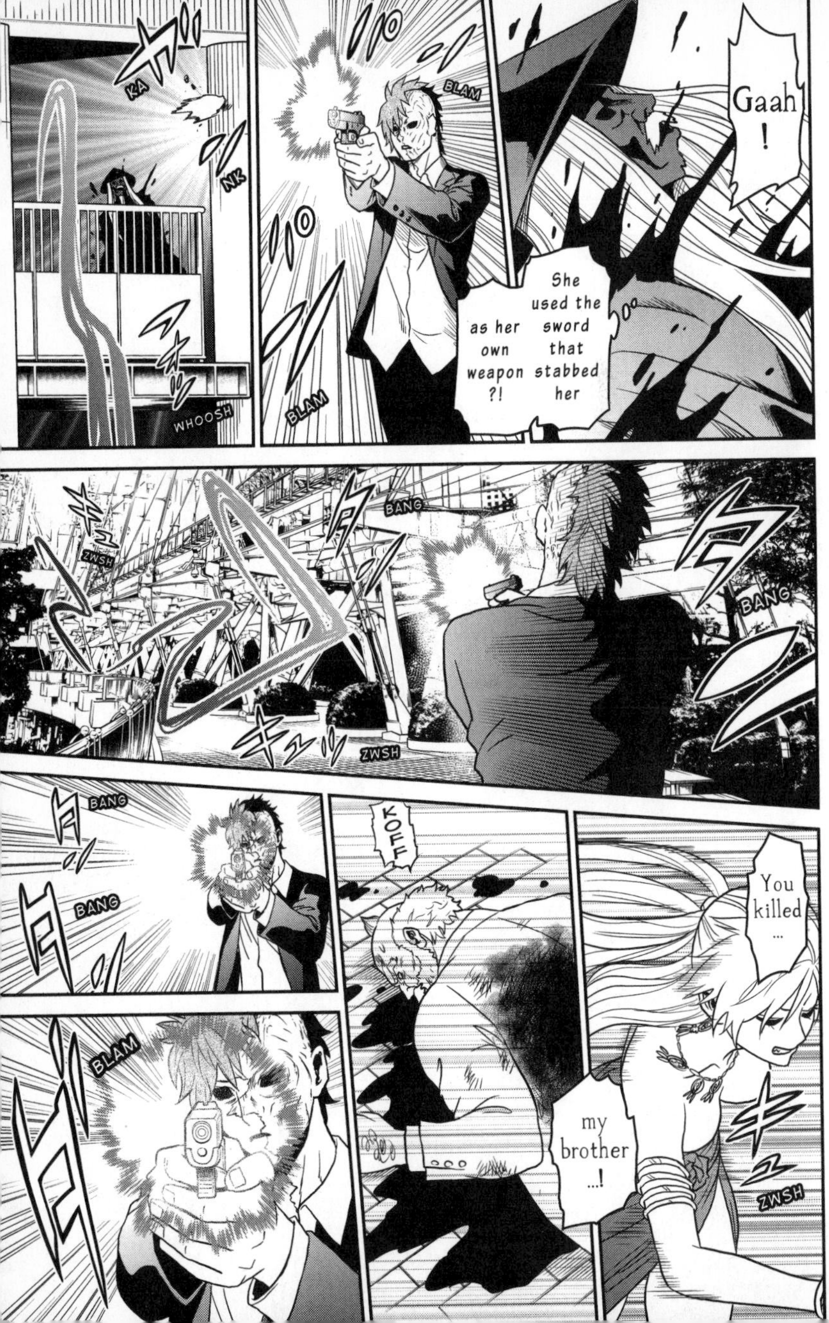
Gaah !
She used the sword that stabbed her as her own weapon ?!
BLAM
BLAM
KA
NK
WHOOSH
BANG
BANG
ZWSH
ZWSH
You killed ...
my brother ...!
ZWSH
KOFF
BANG
BANG
BLAM

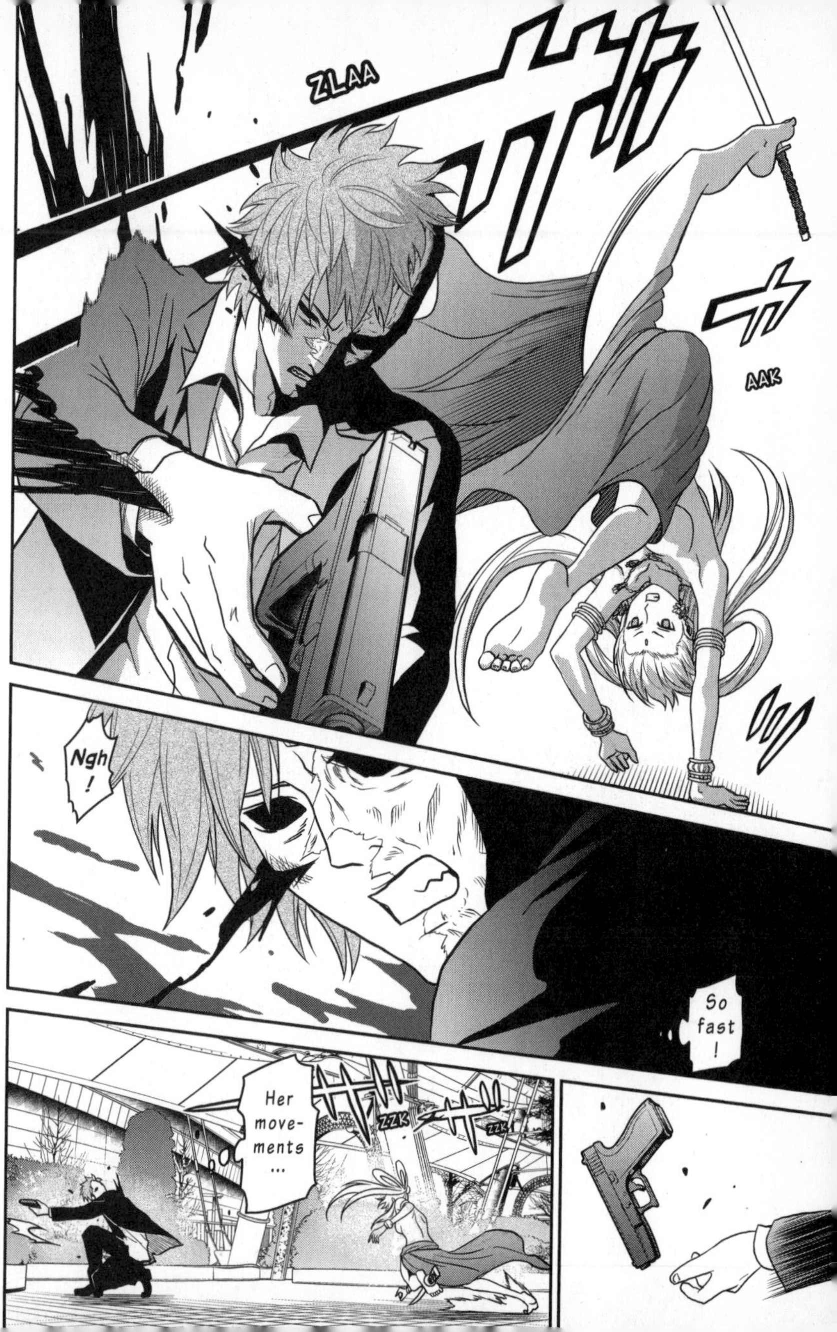
ZLAA
AAK
Ngh!
So fast!
Her movements...
ZZK
ZZK

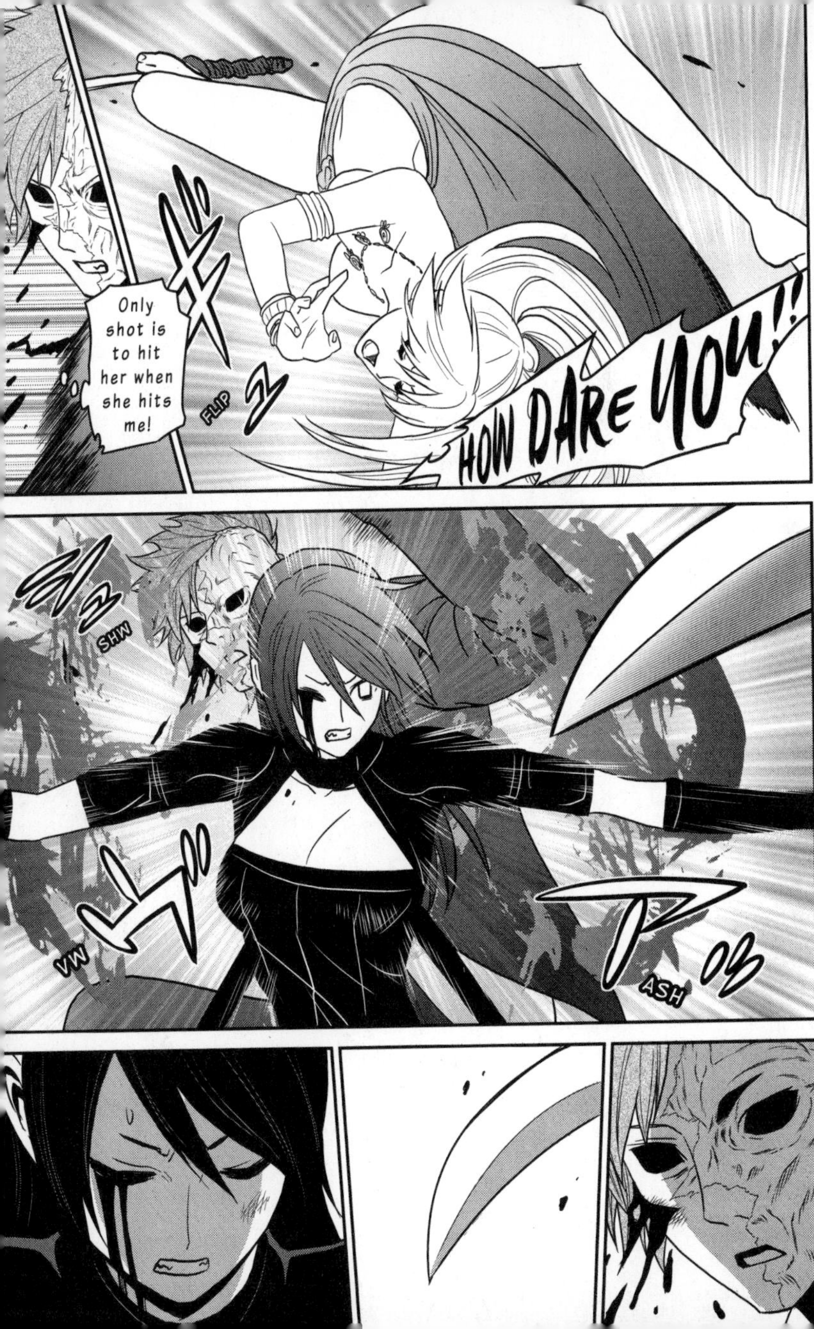
HOW DARE YOU!!
FLIP
Only shot is to hit her when she hits me!
ASH
SHW
VW

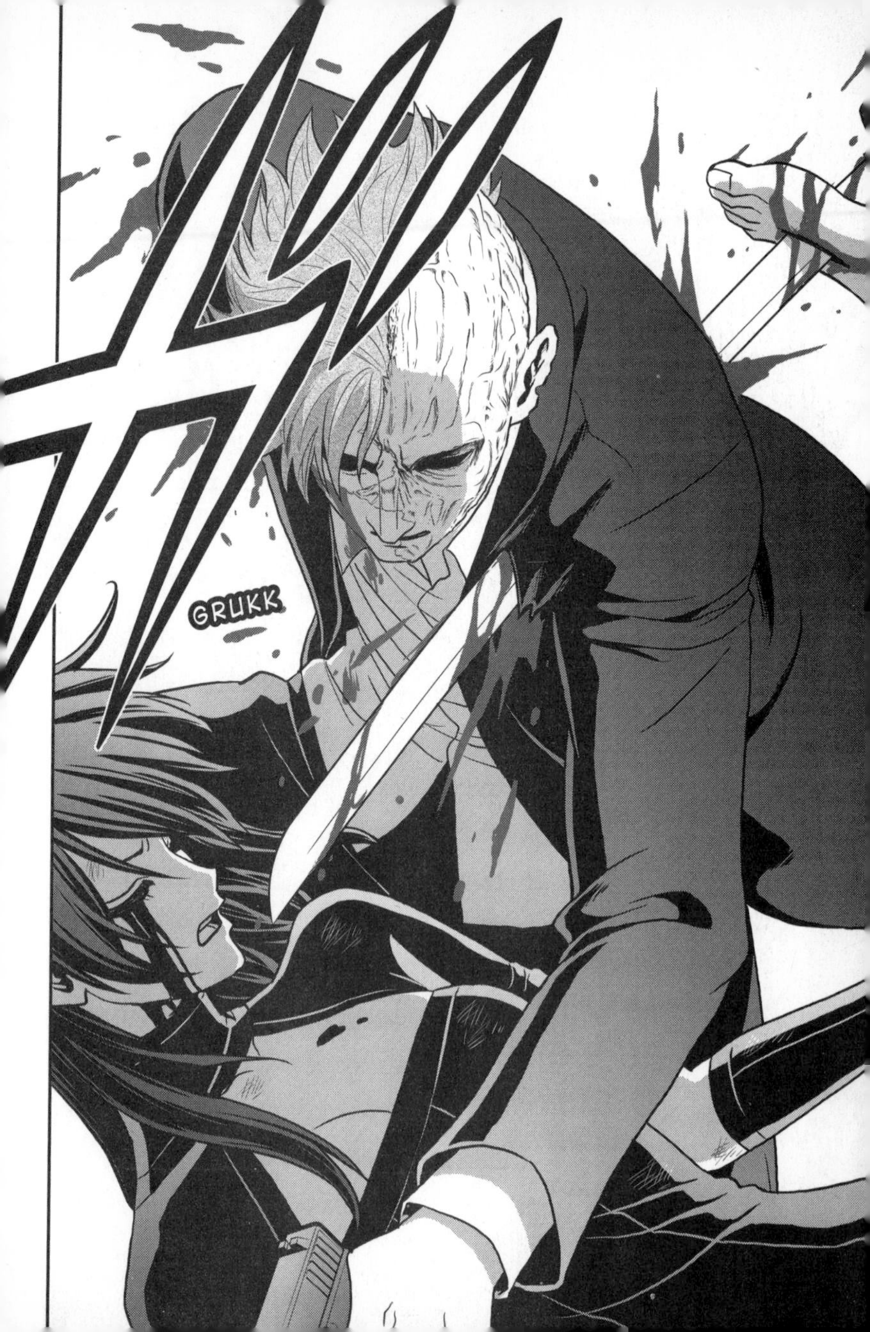
GRUKK

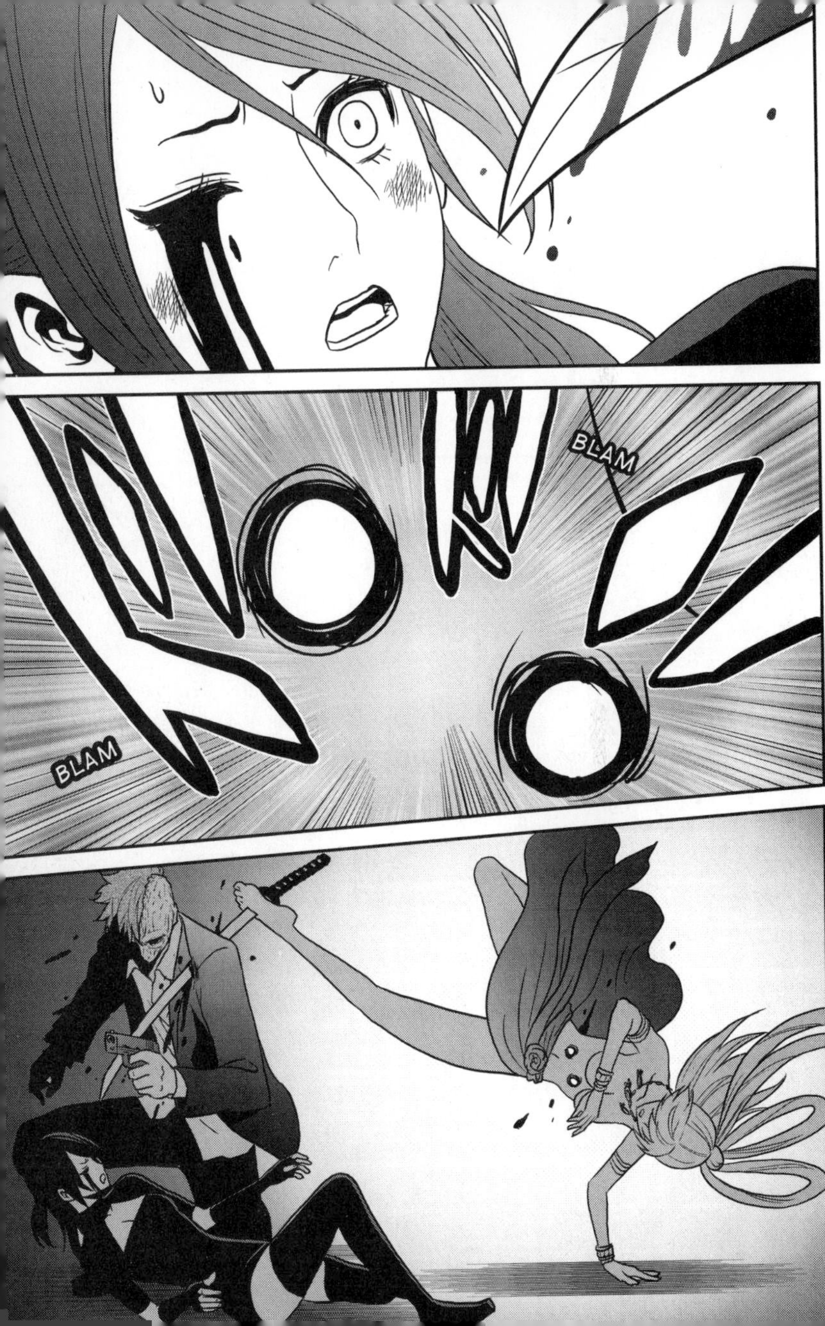
BLAM
BLAM

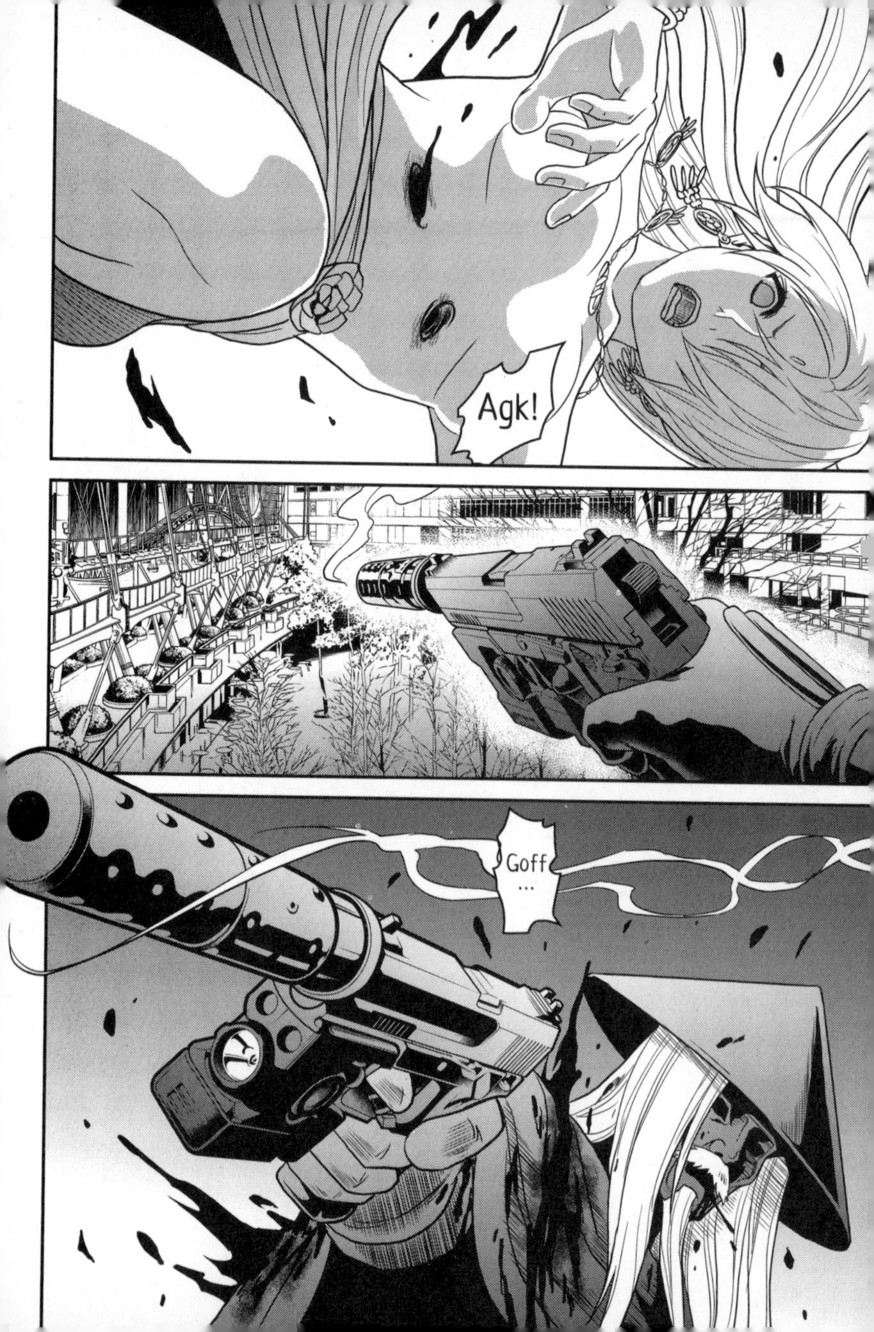
Agk!
Goff
...

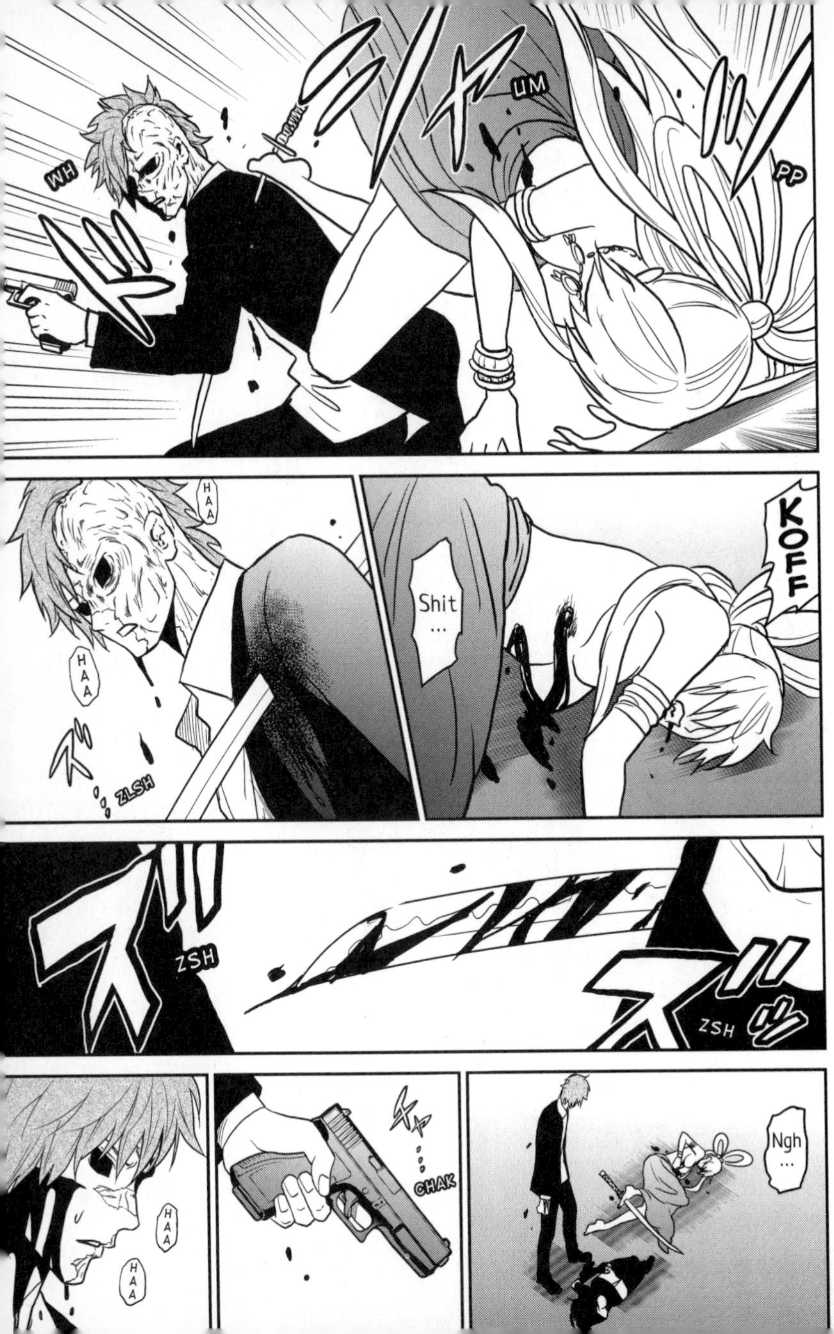
WH
UM
PP
KOFF
Shit ...
HAA
HAA
ZLSH
ZSH
ZSH
Ngh ...
CHAK
HAA
HAA

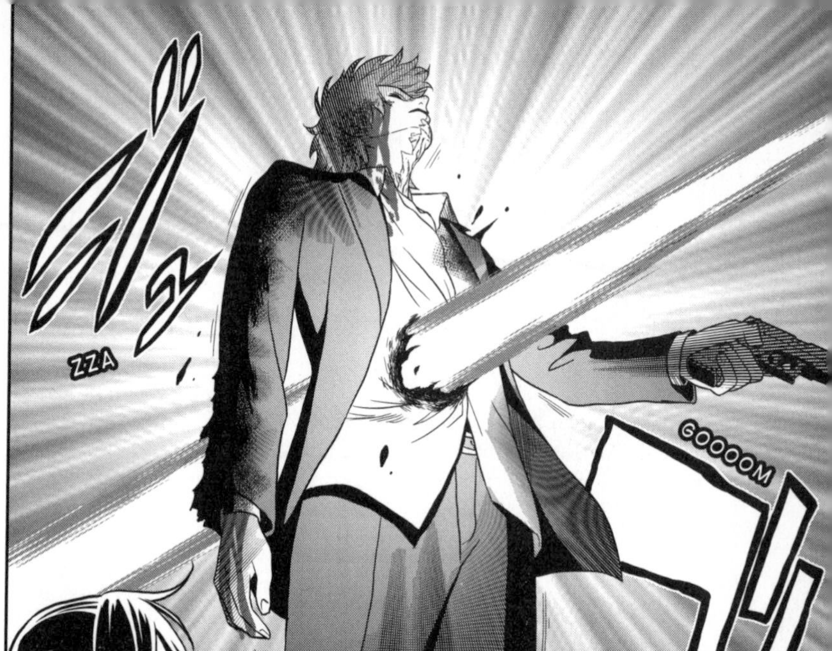
GOOOOM
ZZA
!!
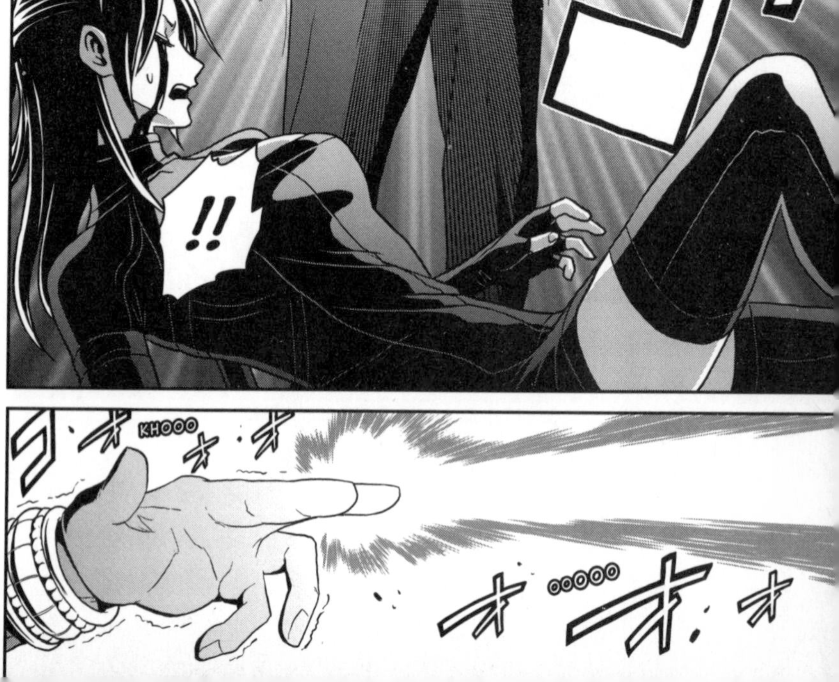
KHOOO
OOOOO

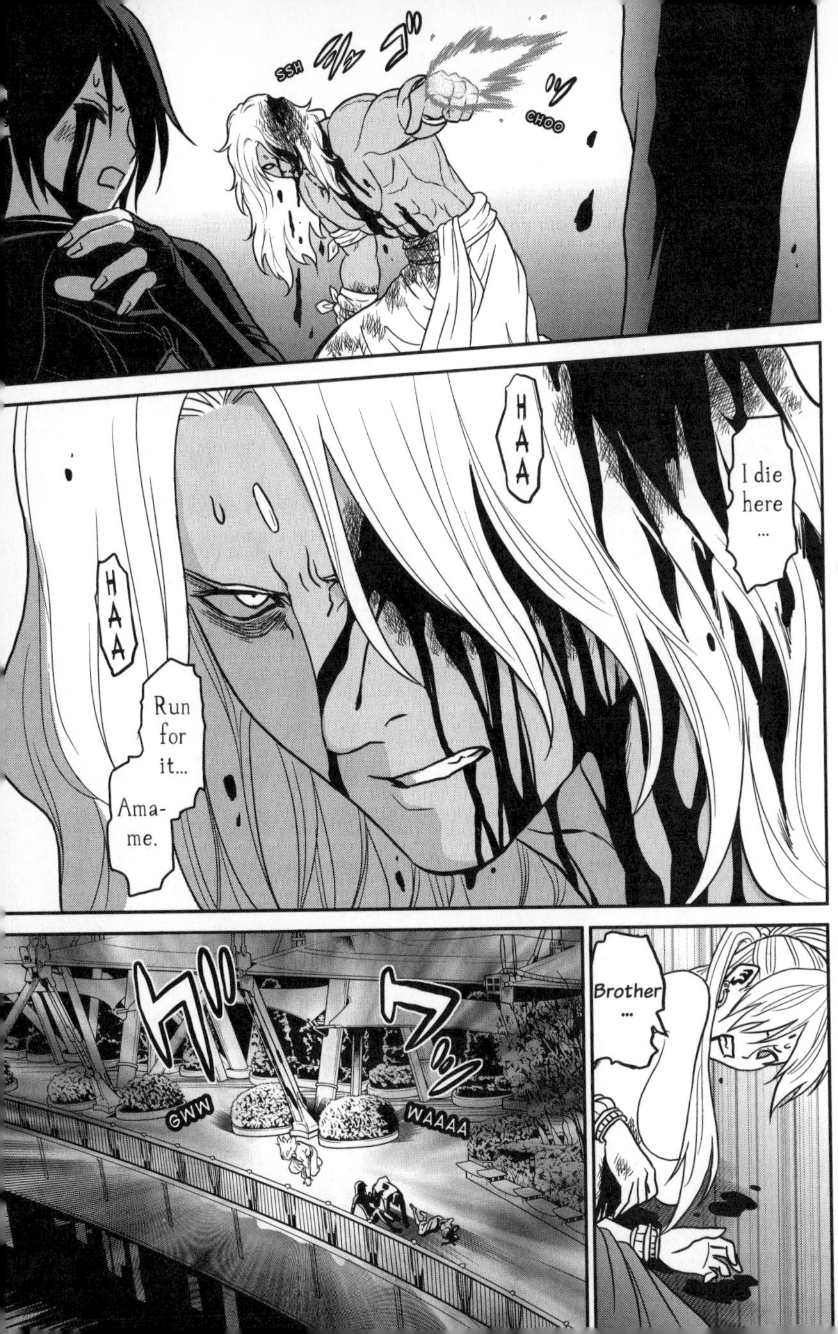
SSH
CHOO
I die here ...
HAA
HAA
Run for it... Ama-me.
Brother ...
WAAAA
GWW

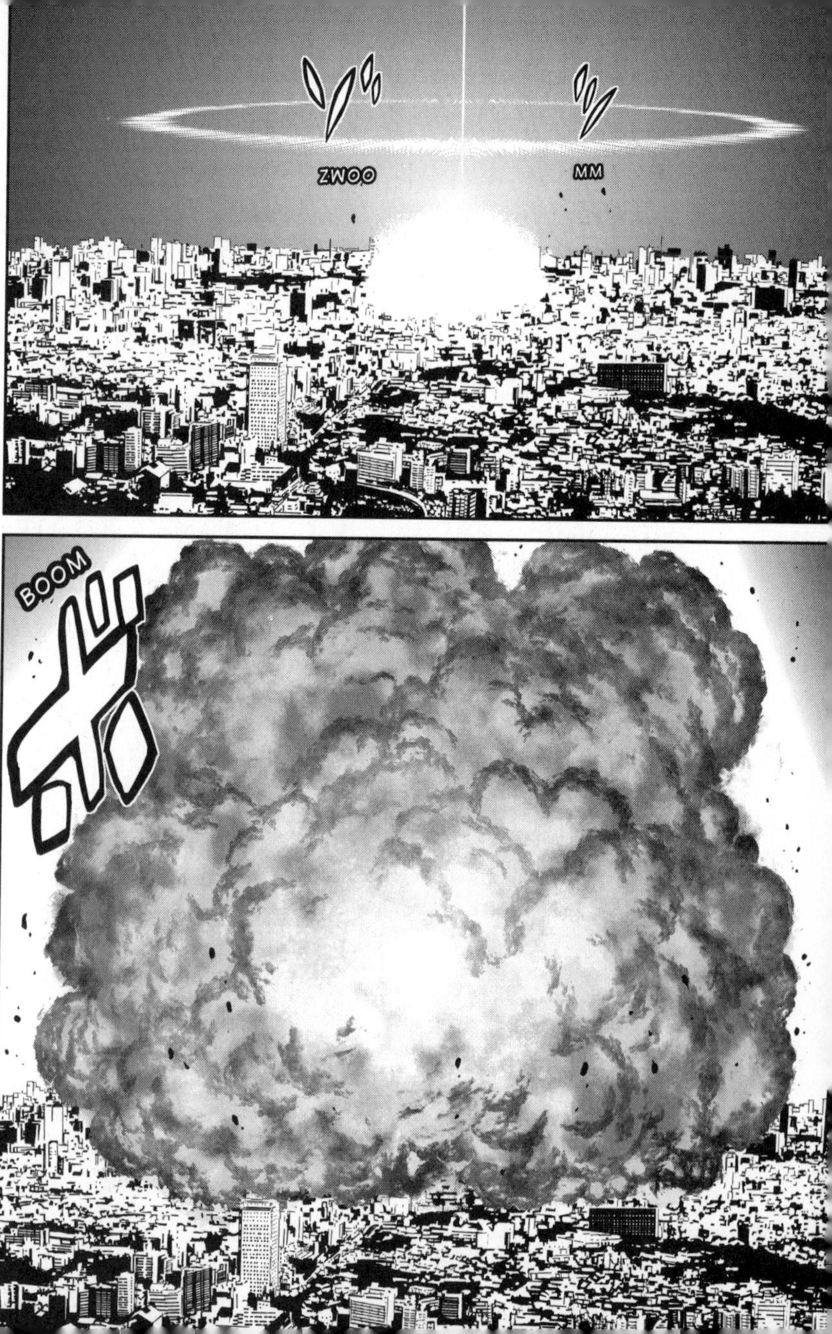
ZWOO
MM
BOOM

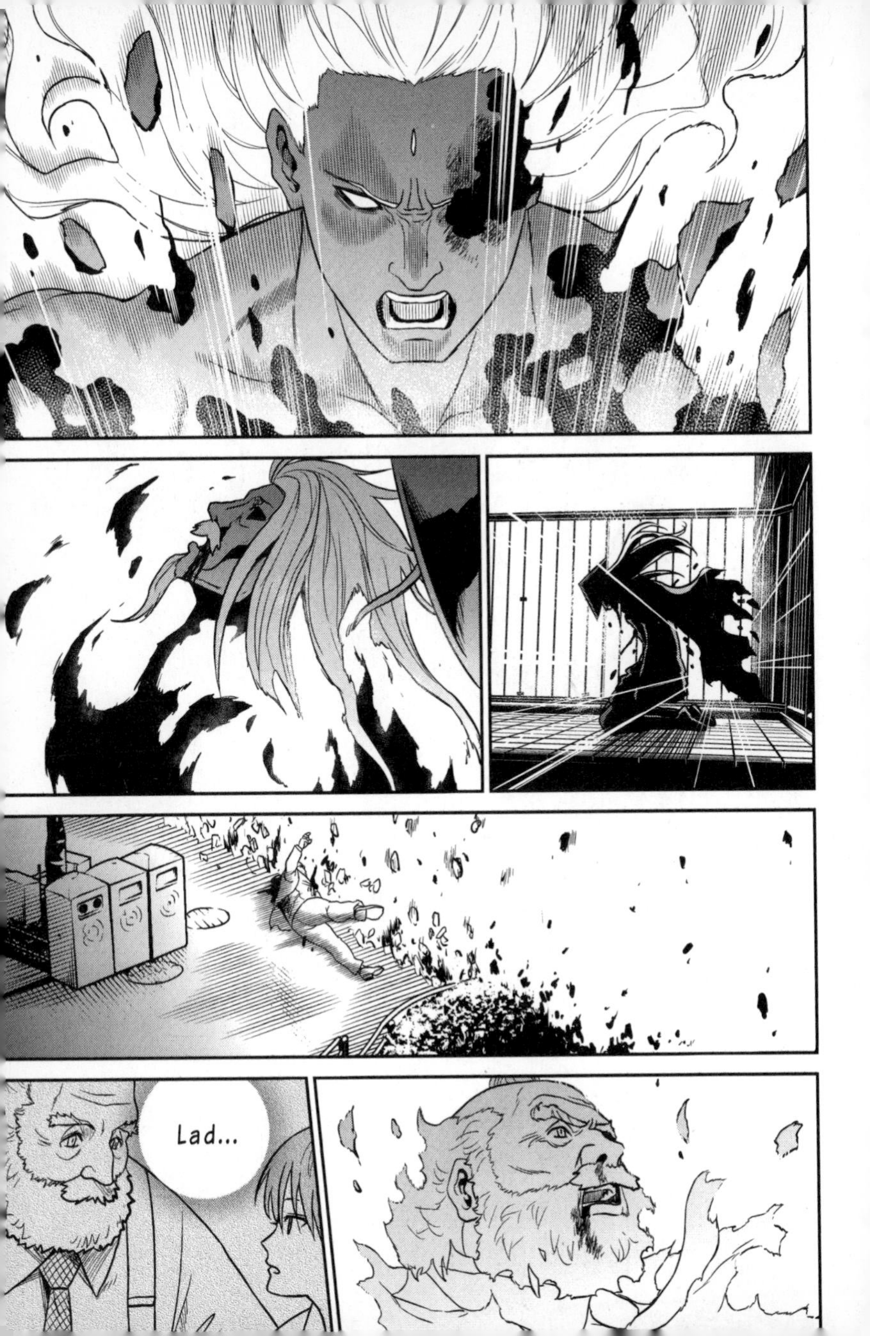
Lad...

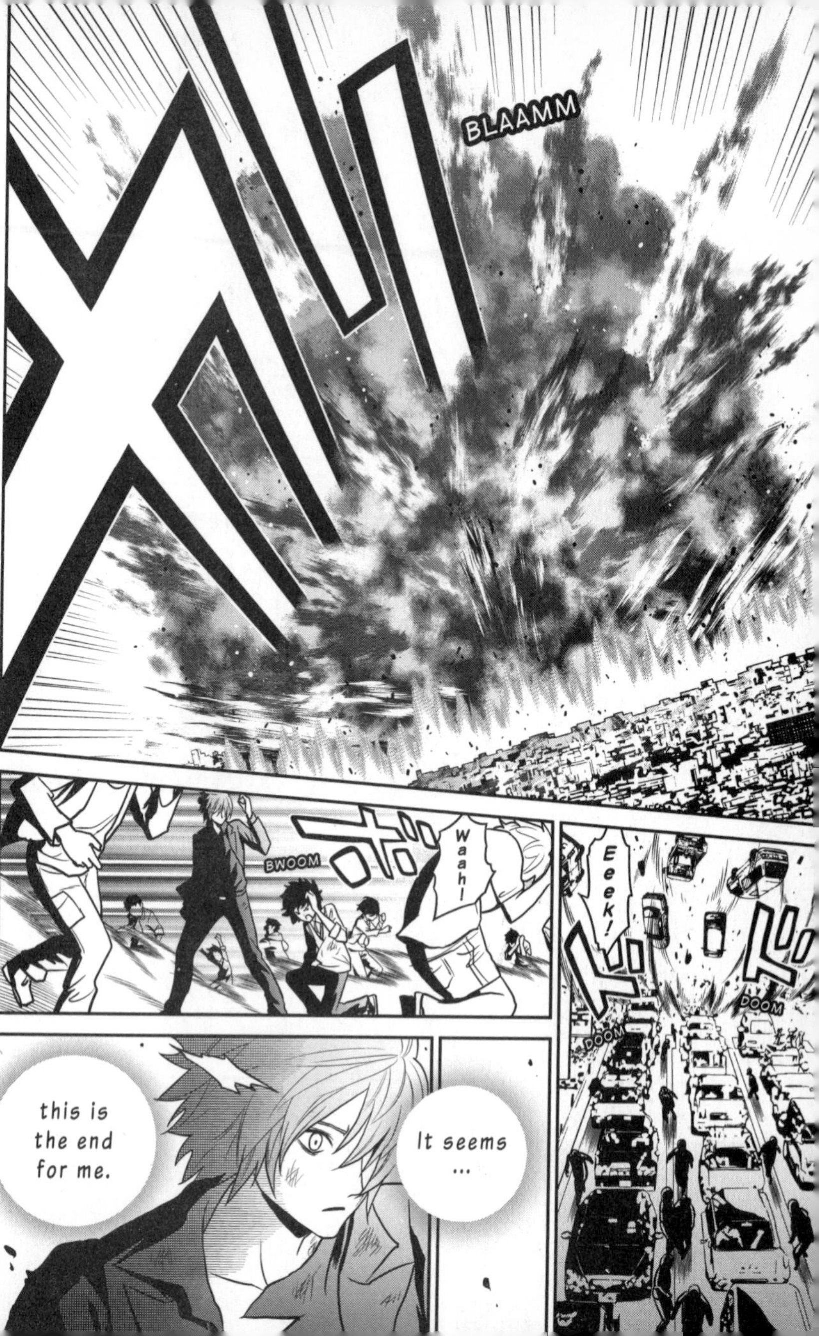
BLAAMM
Eeek!
DOOM
DOOM
Waah!
BWOOM
It seems ...
this is the end for me.

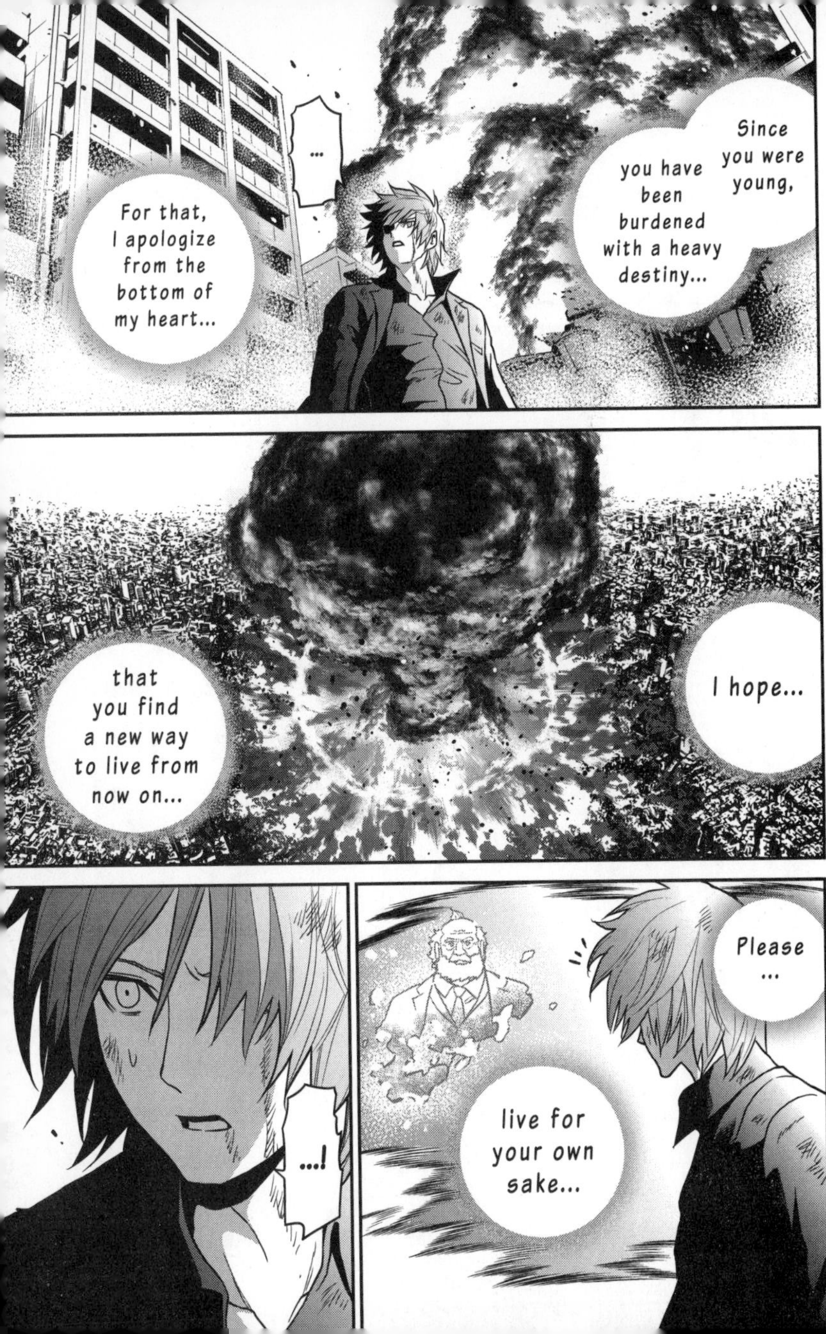
Since you were young,
you have been burdened with a heavy destiny...
...
For that, I apologize from the bottom of my heart...
I hope...
that you find a new way to live from now on...
Please ...
live for your own sake...
...!

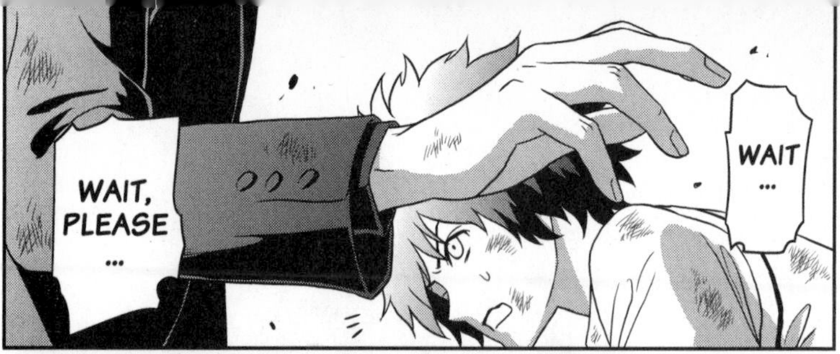
WAIT ...
WAIT, PLEASE ...

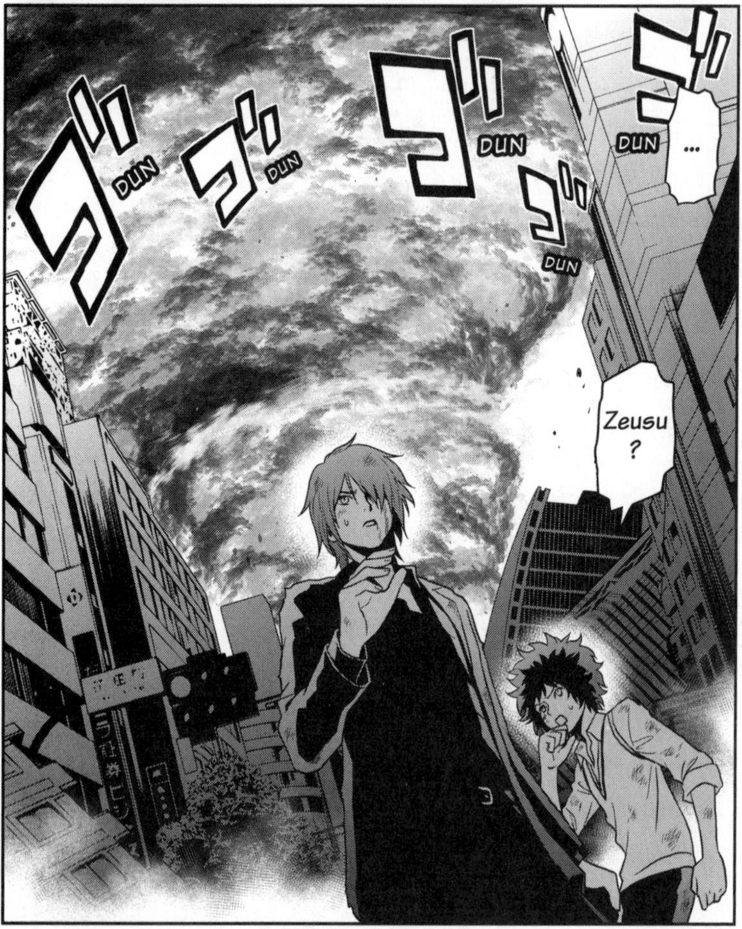
...
DUN
DUN
DUN
DUN
DUN
Zeusu ?

SCENE 71 /// END

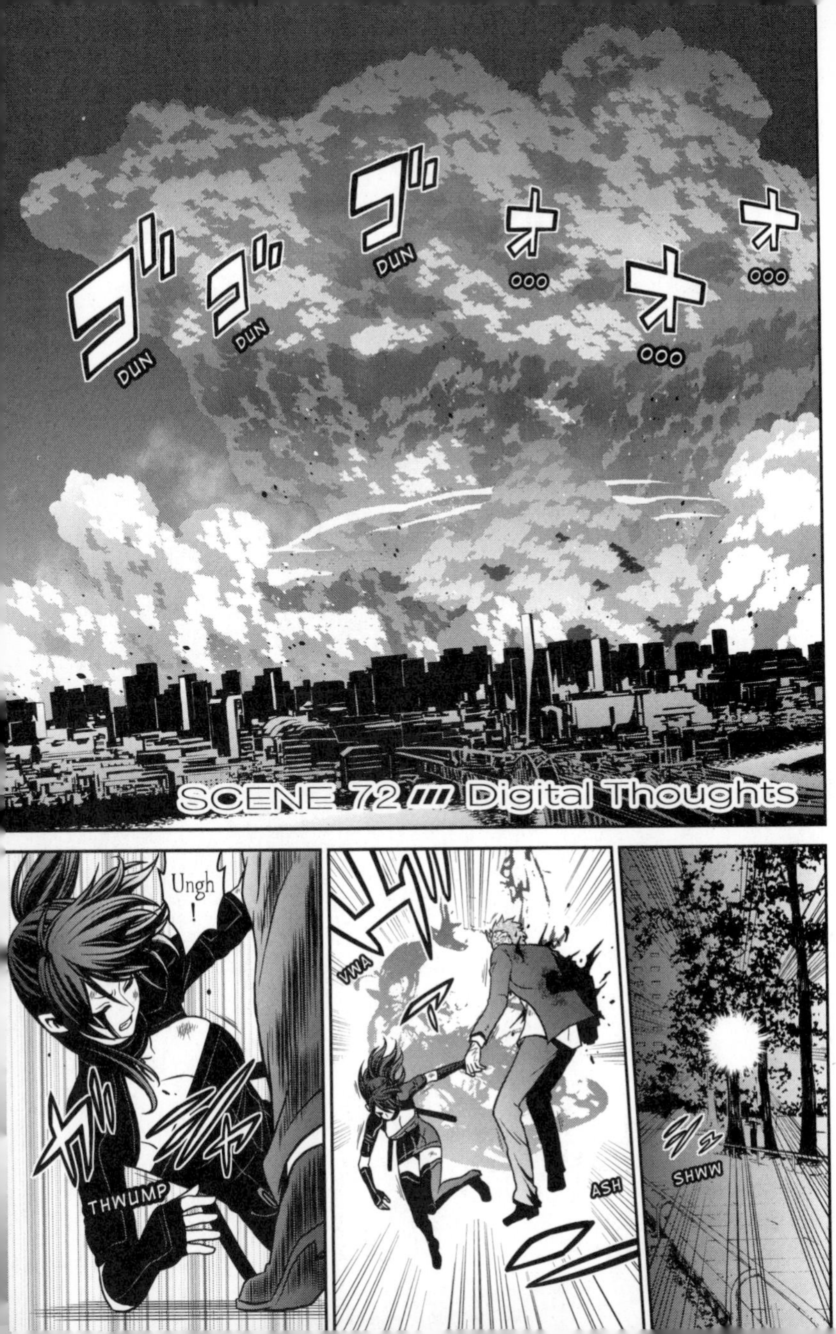
ゴ
DUN
ゴ
DUN
ゴ
DUN
オ
ooo
オ
ooo
オ
ooo
SCENE 72 /// Digital Thoughts
SHWW
VWA
ASH
Ungh!
THWUMP

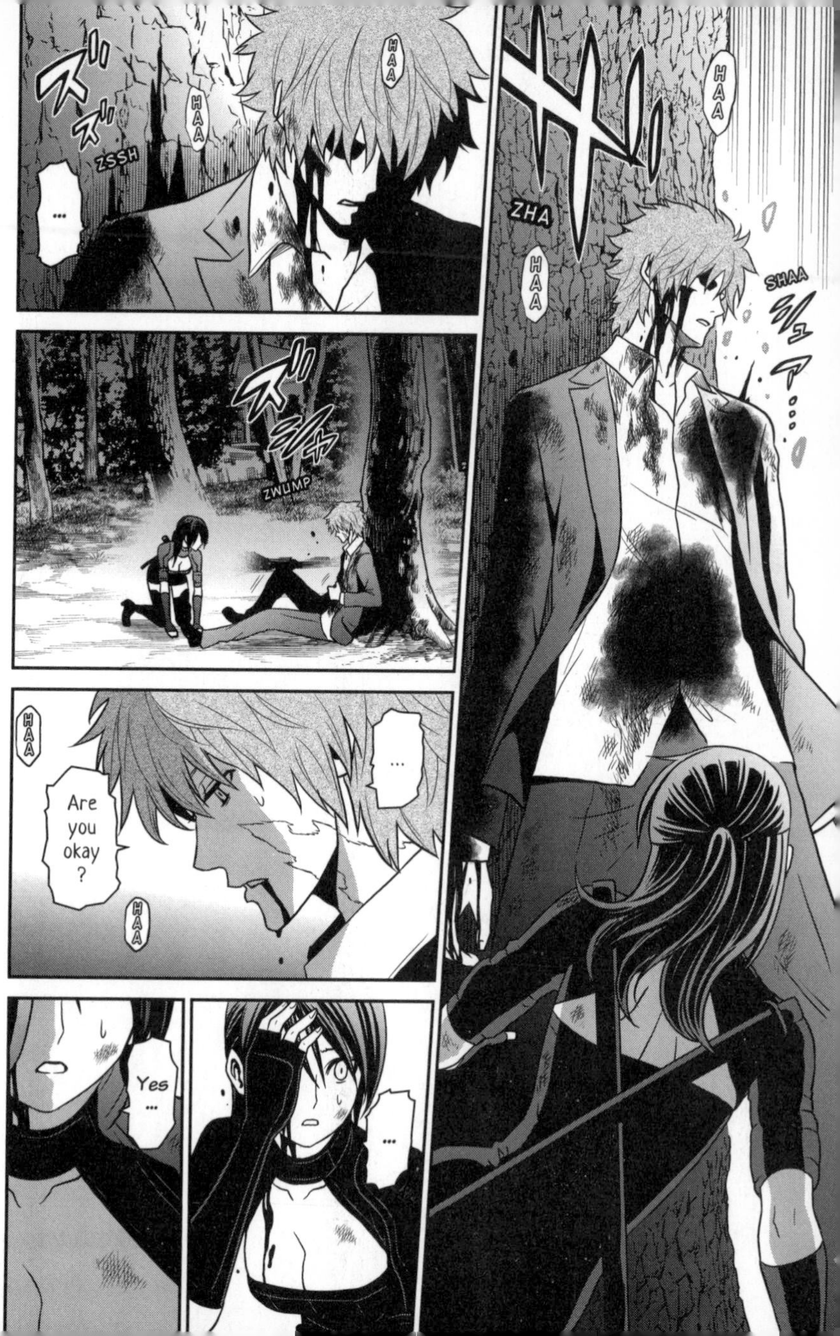
HAA
ZHA
HAA
SHAA
シュア…
ズズ
ZSSH
HAA
HAA
...
ズズ
ZWUMP
...
HAA
Are you okay?
HAA
...
Yes ...

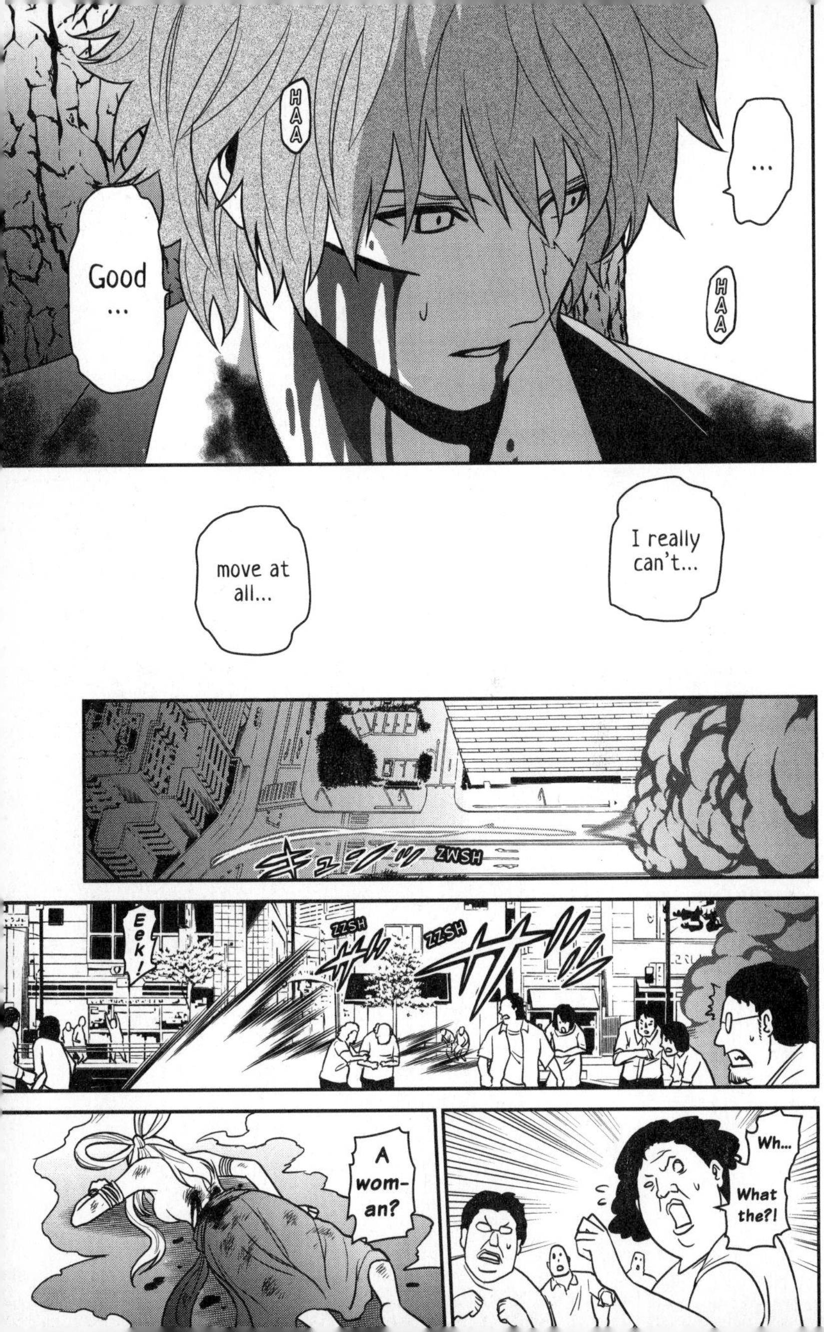
...
HAA
HAA
Good ...
I really can't...
move at all...
ZWSH
ZZSH
ZZSH
Eek!
Wh...
What the?!
A woman?

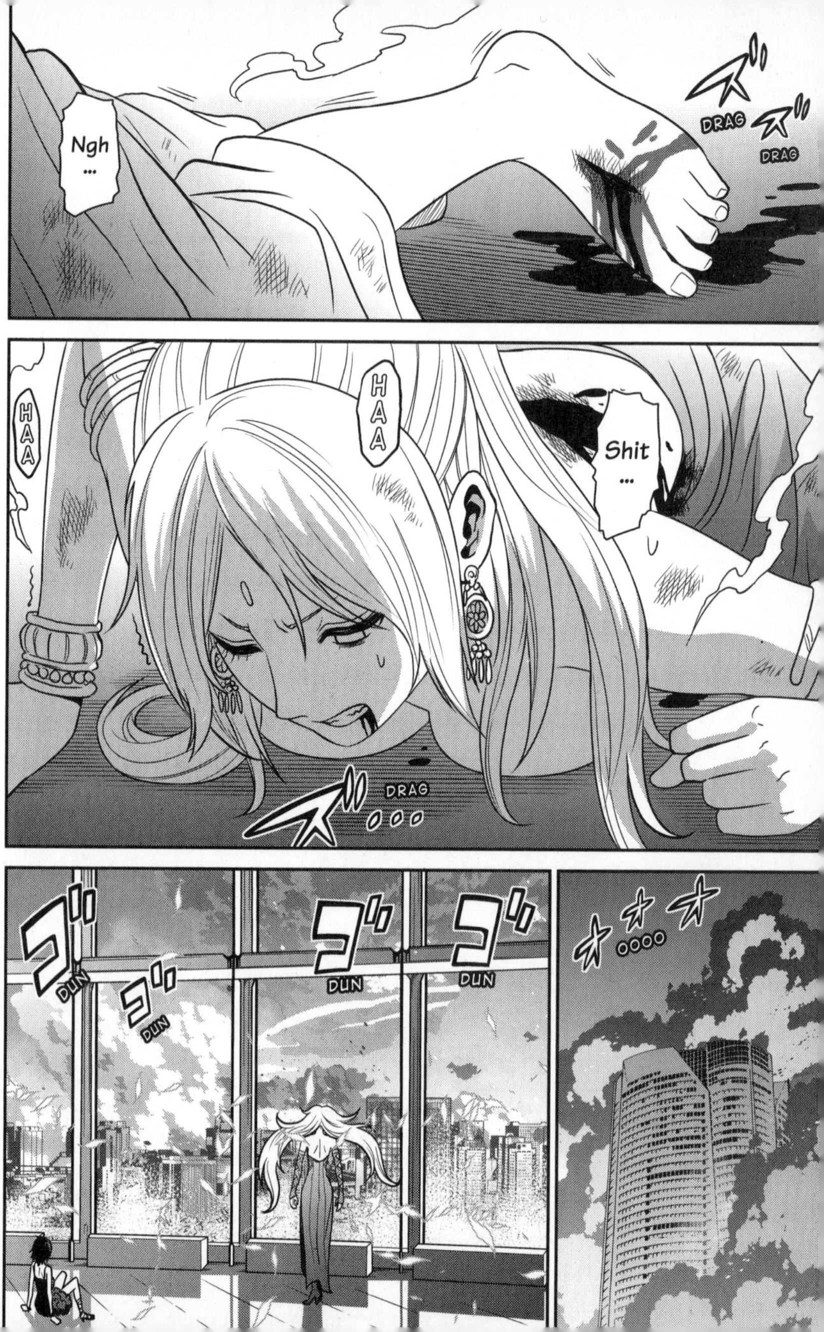
DRAG
DRAG
Ngh...
Shit...
HAA
HAA
DRAG
OOO
OOOO
DUN
DUN
DUN
DUN

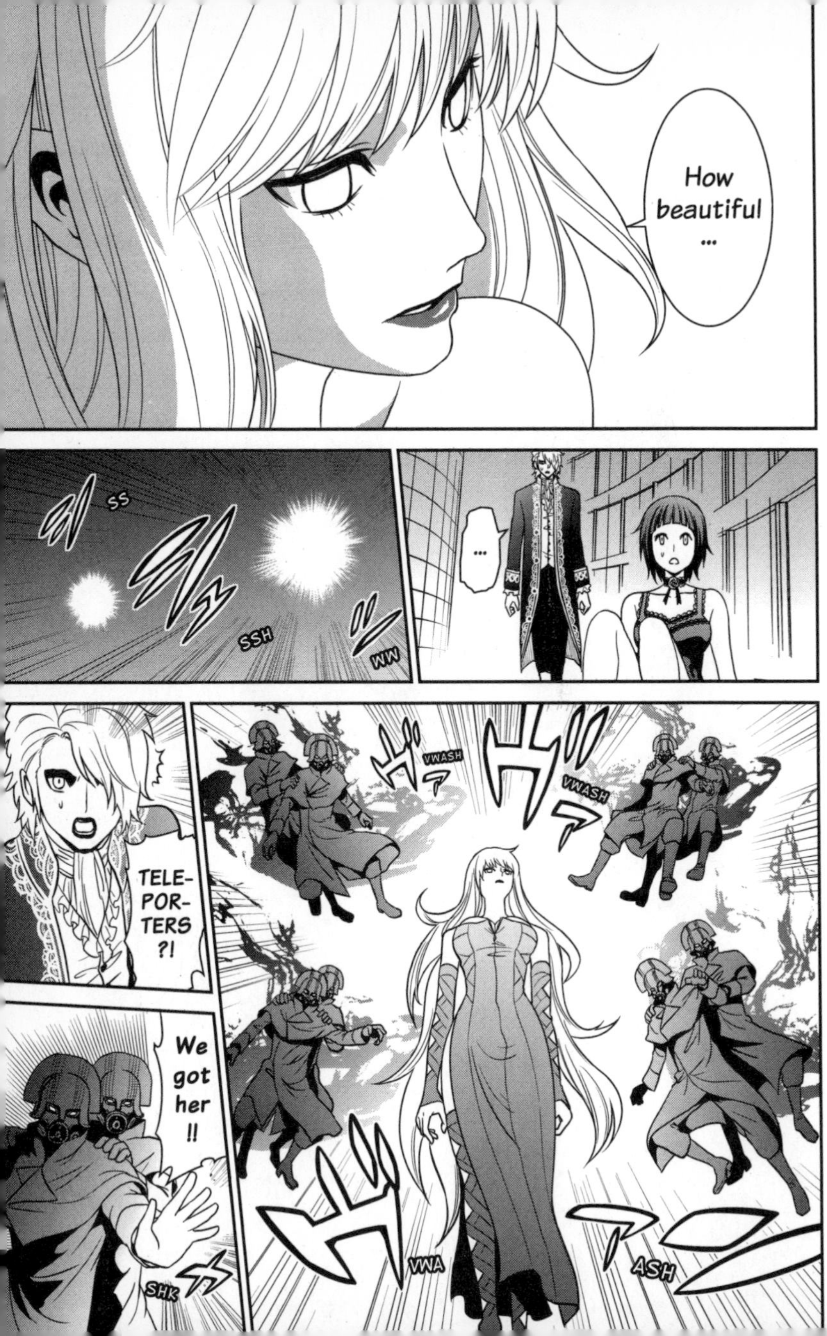
How beautiful ...
...
SS
SSH
WW
VWASH
VWASH
ASH
VWA
TELE-POR-TERS ?!
We got her !!
SHK

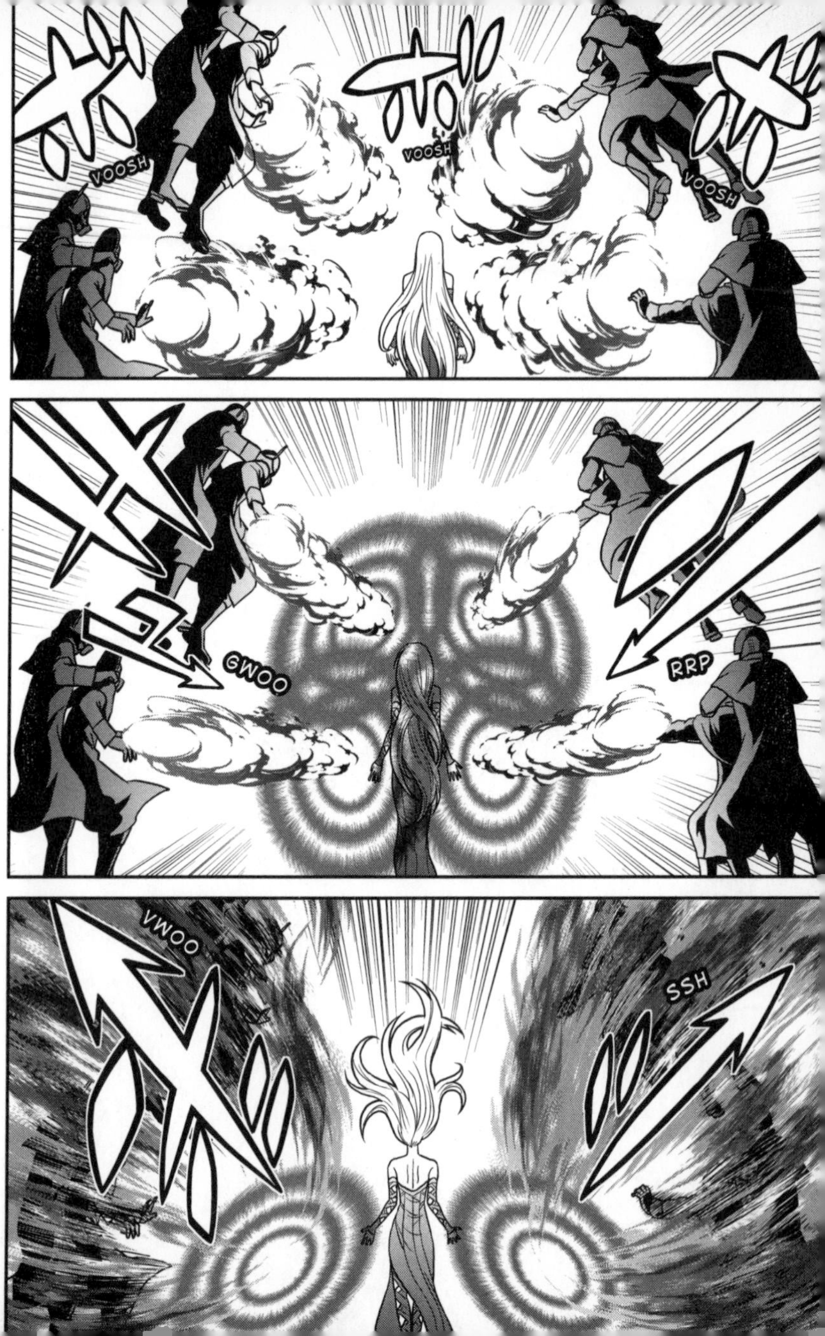
VOOSH
VOOSH
VOOSH
RRP
GWOO
SSH
VWOO

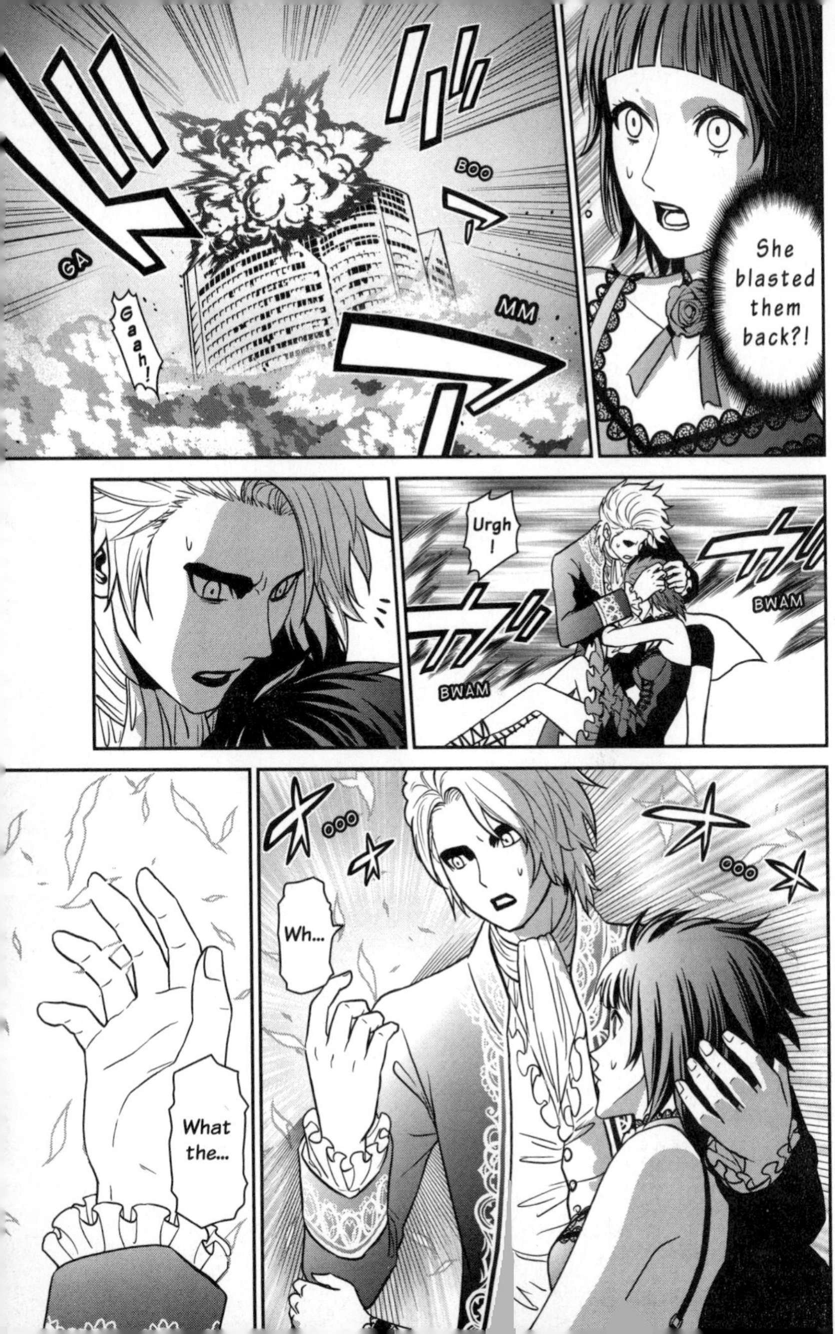
She blasted them back?!
GA
BOO
MM
Gaah!
Urgh!
BWAM
BWAM
ooo
ooo
Wh...
What the...

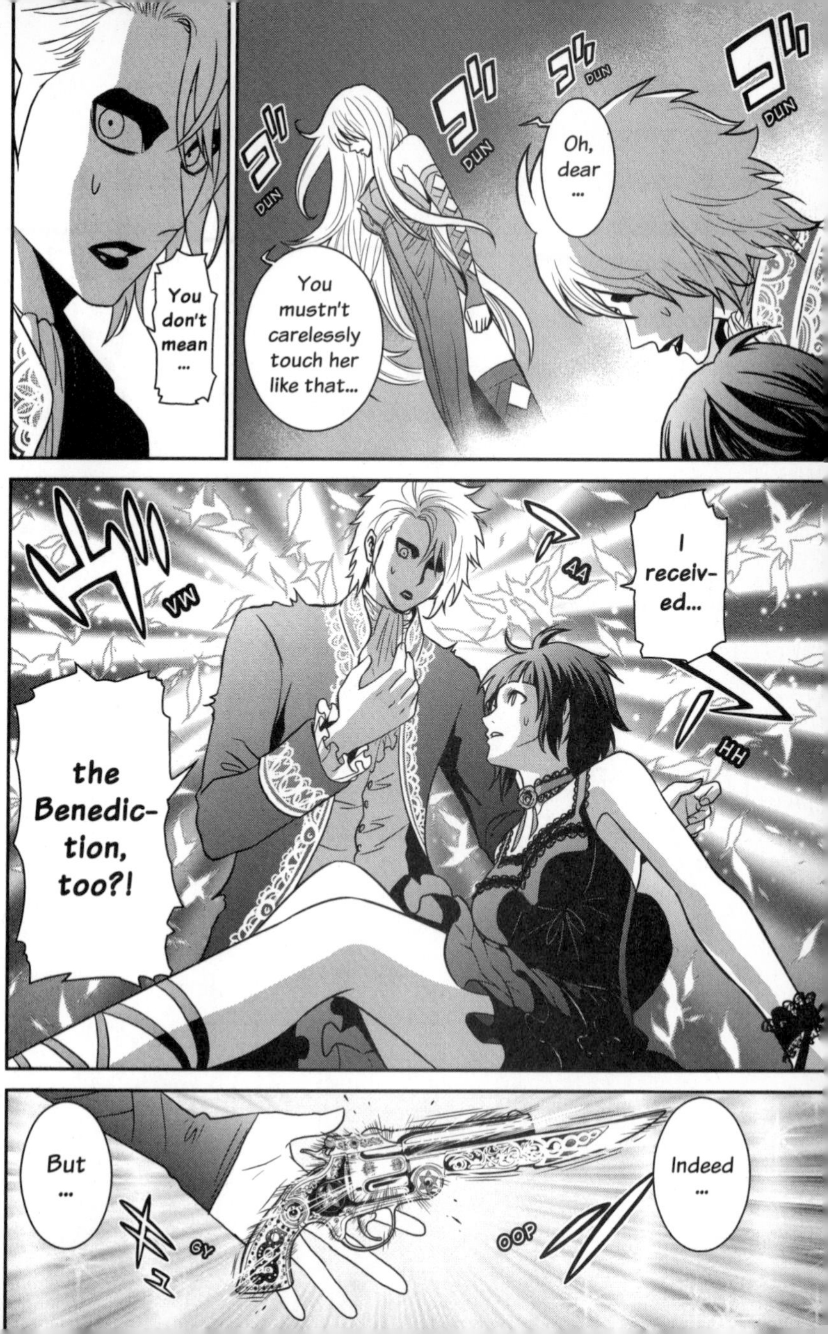
DUN
Oh, dear ...
DUN
DUN
DUN
You mustn't carelessly touch her like that...
You don't mean ...
I receiv-ed...
AA
VW
HH
the Benedic-tion, too?!
Indeed ...
OOP
But ...
GY

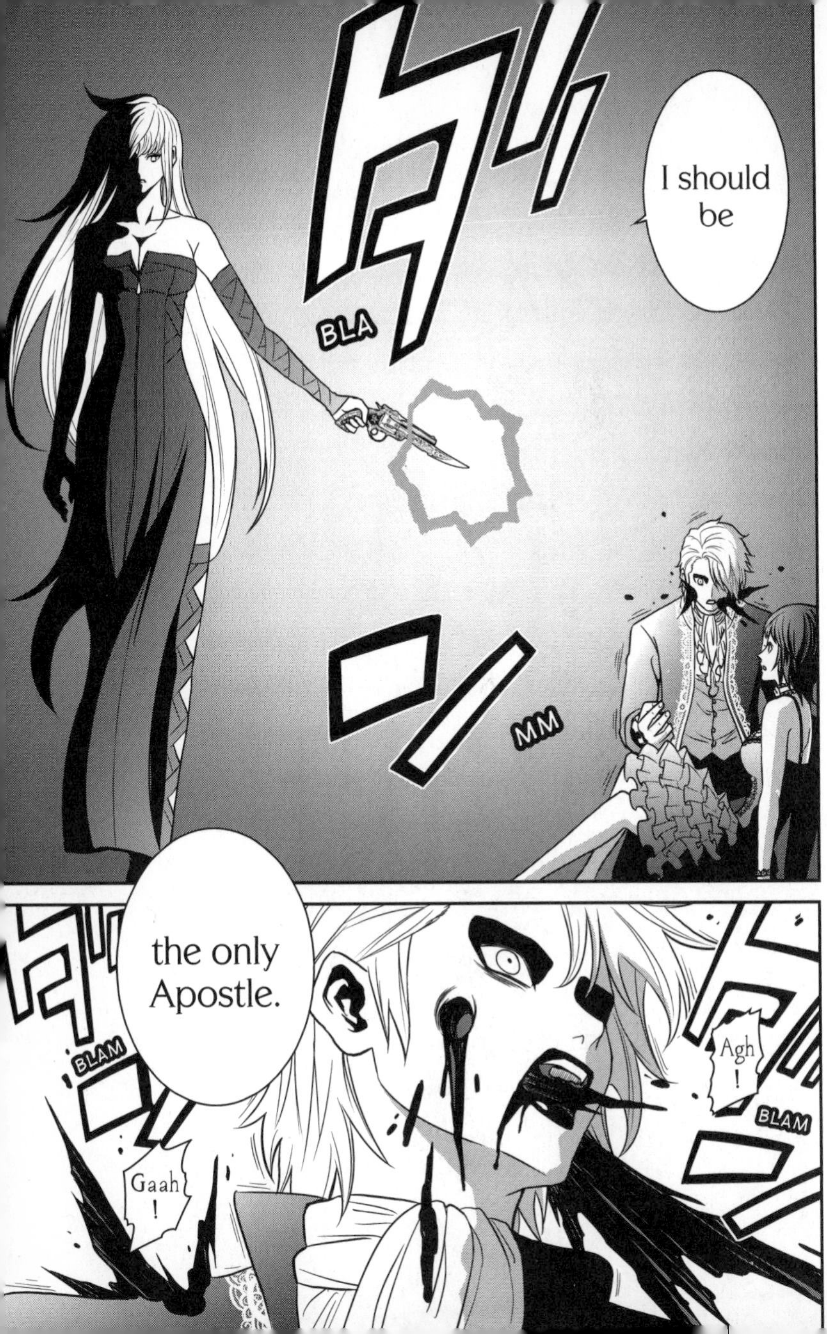
I should be
BLA
MM
Agh!
BLAM
the only Apostle.
BLAM
Gaah!

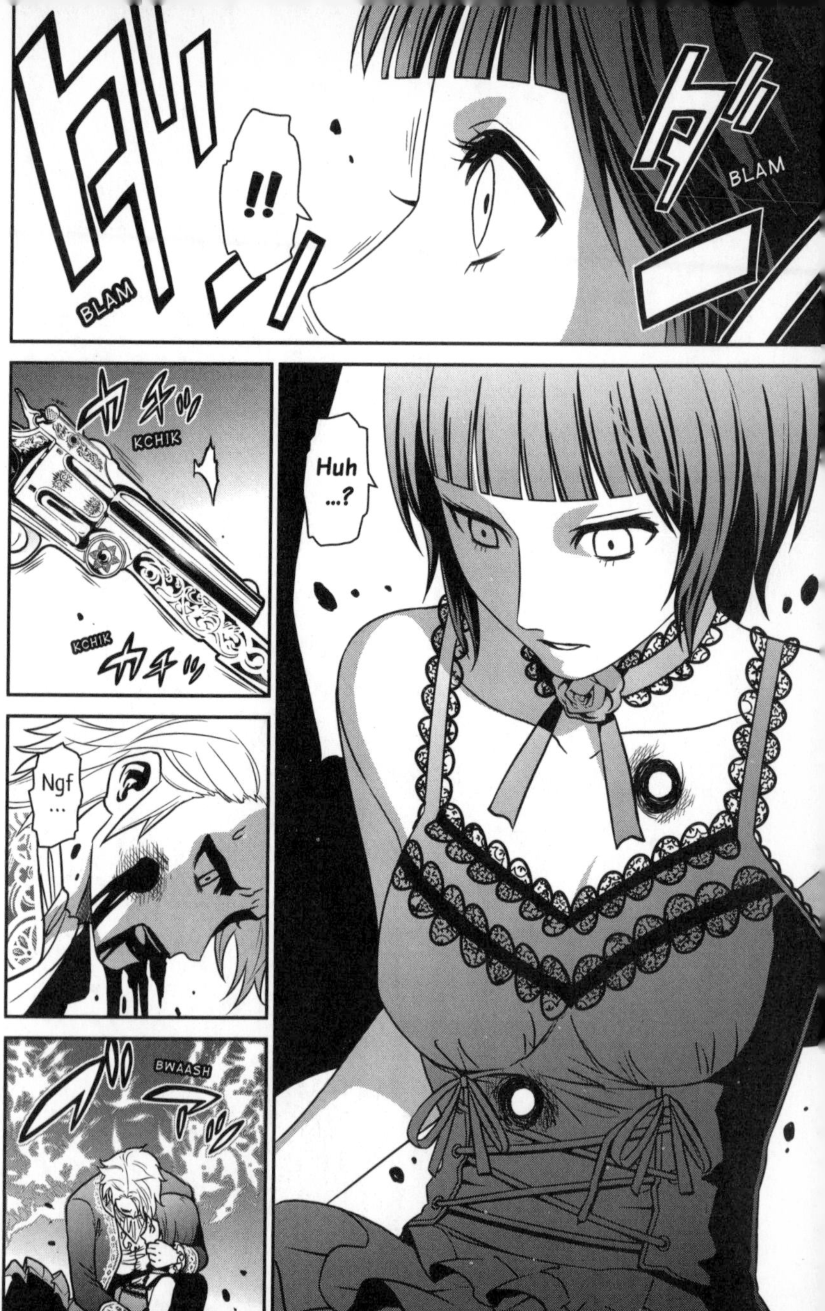
BLAM
!!
BLAM
Huh ...?
KCHIK
KCHIK
Ngf ...
BWAASH

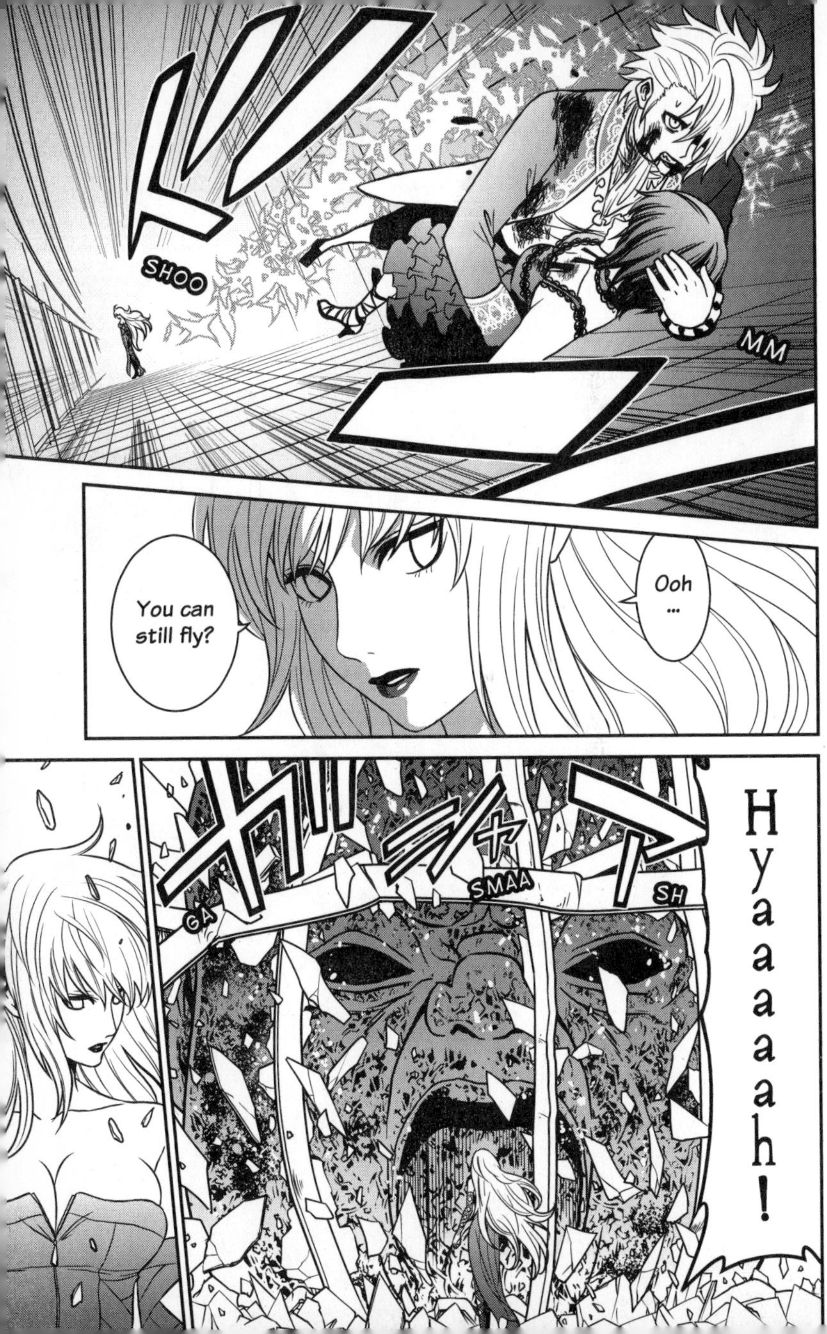
MM
SHOO
Ooh ...
You can still fly?
Hyaaaaaah!
SH
SMAA
GA

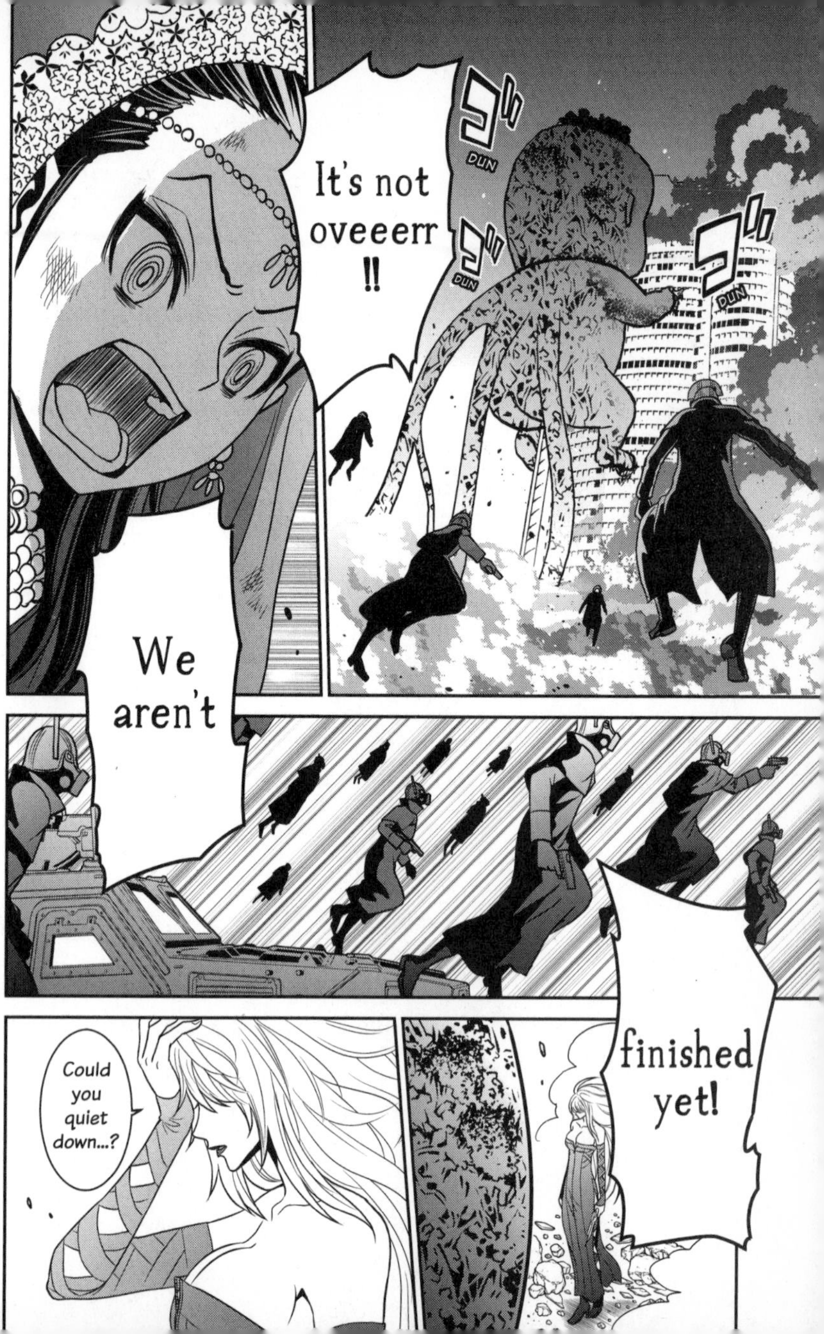

DUN
DUN
DUN
It's not oveeerr!!
We aren't
finished yet!
Could you quiet down...?

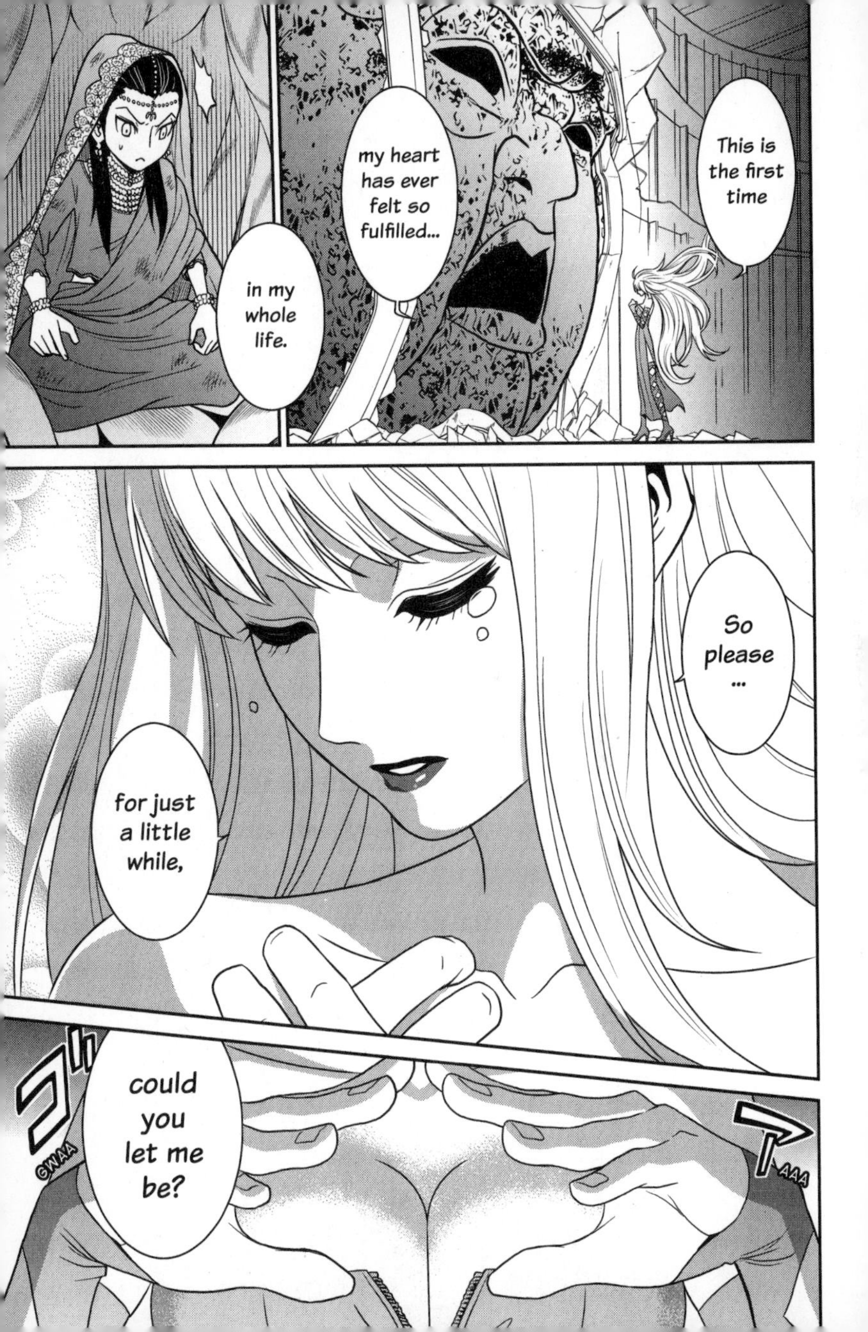
This is the first time
my heart has ever felt so fulfilled...
in my whole life.
So please ...
for just a little while,
could you let me be?
GWAA
AAA

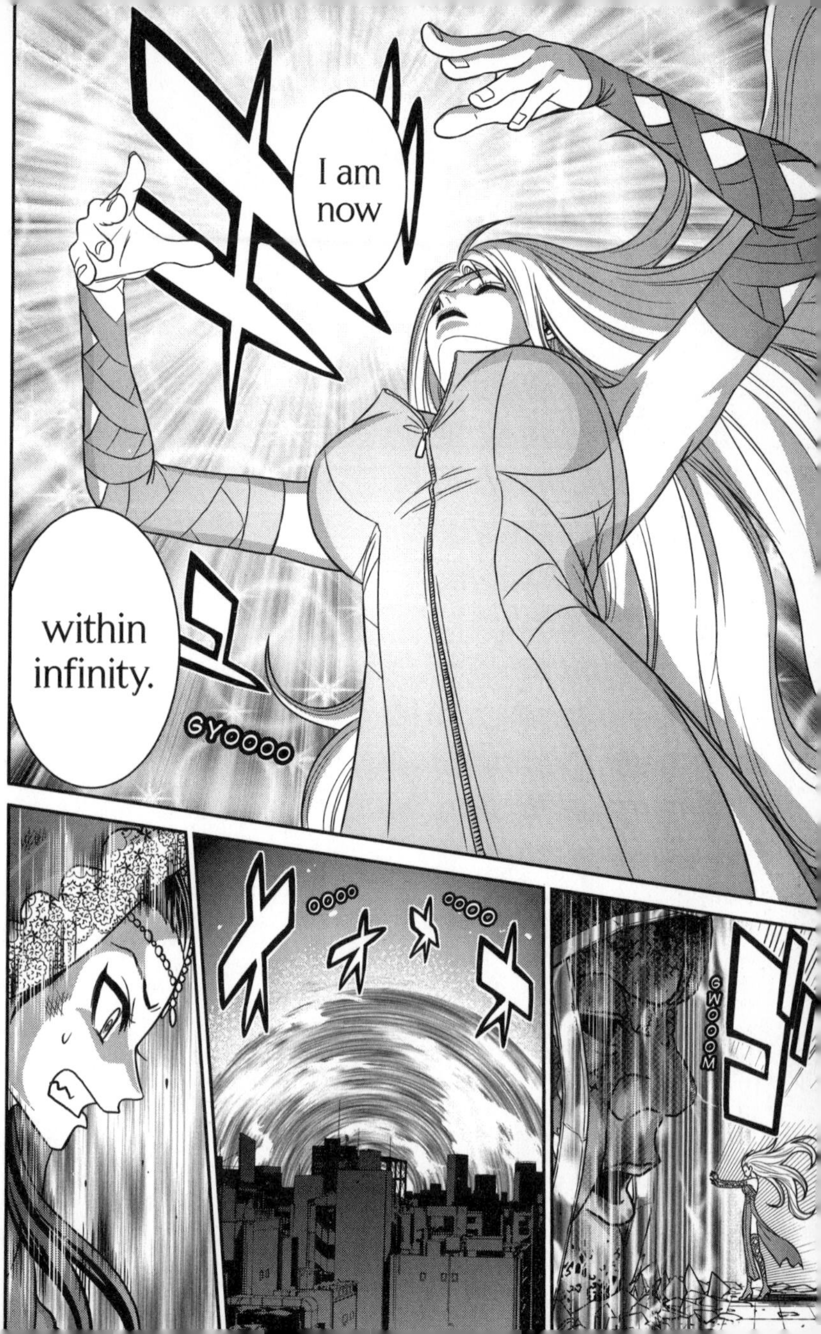
I am now
within infinity.
GYOOOOO
GWOOOOM
OOOO
OOOO

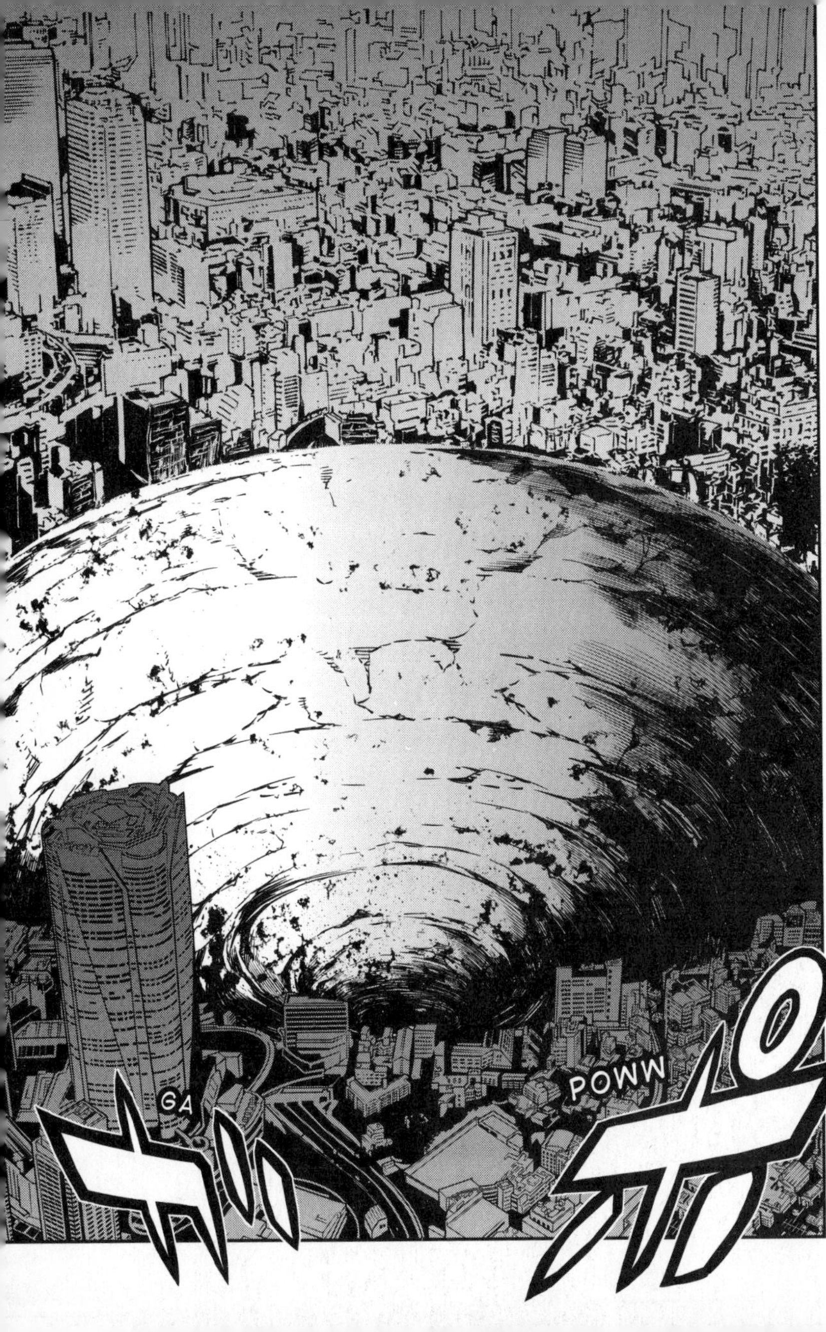
POWW
GA

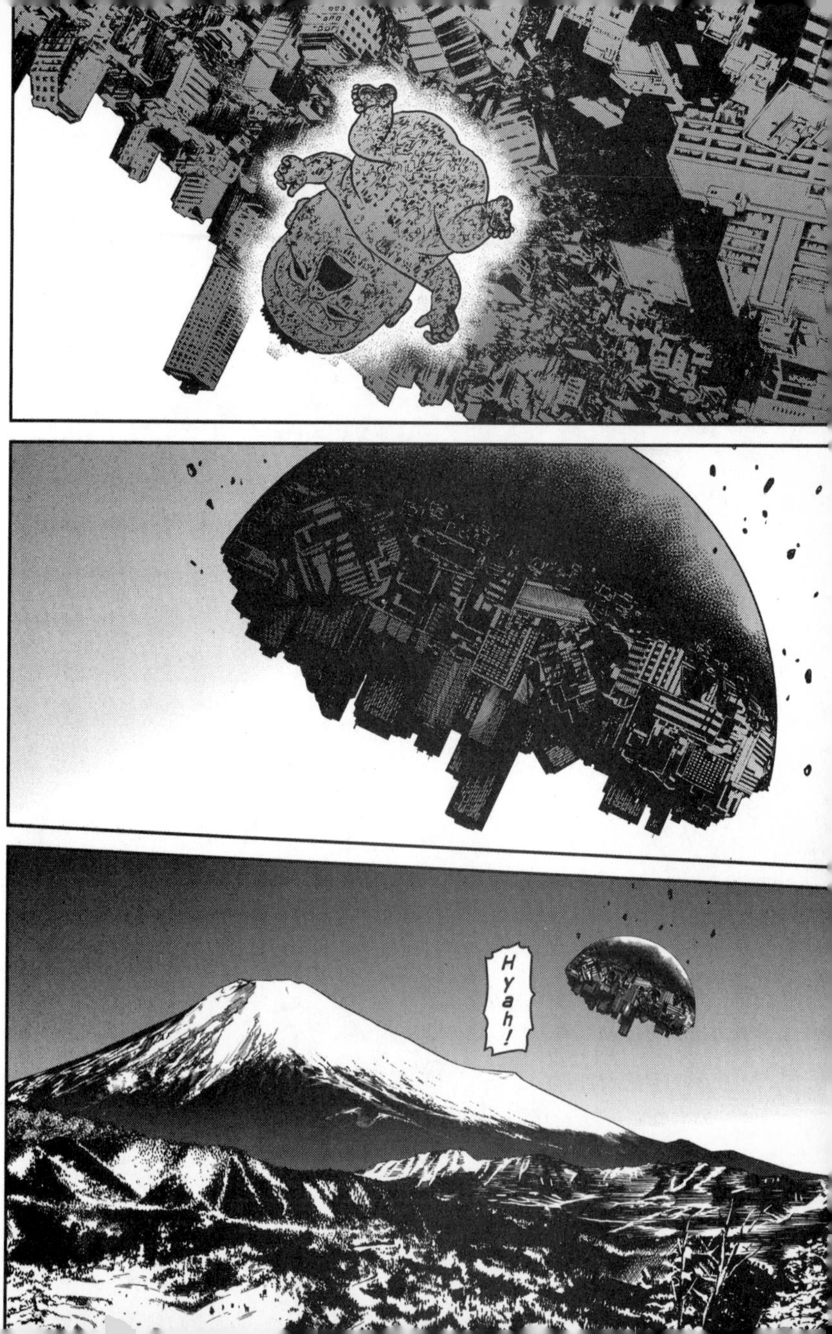
Hyah!

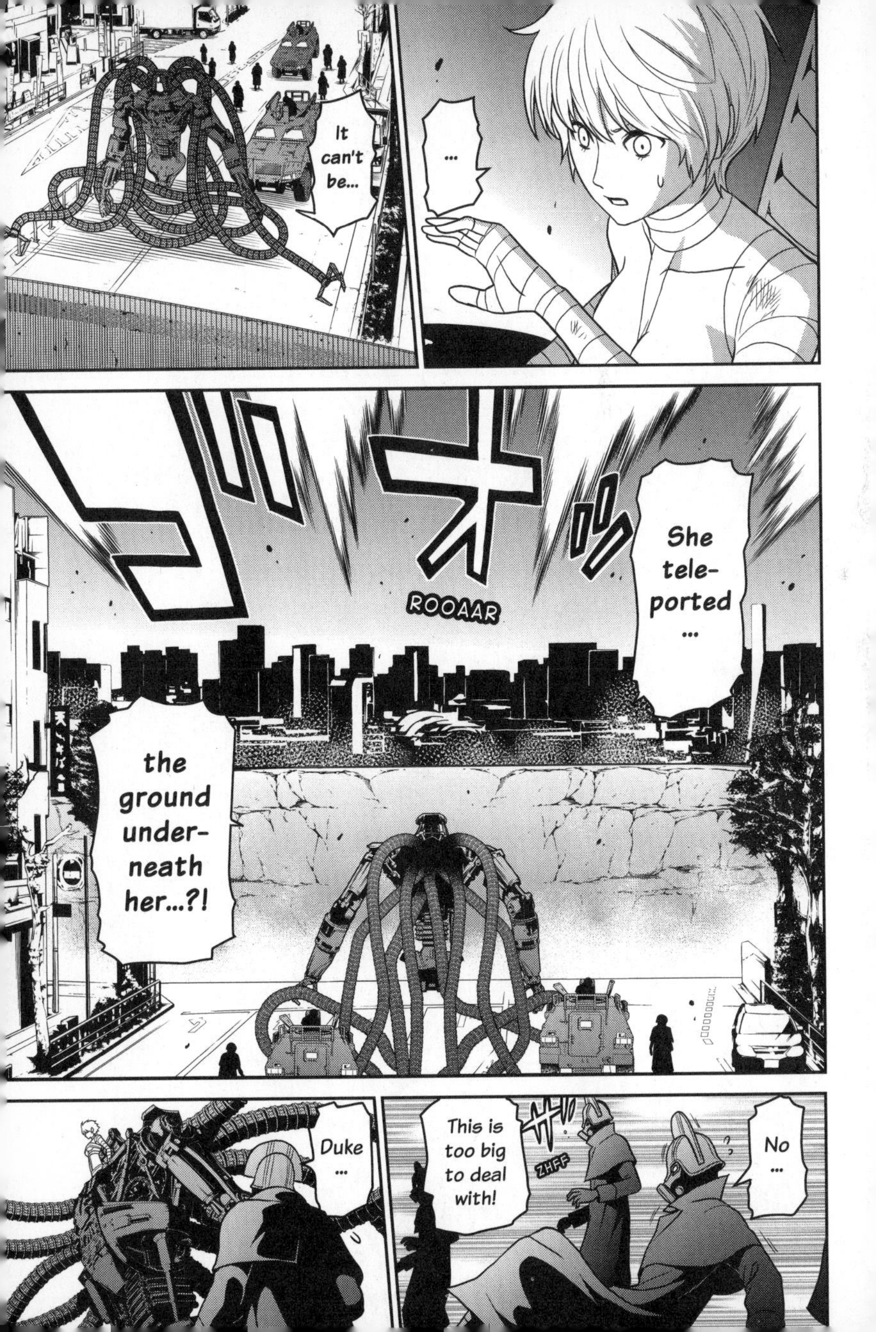
...
It can't be...
She tele-ported...
ROOAAR
the ground under-neath her...?!
No...
This is too big to deal with!
ZHFF
Duke...

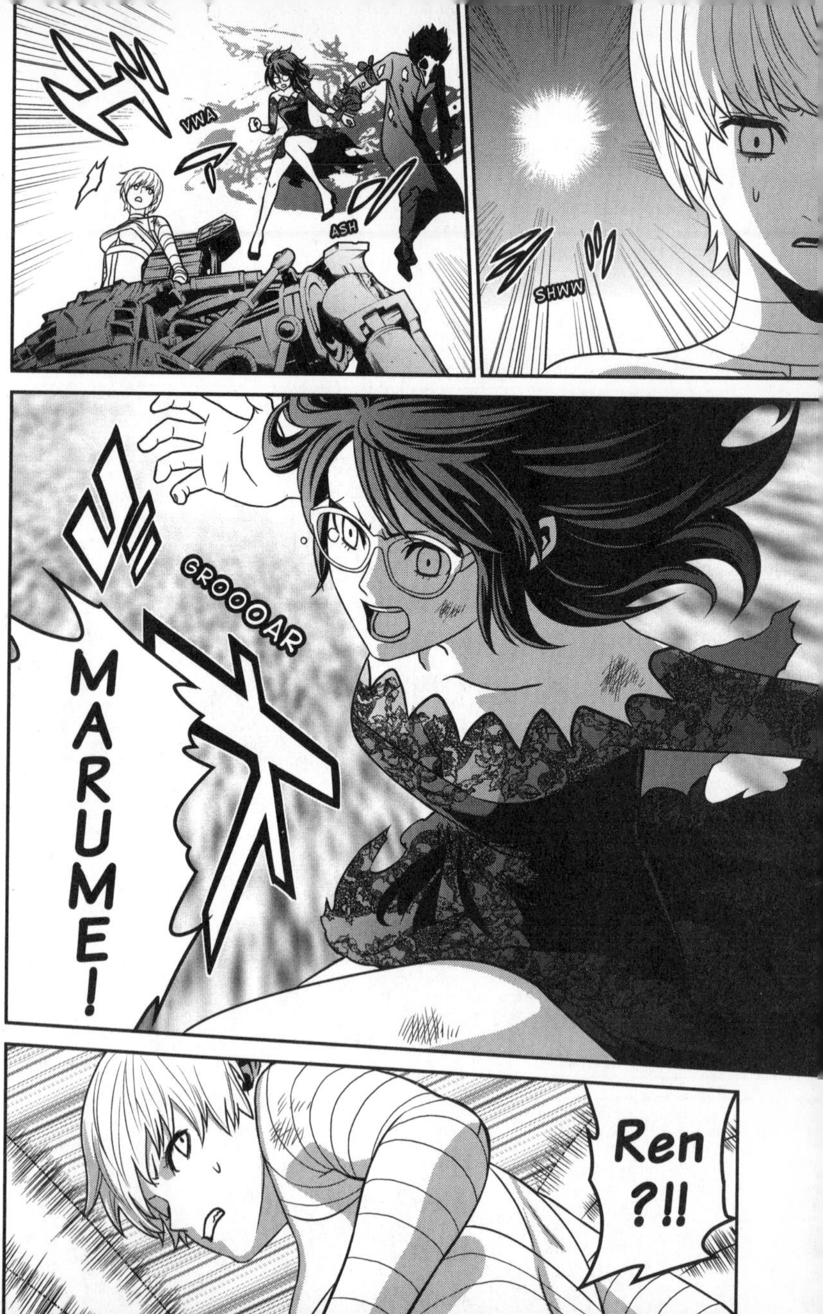
SHWW
VWA
ASH
GROOOOAR
MARUME!
Ren ?!!

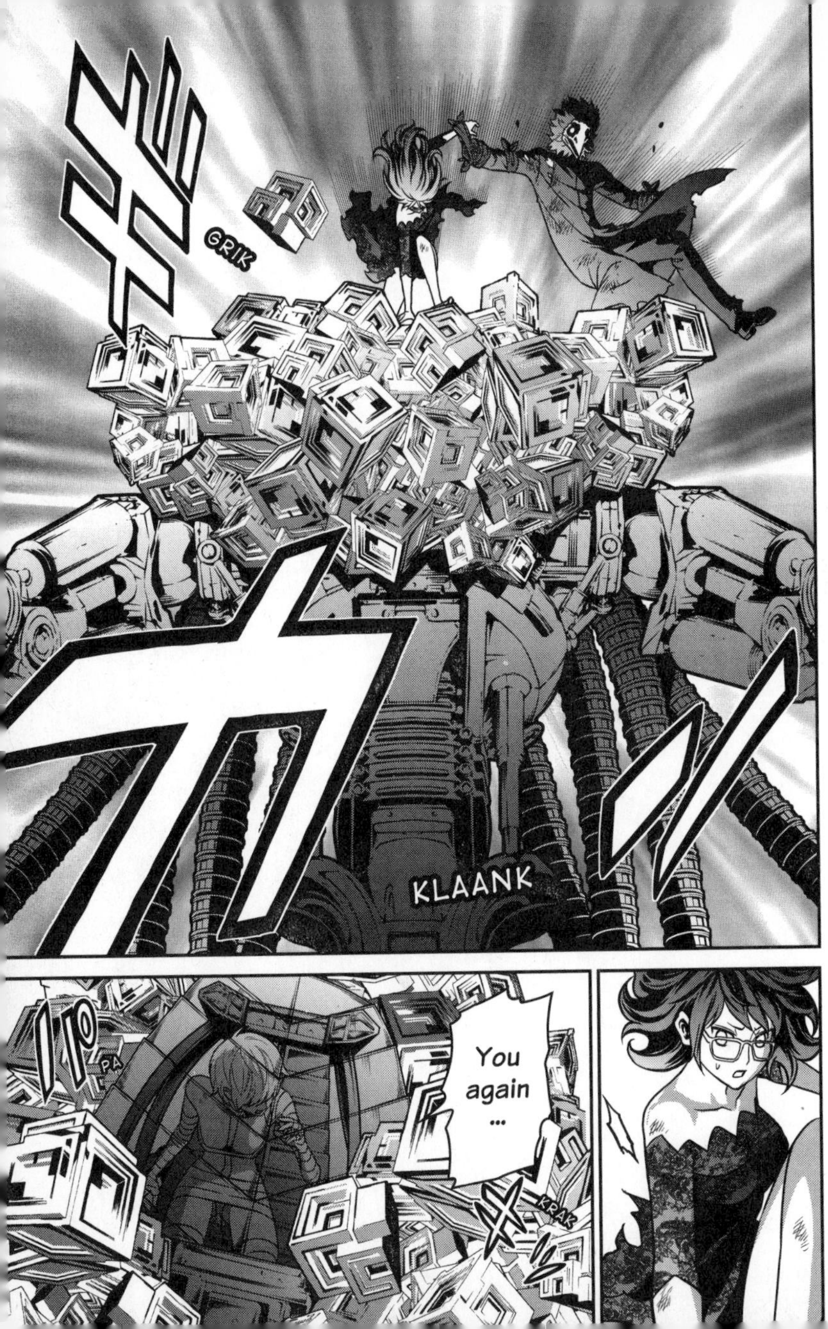
GRIK
KLAANK
You again ...
PA
KRAK

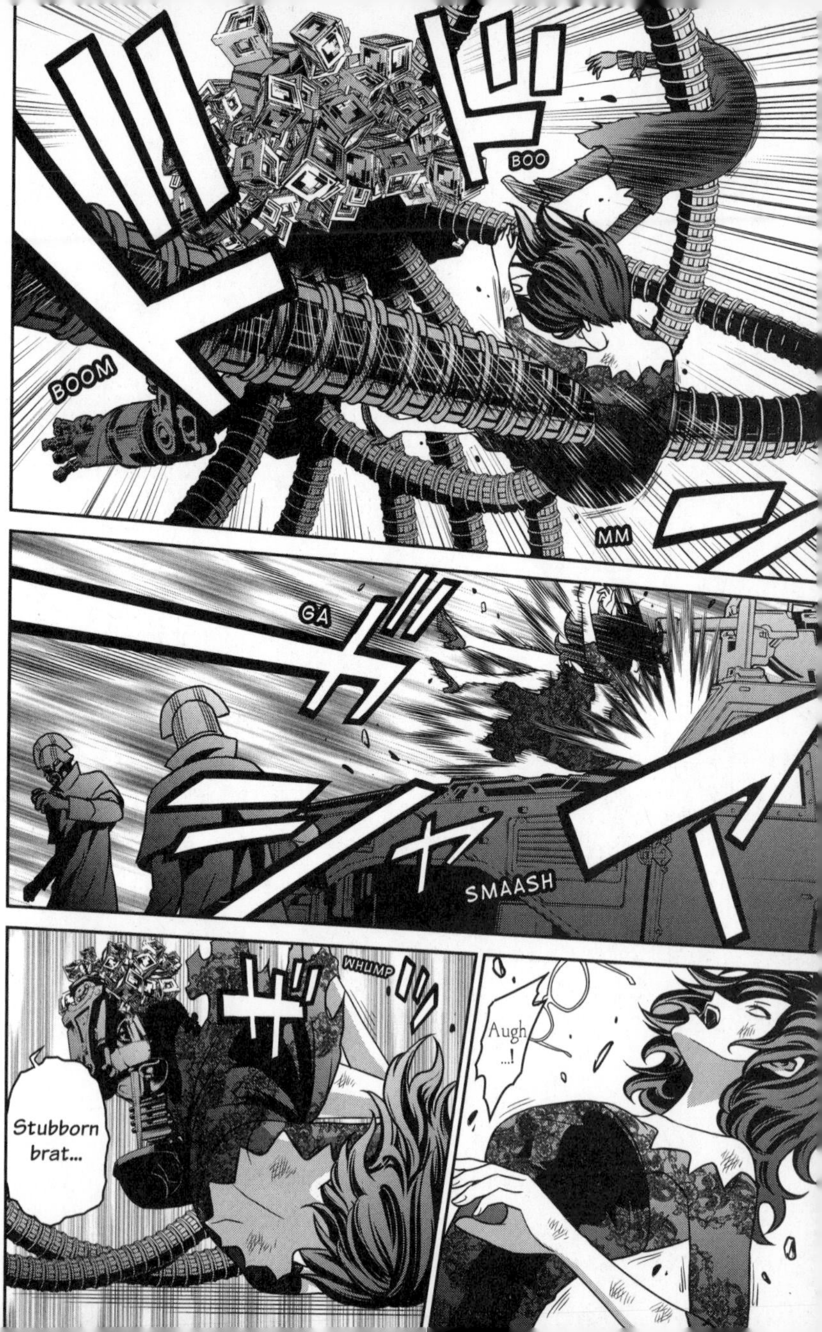
BOO
BOOM
MM
GA
SMAASH
Augh ...!
WHUMP
Stubborn brat...

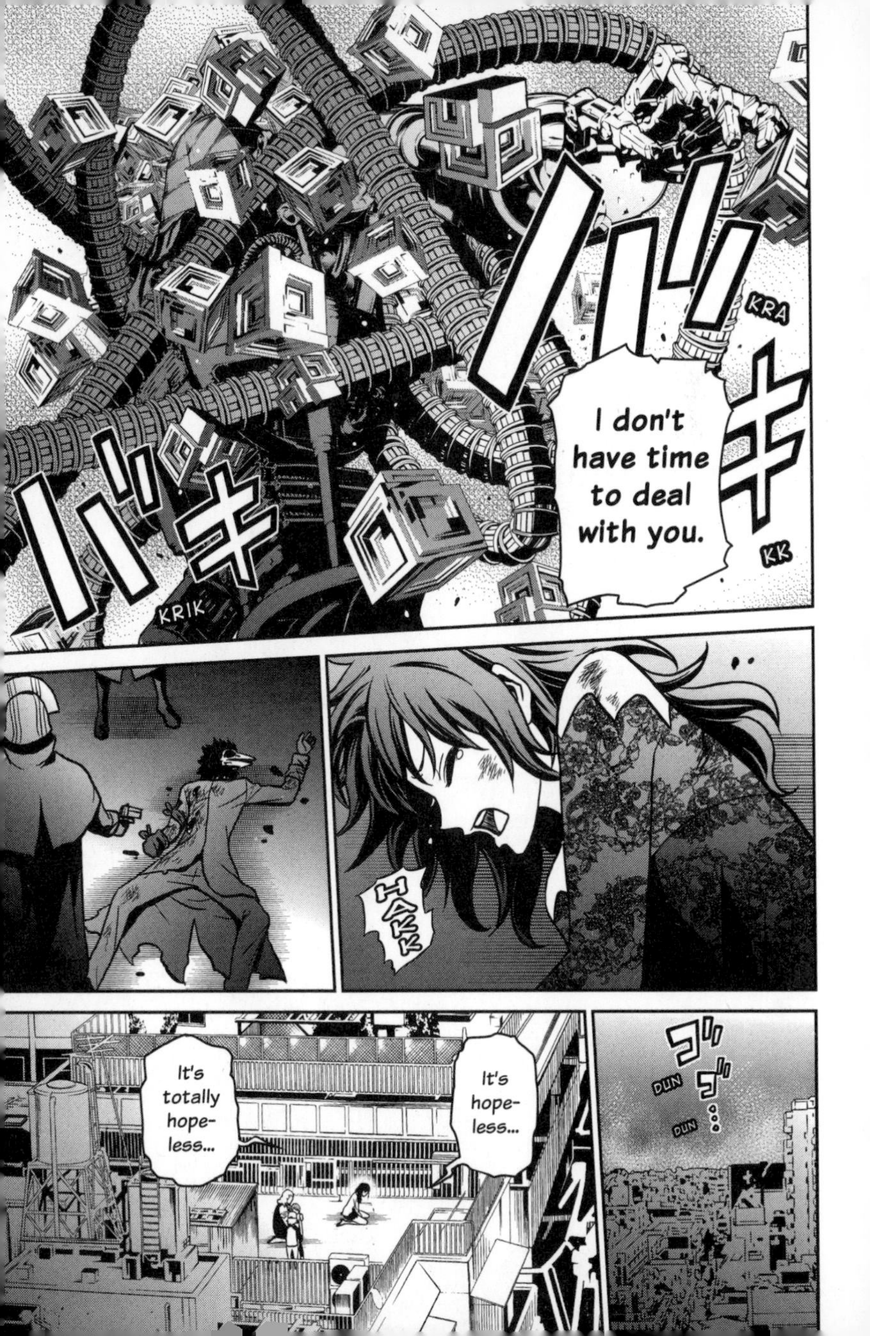
KRA
I don't have time to deal with you.
KK
KRIK
HAKK
DUN
DUN
It's hope-less...
It's totally hope-less...

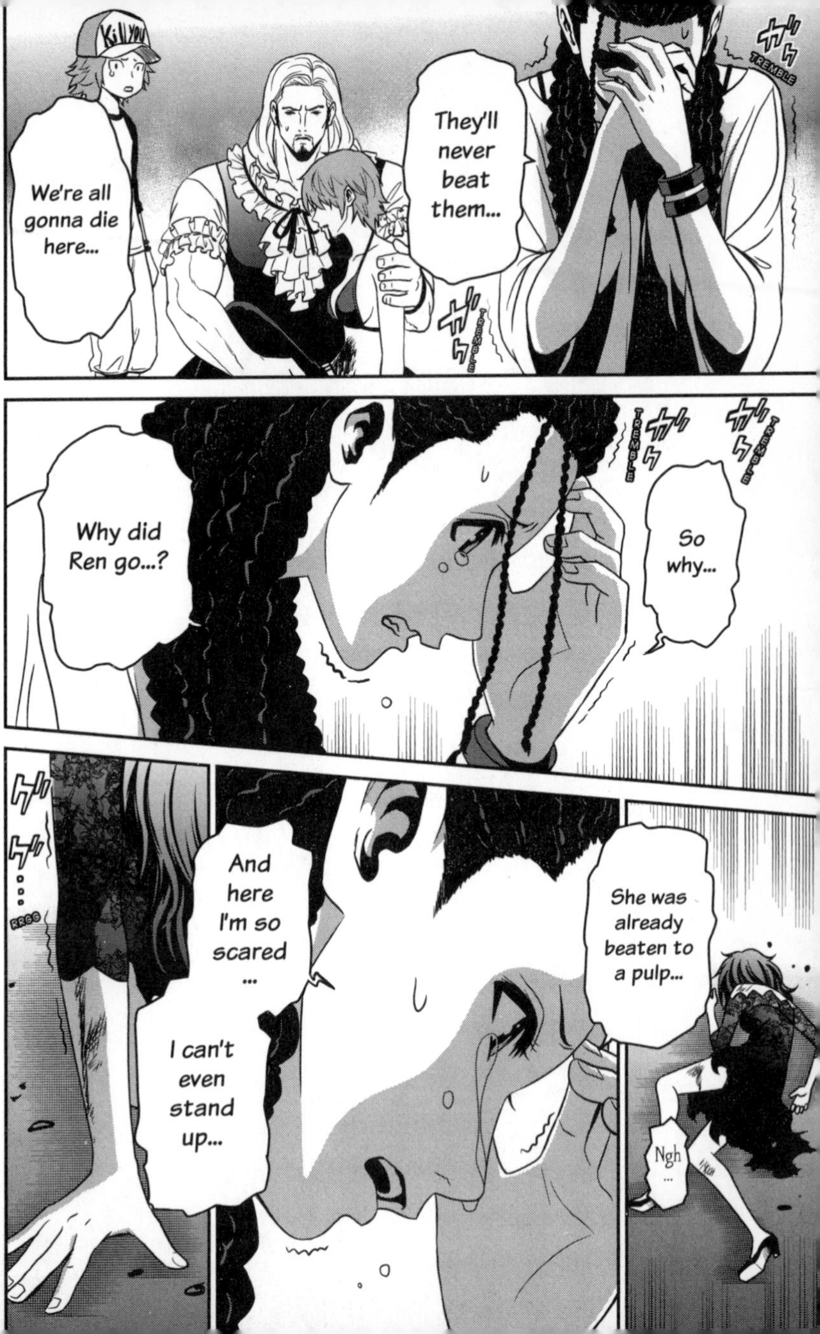
TREMBLE
They'll never beat them...
We're all gonna die here...
Kill YOU
TREMBLE
TREMBLE
TREMBLE
So why...
Why did Ren go...?
She was already beaten to a pulp...
Ngh ...
And here I'm so scared ...
I can't even stand up...
RRGG

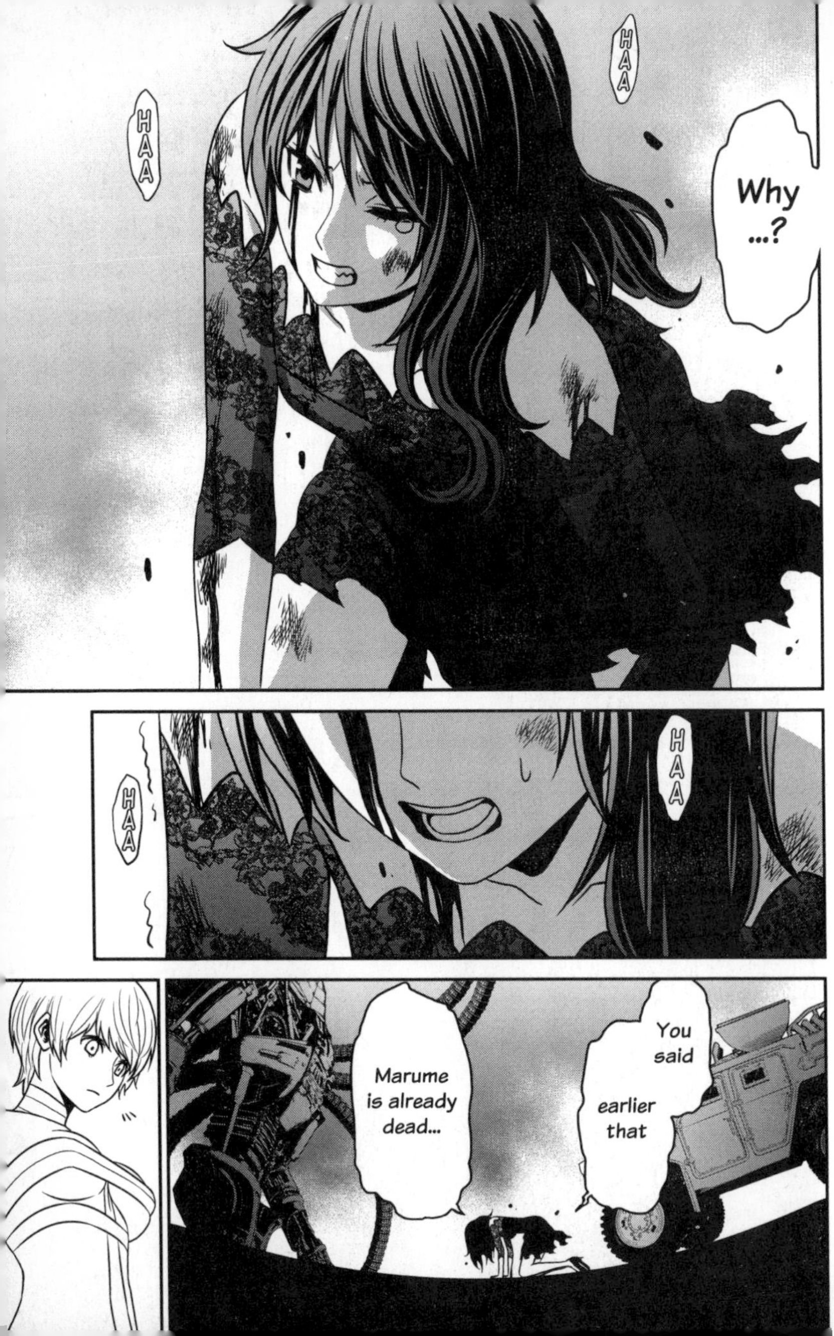
Why ...?
HAA
HAA
HAA
HAA
You said earlier that
Marume is already dead...

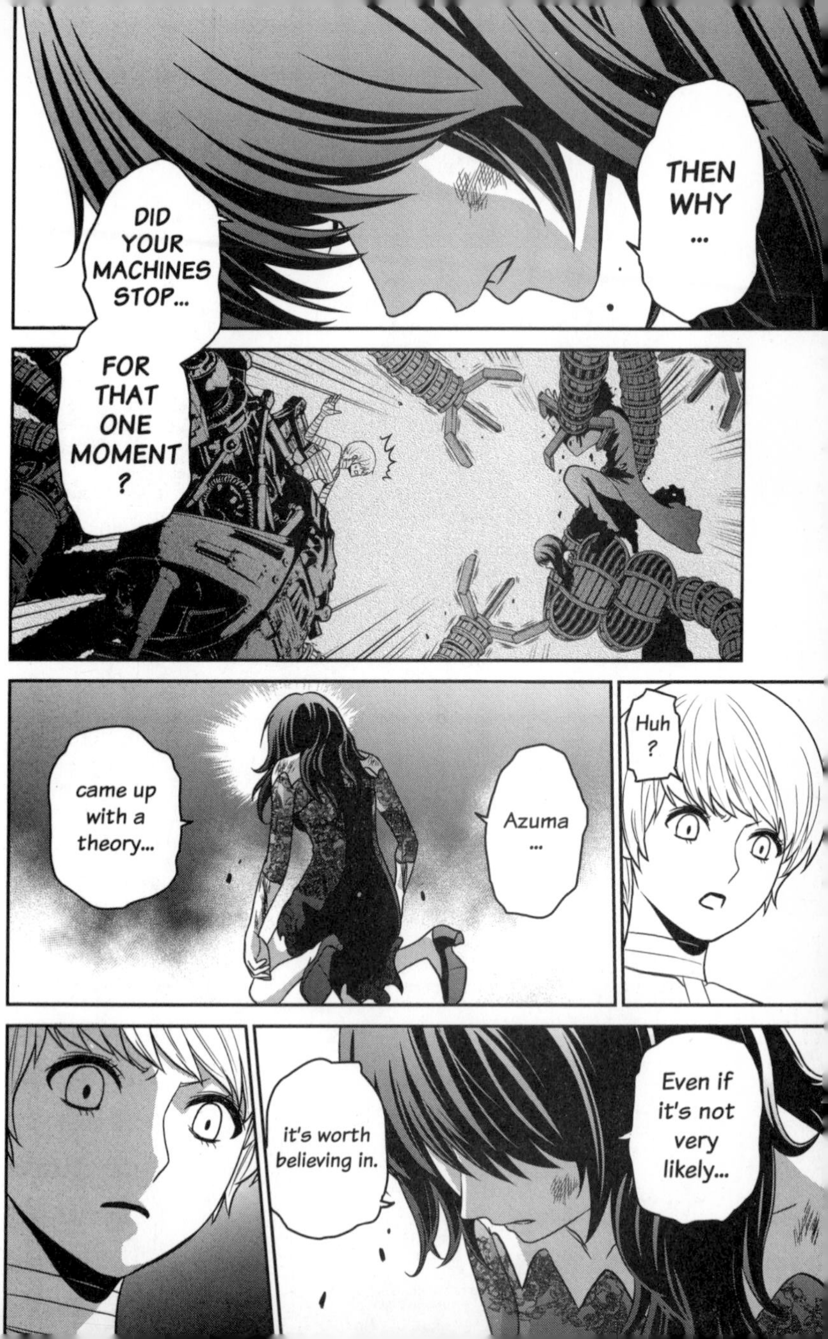
THEN WHY ...
DID YOUR MACHINES STOP...
FOR THAT ONE MOMENT ?
Huh ?
Azuma ...
came up with a theory...
Even if it's not very likely...
it's worth believing in.

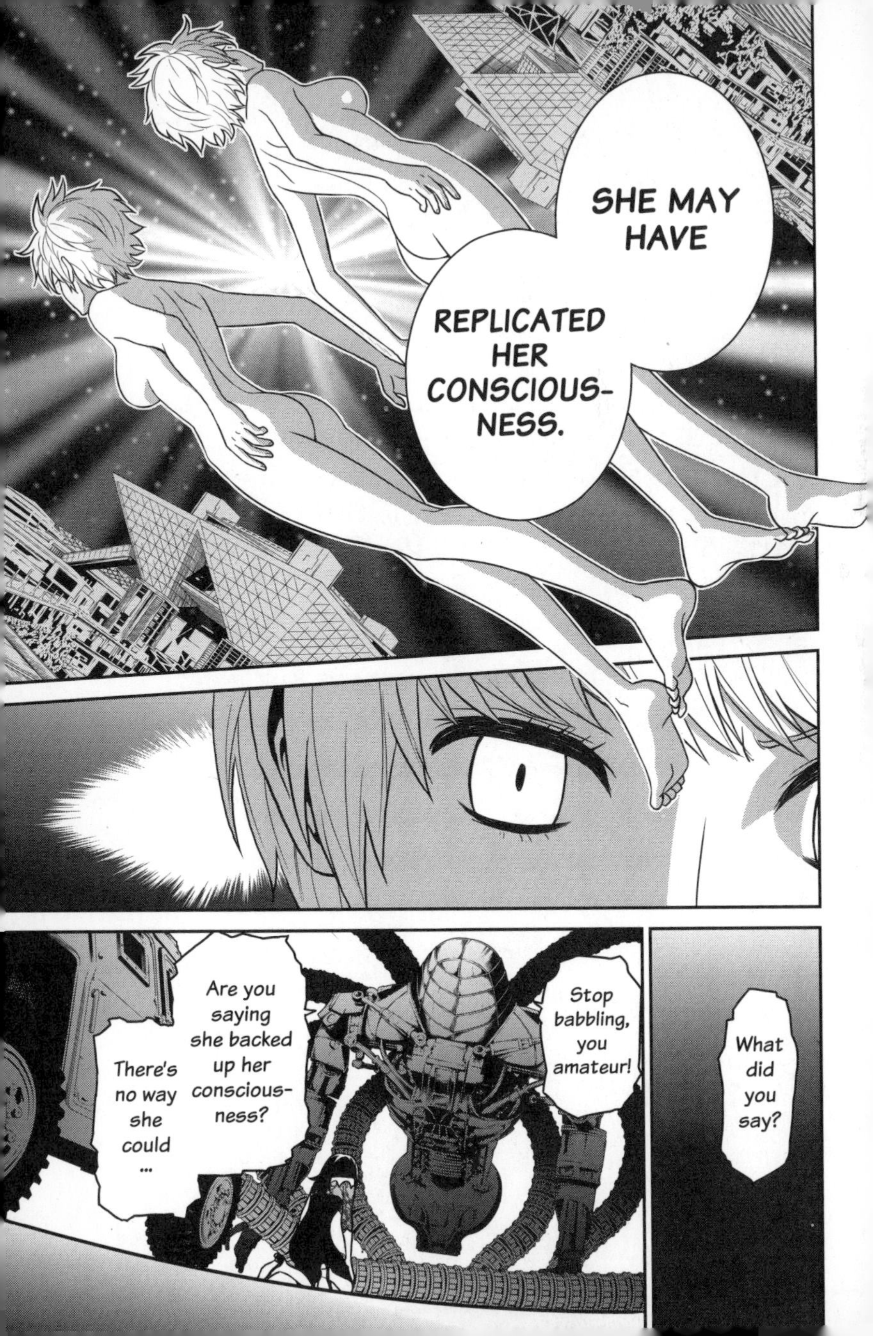
SHE MAY HAVE
REPLICATED HER CONSCIOUS-NESS.
What did you say?
Stop babbling, you amateur!
Are you saying she backed up her conscious-ness?
There's no way she could ...

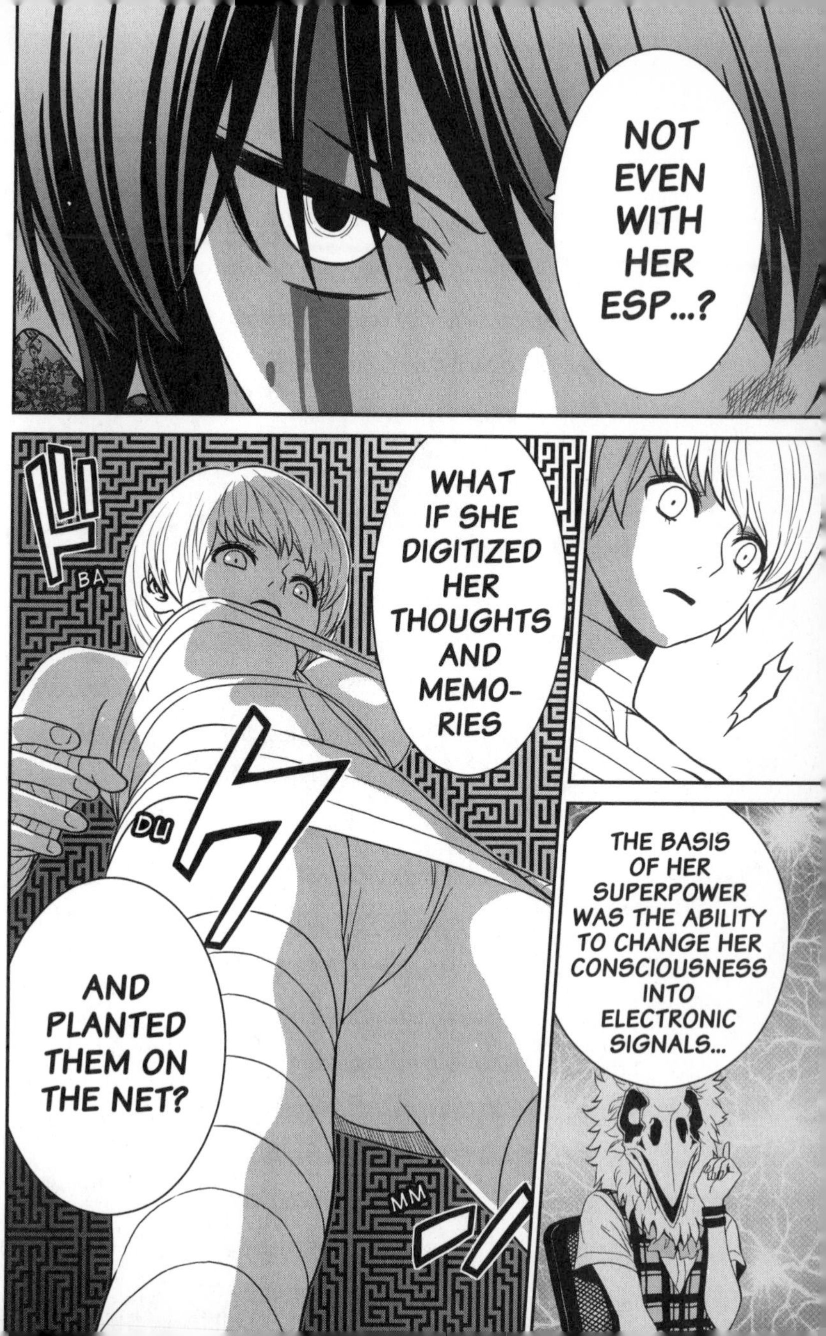
NOT EVEN WITH HER ESP...?
THE BASIS OF HER SUPERPOWER WAS THE ABILITY TO CHANGE HER CONSCIOUSNESS INTO ELECTRONIC SIGNALS...
BA
WHAT IF SHE DIGITIZED HER THOUGHTS AND MEMO-RIES
DU
AND PLANTED THEM ON THE NET?
MM

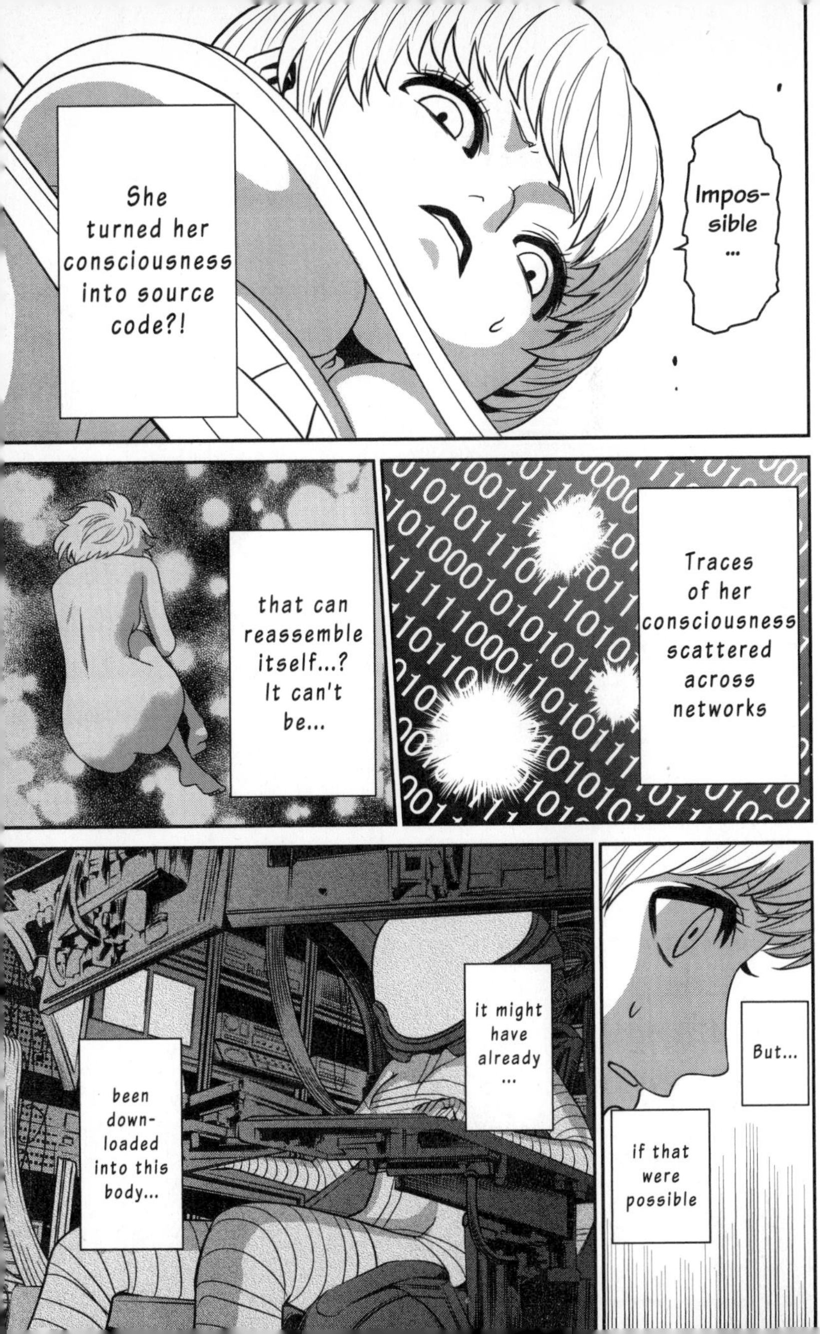

Impos-
sible
...
She turned her consciousness into source code?!
Traces of her consciousness scattered across networks
that can reassemble itself...? It can't be...
But...
if that were possible
it might have already ...
been down-
loaded into this body...

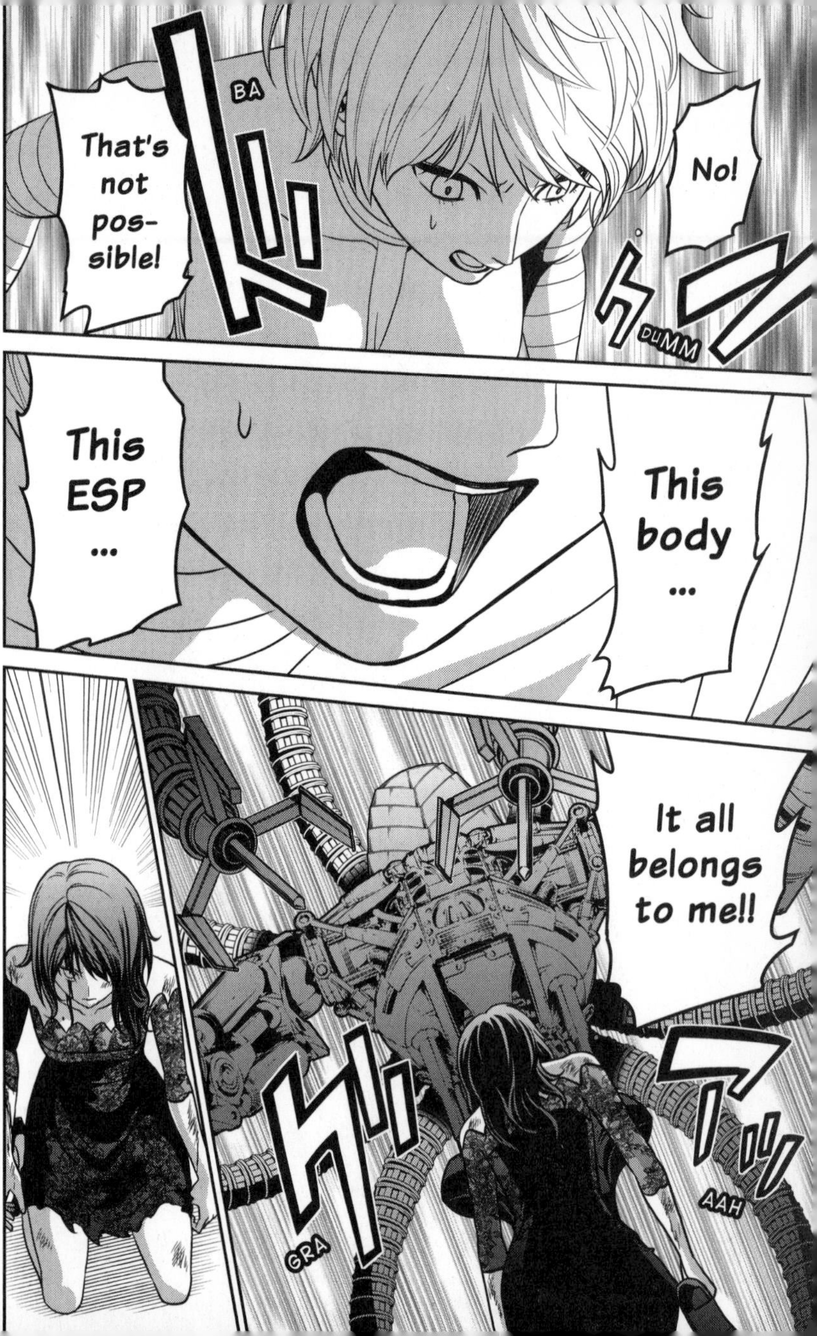
No!
BA
That's not pos-sible!
DUMM
This body ...
This ESP ...
It all belongs to me!!
AAH
GRA

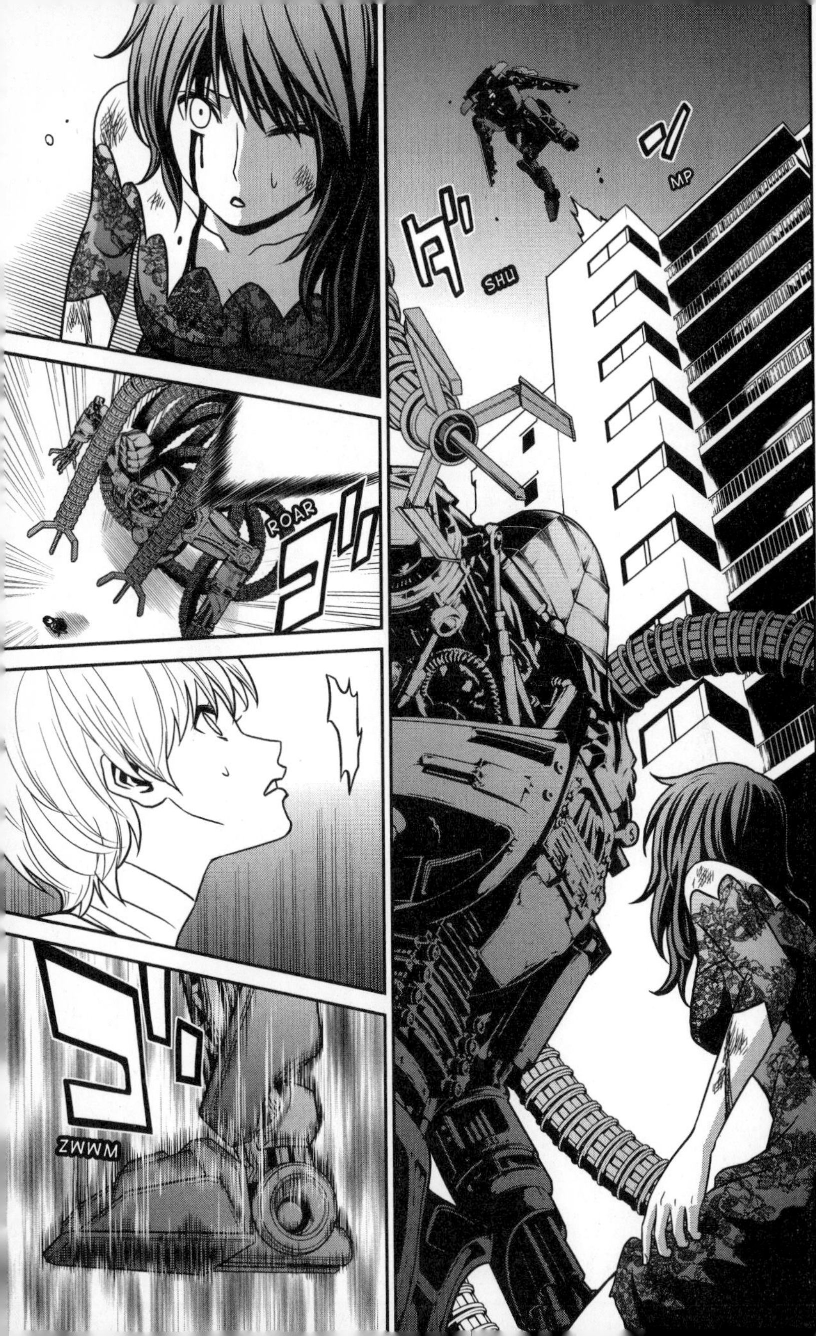
SHU
MP
ROAR
ZWWM

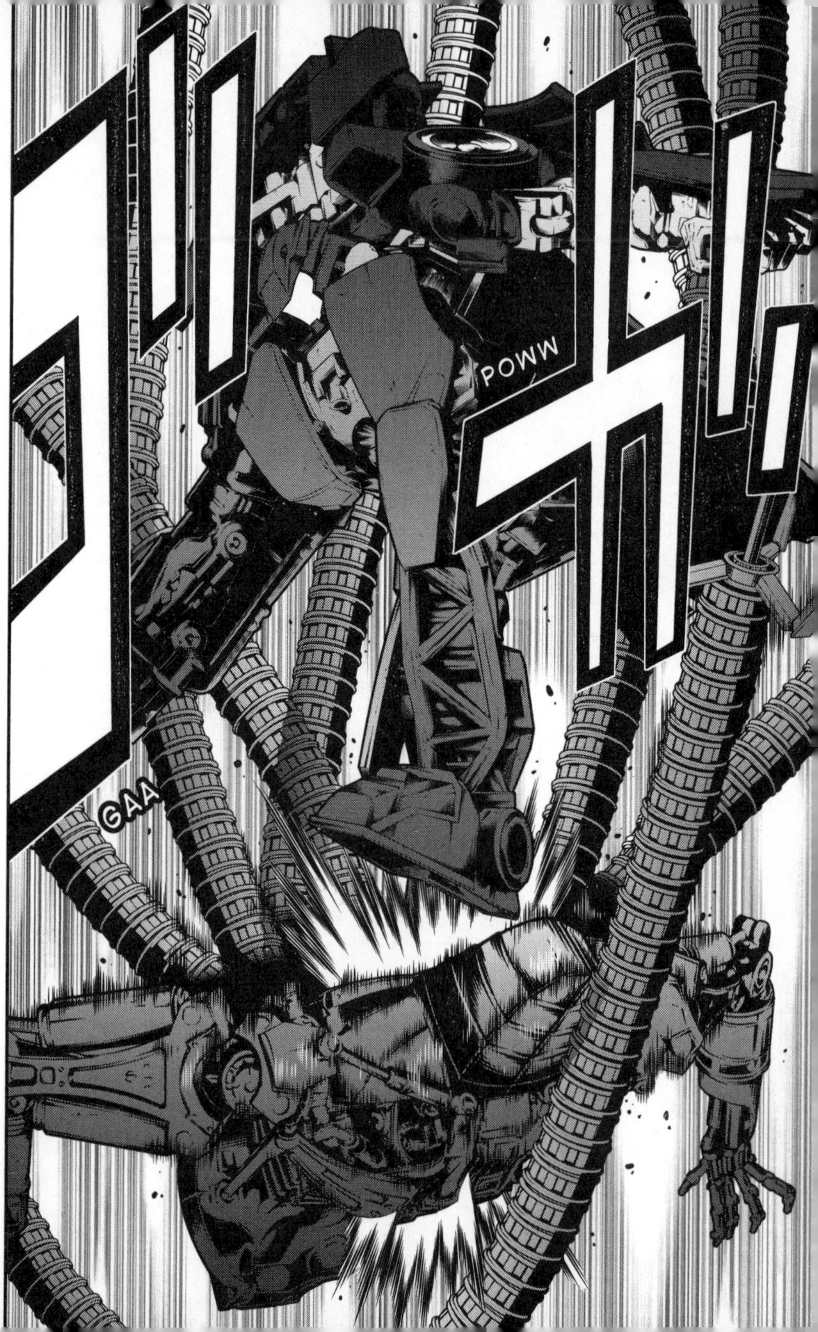
POWW
GAA

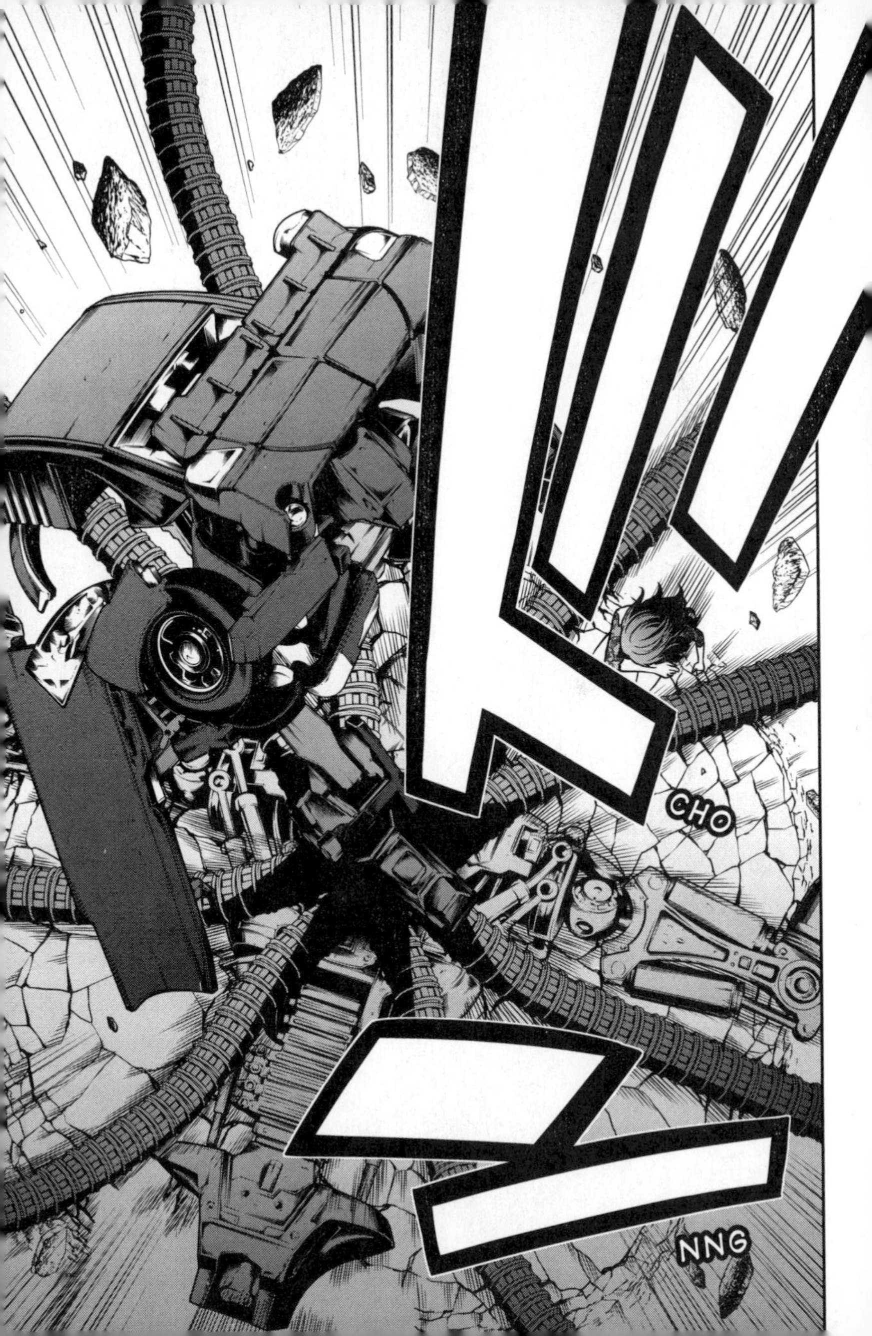
CHO
NNG

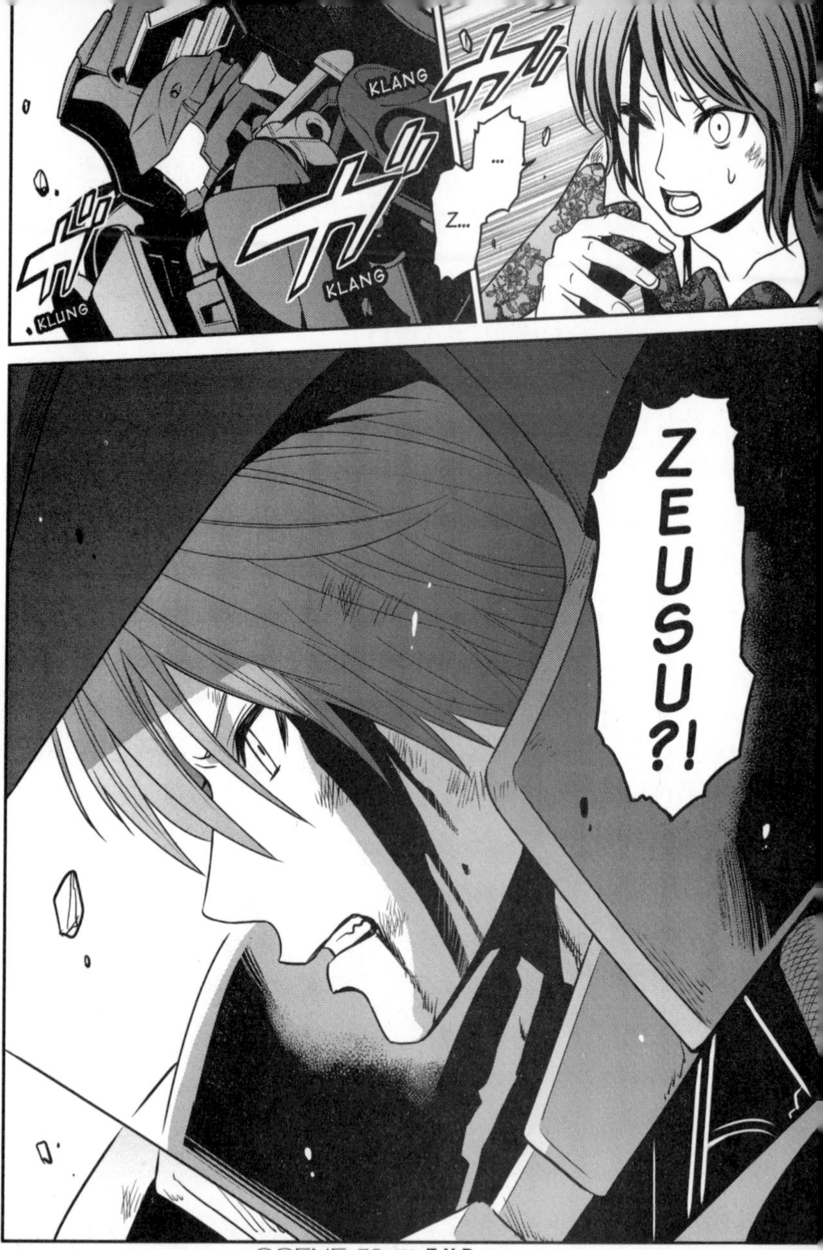
...
Z...
KLANG
KLANG
KLUNG
ZEUSUU?!

SCENE 72 /// END

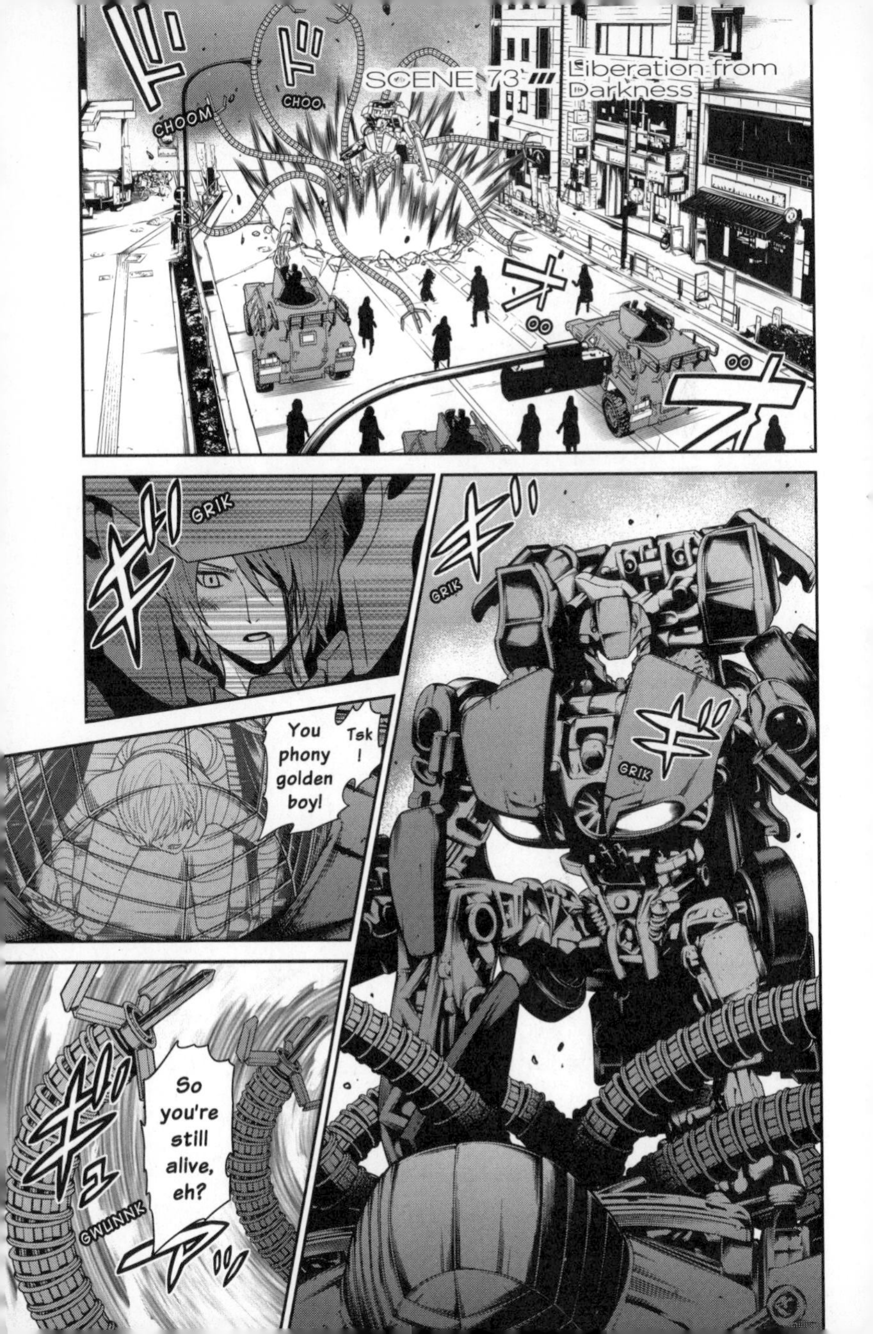
SCENE 73 /// Liberation from Darkness
CHOO
CHOOM
GRIK
GRIK
GRIK
Tsk!
You phony golden boy!
So you're still alive, eh?
GWUNNK

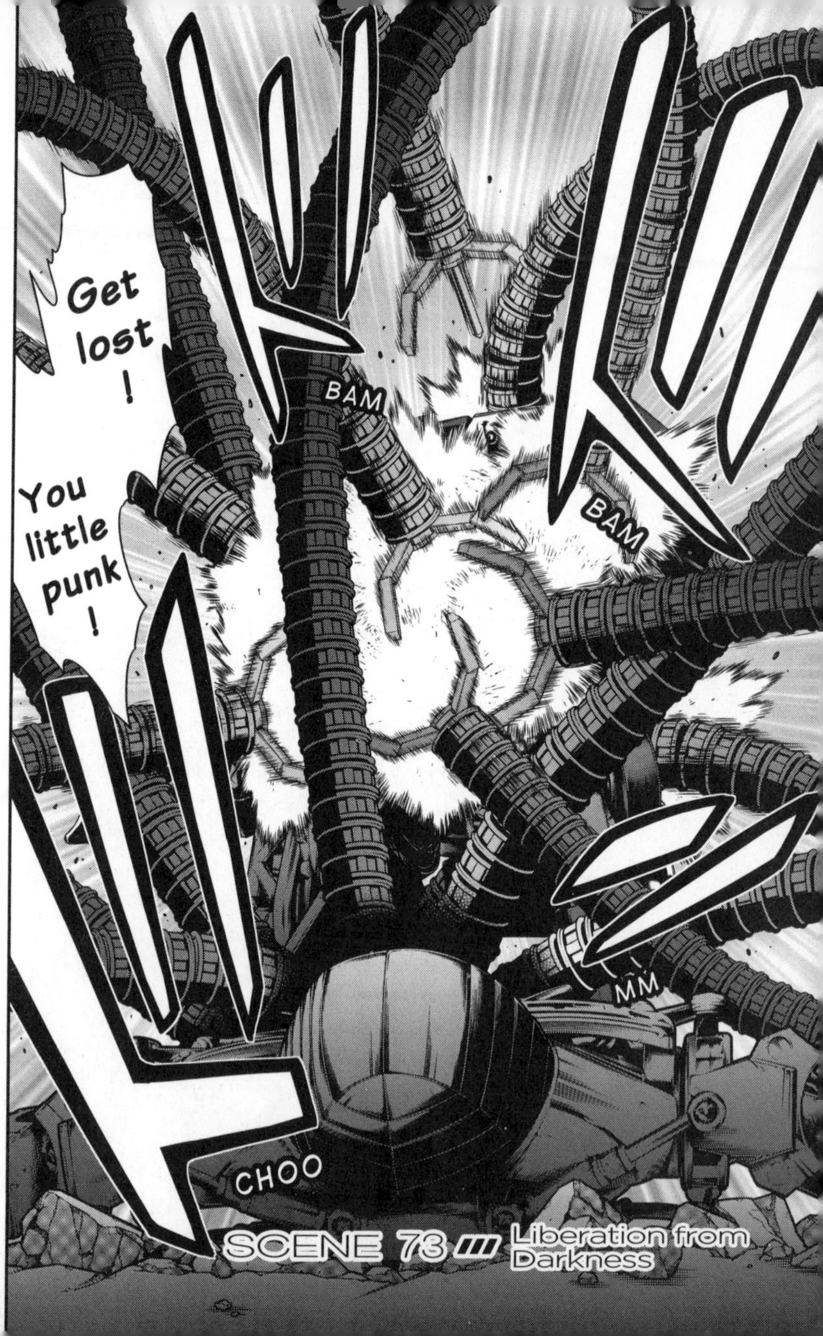
BAM
BAM
Get lost!
You little punk!
MM
CHOO
SCENE 73 /// Liberation from Darkness

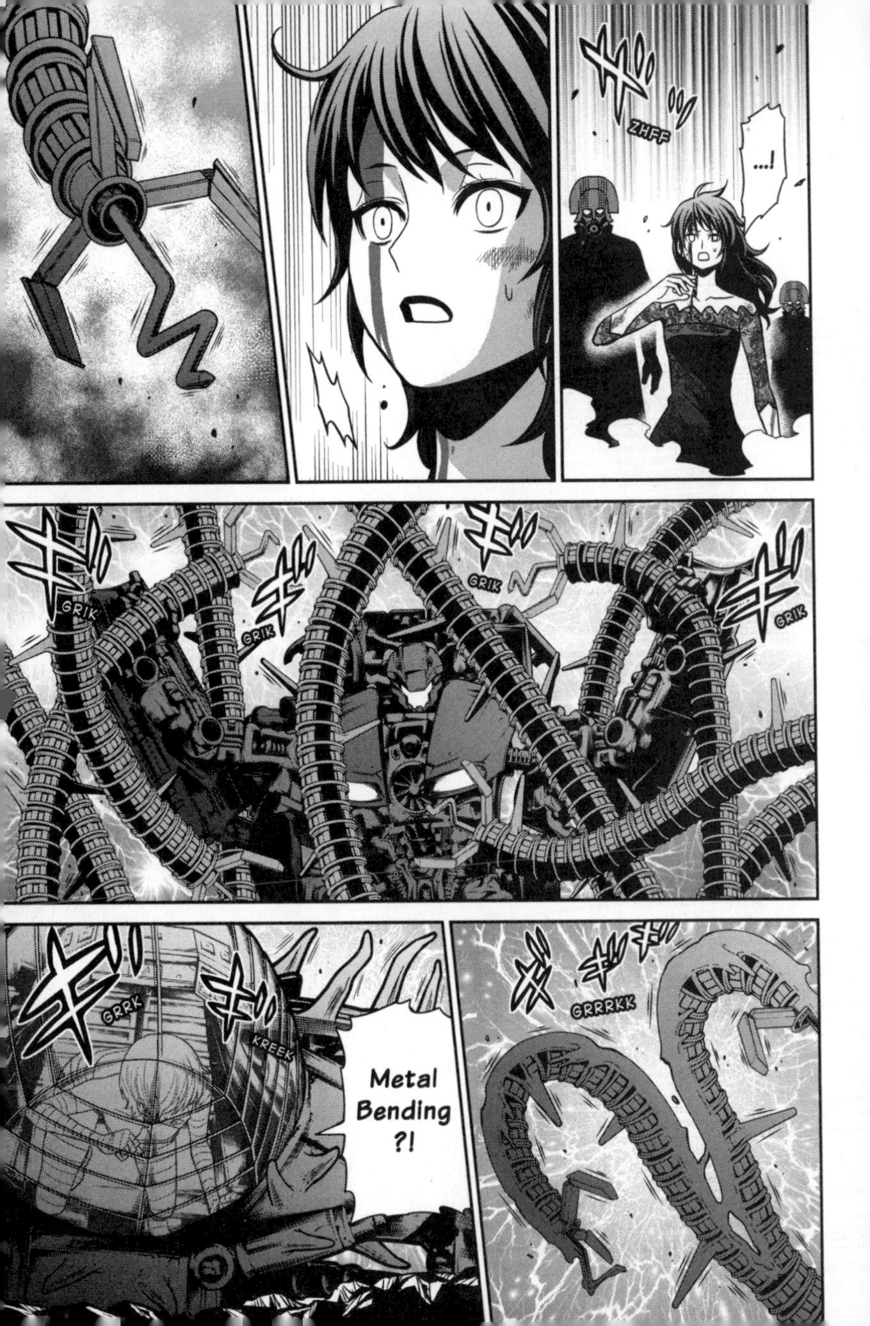
ZHFF
...!
GRIK
GRIK
GRIK
GRIK
GRRRKK
GRRK
KREEK
Metal Bending ?!

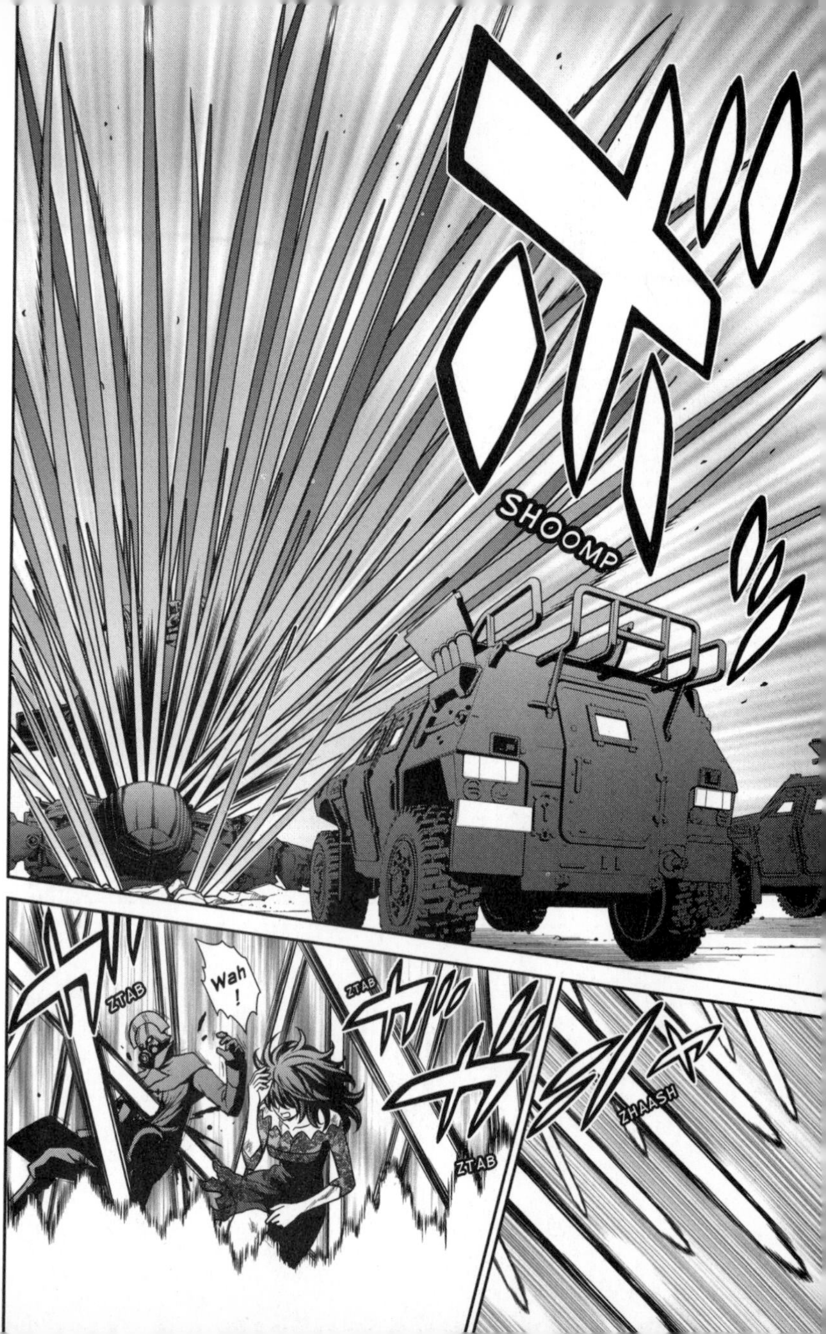
SHOOMP
ZHAASH
ZTAB
ZTAB
Wah!
ZTAB

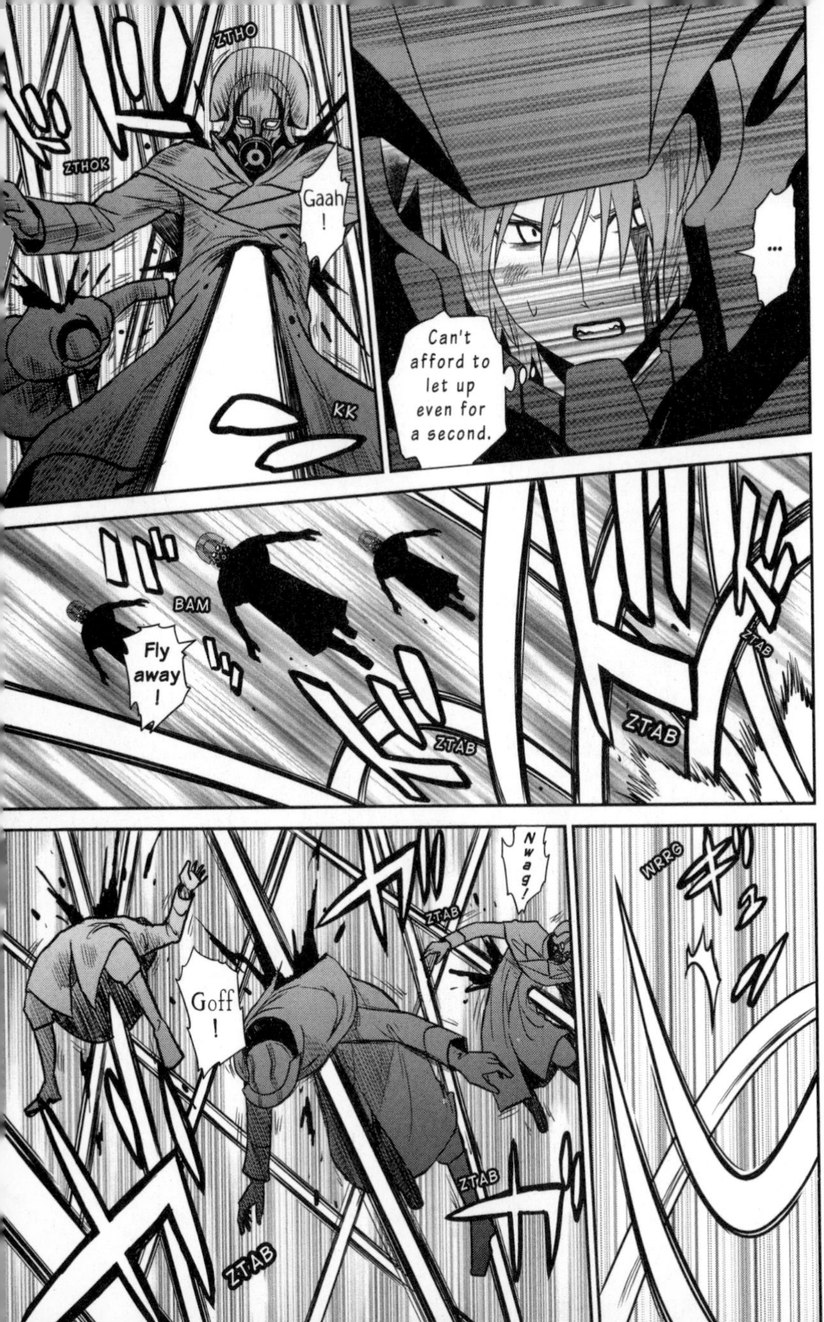
...
Can't afford to let up even for a second.
ZTHO
Gaah!
ZTHOK
KK
ZTAB
ZTAB
ZTAB
BAM
Fly away!
WRRG
Nwag!
ZTAB
Goff!
ZTAB
ZTAB

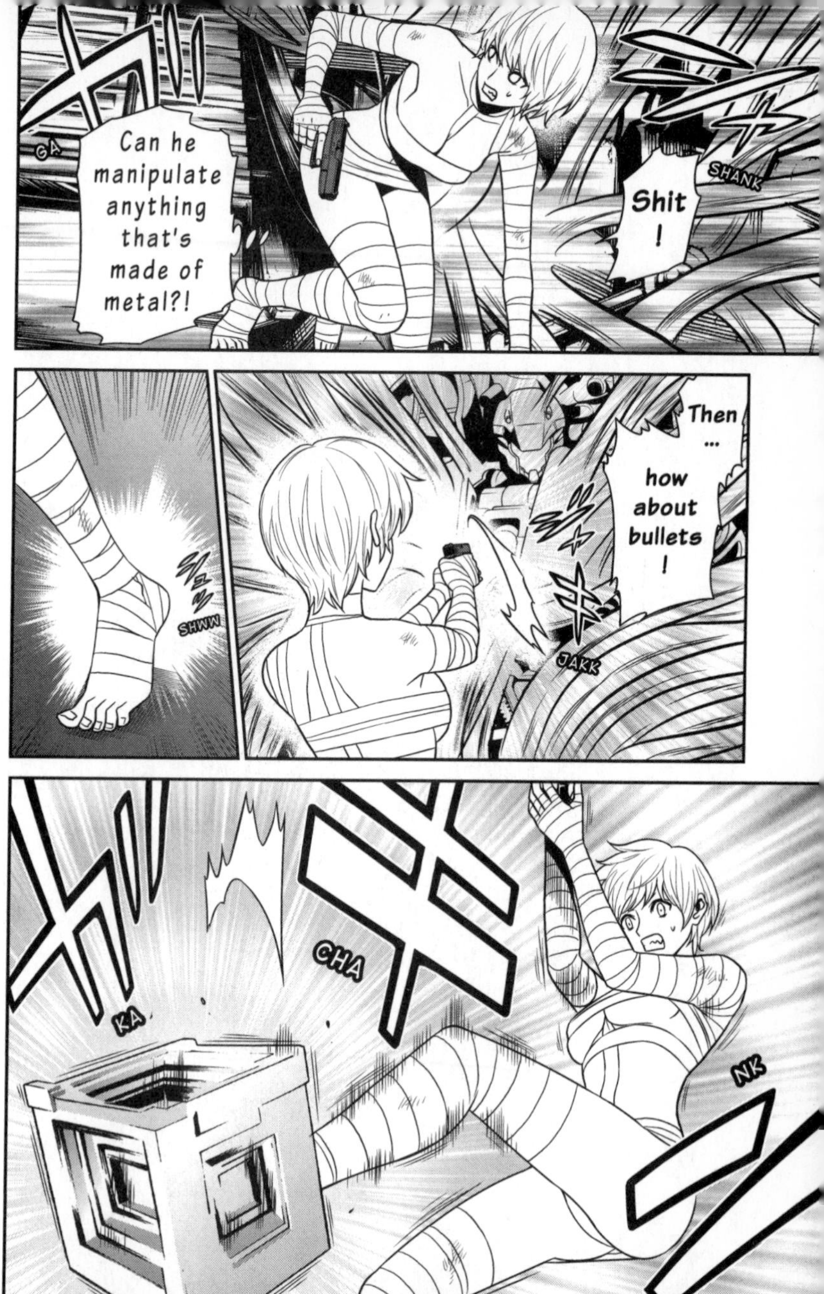
SHANK
Shit!
GA
Can he manipulate anything that's made of metal?!
Then... how about bullets!
JAKK
SHWW
NK
CHA
KA

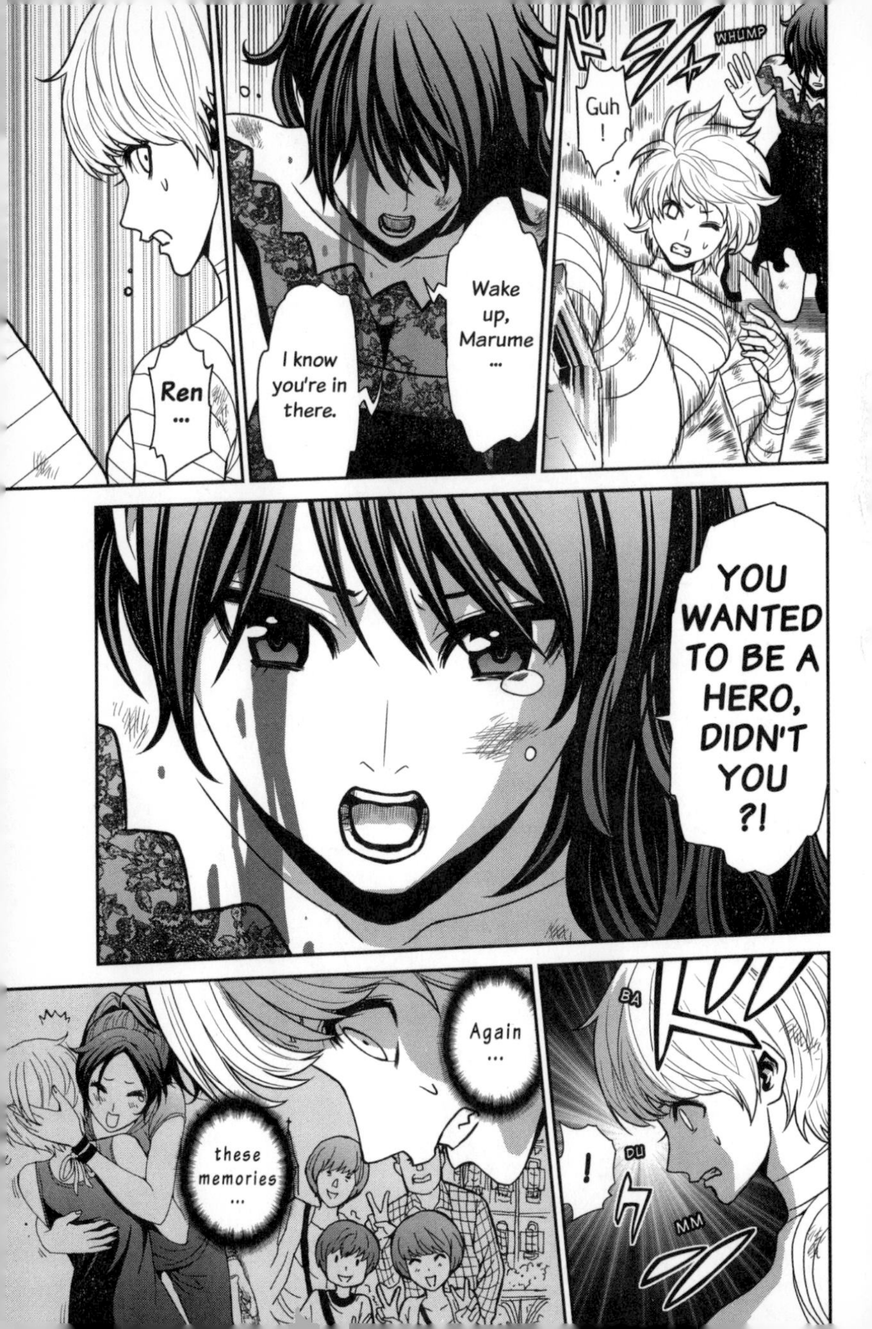
WHUMP
Guh!
Wake up, Marume...
I know you're in there.
Ren...
YOU WANTED TO BE A HERO, DIDN'T YOU?!
BA
!
DU
MM
Again...
these memories...

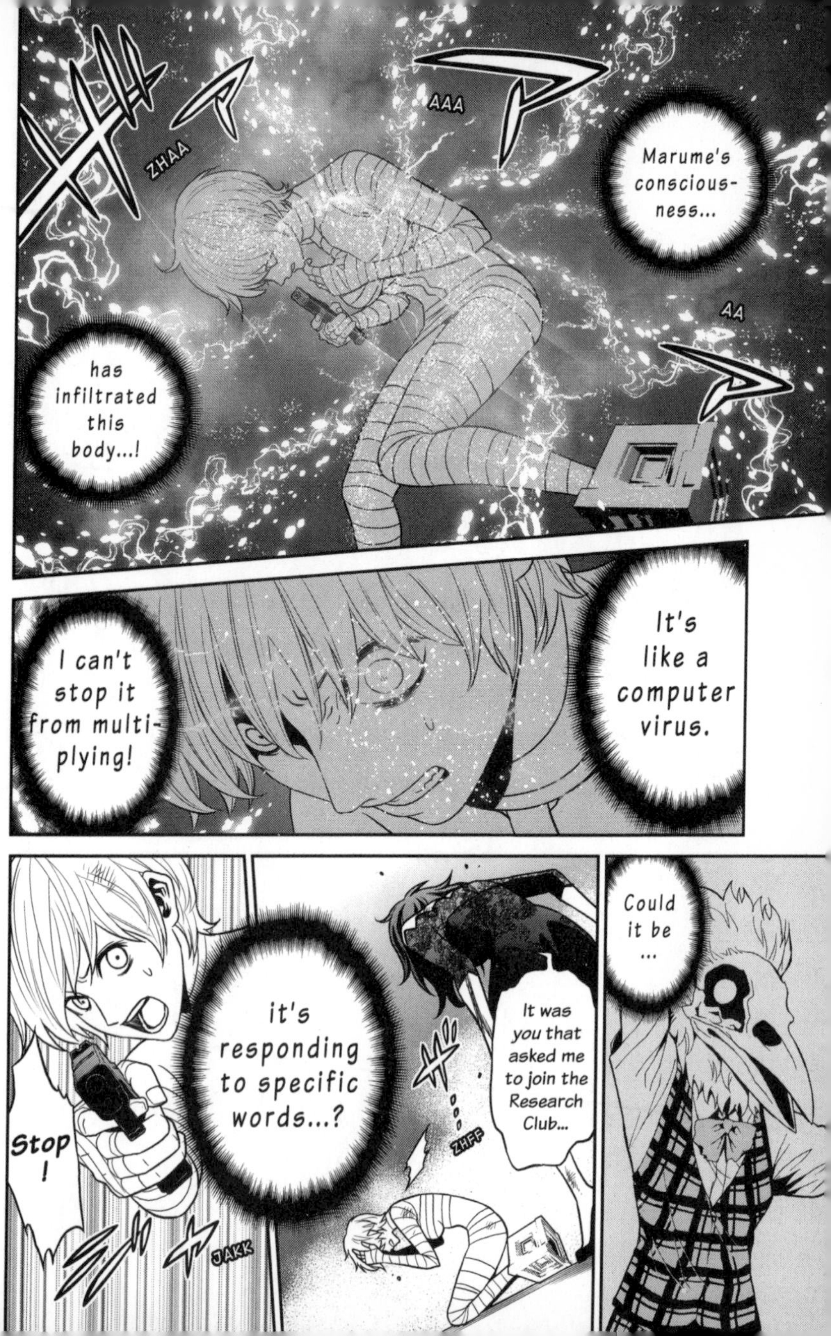
AAA
Marume's consciousness...
ZHAA
AA
has infiltrated this body...!
It's like a computer virus.
I can't stop it from multiplying!
Could it be ...
It was you that asked me to join the Research Club...
ZHFF
it's responding to specific words...?
Stop!
JAKK

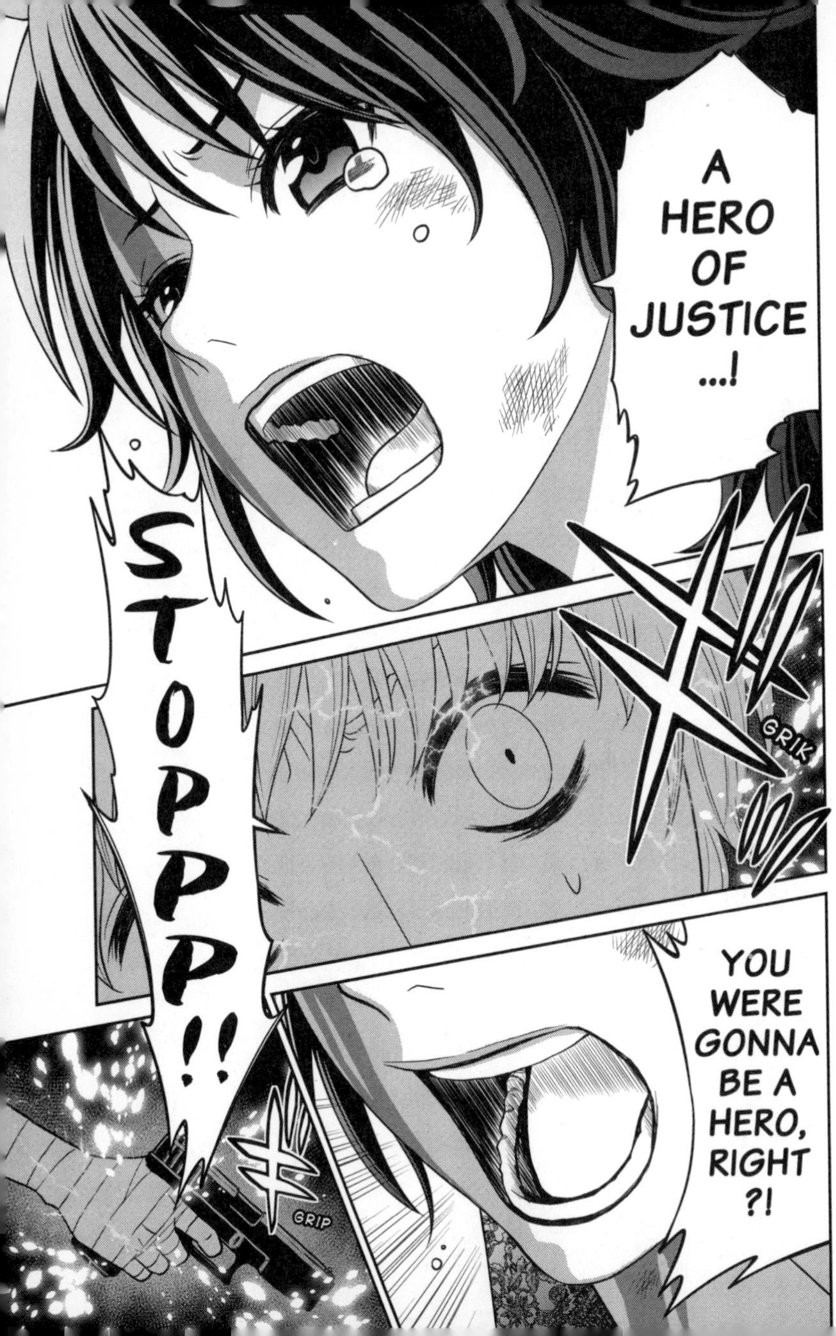
A HERO OF JUSTICE ...!
STOPP!!
GRIK
YOU WERE GONNA BE A HERO, RIGHT?!
GRIP

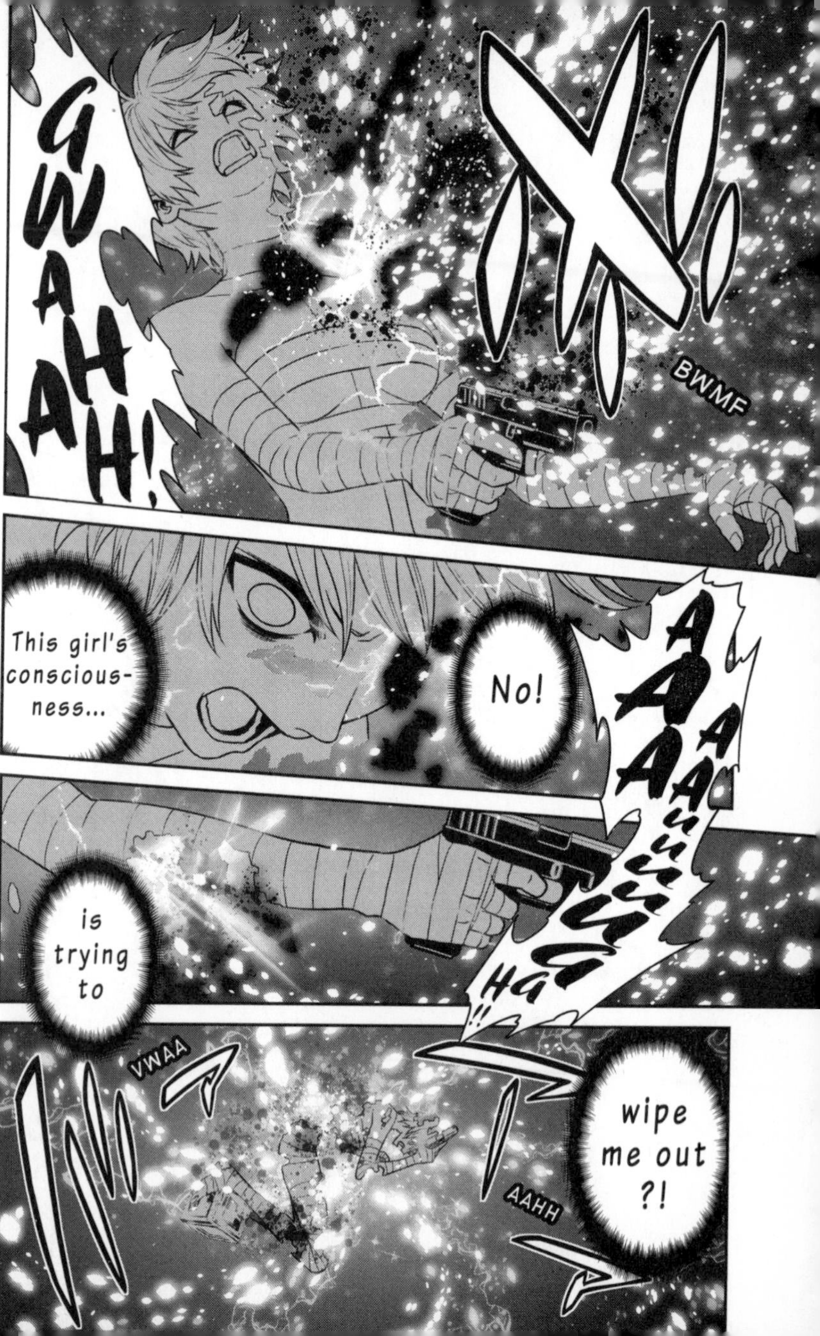
BWMF
GWAAHAH!
No!
This girl's consciousness...
AAAAAUUUUUUGHA!!
is trying to
wipe me out?!
AAHH
VWAA

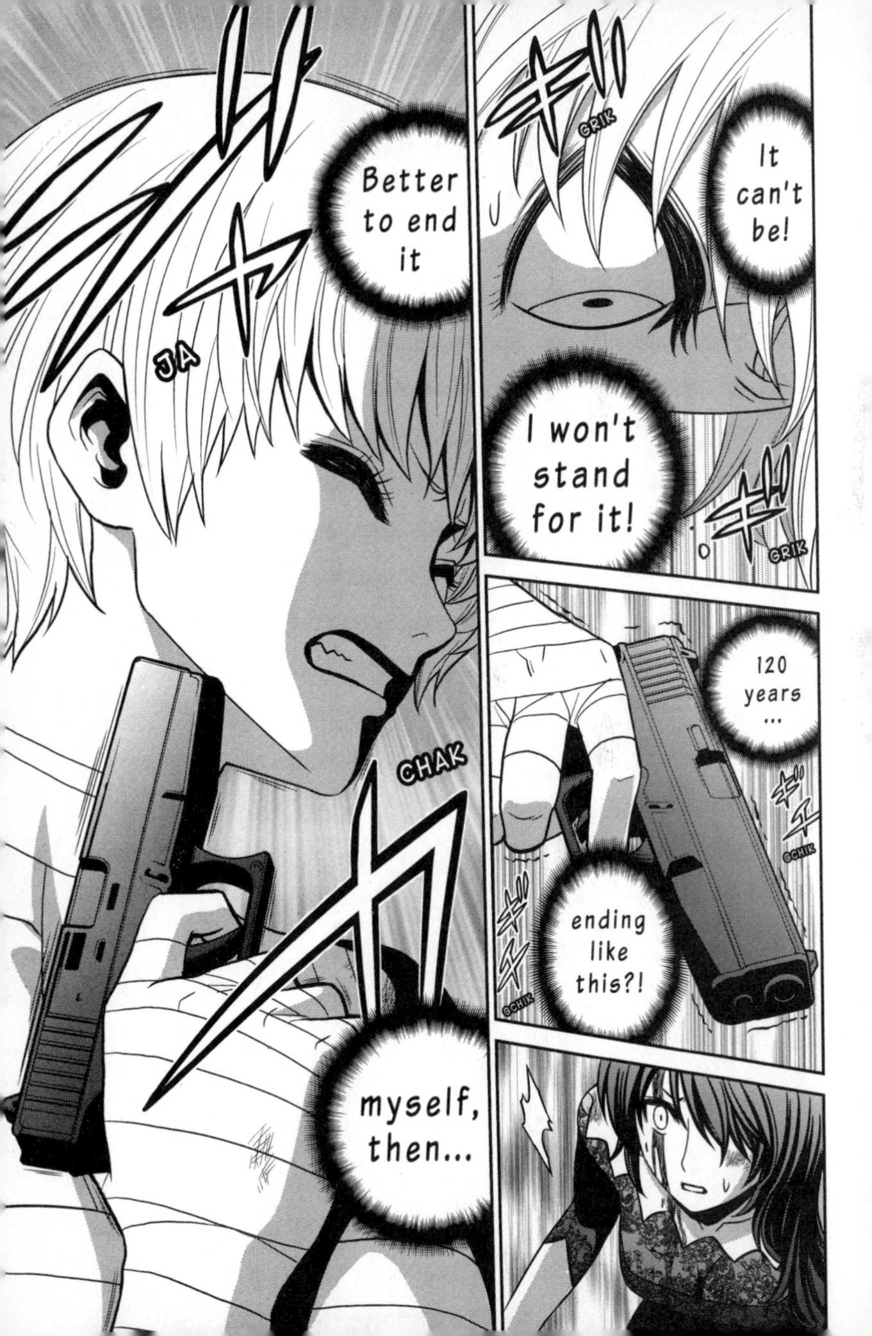
GRIK
It can't be!
I won't stand for it!
GRIK
120 years...
GCHIK
ending like this?!
GCHIK
Better to end it
JA
CHAK
myself, then...

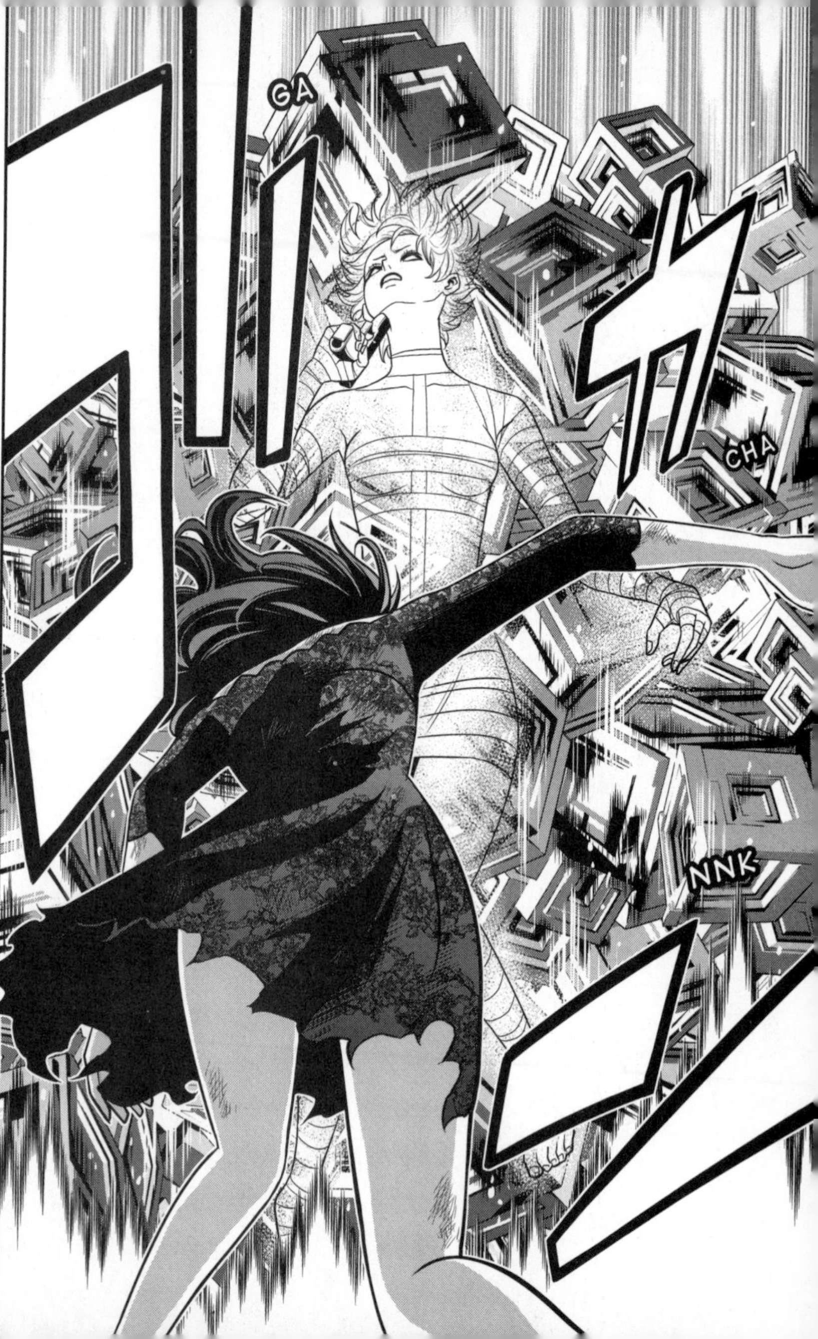
GA
CHA
NNK

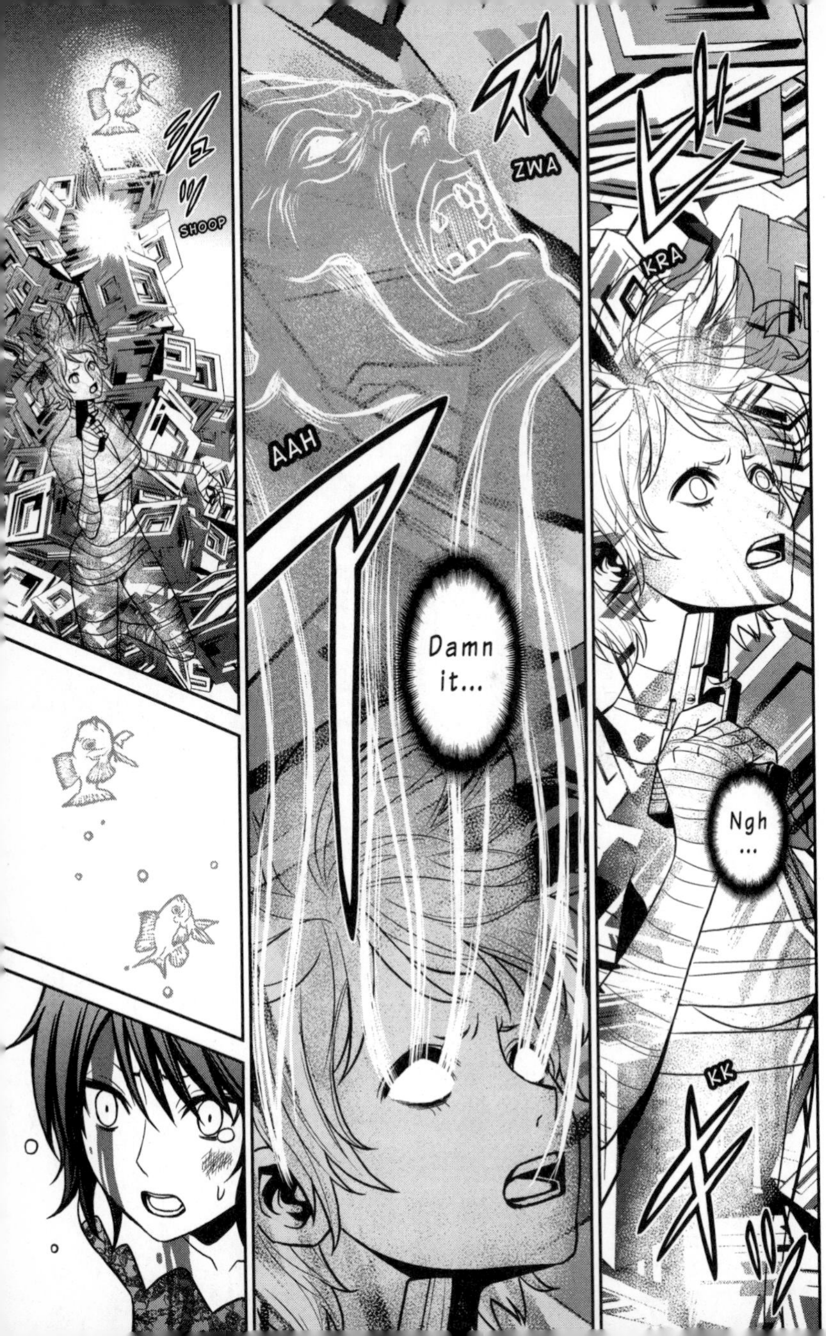
KRA
Ngh ...
KK
ZWA
AAH
Damn it...
SHOOP

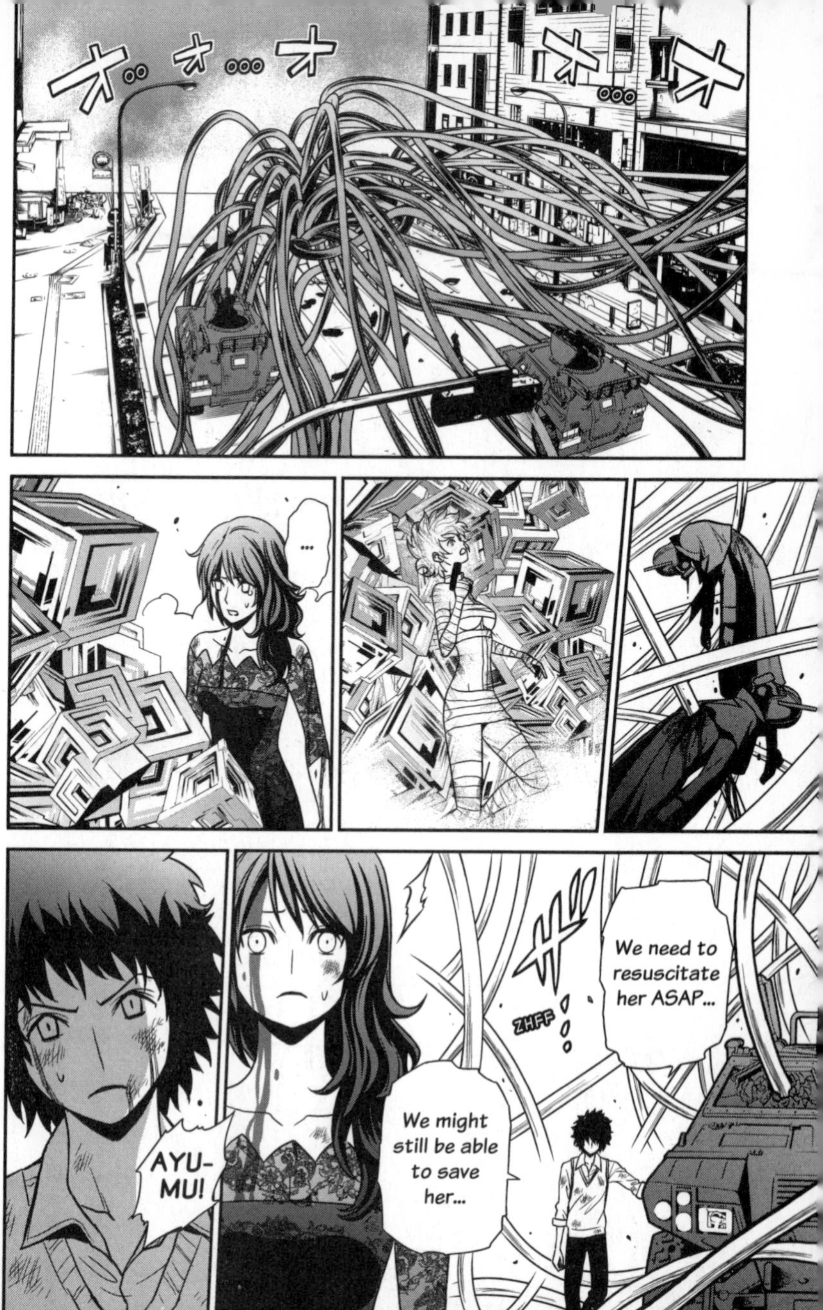

オ
○○○
オ
オ
オ。。オ。。。オ
...
We need to resuscitate her ASAP...
ZHFF
We might still be able to save her...
AYU-MU!

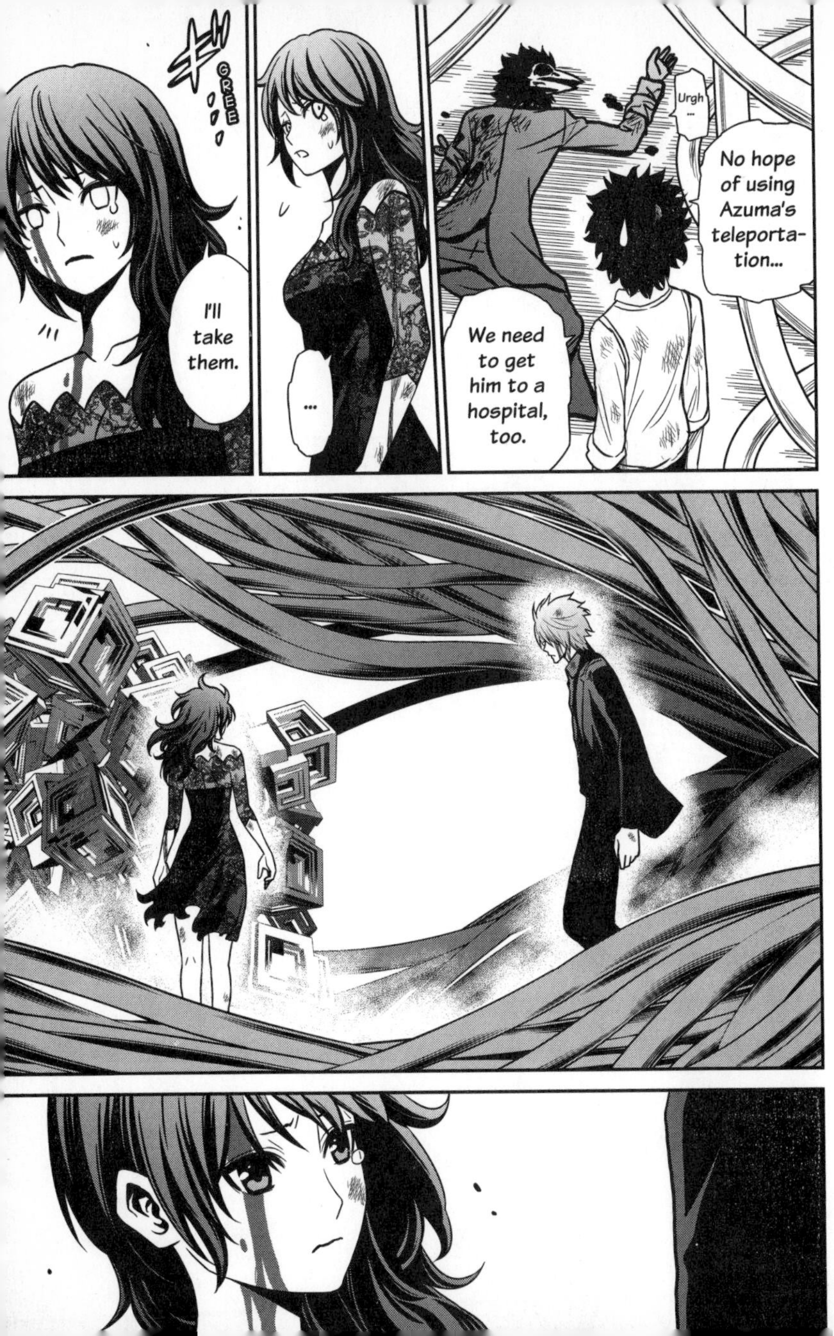
Urgh ...
No hope of using Azuma's teleportation...
We need to get him to a hospital, too.
...
GREE
I'll take them.

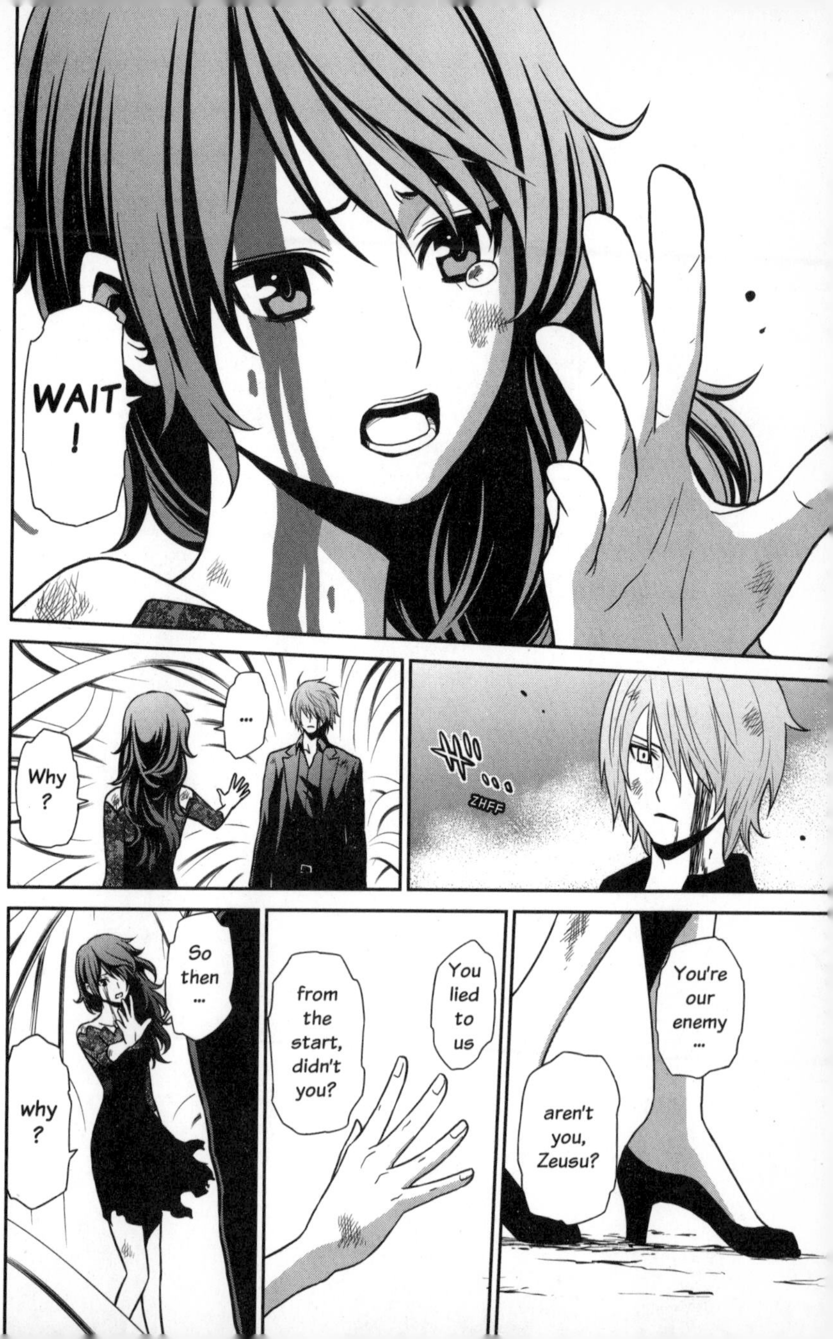
WAIT !
ZHFF
...
Why ?
You're our enemy ...
aren't you, Zeusu?
You lied to us
from the start, didn't you?
So then ...
why ?

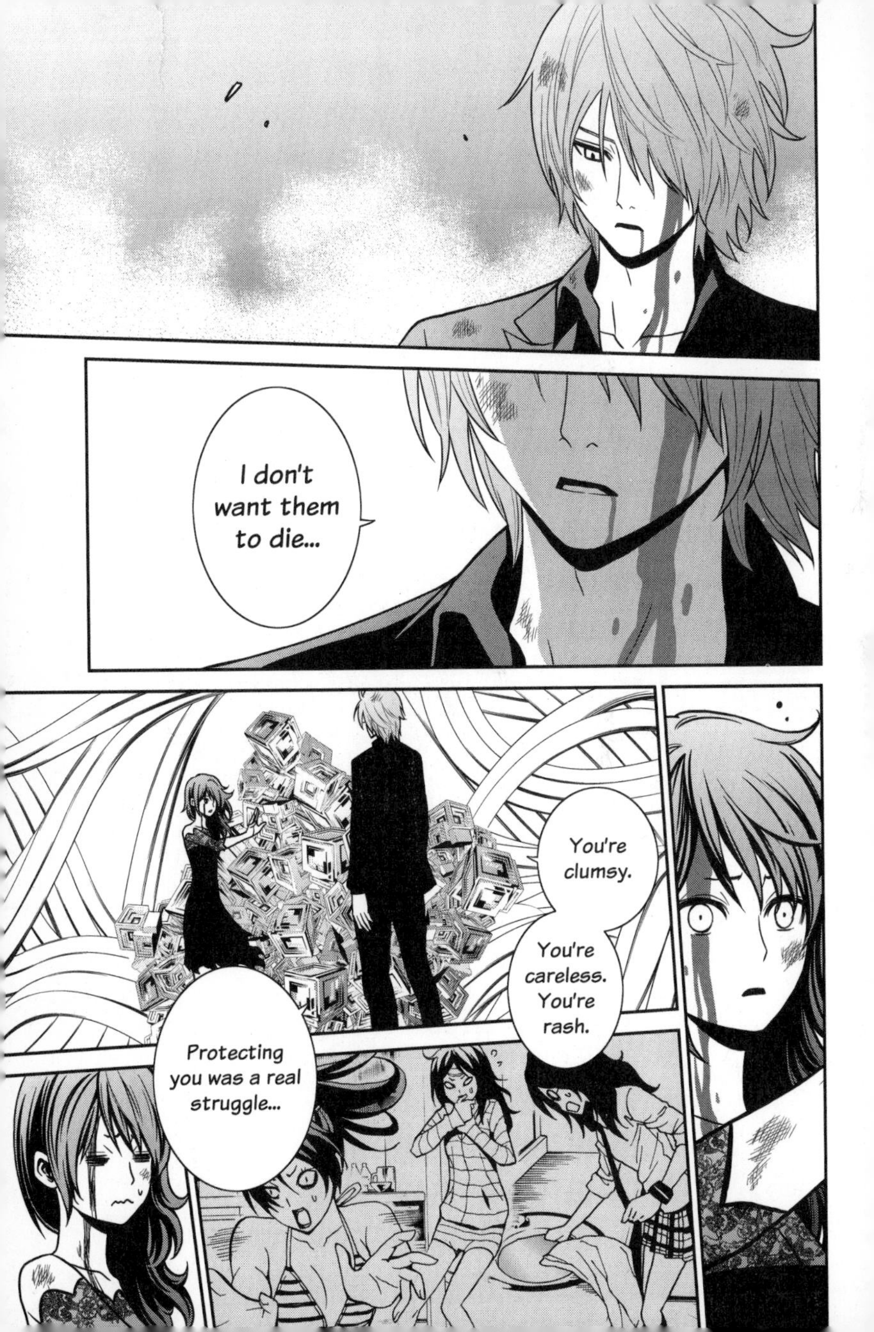
I don't want them to die...
You're clumsy.
You're careless. You're rash.
Protecting you was a real struggle...

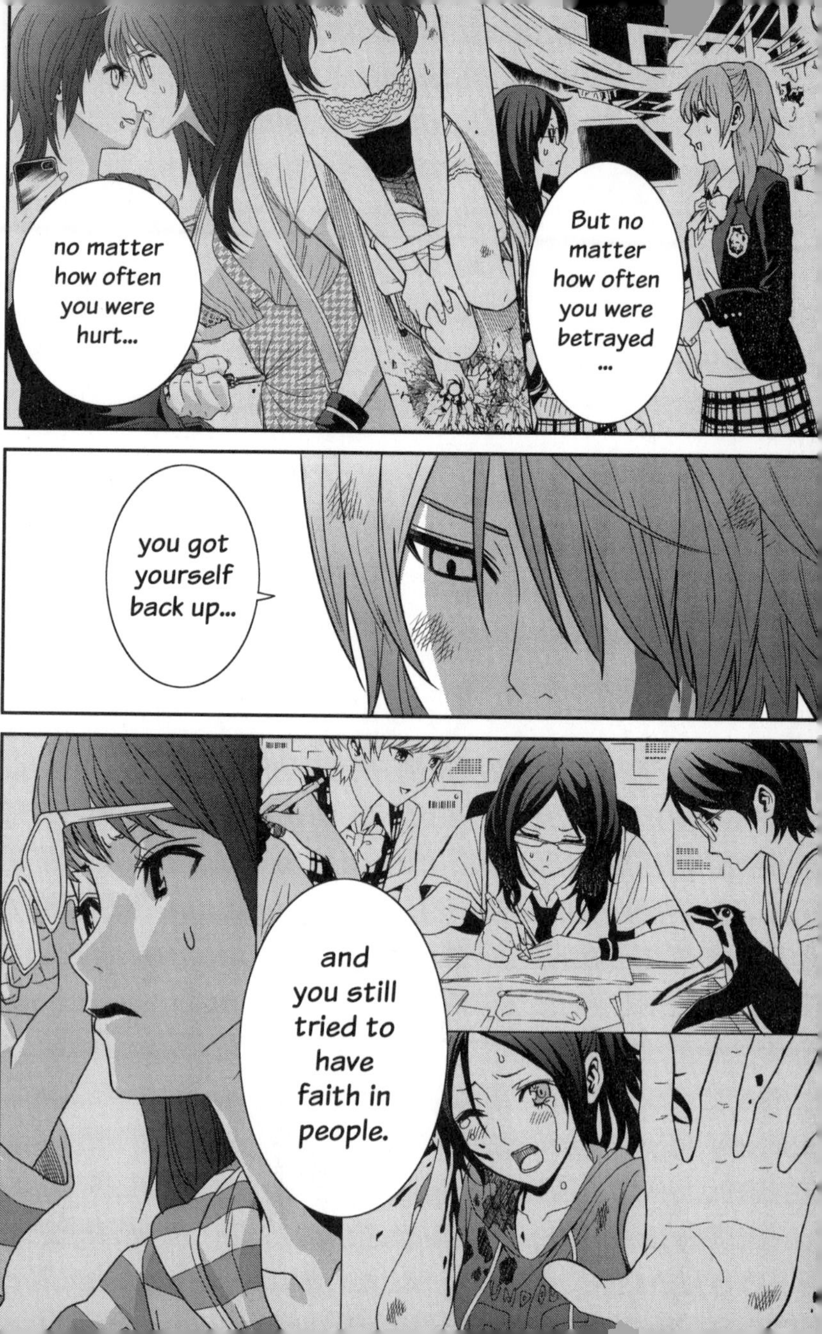
But no matter how often you were betrayed...
no matter how often you were hurt...
you got yourself back up...
and you still tried to have faith in people.

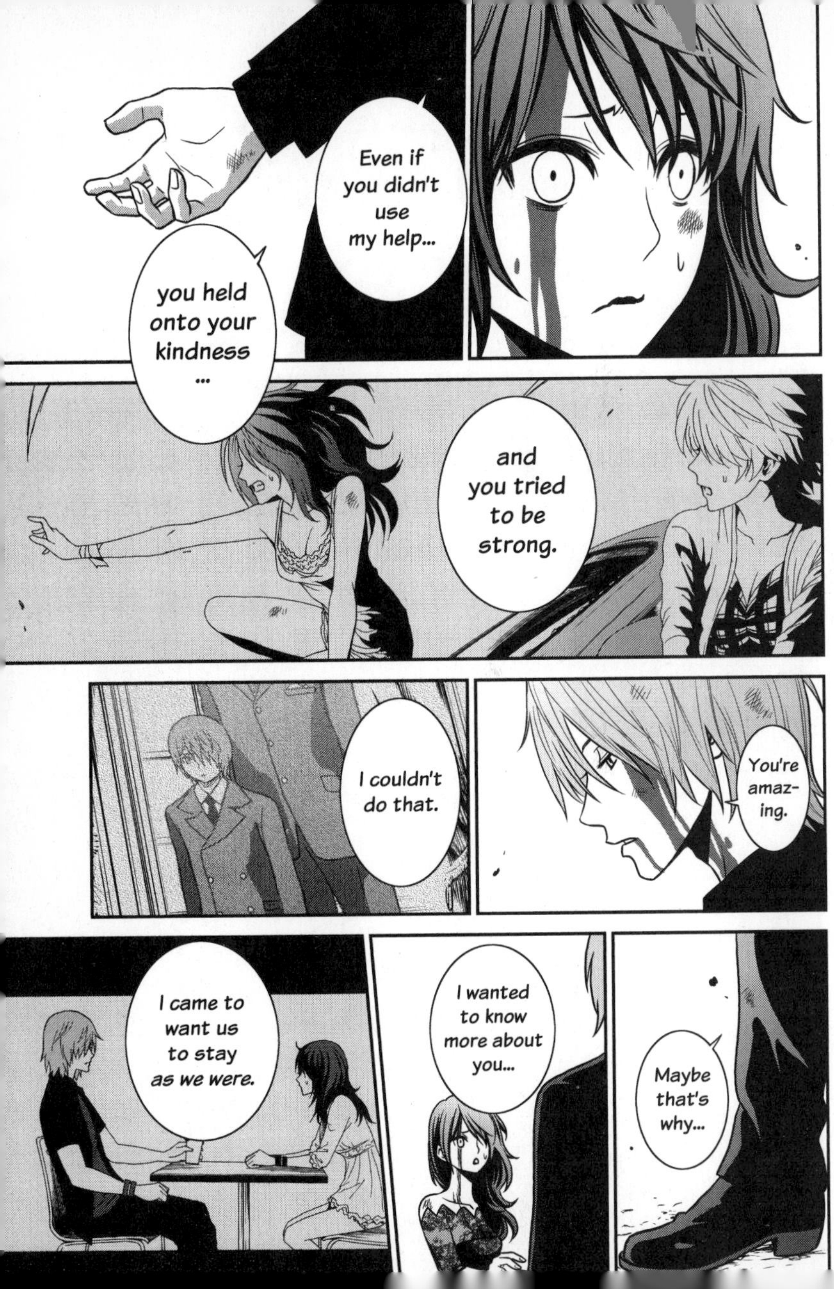
Even if you didn't use my help...
you held onto your kindness ...
and you tried to be strong.
You're amaz-ing.
I couldn't do that.
Maybe that's why...
I wanted to know more about you...
I came to want us to stay as we were.

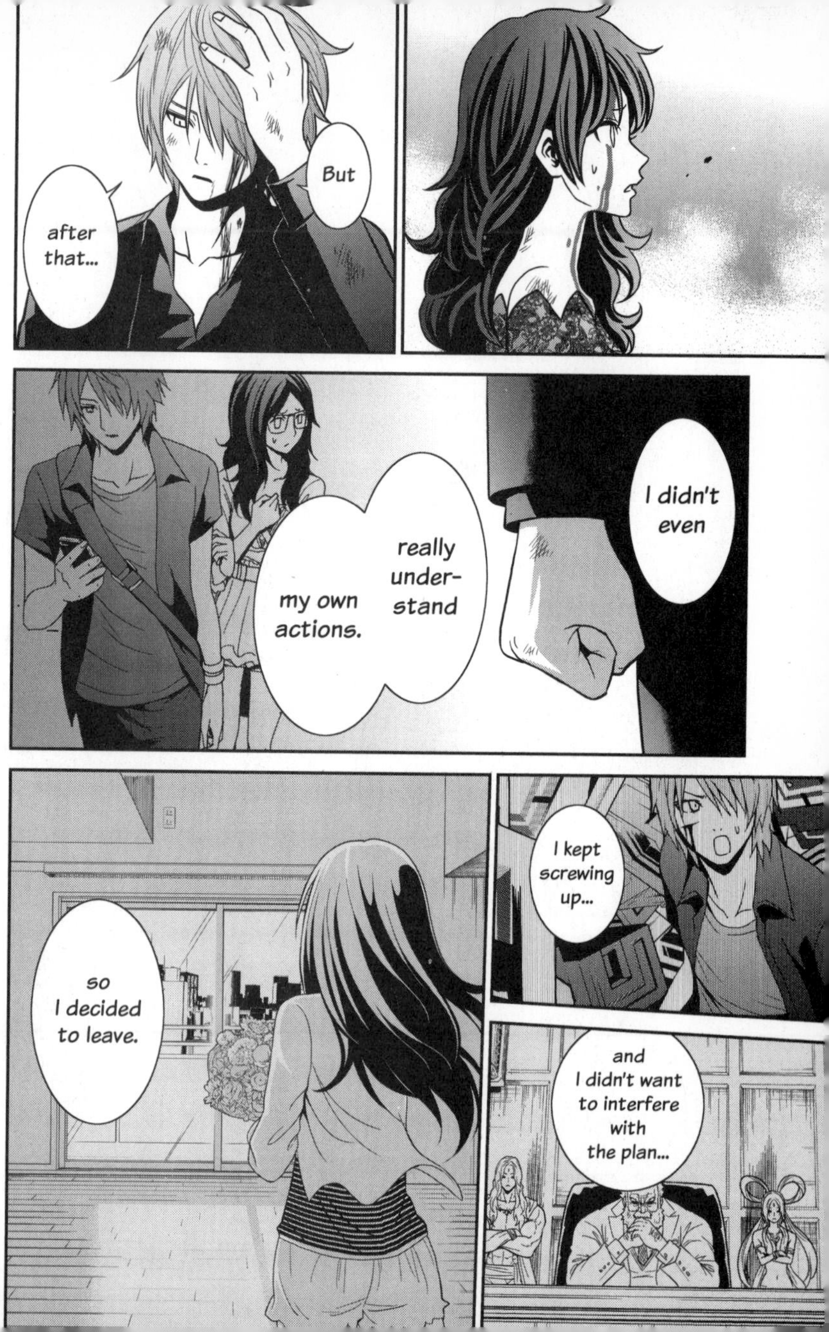
But
after that...
I didn't even
really under-stand
my own actions.
I kept screwing up...
and I didn't want to interfere with the plan...
so I decided to leave.

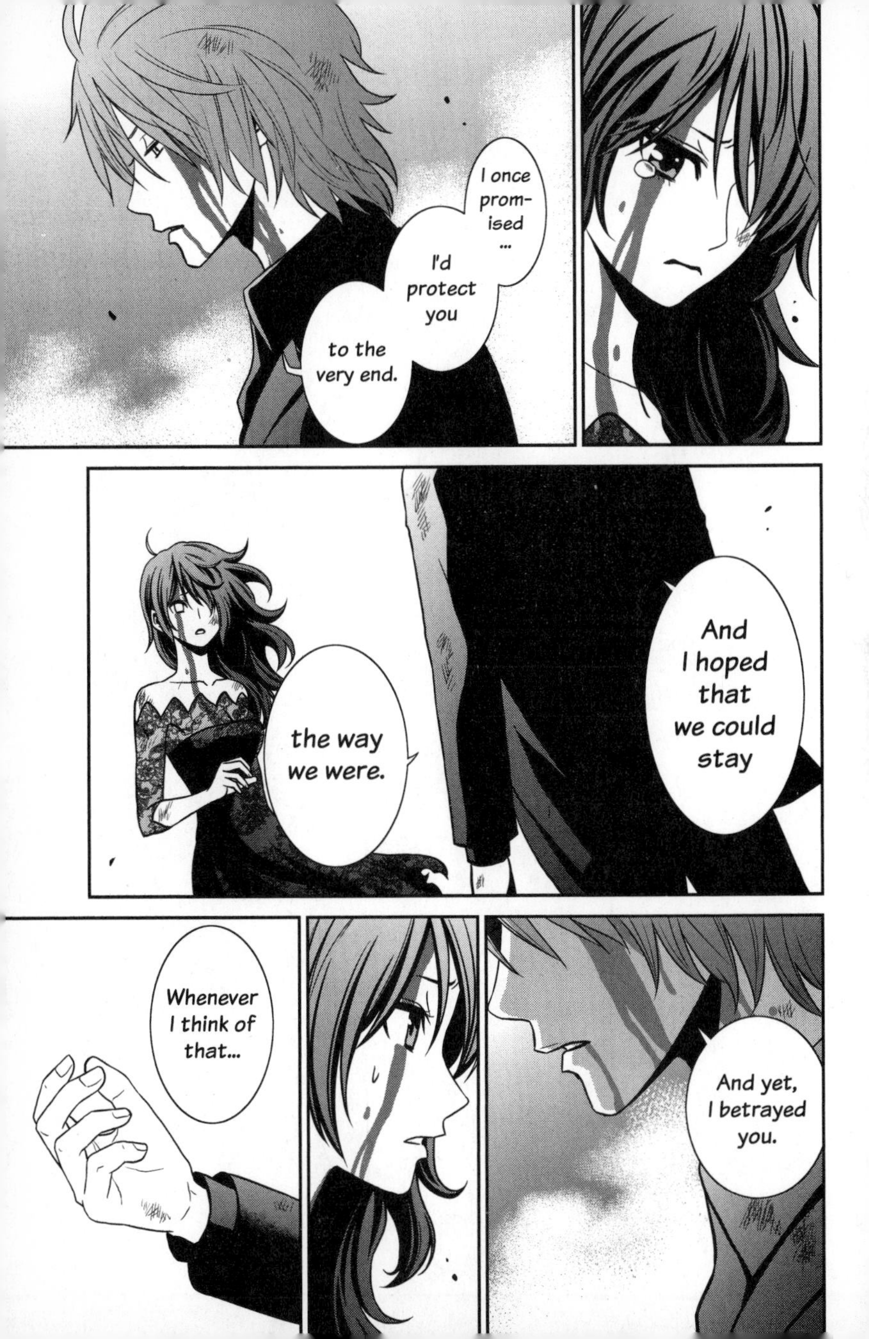
I once prom-ised ...
I'd protect you
to the very end.
And I hoped that we could stay
the way we were.
And yet, I betrayed you.
Whenever I think of that...

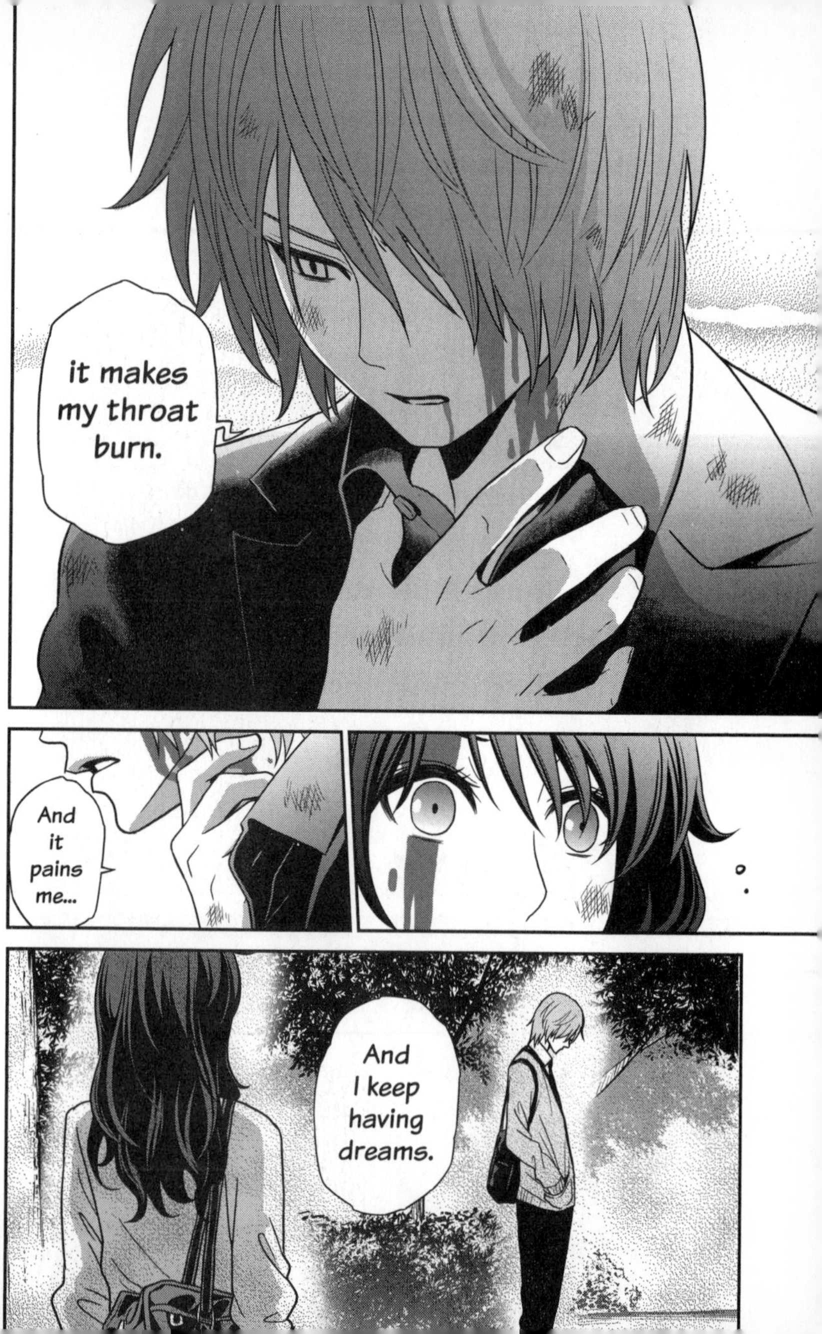
it makes my throat burn.
And it pains me...
And I keep having dreams.

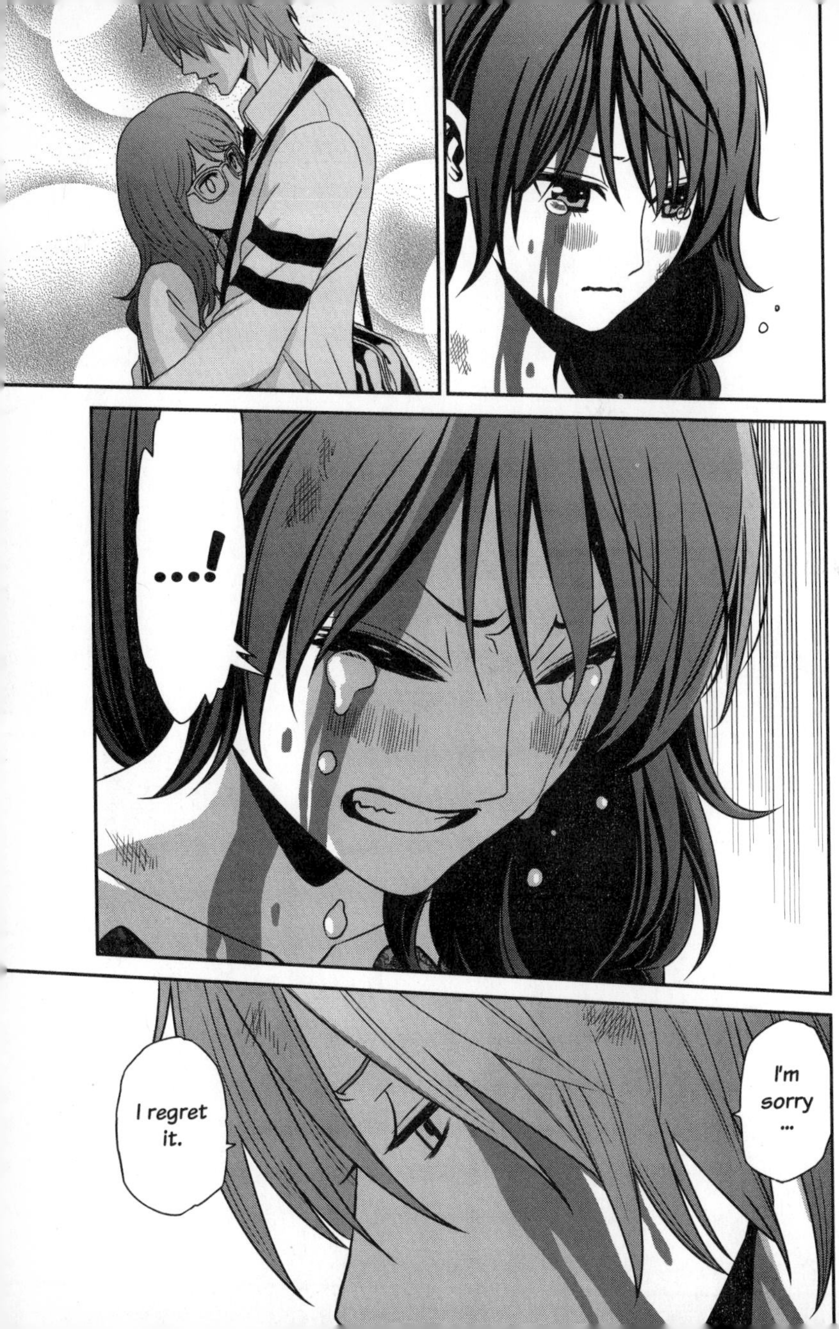
...!
I'm sorry ...
I regret it.

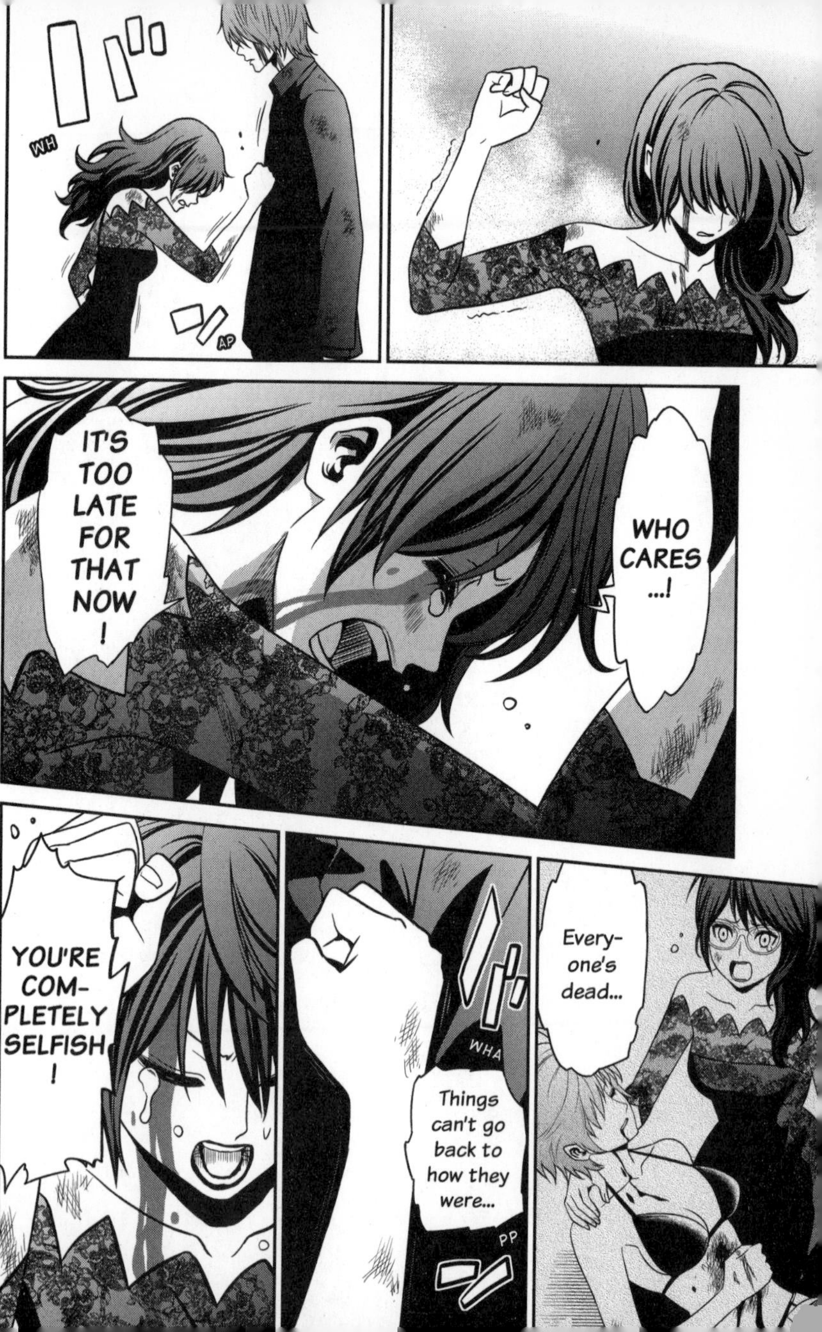
WH
AP
WHO CARES ...!
IT'S TOO LATE FOR THAT NOW!
Everyone's dead...
WHA
Things can't go back to how they were...
PP
YOU'RE COMPLETELY SELFISH!

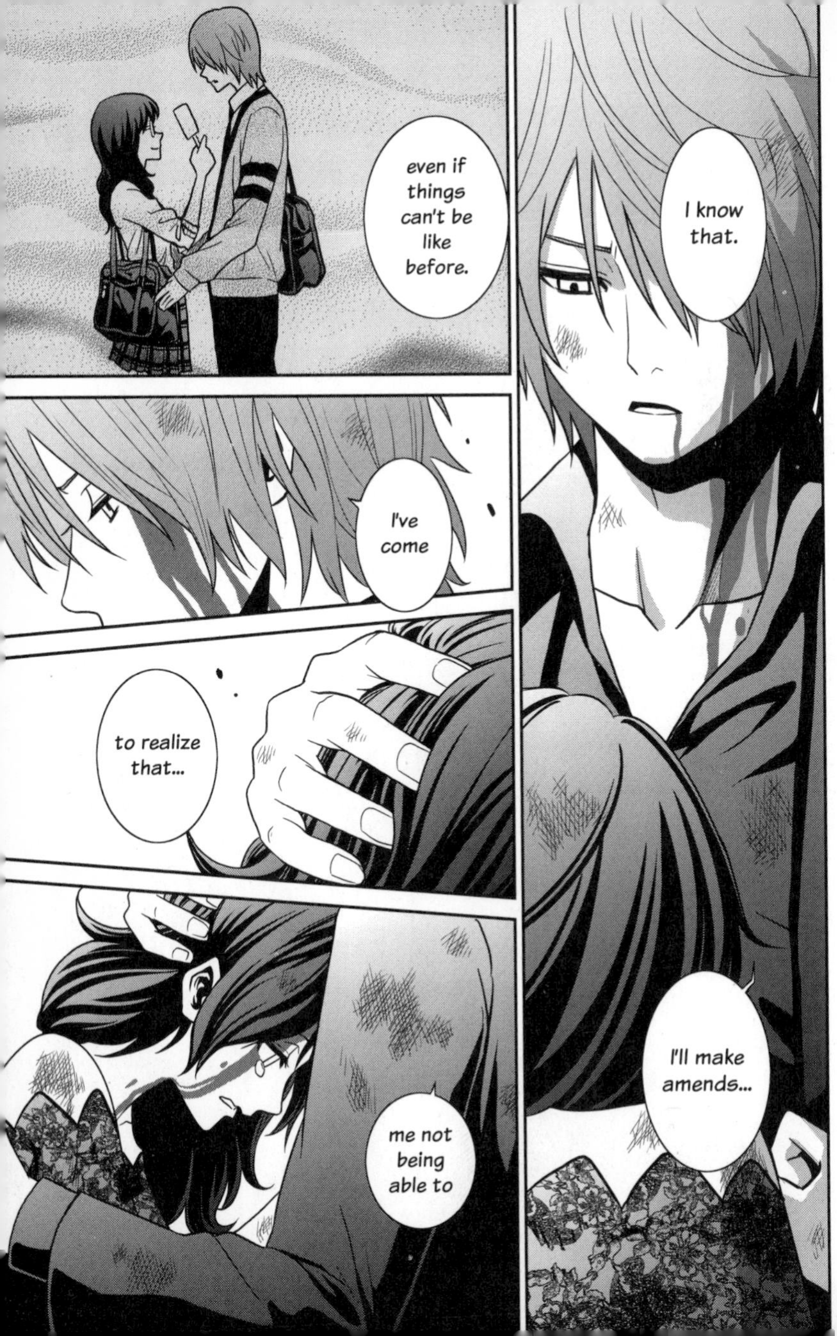

I know that.
I'll make amends...
even if things can't be like before.
I've come
to realize that...
me not being able to

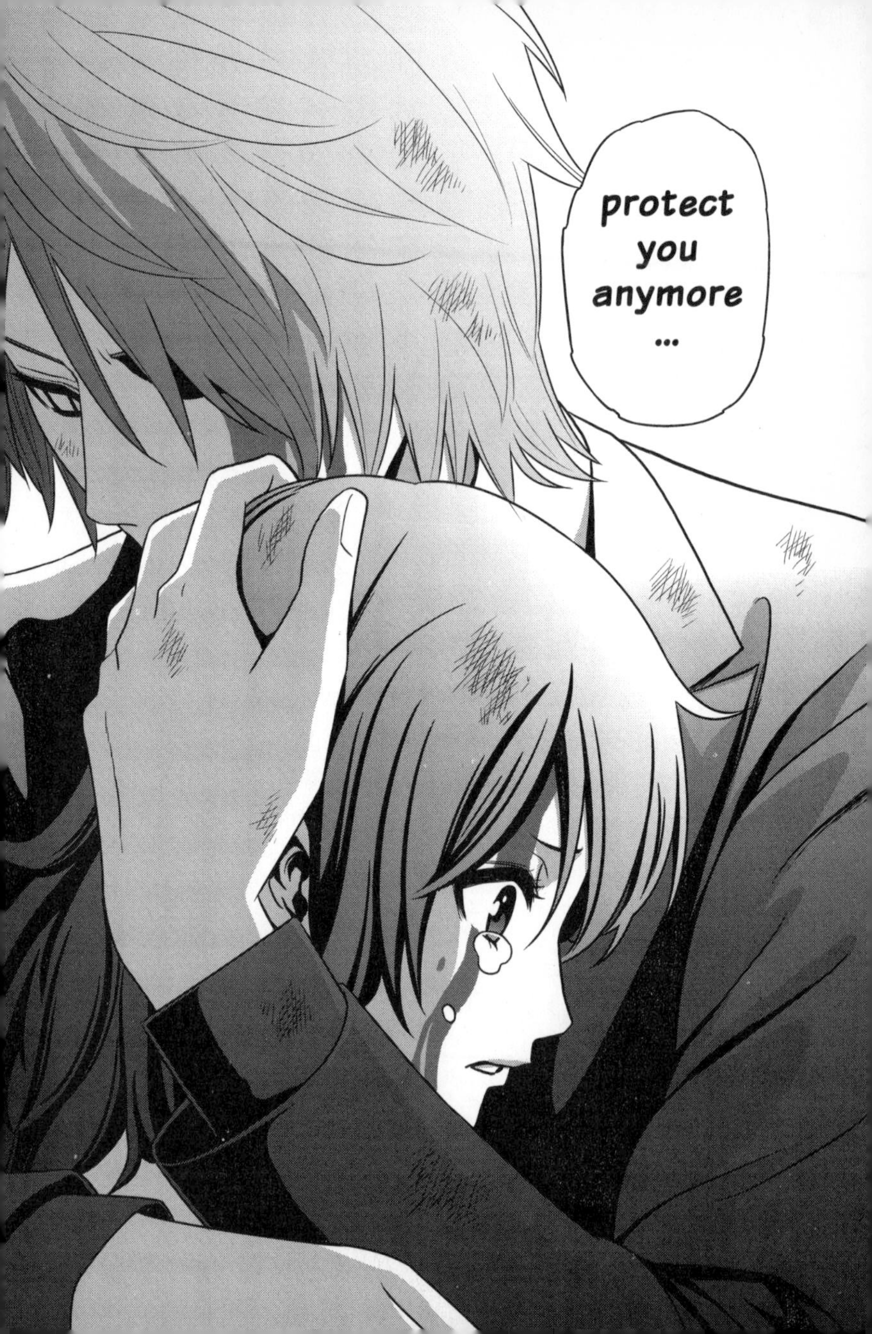
protect you anymore ...

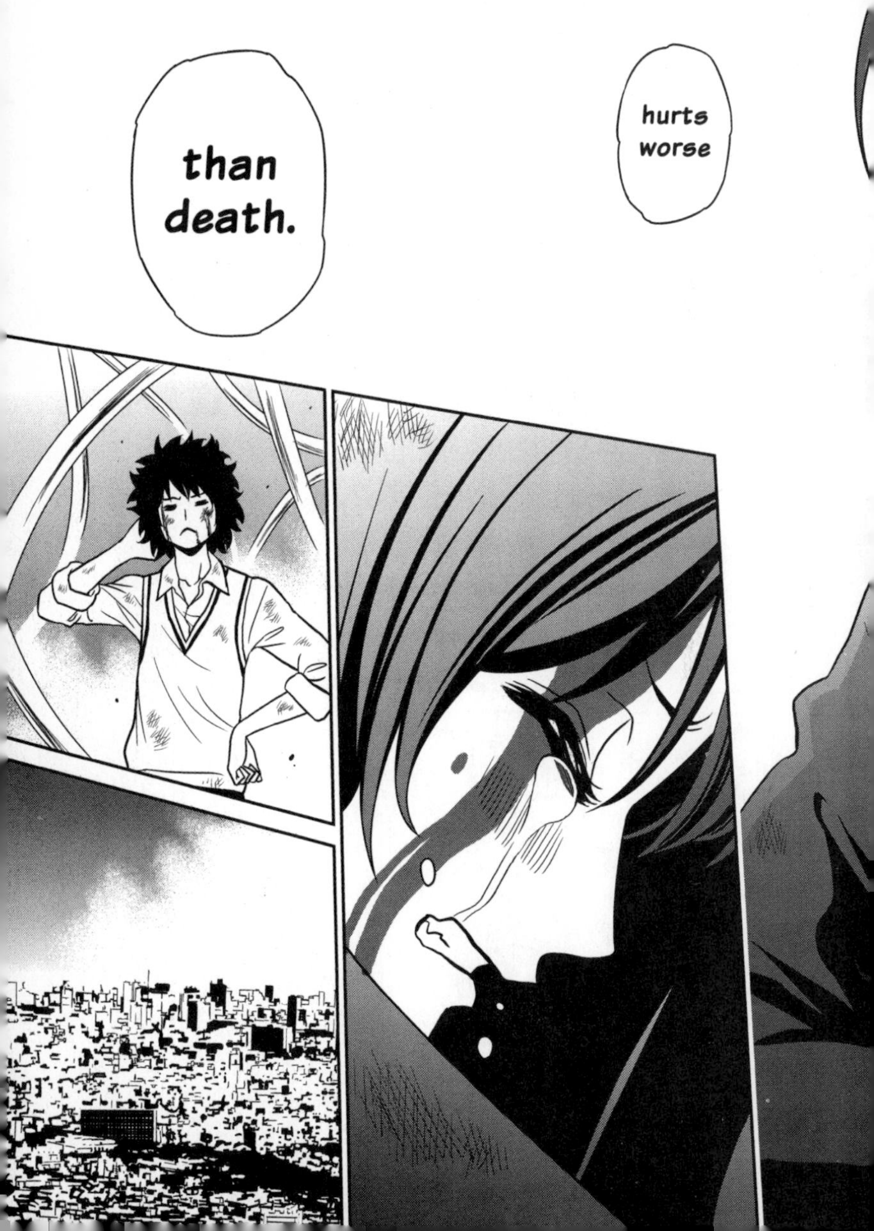
hurts worse
than death.

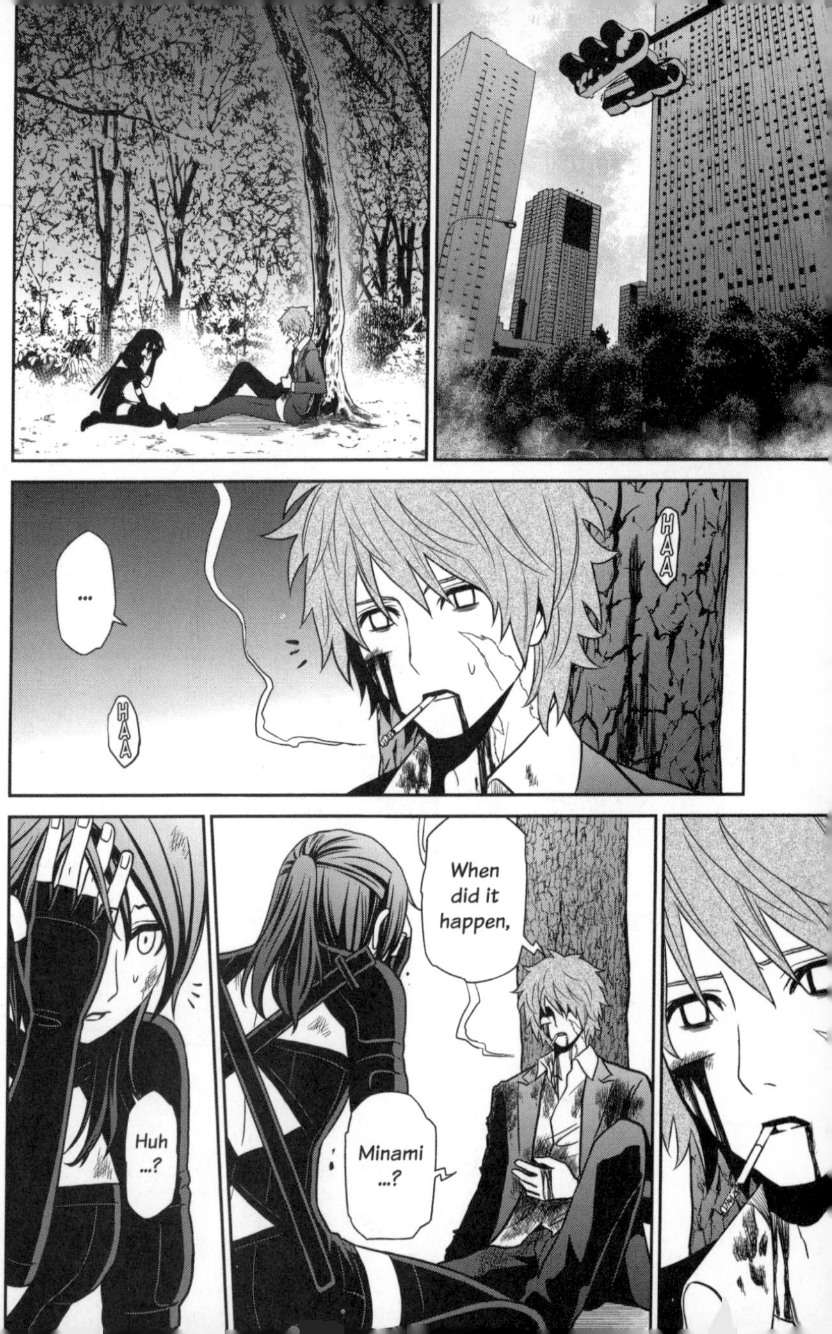
HAA
...
HAA
When did it happen,
Minami ...?
Huh ...?

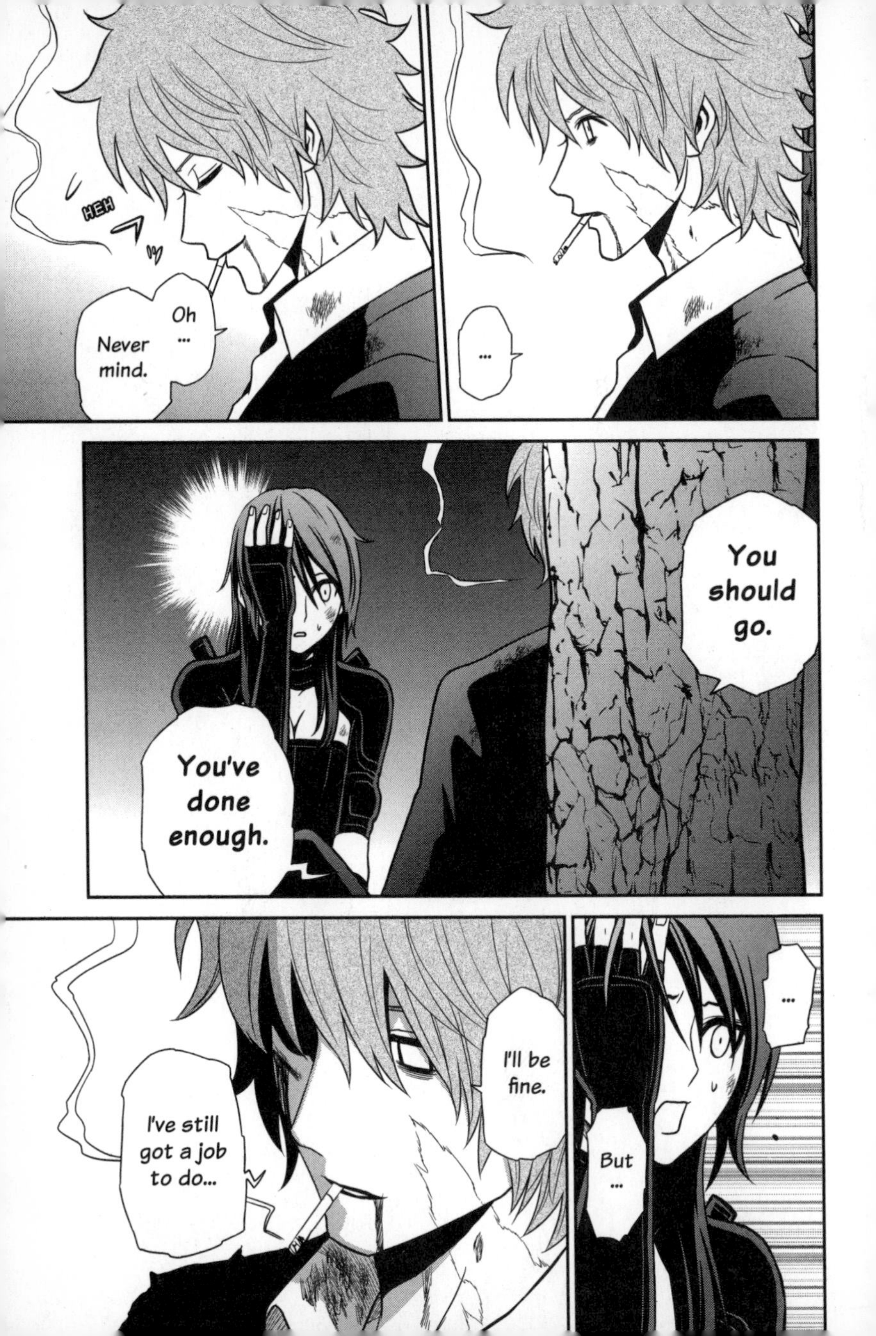
...
HEH
Oh ...
Never mind.
You should go.
You've done enough.
...
But ...
I'll be fine.
I've still got a job to do...

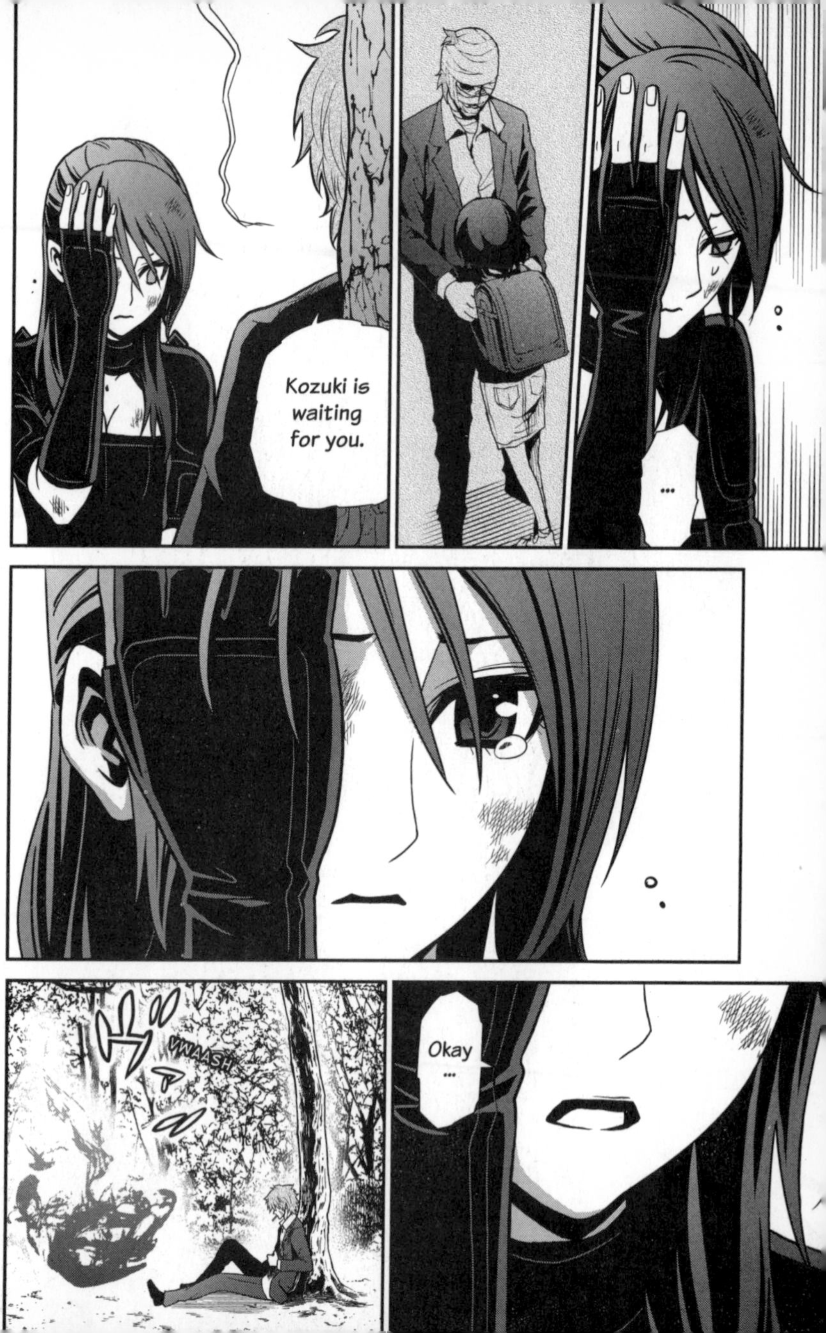
...
Kozuki is waiting for you.
Okay ...
VWAASH

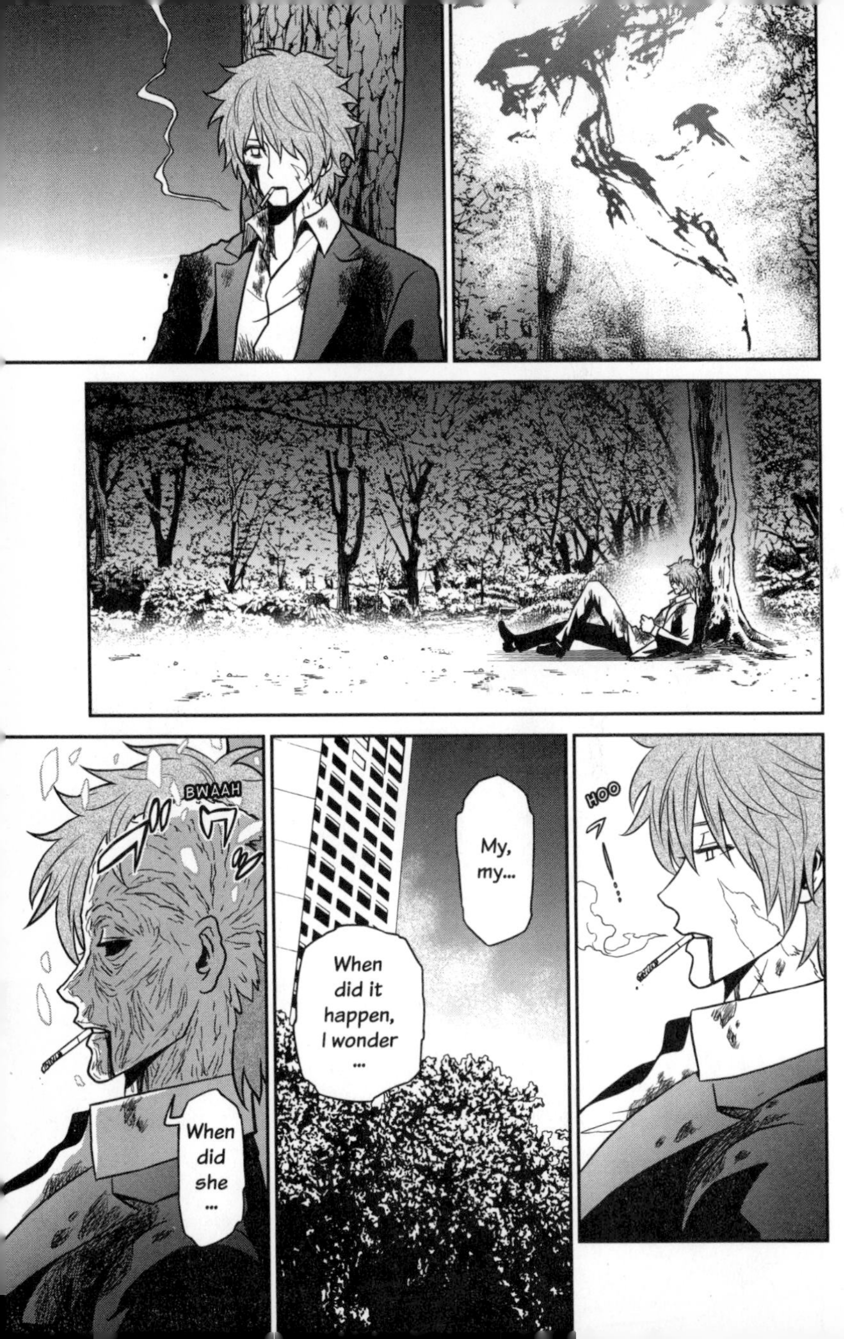
HOO
My, my...
When did it happen, I wonder ...
BWAAH
When did she ...

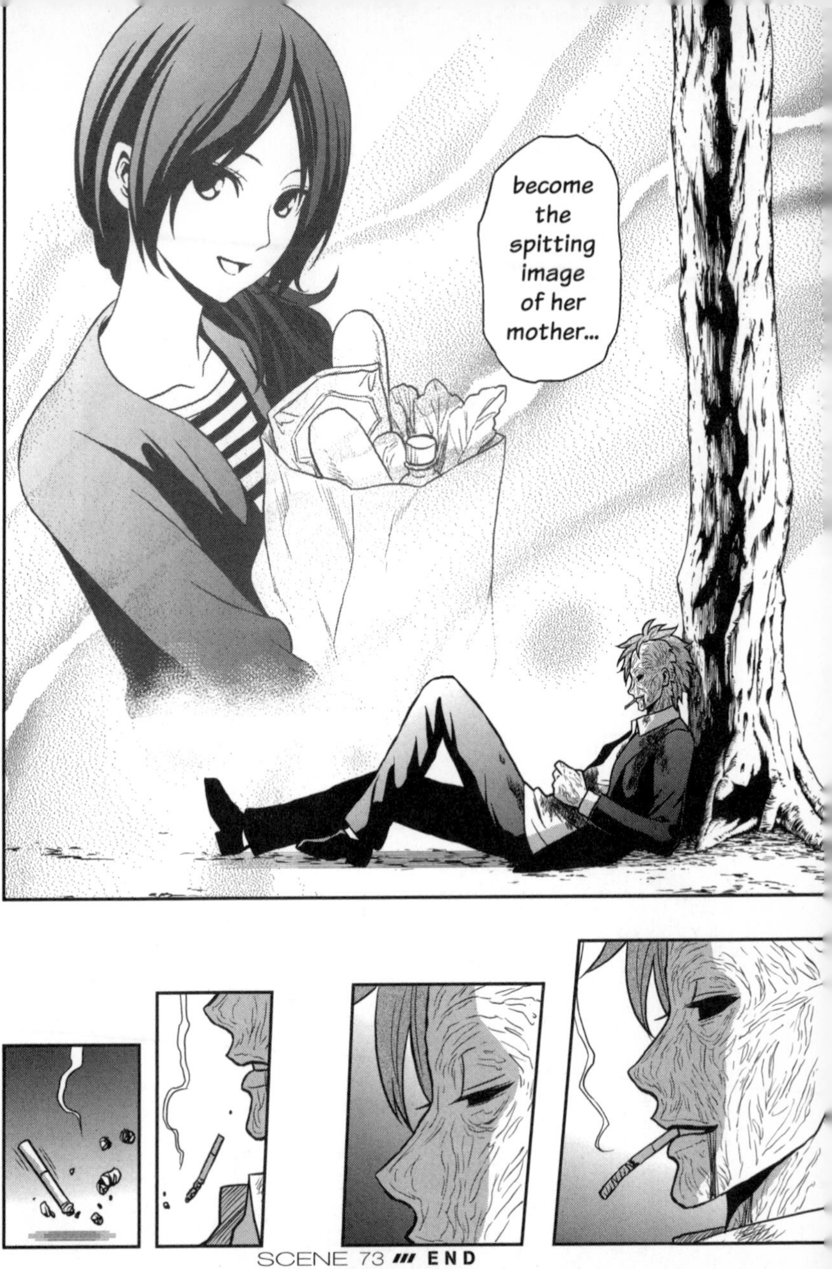
become the spitting image of her mother...

SCENE 73 /// END

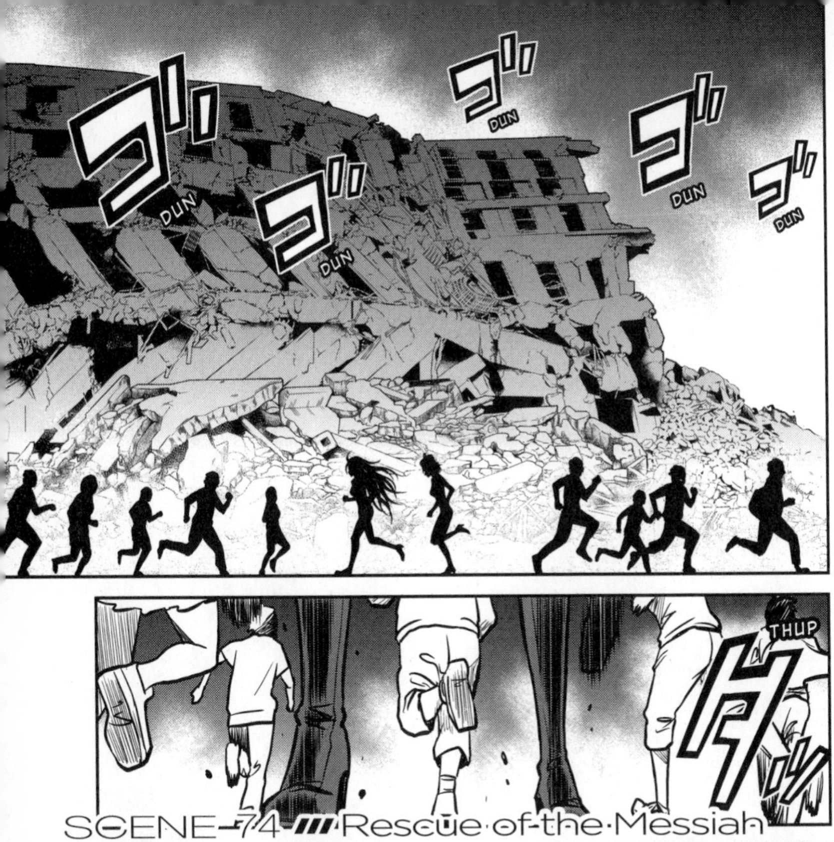
DUN
DUN
DUN
DUN
DUN
THUP

SCENE-74 /// Rescue of the Messiah

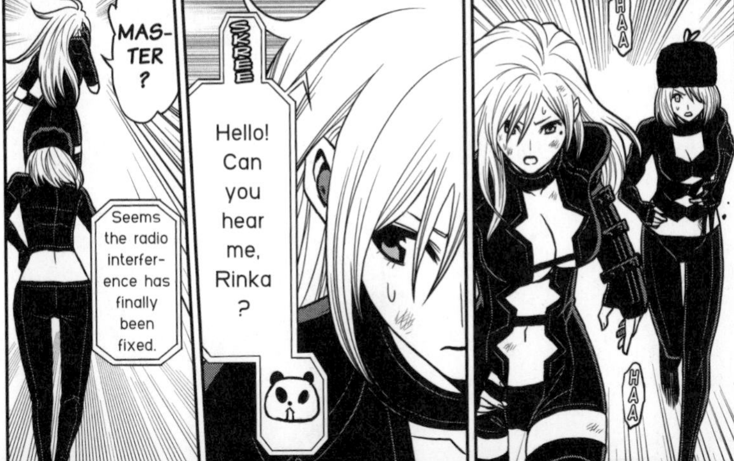
HAA
HAA
SKREE
Hello! Can you hear me, Rinka?
MAS-TER?
Seems the radio interfer-ence has finally been fixed.

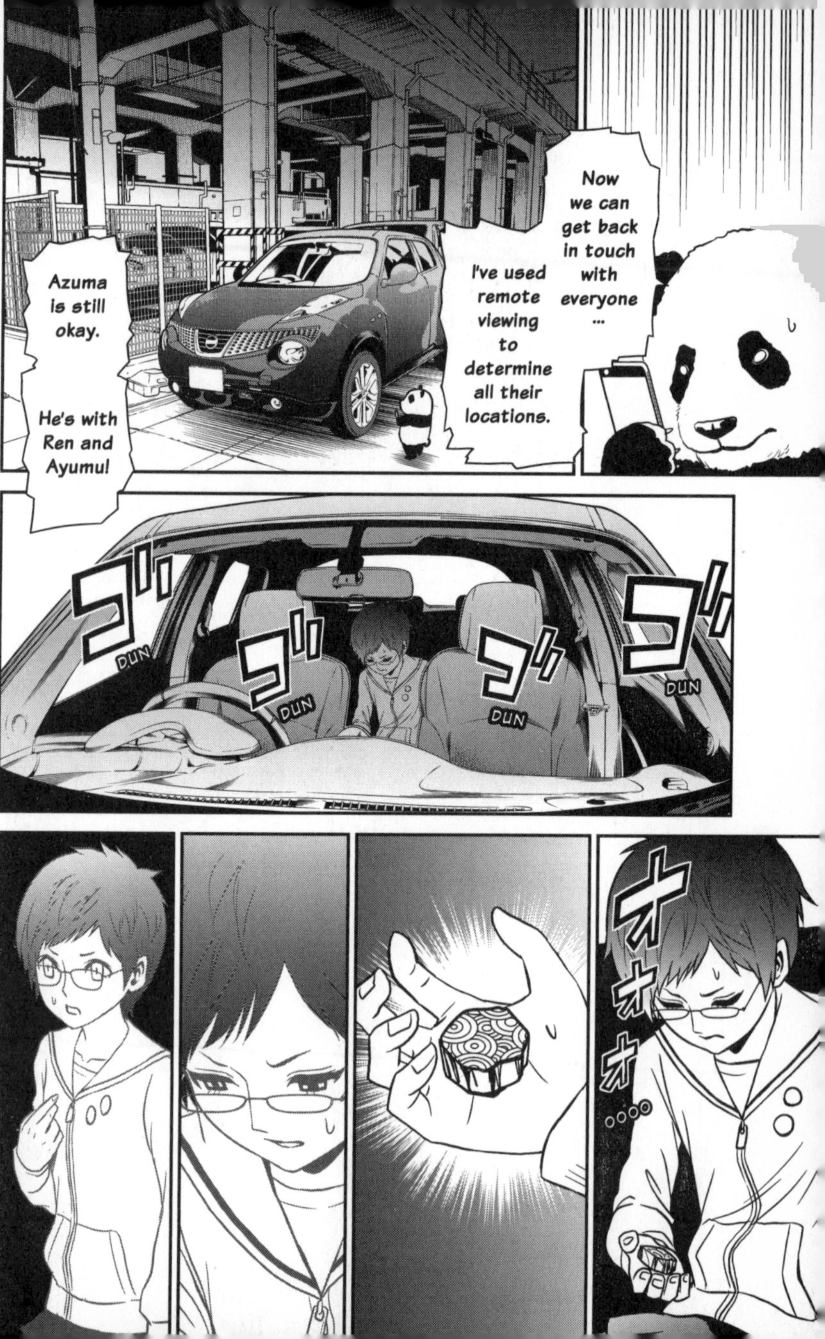
Now we can get back in touch with everyone ...
I've used remote viewing to determine all their locations.
Azuma is still okay.
He's with Ren and Ayumu!
DUN
DUN
DUN
DUN
oooo

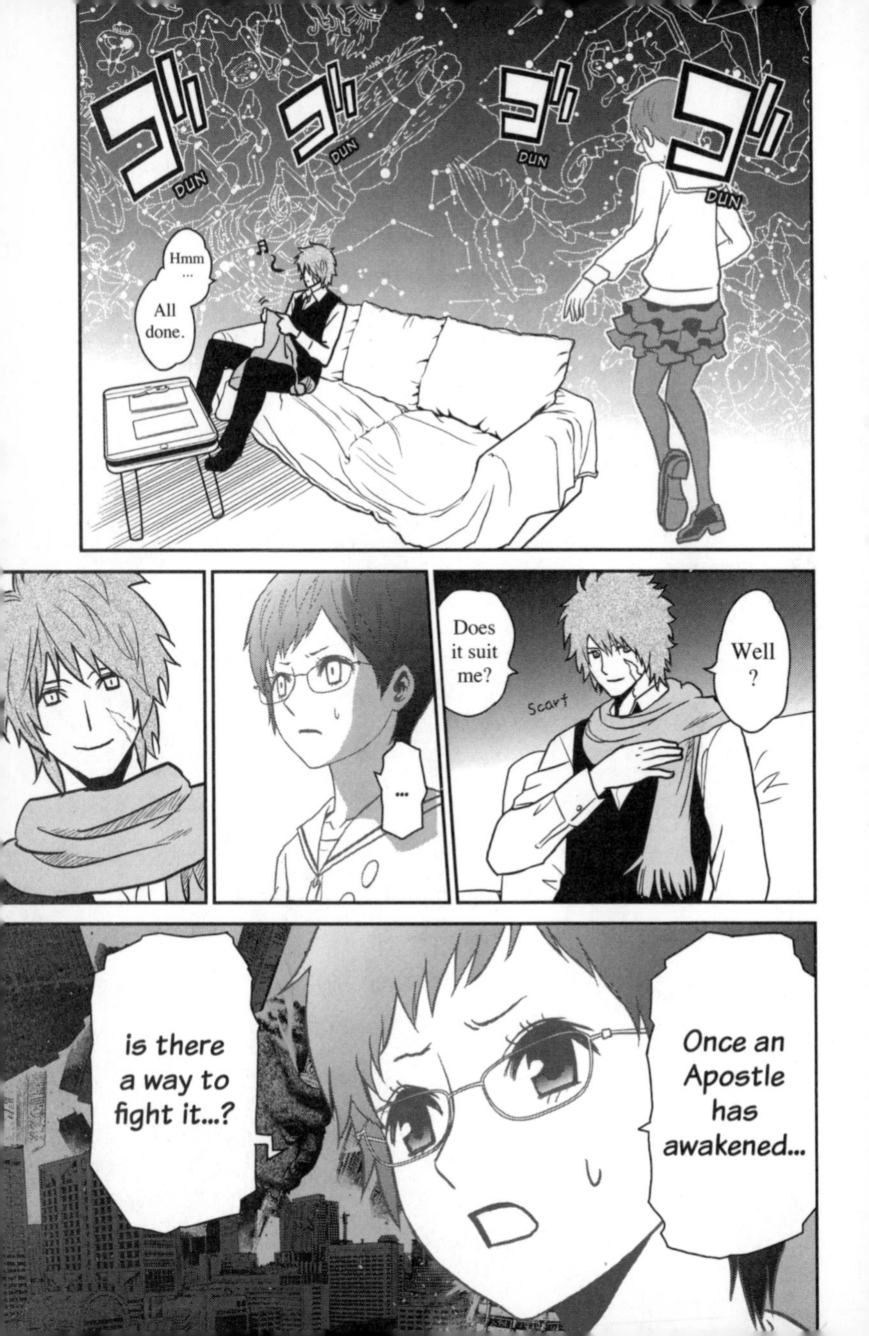
DUN
DUN
DUN
DUN
Hmm ...
All done.
Well ?
Does it suit me?
Scarf
...
Once an Apostle has awakened...
is there a way to fight it...?

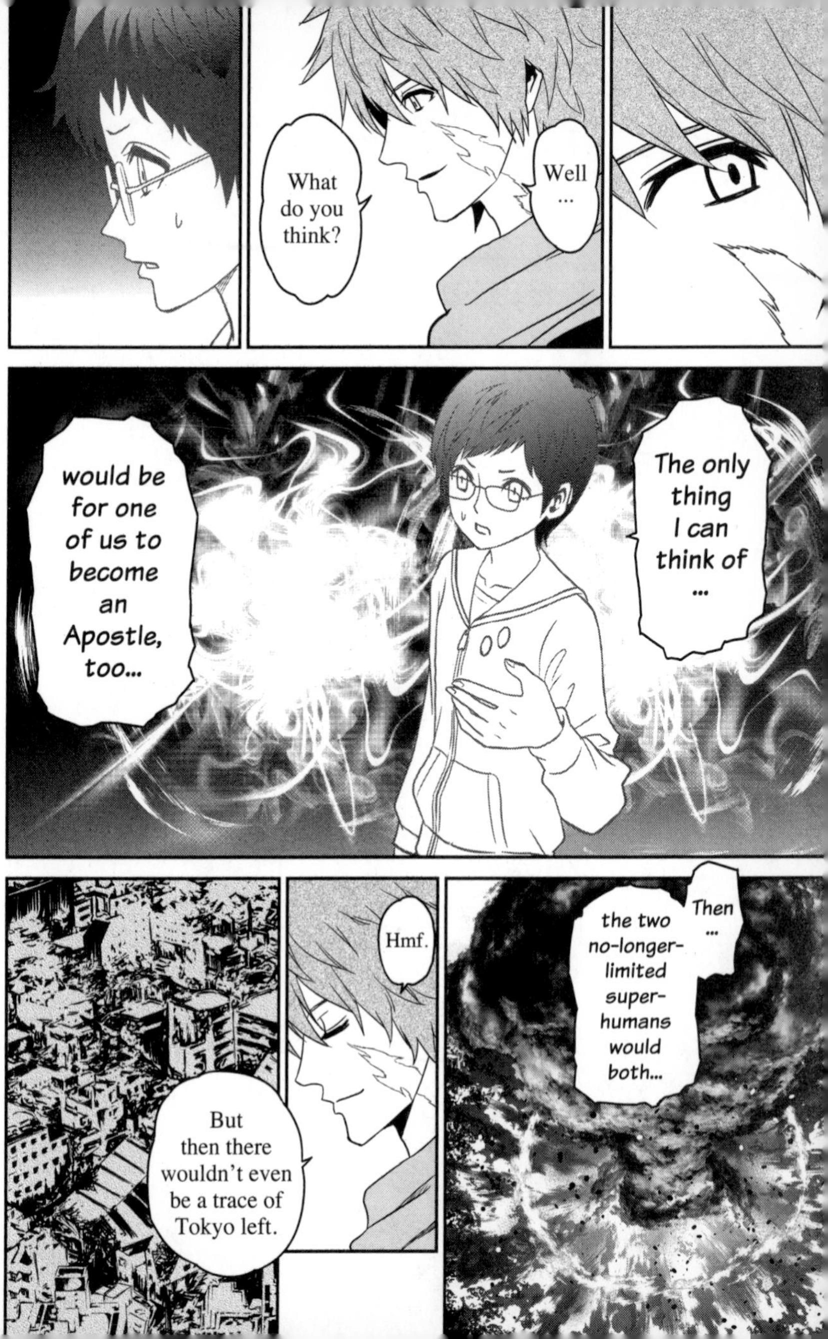
Well …
What do you think?
The only thing I can think of …
would be for one of us to become an Apostle, too…
Then …
the two no-longer-limited super-humans would both…
Hmf.
But then there wouldn't even be a trace of Tokyo left.

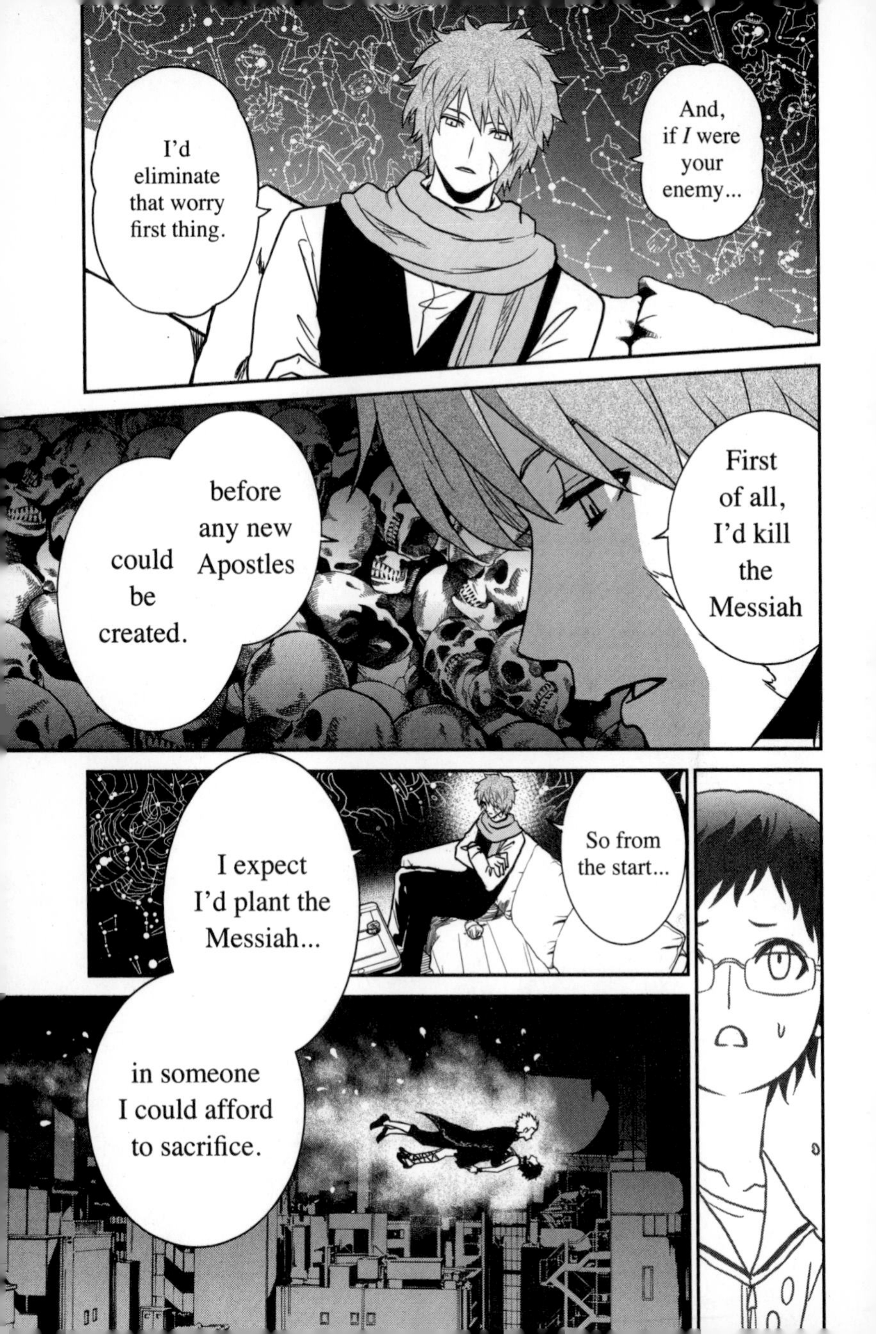
And, if *I* were your enemy...
I'd eliminate that worry first thing.
First of all, I'd kill the Messiah
before any new Apostles could be created.
So from the start...
I expect I'd plant the Messiah...
in someone I could afford to sacrifice.

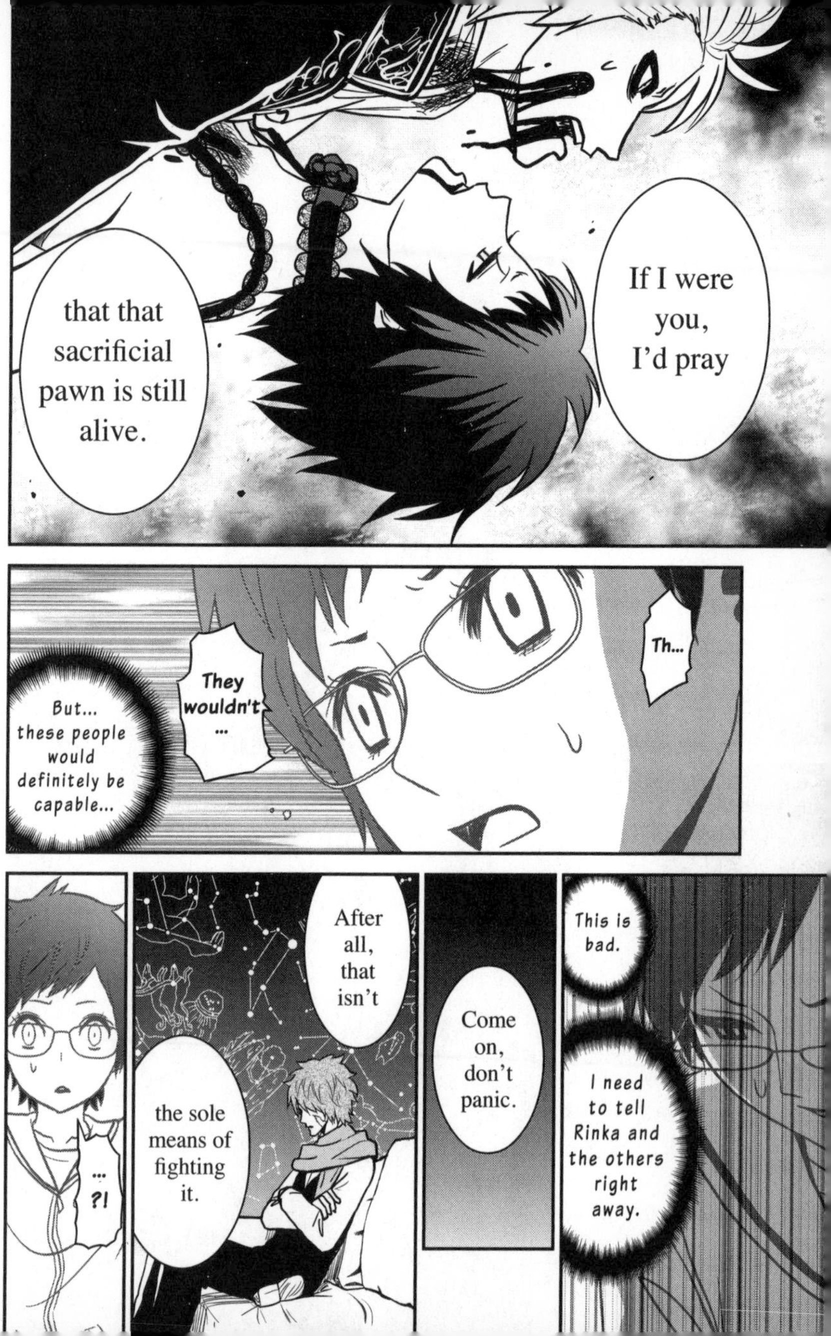

If I were you, I'd pray
that that sacrificial pawn is still alive.
Th...
They wouldn't ...
But... these people would definitely be capable...
This is bad.
I need to tell Rinka and the others right away.
Come on, don't panic.
After all, that isn't
the sole means of fighting it.
...?!

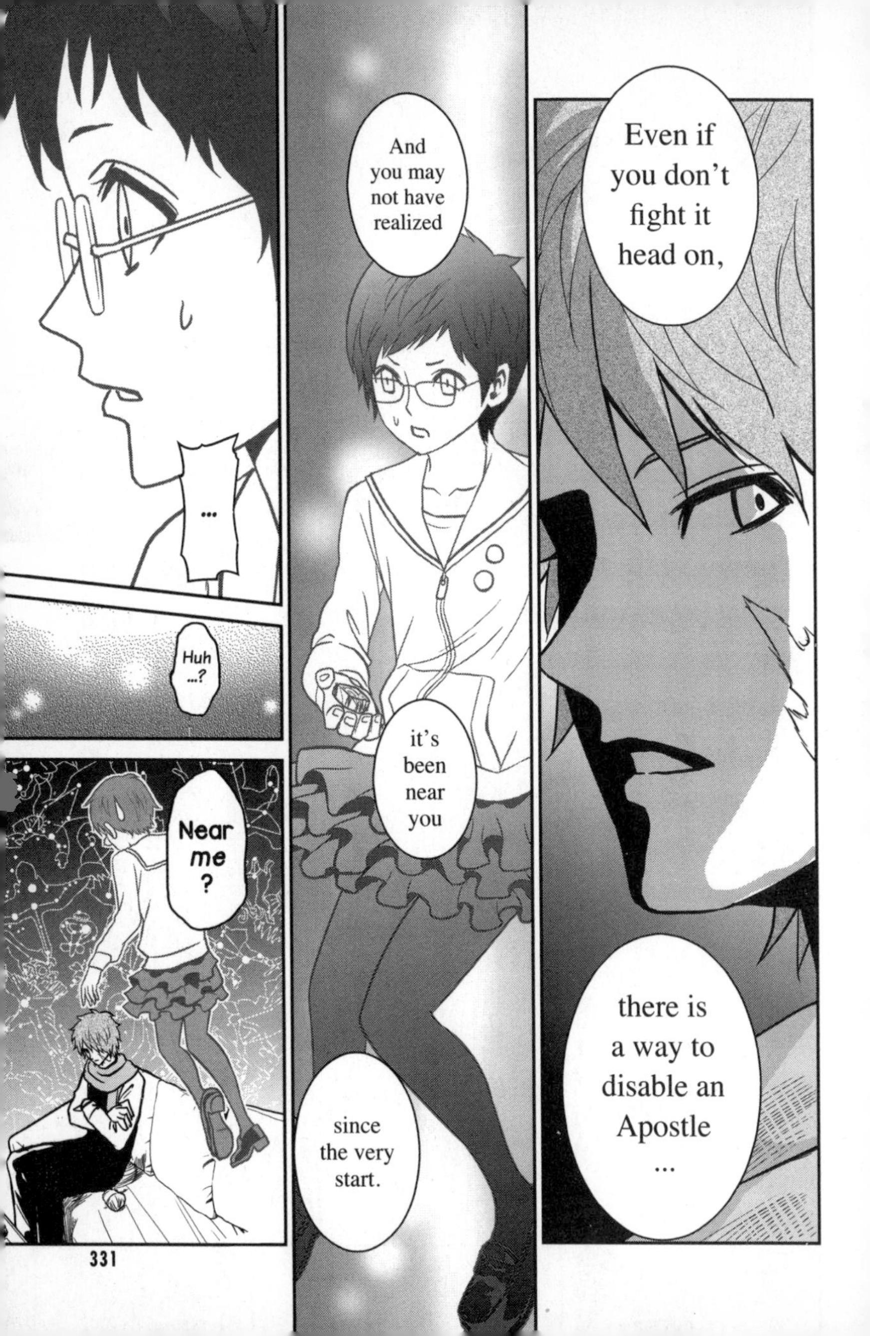
Even if you don't fight it head on,
there is a way to disable an Apostle ...
And you may not have realized
it's been near you
since the very start.
...
Huh ...?
Near me ?

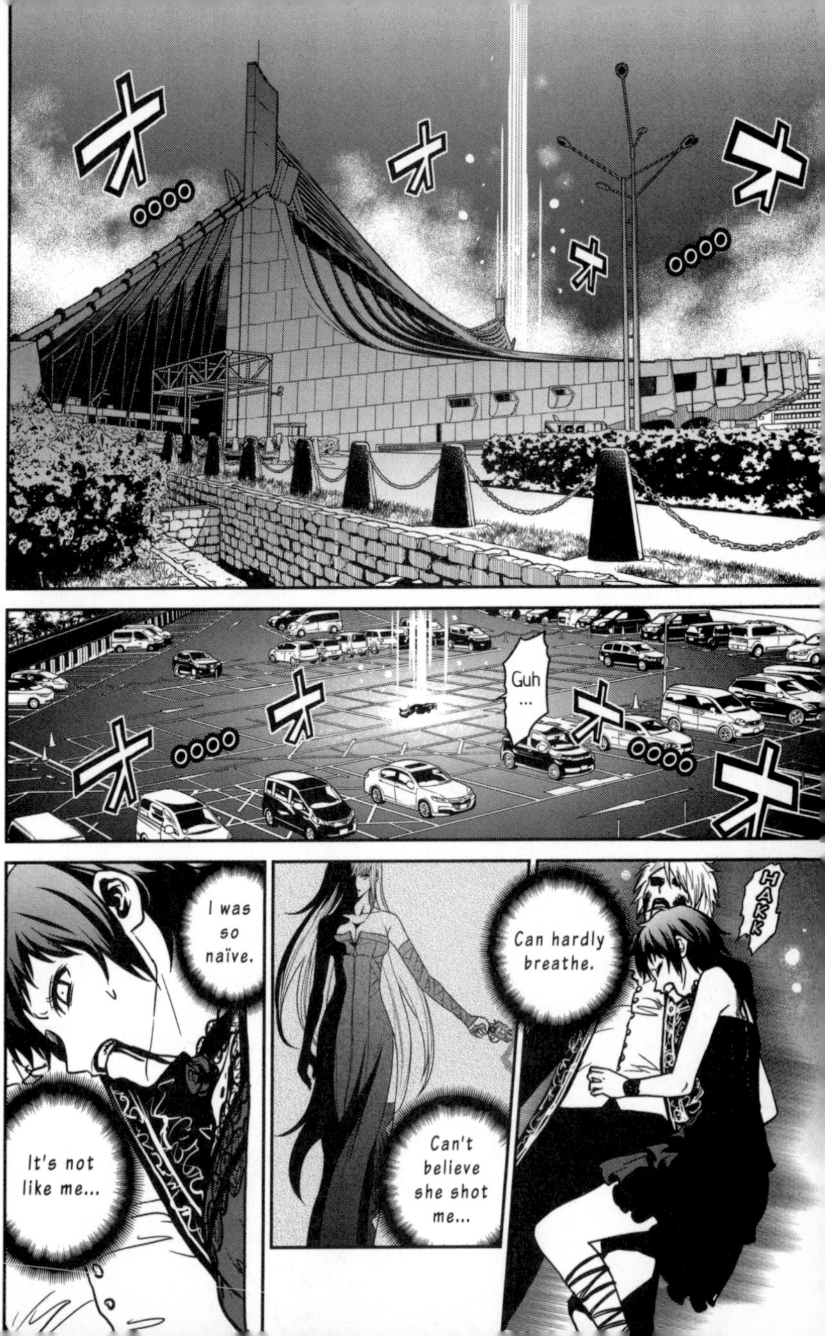

オ
oooo
オ
オ
oooo
オ
oooo
オ
Guh ...
オ
oooo
オ
HAKK
Can hardly breathe.
Can't believe she shot me...
I was so naïve.
It's not like me...

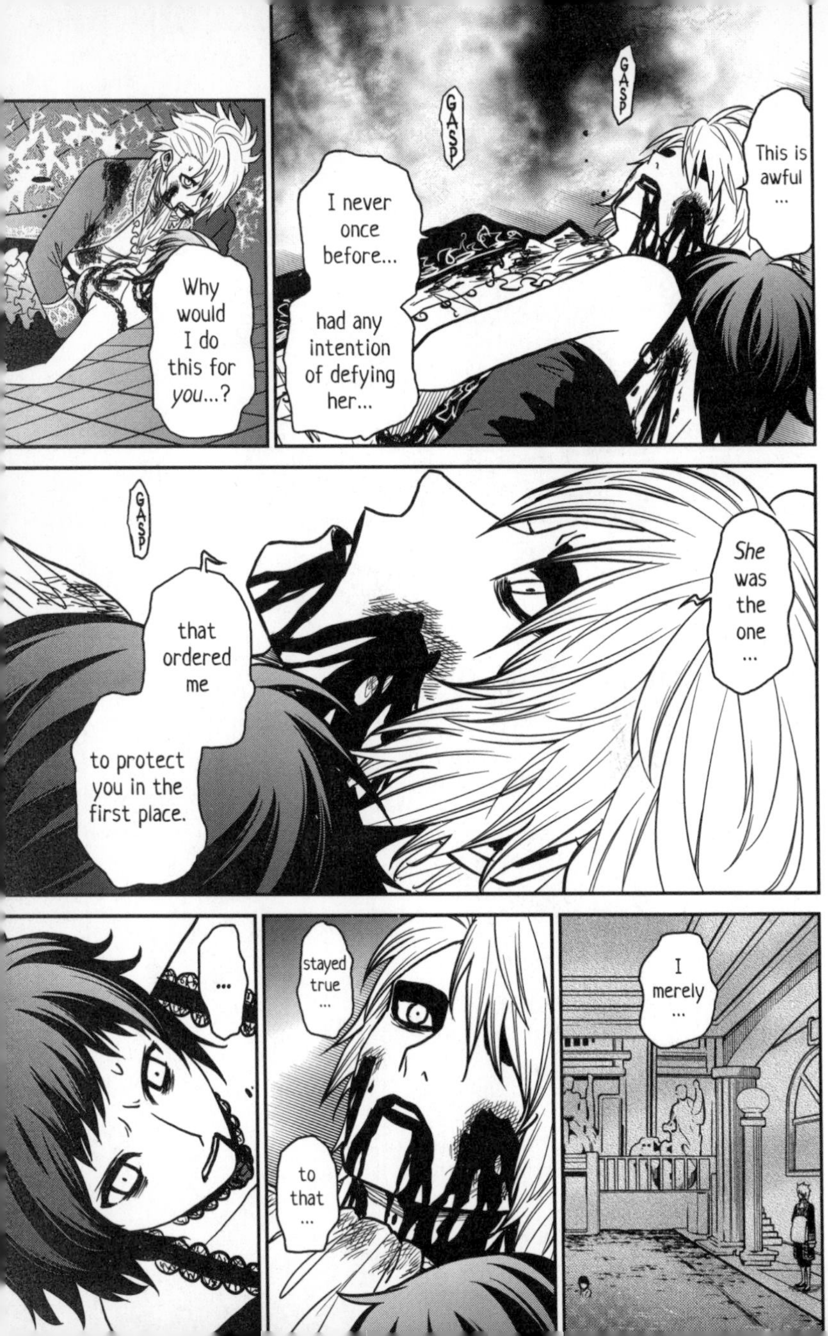
This is awful ...
GASP
GASP
I never once before...
had any intention of defying her...
Why would I do this for *you*...?
She was the one ...
GASP
that ordered me
to protect you in the first place.
I merely ...
stayed true ...
to that ...
...

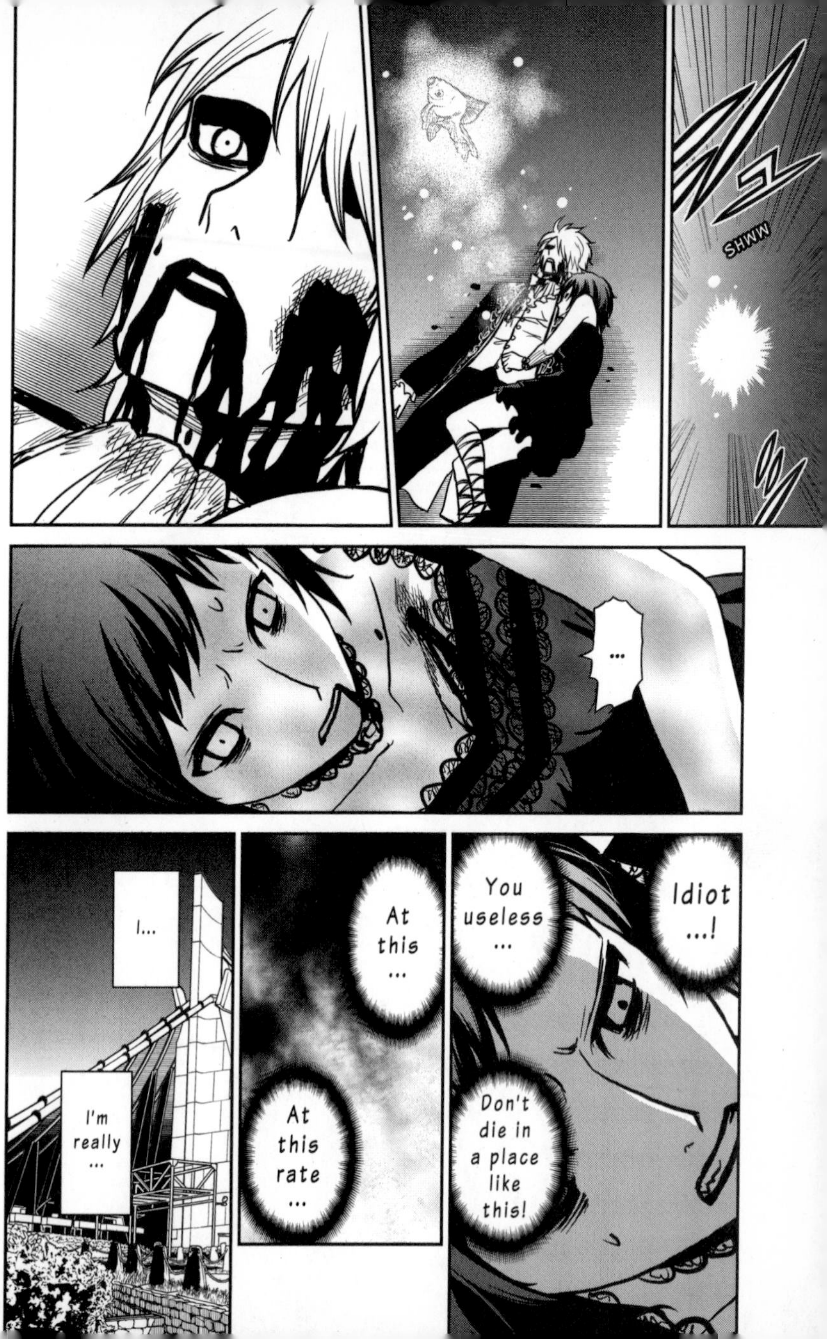
SHWW
...
Idiot ...!
You useless ...
Don't die in a place like this!
At this ...
At this rate ...
I...
I'm really ...

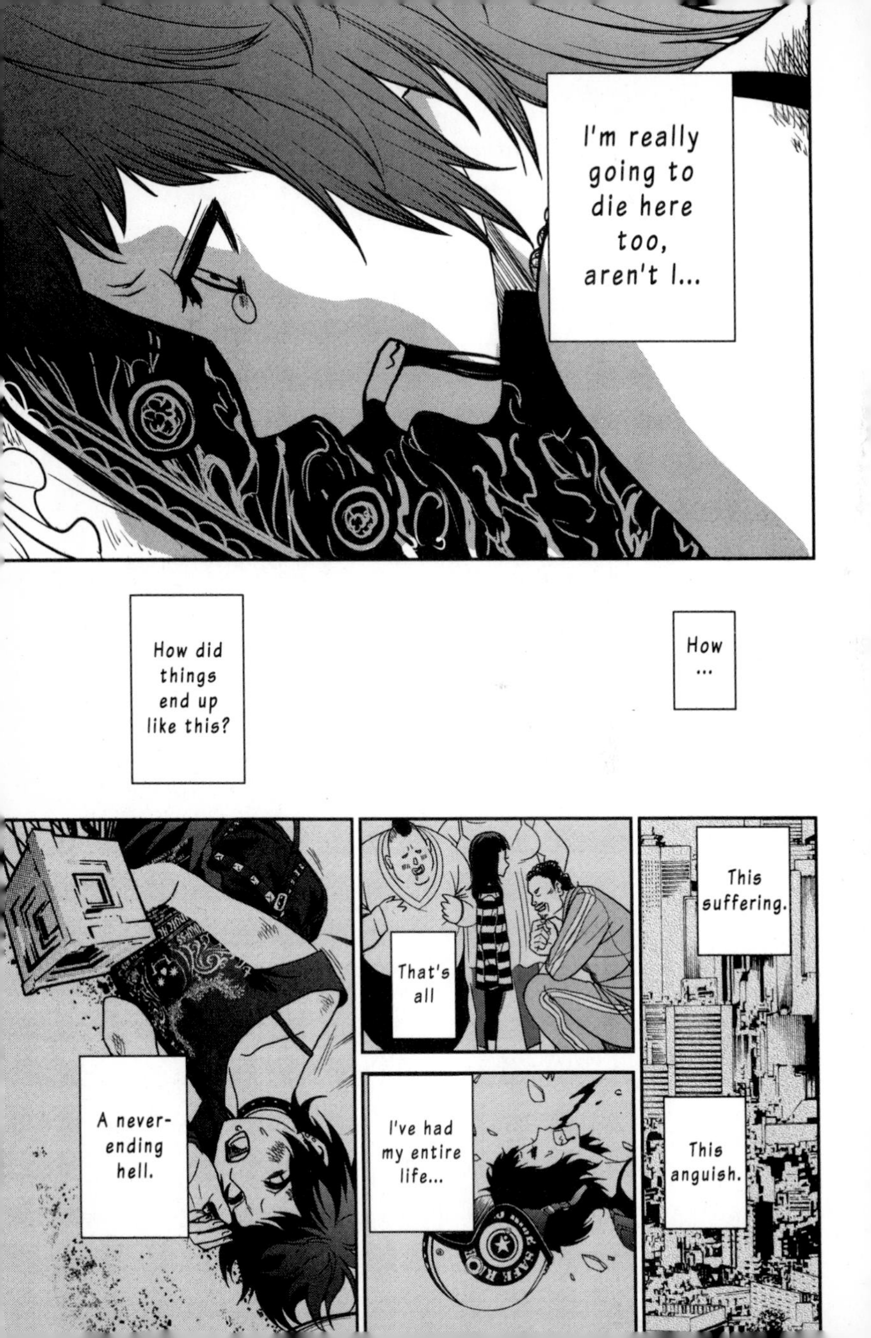
I'm really going to die here too, aren't I...
How ...
How did things end up like this?
This suffering.
This anguish.
That's all
I've had my entire life...
A never-ending hell.

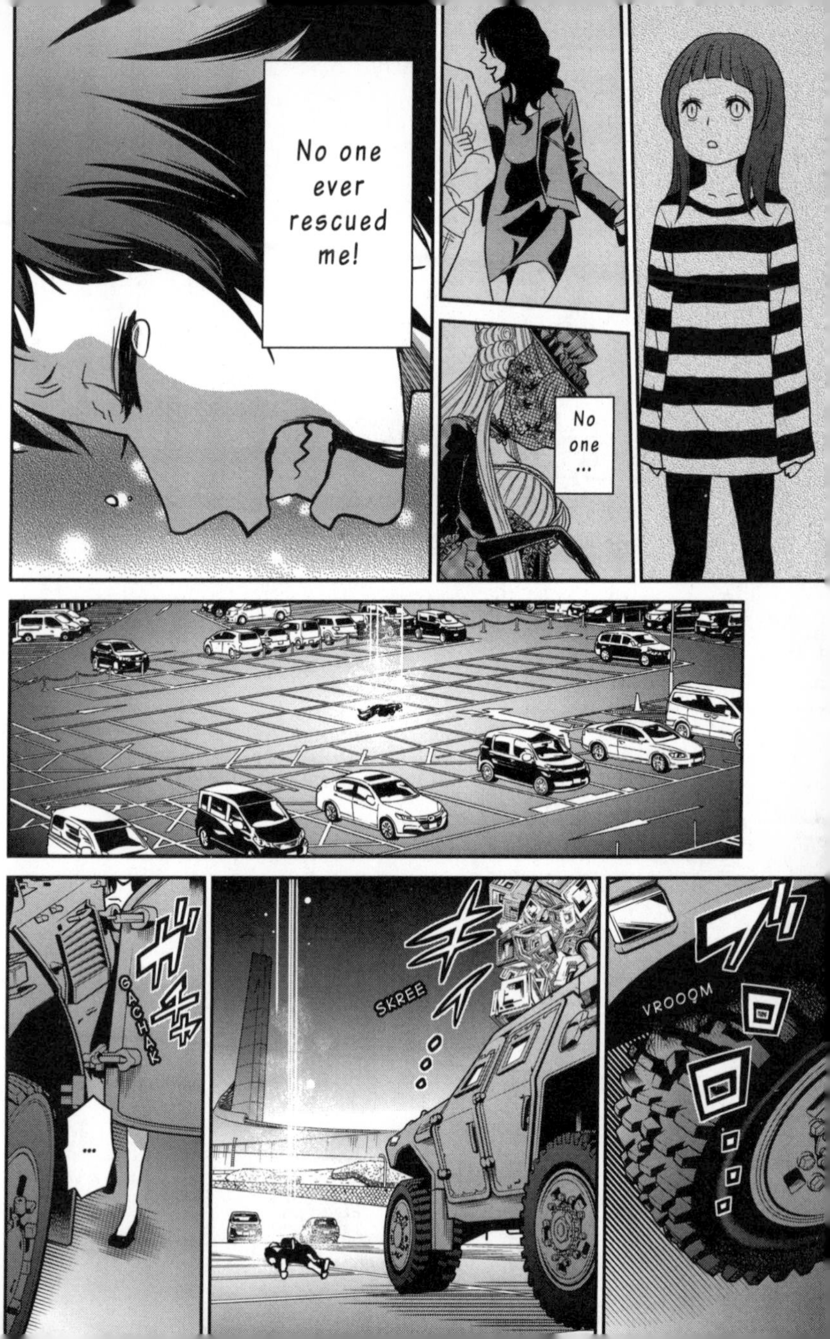
No one ...
No one ever rescued me!
VROOOM
SKREE
GACHAK
...

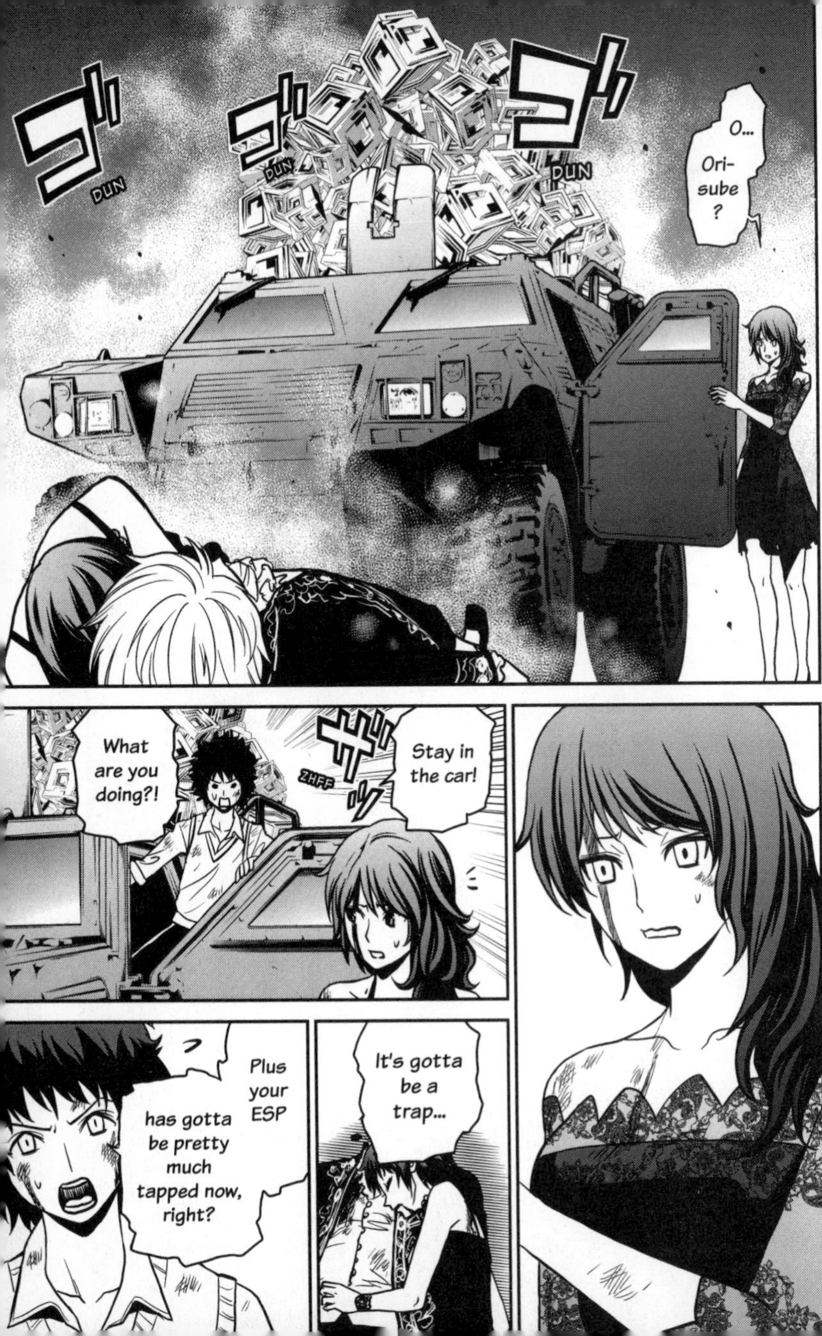
O... Ori-sube ?
DUN
DUN
DUN
Stay in the car!
ZHFF
What are you doing?!
It's gotta be a trap...
Plus your ESP has gotta be pretty much tapped now, right?

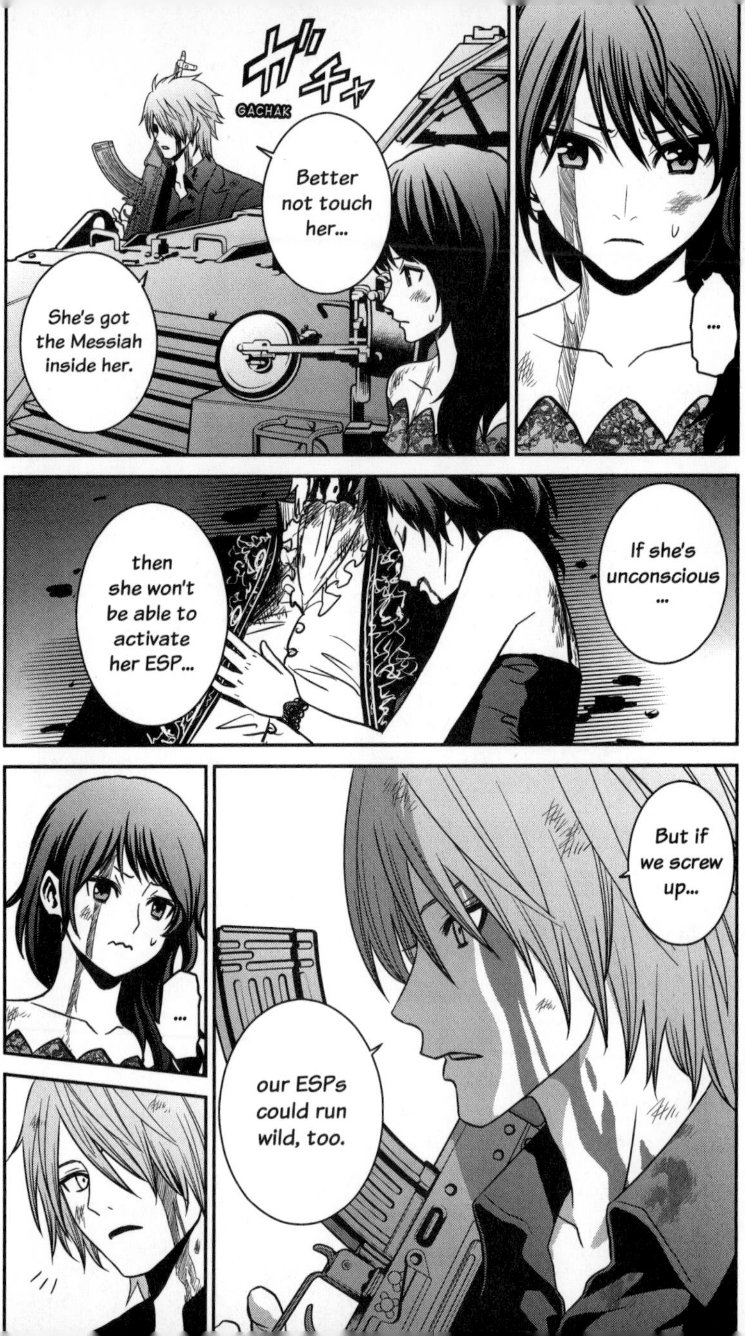
...
GACHAK
Better not touch her...
She's got the Messiah inside her.
If she's unconscious ...
then she won't be able to activate her ESP...
But if we screw up...
our ESPs could run wild, too.
...

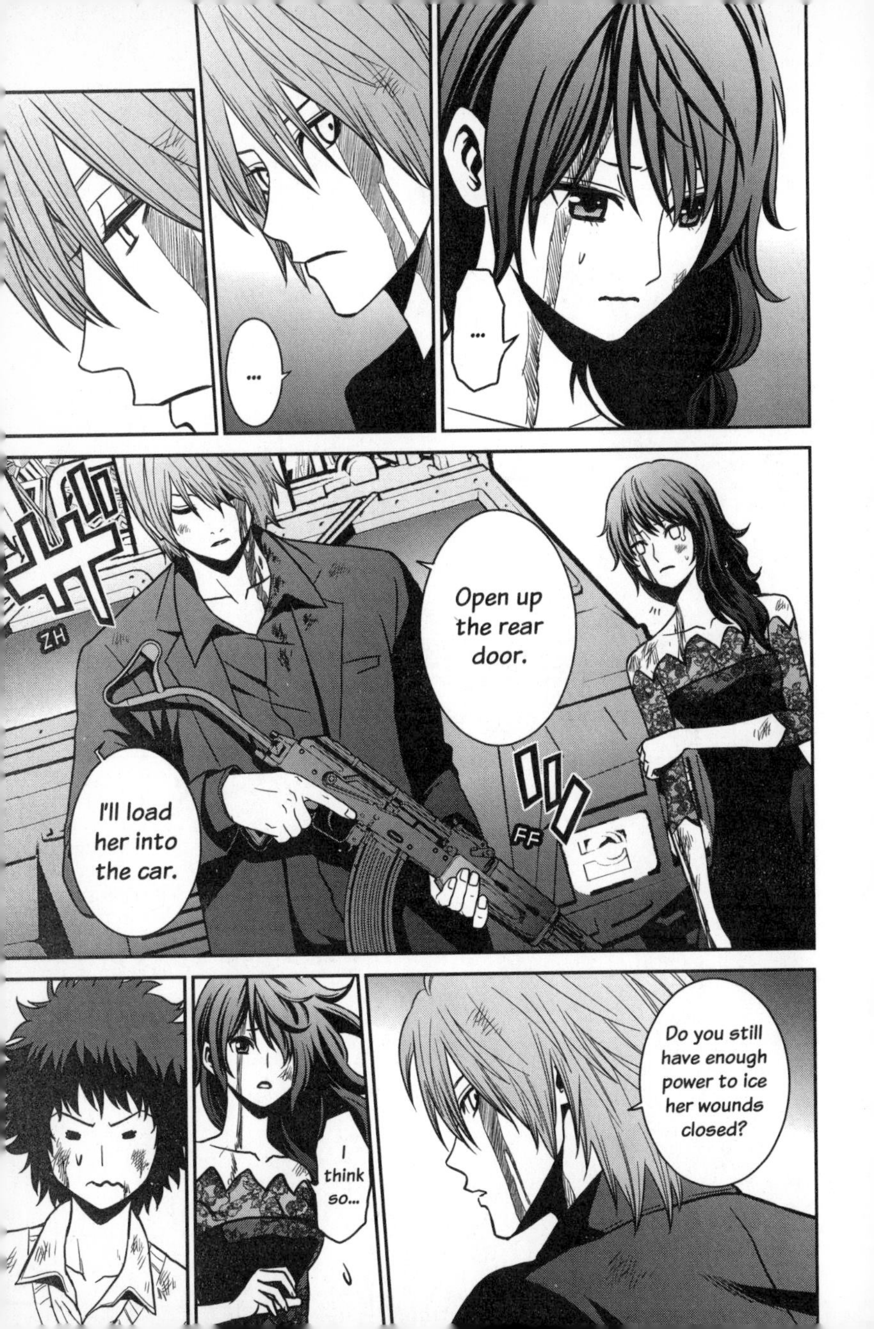
...
...
Open up the rear door.
ZH
FF
I'll load her into the car.
Do you still have enough power to ice her wounds closed?
I think so...

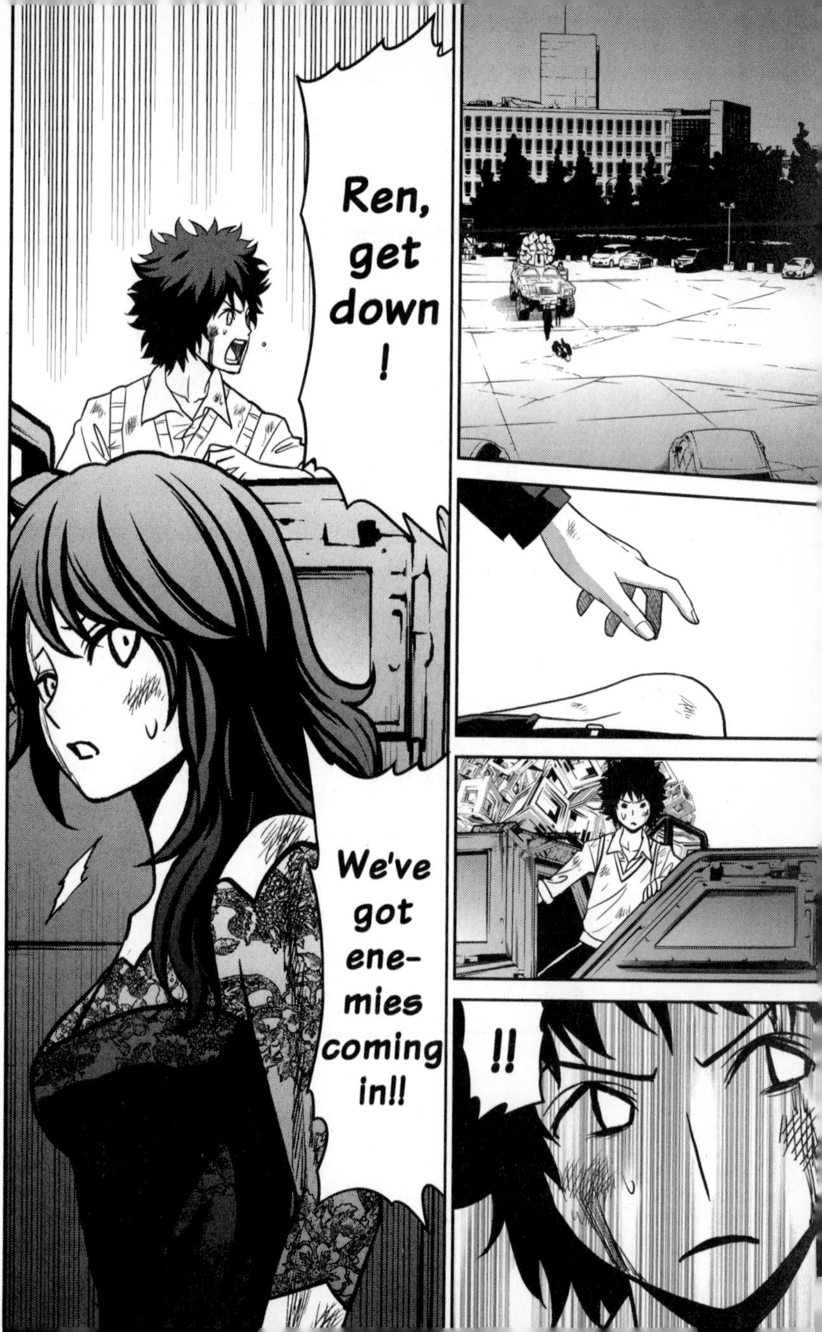
!!
Ren, get down!
We've got enemies coming in!!

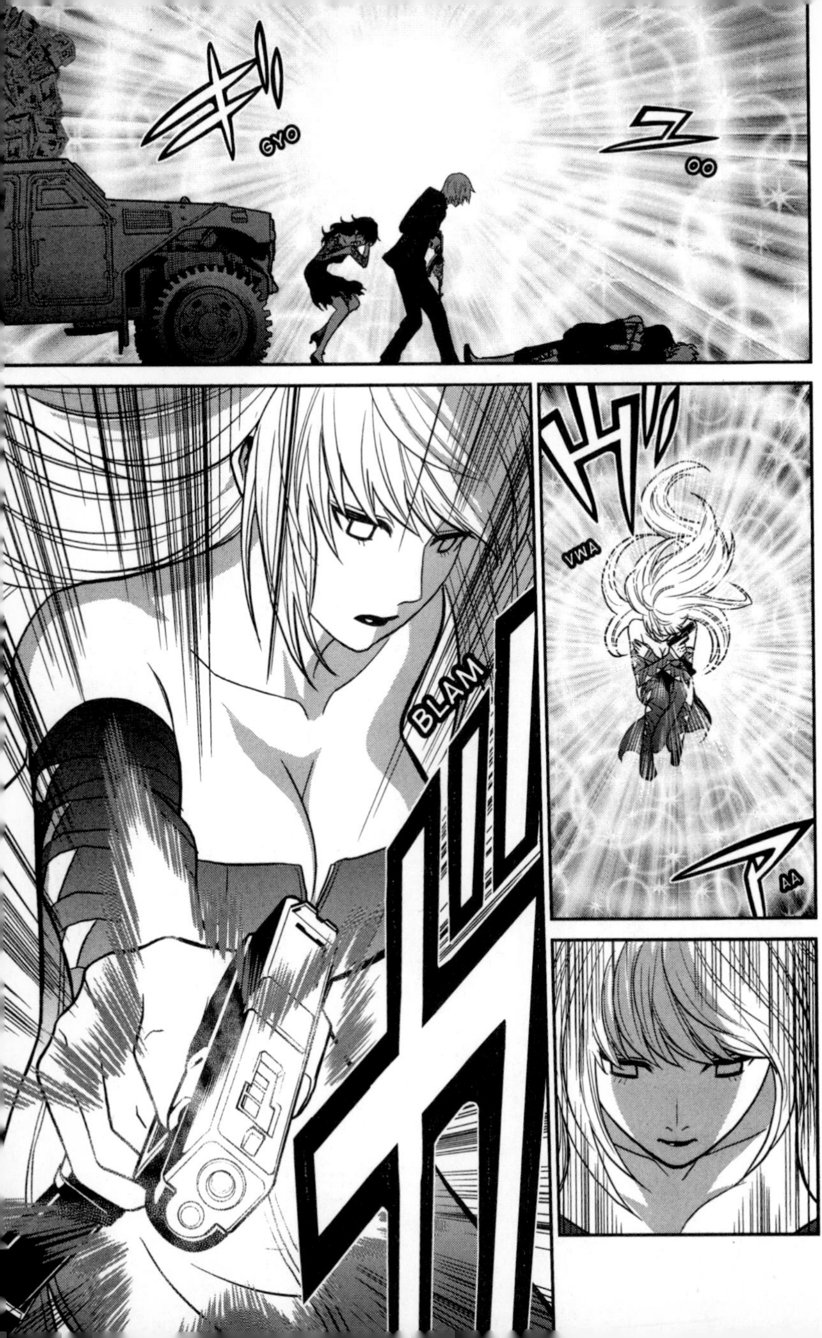
OO
GYO
VWA
AA
BLAM

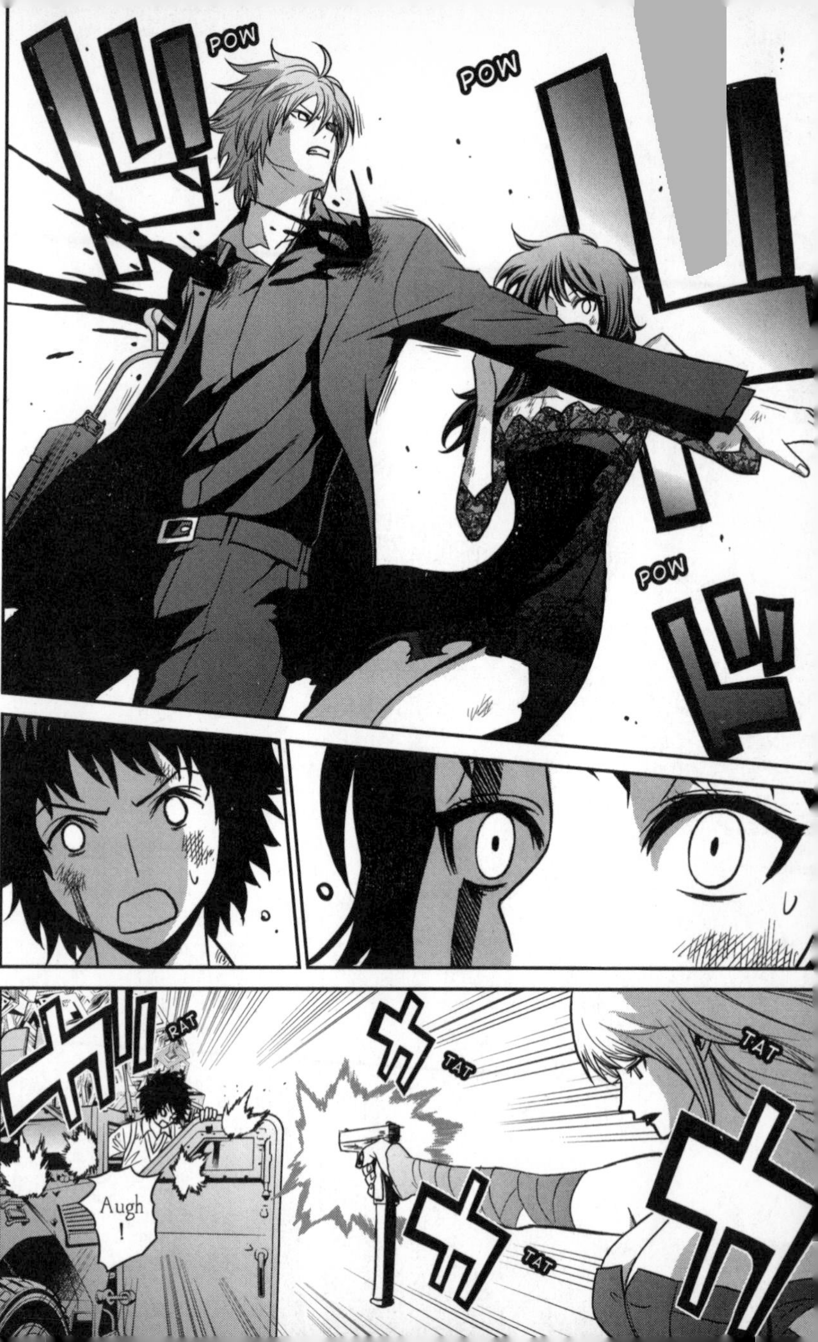
POW
POW
POW
TAT
TAT
TAT
RAT
Augh!

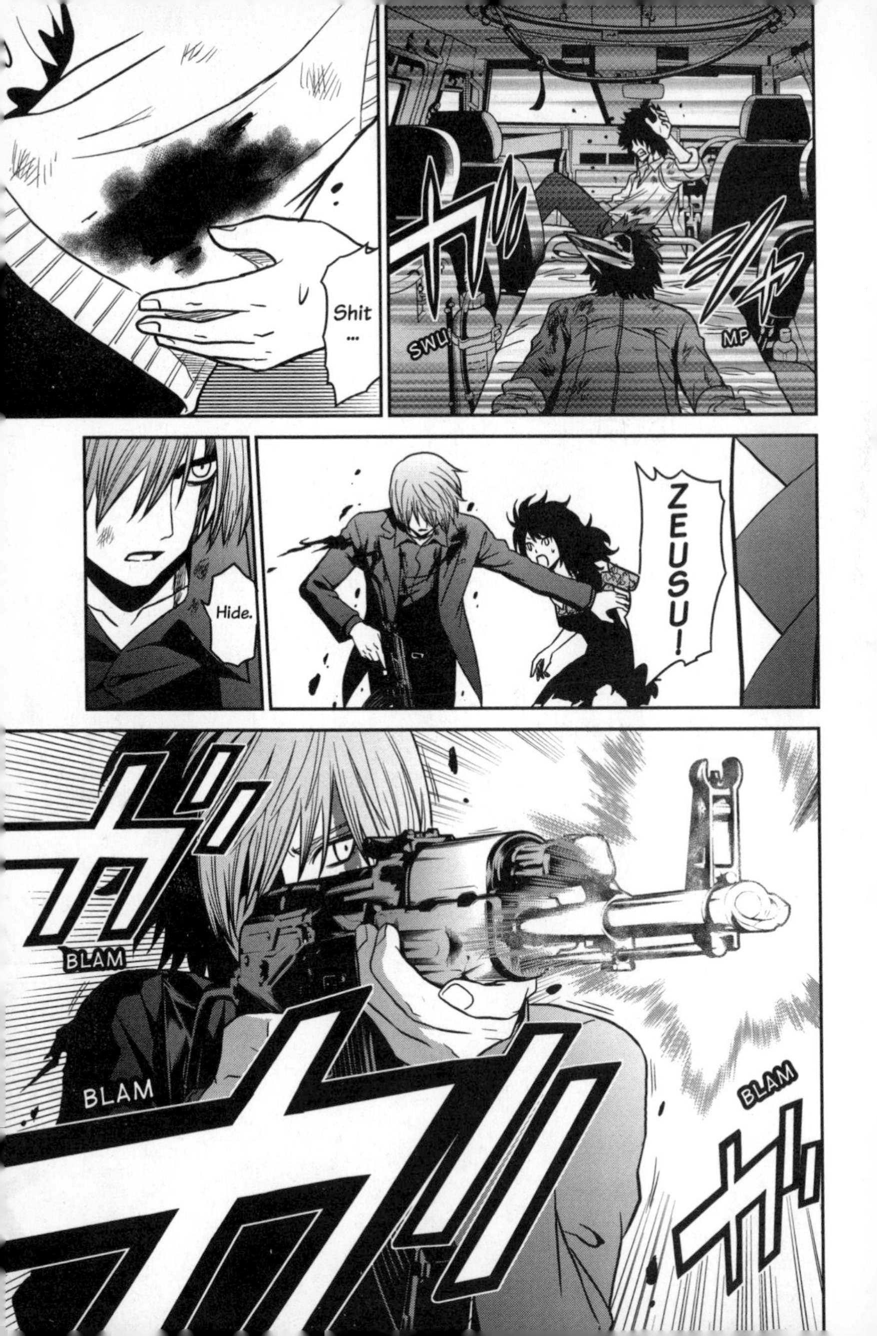
SWU
MP
Shit ...
ZEUSU!
Hide.
BLAM
BLAM
BLAM

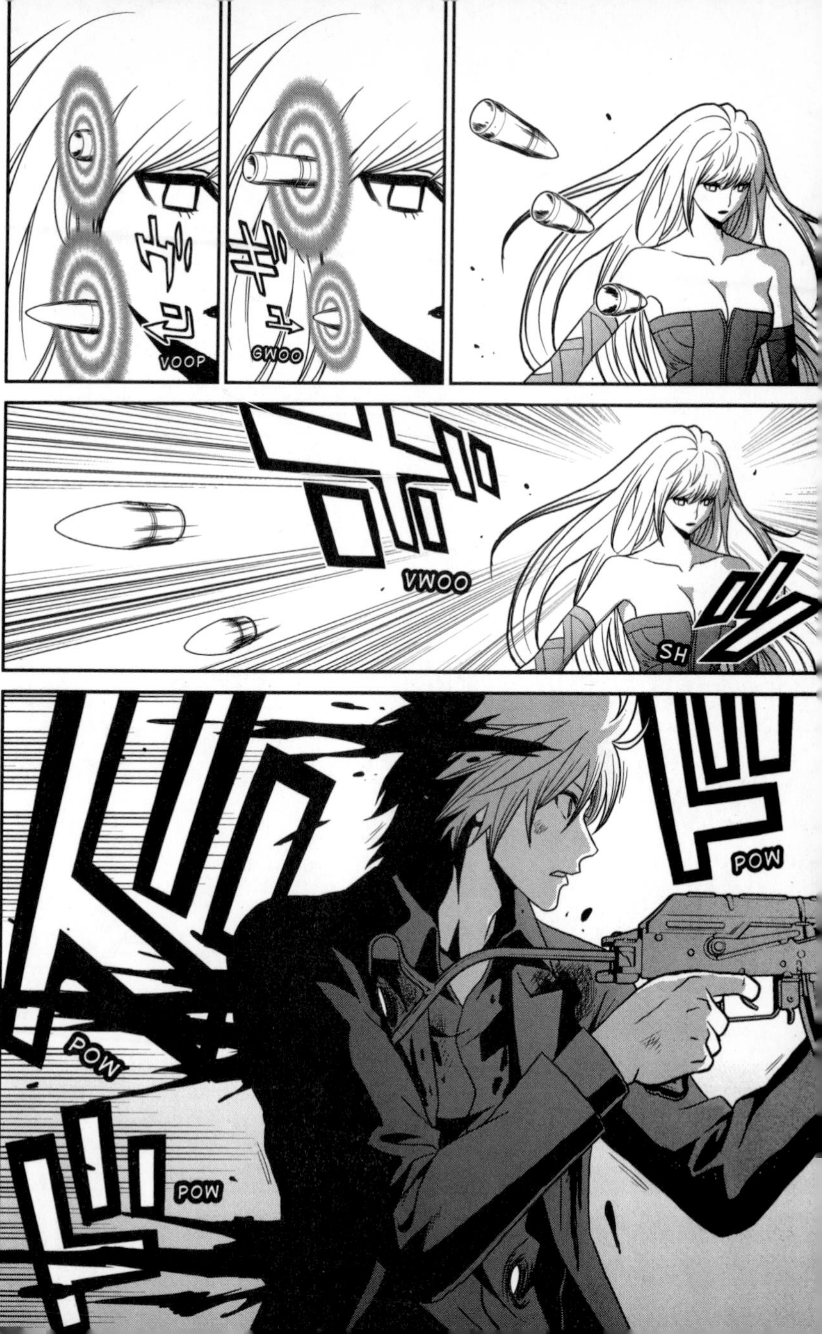
GWOO
VOOP
VWOO
SH
POW
POW
POW

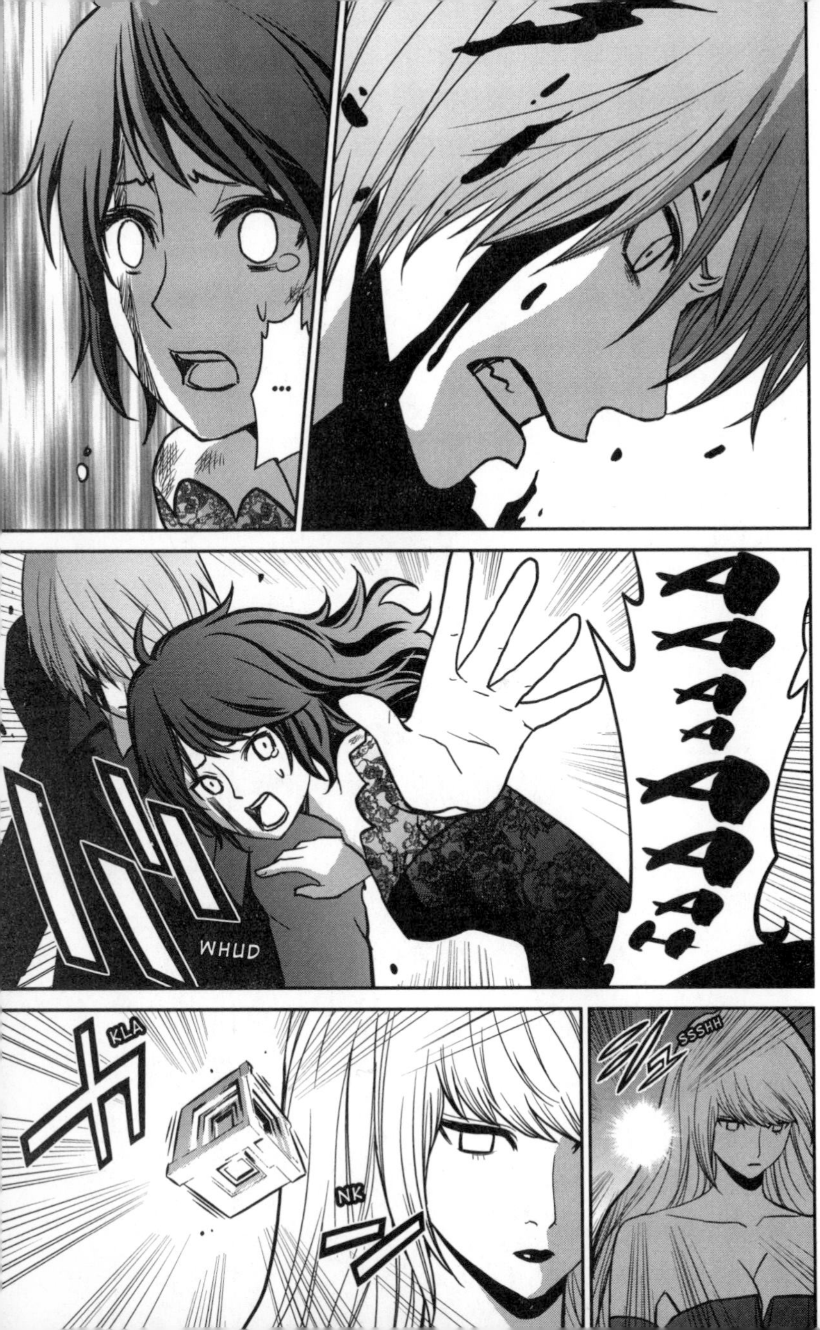
...
AAAAAAAA!!
WHUD
SSSHH
KLA
NK

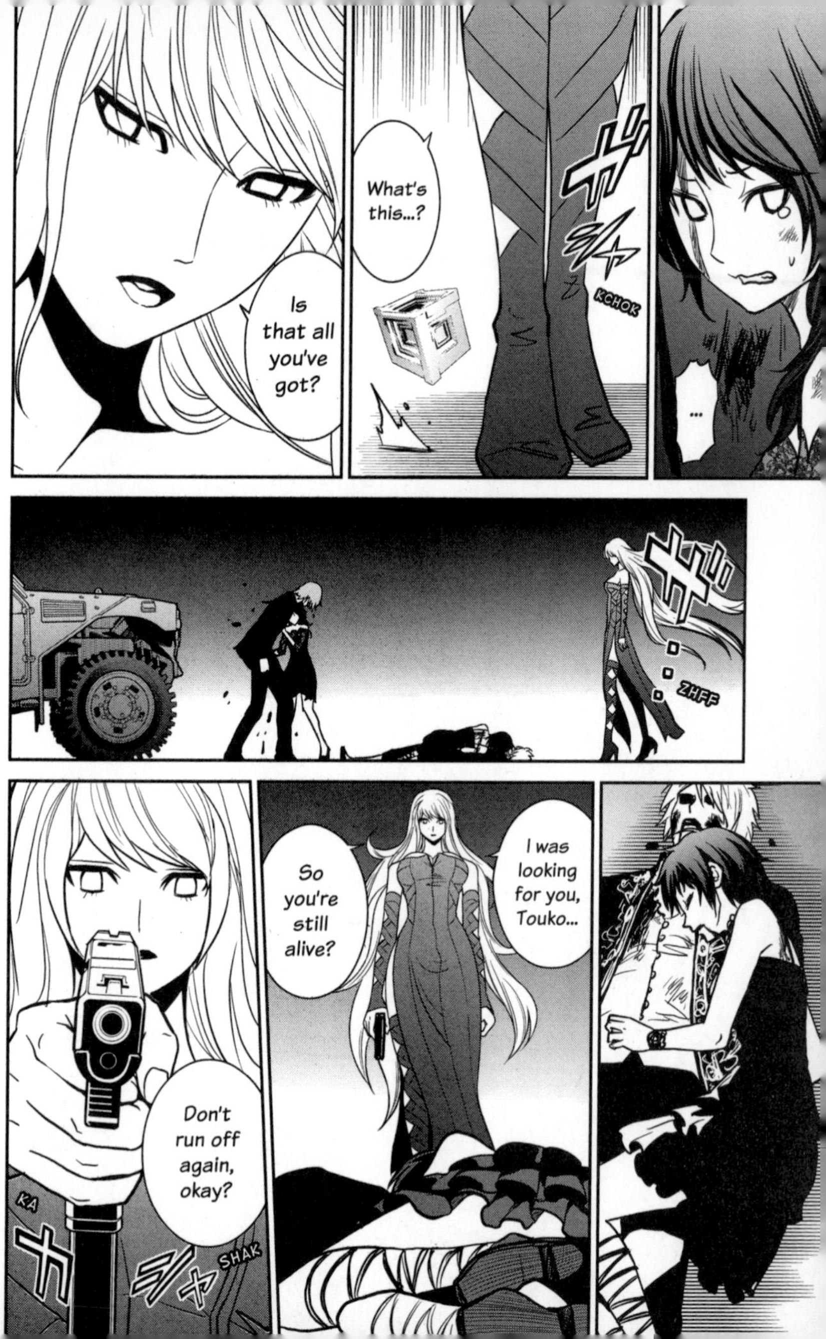
KCHOK
...
What's this...?
Is that all you've got?
ZHFF
I was looking for you, Touko...
So you're still alive?
Don't run off again, okay?
KA
SHAK

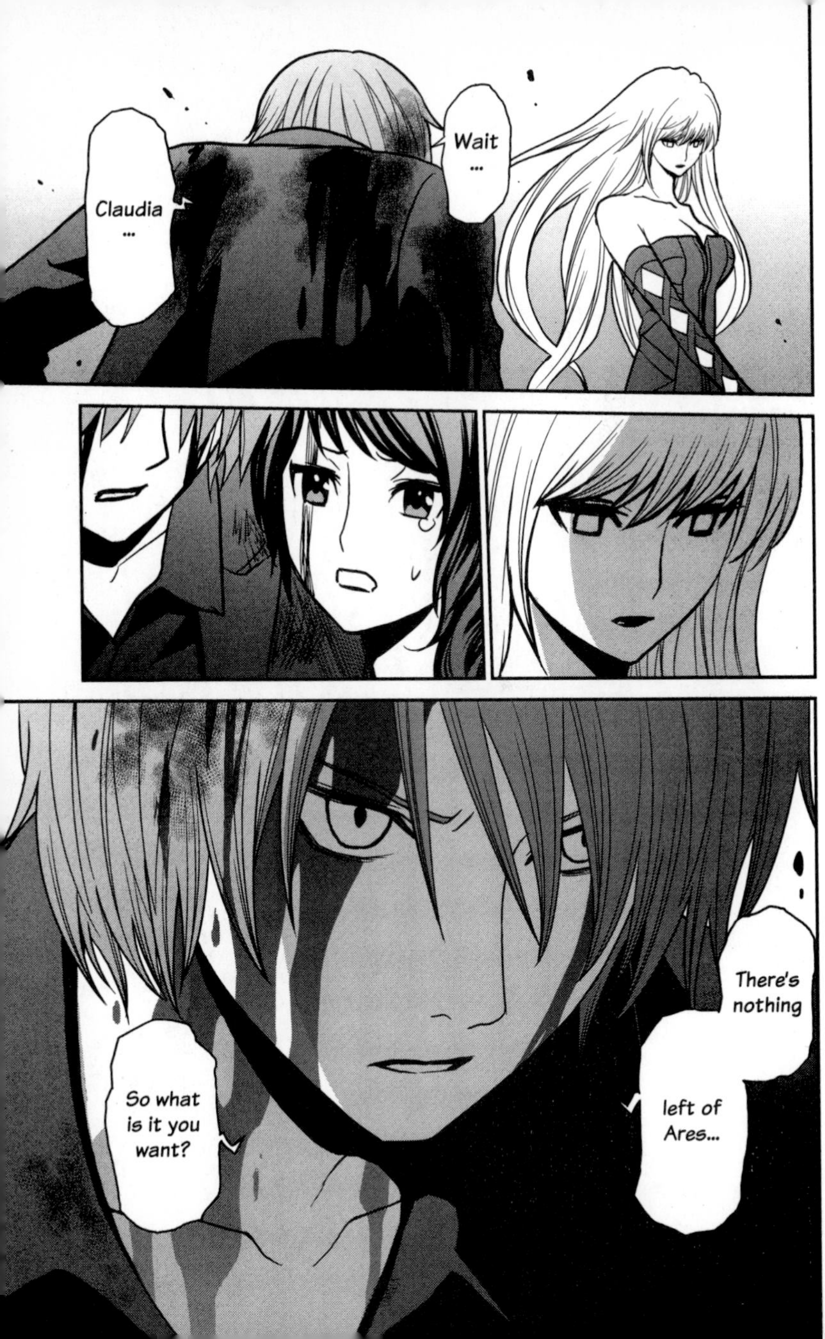
Wait ...
Claudia ...
There's nothing
left of Ares...
So what is it you want?

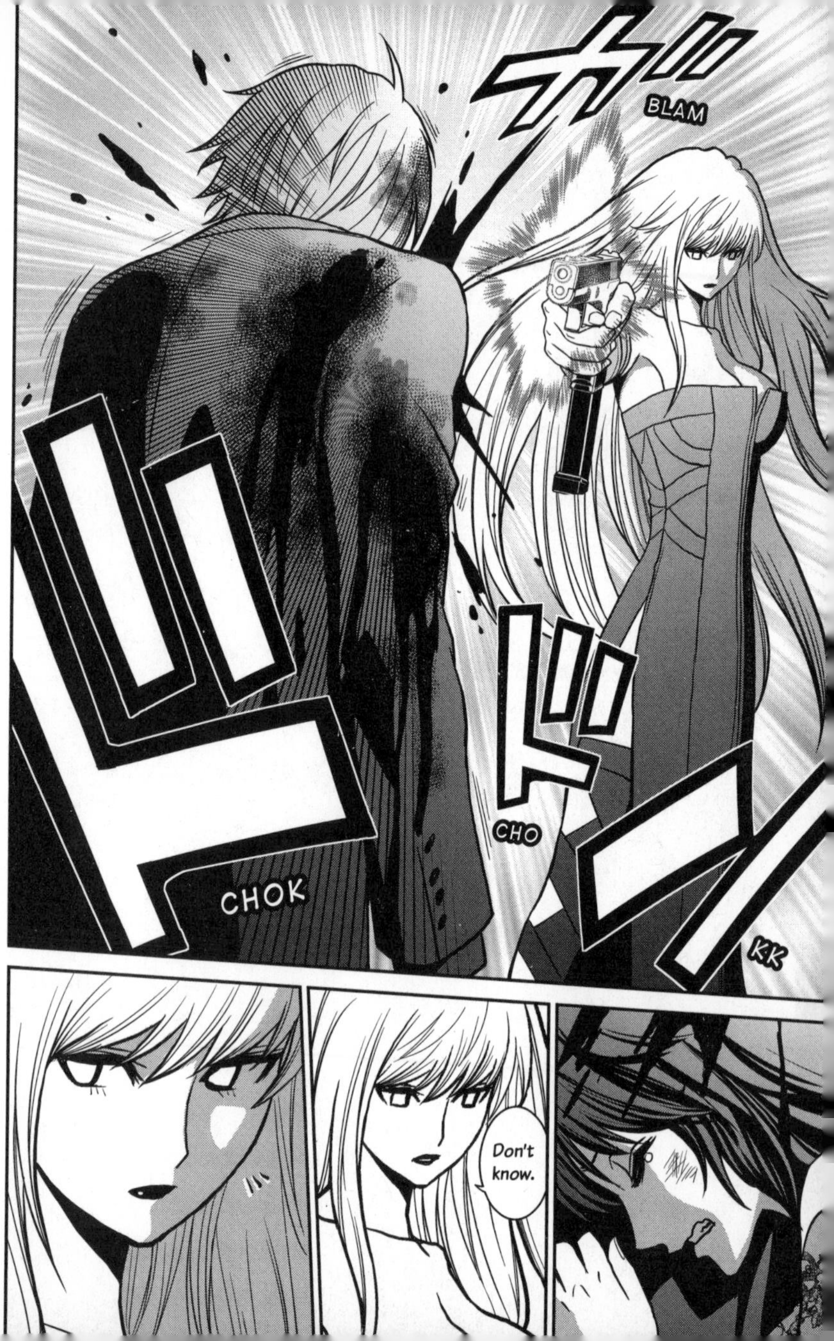
BLAM
CHO
KK
CHOK
Don't know.

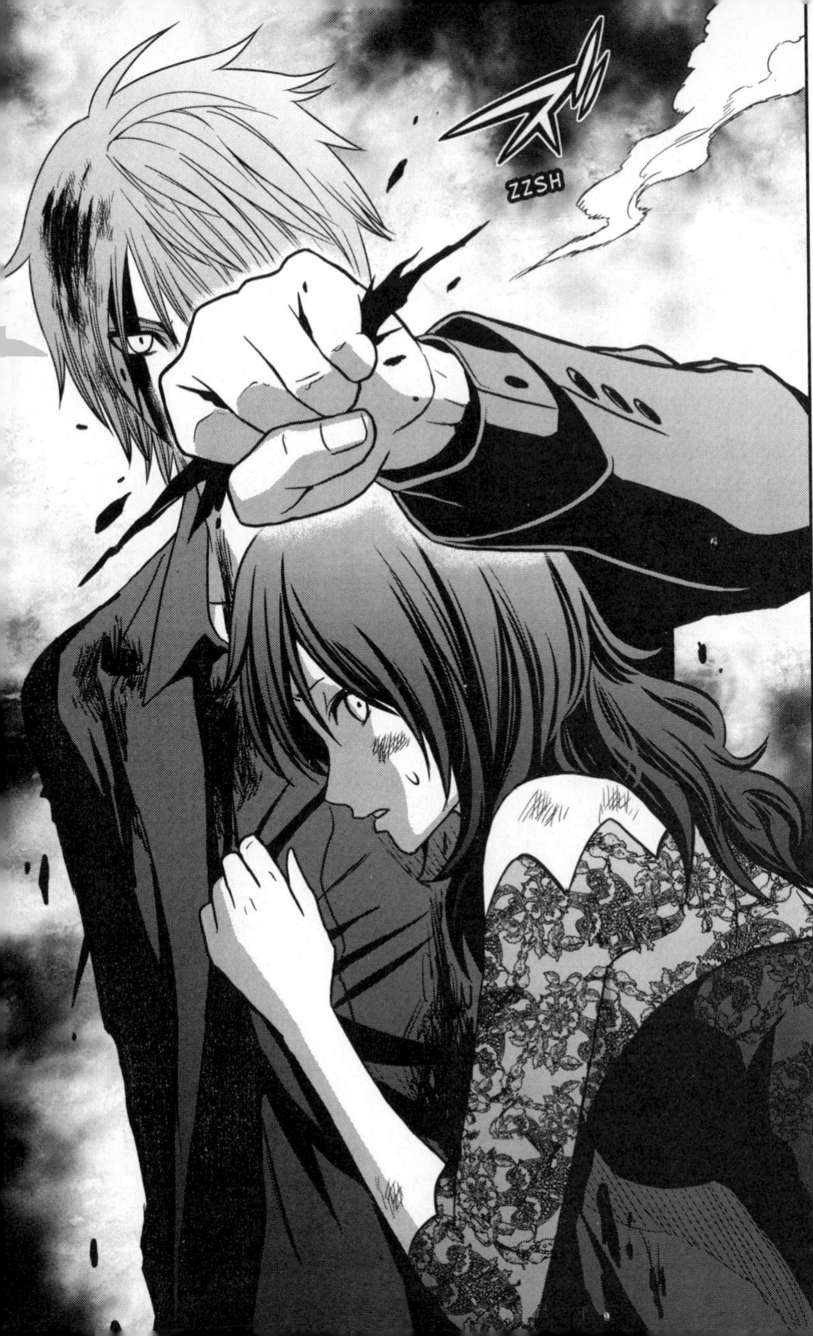
ZZSH

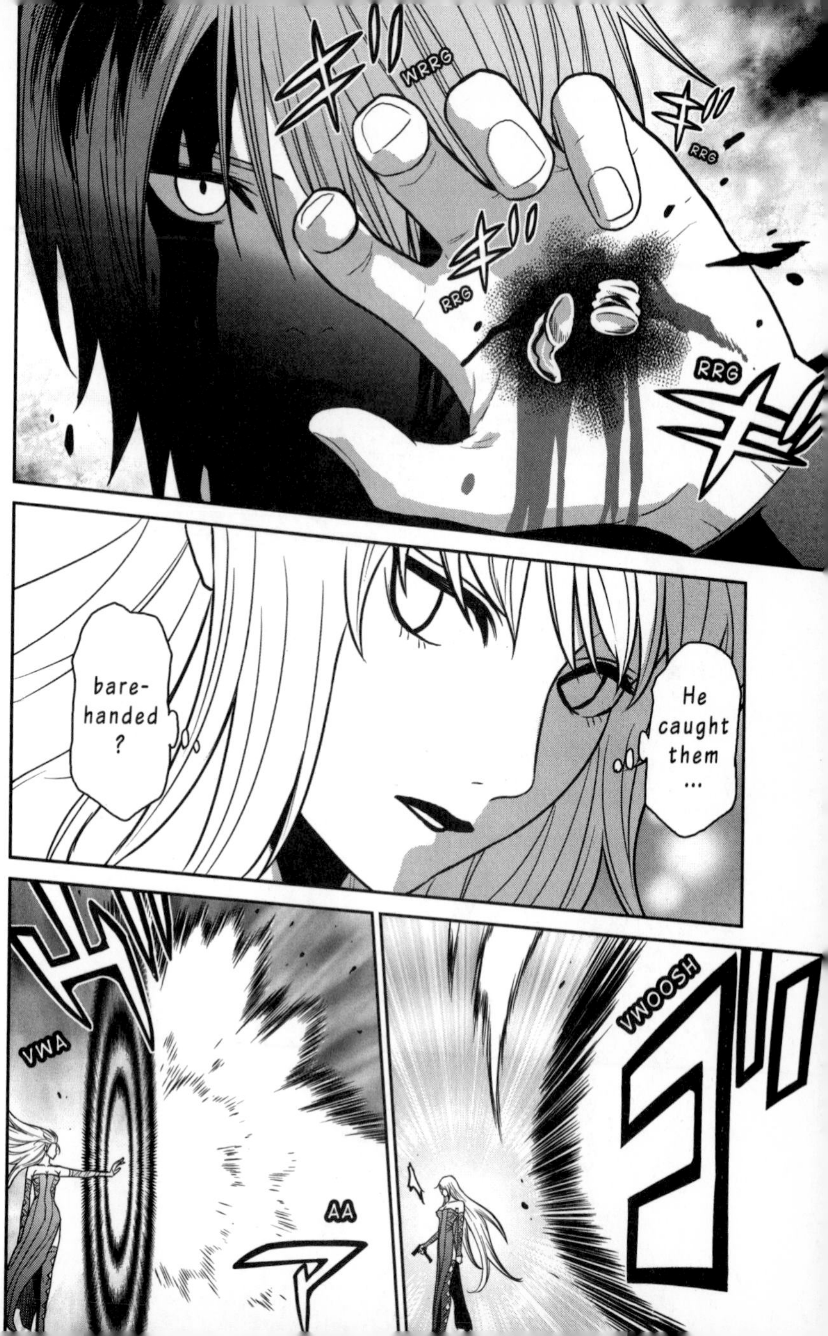

WRRG
RRG
RRG
RRG
He caught them ...
bare-handed?
VWOOSH
VWA
AA

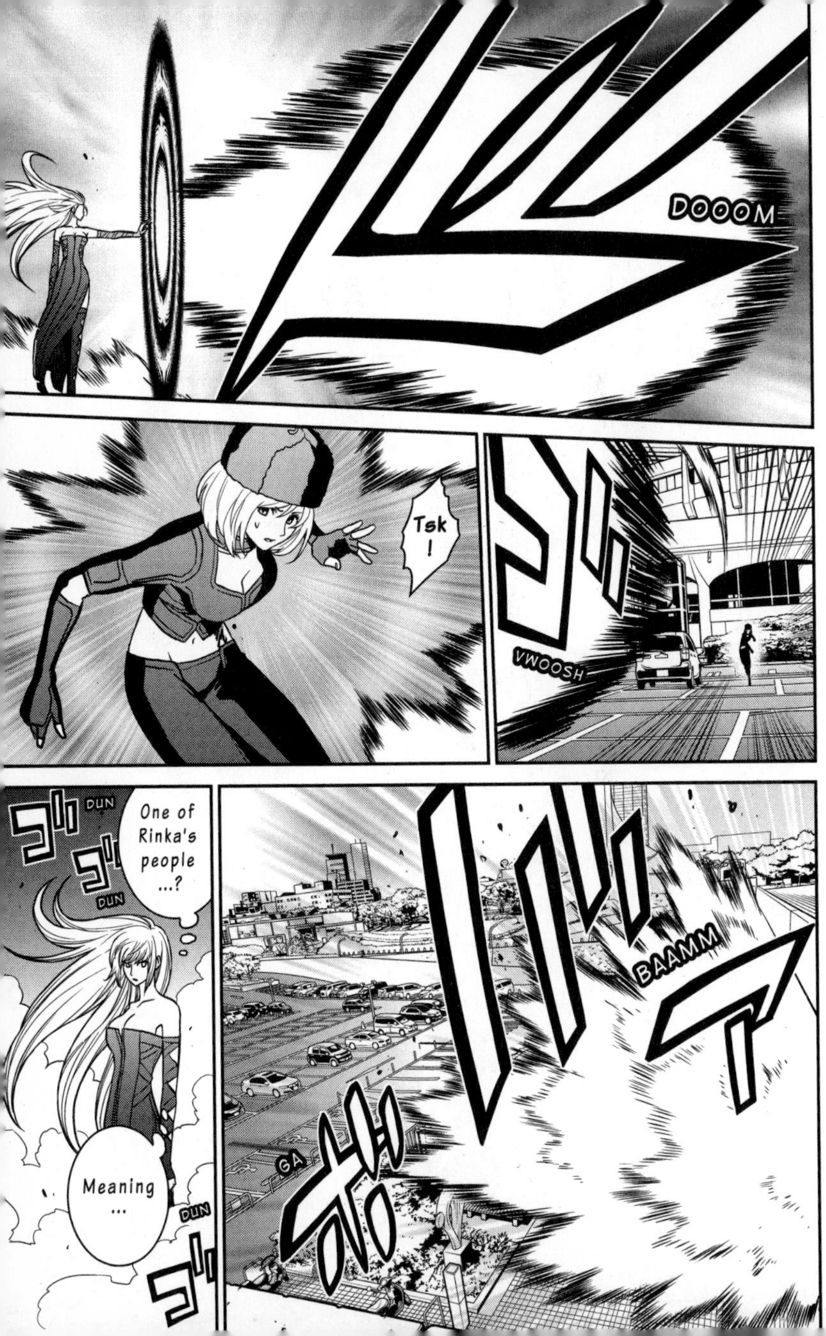
DOOOM
VWOOSH
Tsk !
BAAMM
GA
DUN
One of Rinka's people ...?
DUN
Meaning ...
DUN

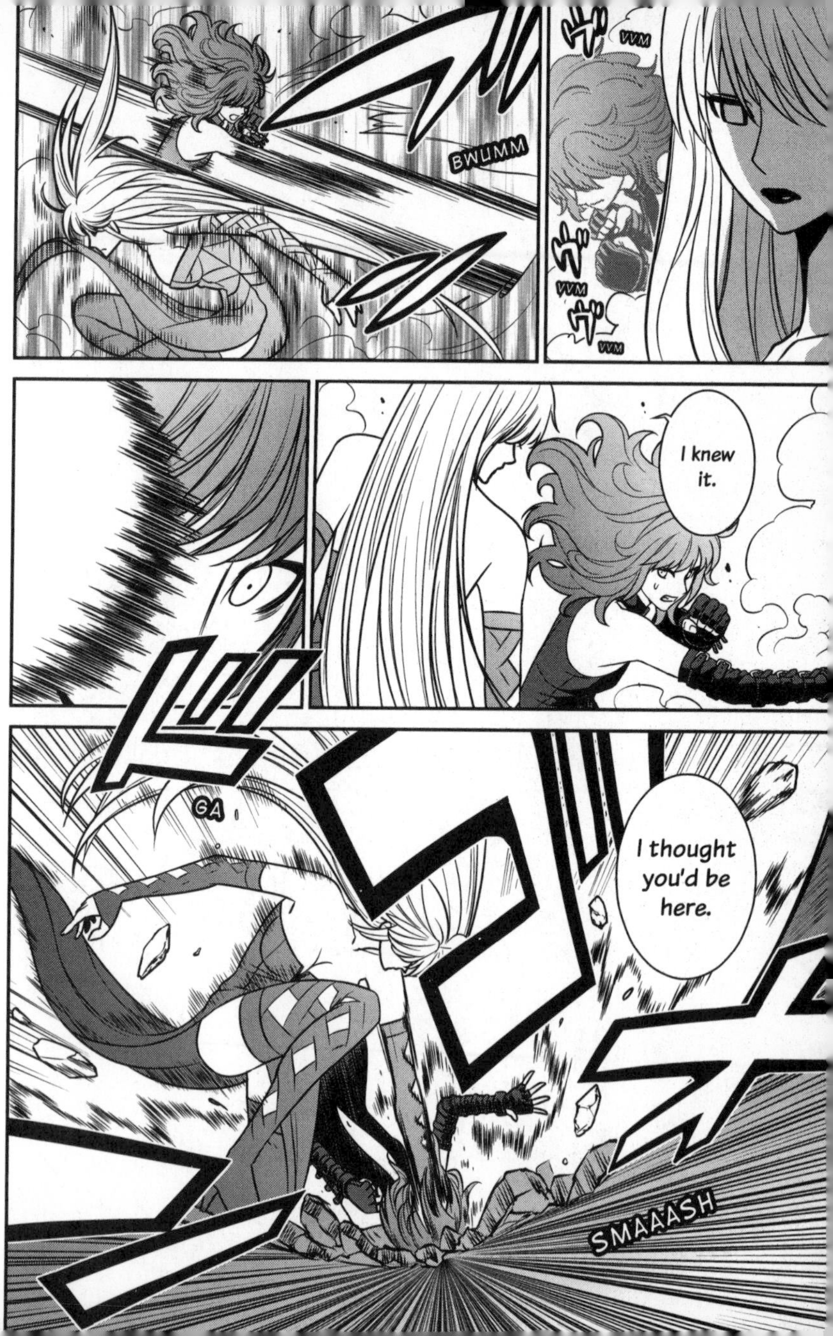

VVM
VVM
VVM
BWUMM
I knew it.
GA
I thought you'd be here.
SMAAASH

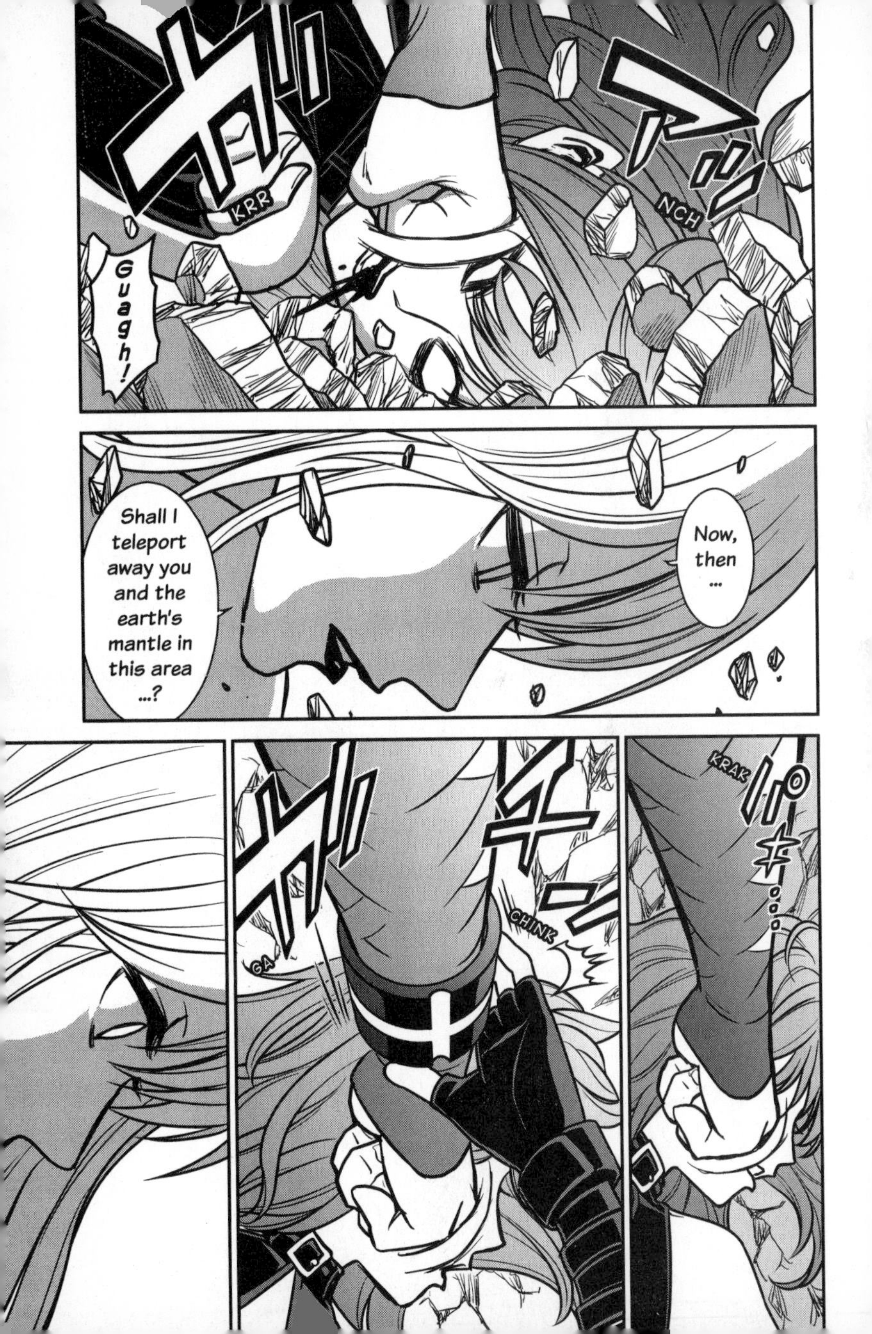
NCH
KRR
Guagh!
Now, then ...
Shall I teleport away you and the earth's mantle in this area ...?
KRAK
CHINK
GA

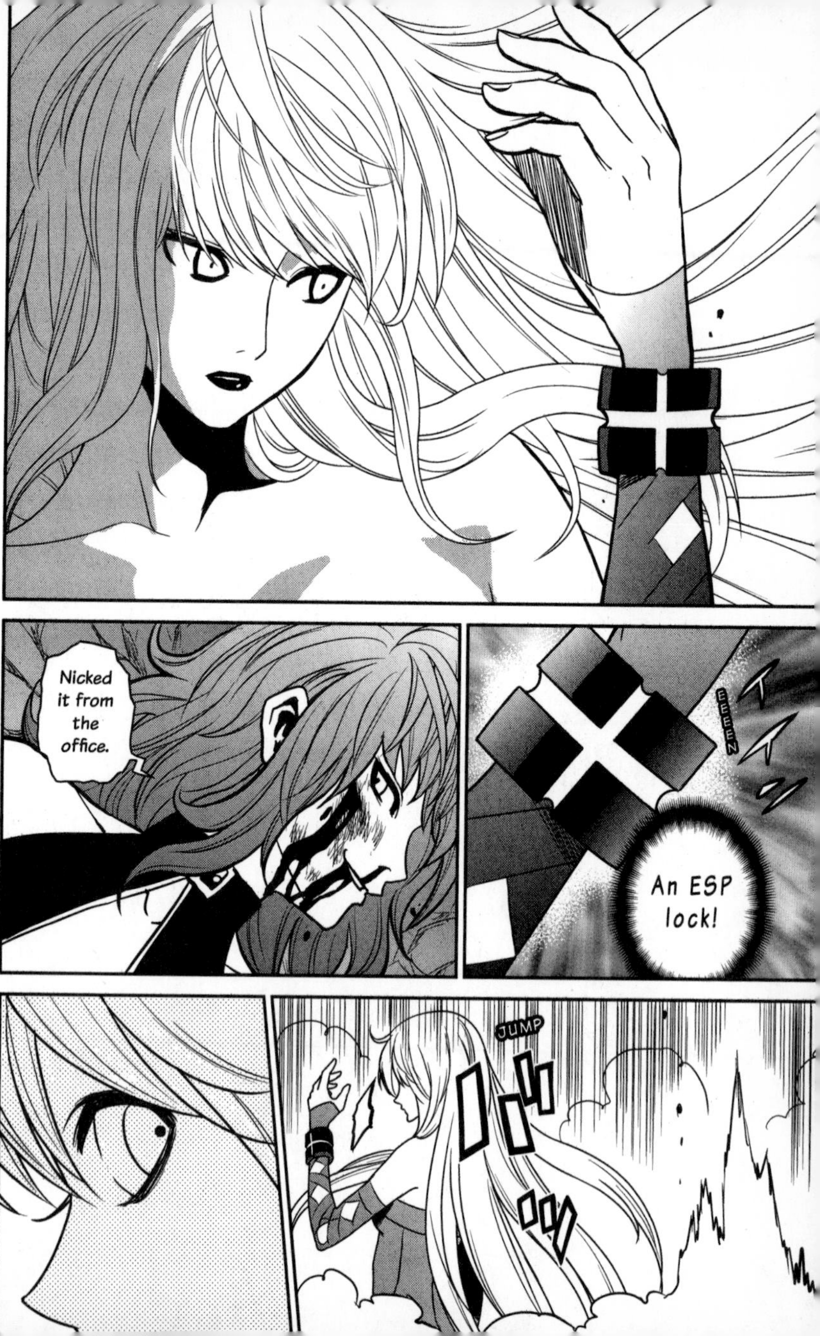
EEEEN
An ESP lock!
Nicked it from the office.
JUMP

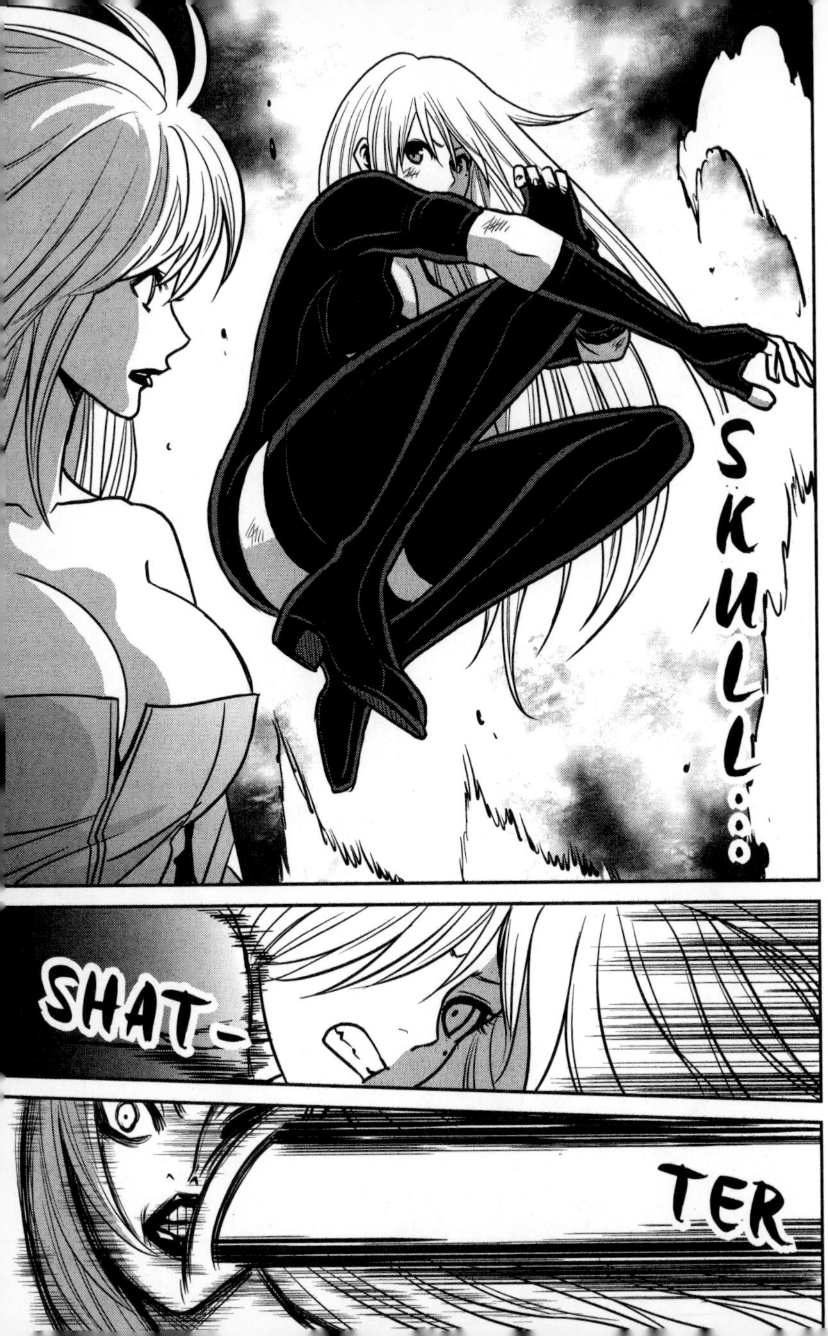
SKULL...
SHAT-
TER

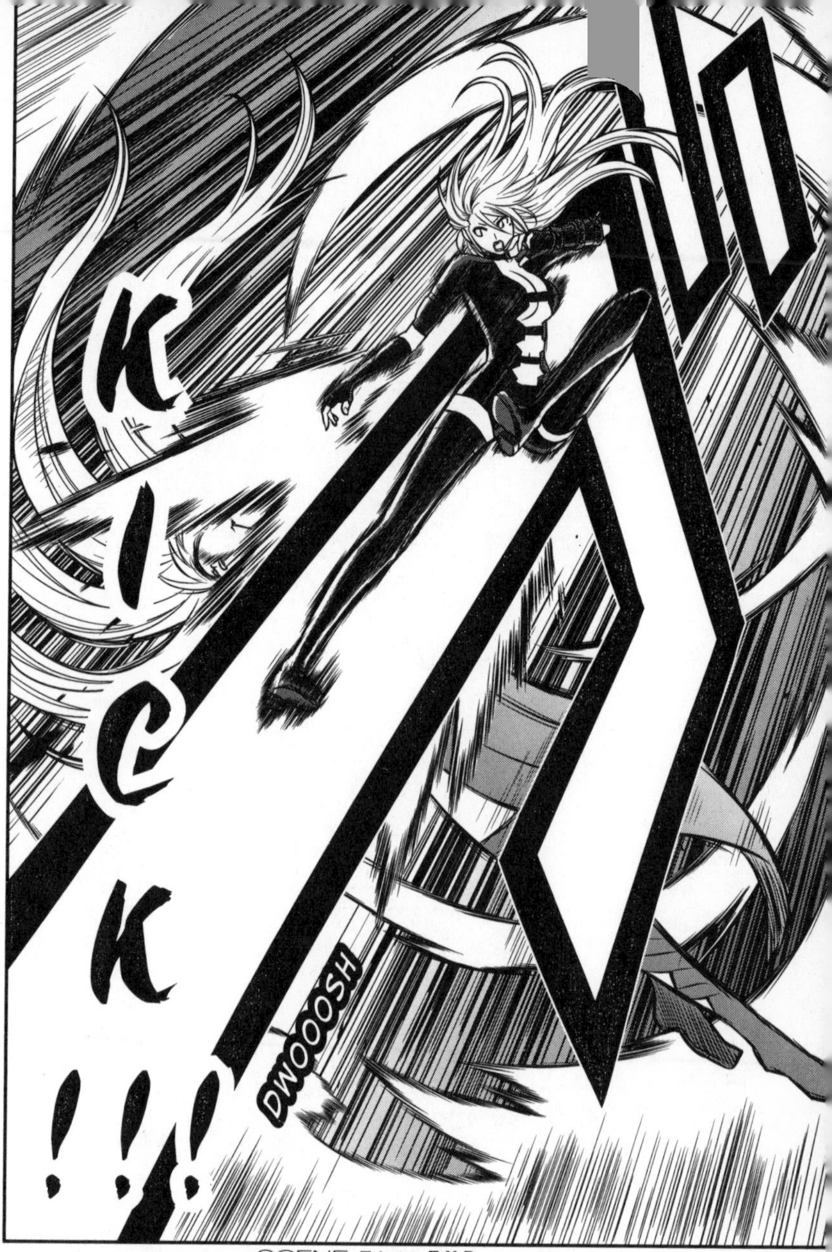
KICK!!!
DWOOOSH

SCENE 74 /// END

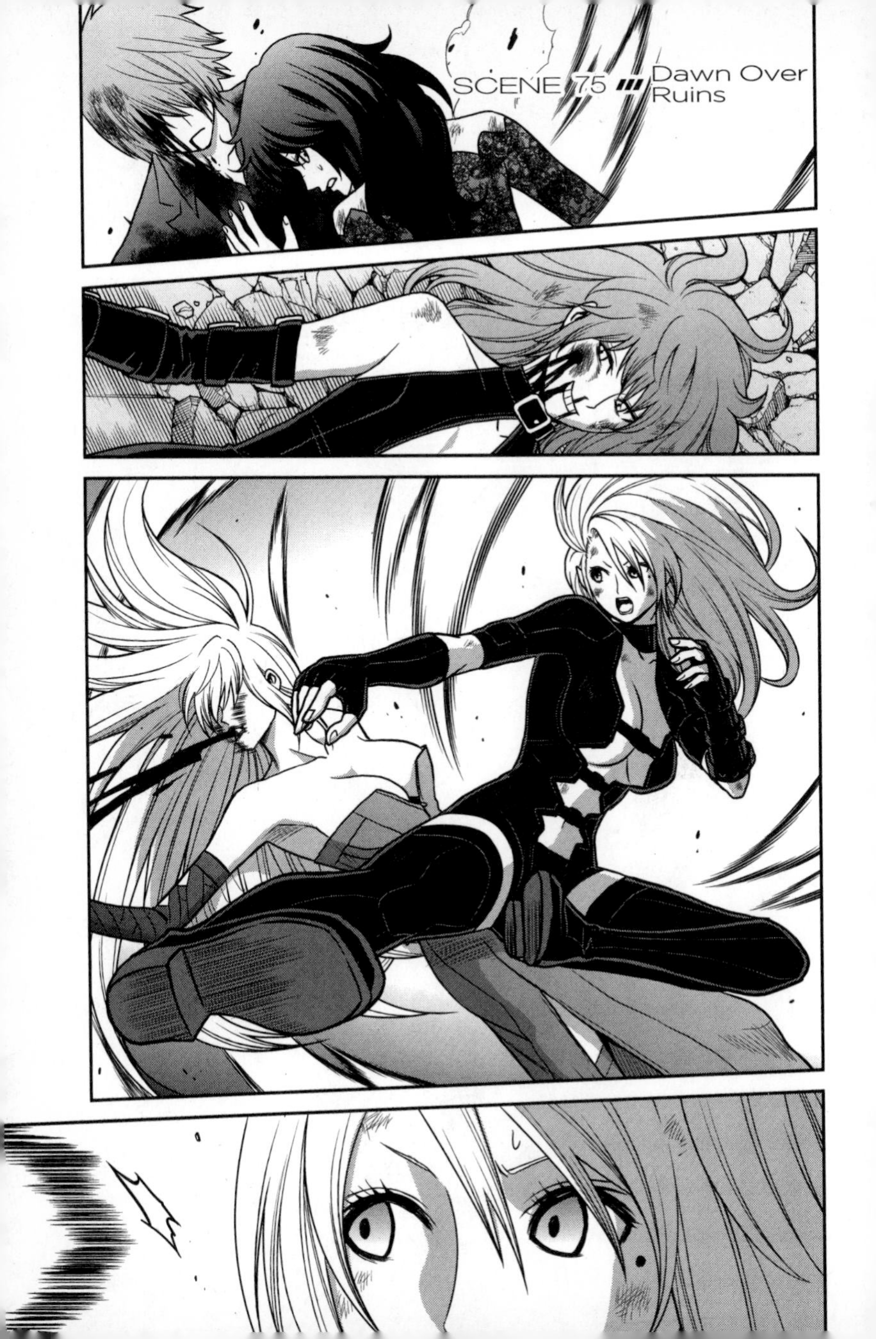
SCENE 75 /// Dawn Over Ruins

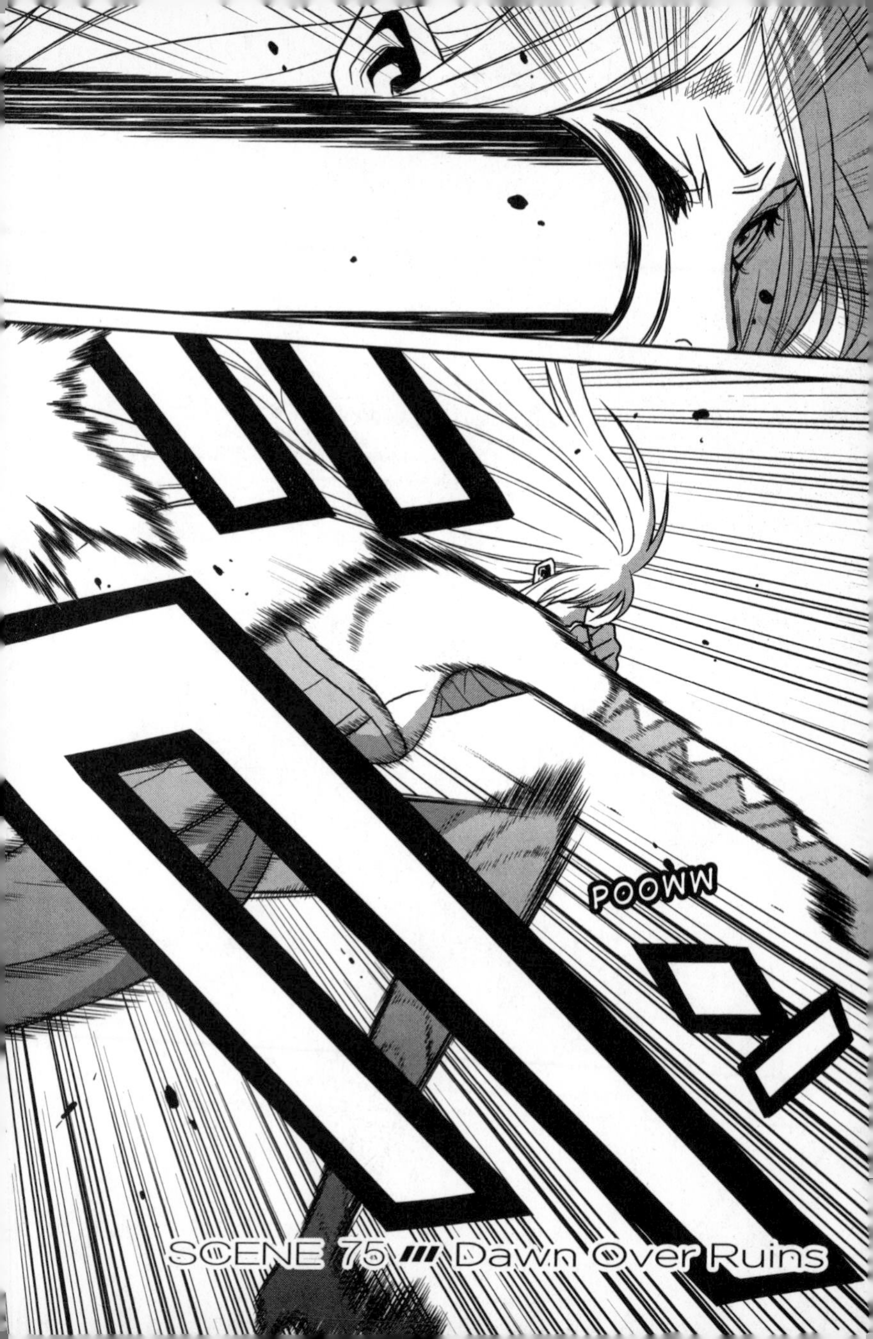
POOWW

SCENE 75 /// Dawn Over Ruins

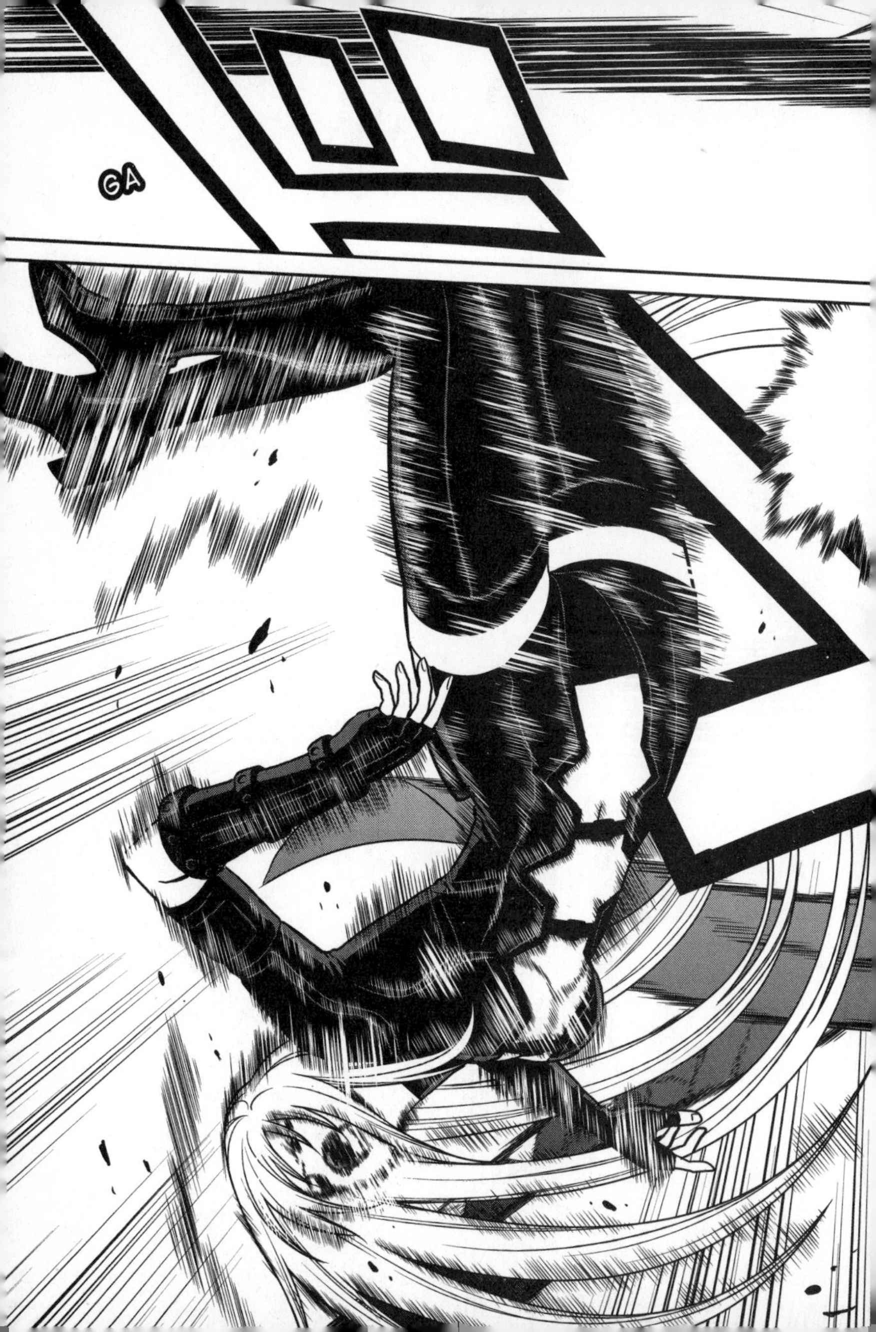
GA

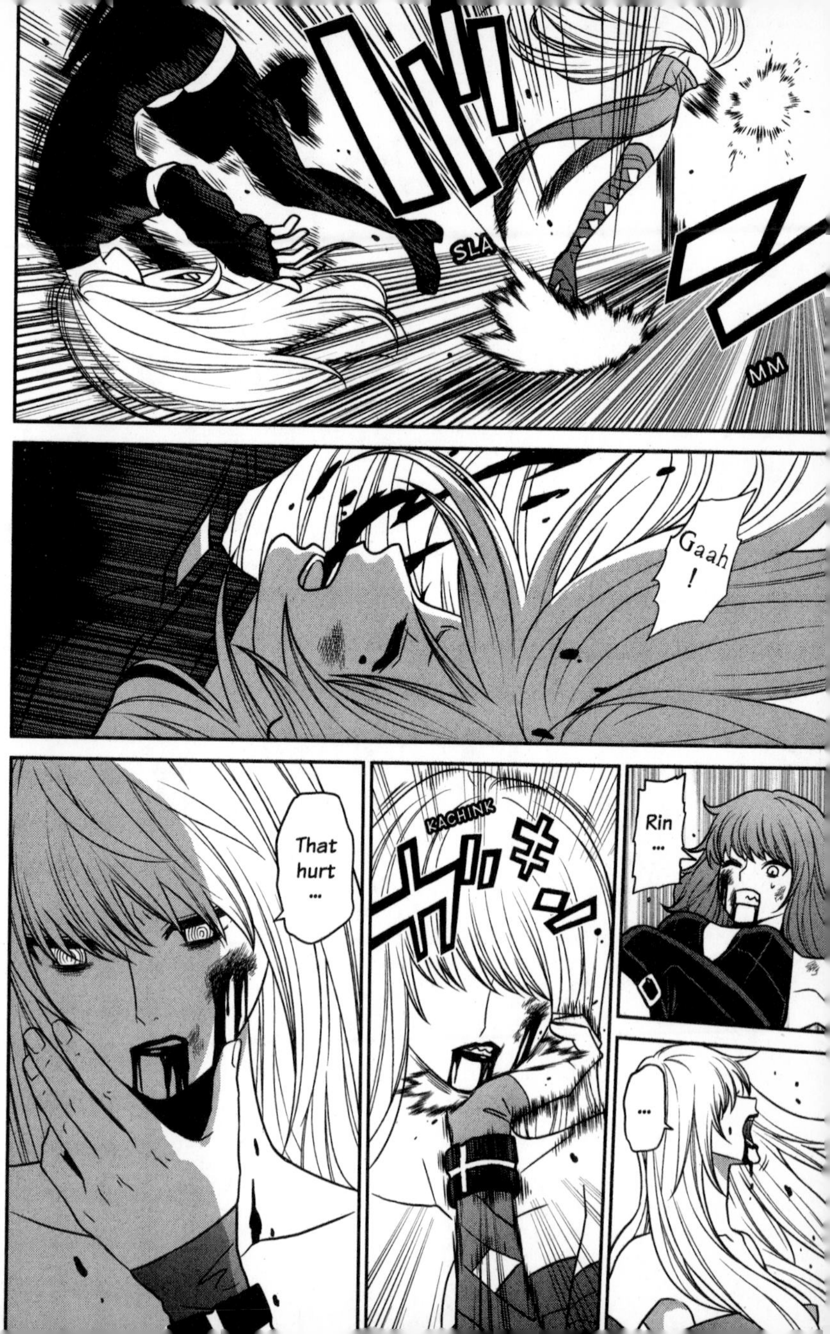
SLA
MM
Gaah !
Rin ...
...
KACHINK
That hurt ...

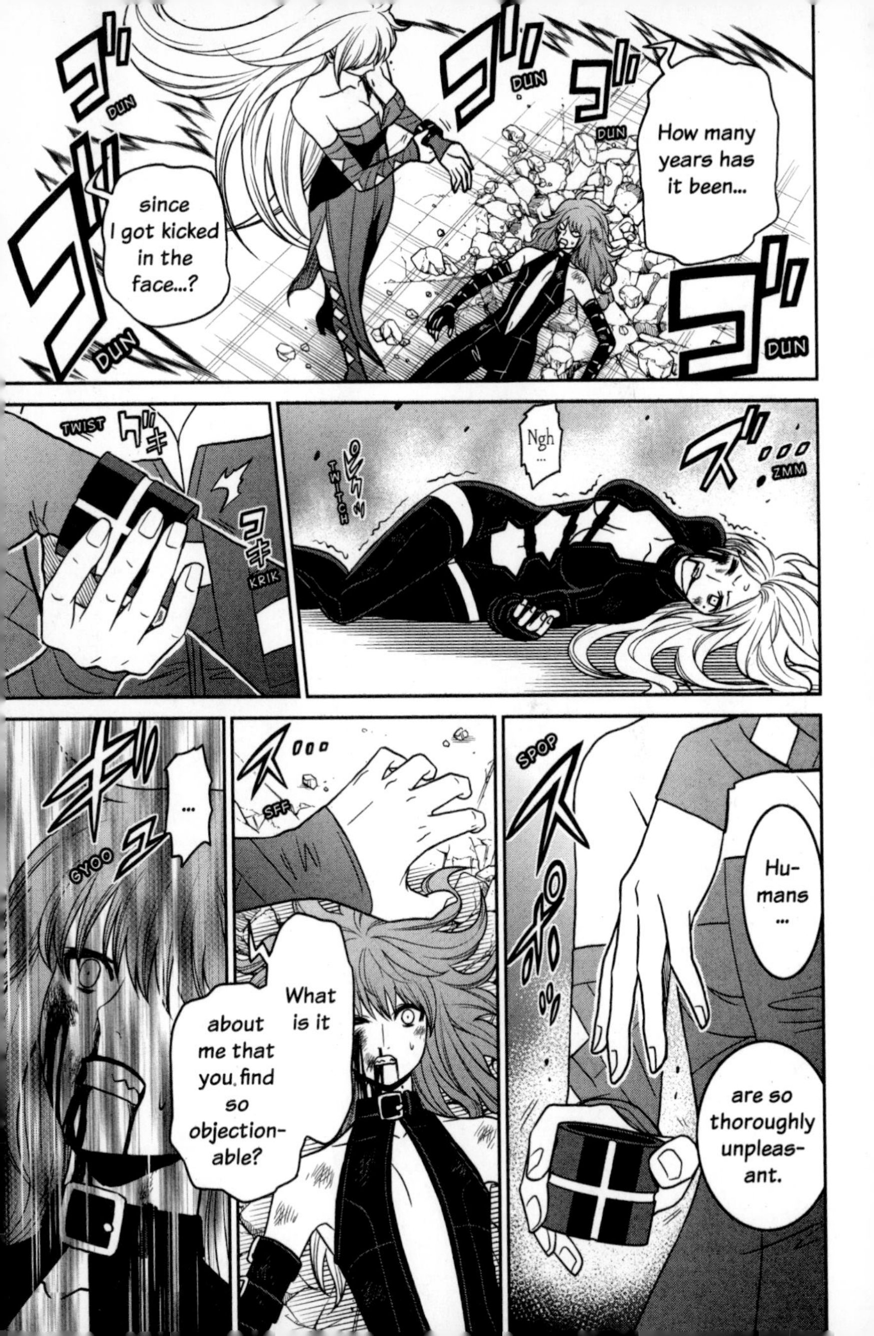
How many years has it been...
DUN
DUN
DUN
since I got kicked in the face...?
DUN
DUN
ZMM
Ngh...
TWITCH
TWIST
KRIK
SPOP
Humans...
are so thoroughly unpleas-ant.
SFF
What is it about me that you find so objectionable?
...
GYOO

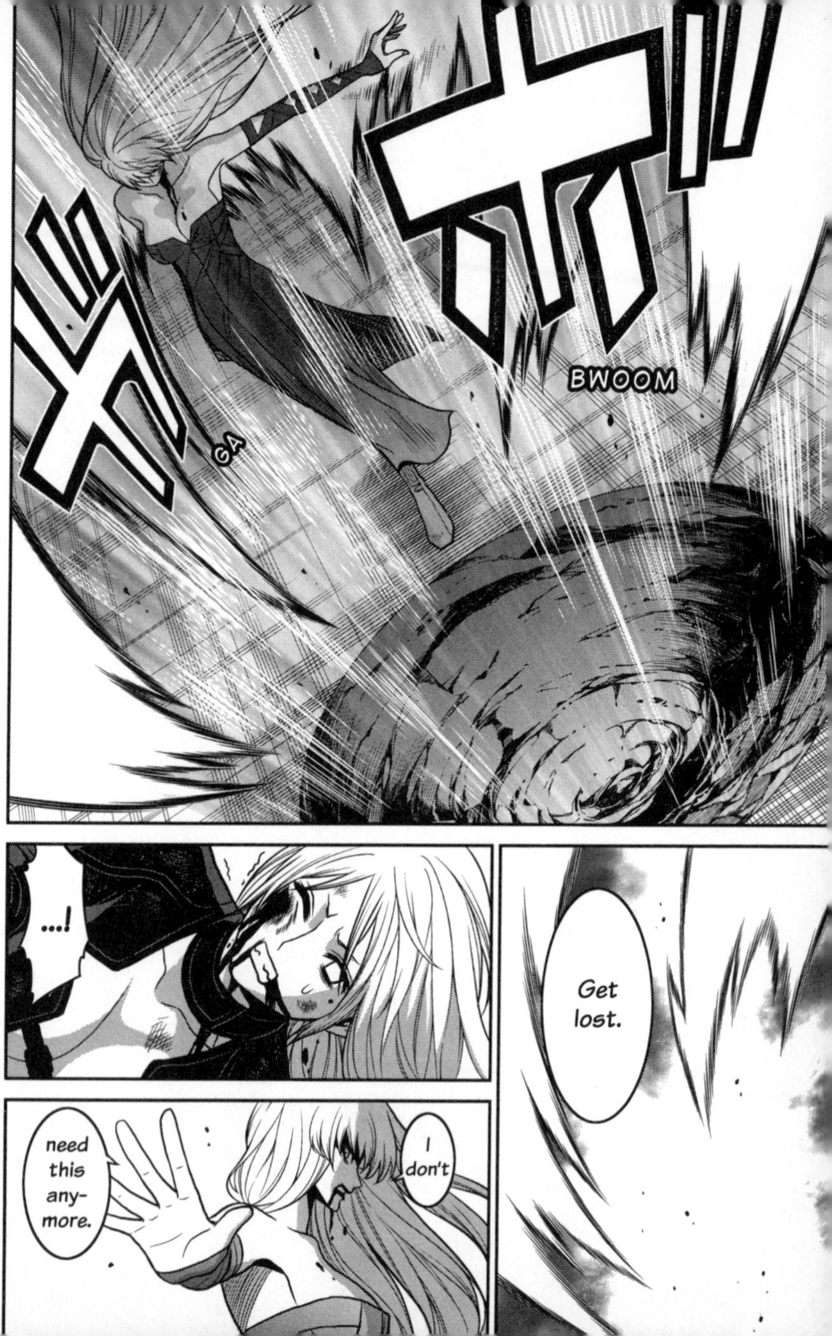
BWOOM
GA
Get lost.
...!
I don't
need this any-more.

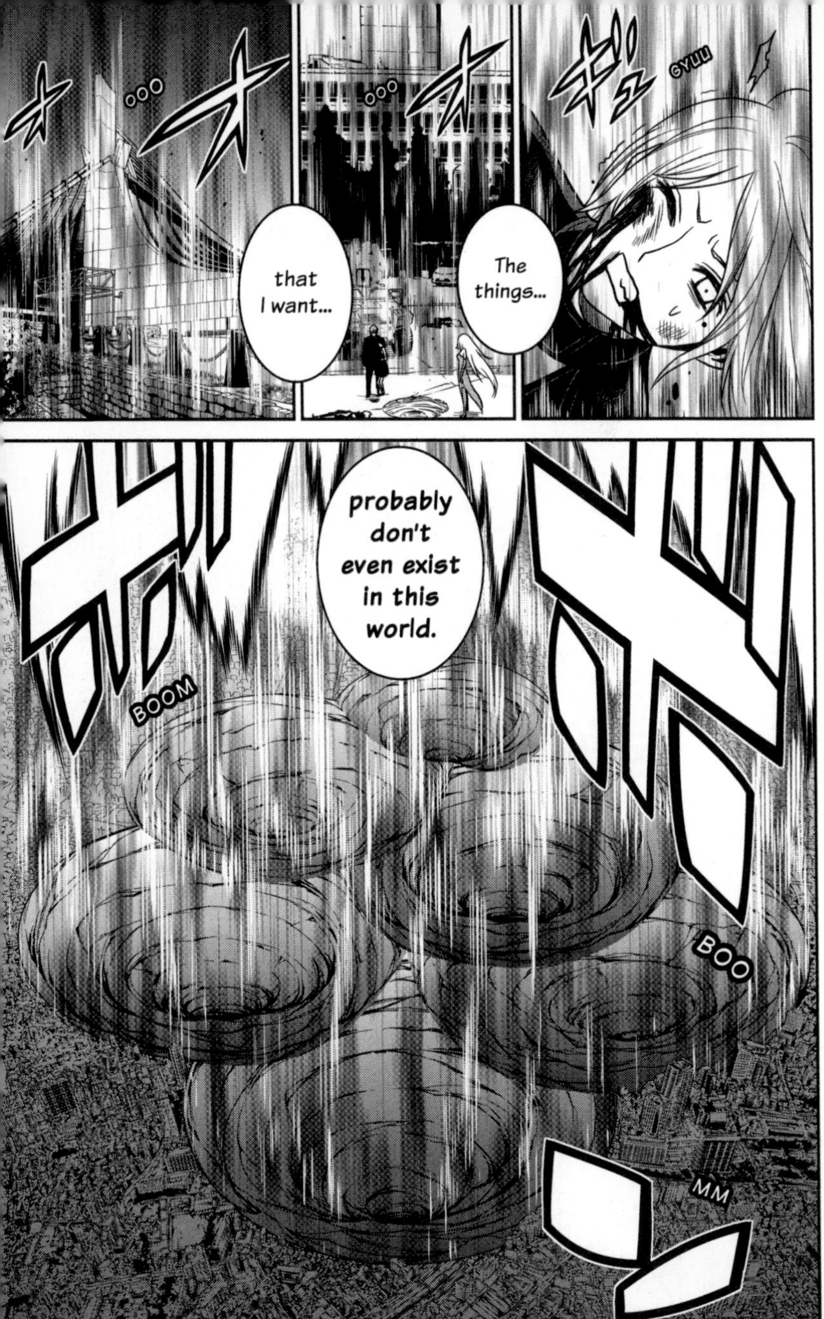
GYUU
The things...
ooo
that I want...
ooo
probably don't even exist in this world.
BOOM
BOO
MM

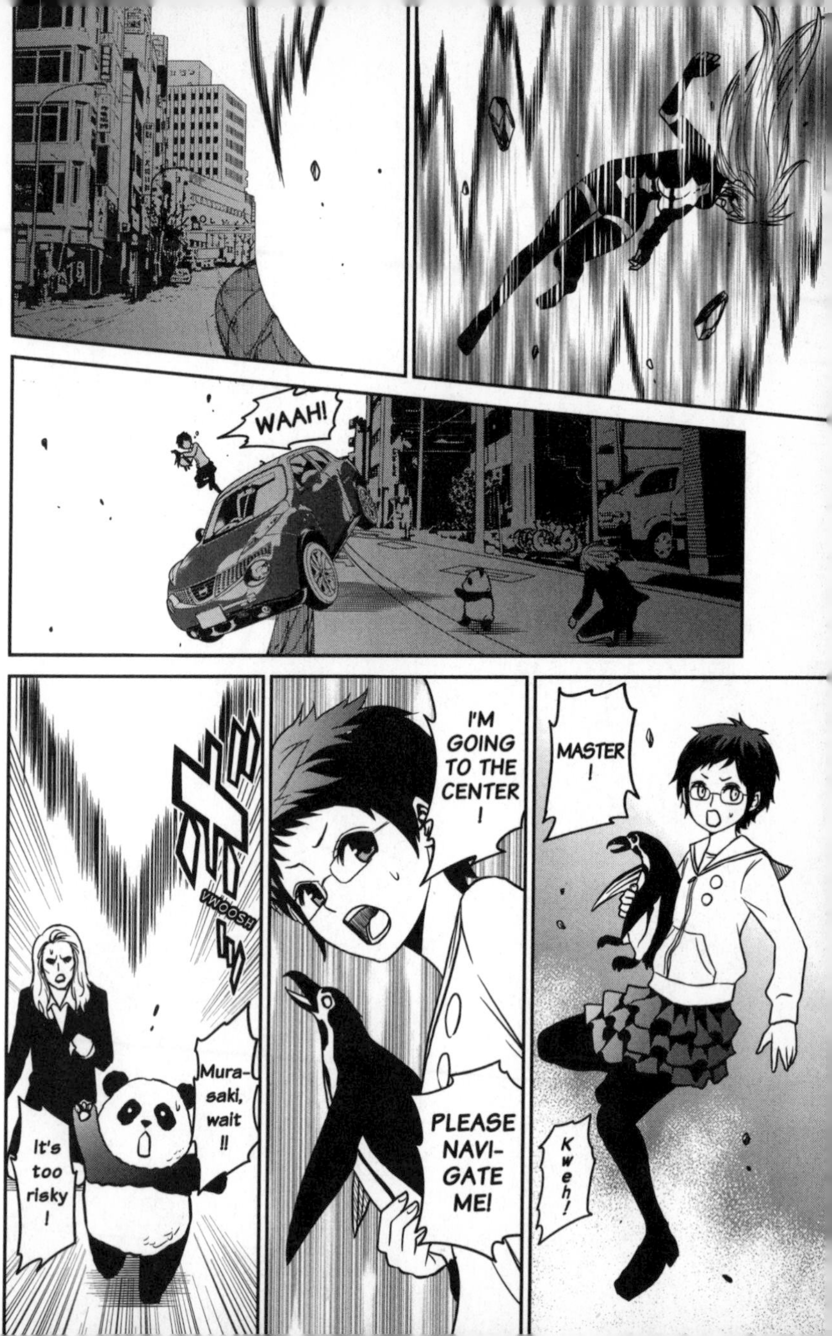
WAAH!
MASTER!
Kweh!
I'M GOING TO THE CENTER!
PLEASE NAVIGATE ME!
VWOOSH
Murasaki, wait!!
It's too risky!

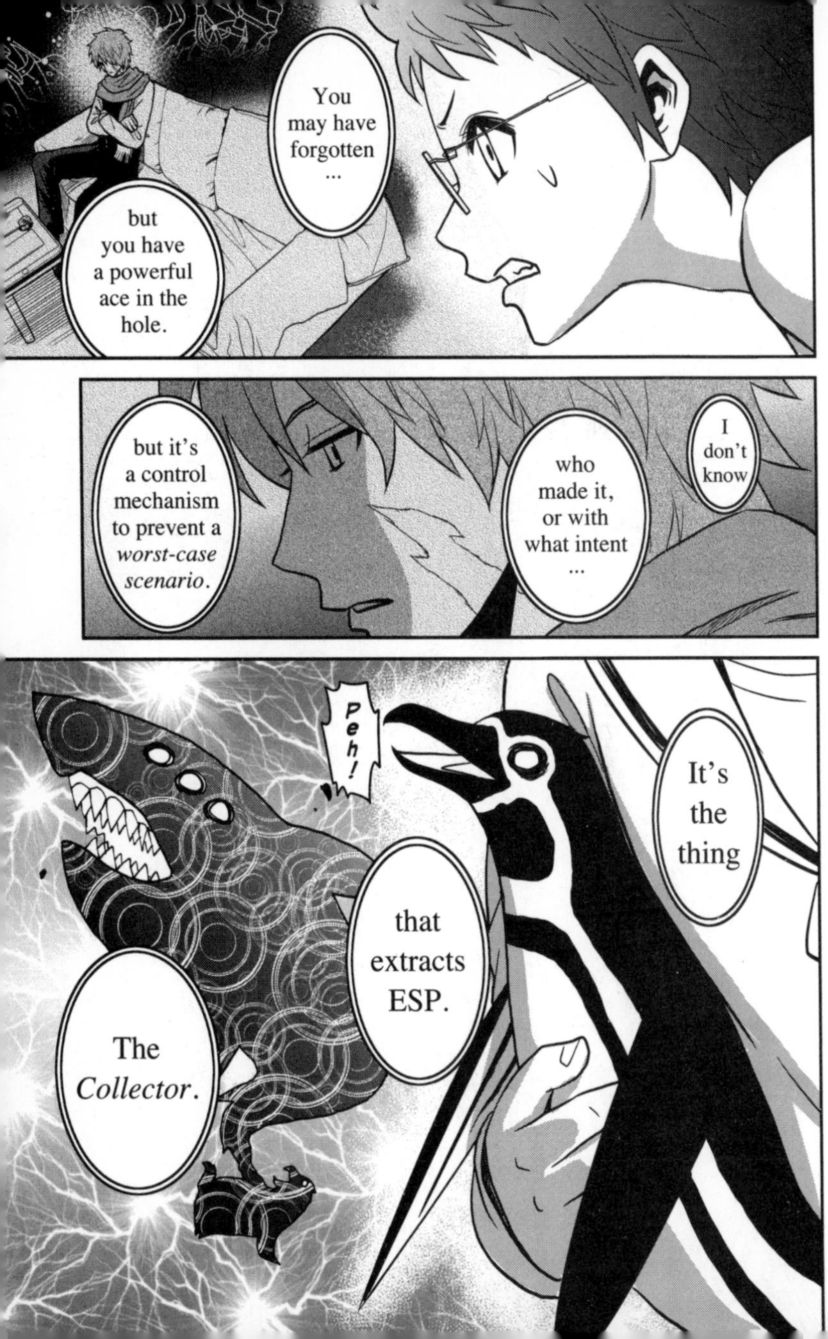
You may have forgotten ...
but you have a powerful ace in the hole.
I don't know
who made it, or with what intent ...
but it's a control mechanism to prevent a *worst-case scenario*.
It's the thing
Peh!
that extracts ESP.
The *Collector*.

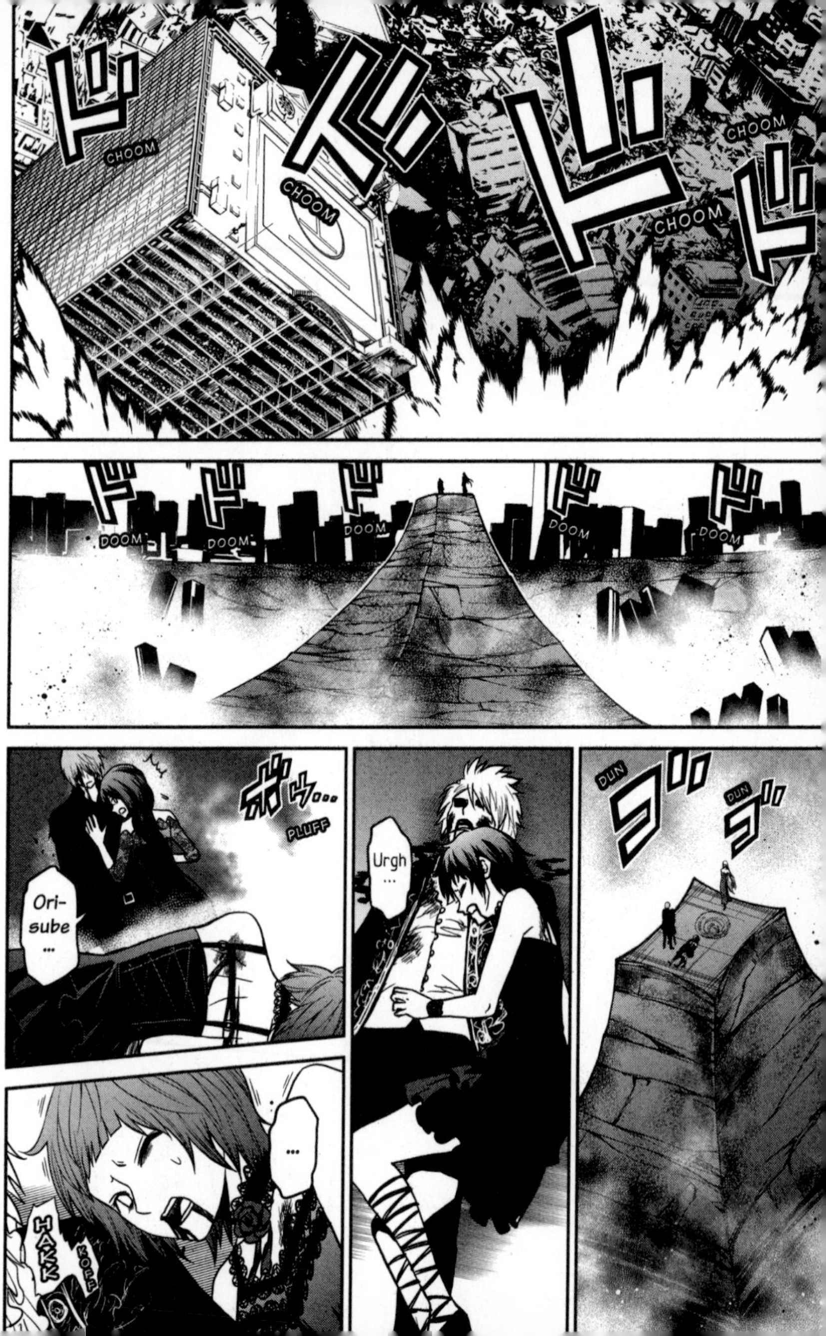
CHOOM
CHOOM
CHOOM
CHOOM
DOOM
DOOM
DOOM
DOOM
DOOM
DUN
DUN
Urgh...
PLUFF
Ori-sube...
...
HAKK
KOFF

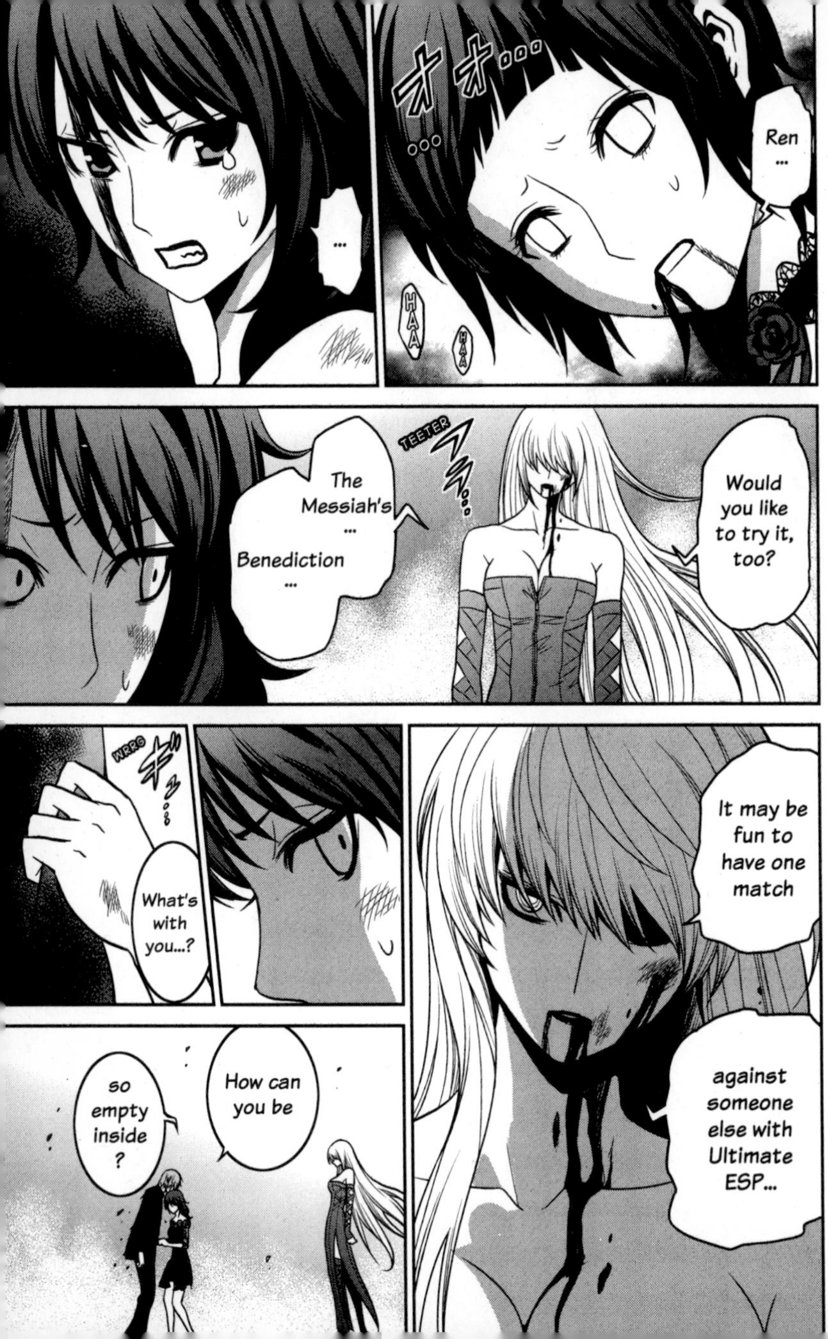

オオ...
...
Ren ...
HAA
HAA
...
Would you like to try it, too?
TEETER
The Messiah's ... Benediction ...
It may be fun to have one match
against someone else with Ultimate ESP...
WRRG
What's with you...?
How can you be
so empty inside ?

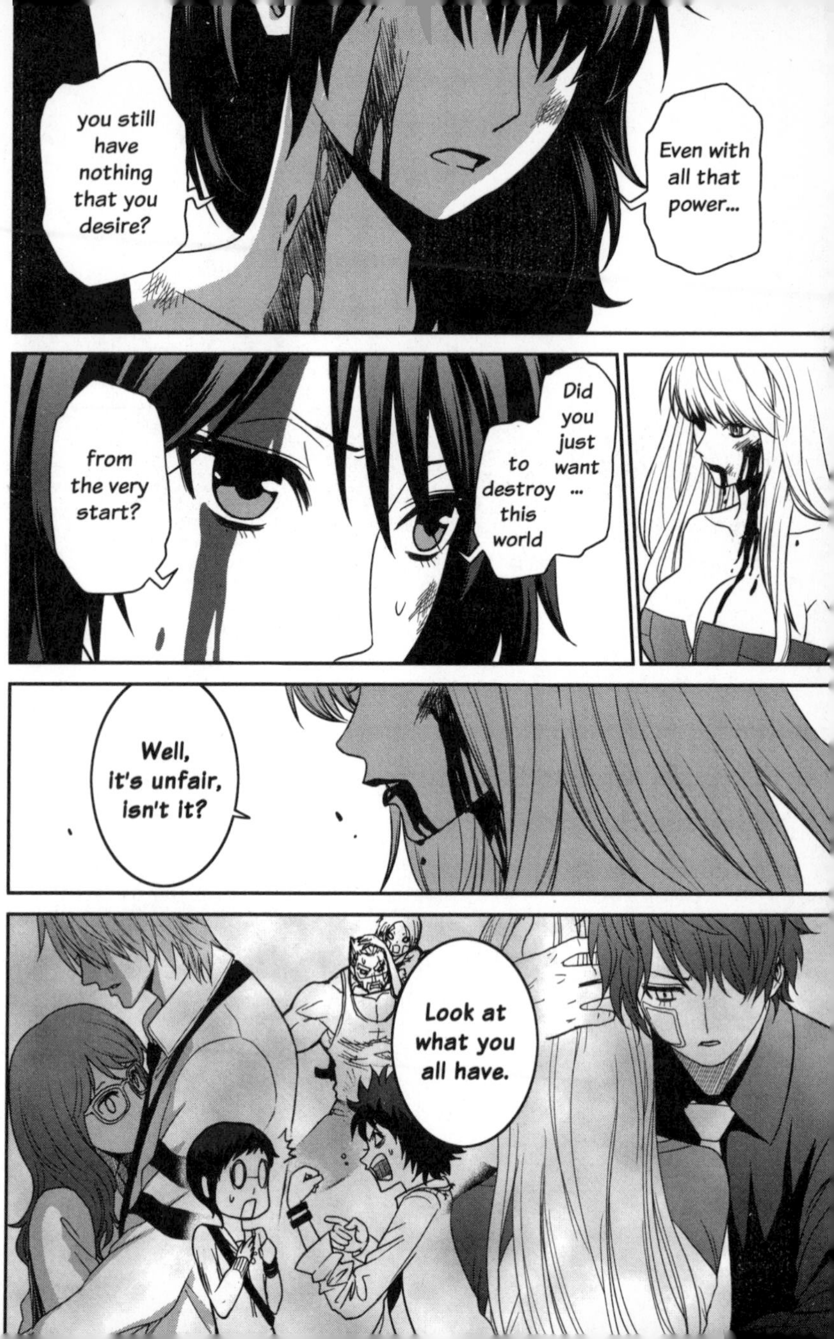
Even with all that power...
you still have nothing that you desire?
Did you just want ... to destroy this world
from the very start?
Well, it's unfair, isn't it?
Look at what you all have.

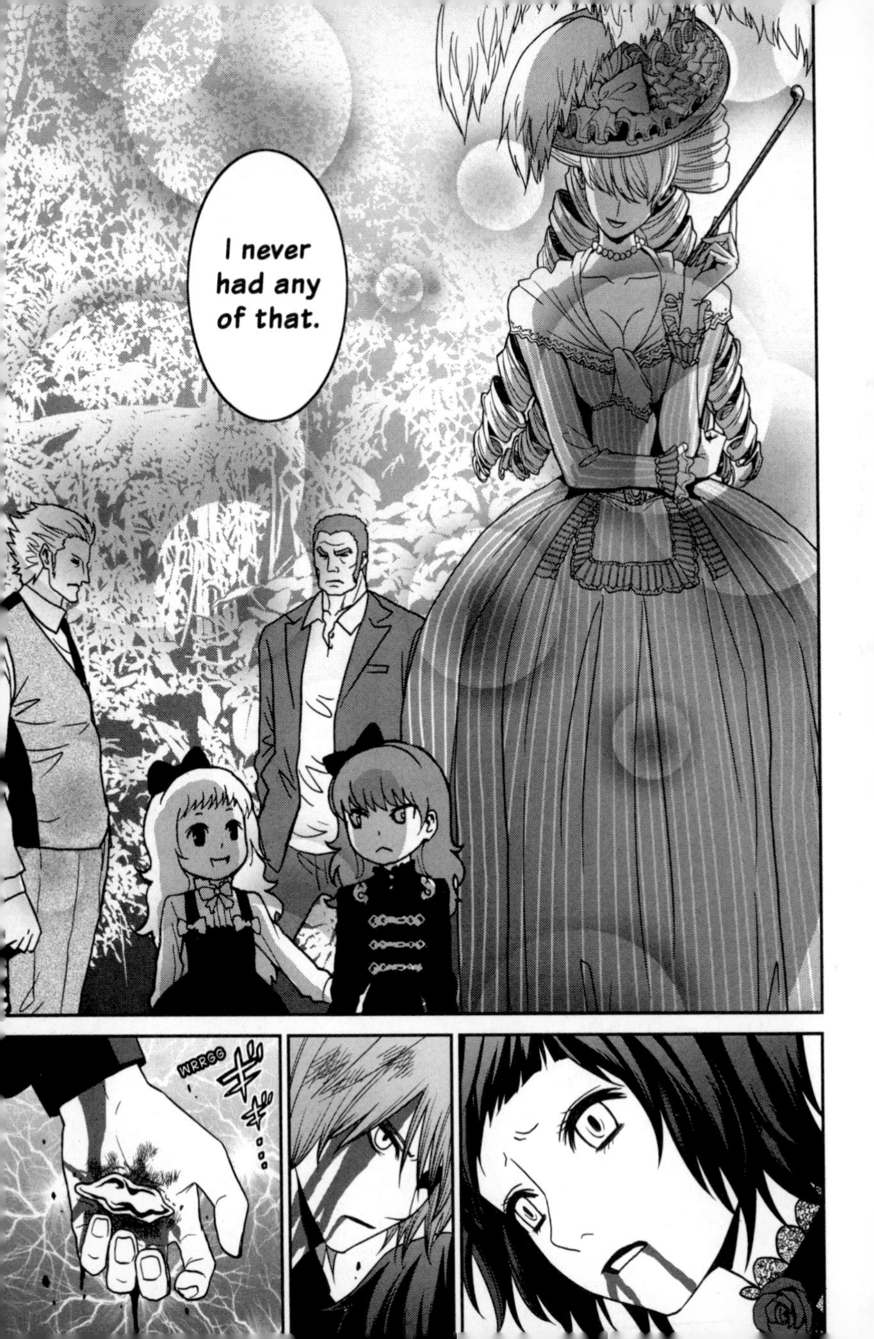
I never had any of that.
WRRGG

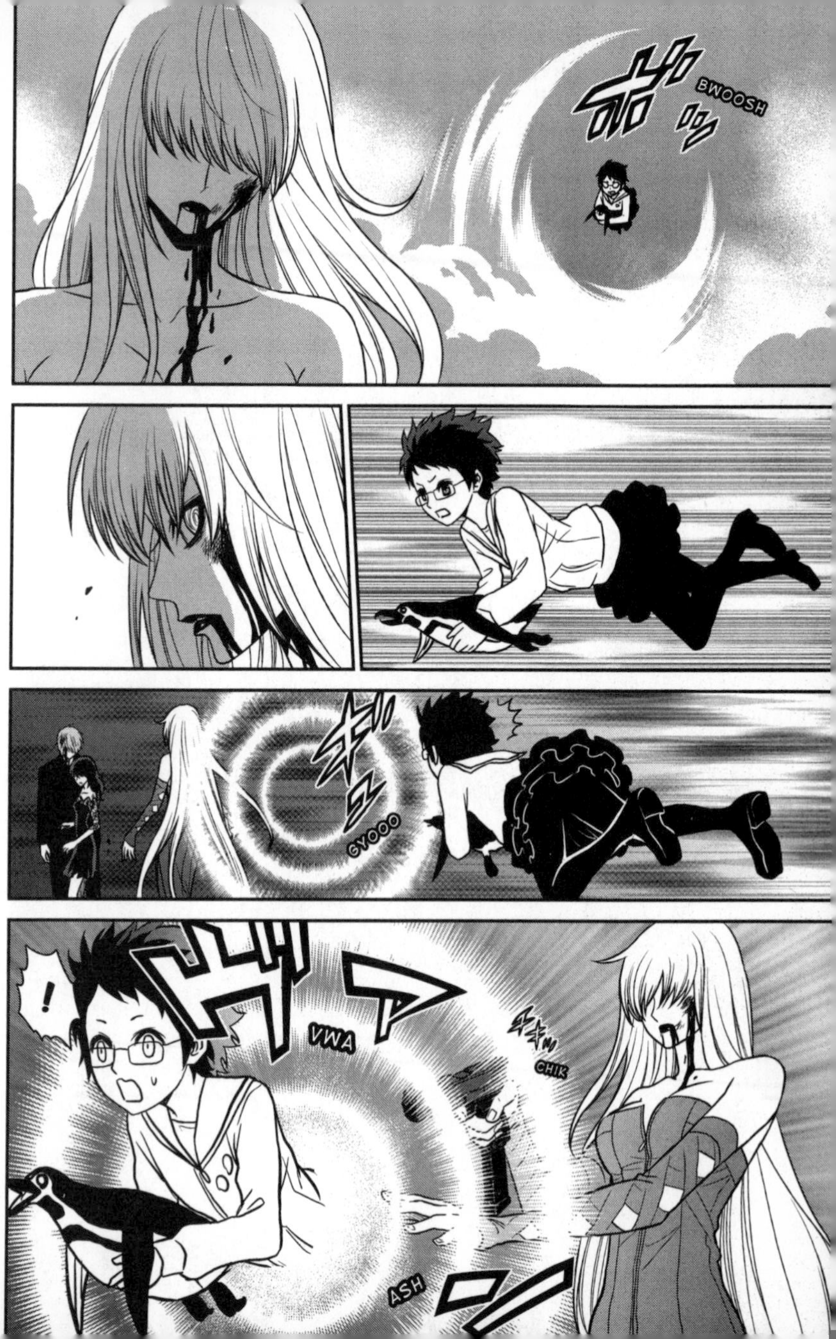
BWOOSH
GYOOO
CHIK
VWA
!
ASH

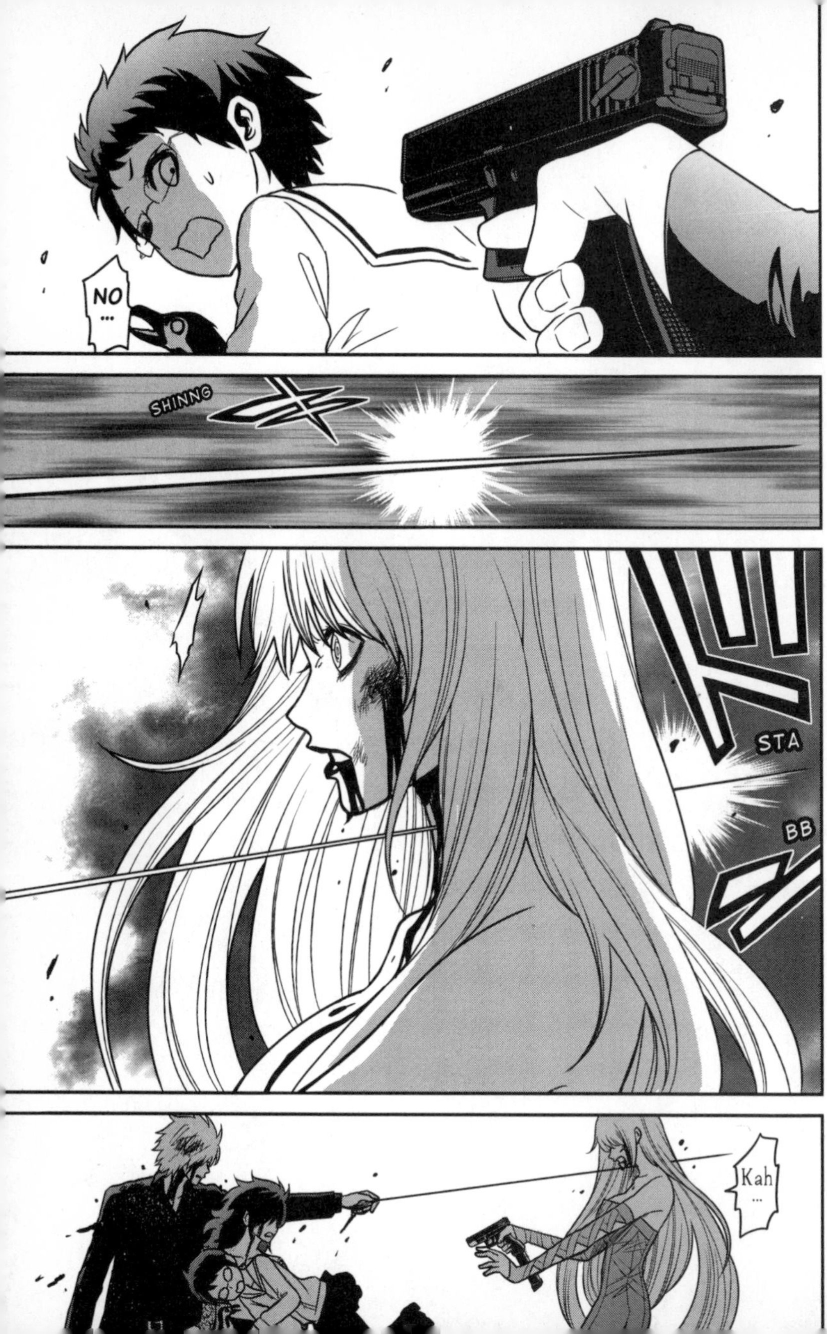
NO
...
SHINNG
STA
BB
Kah
...

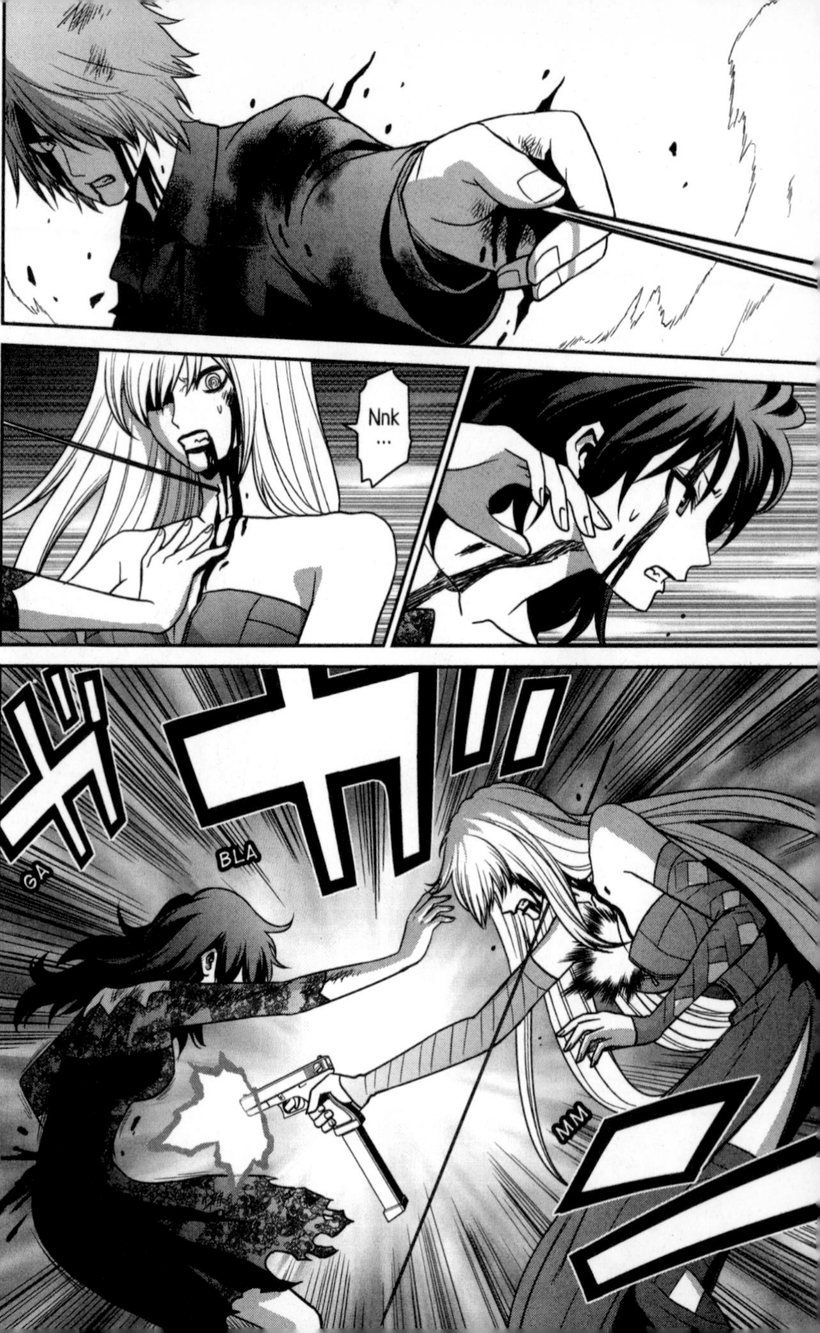
Nnk
...
GA
BLA
MM

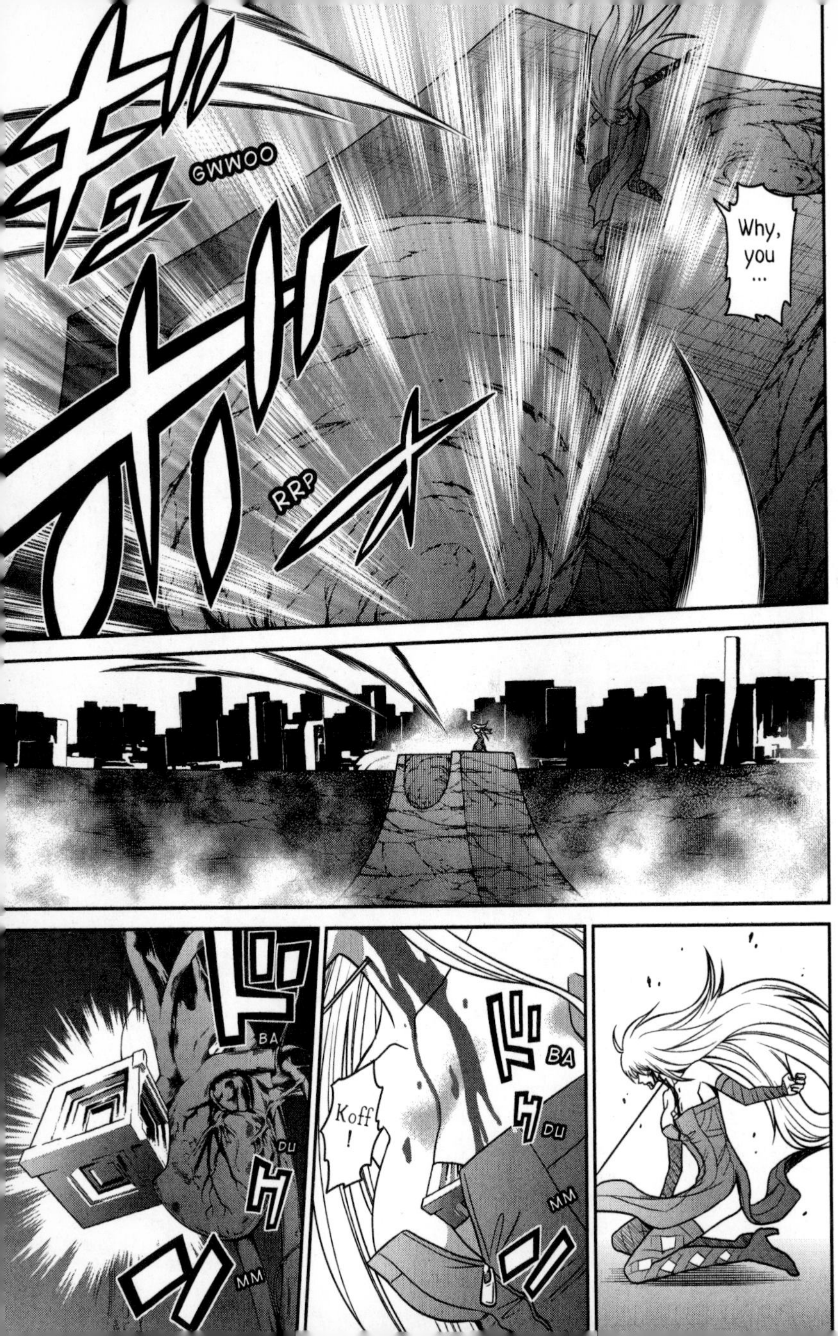
Why, you ...
GWWOO
RRP
BA
DU
MM
Koff!
BA
DU
MM

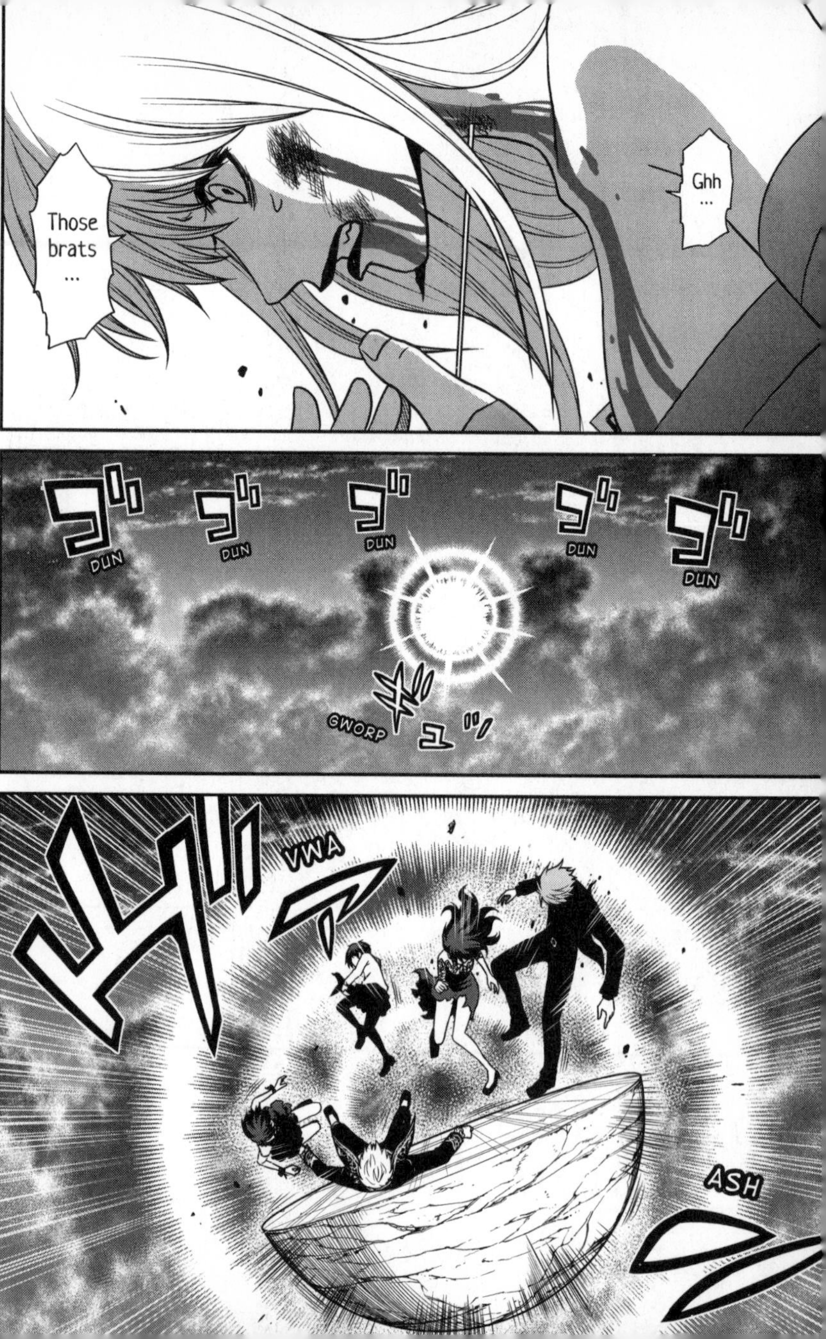
Ghh ...
Those brats ...
DUN
DUN
DUN
DUN
DUN
GWORP
VWA
ASH

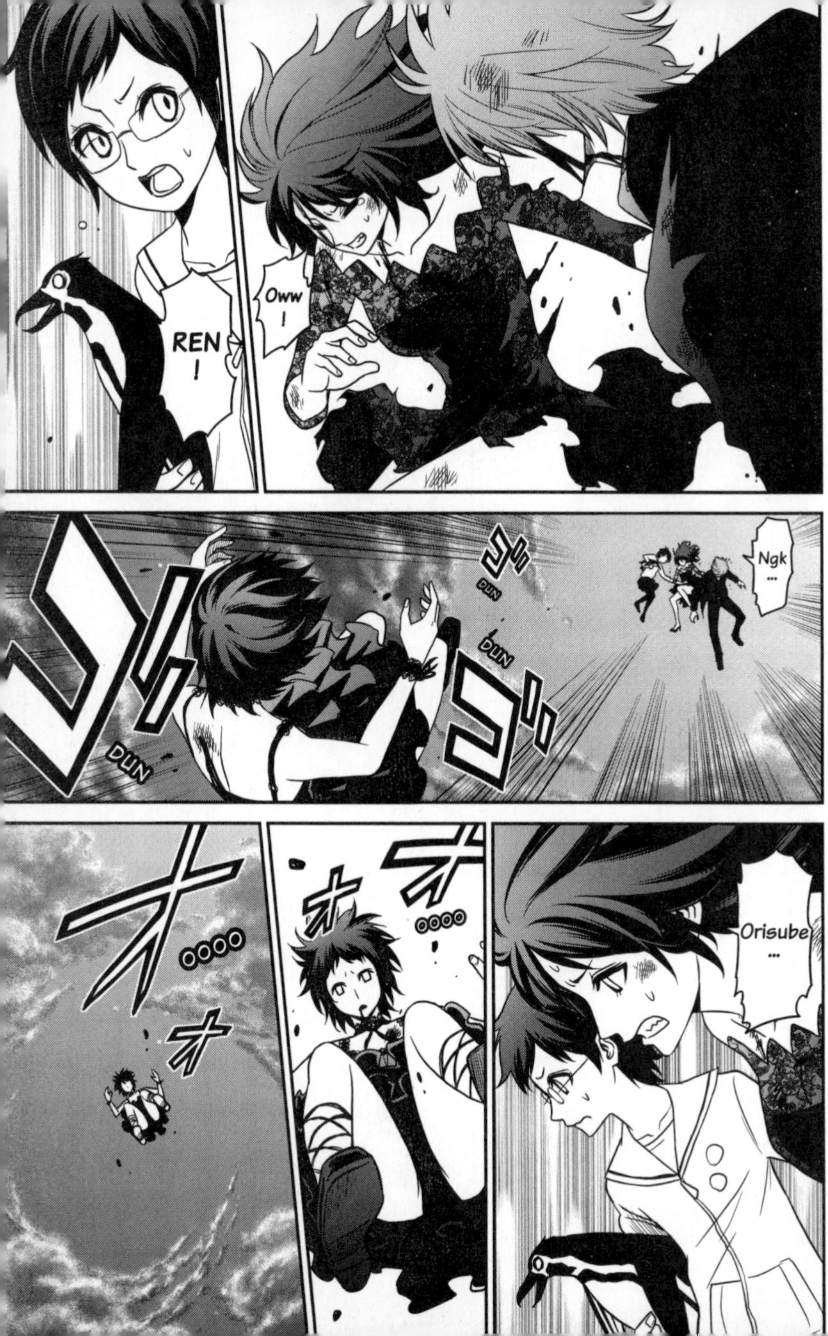
Oww !
REN !
Ngk ...
DUN
DUN
DUN
Orisube ...
oooo
oooo

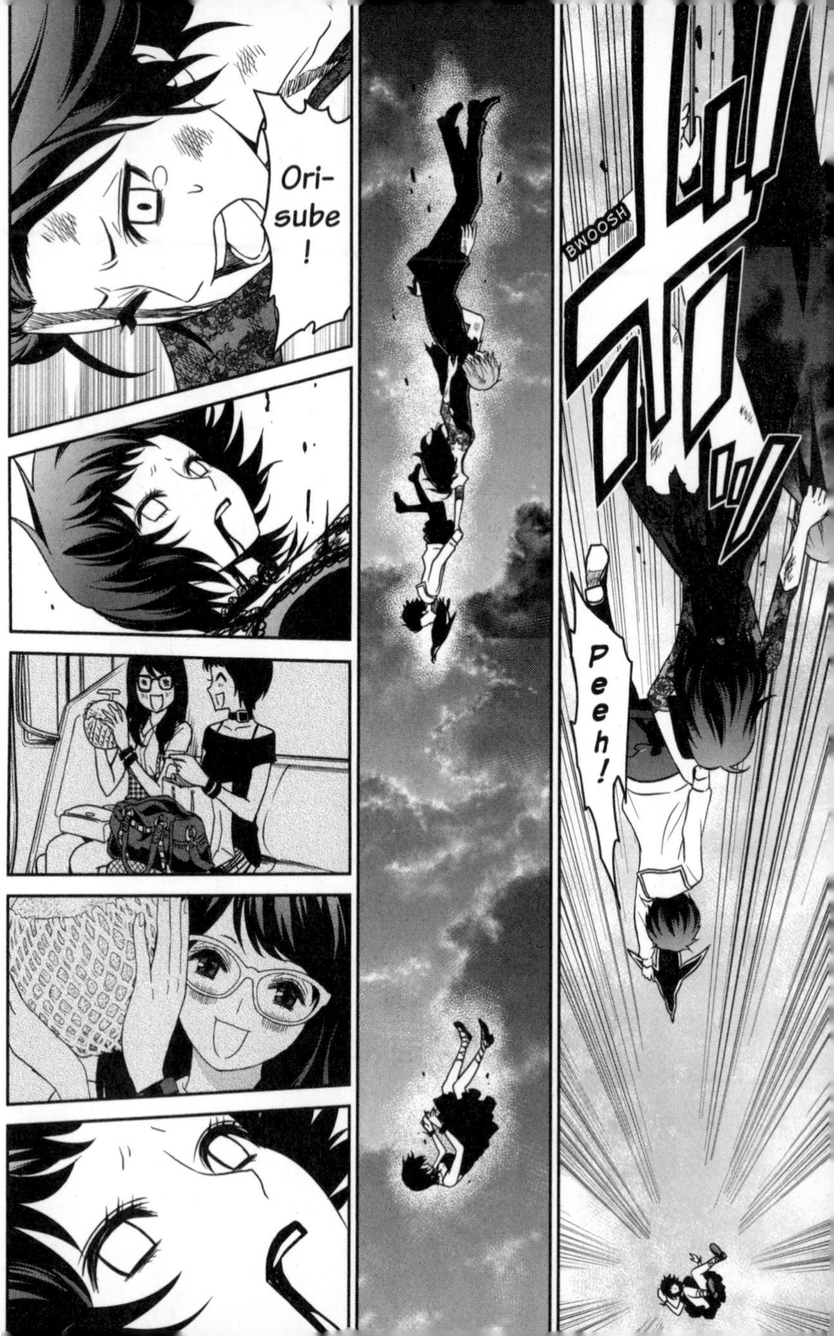
BWOOSH
Peeh!
Ori-sube!

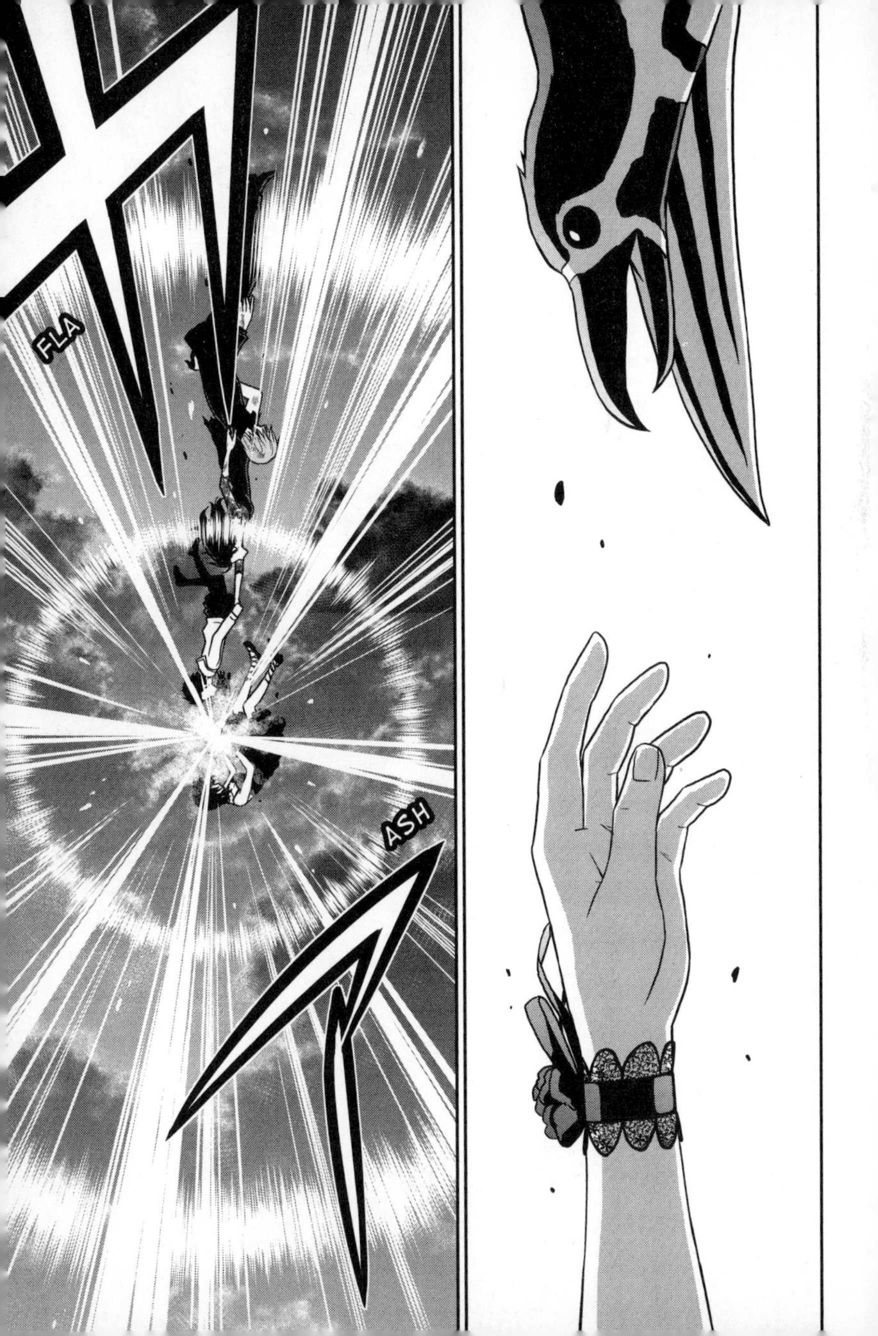
FLA
ASH

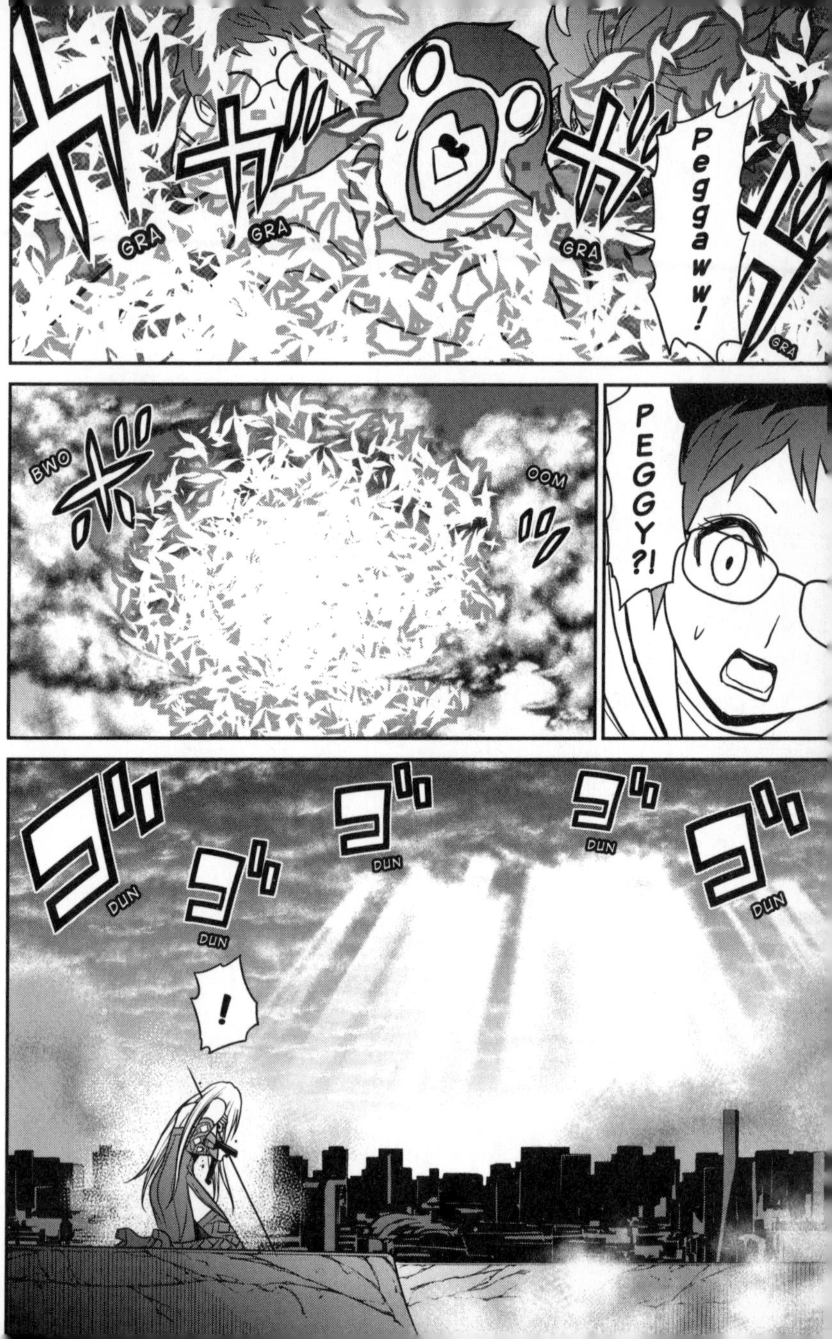
Peggaww!
GRA
GRA
GRA
GRA
PEGGY?!
BWO
OOM
DUN
DUN
DUN
DUN
DUN
!

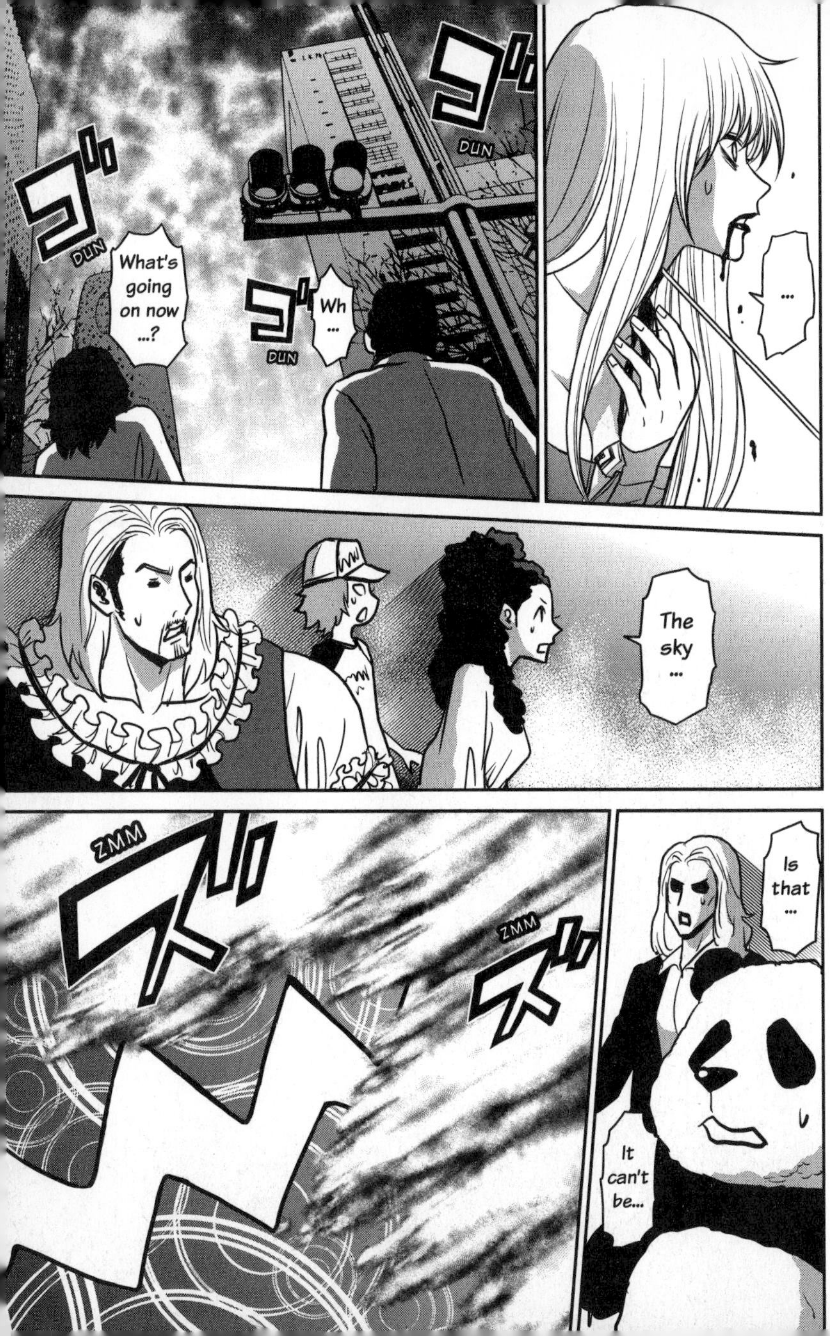
...
DUN
Wh ...
DUN
DUN
What's going on now ...?
The sky ...
Is that ...
It can't be...
ZMM
ZMM

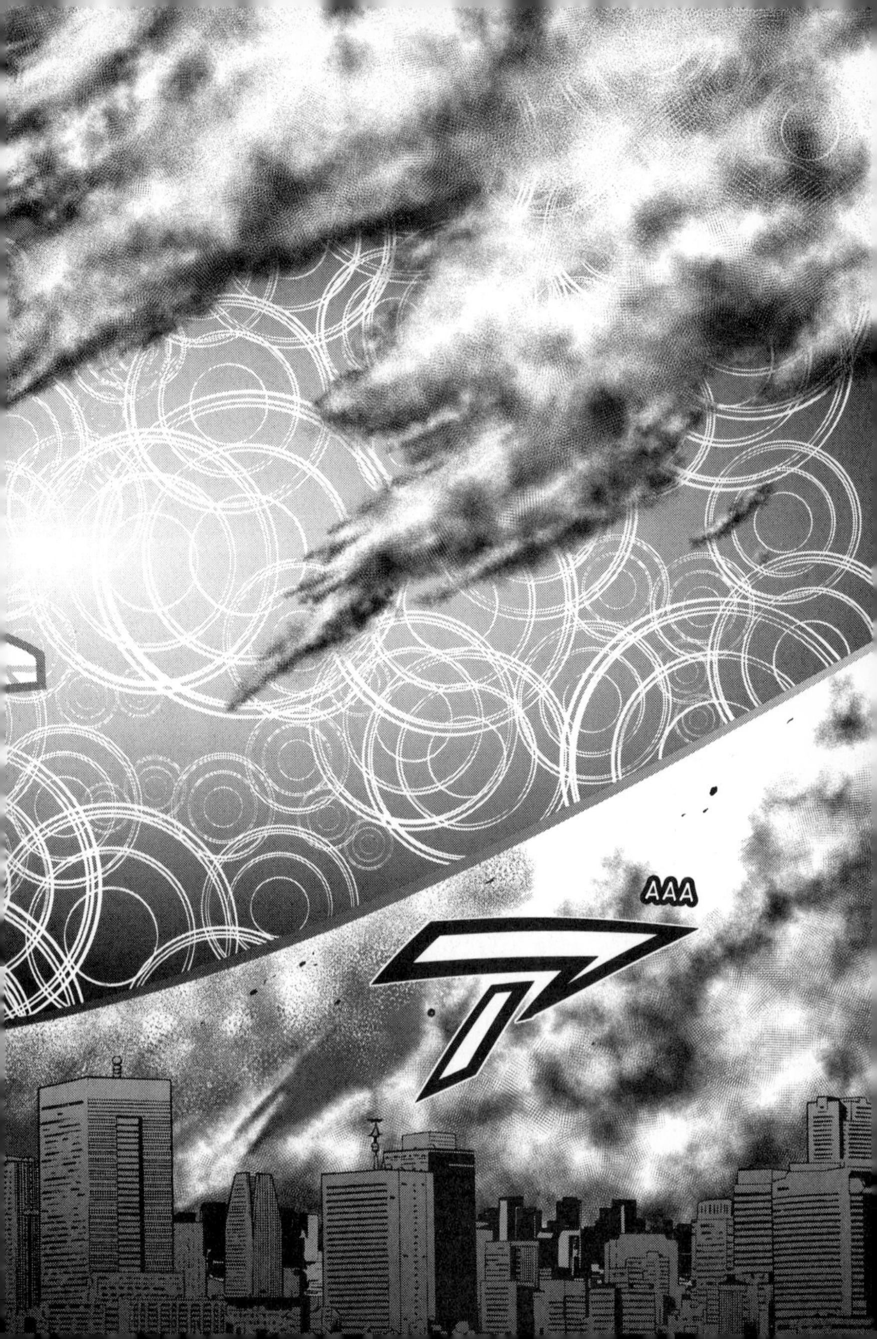
AAA

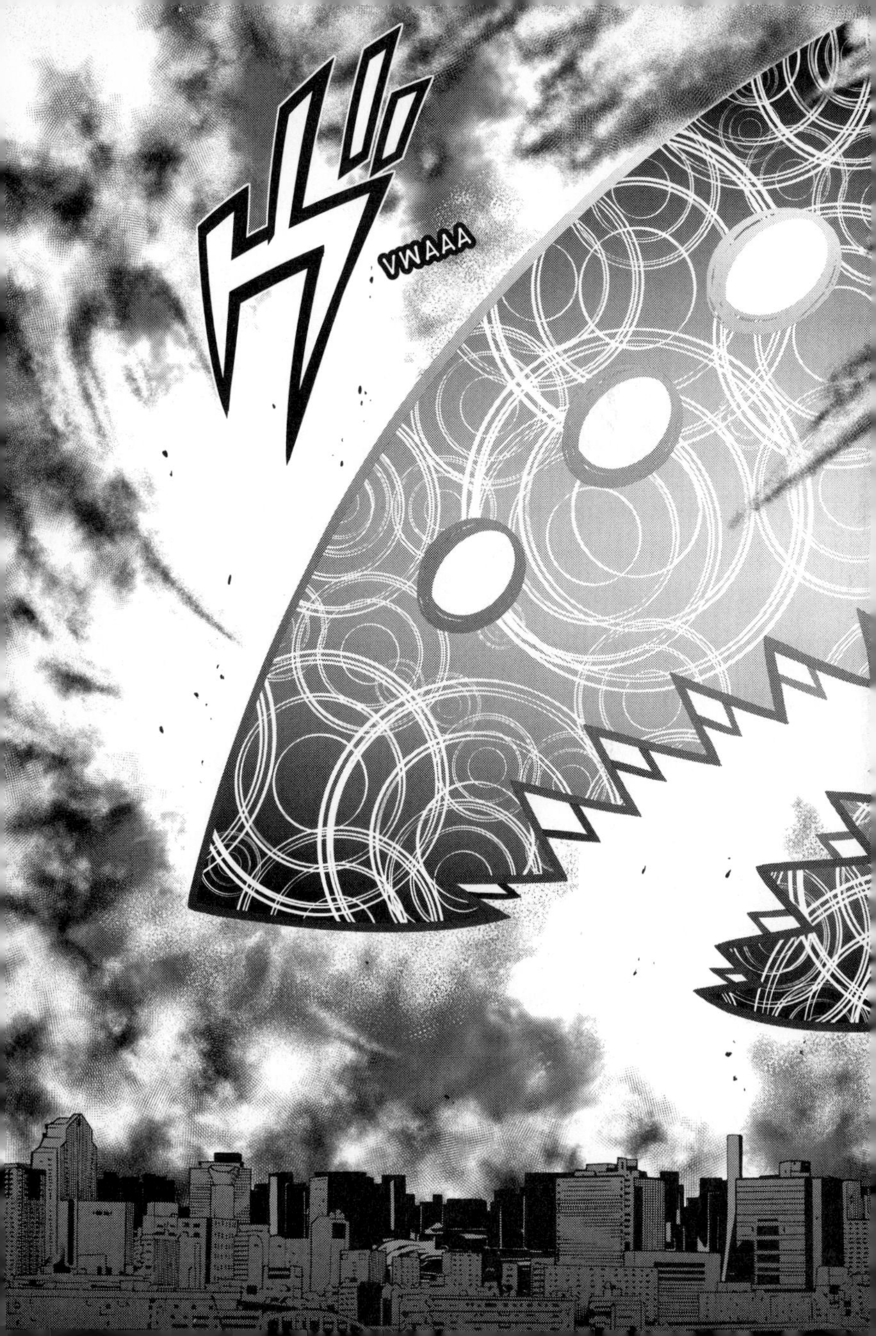
VWAAA

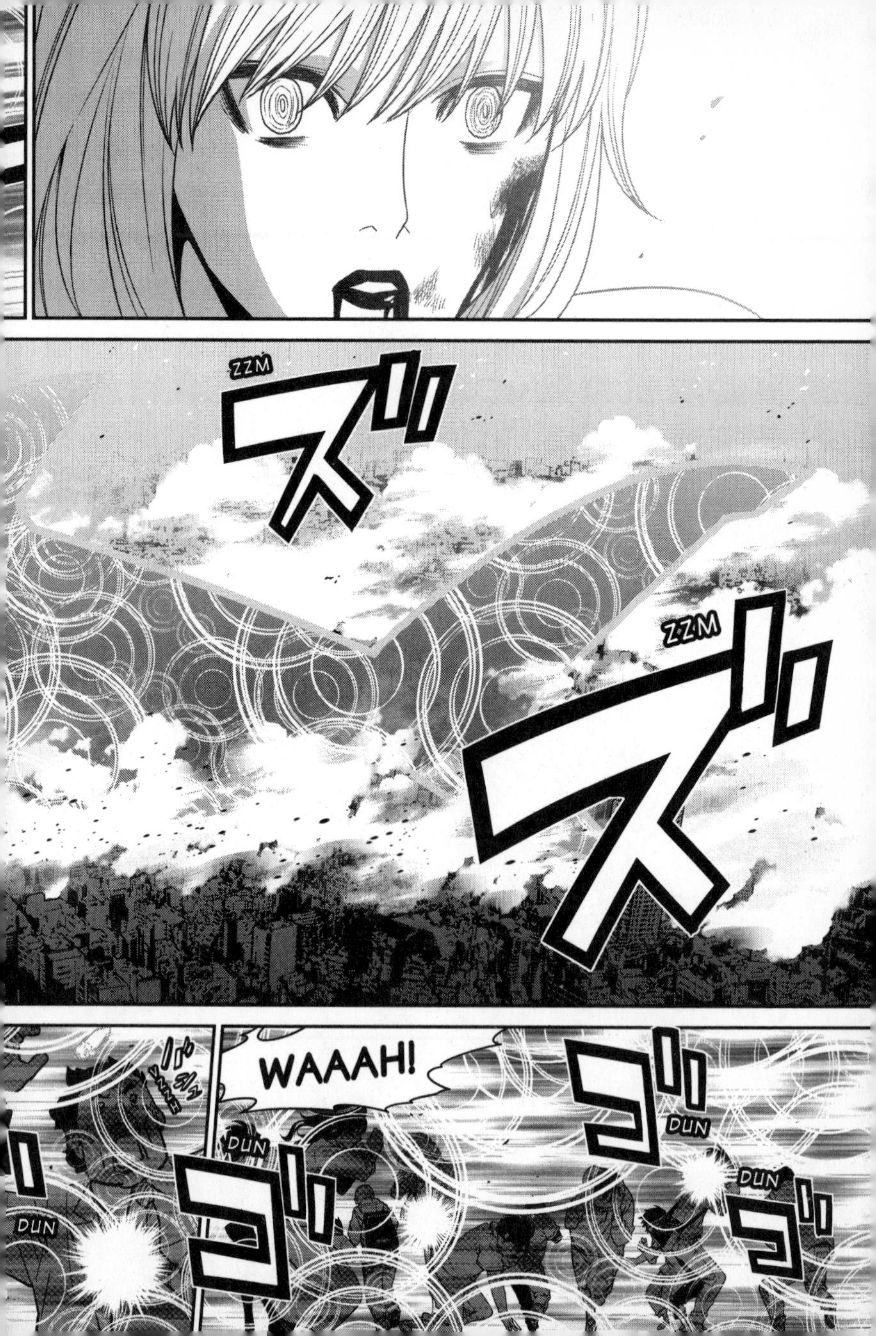
ZZM
ZZM
WAAAH!
DUN
DUN
DUN
VNNH
DUN

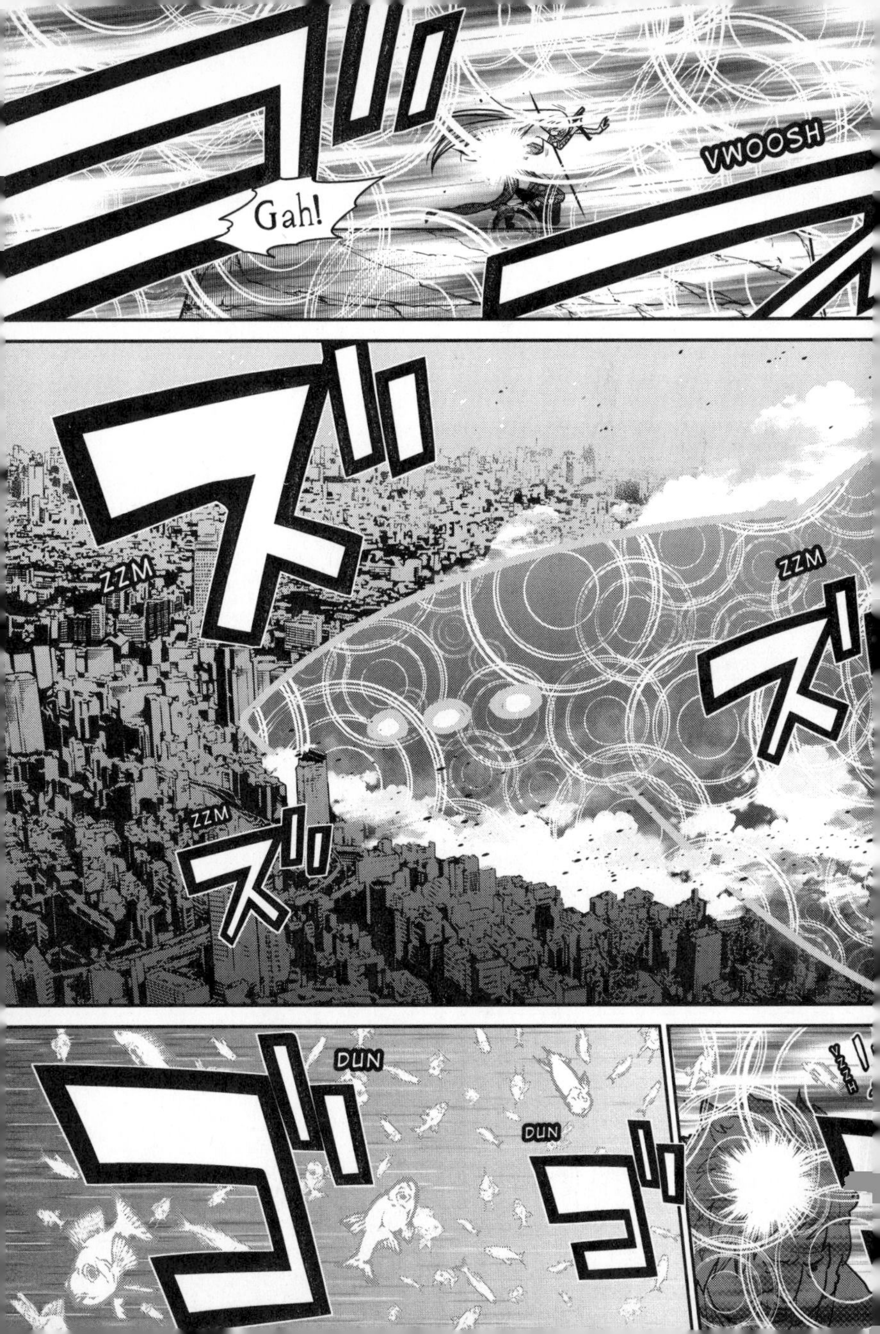
VWOOSH
Gah!
ZZM
ZZM
ZZM
VZZH
DUN
DUN

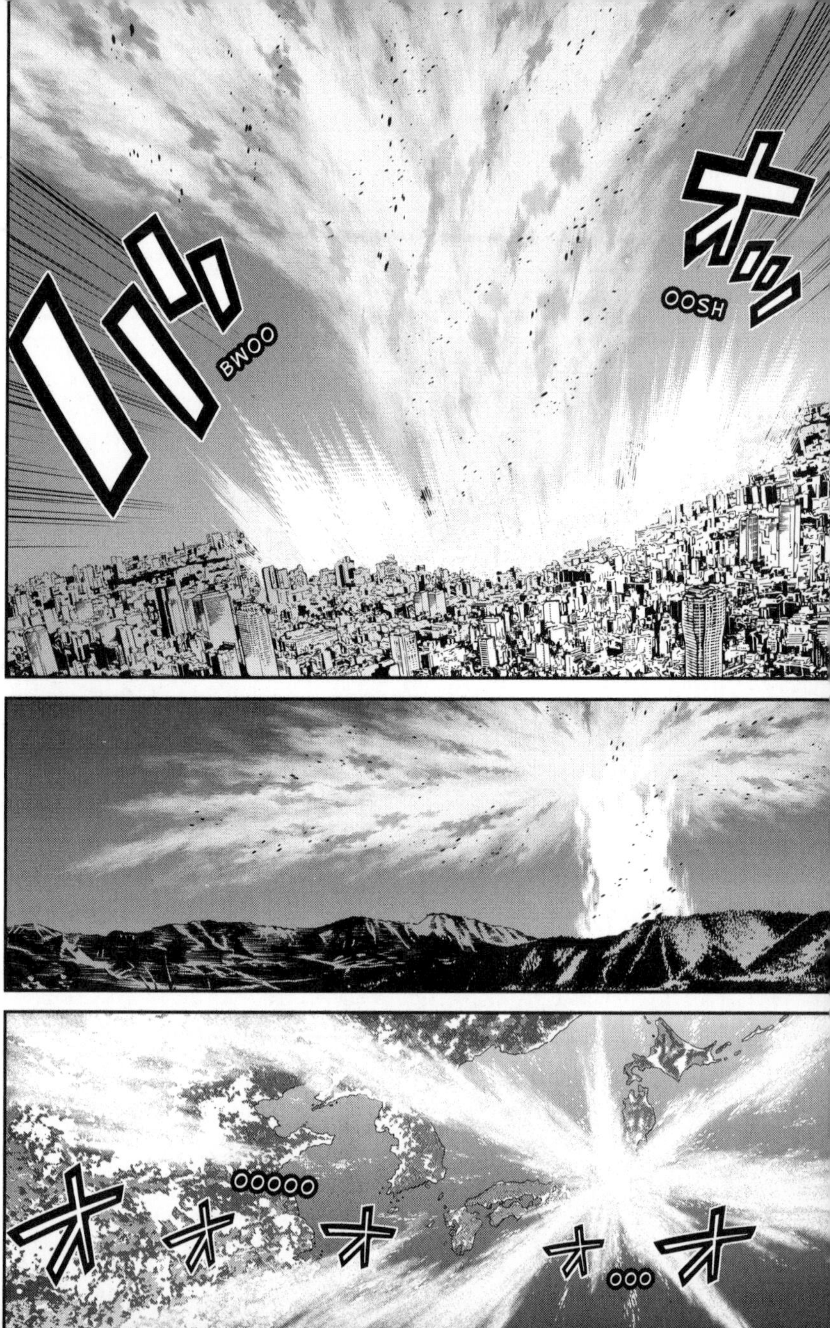

OOSH
BWOO
OOO
OOOOO

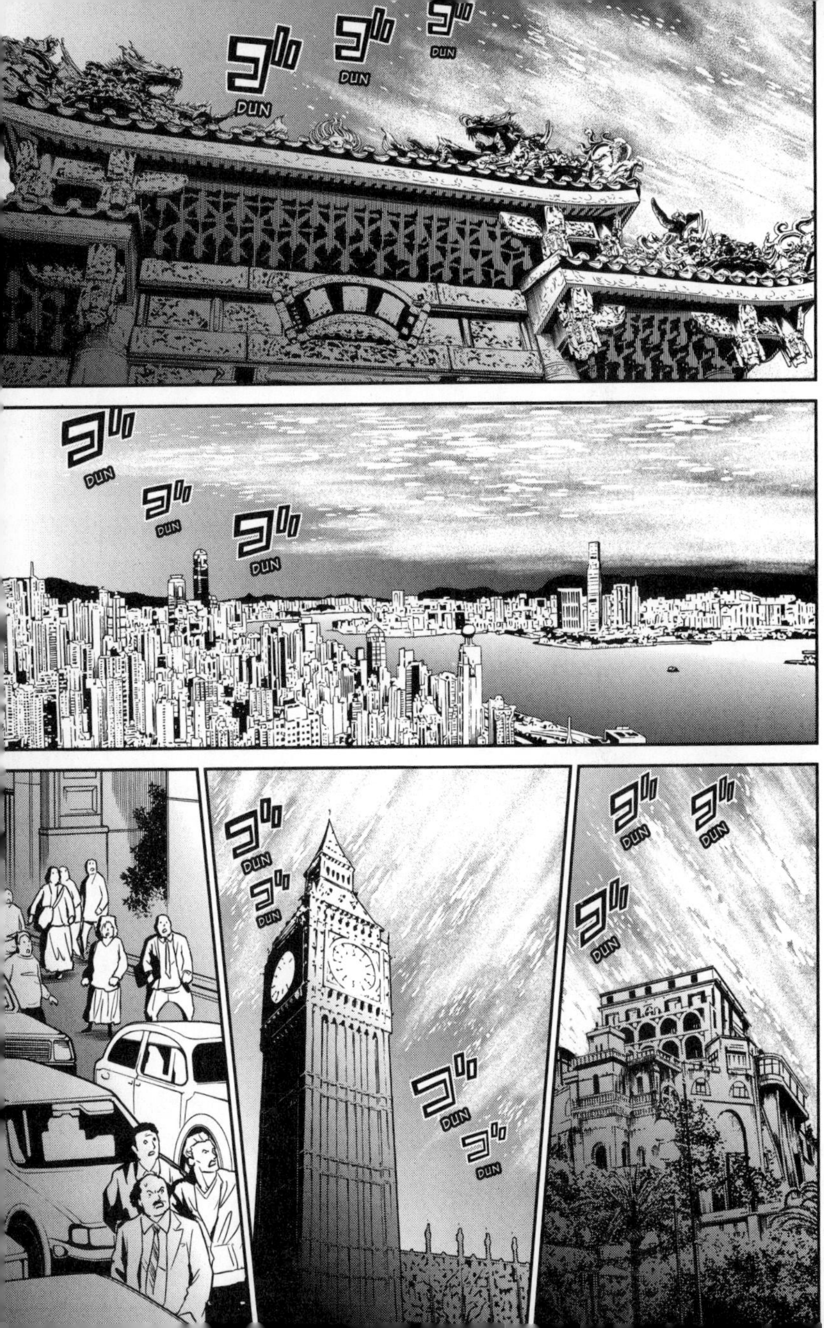

ゴ DUN
ゴ DUN
ゴ DUN
ゴ DUN
ゴ DUN
ゴ DUN
ゴ DUN
ゴ DUN
ゴ DUN
ゴ DUN
ゴ DUN
ゴ DUN
ゴ DUN

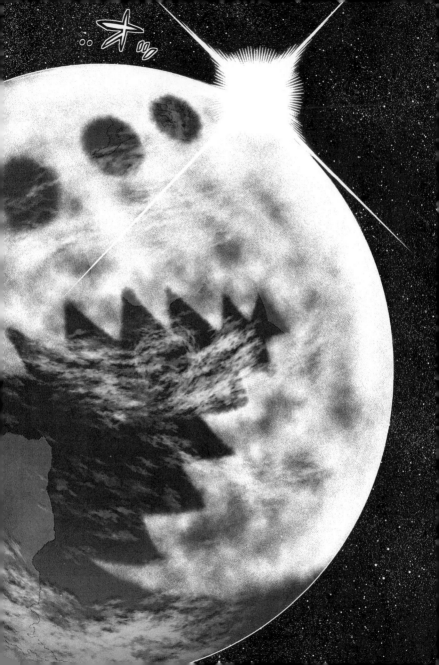

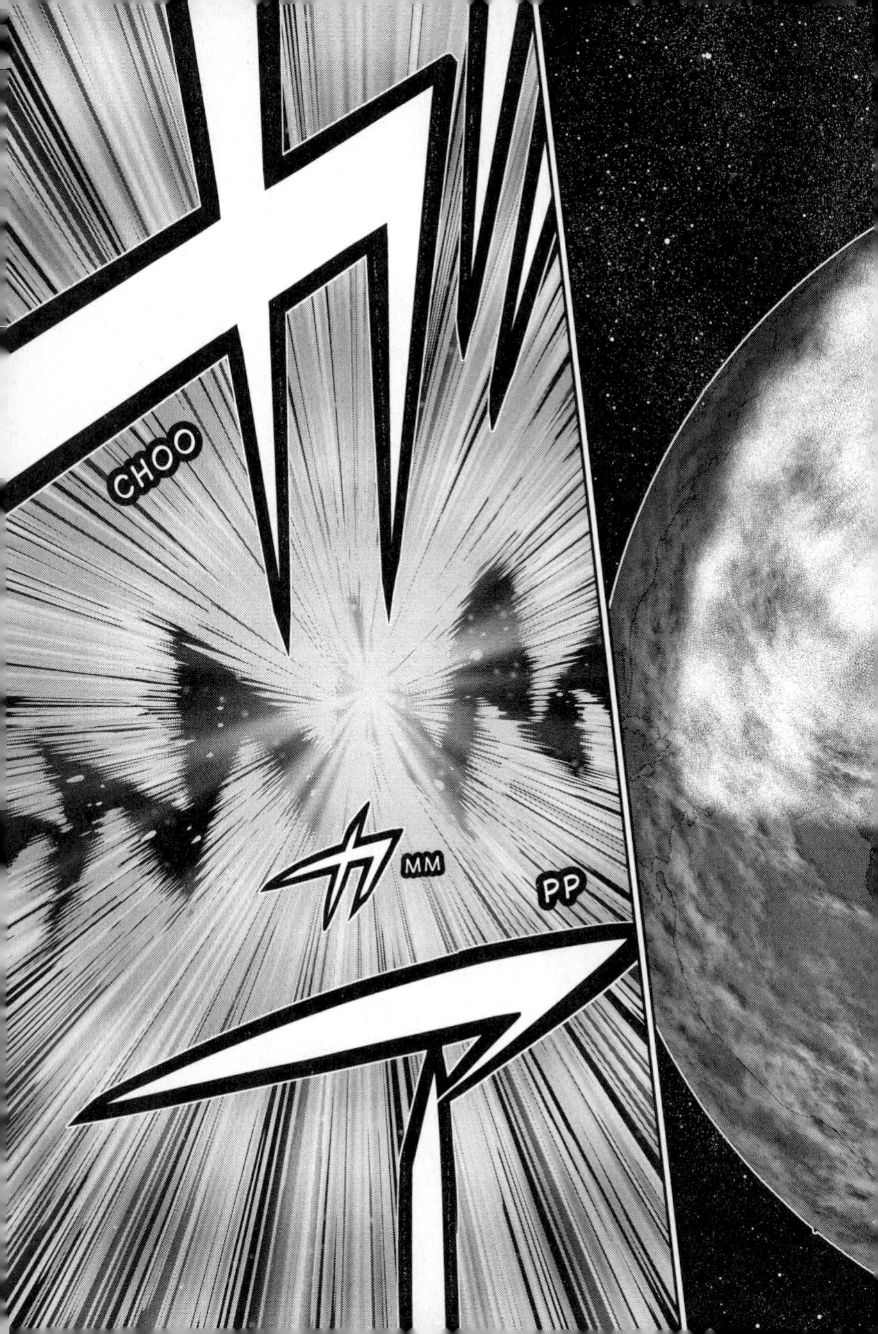
CHOO
MM
PP

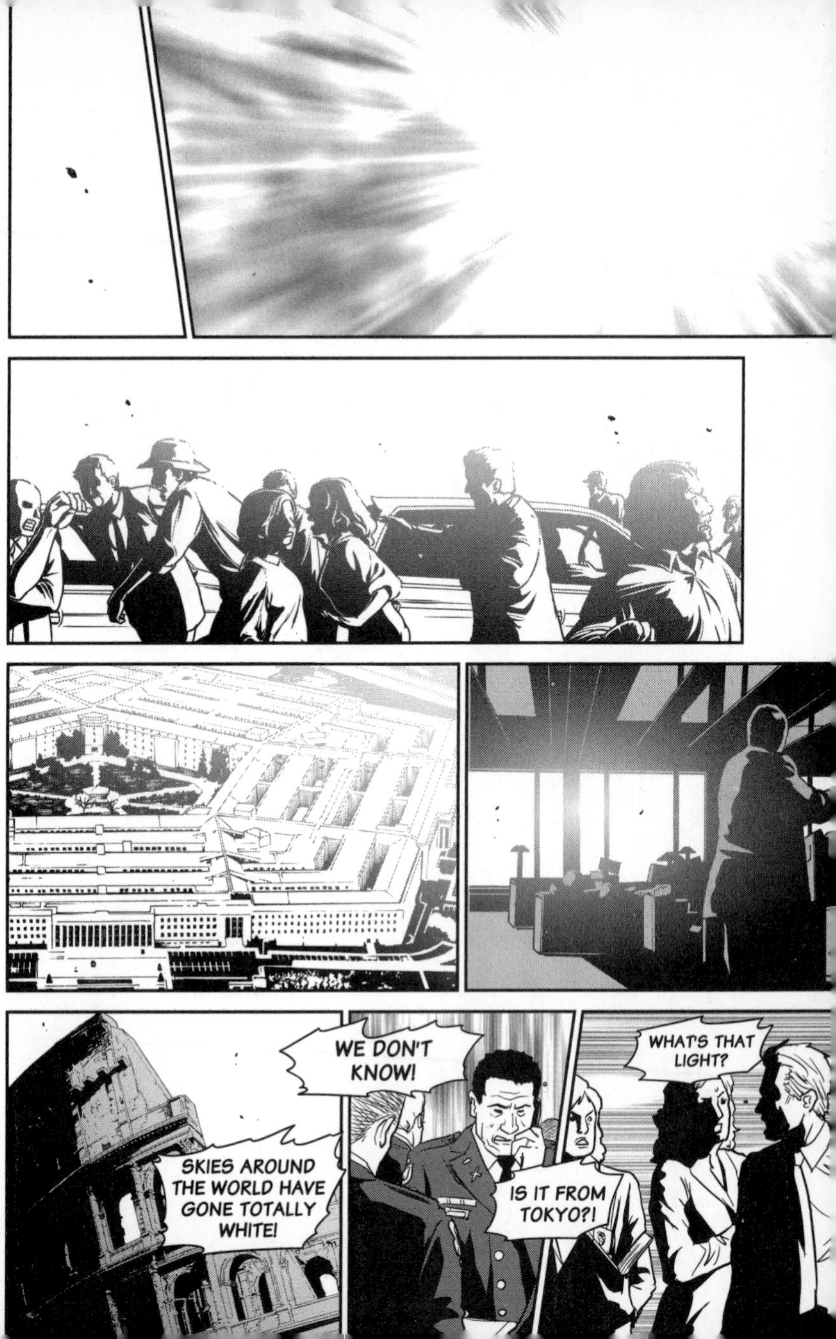
WHAT'S THAT LIGHT?
WE DON'T KNOW!
IS IT FROM TOKYO?!
SKIES AROUND THE WORLD HAVE GONE TOTALLY WHITE!

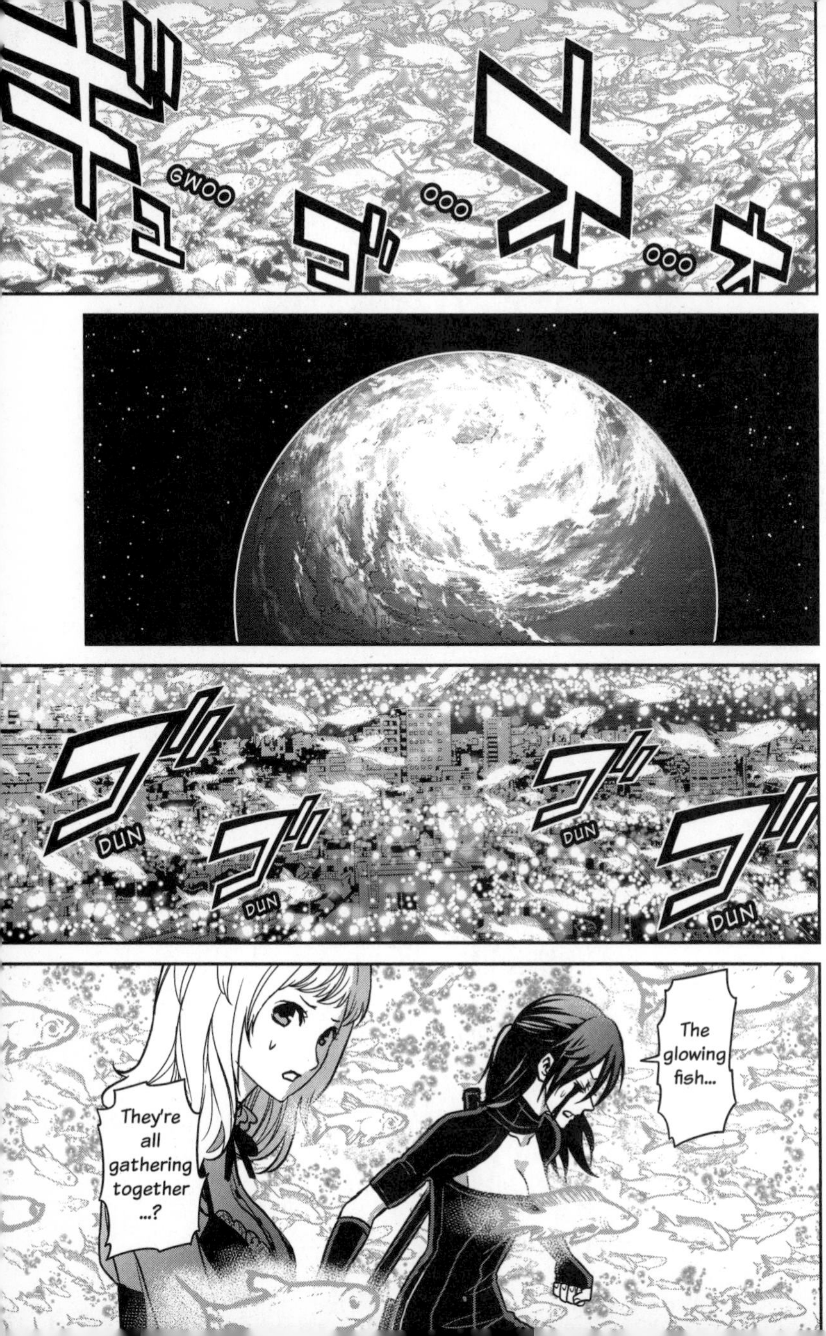
ooo
ooo
GWOO
DUN
DUN
DUN
DUN
The glowing fish...
They're all gathering together ...?

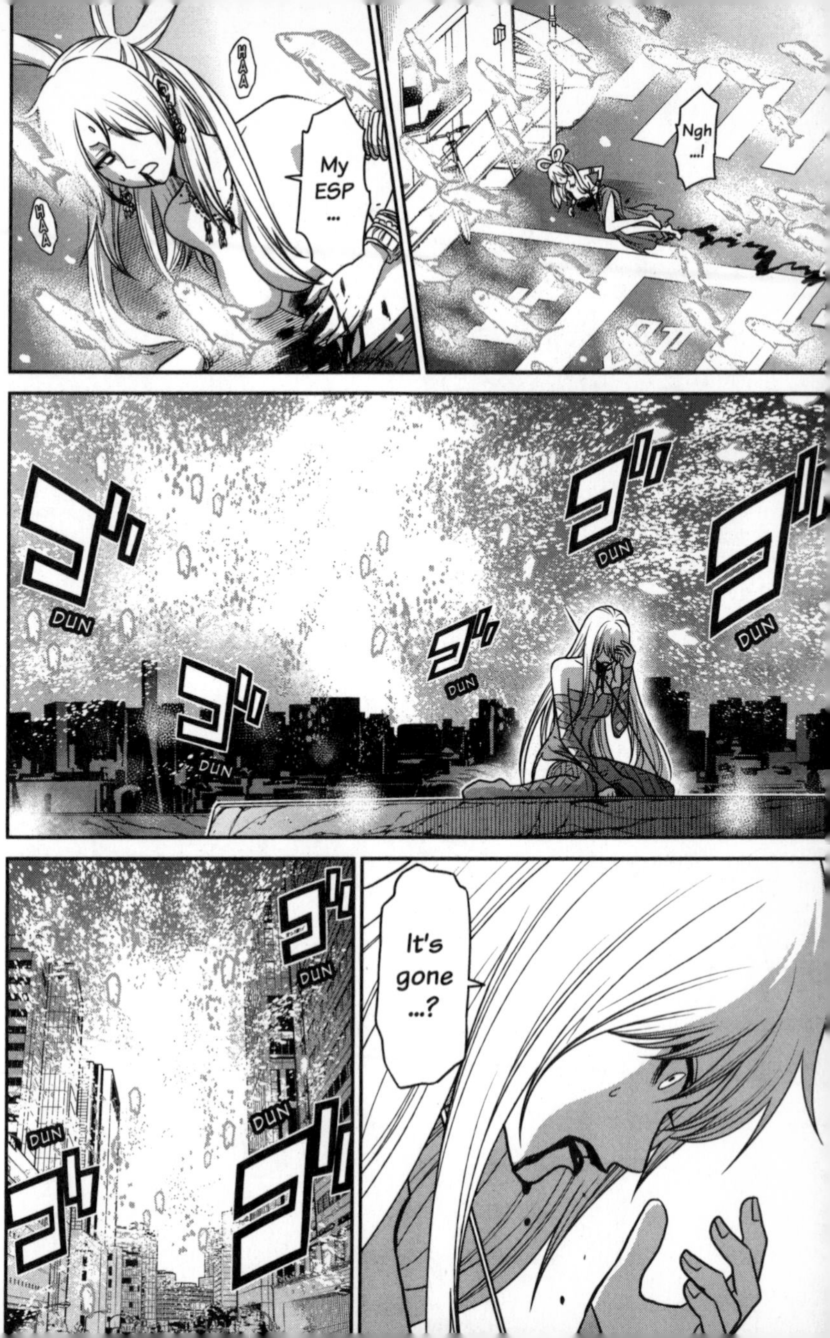
Ngh ...!
My ESP ...
HAA
HAA
DUN
DUN
DUN
DUN
DUN
It's gone ...?
DUN
DUN
DUN

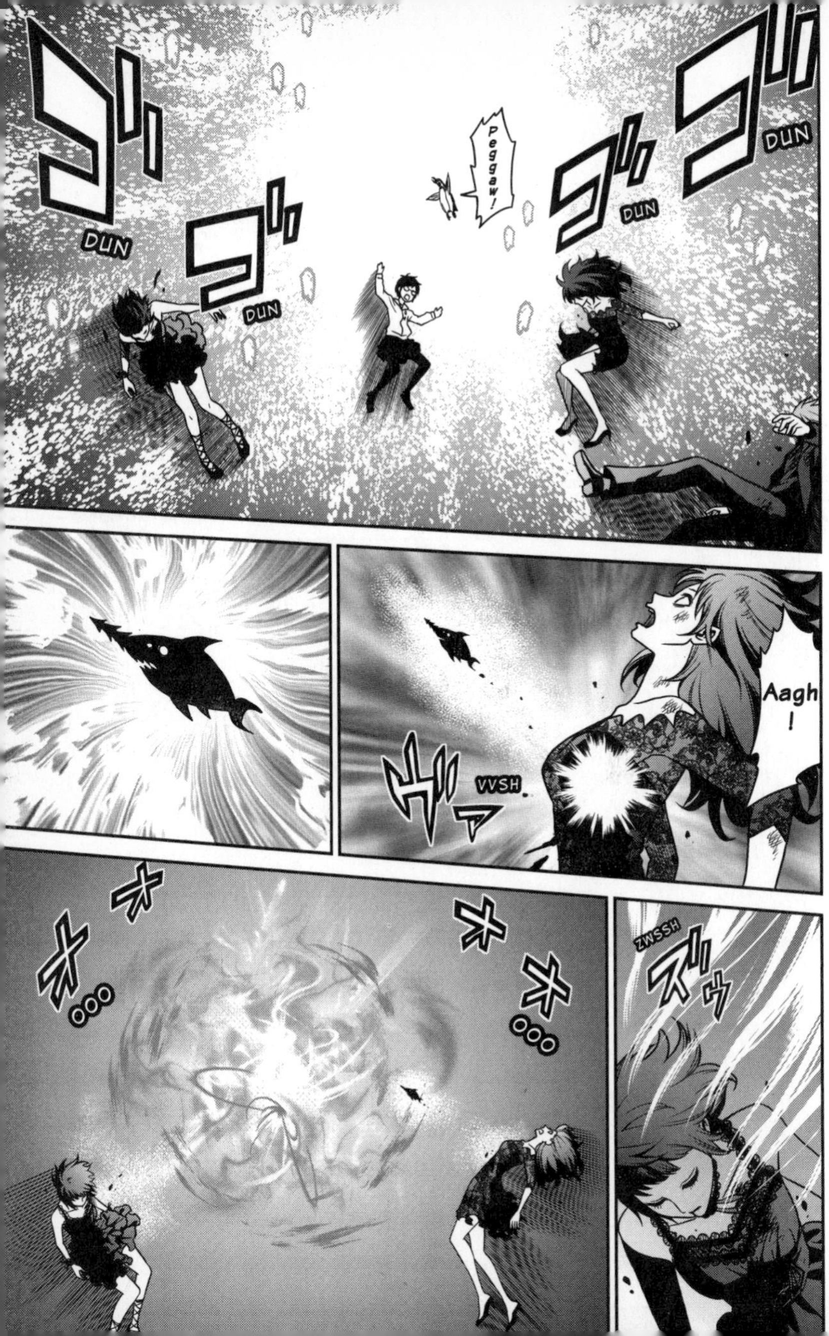
DUN
DUN
Peggaw!
DUN
DUN
Aagh!
VVSH
ZWSSH
OOO
OOO

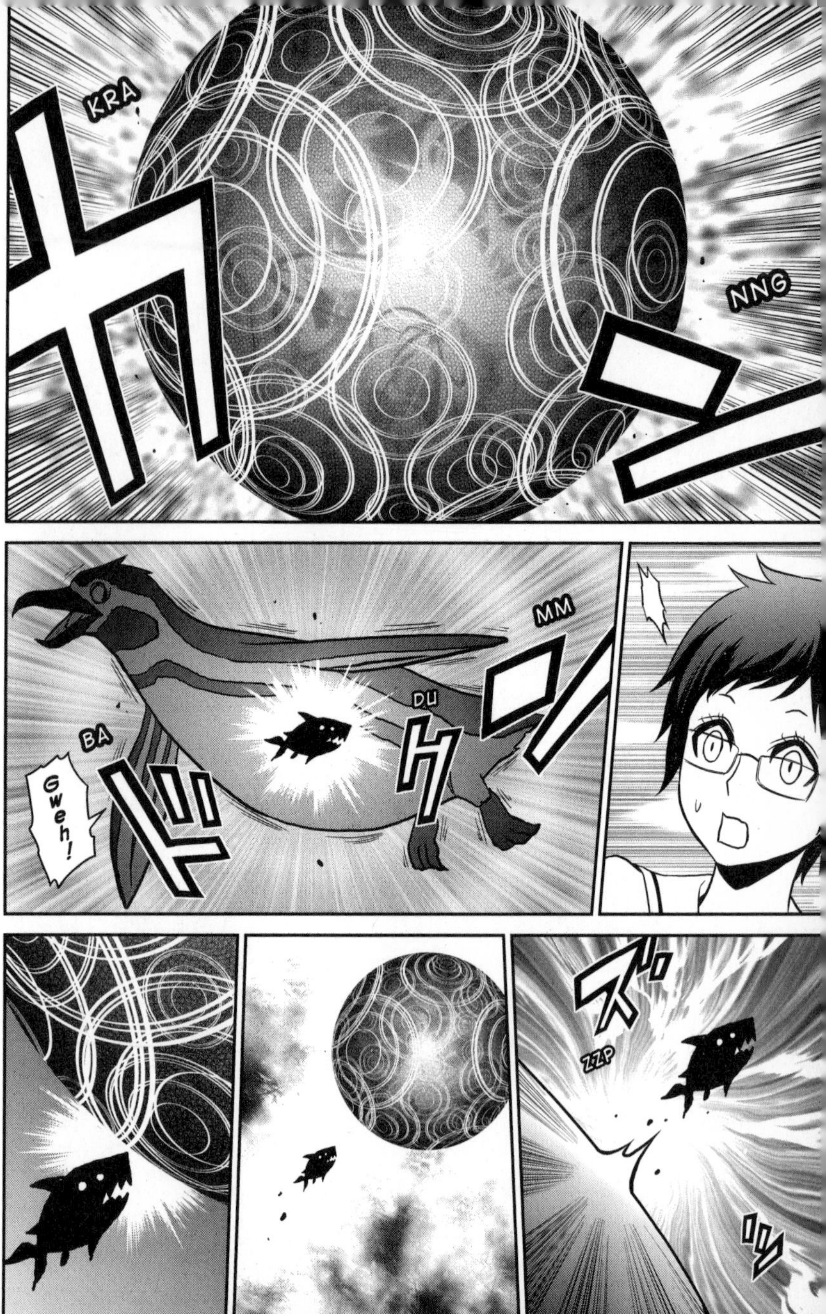
KRA
NNG
MM
DU
BA
Gweh!
ZZP

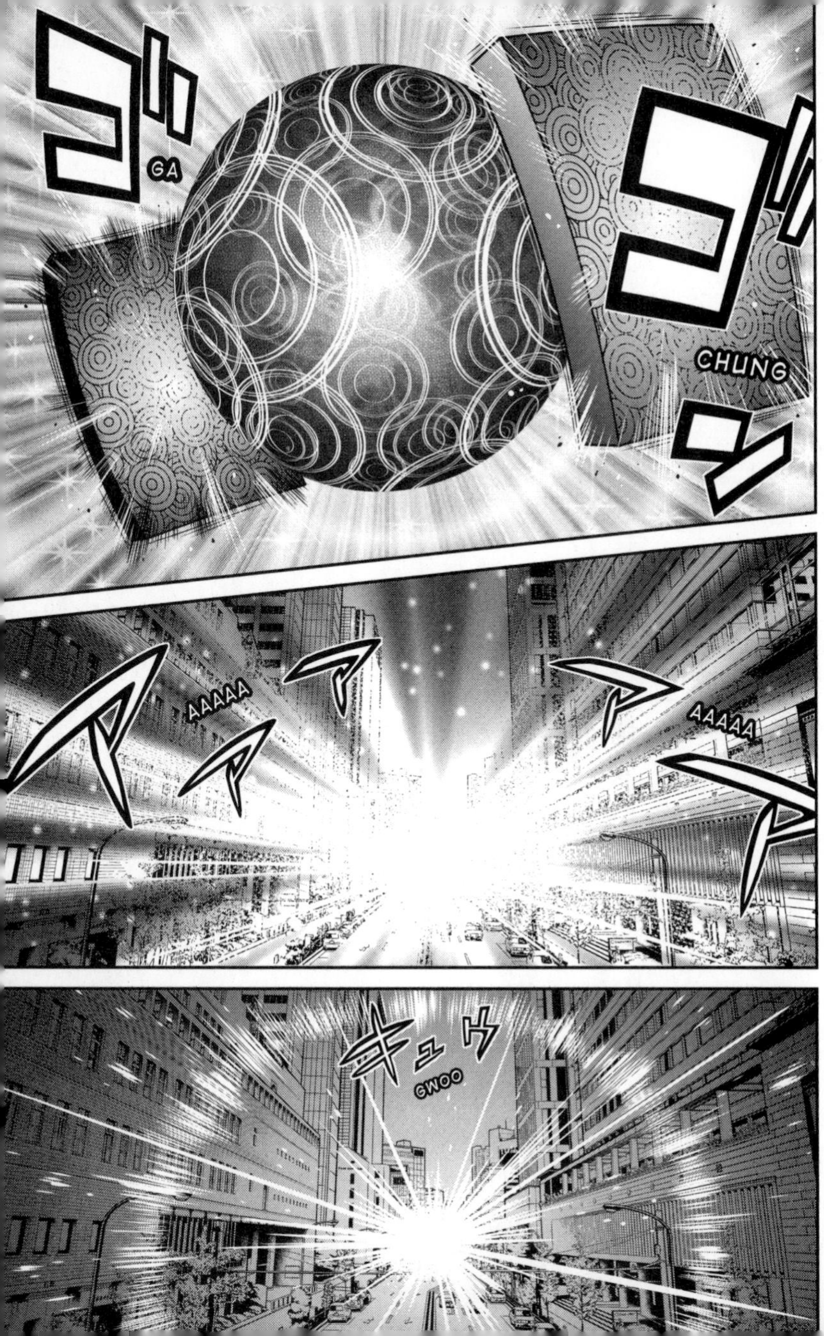
CHUNG
GA
AAAAA
AAAAA
GWOO

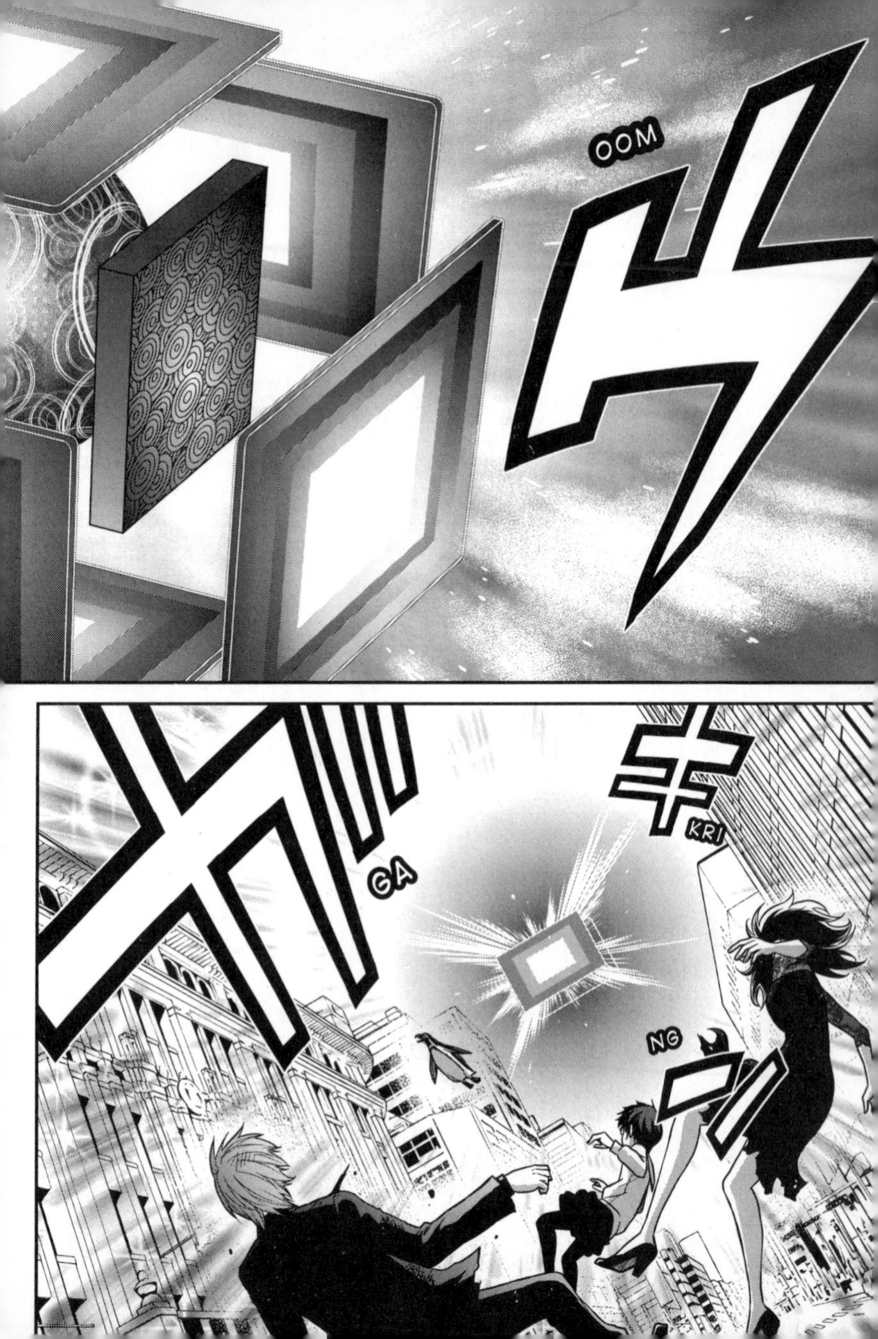
OOM
KRI
GA
NG

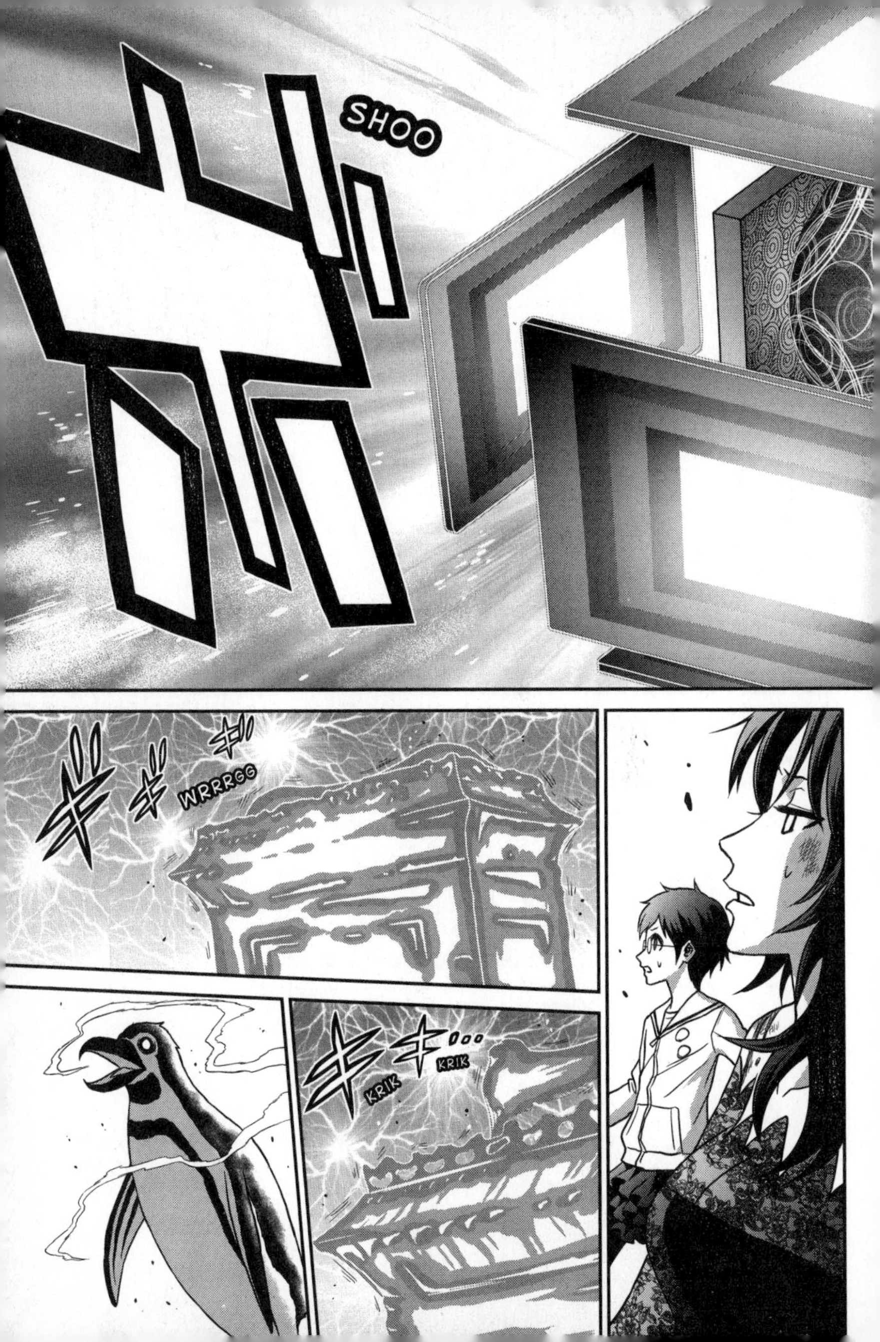
SHOO
WRRRGG
KRIK
KRIK

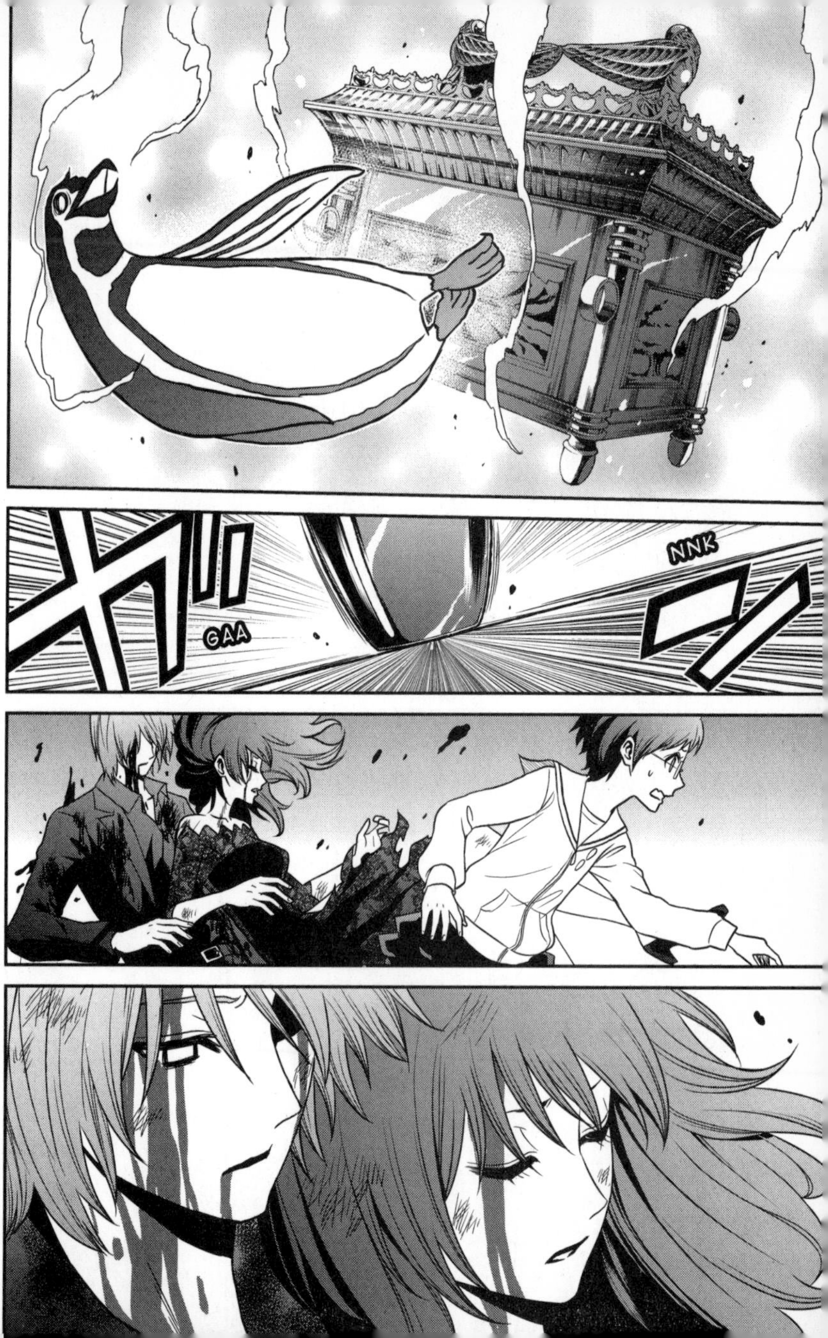
NNK
GAA

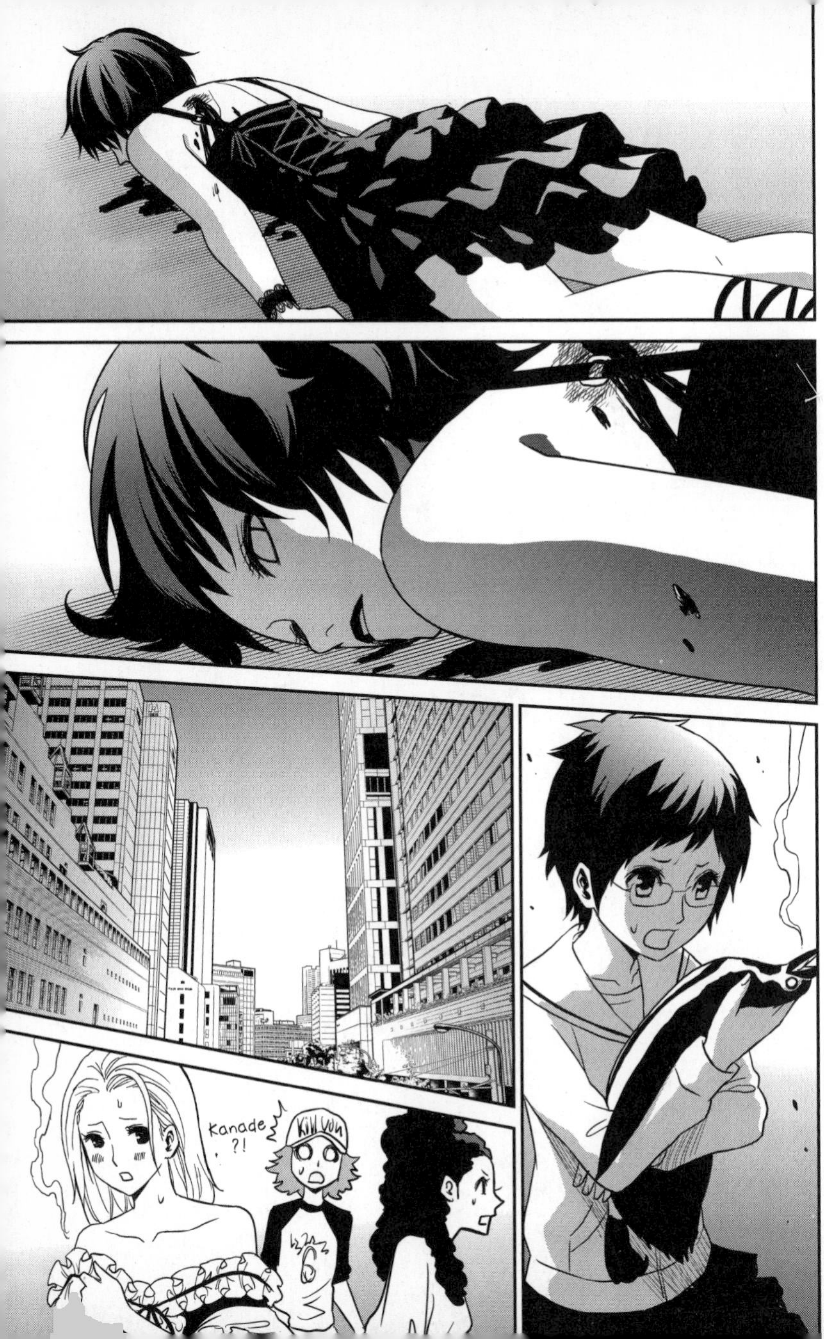
Kanade ?!

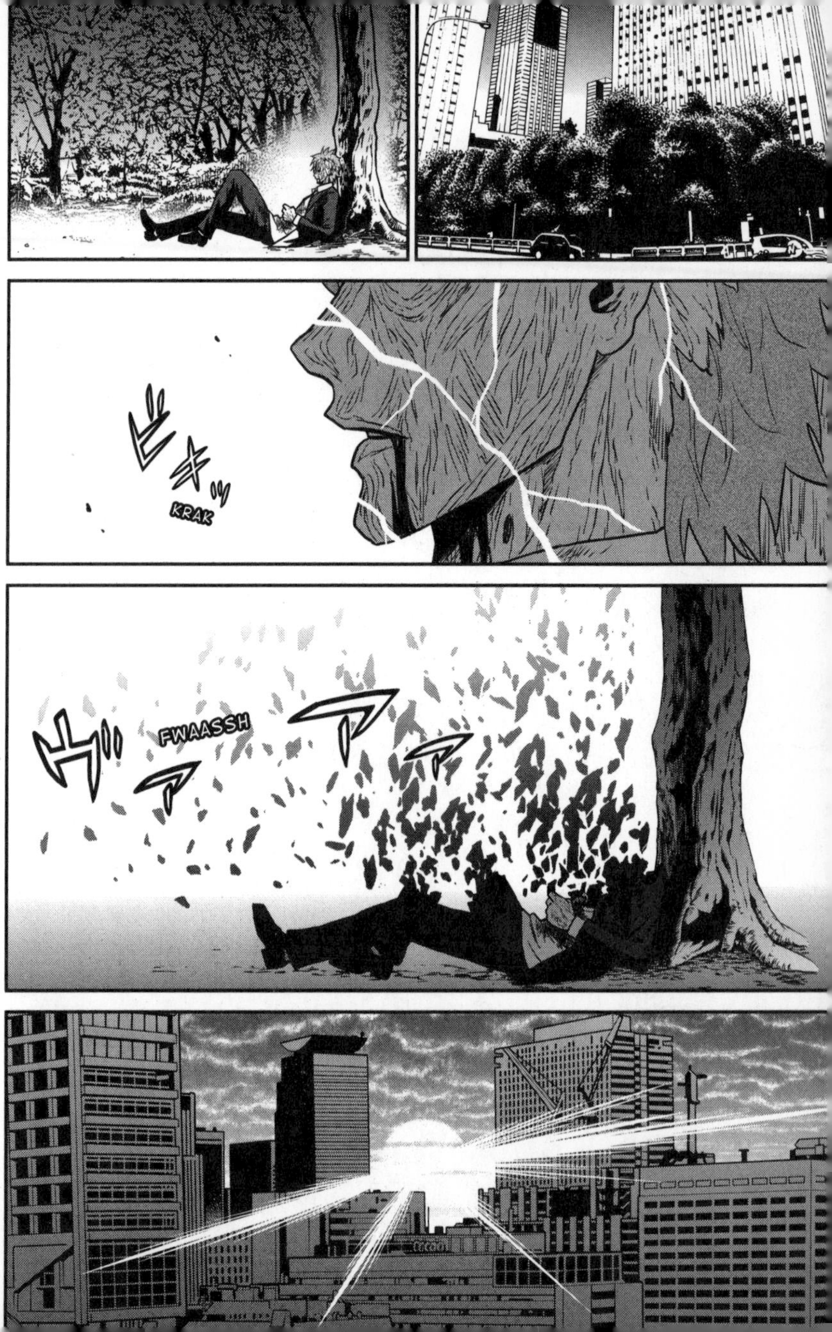
ビキッ
KRAK
FWAASSH

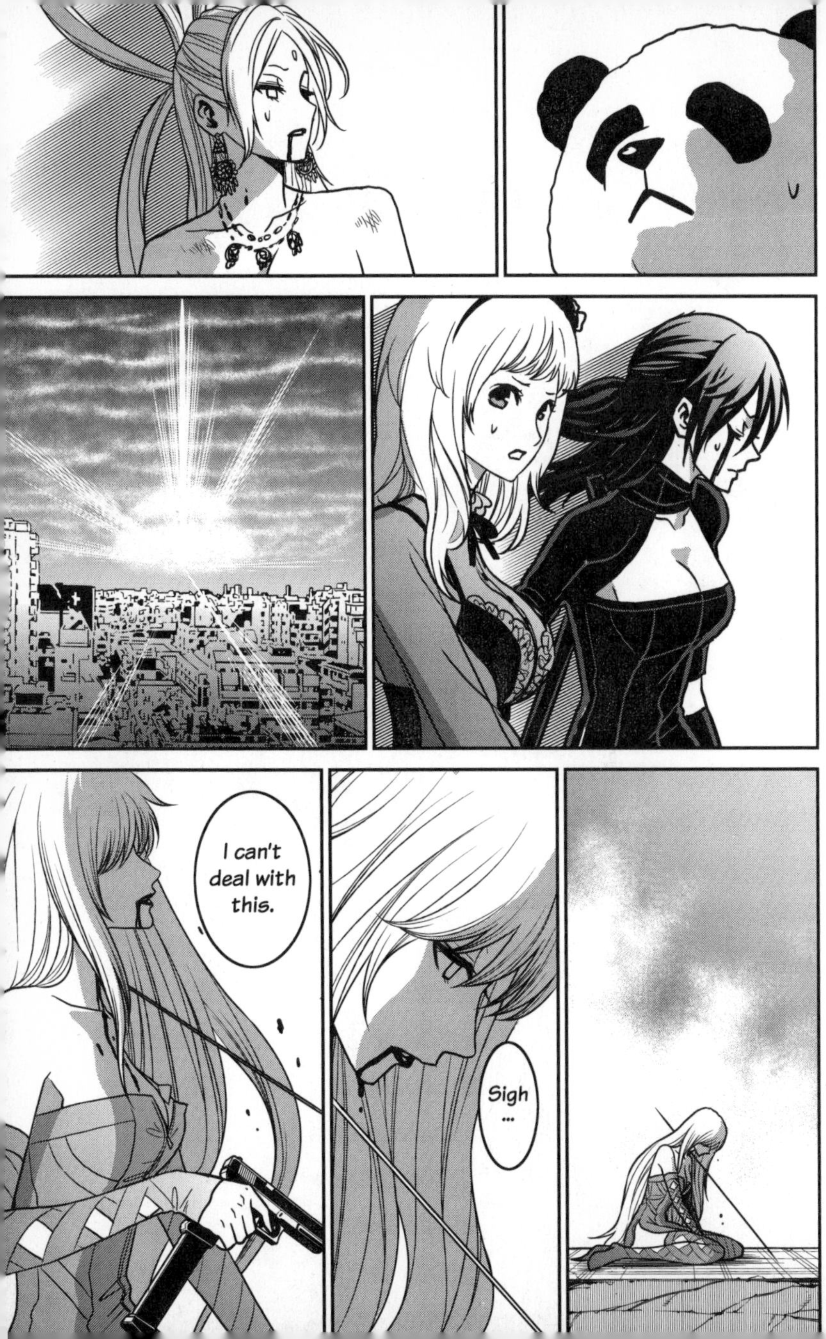
Sigh ...
I can't deal with this.

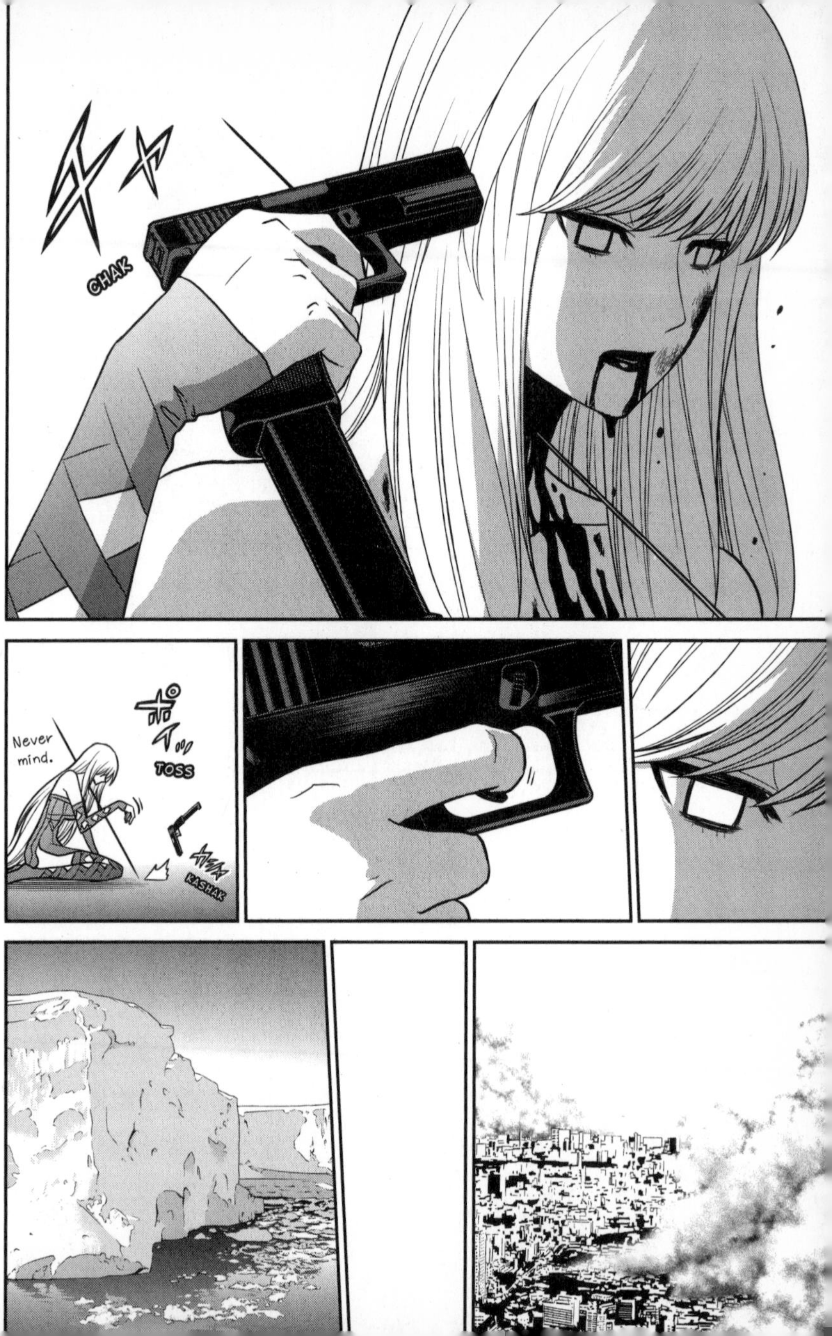
CHAK
Never mind.
TOSS
KASHAK

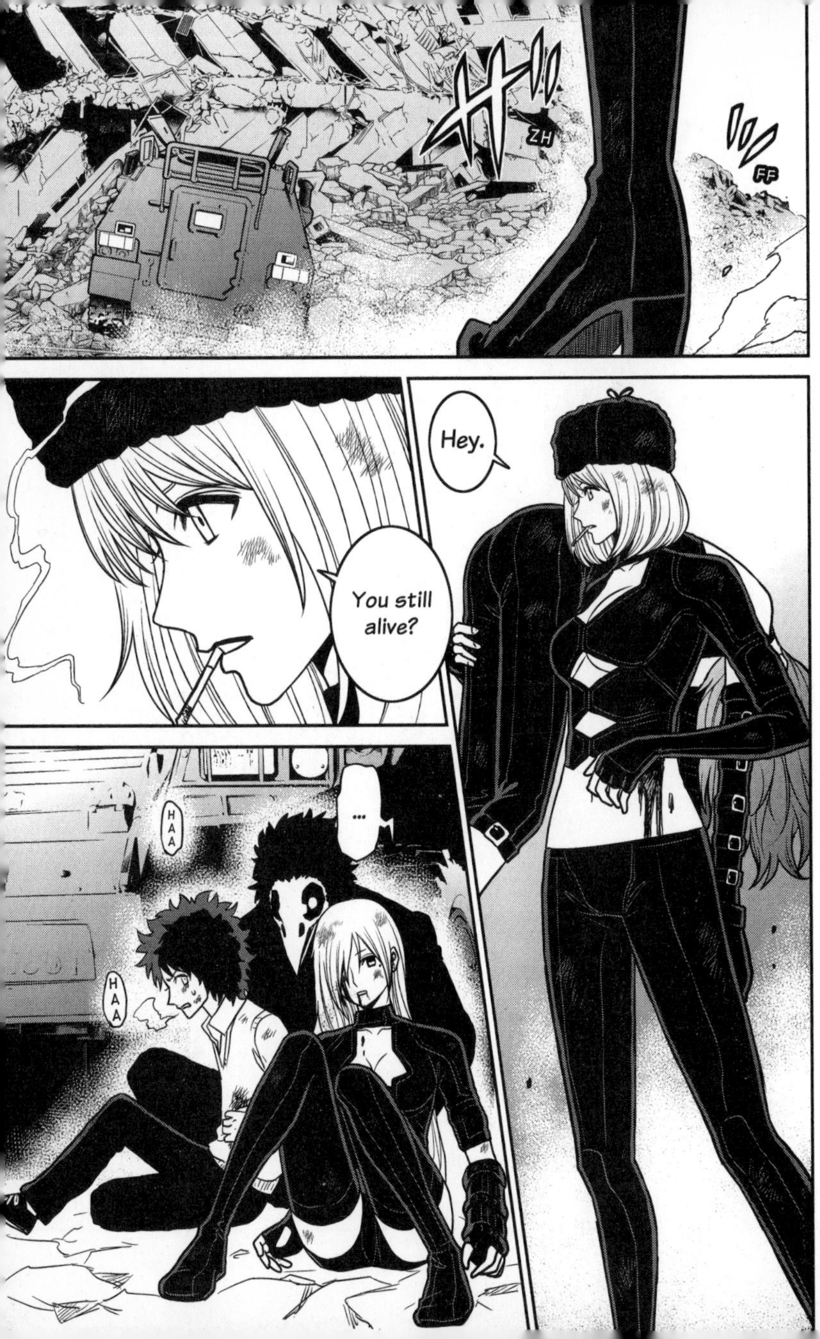
FF
ZH
Hey.
You still alive?
...
HAA
HAA

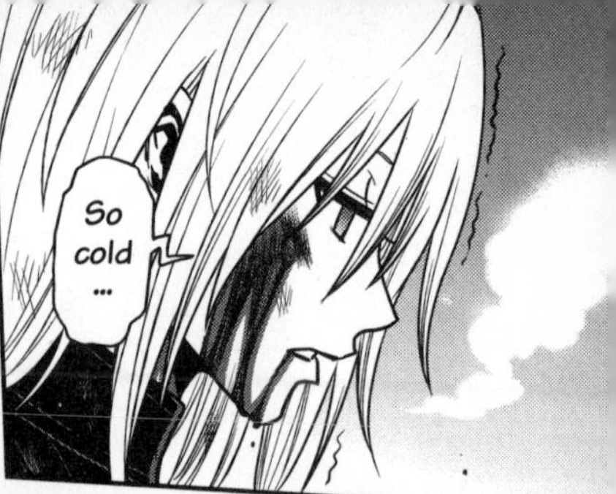
So cold ...

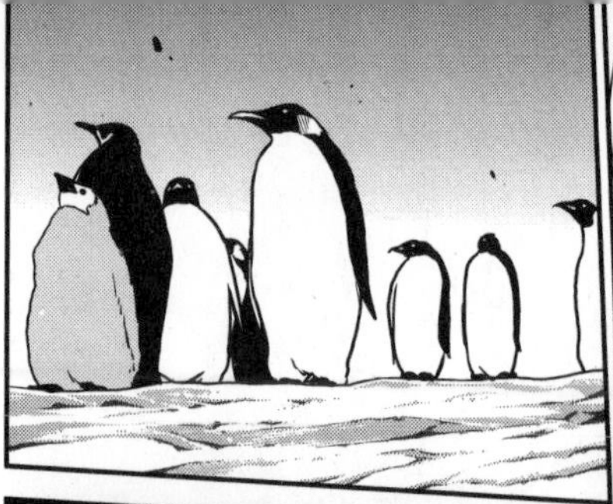

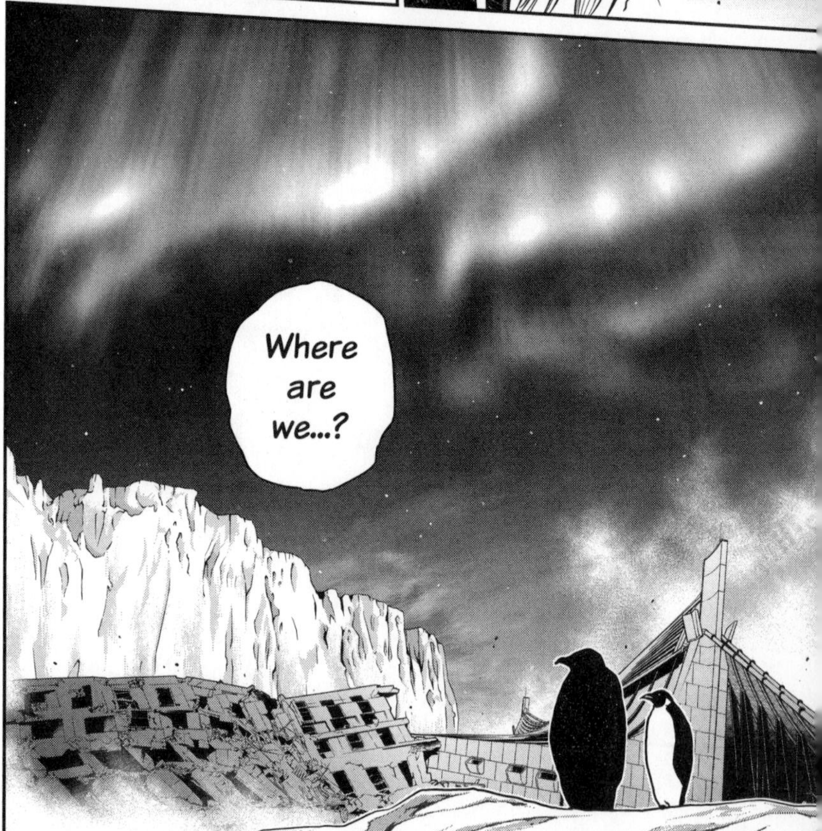
Where are we...?

SCENE 75 /// **END**

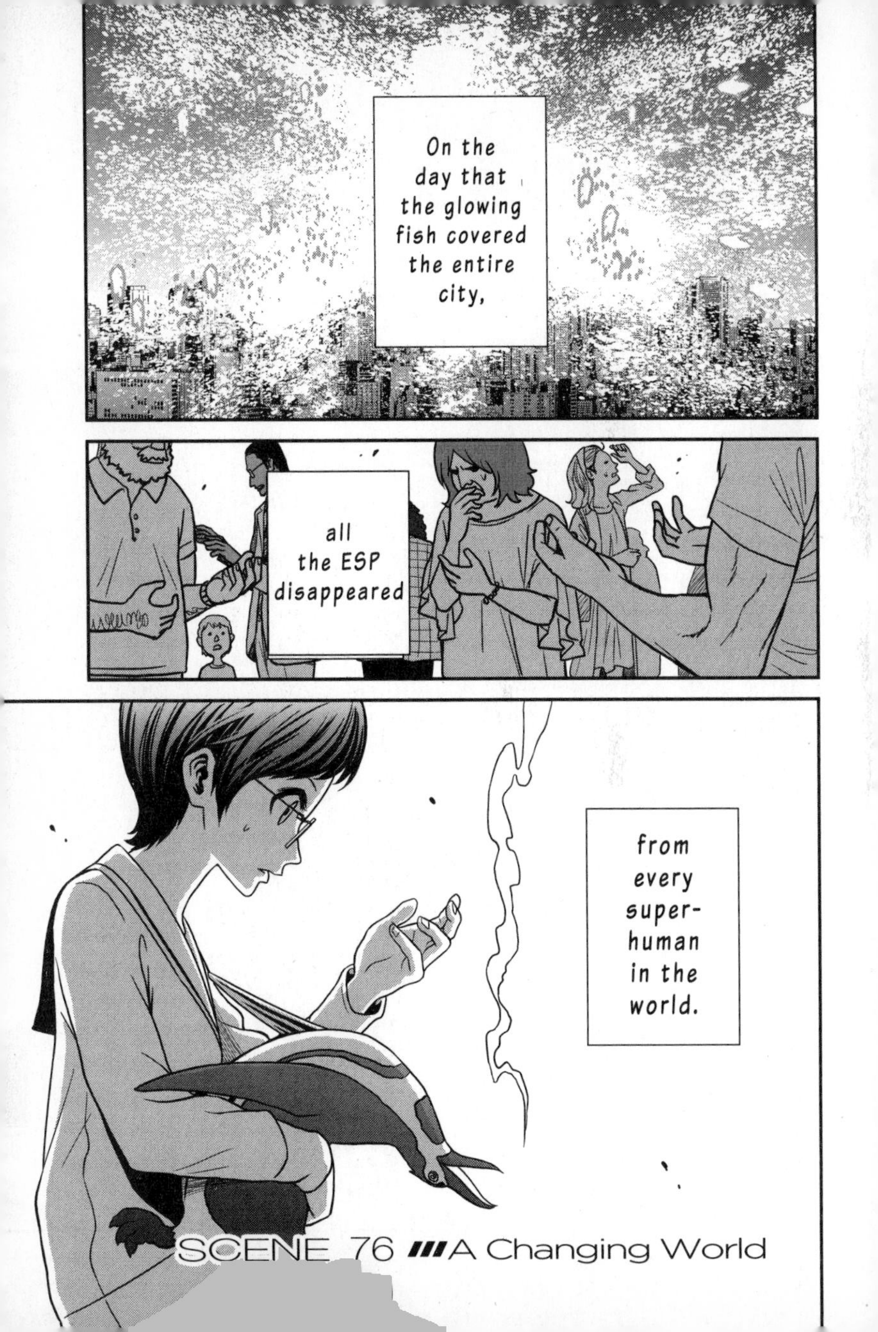
On the day that the glowing fish covered the entire city,
all the ESP disappeared
from every super-human in the world.
SCENE 76 ///A Changing World

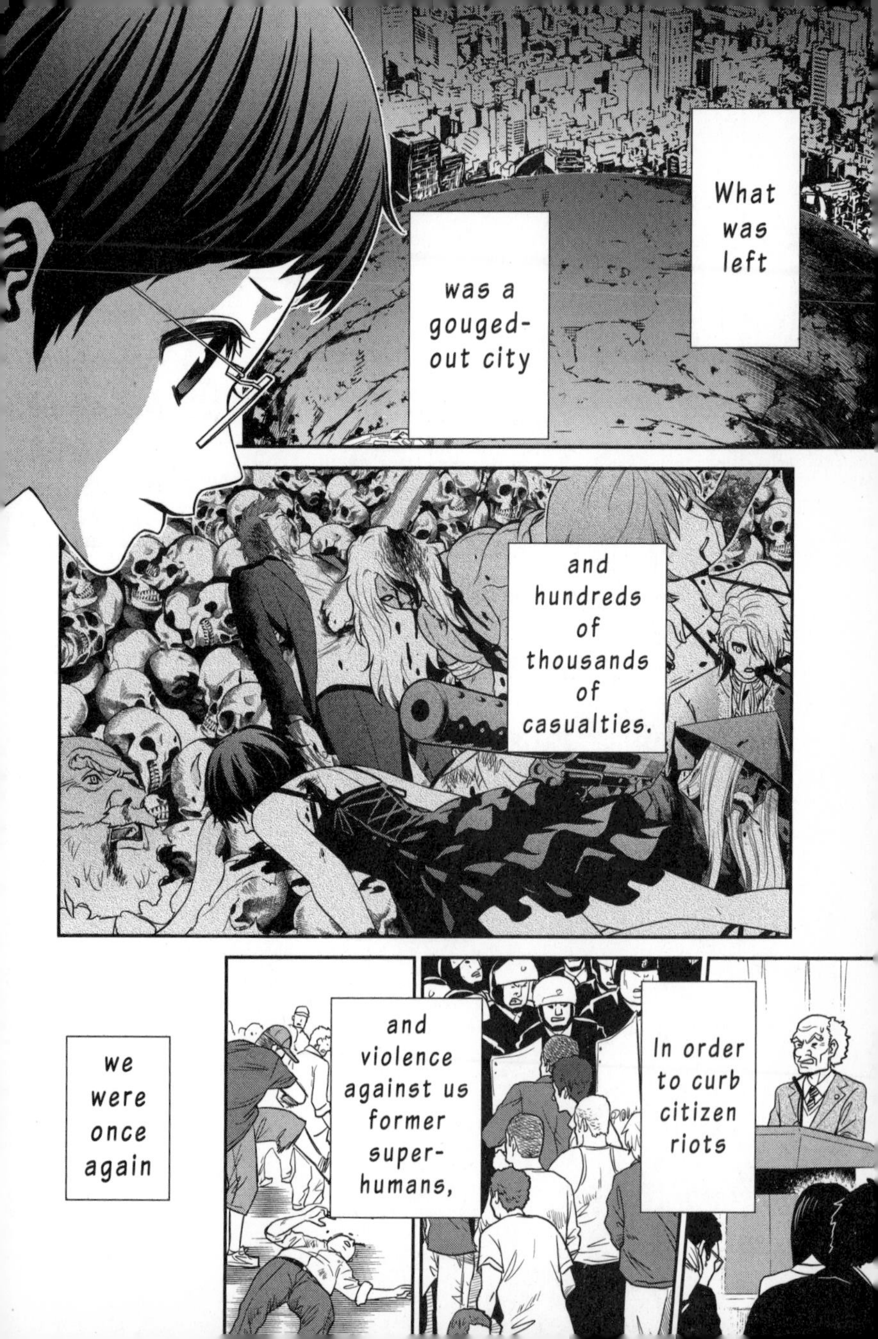
What was left
was a gouged-out city
and hundreds of thousands of casualties.
In order to curb citizen riots
and violence against us former super-humans,
we were once again

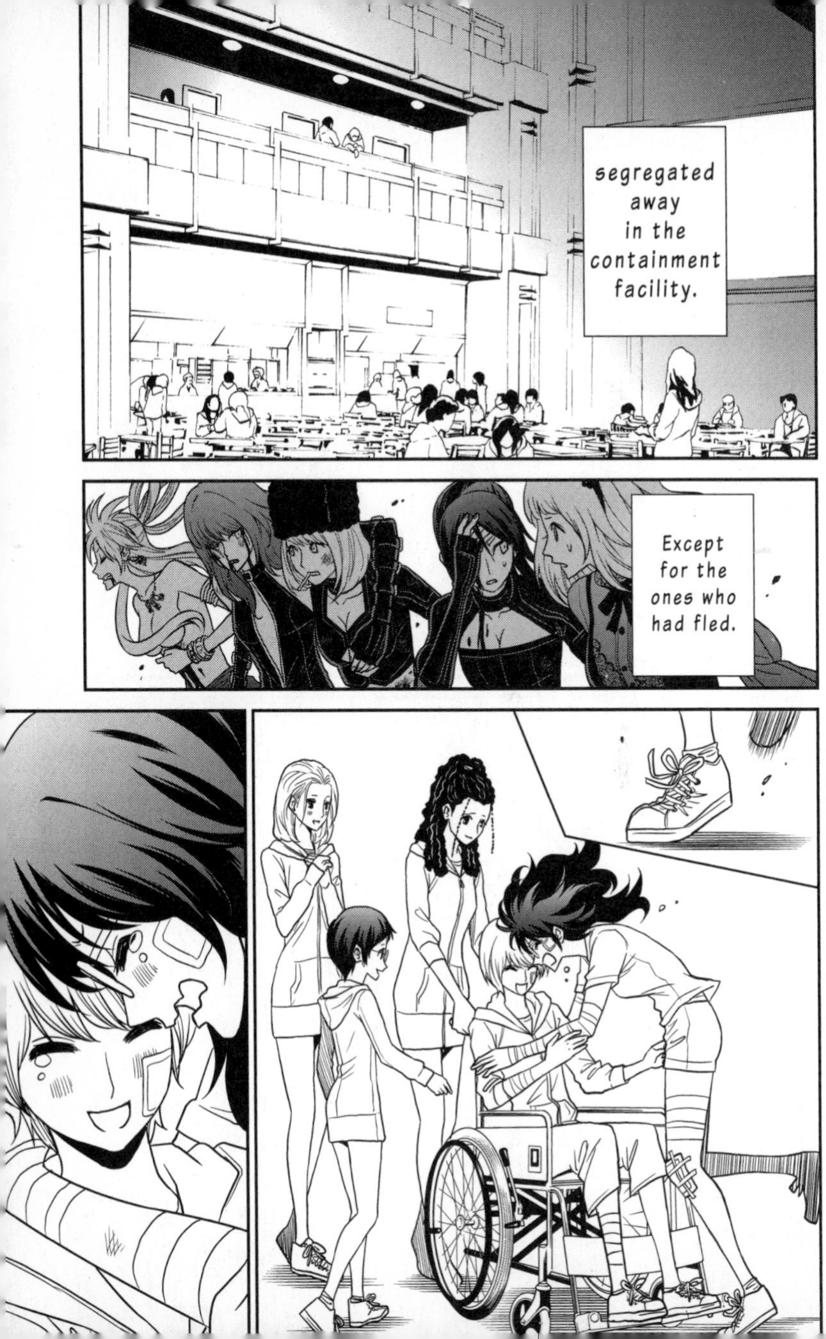
segregated away in the containment facility.
Except for the ones who had fled.

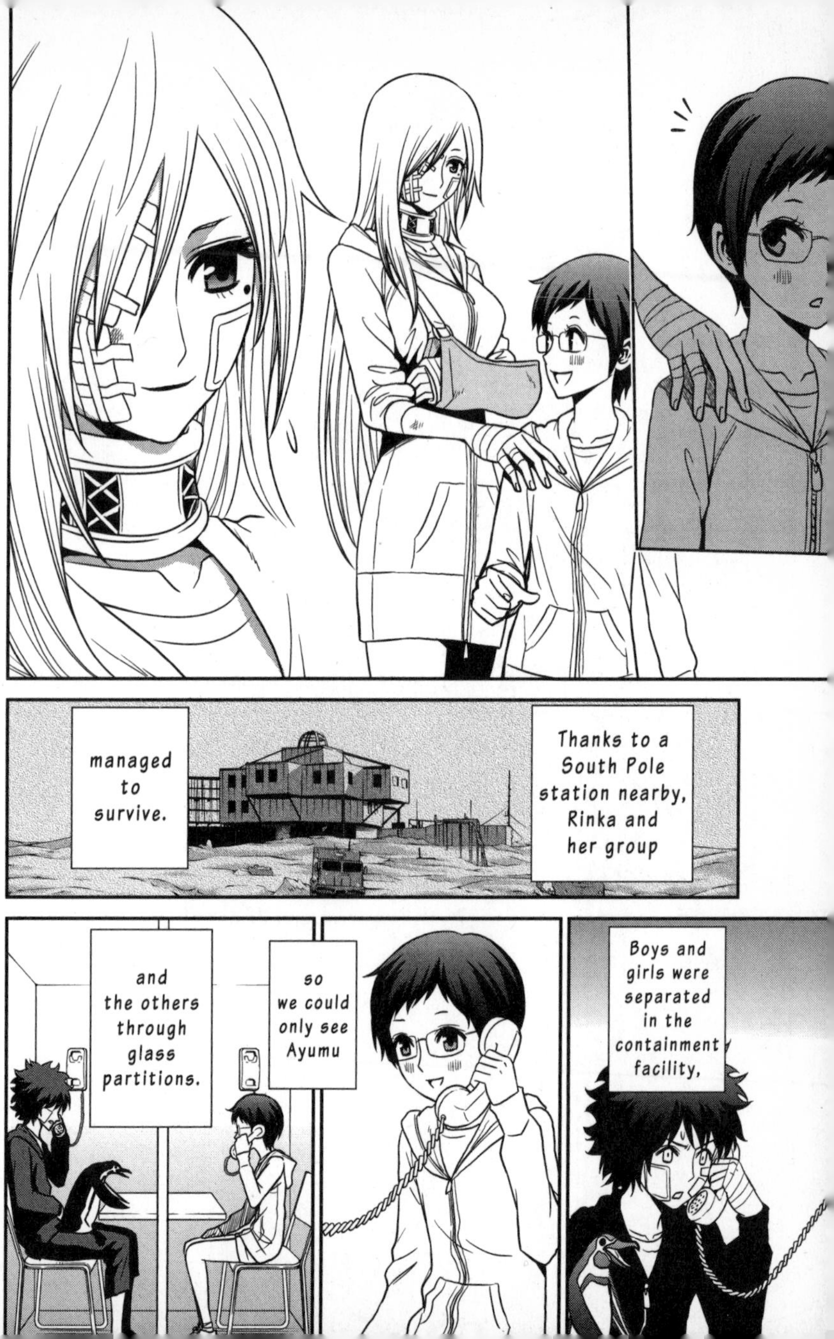
Thanks to a South Pole station nearby, Rinka and her group
managed to survive.
Boys and girls were separated in the containment facility,
so we could only see Ayumu
and the others through glass partitions.

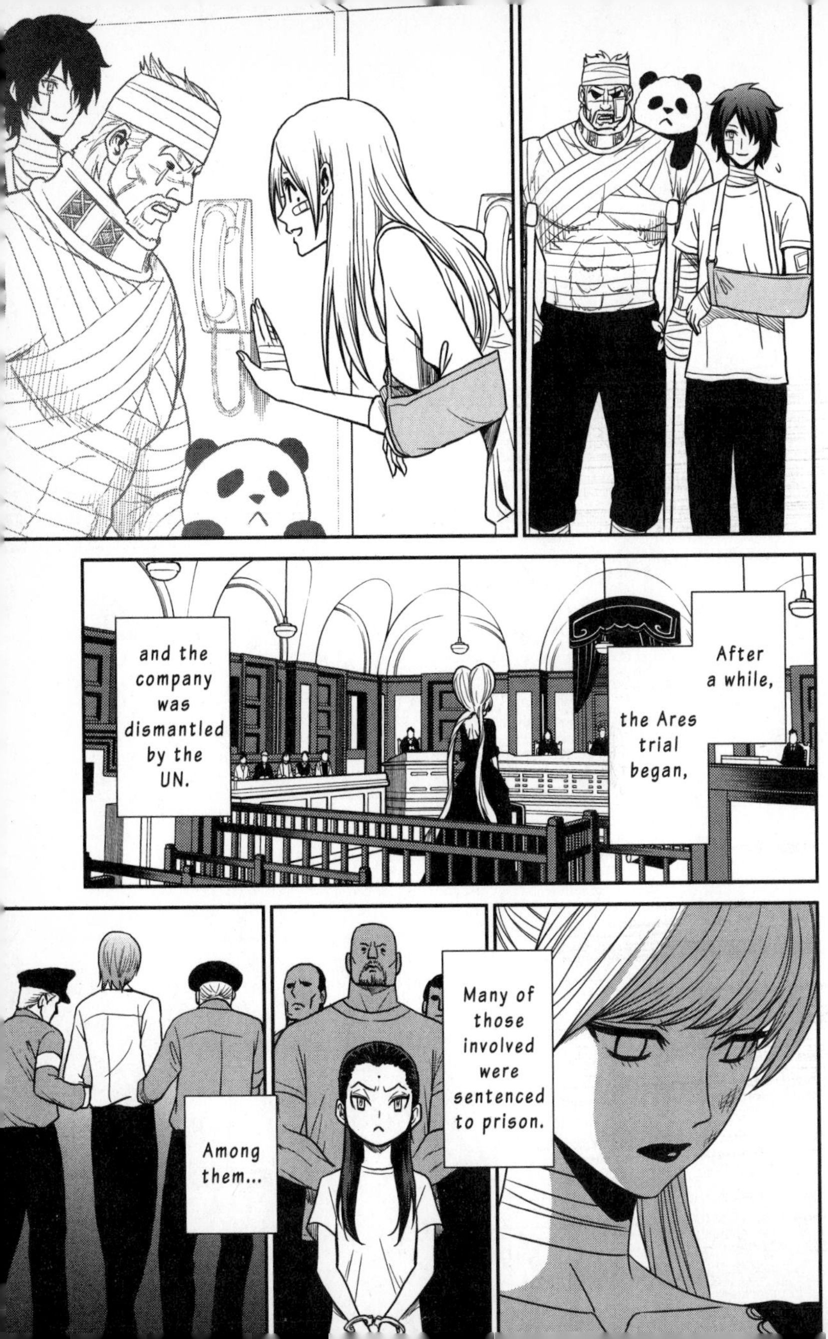
After a while,
the Ares trial began,
and the company was dismantled by the UN.
Many of those involved were sentenced to prison.
Among them...

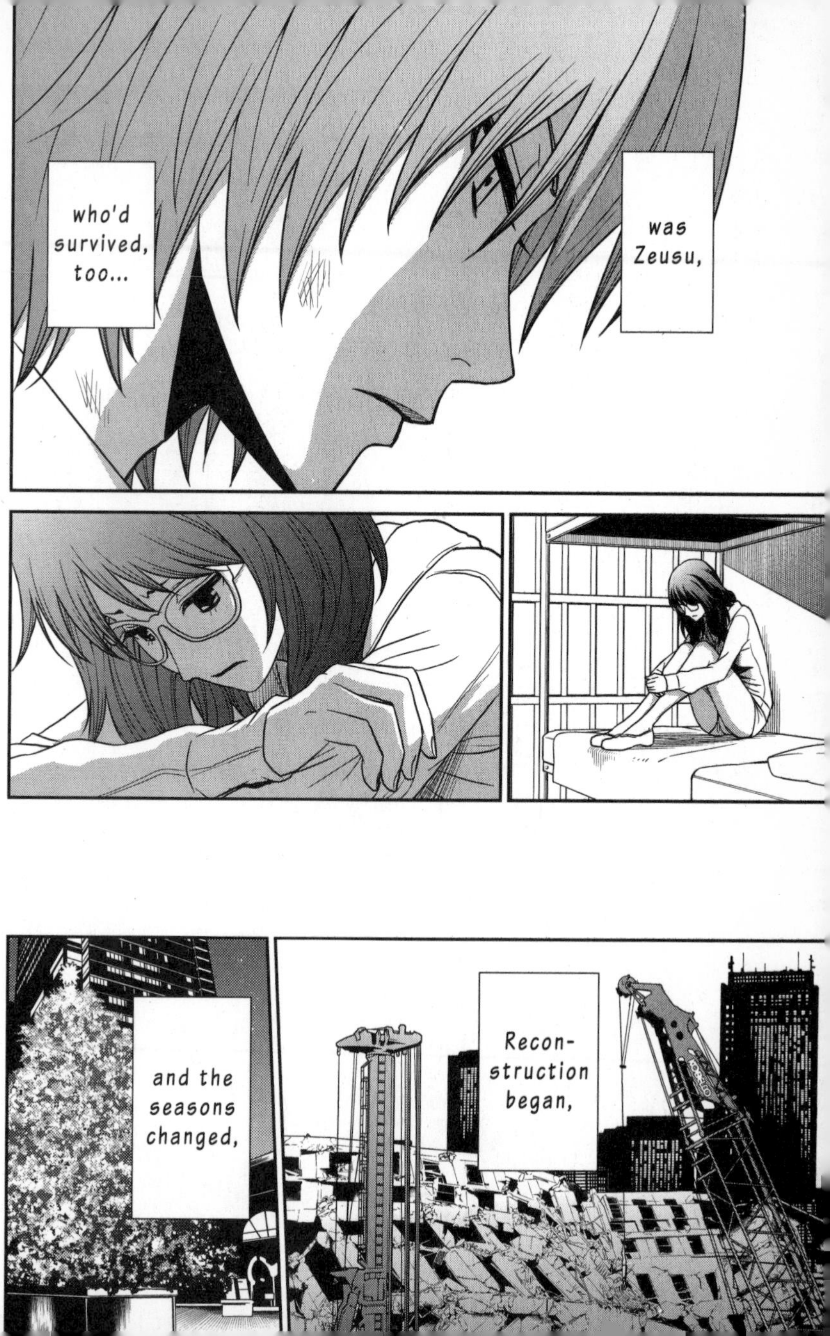
was Zeusu,
who'd survived, too...
Recon-struction began,
and the seasons changed,

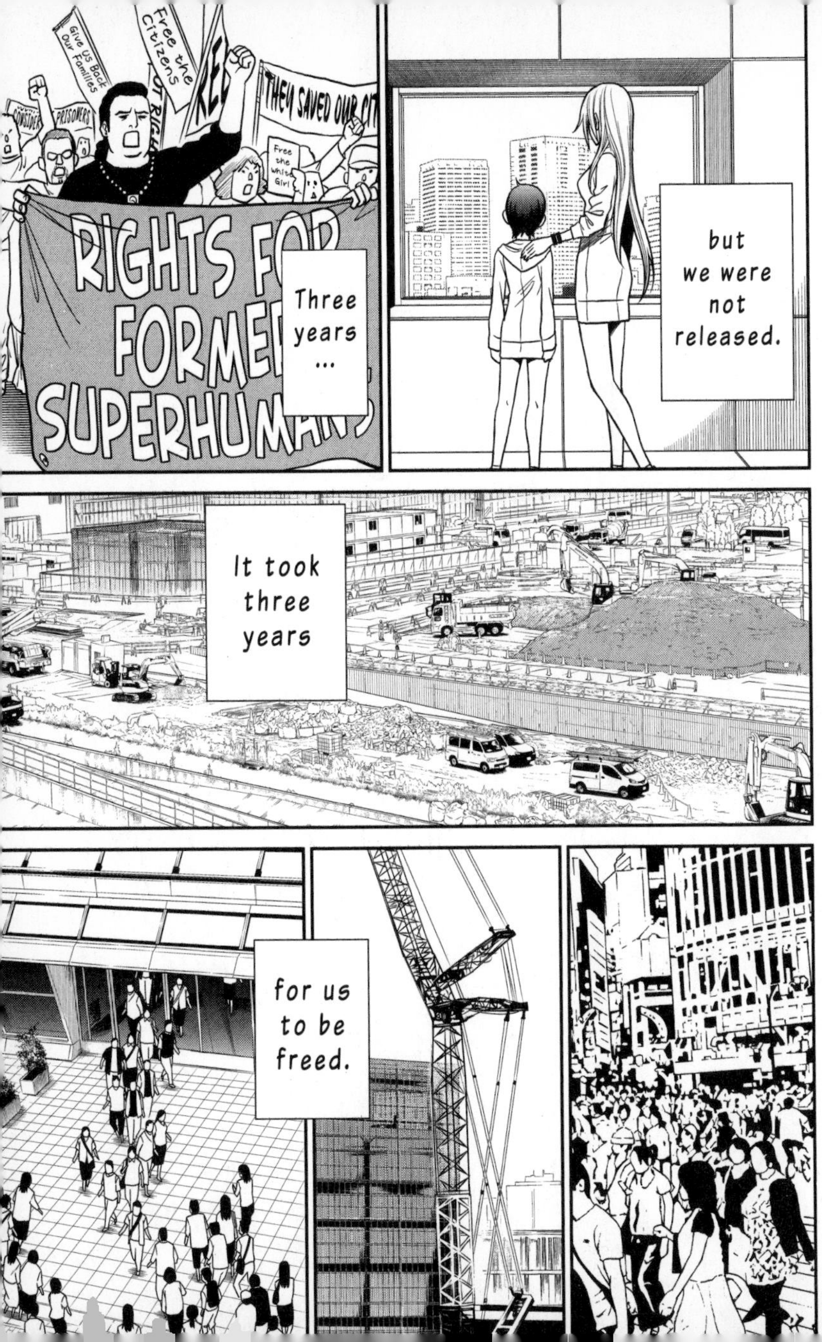
Give Us Back Our Families
Free the Citizens
CONSIDER
PRISONERS
THEY SAVED OUR CIT
Free the White Girl
RIGHTS FO
FORME
SUPERHUMA
Three years ...
but we were not released.
It took three years
for us to be freed.

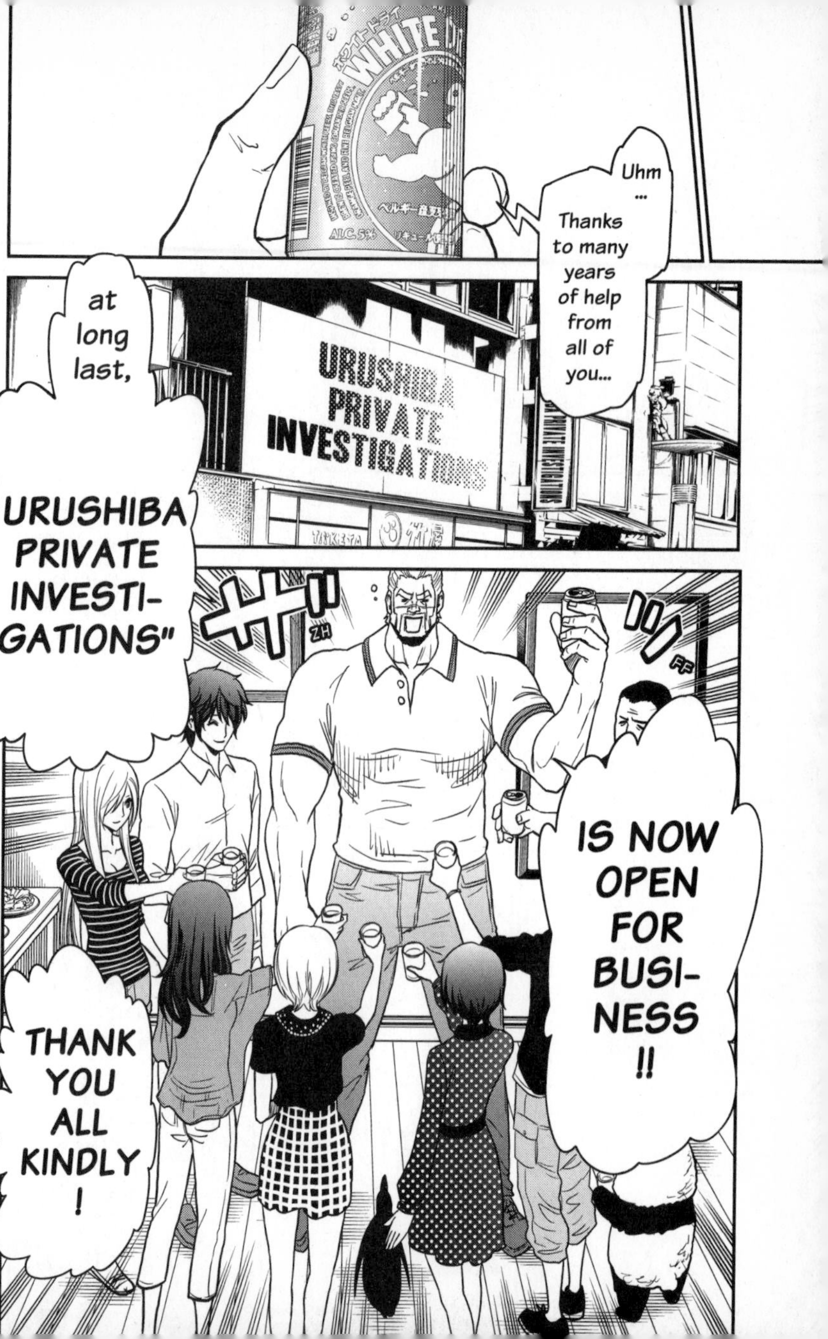
WHITE DR
ALC.5%
Uhm ... Thanks to many years of help from all of you...
at long last,
URUSHIBA PRIVATE INVESTIGATIONS
"URUSHIBA PRIVATE INVESTI-GATIONS"
FF
ZH
IS NOW OPEN FOR BUSI-NESS !!
THANK YOU ALL KINDLY !

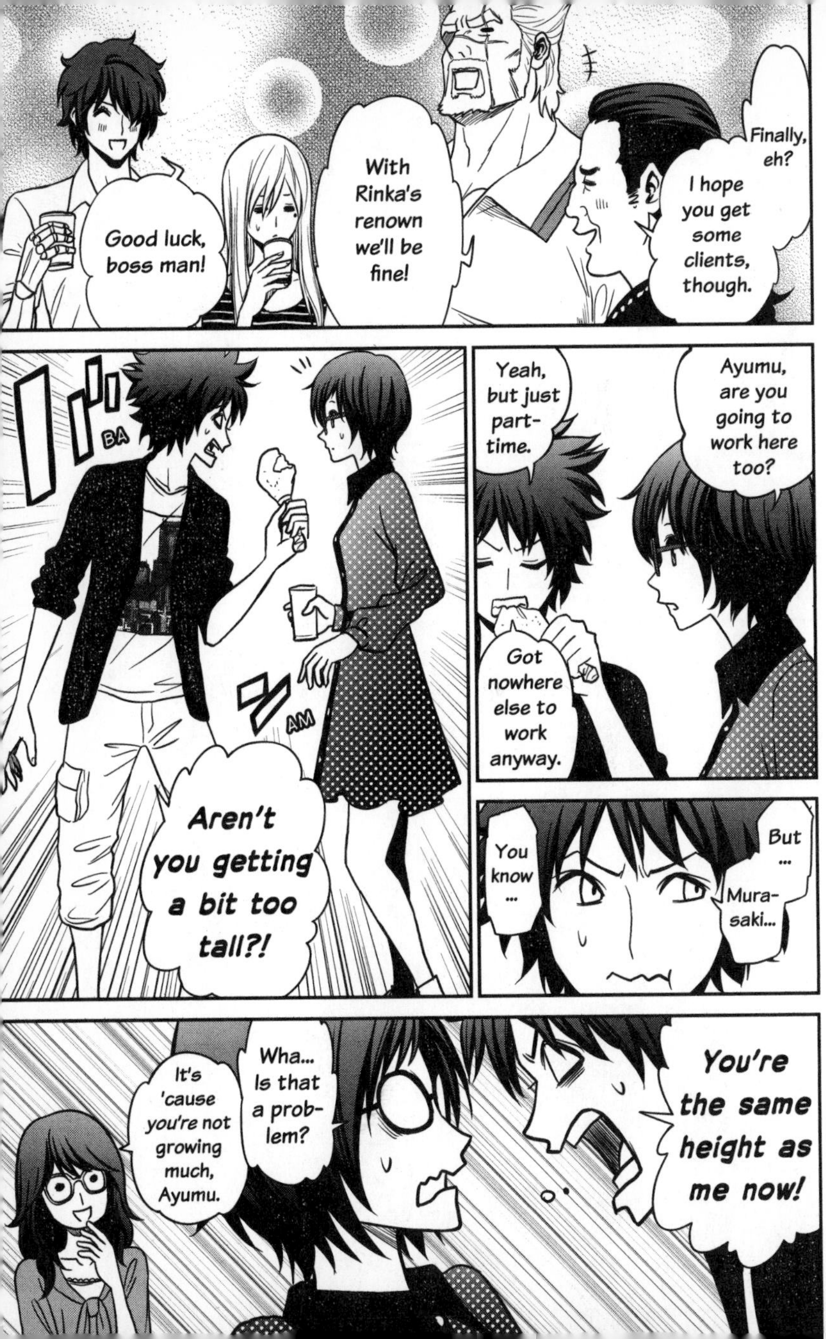
Finally, eh?
I hope you get some clients, though.
With Rinka's renown we'll be fine!
Good luck, boss man!
Ayumu, are you going to work here too?
Yeah, but just part-time.
Got nowhere else to work anyway.
But ... Mura-saki...
You know ...
BA
AM
Aren't you getting a bit too tall?!
You're the same height as me now!
Wha... Is that a prob-lem?
It's 'cause you're not growing much, Ayumu.

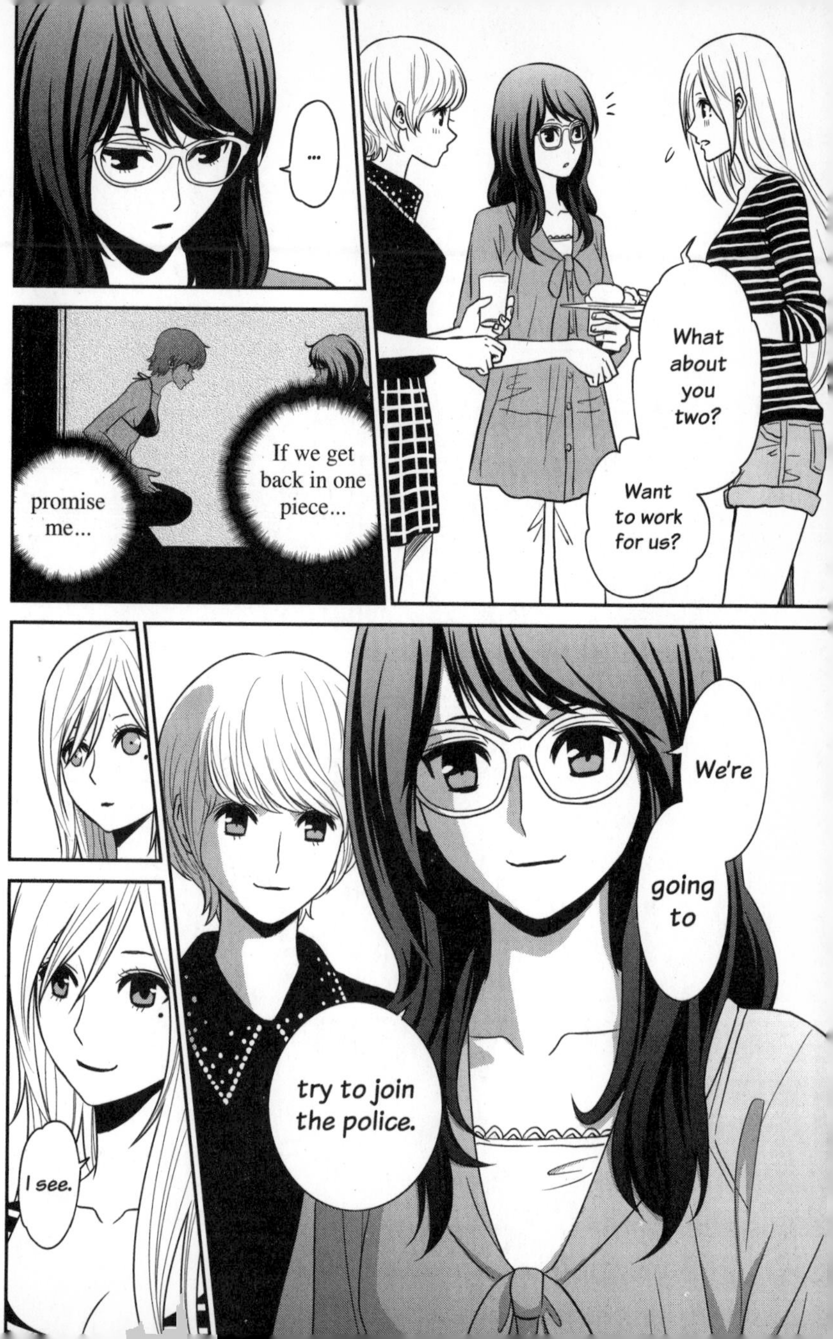
What about you two?
Want to work for us?
...
If we get back in one piece...
promise me...
We're going to
try to join the police.
I see.

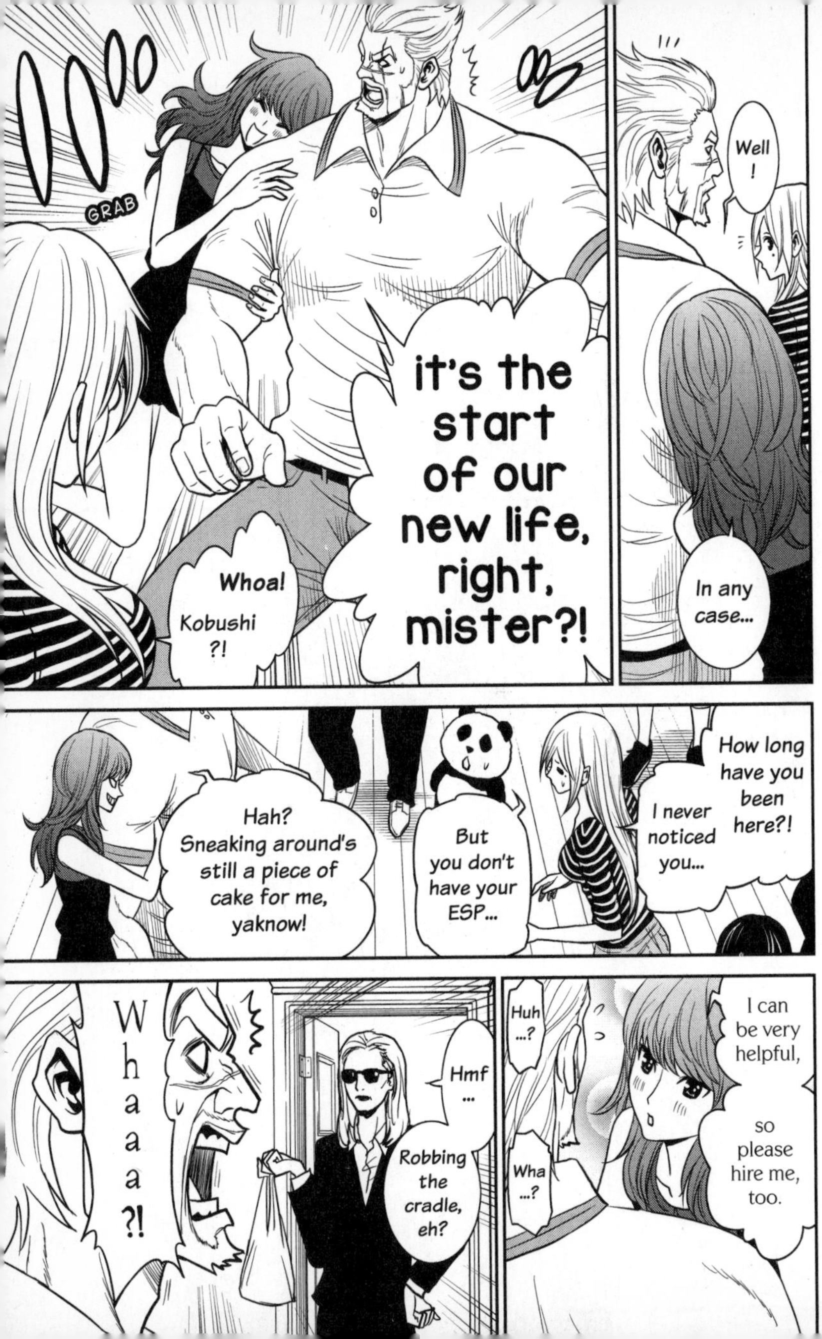
Well !
In any case...
it's the start of our new life, right, mister?!
GRAB
Whoa!
Kobushi ?!
How long have you been here?!
I never noticed you...
But you don't have your ESP...
Hah? Sneaking around's still a piece of cake for me, yaknow!
I can be very helpful,
Huh ...?
so please hire me, too.
Wha ...?
Hmf ...
Robbing the cradle, eh?
Whaaaa ?!

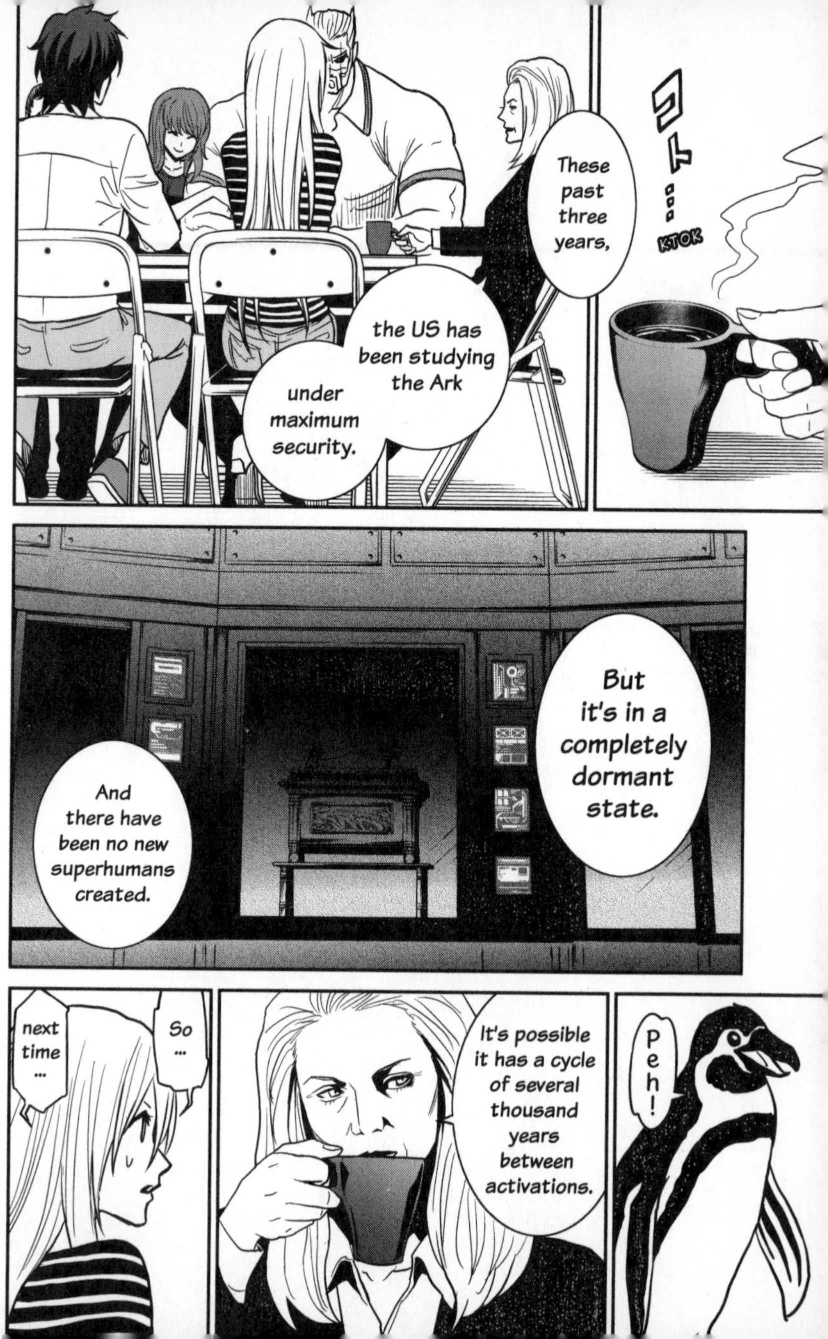
コト…
KTOK
These past three years,
the US has been studying the Ark
under maximum security.
But it's in a completely dormant state.
And there have been no new superhumans created.
Peh!
It's possible it has a cycle of several thousand years between activations.
So ...
next time ...

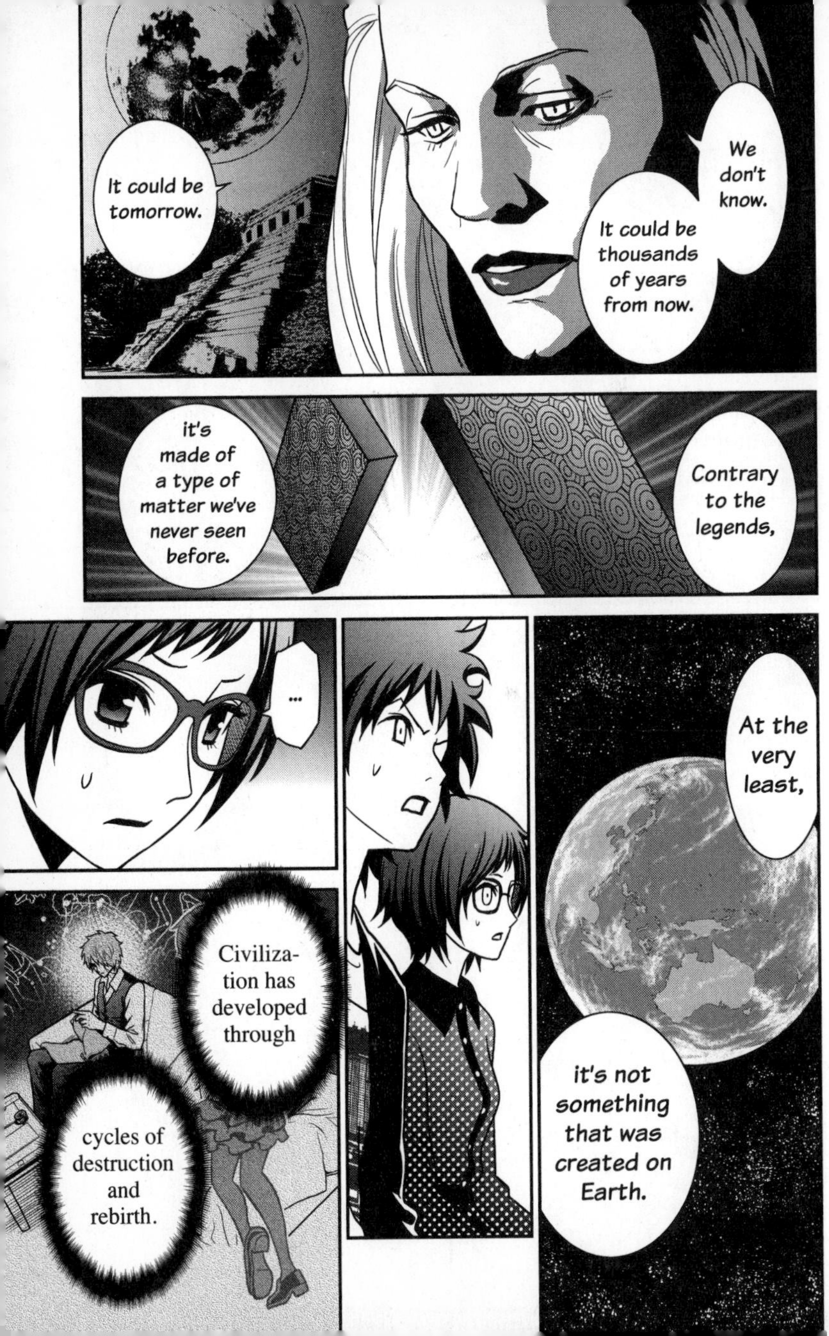
We don't know.
It could be thousands of years from now.
It could be tomorrow.
Contrary to the legends,
it's made of a type of matter we've never seen before.
At the very least,
it's not something that was created on Earth.
...
Civiliza-tion has developed through
cycles of destruction and rebirth.

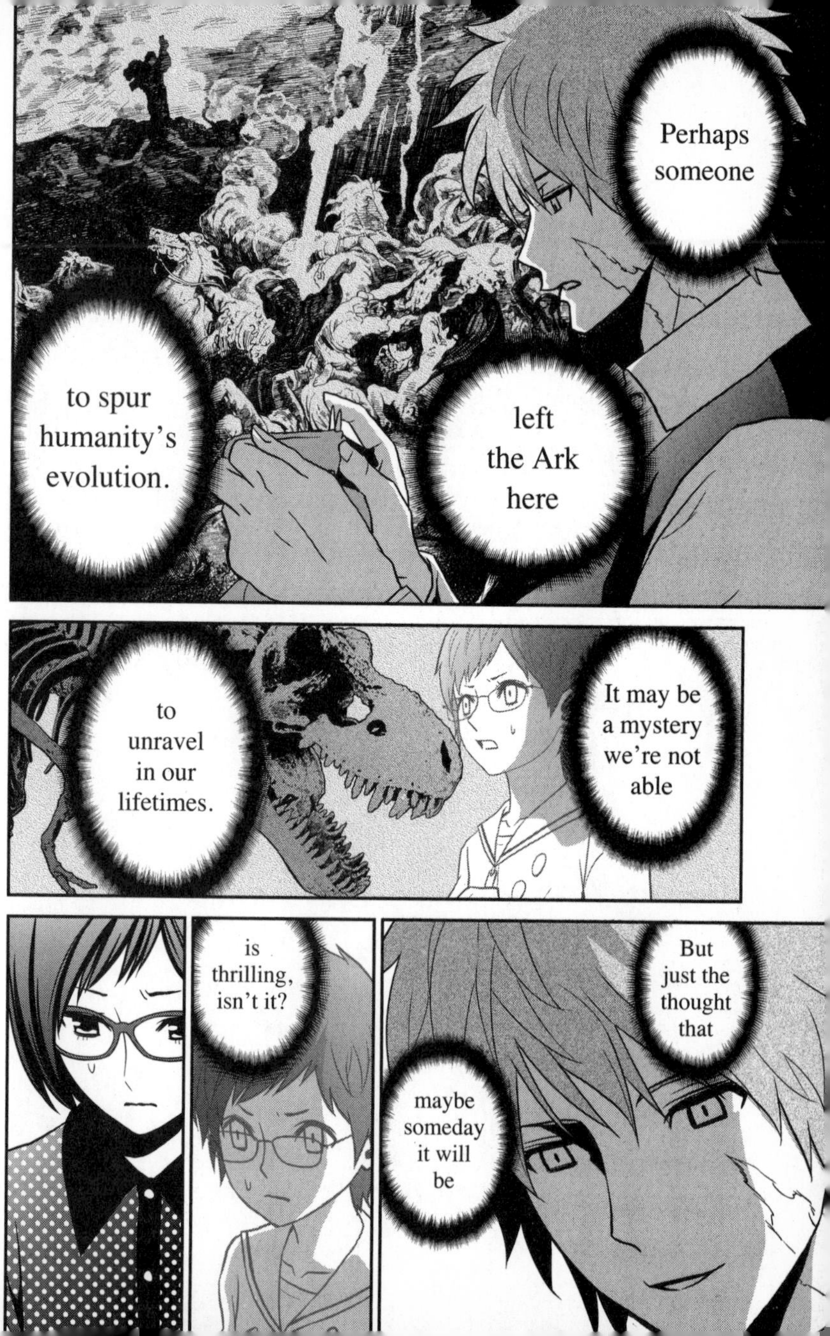
Perhaps someone
left the Ark here
to spur humanity's evolution.
It may be a mystery we're not able
to unravel in our lifetimes.
But just the thought that
maybe someday it will be
is thrilling, isn't it?

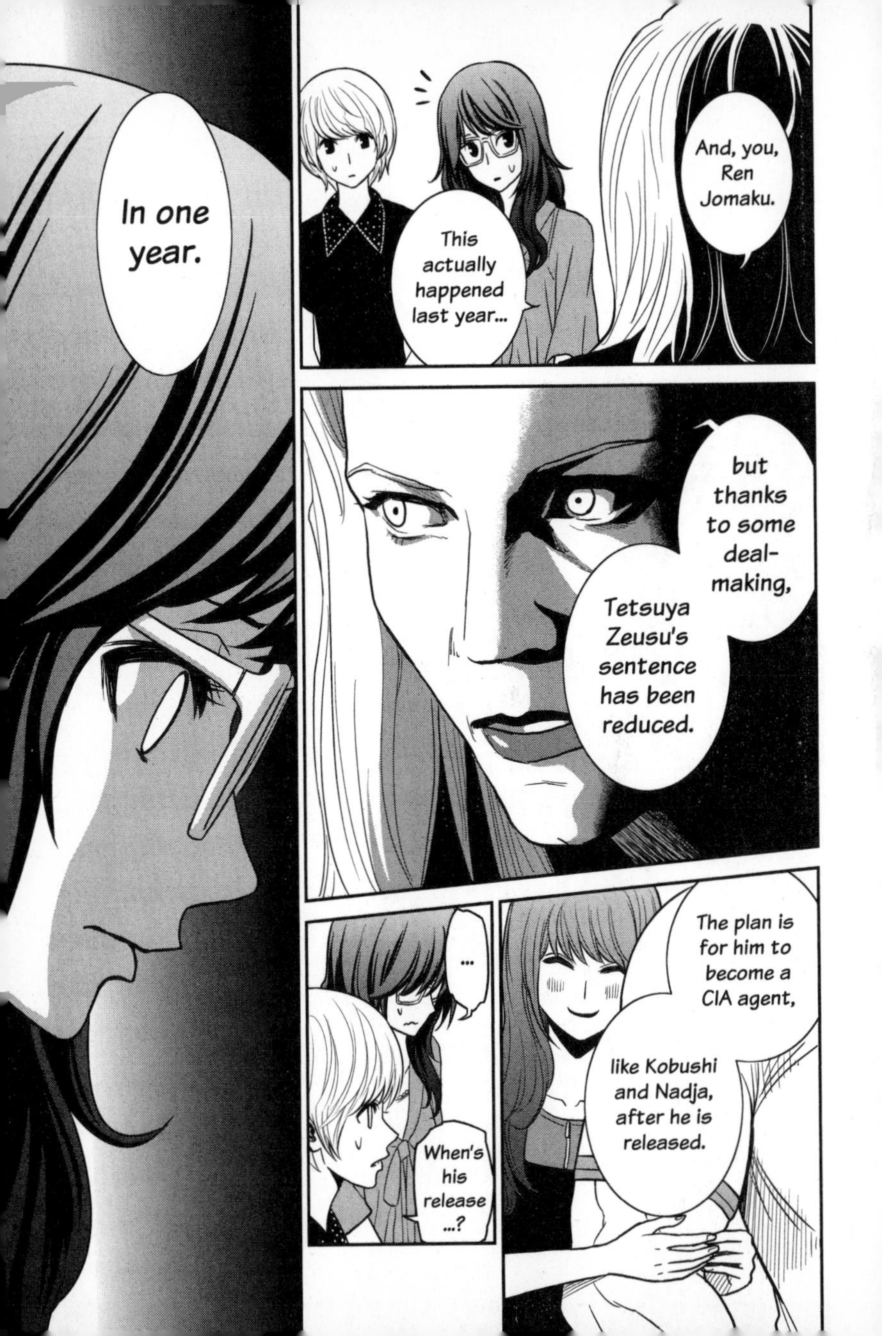
And, you, Ren Jomaku.
This actually happened last year...
but thanks to some deal-making,
Tetsuya Zeusu's sentence has been reduced.
The plan is for him to become a CIA agent,
like Kobushi and Nadja, after he is released.
...
When's his release ...?
In one year.

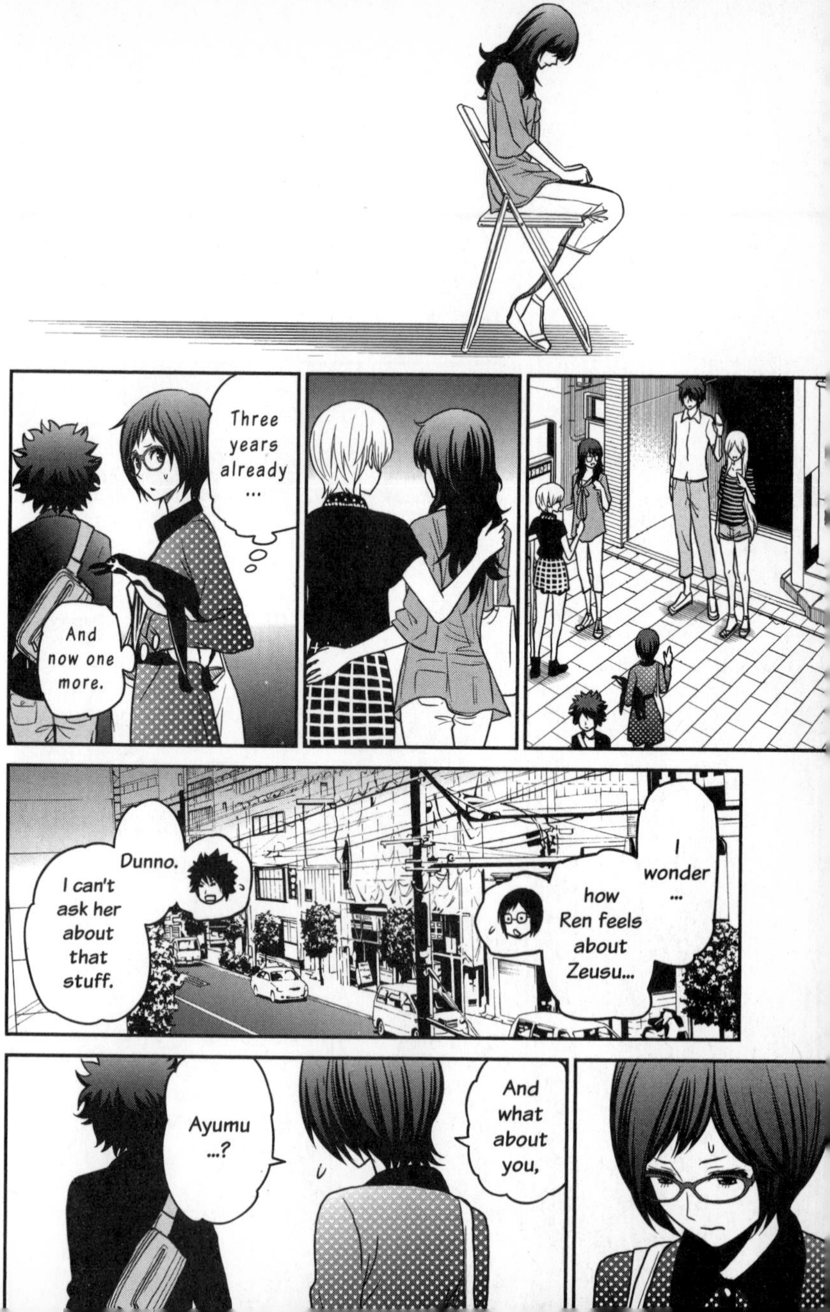
Three years already ...
And now one more.
I wonder ... how Ren feels about Zeusu...
Dunno. I can't ask her about that stuff.
And what about you,
Ayumu ...?

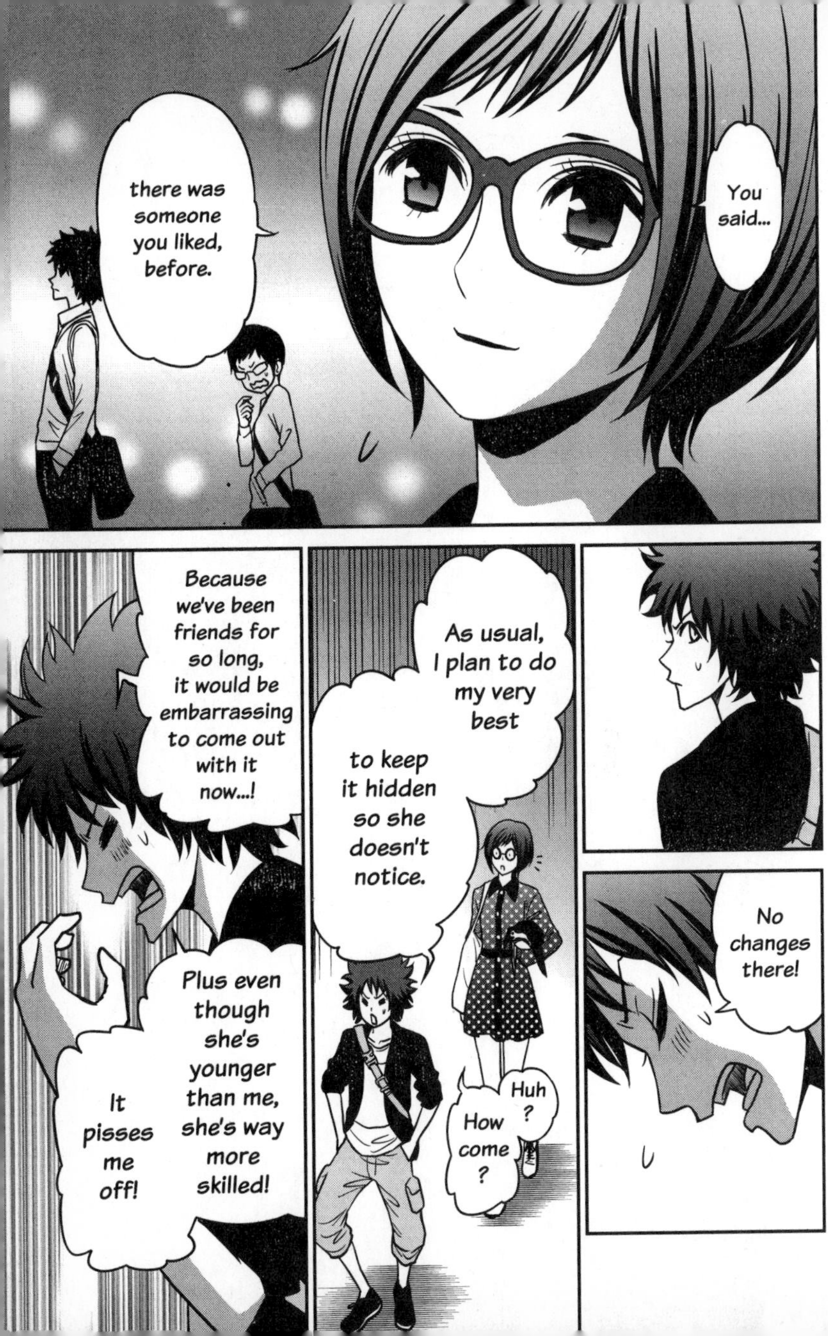
You said...
there was someone you liked, before.
No changes there!
As usual, I plan to do my very best
to keep it hidden so she doesn't notice.
Huh?
How come?
Because we've been friends for so long, it would be embarrassing to come out with it now...!
Plus even though she's younger than me, she's way more skilled!
It pisses me off!

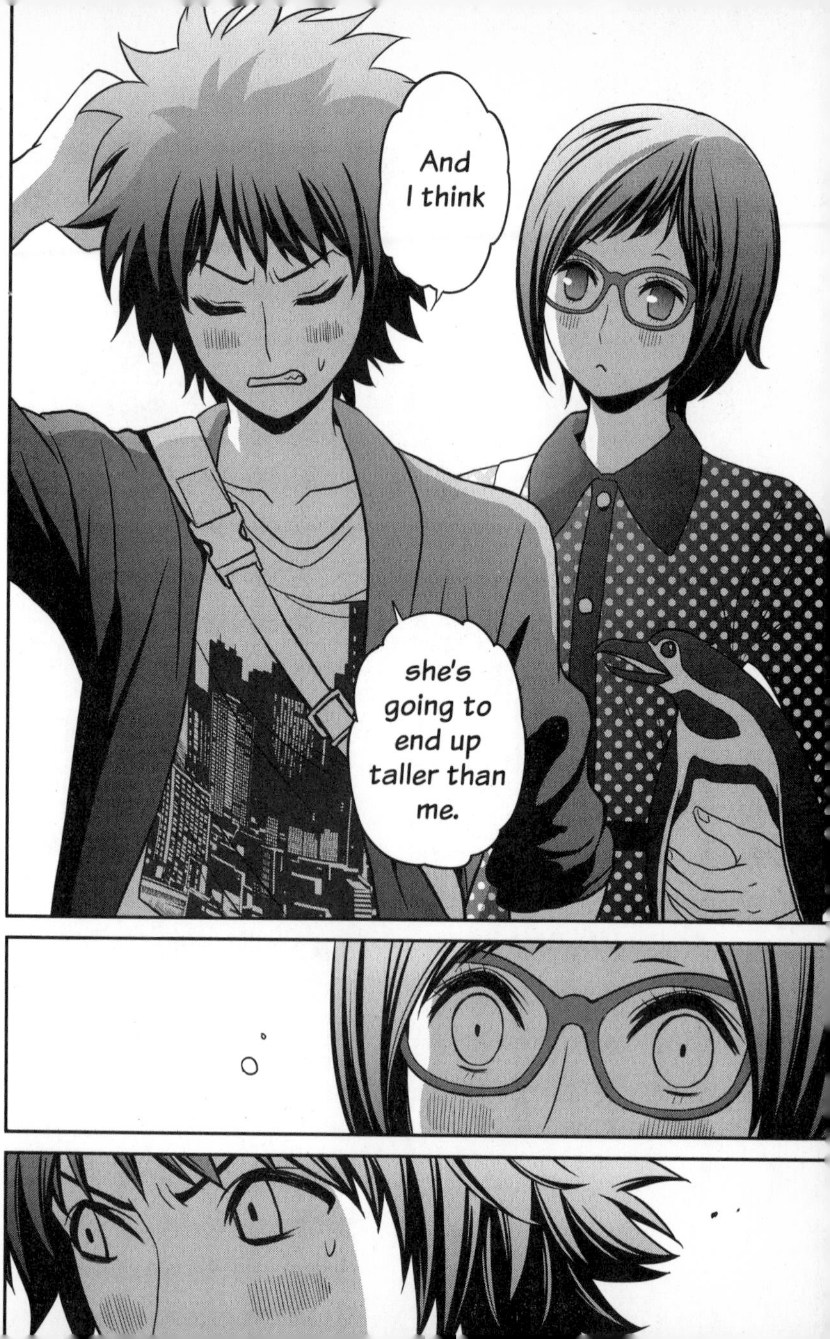
And I think
she's going to end up taller than me.

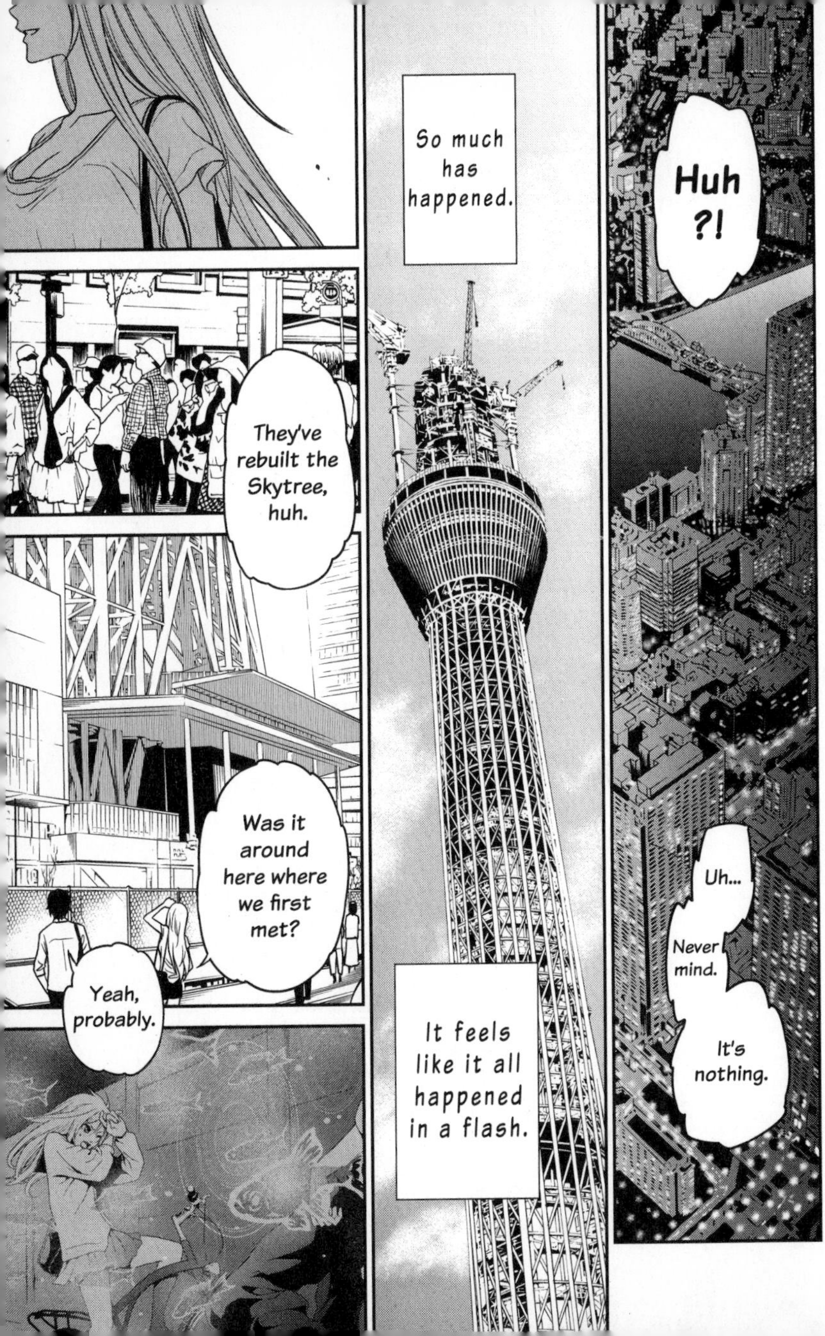
Huh ?!
Uh...
Never mind.
It's nothing.
So much has happened.
It feels like it all happened in a flash.
They've rebuilt the Skytree, huh.
Was it around here where we first met?
Yeah, probably.

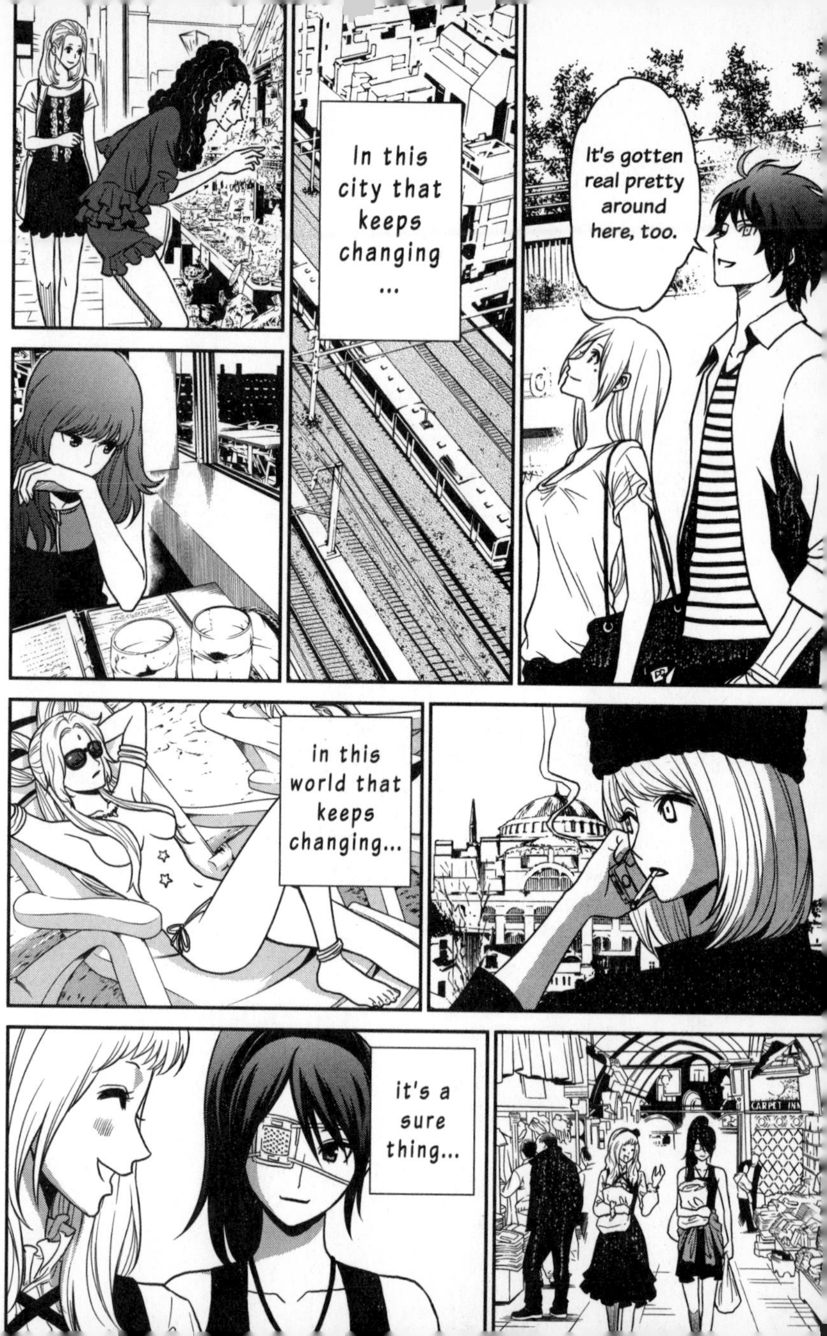
It's gotten real pretty around here, too.
In this city that keeps changing ...
in this world that keeps changing...
it's a sure thing...

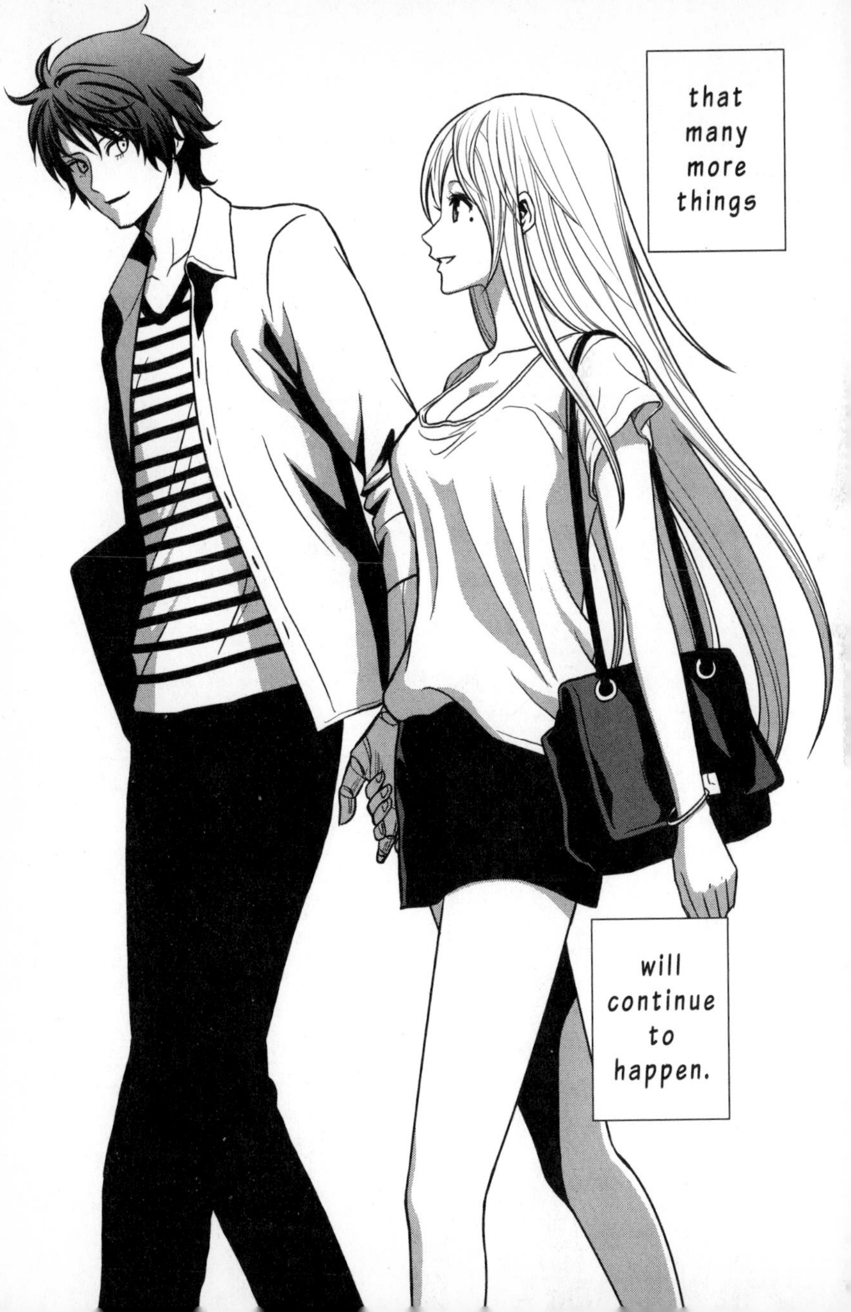
that many more things
will continue to happen.

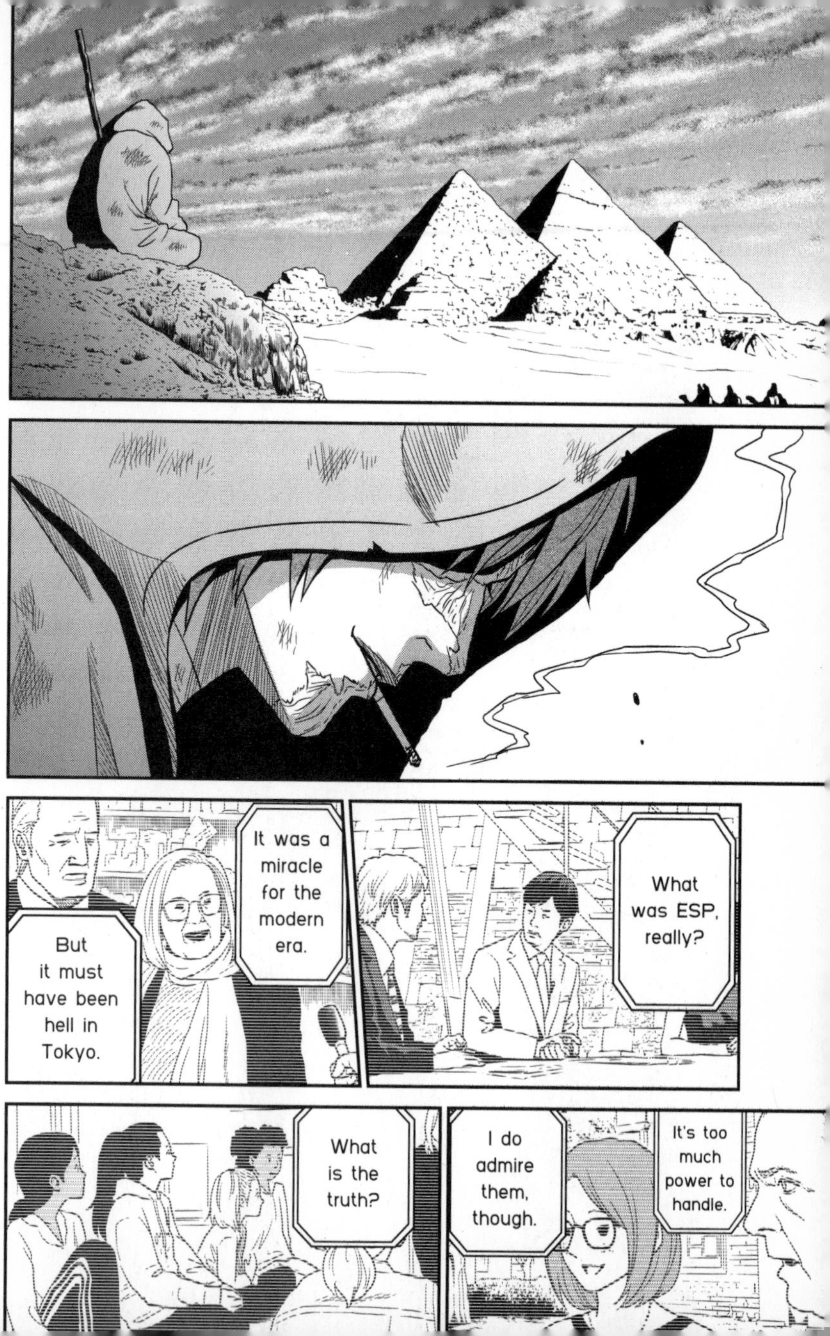
What was ESP, really?
It was a miracle for the modern era.
But it must have been hell in Tokyo.
It's too much power to handle.
I do admire them, though.
What is the truth?

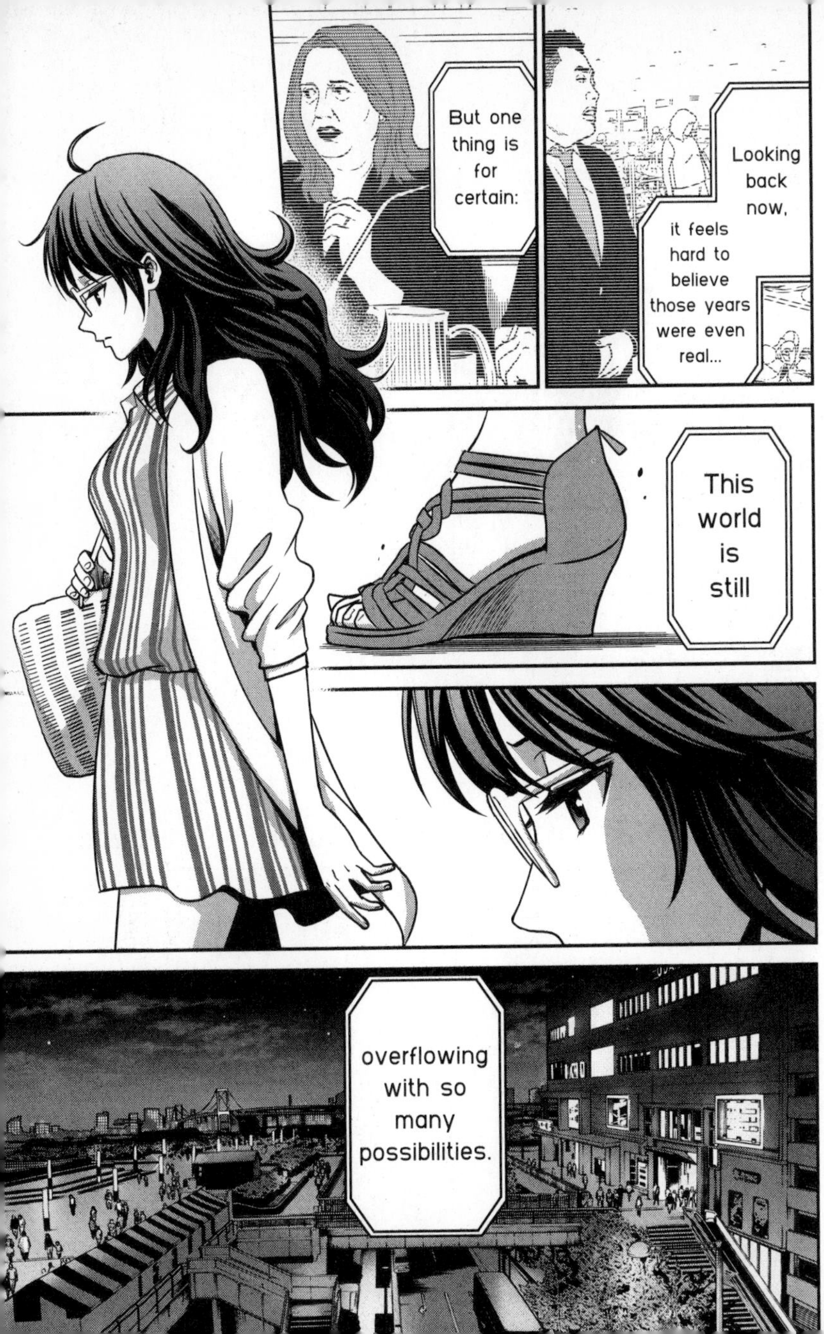
Looking back now, it feels hard to believe those years were even real...
But one thing is for certain:
This world is still
overflowing with so many possibilities.

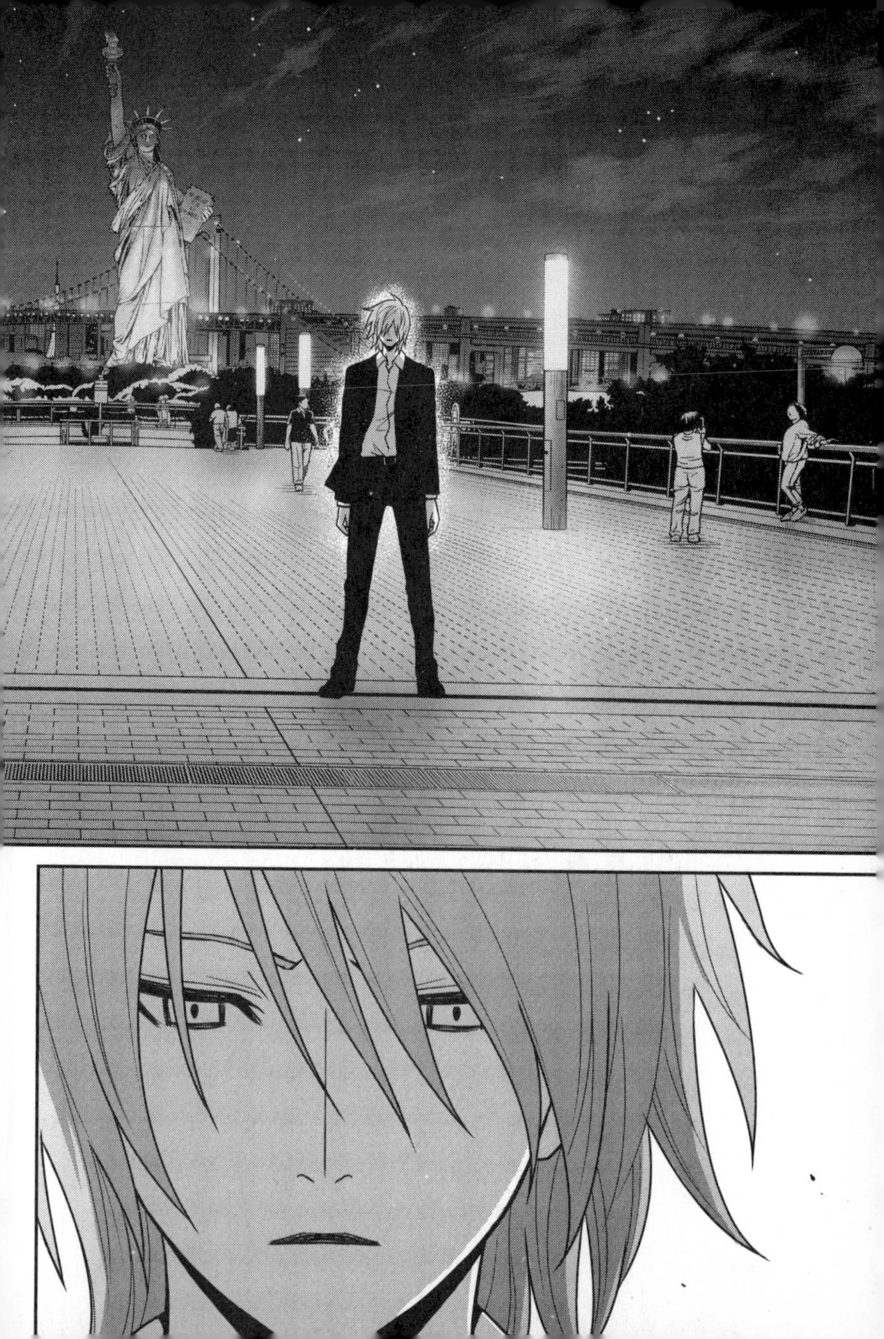

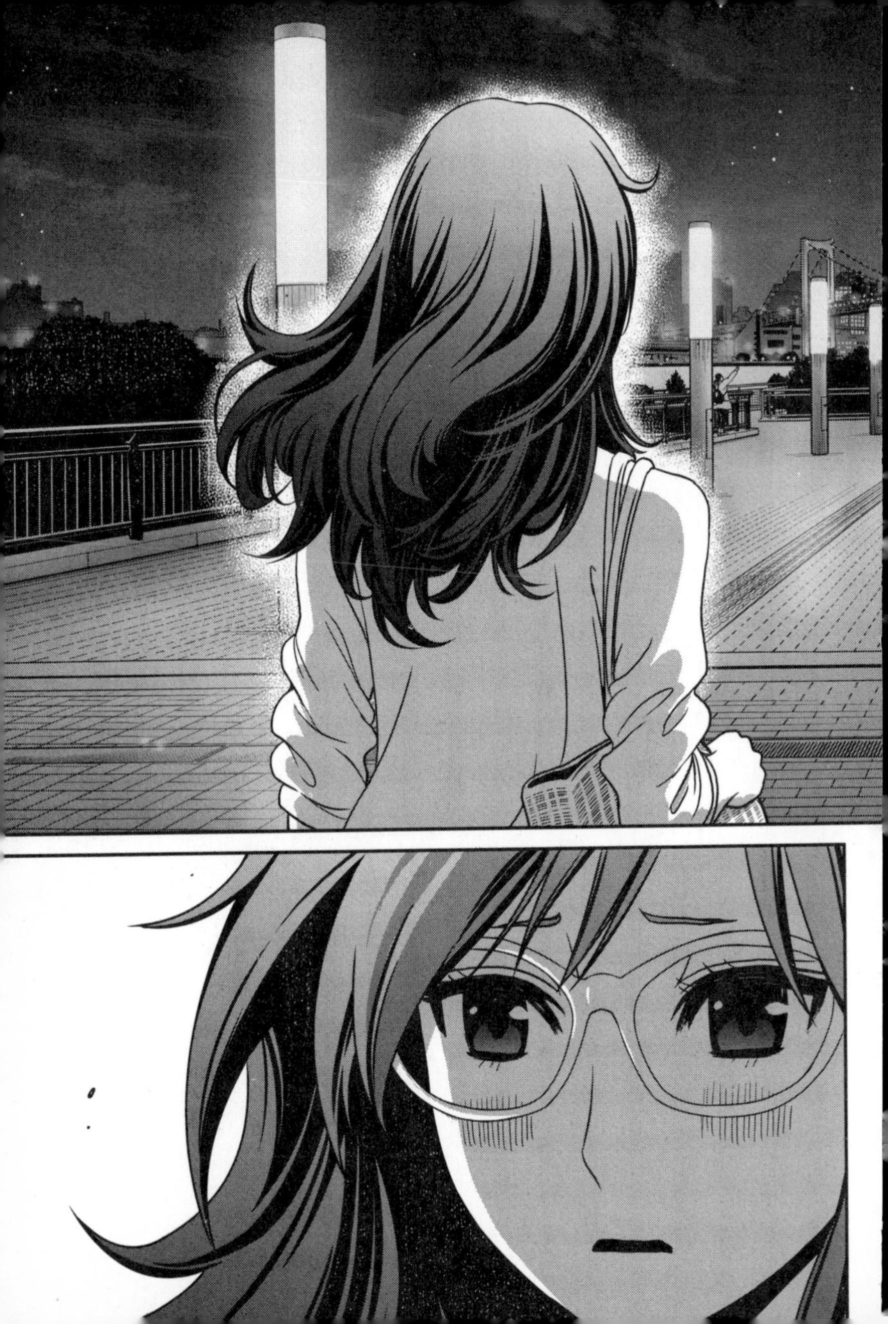

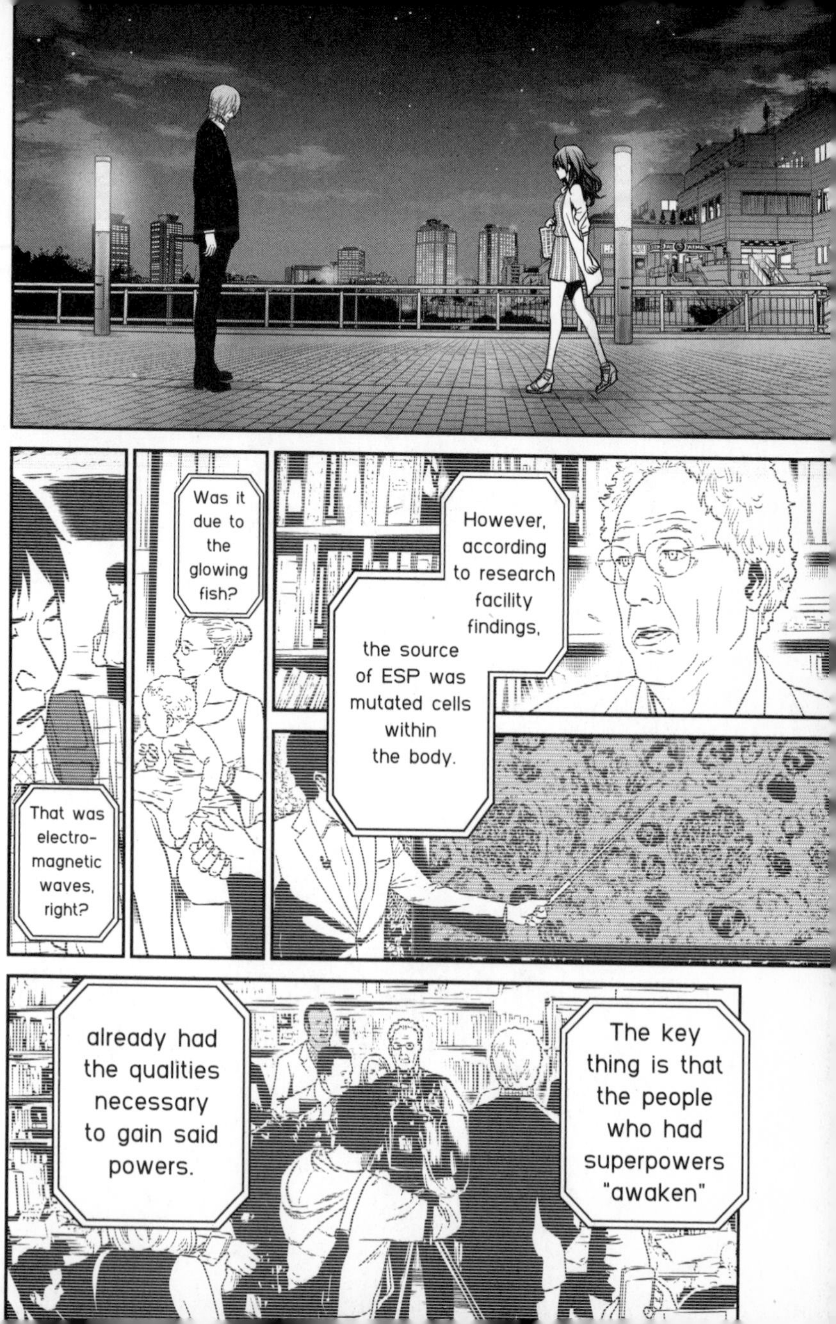
However, according to research facility findings,
the source of ESP was mutated cells within the body.
Was it due to the glowing fish?
That was electro-magnetic waves, right?
The key thing is that the people who had superpowers "awaken"
already had the qualities necessary to gain said powers.

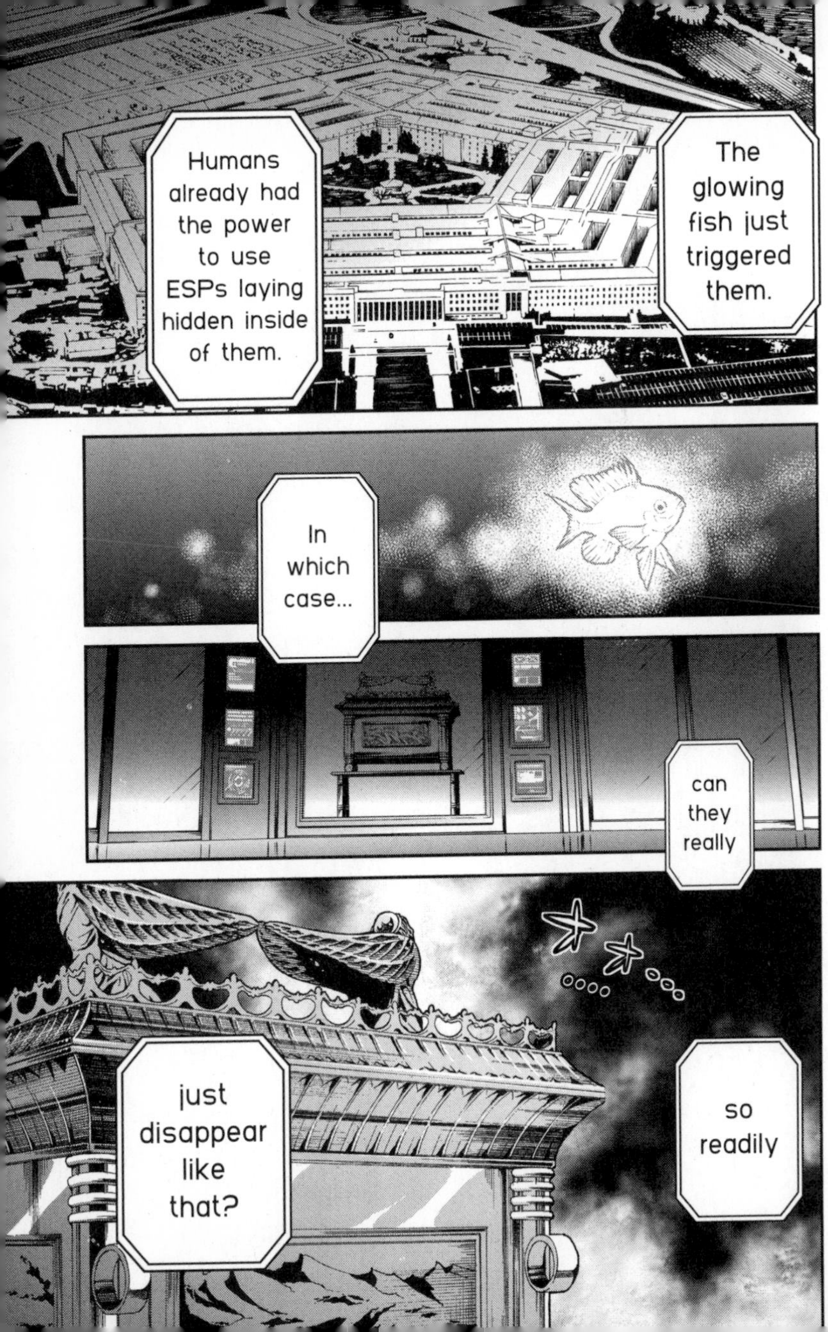
The glowing fish just triggered them.
Humans already had the power to use ESPs laying hidden inside of them.
In which case...
can they really
so readily
just disappear like that?

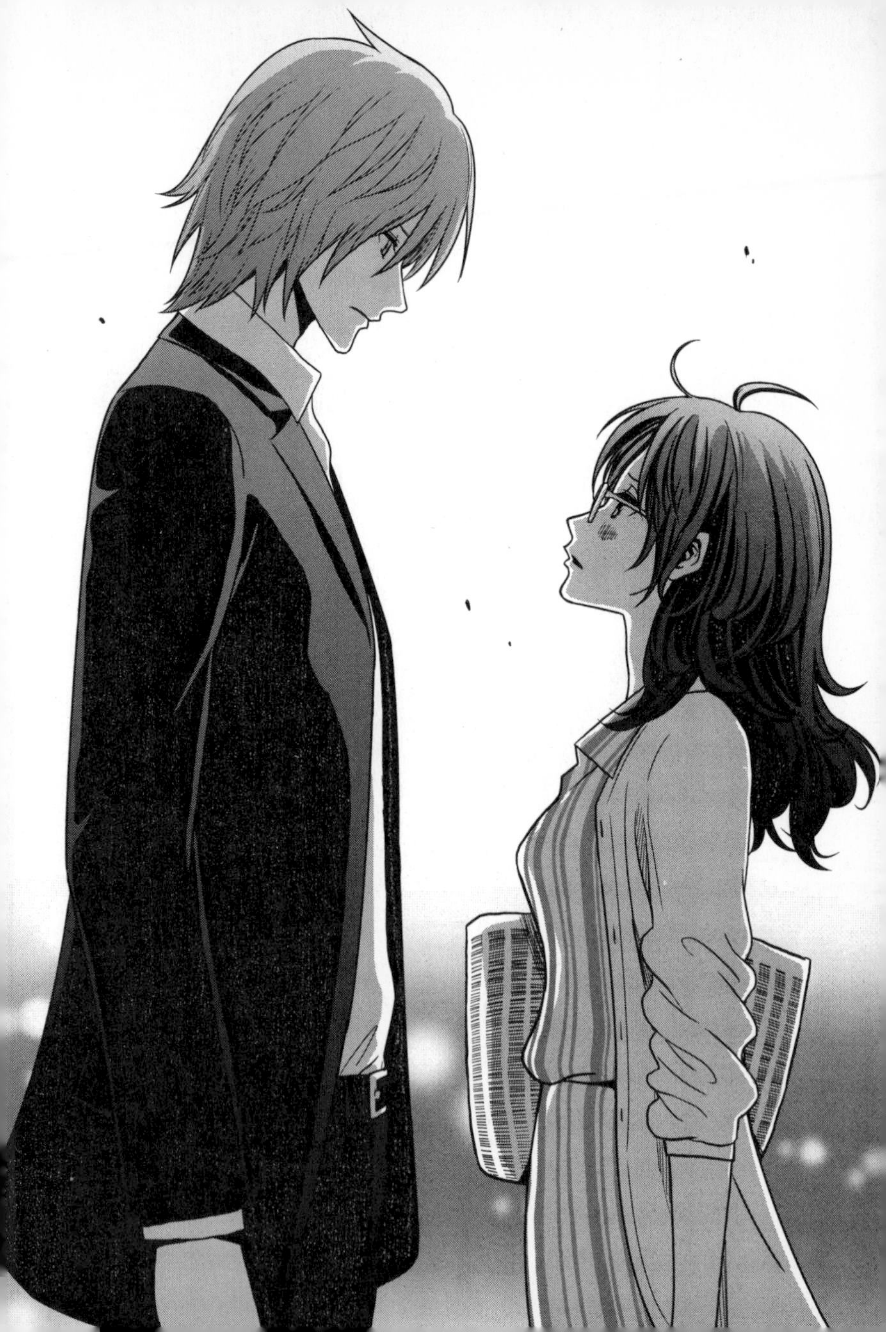

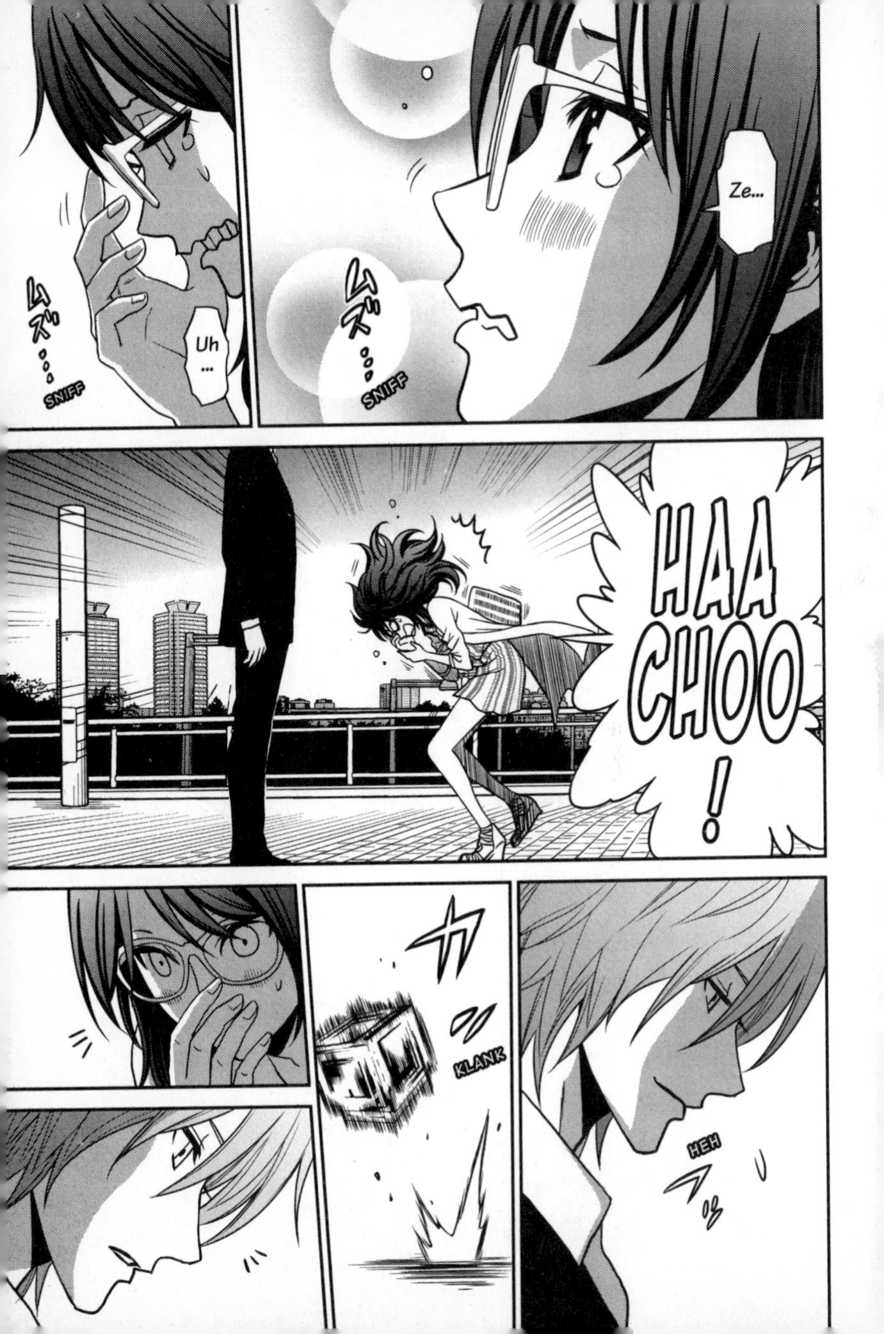

Ze...
ムズ...
SNIFF
Uh...
ムズ...
SNIFF
HAA CHOO!
HEH
へっ
カン
KLANK

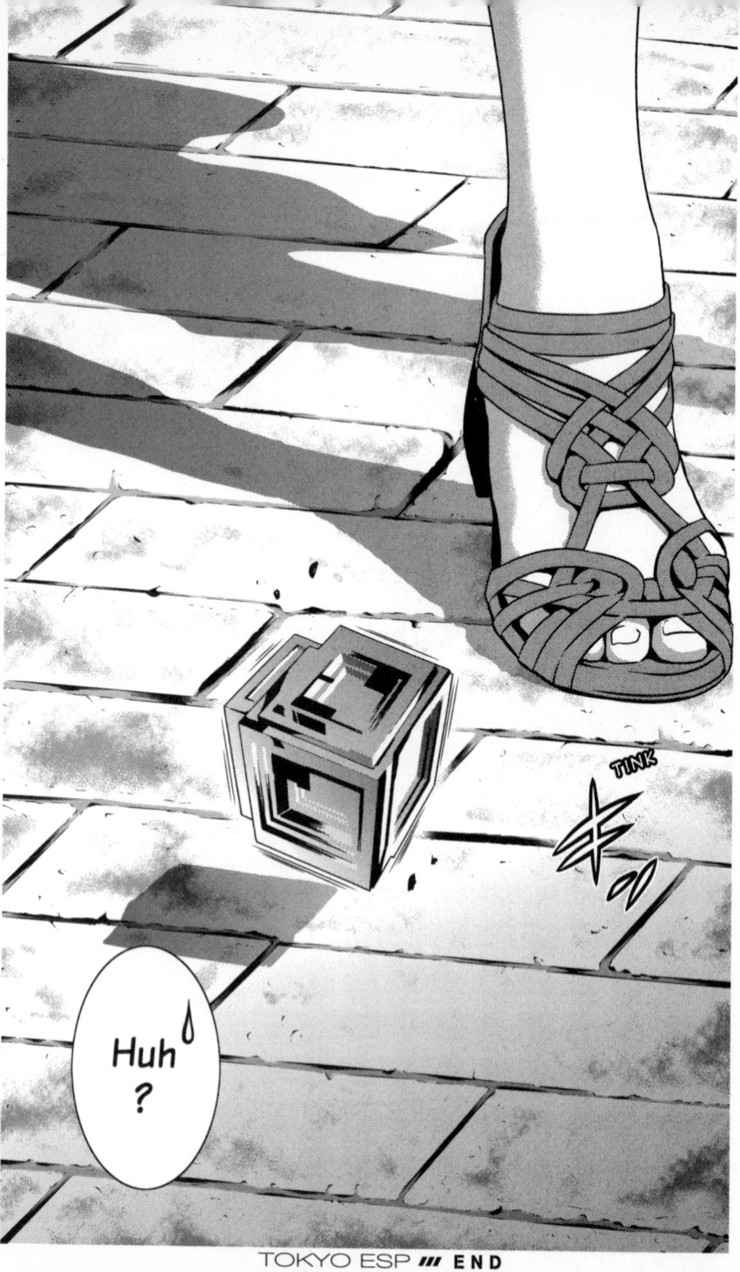
TINK
Huh ?

TOKYO ESP /// END

Hajime Segawa Presents

TOKYO ESP

END

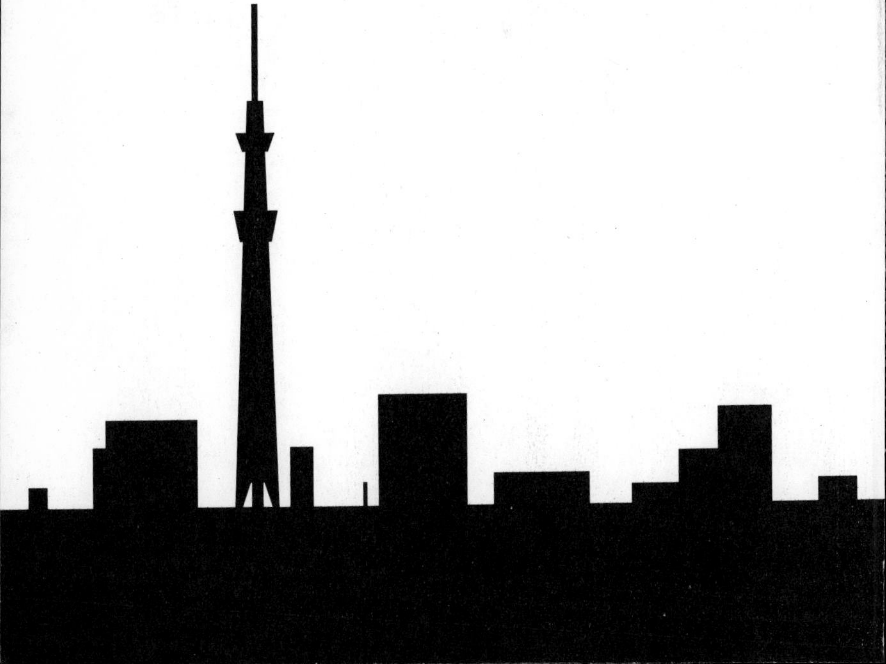

End of Book Bonus

UNUSED SCENE COLLECTION

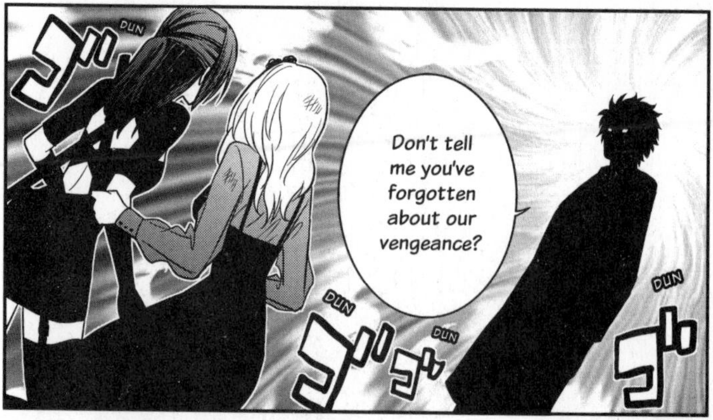
DUN
Don't tell me you've forgotten about our vengeance?
DUN
DUN
DUN

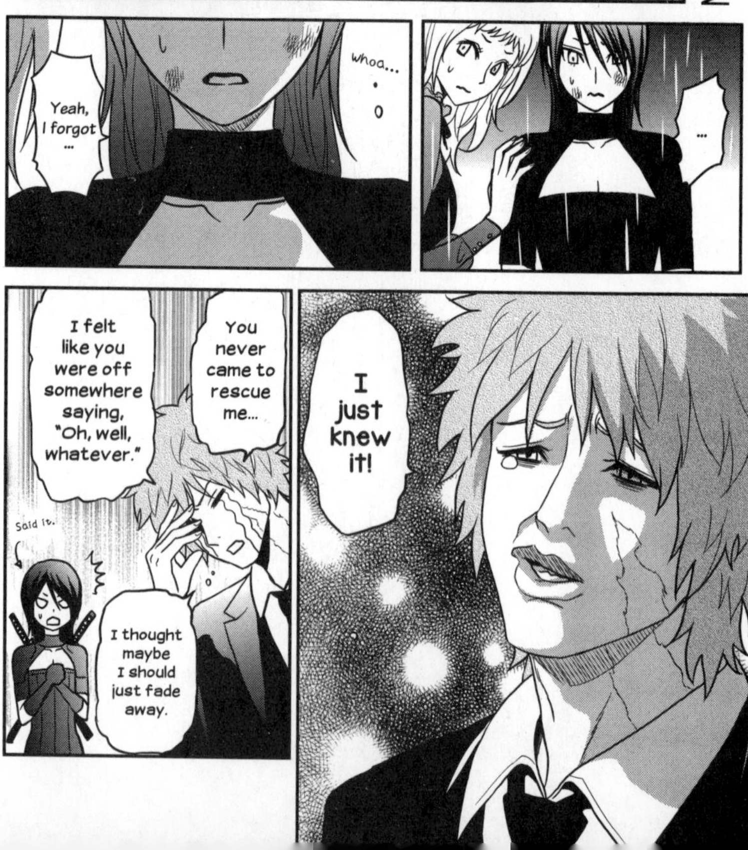
...
whoa...
Yeah, I forgot ...
I just knew it!
You never came to rescue me...
I felt like you were off somewhere saying, "Oh, well, whatever."
Said it.
I thought maybe I should just fade away.

TOKYO ESP

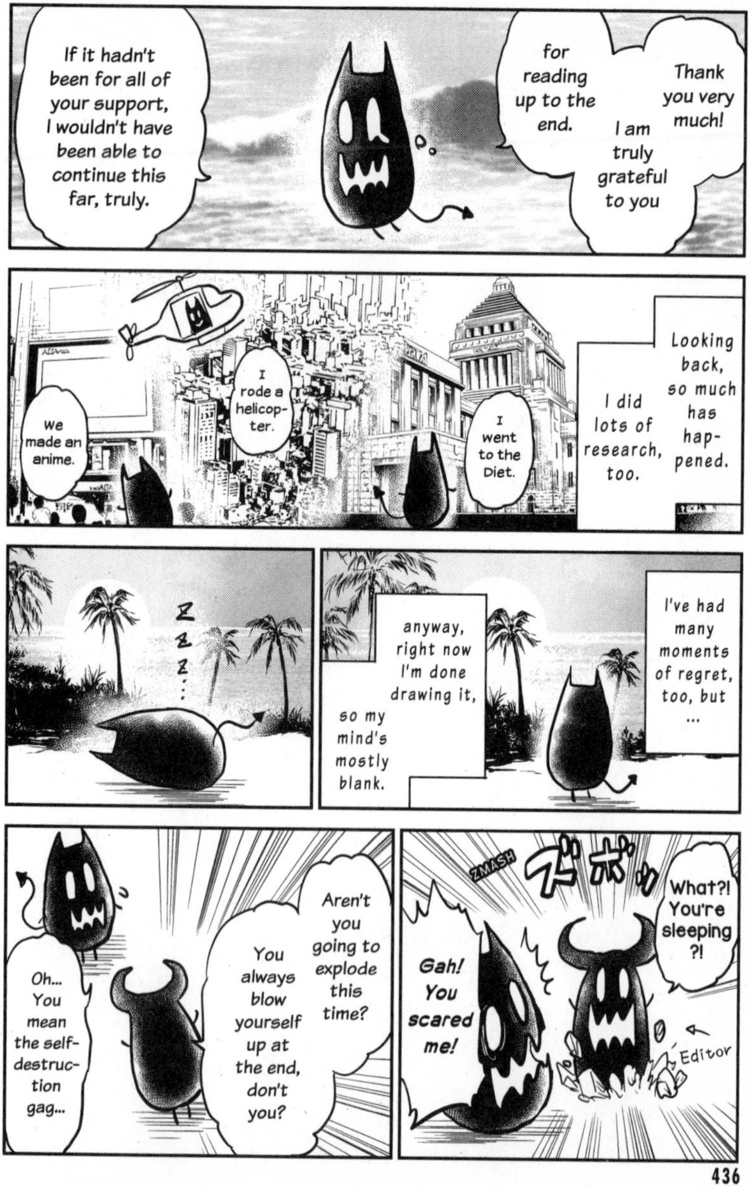

Thank you very much!
I am truly grateful to you
for reading up to the end.
If it hadn't been for all of your support, I wouldn't have been able to continue this far, truly.
Looking back, so much has hap-pened.
I did lots of research, too.
I went to the Diet.
I rode a helicop-ter.
we made an anime.
I've had many moments of regret, too, but ...
anyway, right now I'm done drawing it,
so my mind's mostly blank.
Z Z Z...
ズボッ
ZMASH
What?! You're sleeping?!
Gah! You scared me!
Editor
Aren't you going to explode this time?
You always blow yourself up at the end, don't you?
Oh... You mean the self-destruc-tion gag...